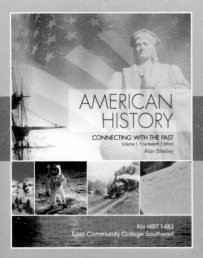

AMERICAN HISTORY
CONNECTING WITH THE PAST
Volume I, Fourteenth Edition
Alan Brinkley

For HIST 1483
Tulsa Community College Southeast

CONNECT TO YOUR COURSEWORK ONLINE.
ANYWHERE, ANY TIME.

With McGraw-Hill *Connect™ Plus*, engage with your coursework efficiently with learning personalized for you. Get an online eBook and immediate feedback on online assignments, quizzes and practice tests. Even access your instructor's class lecture online. Connect to learning and to what you need for future success!

Access Code to accompany

American History: Connecting with the Past
Volume I
Fourteenth Edition
Brinkley

For HIST 1483
Tulsa Community College Southeast

D1066601

To register and activate your *Connect Plus* account, simply follow these three easy steps:

1. Go to the **Connect Plus** course URL provided by your instructor.
2. Click on the link to register.
3. When prompted, enter the registration code listed below. Complete the brief registration form that follows online.

This code is unique and not related to any other registration number or ID you may have. The registration code is good for one-time use.

Suggestion: Bookmark your instructor's Connect course URL for fast, easy access.

Questions? Need Help? Visit **www.mhhe.com/support**

REGISTRATION CODE

ONLINE ACCESS CARD FOR CONNECT PLUS

Students: Do Not Throw Away. This is your personalized registration card for online access to assignment material.

Mc Graw Hill **Learning Solutions**

The McGraw-Hill Companies

ISBN-13: 978-0-07-758494-8
ISBN-10: 0-07-758494-5

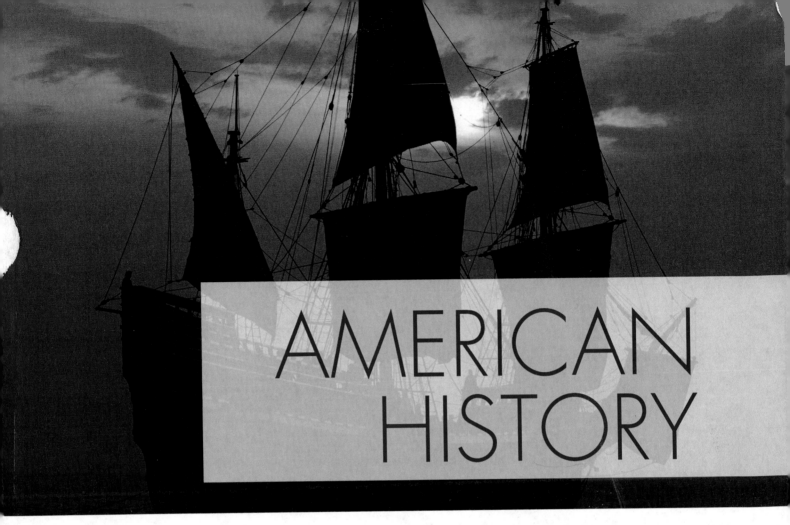

AMERICAN HISTORY

CONNECTING WITH THE PAST
Volume I, Fourteenth Edition

Alan Brinkley
Columbia University

For HIST 1483
Tulsa Community College Southeast

Boston   Burr Ridge, IL   Dubuque, IA   New York   San Francisco
St. Louis   Bangkok   Bogotá   Caracas   Lisbon   London   Madrid
Mexico City   Milan   New Delhi   Seoul   Singapore   Sydney   Taipei   Toronto

The McGraw·Hill Companies

AMERICAN HISTORY: CONNECTING WITH THE PAST, Volume 1, Fourteenth Edition
For HIST 1483
Tulsa Community College Southeast

This book is a McGraw-Hill Learning Solutions textbook and contains select material from *America History: Connecting With the Past, Volume 1,* Fourteenth Edition by Alan Brinkley. Copyright © 2012, 2009, 2007, 2003, 1999, 1995, 1991, 1979, 1971, 1966, 1964, 1961, 1959 by The McGraw-Hill Companies, Inc. Reprinted with permission of the publisher. Many custom published texts are modified versions or adaptations of our best-selling textbooks. Some adaptations are printed in black and white to keep prices at a minimum, while others are in color.

1 2 3 4 5 6 7 8 9 0 DIG DIG 13 12 11

ISBN-13: 978-0-07-754104-0
ISBN-10: 0-07-754104-9
part of
ISBN-13: 978-0-07-754285-6
ISBN-10: 0-07-754285-1

Learning Solutions Manager: Darlene Bahr
Production Editor: Lynn Nagel
Cover Design: Caitlin Anderson
Printer/Binder: Digital Impressions

ABOUT THE AUTHOR

ALAN BRINKLEY is the Allan Nevins Professor of History at Columbia University. He served as University Provost at Columbia from 2003–2009. He is the author of *Voices of Protest: Huey Long, Father Coughlin, and the Great Depression,* which won the 1983 National Book Award; *The Unfinished Nation: A Concise History of the American People; The End of Reform: New Deal Liberalism in Recession and War; Liberalism and Its Discontents; Franklin D. Roosevelt;* and *The Publisher: Henry Luce and His American Century.* He is the chair of the board of the National Humanities Center, the chair of the board of the Century Foundation, and a trustee of Oxford University Press. He is a member of the Academy of Arts and Sciences. In 1998–1999, he was the Harmsworth Professor of History at Oxford University, and in 2011–2012, the Pitt Professor at the University of Cambridge. He won the Joseph R. Levenson Memorial Teaching Award at Harvard, and the Great Teacher Award at Columbia. He was educated at Princeton and Harvard.

BRIEF CONTENTS

1 THE COLLISION OF CULTURES 1

2 TRANSPLANTATIONS AND BORDERLANDS 35

3 SOCIETY AND CULTURE IN PROVINCIAL AMERICA 66

4 THE EMPIRE IN TRANSITION 100

5 | THE AMERICAN REVOLUTION 130

8 VARIETIES OF AMERICAN NATIONALISM 217

9 JACKSONIAN AMERICA 234

10 AMERICA'S ECONOMIC REVOLUTION 260

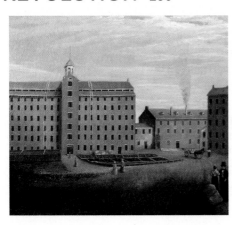

11 COTTON, SLAVERY, AND THE OLD SOUTH 297

12 | ANTEBELLUM CULTURE AND REFORM 320

13 THE IMPENDING CRISIS 346

14 THE CIVIL WAR 373

15 | RECONSTRUCTION AND THE NEW SOUTH 410

WHY do so many people take an interest in history? It is, I think, because we know that we are the products of the past—that everything we know, everything we see, and everything we imagine is rooted in our history. It is not surprising that there have been historians throughout almost all of recorded time. It is only natural that we are interested in what the past was like. Whether we study academic history or not, we all are connected to the past.

Americans have always had a love of their own history. It is a daunting task to attempt to convey the long and remarkable story of America in a single book, but that is what this volume attempts to do. The new subtitle of this book, "Connecting with the Past," describes this edition's focus on encouraging readers to be aware of the ways in which our everyday experiences are rooted in our history.

Like any history, this book is a product of its time and reflects the views of the past that historians of recent generations have developed. A comparable book published decades from now will likely seem as different from this one as this book appears different from histories written a generation or more ago. The writing of history changes constantly—not, of course, because the past changes, but because of shifts in the way historians, and the publics they serve, ask and answer questions about the past.

There are now, as there have always been, critics of changes in historical understanding. Many people argue that history is a collection of facts and should not be subject to "interpretation" or "revision." But historians insist that history is not and cannot be simply a collection of facts. They are only the beginning of historical understanding. It is up to the writers and readers of history to try to interpret the evidence before them; and in doing so, they will inevitably bring to the task their own questions, concerns, and experiences.

Our history requires us to examine the experience of the many different peoples and ideas that have shaped American society. But it also requires us to understand that the United States is a nation whose people share many things: a common political system, a connection to an integrated national (and now international) economy, and a familiarity with a shared and enormously powerful mass culture. To understand the American past, it is necessary to understand both the forces that divide Americans and the forces that draw them together.

Among the changes in the fourteenth edition of *American History: Connecting to the Past* are a new set of primary-source features titled "Consider the Source." By juxtaposing historical and more current sources, my hope is that these features will prompt students to not only consider the way that historians read historical documents but also to think carefully about the many current sources of information they encounter on a daily basis. A new pedagogical program integrated throughout the text further prompts students to engage with our history, at both the levels of basic understanding and more complex analysis. All content is now reinforced and supplemented by a rich set of online practice and assessment resources, housed within the Connect platform. It is not only the writing of history that changes with time—the tools and technologies through which information is delivered change as well.

I am grateful to many people for their help on this book—especially the people at McGraw-Hill who have supported and sustained this book so well for many years. I am grateful to Matt Busbridge, Stacy Ruel, Emily Pecora, and Jasmin Tokatlian. I am grateful, too, to Deborah Bull for her help with photographs. I also appreciate the many suggestions and corrections I have received from students over the last several years, as well as the reviews provided by a group of talented scholars and teachers.

Alan Brinkley
Columbia University
New York, NY

EXPERIENCE *SUCCESS* IN HISTORY

American History connects students
to the relevance of history through
a series of engaging features:

CONSIDER THE SOURCE

TEA PARTIES

THE BOSTON Tea Party of 1773 was a revolt against "taxation without representation." The poem "Ye glorious sons of freedom" celebrates the action of the Boston Tea Party, expresses the colonists' resentments and complaints against the distant London government, and calls upon Boston patriots to continue to resist British actions.

The twenty-first century Tea Party movement became prominent in 2009. Although not an official political party, members tend to endorse Republican candidates. The modern Tea Party movement has borrowed its name from the Boston event that took place more than two hundred years ago, and has picked up some (although not all) of the ideas of the 1773 Boston Tea Party: hostility to distant authority (London then, Washington now) and resentment of taxes (imposed by Britain then, and by Washington now). Although taxation in our time does not really take place "without representation," today's Tea Partiers certainly feel that contemporary taxation is as illegitimate as the Bostonians felt it was in 1773.

New > *Consider the Source* Features

These features guide students through careful analysis of historical documents, both textual and visual, and prompt them to make connections with contemporary events. Among the twelve topics covered are Tea Parties, the Rise of Feminism, Nativism and Anti-Immigration Sentiment, and Banking Crises.

DEBATING THE PAST

THE CAUSES OF THE CIVIL WAR

IN his second inaugural address in March 1865, Abraham Lincoln looked back at the beginning of the Civil War four years earlier. "All knew," he said, that slavery "was somehow the cause of the war." Few historians doubt the basic truth of Lincoln's

"ON TO FREEDOM" This painting by Theodore Kaufmann shows a group of fugitive slaves escaping from the South in the late years of the Civil War. Thousands of former slaves crossed the Union lines, where they were given their freedom. Many of them joined the Union Army. (The Granger Collection, New York)

statement, but they have disagreed sharply about whether slavery was the only, or even the principal, cause of the war.

This debate began even before the war itself. In 1858, Senator William H. Seward of New York took note of two competing explanations of the sectional tensions that were then inflaming the nation. On one side, he claimed, stood those who believed the sectional hostility to be "accidental, unnecessary, the work of interested or fanatical agitators." Opposing them stood those (like Seward himself) who believed there to be "an irrepressible conflict between opposing and enduring forces."

The "irrepressible conflict" argument dominated historical discussion of the war from the 1860s to the 1920s. Because the North and the South had reached positions on the issue of slavery that were both irreconcilable and seemingly unalterable, some historians claimed, the conflict had become "inevitable." James Rhodes, in his seven-volume *History of the United States from the Compromise of 1850 . . .* (1893–1900), placed greatest emphasis on the moral conflict over slavery, but he suggested as well that the struggle also reflected fundamental differences between the Northern and Southern economic systems. Charles and Mary Beard in *The Rise of American Civilization*

DEBATING THE PAST ESSAYS

Twenty-five essays introduce students to the contested quality of much of the American past, and provide a sense of the evolving nature of historical scholarship. From addressing the question of "Why do historians so often disagree?" to examining specific differences in historical understandings of the Constitution, the character of slavery, and the causes of the Great Depression, these essays familiarize students with the interpretive character of historical understanding.

UNDERSTAND, ANALYZE, AND EVALUATE

1. How did the problems facing Bismarck differ from those facing Lincoln?
2. Which man—Mazzini, Cavour, or Garibaldi—in the struggle to achieve the unification of Italy most closely parallels Lincoln and the fight to preserve the Union?
3. Does Mazzini's argument—that peoples with common language, culture, and tradition should be free to unite and govern themselves—apply to the North's attempt to preserve the Union, or does it better fit the South's attempt to secede and form a separate nation?

NEW > *UNDERSTAND, ANALYZE, AND EVALUATE* REVIEW QUESTIONS

Appearing at the end of every feature essay, these questions encourage students to move beyond memorization of facts and names to explore the importance and significance of the featured content.

UNDERSTAND, ANALYZE, AND EVALUATE

1. Some arguments regarding the [Civil War] as inevitable focus on economic differences between the North and the South. What were these differences and how might they have led—inevitably—to war?
2. Some revisionist scholars attribute the Civil War to a "blundering generation" of political leaders. Who were these leaders and what blunders did they make? Could better decisions have avoided war?
3. According to the ethnoculturalists, what was the role of political parties in the coming of the Civil War?

AMERICA IN THE WORLD

THE CONSOLIDATION OF NATIONS

The American Civil War was an event largely rooted in conditions particular to the United States. But it was also a part of a worldwide movement in the nineteenth century to create large, consolidated nations. A commitment to preserving the Union—to consolidating, rather than dismantling, the nation—was one of the principal motives for the North's commitment to fighting a war against the seceding states. Similar efforts at expansion, consolidation, and unification were occurring in many other nations around the same time.

The consolidation of nation-states was, of course, not new to the nineteenth century. The revolutions in America and France in the late eighteenth century—and the subsequent strengthening of the French concept of nationhood under Napoleon in the early nineteenth century—inspired new nationalist enthusiasms in other parts of Europe. Nationalist sentiment also grew among peoples who shared language, culture, ethnicity, and tradition and who came to believe that a consolidated nation was the best vehicle for strengthening their common bonds.

THE UNIFICATION OF ITALY This painting shows a climactic moment in the history of Italian unification. Garibaldi, the great leader of independence forces in southern Italy, greets King Victor Emmanuel of the Piedmont, the leader of independence forces in the North. Garibaldi greeted him by saying, "Saluto il primo Re d'Italia" ("I hail the first king of Italy"). The moment was significant both practically—it demonstrated Garibaldi's willingness to accept Victor Emmanuel's authority—and symbolically, as the triumph of nationalist sentiment in this once-decentralized country. *(Museo del Risorgimento, Milan/Index S.A.S.)*

In 1848, a wave of nationalist revolutions erupted in Italy, France, and Austria, challenging the imperial powers that many Europeans believed were subjugating national cultures. Those revolutions failed, but they helped lay the groundwork for the two most important national consolidations of nineteenth-century Europe.

One of these consolidations occurred in Germany, which was divided into numerous small, independent states in the early nineteenth century but where popular sentiment for German unification had been growing for decades. It was spurred in part by new histories of the German *Volk* (people) and by newly constructed images of German traditions, visible in such literature as the Grimms' fairy tales—an effort to record and popularize German folk traditions and make them the basis of a shared sense of a common past. In 1862, King Wilhelm I of Prussia—the leader of one of the most powerful of the scattered German states—appointed an aristocratic landowner, Otto von Bismarck, as his prime minister. Bismarck exploited the growing nationalism throughout the various German states and helped develop a strong popular base for unification. He did so in part by launching Prussian wars against Denmark, Austria, and France—wars Prussia easily won, inspiring pride in German power that extended well beyond Prussia itself. The Franco-Prussian War of 1870 was particularly important, because Prussia fought it to take possession of the French provinces of Alsace and Lorraine—provinces the Prussians claimed were part of the German "national community" because its people, although legally French citizens, were ethnically and linguistically German. In 1871, capitalizing on the widespread nationalist sentiment the war had created throughout the German-speaking states, Bismarck persuaded the German king to proclaim himself emperor (or *Kaiser*) of a new empire that united all German peoples except those in Austria and Switzerland.

The second great European movement for national unification occurred in Italy, which had

AMERICA IN THE WORLD ESSAYS

These fifteen essays focus on specific parallels between American history and those of other nations, and demonstrate the importance of the many global influences on the American story. Topics like the global industrial revolution, the abolition of slavery, and the origins of the Cold War provide concrete examples of the connections between the history of the United States and the history of other nations.

PATTERNS OF POPULAR CULTURE

BASEBALL AND THE CIVIL WAR

LONG before the great urban stadiums, long before the lights and the cameras and the multimillion-dollar salaries, long before the Little Leagues and the high school and college teams, baseball was the most popular game in America. And during the Civil War, it was a treasured pastime for soldiers, and for thousands of men (and some women) behind the lines, in both North and South.

The legend that baseball was invented by Abner Doubleday, who probably never even saw the game, came from Albert G. Spalding, a patriotic sporting-goods manufacturer eager to prove that the game had purely American origins and to dispel the notion that it came from England. In fact, baseball was derived from a variety of earlier games, especially the English pastimes of cricket and rounders. American baseball took its own distinctive form beginning in the 1840s, when Alexander Cartwright, a shipping clerk, formed the New York Knickerbockers, laid out a diamond-shaped field with four bases, and declared that batters with three strikes were out and that teams with three outs were retired.

Cartwright moved west in search of gold in 1849, ultimately grew rich, and settled finally in Hawaii (where he brought the game to Americans in the Pacific). But the game did not languish in his absence. Henry Chadwick, an English-born journalist, spent much of the 1850s popularizing the game (and regularizing its rules). By 1860, baseball was being played by college students and Irish workers, by urban elites and provincial farmers, by people of all classes and ethnic groups from New England to Louisiana. It was also attracting the attention of women. Students at Vassar College formed "ladies" teams in the 1860s, and in Philadelphia, free black men formed the first of what was to become a great network of African American baseball teams, the Pythians. From the beginning, they were barred from playing against most white teams.

When young men marched off to war in 1861, some took their bats and balls with them. Almost from the start of the fighting, soldiers in both armies took advantage of

idle moments to lay out baseball diamonds and organize games. There were games in prison camps; games on the White House lawn (where Union soldiers were sometimes billeted); and games on battlefields that were sometimes interrupted by gunfire and cannonfire. "It is astonishing how indifferent a person can become to danger," a soldier wrote home to Ohio in 1862. "The report of musketry is heard but a very little distance from us, . . . yet over there on the other side of the road is most of our company, playing Bat Ball." After a skirmish in Texas, another Union soldier lamented that, in addition to casualties, his company had lost "the only baseball in Alexandria, Texas." Far from discouraging baseball, military commanders—and the United States Sanitary Commission, the Union army's medical arm—actively encouraged the game during the war. It would, they believed, help keep up the soldiers' morale.

Away from the battlefield, baseball continued to flourish. In New York City, games between local teams drew crowds of ten or twenty thousand. The National Association of Baseball Players (founded in 1859) had recruited ninety-one clubs in ten northern states by 1865; a North

PATTERNS OF POPULAR CULTURE FEATURES

These twenty-six features bring fads, crazes, hang-outs, hobbies, and entertainment into the story of American history, encouraging students to expand their definition of what constitutes history, and to think about how we can best understand the lived experience of past lives.

American History ensures student success through review features and an exciting digital program, *Connect History*.

End-of-chapter review content, consisting of Recall and Reflect questions, key term lists, and significant events timelines, provide effective tools for reviewing content. With *Connect History,* a groundbreaking digital program, students study more effectively by confirming what they know and learning what they don't through engaging activities and review questions. Plus, each student receives a personalized study plan for every chapter. Additionally, *Connect History* builds critical thinking skills by placing students in a "critical mission" scenario and asking them to examine, evaluate, and analyze data.

McGraw-Hill's **Primary Source Investigator** is available online at www.mhhe.com/psi and gives students and instructor access to more than 650 primary and secondary sources including documents, images, maps, and videos.

Chapter 1

Expanded discussion of the peoples of pre-contact Americas

New America in the World essay, "Mercantilism and Colonial Commerce"

Revised coverage of religion in England at the time of American colonization

Chapter 2

Expanded discussion of the Puritans' religious practices and beliefs

Chapter 3

Revised discussion of the agricultural base of the early Northern economy

Revised discussion of the rise of consumerism

New coverage of the "halfway covenant"

New coverage of economic stratification in early New England

Chapter 4

New America in the World essay, "The First Global War"

New coverage of internal challenges to power in the American colonies

New Consider the Source feature, "Tea Parties"

Chapter 5

Revised discussion of Native Americans and the American Revolution

Chapter 6

New section, "The Limits of the Constitution"

Expanded coverage of the Republican opposition to the Constitution

Chapter 7

Expanded coverage of Tenskwatawa and Tecumseh

Revised discussion of the War of 1812 peace settlement

New Consider the Source essay, "Religious Revivals"

Chapter 8

Revised discussion of trading and trapping in the Far West

Chapter 9

New section on Tocqueville and *Democracy in America*

New maps on the elections of 1836 and 1840

Chapter 10

New Consider the Source feature, "Nativism and Anti-Immigration Sentiment"

New section on the concept of "free labor"

New Consider the Source feature, "Rules for Employees"

Chapter 11

Expanded coverage on slave resistance and slave revolts

Chapter 12

Expanded coverage of abolitionism

New Consider the Source feature, "The Rise of Feminism"

Chapter 13

Revised discussion of the conflict between Mexico and the United States in the 1830s

Expanded coverage of the Mexican War

Expanded coverage of Douglass's and Lincoln's views on slavery

Chapter 14

New coverage of photography and the Civil War

New Consider the Source feature, "Suspending the Writ of Habeas Corpus"

Expanded discussion of African American soldiers

New section on the Union's slow progress during the first two years of the war

BRINKLEY
HISTORY
14TH EDITION

the 14th EDITION

Chapter 15
Expanded discussion of Reconstruction and partisan politics

Chapter 16
Revised discussion of the mining boom in the West

Revised discussion of the "cattle kingdom"

Chapter 17
New Consider the Source feature, "Philanthropy"

Chapter 18
Streamlined discussion of "the ethnic city"

Streamlined discussion of leisure and consumer society

Chapter 19
Expanded coverage of the Spanish-American conflict

New Consider the Source feature, "Memorializing National History"

Chapter 20
Refined discussion of the settlement house movement

New coverage on the decline in voter turnout in the early twentieth century

New Consider the Source feature, "Conservation"

Chapter 21
Refined discussion of the post-WWI search for social unity

New section, "Refuting the Red Scare"

Chapter 22
Refined discussion of "the disenchanted"

Refined discussion of nativism in the 1920s

New Consider the Source feature, "Communications Technology"

Chapter 23
Refined discussion on the causes of the Great Depression

Chapter 24
New Consider the Source feature, "Banking Crises"

Chapter 25
Refined coverage of Pearl Harbor

Chapter 26
New Consider the Source feature, "The Face of the Enemy"

Revised discussion of the Pacific offensive

Chapter 27
Expanded coverage of the post-WWII "China problem"

Refined discussion of the Korean War

Chapter 28
Refined discussion of France, America, and Vietnam in the 1950s

Chapter 29
Streamlined discussion of the Vietnam War

Chapter 30
New America in the World essay, "The End of Colonialism"

Streamlined discussion of the Nixon presidency

New Section on inequality in America

Chapter 31
Expanded coverage of the first Gulf War

Chapter 32
Expanded coverage of the war on terrorism

New America in the World essay, "The Global Environmental Movement"

New section on the Obama presidency

ACKNOWLEDGMENTS

We are grateful to the many advisors and reviewers who generously offered comments, suggestions, and ideas at various stages in the development of this project.

Academic Reviewers

Eirlys Barker, *Thomas Nelson Community College*
Cathy Briggs, *Northwest Vista College*
Jeff Carlisle, *Oklahoma City Community College*
Mike Downs, *University of Texas—Arlington*
John Ehrhardt, *Oklahoma City Community College*
Mary Farmer-Kaiser, *University of Louisiana at Lafayette*
Linda Foutch, *Walters State Community College*
Brandon Franke, *Blinn College*
Keith Freese, *Itawamba Community College*
Wendy Gunderson, *Collin County Community College*
Michael Harkins, *William Rainey Harper College*
Timothy Holder, *Walters State Community College*
Bruce Ingram, *Itawamba Community College*
Greg Kelm, *Dallas Baptist University*
Wendy Kline, *University of Cincinnati*
Jennifer Lawrence, *Tarrant County College*
Pat Ledbetter, *North Central Texas College*
John W. Meador, *Central New Mexico Community College*
Rachel Mitchell, *Itawamba Community College*
Michael Namorato, *University of Mississippi*
Jessica Patton, *Tarrant County College*
Susan Richards, *Central New Mexico Community College*
Esther Robinson, *Lone Star College—Cyfair*
Erik Schmeller, *Tennessee State University*
Manfred Silva, *El Paso Community College*
Armando Villarreal, *Tarrant County College South*
Roger Ward, *Collin County Community College*
Bill Zeman, *Citrus Community College*

Connect Consultants

Charles Ambler, *University of Texas—El Paso*
Tramaine Anderson, *Tarrant County College*
Mario Bennekin, *Georgia Perimeter College*
Cassandra Cookson, *Lee College*
Nancy Duke, *Daytona State College*
Wendy Gunderson, *Collin County Community College*
Aimee Harris, *El Paso Community College*
Stephen Lopez, *San Jacinto College*
Mark Newell, *Ramapo College of New Jersey*
Jessica Patton, *Tarrant County College*
Penne Restad, *University of Texas—Austin*
Manfred Silva, *El Paso Community College*
Richard Straw, *Radford University*
David Stricklin, *Dallas Baptist University*
Paddy Swiney, *Tulsa Community College Southeast*
Teresa Thomas, *Austin Community College*
Armando Villarreal, *Tarrant County College South*
Roger Ward, *Collin County College*

Digiposium Attendees

Salvadore Anselmo, *Delgado Community College*
Olwyn Blouet, *Virginia State University*
Roger Chan, *Washington State University*
Laura Dunn, *Brevard Community College*
Arthur Durand, *Metropolitan Community College*
R. David Goodman, *Pratt Institute*
John Hosler, *Morgan State University*
James Jones, *Prairie View A&M University*
Philip Kaplan, *University of North Florida*
Michael Kinney, *Calhoun Community College*
Sandra Norman, *Florida Atlantic University*
Linda Scherr, *Mercer County Community College*
Carlton Wilson, *North Carolina Central College*

Focus Group Participants

Javier Aguirre, *Northeast Lakeview College*
Steven Boyd, *University of Texas—San Antonio*
Kathleen Brosnan, *University of Houston*
June Cheatham, *Richland College*
Andrea Crosson, *University of Texas—San Antonio*
Kevin Davis, *North Central Texas College*
Ambronita Douzart, Ph.D., *Richland College*
Mike Downs, *University of Texas—Arlington*
Rex Field, *Palo Alto College*
Ronald Goodwin, *Prairie View A&M University*
Devethia Guillory, *Prairie View A&M University*
David Hansen, *University of Texas—San Antonio*
Scott Hickle, *Blinn College—Bryan*
Matt Hinkley, *Eastfield College*
Valerie Hinton, *Richland College*
Alan Johnson, *HCC—Northeast College*
James Jones, *Prairie View A&M University*
Carol Keller, *San Antonio College*
Gregory Kosc, *University of Texas—Arlington*
Karen Marcotte, *Palo Alto College*
Linda McCabe, *Tarrant County College Northeast*
Suzanne McFadden, *Austin Community College—Riverside*
Peter Myers, *Palo Alto College*
Michelle Novak, *HCC—Southeast College*
Darren Pierson, *Blinn College—Bryan*
Linda Reed, *University of Houston*
Beverly Tomek, *Wharton County Junior College*
Joel Tovanche, *Tarrant County College*
Victor Vigorito, *Austin Community College—Rio Grande*
Armando Villarreal, *Tarrant County College South*
Rudy Villarreal, *HCC—Northeast College*
Eric Walther, *University of Houston*
Roger Ward, *Collin College—Plano*
Christopher Whitaker, *Lee College*
Laura Matysek Wood, *Tarrant County College Northwest*

FIRST ENCOUNTERS WITH NATIVE AMERICANS This 1505 engraving is one of the earliest European images of the way Native Americans lived in the Americas. It also represents some of the ways in which white Europeans would view the people they called Indians for many generations. Native Americans here are portrayed as exotic savages, whose sexuality was not contained within stable families and whose savagery was evidenced in their practice of eating the flesh of their slain enemies. In the background are the ships that have brought the European visitors who recorded these images. (The Granger Collection, New York)

1 THE COLLISION OF CULTURES

THE DISCOVERY OF THE AMERICAS did not begin with Christopher Columbus in 1492. It began many thousands of years earlier when human beings first crossed into the American continents and began to people them. By the end of the fifteenth century A.D., when the first important contact with Europeans occurred, the Americas were the home of millions of men and women.

These ancient civilizations experienced many changes and many catastrophes during their long history. But none of these experiences was likely as tragically transforming as the arrival of Europeans. In the short term—in the first violent years of Spanish and Portuguese exploration and conquest—the impact of the new arrivals was profound. Europeans brought with them diseases (most notably smallpox) to which natives, unlike the invaders, had no immunity. The result was a great demographic catastrophe that killed millions of people, weakened existing societies, and greatly aided the Spanish and Portuguese in their rapid and devastating conquest of the existing American empires. Although in the long term European settlers came to dominate most areas of the Americas, the Europeans were never able to eliminate the influence of the existing

SETTING THE STAGE

peoples (whom they came to call "Indians"). Battles

between natives and Europeans continued into the late nineteenth century and beyond. But there were also more productive interactions through which these very different civilizations shaped one another, learned from one another, and changed each other permanently and profoundly.

LOOKING AHEAD

1. How did the societies of native peoples in the south differ from those in the north in the precontact period (before the arrival of the Europeans)?
2. What effects did the arrival of Europeans have on the native peoples of the Americas?
3. How did patterns of settlement differ among the Spanish, English, French, and Dutch immigrants to the Americas?

AMERICA BEFORE COLUMBUS

We know relatively little about the first peoples in the Americas. What we do know comes from scattered archaeological discoveries—new evidence from artifacts that have survived over many millennia.

THE PEOPLES OF THE PRECONTACT AMERICAS

For many decades, scholars believed that all early migrations into the Americas came from humans crossing an ancient land bridge over the Bering Strait into what is now Alaska, approximately 11,000 years ago. These migrants then traveled from the glacial north, through an unfrozen corridor between two great ice sheets, until they reached the nonglacial lands to the south. The migrations were probably a result of the development of new stone tools—spears and other hunting implements—with which it became possible to pursue the large animals that regularly crossed between Asia and North America. All of these land-based migrants are thought to have come from a Mongolian stock related to that of modern-day Siberia. They are known to scholars as the "Clovis" people, named for a town in New Mexico where archaeologists first discovered evidence of their tools and weapons in the 1930s.

THE "CLOVIS" PEOPLE

More recent archaeological evidence, however, suggests that not all the early migrants came across the Bering Strait. Some migrants from Asia appear to have settled as far south as Chile and Peru even before people began moving into North America by land. This suggests that these first South Americans may have come not by land but by sea, using boats. Other discoveries on other continents have made clear that migrants had traveled by water much earlier to populate Japan, Australia, and other areas of the Pacific. Those discoveries suggest that migrants were capable of making long ocean voyages—long enough perhaps to bring them to the American coasts.

ARCHAEOLOGISTS AND POPULATION DIVERSITY

This new evidence suggests, therefore, that the early population of the Americas was much more diverse and more scattered than scholars used to believe. Some people came to the Americas from farther south in Asia than Mongolia—perhaps Polynesia and Japan. Recent DNA evidence has identified what may have been yet another population group that, unlike most other American groups, does not seem to have Asian characteristics. Thus it is also possible that, thousands of years before Columbus, there may have been some migration from Europe or Africa. Most Indians in the Americas today share relatively similar characteristics, and those characteristics link them to modern Siberians and Mongolians. But that does not prove that Mongolian migrants were the first and only immigrants to the Americas. It suggests, rather, that Mongolian migrants eventually came to dominate and perhaps eliminate earlier population groups.

THE "ARCHAIC" PERIOD

The "Archaic" period is a scholarly term for the history of humans in America during a period of about 5,000 years beginning around 8000 B.C. In the first part of this period, most humans continued to support themselves through hunting and gathering, using the same stone tools that earlier Americans had brought with them from Asia. Some of the largest animals that the earliest humans in America once hunted became extinct during the Archaic period. But people continued to hunt with spears—for example, the Indians in the area later known as the Great Plains of North America who, then as centuries later, pursued bison (also known as buffalo). Bows and arrows were unknown in most of North America until 400–500 A.D.

Later in the Archaic period, population groups also began to expand their activities and to develop new tools to facilitate them. Among them were nets and hooks for fishing, traps for the smaller animals that they gradually began to pursue, and baskets for gathering berries, nuts, seeds, and other plants. Still later, some groups began to farm. Through much of the Americas, the most important farm crop was corn, but many agricultural communities also grew other crops such as beans and squash. Farming, of course, requires people to stay in one place. In agricultural areas, the first sedentary settlements slowly began to form, creating the basis for larger civilizations.

THE GROWTH OF CIVILIZATIONS: THE SOUTH

The most elaborate early civilizations emerged south of what is now the United States—in South and Central America and in what is now Mexico. In Peru, the Incas created the largest empire in the Americas. They began as a small tribe in the mountainous region of Cuzco, in the early fifteenth century—spurred by a powerful leader, Pachacuti (whose name meant "world shaker"). He incorporated into his empire lands stretching along almost 2,000 miles of western South America. It was an empire created as much by persuasion as by force. Pachacuti's agents fanned out around the region and explained the benefits of the empire to people in the areas the Incas hoped to control. Most local leaders eventually agreed to ally themselves with the Incas. The empire was sustained by innovative administrative systems and by the creation of a large network of paved roads.

Another great civilization emerged from the so-called Meso-Americans, the peoples of what is now Mexico and much of Central America. Organized societies emerged in these regions as early as 10,000 B.C. and the first truly complex society in the Americas—of the Olmec people—began in approximately 1000 B.C. A more sophisticated culture emerged beginning around 800 A.D. in parts of Central America and in the Yucatán peninsula of Mexico, in an area known as Maya (a term subsequently used to describe the various tribes who populated the region). Mayan civilization developed a written language, a numerical system similar to the Arabic, an accurate calendar, an advanced agricultural system, and important trade routes into other areas of the continents.

NORTH AMERICAN MIGRATIONS This map tracks some of the early migrations into, and within, North America in the centuries preceding contact with Europe. The map shows the now-vanished land bridge between Siberia and Alaska over which thousands, perhaps millions, of migrating people passed into the Americas. It also shows the locations of some of the earliest settlements in North America.

• *What role did the extended glacial field in what is now Canada have on residential patterns in the ancient American world?*

Gradually, the societies of the Maya regions were superseded by other Meso-American tribes, who have become known collectively (and somewhat inaccurately) as the Aztec. They called themselves Mexica, a name that eventually came to describe people of a number of different tribes. In about 1300 A.D., the Mexica established a city, which they named Tenochtitlán, on a large island in a lake in central Mexico, the site of present-day Mexico City. The Mexica soon incorporated the peoples of other tribes into their society as well. It became by far the greatest city ever created in the Americas to that point, with a population as high as 100,000 by 1500, connected to water supplies from across the region by aqueducts. The residents of Tenochtitlán also created large and impressive public buildings, schools that all male children attended, an organized military, a medical system, and a slave workforce drawn from conquered tribes. They gradually established their

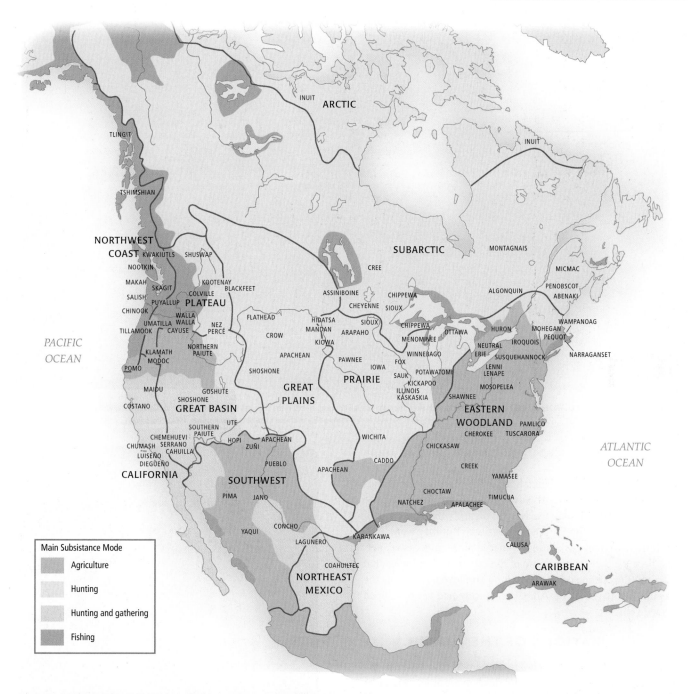

HOW THE EARLY NORTH AMERICANS LIVED This map shows the various ways in which the native tribes of North America supported themselves before the arrival of European civilization. Like most precommercial peoples, the native Americans survived largely on the resources available in their immediate surroundings. Note, for example, the reliance on the products of the sea of the tribes along the northern coastlines of the continent, and the way in which tribes in relatively inhospitable climates in the North—where agriculture was difficult—relied on hunting large game. Most native Americans were farmers.

• *What different kinds of farming would have emerged in the very different climates of the agricultural regions shown on this map?*

dominance over almost all of central Mexico, and beyond, through a system of tribute (in essence a heavy tax paid in such goods as crops or cloth or animals) enforced by military power. The peoples ruled by the Mexica maintained a significant element of independence nevertheless, and many of them always considered the Mexica to be tyrannical rulers, but too powerful to resist.

Like other Meso-American societies, the Mexica developed a religion based on the belief that the gods drew their subsidence from human sacrifice. Unlike earlier societies in the Americas, whose sacrifices to the gods emphasized blood-letting and other mostly nonfatal techniques, the Mexica believed that the gods could be satisfied only by being fed the living hearts of humans. As a result, they sacrificed people—largely prisoners

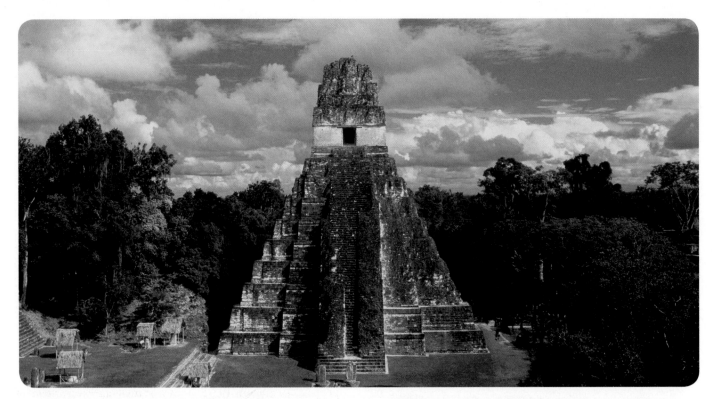

MAYAN TEMPLE, TIKAL Tikal was the largest city in what was then the vast Mayan Empire. It extended through what is now Mexico, Guatemala, and Belize. The temple shown here was built before 800 A.D and was one of many pyramids created by the Mayas. Only a few of these pyramids now survive. (M.L. Sinibaldi/Corbis)

captured in combat—on a scale unknown in other American civilizations.

The Meso-American civilizations were for many centuries the center of civilized life in North and Central America—the hub of culture and trade. Disease and disunity made it difficult for them to survive the European invasions. But they were, nevertheless, very great civilizations—all the more impressive, perhaps, because they lacked some of the crucial technologies that Asian and European societies had long employed. As late as the sixteenth century A.D., no American society had yet developed wheeled vehicles.

THE CIVILIZATIONS OF THE NORTH

The peoples north of Mexico—in the lands that became the United States and Canada—did not develop empires as large or political systems as elaborate as those of the Incas, Mayas, and Mexica. They did, however, build complex civilizations of great variety. Societies that subsisted on hunting, gathering, fishing, or some combination of the three emerged in the northern regions of the continent. The Eskimos of the Arctic Circle fished and hunted seals; their civilization spanned thousands of miles of largely frozen land, which they traversed by dogsled. The big-game hunters of the northern forests led nomadic lives based on pursuit of moose and caribou. The tribes of the Pacific Northwest, whose principal occupation was salmon fishing, created substantial permanent settlements along the coast and engaged in constant and often violent competition with one another for access to natural resources.

COMPLEX AND VARIED CIVILIZATIONS

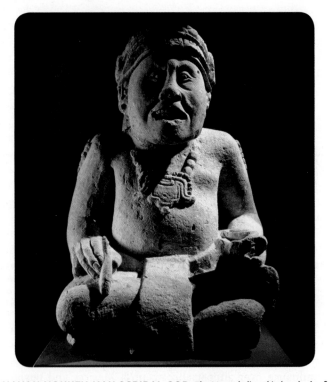

MAYAN MONKEY-MAN SCRIBAL GOD The Mayas believed in hundreds of different gods, and they attempted to personify many of them in sculptures such as the one depicted here, which dates from before 900 A.D. The monkey gods were believed to be twins who took the form of monkeys after being lured into a tree from which they could not descend. According to legend, they abandoned their loincloths, which then became tails, which they then used to move more effectively up and down trees. The monkey-men were the patrons of writing, dancing, and art. (The Art Archive/Archaeological Museum Copán Honduras/Alfredo Dagli Orti)

CAHOKIA An artist's rendition of the city of Cahokia circa 1100 A.D. Its great earthen mounds, constructed by the Cahokia Indians near present-day St. Louis, have endured into modern times as part of the Missouri landscape. (Courtesy of Cahokia Mounds State Historic Site, Collinsville, Illinois. Painting by William R. Iseminger)

Another group of tribes spread through relatively arid regions of the Far West and developed successful communities—many of them quite wealthy and densely populated—based on fishing, hunting small game, and gathering. Other societies in North America were primarily agricultural. Among the most elaborate were those in the Southwest. The people of that region built large irrigation systems to allow farming on their relatively dry land, and they constructed substantial towns that became centers of trade, crafts, and religious and civic ritual. Their densely populated settlements at Chaco Canyon and elsewhere consisted of stone and adobe terraced structures, known today as pueblos, many of which resembled the large apartment buildings of later eras in size and design. In the Great Plains region, too, most tribes were engaged in sedentary farming (corn and other grains) and lived in substantial permanent settlements, although there were some small nomadic tribes that subsisted by hunting buffalo. (Only in the eighteenth century, after Europeans had introduced the horse to North America, did buffalo hunting begin to support a large population in the region; at that point, many once-sedentary farmers left the land to pursue the great migratory buffalo herds.)

The eastern third of what is now the United States—much of it covered with forests and inhabited by people who have thus become known as the Woodland Indians—had the greatest food resources of any region of the continent. Many tribes lived there, and most of them engaged simultaneously in farming, hunting, gathering, and fishing. In the South there were for a time substantial permanent settlements and large trading networks based on corn and other grains grown in the rich lands of the Mississippi River valley. Among the major cities that emerged as a result of trade was Cahokia (near present-day St. Louis), which at its peak in 1200 A.D. had a population of about 10,000 and contained a great complex of large earthen mounds.

The agricultural societies of the Northeast were more nomadic than those in other regions. Much of the land in the region was less fertile than other regions because farming was newer and less established. Most tribes combined farming with hunting. Farming techniques in the Northeast were usually designed to exploit the land quickly rather than to develop permanent settlements. Natives often cleared the land by setting forest fires or cutting into trees to kill them. They then planted crops—corn, beans, squash, pumpkins, and others—among the dead or blackened trunks. After a few years, when the land became exhausted or the filth from a settlement began to accumulate, they moved on and established themselves elsewhere. In some parts of eastern North America, villages dispersed every winter and families foraged for themselves in the wilderness until warm weather returned; those who survived then reassembled to begin farming again.

Many of the tribes living east of the Mississippi River were linked together loosely by common linguistic roots. The largest of the language groups was the Algonquian, which dominated the Atlantic seaboard from Canada to Virginia. Another important language group was the Iroquoian, centered in what is now upstate New York. The Iroquois included at least five distinct northern "nations"—the Seneca, Cayuga, Onondaga, Oneida, and Mohawk—and had links as well with the Cherokees and the Tuscaroras farther south, in the Carolinas and Georgia. The third-largest language group—the Muskogean—included the tribes in the southernmost region of the eastern seaboard: the Chickasaws, Choctaws, Creeks, and Seminoles. Alliances among the various Indian societies (even among those with common languages) were fragile, since the peoples of the

MOBILE SOCIETIES

WHY DO HISTORIANS SO OFTEN DIFFER?

EARLY in the twentieth century, when the professional study of history was still relatively new, many historians believed that questions about the past could be answered with the same certainty and precision that questions in other, more scientific fields could be answered. By sifting through available records, using precise methods of research and analysis, and producing careful, closely argued accounts of the past, they believed they could create definitive histories that would survive without controversy. Scholars who adhered to this view and

GEORGE BANCROFT (© Corbis)

RICHARD HOFSTADTER (© Bernard Gotfryd/ Getty Images)

Americas did not think of themselves as members of a single civilization. When Europeans arrived and began to threaten their way of life, Indians generally viewed the intruders as another tribe to be resisted. Only rarely did native tribes unite in opposition to challenges from whites.

TRIBAL CULTURES

The enormous diversity of economic, social, and political structures among the North American Indians makes large generalizations about their cultures difficult. In the last centuries before the arrival of Europeans, however, Native Americans—like peoples in other areas of the world—were experiencing an agricultural revolution. In all

> WHEN EUROPEANS ARRIVED AND BEGAN TO THREATEN THEIR WAY OF LIFE, INDIANS GENERALLY VIEWED THE INTRUDERS AS ANOTHER TRIBE TO BE RESISTED.

AGRICULTURAL REVOLUTION

regions of the United States (if in varying degrees from place to place), tribes were becoming more sedentary and were developing new sources of food, clothing, and shelter. Most regions were experiencing significant population growth. Virtually all were developing the sorts of elaborate social customs and rituals that only relatively stationary societies can produce. Religion was as important to Indian society as it was to most other cultures, and it was usually closely bound up with the natural world on which the tribes depended. Native Americans worshiped many gods, whom they associated variously with crops, game, forests, rivers, and other elements of nature. Some tribes believed that real knowledge can be derived only from direct, scientific observation of clear "facts" were known as "positivists."

Although a vigorous debate continues to this day over whether historical research can or should be truly objective, almost no historian any longer accepts the "positivist" claim that history could ever be an exact science. Disagreement about the past is, in fact, at the heart of the effort to understand history. Critics of contemporary historical scholarship often denounce the way historians are constantly revising earlier interpretations; some denounce the act of interpretation itself. History, they claim, is "what happened." Historians should "stick to the facts."

Historians, however, continue to differ with one another both because the "facts" are seldom as straightforward as their critics claim and because facts by themselves mean almost nothing without an effort to assign meaning to them. Some historical "facts," of course, are not in dispute. Everyone agrees, for example, that the Japanese bombed Pearl Harbor on December 7, 1941, and that Abraham Lincoln was elected president in 1860. But many other "facts" are much harder to determine—among them, for example, the question of how large the American population was before the arrival of Columbus, which is discussed later in this chapter. How many slaves resisted slavery? This sounds like a reasonably straightforward question, but it is almost impossible to answer with any certainty—because the records of slave resistance are spotty and the definition of "resistance" is a matter of considerable dispute.

Even when a set of facts is clear and straightforward, historians disagree—sometimes quite radically—over what they mean. Those disagreements can be the result of political and ideological disagreements. Some of the most vigorous debates in recent decades have been between scholars who believe that economic interests and class divisions are the key to understanding the past, and those who believe that ideas and culture are at least as important as material interests. The disagreements can be a result of the particular perspectives that people of different backgrounds bring to the study of the past. Whites and people of color, men and women, people from the American South and people from the North, young people and older people: these and many other points of difference find their way into scholarly disagreements. Debates can also occur over differences in methodology—between those who believe that quantitative studies can answer important historical questions and those who believe that other methods come closer to the truth.

Most of all, perhaps, historical interpretation changes in response to the time in which it is written. Historians may strive to be "objective" in their work, but no one can be entirely free from the assumptions and concerns of the present. In the 1950s, the omnipresent shadow of the Cold War had a profound effect on the way most historians viewed the past. In the 1960s, concerns about racial justice and disillusionment with the Vietnam War altered the way many historians viewed the past. Those events introduced a much more critical tone to scholarship and turned the attention of scholars away from politics and government and toward the study of society and culture.

Many areas of scholarship in recent decades are embroiled in a profound debate over whether there is such a thing as "truth." The world, some scholars argue, is simply a series of "narratives" constructed by people who view life in very different and often highly personal ways. "Truth" does not really exist. Everything is a product of interpretation. Not many historians embrace such radical ideas; most would agree that interpretations, to be of any value, must rest on a solid foundation of observable facts. But historians do recognize that even the most compelling facts are subject to many different interpretations and that the process of understanding the past is a forever continuing—and forever contested—process. •

UNDERSTAND, ANALYZE, AND EVALUATE

1. What are some of the reasons historians so often disagree?
2. Is there ever a "right" or "wrong" in historical interpretation? What value might historical inquiry have other than reaching a "right" or "wrong" conclusion?
3. If historians so often disagree, how should a student of history approach historical content? How might disagreement expand our understanding of history?

created elaborate, brightly colored totems as part of their religious ritual; most staged large festivals on such important occasions as harvests or major hunts.

As in other parts of the world, the societies of North America tended to divide tasks according to gender. All tribes assigned women the jobs of caring for children, preparing meals, and gathering certain foods. But the allocation of other tasks varied from one society to another. Some tribal groups (notably the Pueblos of the Southwest) reserved farming tasks almost entirely for men. Among others (including the Algonquins, the Iroquois, and the Muskogees), women tended the fields, while men engaged in hunting, warfare, or clearing land. Iroquois women and children were often left alone for extended periods while men were away hunting or fighting battles. As a result, women tended to control the social and economic organization of the settlements and played powerful roles within families.

EUROPE LOOKS WESTWARD

Europeans were almost entirely unaware of the existence of the Americas before the fifteenth century. A few early wanderers—Leif Eriksson, an eleventh-century Norse seaman, and perhaps others—had glimpsed parts of the New World and had demonstrated that Europeans were capable of crossing the ocean to reach it. But even if their discoveries had become common knowledge (and they had not), there would have been little incentive for others to follow. Europe in the Middle Ages (roughly 500–1500 A.D.) was not an adventurous civilization. Divided into innumerable small duchies and kingdoms, Europe had an overwhelmingly provincial outlook. Subsistence agriculture predominated, and commerce was limited; few merchants looked beyond the boundaries of their own regions. The Roman Catholic Church exercised a measure of spiritual authority over

THE AMERICAN POPULATION BEFORE COLUMBUS

NO one knows how many people lived in the Americas in the centuries before Columbus. But scholars and other researchers have spent more than a century and have written many thousands of pages debating the question nevertheless. Interest in this question survives, despite the near impossibility of answering it, because the debate over the pre-Columbian population is closely connected to the much larger debate over the consequences of European settlement of the Western Hemisphere.

Throughout the nineteenth century, Native Americans spoke often of the great days before Columbus when there were many more people in their tribes. They drew from their own rich tradition of oral history handed down through storytelling from one generation to another. The painter and ethnographer George Catlin, who spent much time among the tribes in the 1830s painting portraits of a race that he feared was "fast passing to extinction," listened to these oral legends and estimated that there had been 16 million Indians in North America before the Europeans came. Other white Americans dismissed such claims as preposterous, insisting that Indian civilization was far too primitive to have been able to sustain so large a population.

In 1928, James Mooney, an ethnologist at the Smithsonian Institution, drew from early accounts of soldiers and missionaries in the sixteenth century and came up with the implausibly precise figure of 1.15 million natives who lived north of Mexico in the

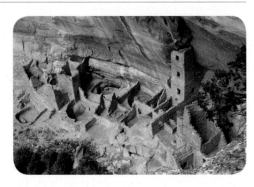

(Wil Meinderts/Foto Natura/Getty Images)

early sixteenth century. That was a larger figure than nineteenth-century writers had suggested, but still much smaller than the Indians themselves claimed. A few years later, the anthropologist Alfred Kroeber used many of Mooney's

most of the continent, and the Holy Roman Empire provided at least a nominal political center. Even so, real power was for the most part widely dispersed; only rarely could a single leader launch a great venture. Gradually, however, conditions in Europe changed so that by the late fifteenth century, interest in overseas exploration had grown.

COMMERCE AND NATIONALISM

Two important and related changes provided the first incentive for Europeans to look toward new lands. One was a result of the significant population growth in fifteenth-century Europe. The Black Death, a catastrophic epidemic of the bubonic plague that began in Constantinople in 1347, had decimated Europe, killing (according to some estimates) more than a third of the people of the continent and debilitating its already limited economy. But a century and a half later, the population had rebounded. With

A REAWAKENING
OF COMMERCE

that growth came a rise in land values, a reawakening of commerce, and a general increase in prosperity. Affluent landlords became eager to purchase goods from distant regions, and a new merchant class emerged to meet their demand. As trade increased, and as advances in navigation and shipbuilding made long-distance sea travel more feasible, interest in developing new markets, finding new products, and opening new trade routes rapidly increased.

Paralleling the rise of commerce in Europe, and in part responsible for it, was the rise of new governments that were more united and powerful than the feeble political entities of the feudal past. In the western areas of Europe, the authority of the distant pope and the even more distant Holy Roman Emperor was necessarily weak. As a result, strong new monarchs emerged and created centralized nation-states, with national courts, national armies, and—perhaps most important— national tax systems. As these ambitious kings and queens consolidated their power and increased their wealth, they became eager to enhance the commercial growth of their nations.

CENTRALIZED
NATION-STATES

Ever since the early fourteenth century, when Marco Polo and other adventurers had returned from Asia bearing exotic goods (spices, fabrics, dyes) and even more exotic tales, Europeans who hoped for commercial glory had dreamed above all of trade with the East. For two centuries, that trade had been limited by the difficulties of the long, arduous overland journey to the Asian courts. But in the fourteenth century, as the maritime capabilities of several western European societies increased and as Muslim societies seized control of the eastern routes to Asia, there began to be serious talk of finding a faster, safer sea route to Asia. Such dreams found a receptive audience in the courts of the new monarchs. By the late fifteenth century, some of them were ready to finance daring voyages of exploration.

methods to come up with an estimate of the population of the entire Western Hemisphere—considerably larger than Mooney's, but much lower than Catlin's. He concluded in 1934 that there were 8.4 million people in the Americas in 1492, half in North America and half in the Caribbean and South America.

These low early estimates reflected, more than anything else, an assumption that the arrival of the Europeans did not much reduce the native population. But in the 1960s and 1970s, scholars discovered that the early tribes had been catastrophically decimated by European plagues not long after the arrival of Columbus—meaning that the numbers Europeans observed even in the late 1500s were already dramatically smaller than the numbers in 1492. Drawing on early work by anthropologists and others who discovered evidence of widespread deaths by disease, historians William McNeill in 1976 and Alfred Crosby a decade later, as well as other scholars, produced powerful accounts of the near extinction of some tribes and the dramatic depopulation of others in a pestilential catastrophe with few parallels in history. Almost all scholars now accept that much, perhaps most, of the native population was wiped out by disease—smallpox, measles, tuberculosis, and other plagues imported from Europe.

The belief that the native population was much bigger in 1492 than it would be a few decades later has helped spur much larger estimates of how many people were in America before Columbus. Henry Dobyns, an anthropologist who was one of the earliest scholars to challenge the early, low estimates, claimed in 1966 that in 1492 there were between 10 and 12 million people north of Mexico and between 90 and 112 million in all of the Americas. No subsequent scholar has made so high a claim, but most estimates that followed have been much closer to Dobyns's than to Kroeber's. The geographer William M. Denevan, for example, argued in 1976 that the American population in 1492 was around 55 million and that the population north of Mexico was under 4 million. Those are among the lowest of modern estimates, but still dramatically higher than the nineteenth-century numbers.

The vehemence with which scholars, and at times the larger public, have debated these figures is not just because it is very difficult to determine population size. It is also because the debate over the population is part of the debate over whether the arrival of Columbus—and the millions of Europeans who followed him—was a great advance in the history of civilization or an unparalleled catastrophe that virtually exterminated a large and flourishing native population. How to balance the many achievements of European civilization in the New World after 1492 against the terrible destruction of native peoples that accompanied it is, in the end, less a historical question, perhaps, than a moral one. •

UNDERSTAND, ANALYZE, AND EVALUATE

1. Why is there such interest in and such vehement disagreement about the population of native peoples of the Americas in the pre-contact period?
2. What are some of the difficulties in trying to determine the size of the pre-Columbian population?
3. What are the advantages and disadvantages of using oral history as a source of information about the past?

The first to do so were the Portuguese. They were the pre-eminent maritime power in the fifteenth century, in large part

PRINCE HENRY THE NAVIGATOR

because of the work of one man, Prince Henry the Navigator. Henry's own principal interest was not in finding a sea route to Asia, but in exploring the western coast of Africa. He dreamed of establishing a Christian empire there to aid in his country's wars against the Moors of northern Africa; and he hoped to find new stores of gold. The explorations he began did not fulfill his own hopes, but they ultimately led farther than he had dreamed. Some of Henry's mariners went as far south as Cape Verde, on Africa's west coast. In 1486 (six years after Henry's death), Bartholomeu Dias rounded the southern tip of Africa (the Cape of Good Hope); and in 1497–1498 Vasco da Gama proceeded all the way around the cape to India. In 1500, the next fleet bound for India, under the command of Pedro Cabral, was blown westward off its southerly course and happened upon the coast of Brazil. But by then another man, in the service of another country, had already encountered the New World.

IROQUOIS WOMEN This 1734 French engraving shows Iroquois women at work in a settlement somewhere in what is now upstate New York. In the foreground, women are cooking. Others are working in the fields. Men spent much of their time hunting and soldiering, leaving the women to govern and dominate the internal lives of the villages. Property in Iroquois society was inherited through the mother, and women occupied positions of great authority within the tribes. (Library of Congress)

THE INDIAN VILLAGE OF SECOTON (C. 1585), BY JOHN WHITE John White created this illustration of life among the Eastern Woodland Indians in coastal North Carolina. It shows the diversified agriculture practiced by the natives: squash, tobacco, and three varieties of corn. The hunters shown in nearby woods suggest another element of the native economy. At bottom right, Indians perform a religious ritual, which White described as "strange gestures and songs."
(British Museum)

CHRISTOPHER COLUMBUS

Christopher Columbus, who was born and reared in Genoa, Italy, obtained most of his early seafaring experience in the service of the Portuguese. As a young man, he became intrigued with the possibility, already under discussion in many seafaring circles, of reaching Asia by going not east but west. Columbus's hopes rested on several basic misconceptions. He believed that the world was far smaller than it actually is. He also believed that the Asian continent extended farther eastward than it actually does. He assumed, therefore, that the Atlantic was narrow enough to be crossed on a relatively brief voyage. It did not occur to him that anything lay to the west between Europe and Asia.

Columbus failed to win support for his plan in Portugal, so he turned to Spain. The Spaniards were not yet as advanced a maritime people as the Portuguese, but they were at least as energetic and ambitious. And in the fifteenth century, the marriage of Spain's two most powerful regional rulers, Ferdinand of Aragon and Isabella of Castile, had produced the strongest monarchy in Europe. Like other young monarchies, Spain soon grew eager to demonstrate its strength by sponsoring new commercial ventures.

Columbus appealed to Queen Isabella for support for his proposed westward voyage. In 1492, Isabella agreed to Columbus's request. Commanding ninety men and three ships—the *Niña,* the *Pinta,* and the *Santa María*—Columbus left Spain in August 1492 and sailed west into the Atlantic on what he thought was a straight course for Japan. Ten weeks later, he sighted land and assumed he had reached his target. In fact, he had landed on an island in the Bahamas. When he pushed on and encountered Cuba, he assumed he had reached China. He returned to Spain in triumph, bringing with him several captured natives as evidence of his achievement. (He called the natives "Indians" because he believed they were from the East Indies in the Pacific.)

> COLUMBUS'S FIRST VOYAGE

But Columbus had not, of course, encountered the court of the great khan in China or the fabled wealth of the Indies. A year later, therefore, he tried again, this time with a much larger expedition. As before, he headed into the Caribbean, discovering several other islands and leaving a small and short-lived colony on Hispaniola. On a third voyage, in 1498, he finally reached the mainland and cruised along the northern coast of South America. When he passed the mouth of the Orinoco River (in present-day Venezuela), he concluded for the first time that what he had discovered was not in fact an island off the coast of China, as he had assumed, but a separate continent; such a large freshwater stream, he realized, could emerge only from a large body of land. Still, he remained convinced that Asia was only a short distance away. And although he failed in his efforts to sail around the northeastern coast of South America to the Indies (he was blocked by the Isthmus of Panama), he returned to Spain believing that he had explored at least the fringes of the Far East. He continued to believe that for the rest of his life.

Columbus's celebrated accomplishments made him a popular hero for a time, but he ended his life in obscurity. When Europeans at last gave a name to the New World, they ignored him. The distinction went instead to a Florentine merchant, Amerigo Vespucci, a member of a later Portuguese expedition to the New World who wrote a series of vivid descriptions of the lands he had visited and who recognized the Americas as new continents.

Columbus has been celebrated for centuries as the "Admiral of the Ocean Sea" (a title he struggled to have officially bestowed on him during his lifetime) and as a representative of the new, secular, scientific impulses of Renaissance Europe. But Columbus was also a deeply religious man, even something of a mystic. His voyages were inspired as much by his conviction that he was fulfilling a divine mission as by his

> RELIGIOUS MOTIVES FOR EXPLORATION

CHRISTOPHER COLUMBUS In this somewhat idealized drawing, created several years after Christopher Columbus's historic voyage to the New World, Columbus stands in the bow of his ship, a suit of armor ready at his feet, approaching a shore in the New World that he believed was in fact part of Asia. (Library of Congress)

interest in geography and trade. A strong believer in biblical prophecies, he came to see himself as a man destined to advance the coming of the millennium. "God made me the messenger of the new heaven and the new earth," Columbus wrote near the end of his life, "and he showed me the spot where to find it." A similar combination of worldly and religious passions lay behind many subsequent efforts at exploration and settlement of the New World.

Partly as a result of Columbus's initiative, Spain began to devote greater resources and energy to maritime exploration and gradually replaced Portugal as the leading seafaring nation. The Spaniard Vasco de Balboa fought his way across the Isthmus of Panama in 1513 and became the first known European to gaze westward upon the great ocean that separated America from China and the Indies. Seeking access to

> **❝ GOD MADE ME THE MESSENGER OF THE NEW HEAVEN AND THE NEW EARTH, AND HE SHOWED ME THE SPOT WHERE TO FIND IT. ❞**
>
> **CHRISTOPHER COLUMBUS**

FERDINAND MAGELLAN

that ocean, Ferdinand Magellan, a Portuguese in the employ of the Spanish, found the strait that now bears his name at the southern end of South America, struggled through the stormy narrows and into the ocean (so calm by contrast that he christened it the "Pacific"), then proceeded to the Philippines. There Magellan died in a conflict with the natives, but his expedition went on to complete the first known circumnavigation of the globe (1519–1522). By 1550, Spaniards had explored the coasts of North America as far north as Oregon in the west and Labrador in the east, as well as some of the interior regions of the continent.

THE CONQUISTADORES

In time, Spanish explorers in the New World stopped thinking of America simply as an obstacle to their search for a route to the East. They began instead to consider it a possible source of wealth rivaling and even surpassing the original Indies. On the basis of Columbus's discoveries, the Spanish claimed for themselves the whole of the New World, except for a piece of it (today's Brazil) that was reserved by a papal decree for the Portuguese. By the mid-sixteenth century, the Spanish were well on their way to establishing a substantial American empire.

The first Spanish colonists, whom Columbus brought on his second voyage, settled on the islands of the Caribbean, where they tried to enslave the Indians and find gold. They had little luck in either effort. But then, in 1518, Hernando Cortés led a small military expedition of about 600 men into Mexico. Cortés had been a Spanish government official in Cuba for fourteen years and to that point had achieved little success. But when he heard stories of great treasures in Mexico, he decided to go in

CORTÉS CONQUERS THE AZTECS

search of them. He met strong and resourceful resistance from the Aztecs and their powerful emperor, Montezuma. But Cortés and his army had, unknowingly, unleashed an assault on the Aztecs far more devastating than military attack: they had exposed the natives to smallpox during an early and relatively peaceful visit to Tenochtitlán. A smallpox epidemic decimated the population and made it possible for the Spanish to triumph in their second attempt at conquest. The Spanish saw the epidemic as vindication of their efforts. When the Christians were exhausted from war, one follower of Cortés said at the time, "God saw fit to send the Indians smallpox." Through his ruthless suppression of the surviving natives, Cortés established a lasting reputation as the most brutal of the Spanish *conquistadores* (conquerors).

The news that silver was to be found in Mexico attracted the attention of other Spaniards. From the island colonies and from Spain itself, a wave of conquistadores descended on the mainland in search of fortune. Francisco Pizarro, who conquered Peru (1532–1538) and revealed to Europeans the wealth of the Incas, opened the way for other advances into South America. His

EUROPEAN EXPLORATION AND CONQUEST, 1492–1583 This map shows the many voyages of exploration and conquest of North America launched by Europeans in the late fifteenth and sixteenth centuries. Note how Columbus and the Spanish explorers who followed him tended to move quickly into the lands of Mexico, the Caribbean, and Central and South America, while the English and French explored the northern territories of North America.

• *What factors might have led these various nations to explore and colonize these different areas of the New World?*

THE MEXICANS STRIKE BACK In this vivid scene from the Duran Codex, Mexican artists illustrate a rare moment in which Mexican warriors gained the upper hand over the Spanish invaders. Driven back by native fighters, the Spanish have taken refuge in a room in the royal palace in Tenochtitlán while brightly attired Mexican warriors besiege them. Although the Mexicans gained a temporary advantage in this battle, the drawing illustrates one of the reasons for their inability to withstand the Spanish in the longer term. The Spanish soldiers are armed with rifles and crossbows, while the Indians carry only spears and shields. (Oronoz Archivo)

onetime deputy Hernando de Soto, in a futile search for gold, silver, and jewels, led several expeditions (1539–1541) through Florida west into the continent and became the first white man known to have crossed the Mississippi River. Francisco Coronado traveled north from Mexico (1540–1542) into what is now New

PIZARRO IN PERU A European artist depicted Pizarro's arrival on the coast of Peru in the early 1530s, where he was greeted by crowds of hostile Indians. By 1538, Pizarro had conquered the empire of the Incas. (Library of Congress)

Mexico in a similarly fruitless search for gold and jewels; in the process, he helped open the Southwest of what is now the United States to Spanish settlement.

The story of the Spanish warriors is one of great military daring and achievement. It is also a story of great brutality and greed—a story that would be repeated time and again over centuries of European conquest of the Americas. The conquistadores subjugated and, in some areas, almost exterminated the native populations through a combination of warfare and disease.

BRUTALITY AND GREED

SPANISH AMERICA

Lured by dreams of treasure, Spanish explorers, conquistadores, and colonists established a vast empire for Spain in the New World. The history of the Spanish Empire spanned three distinct periods. The first was the age of discovery and exploration—beginning with Columbus and continuing through the first two decades of the sixteenth century. The second was the age of the conquest, in which Spanish military forces (aided by the diseases they unleashed) established their dominion over the lands once ruled by natives. The third phase began in the 1570s, when new Spanish laws—the Ordinances of Discovery—banned the most brutal military conquests. From that point on, the Spanish expanded their presence in America through colonization.

ORDINANCES OF DISCOVERY

DE SOTO IN NORTH AMERICA This gruesome drawing portrays Spanish troops under Hernando de Soto massacring a group of Mobile Indians in what is now Alabama, in the winter of 1540–1541. De Soto had been governor of Cuba, but in 1539 he sailed to Florida with 600 troops and for the next several years traveled through large areas of what would later become the southern United States until he died of fever in 1542. Here, as elsewhere, his troops dealt with the Indian tribes they encountered along the way with unrestrained brutality. (Rare Books and Special Collections, Library of Congress)

The first Spaniards to arrive in the New World, the conquistadores, had been interested in only one thing: getting rich. And in that they were fabulously successful. For 300 years, beginning in the sixteenth century, the mines in Spanish America yielded more than ten times as much gold and silver as the rest of the world's mines put together. These riches made Spain the wealthiest and most powerful nation on earth for a time.

After the first wave of conquest, however, most Spanish settlers in America traveled to the New World for other reasons. Many went in hopes of creating a profitable agricultural economy. Unlike the conquistadores, who left little but destruction behind them, these settlers helped establish elements of European civilization in America that permanently altered both the landscape and the social structure.

Another important force for colonization was the Catholic Church. Ferdinand and Isabella, in establishing Spain's claim to most of the Americas from Mexico south, bowed to the wishes of the Church and established the requirement that Catholicism be the only religion of the new territories. Spain abided by that condition. Although the Spanish founded commercial and military centers in the sixteenth century, another common form of settlement by the early seventeenth century

CATHOLIC MISSIONS

was the Catholic mission. Missions had commercial lives. But their primary purpose, at least at first, was converting natives to Catholicism. There were usually military garrisons connected to the missions, to protect the Europeans from hostile natives. *Presidios* (military bases) often grew up nearby to provide additional protection. Indeed, after the era of the conquistadores came to a close in the 1540s, the missionary impulse became one of the most important motives for European emigration to America. Priests or friars accompanied almost all colonizing ventures. Through their zealous work, the gospel of the Catholic Church ultimately extended throughout South and Central America, Mexico, and into the South and Southwest of the present United States.

NORTHERN OUTPOSTS

ST. AUGUSTINE

The Spanish fort established in 1565 at St. Augustine, Florida, became the first permanent European settlement in what is now the United States. It served as a military outpost, an administrative center for Franciscan missionaries, and a headquarters for unsuccessful

SPANISH AMERICA From the time of Columbus's initial voyage in 1492 until the mid-nineteenth century, Spain was the dominant colonial power in the New World. From the southern regions of South America to the northern regions of the Pacific Northwest, Spain controlled one of the world's largest empires. Note how much of the Spanish Empire was simply grafted upon the earlier empires of native peoples—the Incas in what is today Chile and Peru, and the Aztecs across much of the rest of South America, Mexico, and the Southwest of what is now the United States.

• *What characteristics of Spanish colonization would account for Spain's preference for already-settled regions?*

campaigns against North American natives that were ultimately abandoned. But it did not mark the beginning of a substantial effort at colonization in the region.

A more substantial colonizing venture began thirty years later in the Southwest. In 1598, Don Juan de Oñate traveled north from Mexico with a party of 500 men. He claimed for Spain some of the lands of the Pueblo Indians that Coronado had passed through over fifty years before. The Spanish migrants established a colony in what is now New Mexico, modeled roughly on those the Spanish had created farther south. Oñate distributed *encomiendas* to the Spanish settlers. They were licenses to exact labor and tribute from the natives in specific areas (a system first used in dealing with the Moors in Spain). The Spanish demanded tribute from the local Indians (and at times commandeered them as laborers). Spanish colonists founded Santa Fe in 1609.

Oñate's harsh treatment of the natives (who greatly outnumbered the small Spanish population) threatened the stability of the new colony and led to his removal as governor in 1606. Over time, relations between the Spanish and the Pueblos improved. Substantial numbers of Pueblos converted to Christianity under the influence of Spanish missionaries. Others entered into important trading relationships with the Spanish. The colony remained precarious nevertheless because of the danger from Apache and Navajo raiders, who threatened the Spanish and Pueblos alike. Even so, the New Mexico settlement continued to grow. By 1680, there were over 2,000 Spanish colonists living among about 30,000 Pueblos. The economic heart of the colony was not the gold and precious metals the early Spanish explorers had tried in vain to find. It was cattle and sheep, raised on the *ranchos* that stretched out around the small towns Spanish settlers established.

In 1680, the colony was nearly destroyed when the Pueblos rose in revolt. In the 1660s and 1670s, the Spanish priests and the colonial government, which was closely tied to the missionaries, launched efforts to suppress tribal rituals that Europeans considered incompatible with Christianity. The discontent among the natives at this suppression survived for decades. More important as a cause of the Pueblo revolt of 1680, however, was a major drought and a series of raids by neighboring Apache tribes. The instability these events produced sparked the uprising. An Indian religious leader named Pope led an uprising that killed hundreds of European settlers (including twenty-one priests), captured Santa Fe, and drove the Spanish temporarily from the region. But twelve years later the Spanish returned, resumed seizing Pueblo lands, and crushed a last revolt in 1696.

PUEBLO REVOLT OF 1680

Spanish exploitation of the Pueblos did not end. But after the revolts, many Spanish colonists realized that they could not prosper in New Mexico if they remained constantly in conflict with a native population that greatly outnumbered them. They tried to solve the problem in two ways. On the one hand, the Spanish intensified their efforts to assimilate the Indians—baptizing Indian children at birth and enforcing observance of Catholic rituals. On the other hand, they now permitted the Pueblos to own land; they stopped commandeering Indian labor; they replaced the encomienda system with a less demanding and oppressive one; and they tacitly tolerated the practice of tribal religious rituals.

These efforts were at least partially successful. After a while, there was significant intermarriage between Europeans and Indians. Increasingly, the Pueblos came to consider the Spanish their allies in the continuing battles with the Apaches and Navajos. By 1750, the Spanish population had grown modestly to about 4,000. The Pueblo population had declined (through disease, war, and migration) to about 13,000, less than half what it had been in 1680. New Mexico had by then become a reasonably stable but still weak and isolated outpost of the Spanish Empire.

THE EMPIRE AT HIGH TIDE

By the end of the sixteenth century, the Spanish Empire had become one of the largest in the history of the world. It included the islands of the Caribbean and the coastal areas of South America that had been the first targets of the Spanish expeditions. It extended to Mexico and southern North America, where a second wave of colonizers had established outposts. Most of all, the empire spread southward and westward into the vast landmass of South America—the areas that are now Chile, Argentina, and Peru. In 1580, when the Spanish and Portuguese monarchies temporarily united, Brazil came under Spanish jurisdiction as well.

SPAIN'S VAST EMPIRE

It was, however, a colonial empire very different from the one the English would establish in North America beginning in the early seventeenth century. Although the earliest Spanish ventures in the New World had been largely independent of the throne, by the end of the sixteenth century the monarchy had extended its authority directly into the governance of local communities. Colonists had few opportunities to establish political institutions independent of Spain. There was also a significant economic difference between the Spanish Empire and the later British one. The Spanish were far more successful than the British would be in extracting great surface wealth—gold and silver—from their American colonies. But they concentrated relatively less energy on making agriculture and commerce profitable in their colonies. The strict commercial policies of the Spanish government (policies that the British Empire was never strong enough to impose on their colonies to the north) made things worse. To enforce the collection of duties and to provide protection against pirates, the government established rigid and restrictive regulations that required all trade with the colonies to go through a single Spanish port and only a few colonial ports, in fleets making but two voyages a year. The system stifled economic development of the Spanish areas of the New World.

RIGID ROYAL CONTROL

There was also an important difference between the character of the population in the Spanish Empire and that of the colonies to the north. Almost from the beginning, the English, Dutch, and French colonies in North America concentrated on establishing permanent settlement and family life in the

New World. The Europeans in North America reproduced rapidly after their first difficult years and in time came to outnumber the natives. The Spanish, by contrast, ruled their empire but did not people it. In the first century of settlement, fewer than 250,000 settlers in the Spanish colonies were from Spain itself or from any other European country. Only about 200,000 more arrived in the first half of the seventeenth century. Some additional settlers came from various outposts of Spanish civilization in the Atlantic—the Azores, the Cape Verde Islands, and elsewhere; but even with these other sources, the number of European settlers in Spanish America remained very small relative to the native population. Despite the ravages of disease and war, the vast majority of the population of the Spanish Empire continued to consist of natives. The Spanish, in other words, imposed a small ruling class upon a much larger existing population; they did not create a self-contained European society in the New World as the English would attempt to do in the north.

A COLLISION OF CULTURES

BIOLOGICAL AND CULTURAL EXCHANGES

The lines separating the races in the Spanish Empire gradually grew less distinct than they would be in the English colonies to the north. European and native cultures never entirely merged in the Spanish colonies. Indeed, significant differences remain today between European and Indian cultures throughout South and Central America.

Europeans would not have been exploring the Americas at all without their early contacts with the natives. From them, they first learned of the rich deposits of gold and silver. After that, the history of the Americas became one of increasing levels of exchanges—some beneficial, some catastrophic—among different peoples and cultures.

INCREASING LEVELS OF EXCHANGE

The first and most profound result of this exchange was the importation of European diseases to the New World. It would be difficult to exaggerate the consequences of the exposure of Native Americans to such illnesses as influenza, measles, chicken pox, mumps, typhus, and above all smallpox—diseases to which Europeans had over time developed at least a partial immunity but to which Native Americans were tragically vulnerable. Millions died. (See "Debating the Past," pp. 10–11.)

Native groups inhabiting some of the large Caribbean islands and some areas of Mexico were virtually extinct within fifty years of their first contact with whites. On Hispaniola—where the Dominican Republic and Haiti are today and where Columbus landed and established a small, short-lived colony in the 1490s—the native population quickly declined from approximately 1 million to about 500. In the Mayan areas of Mexico, as much as 95 percent of the population perished within a few years of their first contact with the Spanish. Some groups fared better than others; some of the tribes north of Mexico, whose contact with European settlers came later and less

DEMOGRAPHIC CATASTROPHE

intimately, were spared the worst of the epidemics. But most areas of the New World experienced a demographic catastrophe at least as grave as, and in many places far worse than, the Black Death that had killed at least a third of the population of Europe two centuries before.

The decimation of native populations in the southern regions of the Americas was not, however, purely a result of this inadvertent exposure to infection. It was also a result of the conquistadores' quite deliberate policy of subjugation and extermination. Their brutality was in part a reflection of the ruthlessness with which Europeans waged war in all parts of the world. It was also a result of their conviction that the natives were "savages"—uncivilized peoples whom they considered somehow not fully human.

DELIBERATE SUBJUGATION AND EXTERMINATION

Not all aspects of the exchange were so disastrous to the natives. The Europeans introduced important new crops to America (among them sugar and bananas), domestic livestock (cattle, pigs, and sheep), and perhaps most significantly the horse, which had disappeared from the Western Hemisphere in the Ice Age and now returned aboard Spanish ships in the sixteenth century. The Europeans imported these things for their own use. But Indian tribes soon learned to cultivate the new crops, and European livestock proliferated rapidly and

> AGRICULTURAL DISCOVERIES ULTIMATELY PROVED MORE IMPORTANT TO THE FUTURE OF EUROPE THAN THE GOLD AND SILVER THE CONQUISTADORES VALUED SO HIGHLY.

spread widely among natives. In the past, most tribes had possessed no domesticated animals other than dogs. The horse, in particular, became central to the lives of many natives and transformed their societies.

The exchange was at least as important (and far more beneficial) to the Europeans. In both North and South America, the arriving white peoples learned new agricultural techniques from the natives, techniques often better adapted to the character of the new land than those they had brought with them from Europe. They discovered new crops, above all maize (corn), which became an important staple among the settlers. Columbus took corn back to Europe from his first trip to America, and it soon spread through much of Europe as well. Such American foods as squash, pumpkins, beans, sweet potatoes, tomatoes, peppers, and potatoes also found their way back to Europe and in the process revolutionized European agriculture. Agricultural discoveries ultimately proved more important to the future of Europe than the gold and silver the conquistadores valued so highly.

NEW CROPS AND AGRICULTURAL TECHNIQUES

In South America, Central America, and Mexico, societies emerged in which Europeans and natives lived in intimate, if unequal, contact with one another. As a result, Indians adopted many features of European civilization. Many natives gradually came to learn Spanish or Portuguese, but in the process they created a range of dialects, combining the European languages with their own. European missionaries—through both persuasion and coercion—spread Catholicism through most areas of the Spanish Empire. But native Christians tended to connect the new creed with features of their old religions, creating a hybrid of faiths that were, while essentially Christian, nevertheless distinctively American.

Colonial officials were expected to take their wives with them to America, but among the ordinary settlers—the majority—European men outnumbered European women by at least ten to one. Not surprisingly, therefore, the Spanish immigrants had substantial sexual contact with native women. Intermarriage became frequent, and before long the population of the colonies came to be dominated (numerically, at least) by people of mixed race, or *mestizos*. Through much of the Spanish Empire, as a result, an elaborate racial hierarchy developed, with Spanish at the top, natives at the bottom, and people of mixed races in between. Racial categories, however, were much more fluid than the Spanish wanted to believe and did not long

A COMPLEX RACIAL HIERARCHY

SMALLPOX AMONG THE INDIANS Far more devastating to the Indians of America than the military ventures of Europeans were deadly diseases carried to the New World by invaders from the Old World. Natives had developed no immunity to the infectious diseases of Europe, and they died by the hundreds of thousands from such epidemics as measles, influenza, and (as depicted here by a European artist) smallpox. (Firenze, Biblioteca Medicea Laurenziana, Ms. Med. Palat. 220, c. 460v. Su concessione del Ministero per i Beni e le Attività Culturali E' vietata ogni ulteriore riproduzuione con qualsiasi mezzo) remain fixed. Over time, the wealth and influence of a family often came to define its place in the "racial" hierarchy more decisively than race itself. Eventually, a successful or powerful person could become "Spanish" regardless of his or her actual ancestry.

Natives were the principal labor source for the Europeans. Virtually all the commercial, agricultural, and mining enterprises of the Spanish and Portuguese colonists depended on an Indian work force. Different labor systems emerged in different areas of the empire. In some places, Indians were sold into slavery. More often, colonists used a wage system closely related, but not iden-

VARIED LABOR SYSTEMS tical, to slavery, by which Indians were forced to work in the mines and on the plantations for fixed periods, unable to leave without the consent of their employers. Such workforces survived in some areas of the South American mainland for many centuries. So great was the need for native labor that European settlers were less interested in acquiring land than they were in gaining control over Indian villages, which could become a source of labor.

Even so, the native population could not meet all the labor needs of the colonists—particularly since the native population had declined (and in some places virtually vanished) because of disease and war. As early as 1502, therefore, European settlers began importing slaves from Africa.

AFRICA AND AMERICA

Most of the black men and women who were forcibly taken to America came from a large region in west Africa below the Sahara Desert, known as Guinea. It was the home of a wide variety of peoples and cultures. Since over half of all the new arrivals in the New World between 1500 and 1800 were Africans, those cultures greatly affected the character of American civilization. Europeans and white Americans came to portray African society as primitive and uncivilized (in part to justify the enslavement of Africa's people). But most Africans were, in fact, civilized peoples with well-developed economies and political systems.

Humans began settling in west Africa at least 10,000 years ago. By the fifteenth century A.D., they had developed extensive civilizations and complex political systems. The resi-

GHANA AND MALI dents of upper Guinea had substantial commercial contact with the Mediterranean world—trading ivory, gold, and slaves for finished goods. Largely as a result, they became early converts to Islam. After the collapse of the ancient kingdom of Ghana around 1100 A.D., the even larger empire of Mali emerged and survived well into the fifteenth century. Its great city, Timbuktu, became fabled as a trading center and a seat of education.

SINCE OVER HALF OF ALL THE NEW ARRIVALS IN THE NEW WORLD BETWEEN 1500 AND 1800 WERE AFRICANS, THOSE CULTURES, TOO, GREATLY AFFECTED THE CHARACTER OF AMERICAN CIVILIZATION.

BENIN, CONGO AND SONGHAY

Africans farther south were more isolated from Europe and the Mediterranean. They were also more politically fragmented. The central social unit in much of the south was the village, which usually consisted of members of an extended family group. Some groups of villages united in small kingdoms—among them Benin, Congo, and Songhay. But no large empires emerged in the south comparable to the Ghana and Mali kingdoms farther north. Nevertheless, these southern societies also developed extensive trade—in woven fabrics, ceramics, and wooden and iron goods, as well as crops and livestock—both among themselves and, to a lesser degree, with the outside world.

The African civilizations naturally developed economies that reflected the climates and resources of their lands. In upper Guinea, fishing and rice cultivation, supplemented by the extensive trade with Mediterranean lands, were the foundation of the economy. Farther south, Africans grew wheat and other food crops, raised livestock, and fished. There were some more nomadic tribes in the interior, which subsisted largely on hunting and gathering and developed less elaborate social systems. But most Africans were sedentary people, linked by elaborate political, economic, and familial relationships.

SCULPTURE OF DJENNÉ Many of the Africans forcibly exported from their homes to America in the seventeenth and eighteenth centuries were natives of Mali, the seat of an ancient east African civilization. This terra cotta sculpture, discovered in the 1940s, dates from between 600 and 900 years ago. It portrays a prisoner who most likely represented an African enslaved by the Malis. ("Seated Prisoner," 11th/16th Century, Djenné, Founders Society Purchase, Robert H. Tannahill Foundation Fund. Photograph © 1995 The Detroit Institute of the Arts)

The Atlantic Context of Early American History

MOST Americans understand that in the twenty-first century our nation has become intimately bound up with the rest of the world—that we live in a time that is often called the "age of globalization." But globalization long preceded our own time, and historians have recently come to recognize that the "New World" of seventeenth- and eighteenth-century America was part of a vast network of connections that has become known as the "Atlantic World."

The idea of an "Atlantic World" rests in part on the obvious connections between western Europe and the Spanish, British, French, and Dutch colonies in North and South America. The massive European immigration to the Americas beginning in the sixteenth century, the defeat and devastation of native populations, the creation of European agricultural and urban settlements, and the imposition of imperial regulations on trade, commerce, landowning, and political life—all of these forces reveal the influence of Old World imperialism on the history of the New World.

Although some Europeans traveled to the New World to escape oppression or to search for adventure, the great majority of European immigrants were in search of economic opportunity. Not surprisingly, therefore, the European settlements in the Americas were almost from the start intimately connected to Europe through the growth of commerce between them. The commercial relationship between America and Europe was responsible not just for the growth of trade, but also for the increases in migration over time—as the demand for labor in the New World drew more and more settlers from the Old World. Commerce was also the principal reason for the rise of slavery in the Americas, and for the growth of the slave trade between European America and Africa. The Atlantic World, in other words, included not just Europe and the Americas, but Africa as well.

Religion was another force binding together the Atlantic World. The vast majority of people of European descent were Christians, and most of them maintained important religious ties to Europe. Catholics, of course, were part of a hierarchical church based in Rome and maintained close ties with the Vatican. But the Protestant faiths that predominated in North America were intimately linked to their European counterparts as well. New religious ideas and movements spread back and forth across the Atlantic with astonishing speed. Great revivals that began in Europe moved quickly to America. The "Great Awakening" of the mid-eighteenth century, for example, began in Britain and traveled to America in large part through the efforts of the English evangelist George Whitefield. American evangelists later carried religious ideas from the New World back to the Old.

The early history of European America was also closely bound up with the intellectual life of Europe. The Enlightenment—the cluster of ideas that emerged in Europe in the seventeenth and eighteenth centuries emphasizing the power of human reason—moved quickly to the Americas, producing considerable intellectual ferment throughout the New World, but particularly in the British colonies in North America and the Caribbean. Many of the ideas that lay behind the American Revolution were products of British and French philosophy that had traveled across the Atlantic. The reinterpretation of those ideas by Americans to help justify their drive to independence—by, among others, Thomas Paine—moved back across the Atlantic to Europe and helped, among other things, to inspire the French Revolution. Scientific and technological knowledge—another product of the Enlightenment—moved rapidly back and forth across the Atlantic. Americans borrowed industrial technology from Britain.

Like many Native American societies, but unlike those in Europe, African societies tended to be matrilineal—which means that people traced their heredity through, and inherited property from, their mothers rather than their fathers. When a couple married, the husband left his own family to join the family of his wife. Like most other peoples, Africans divided work by gender, but the nature of that division varied greatly **MATRILINEAL SOCIETIES** from place to place. Women played a major role, often the dominant role, in trade; in many areas they were the principal farmers (while the men hunted, fished, and raised livestock); everywhere, they managed child care and food preparation. Most tribes also divided political power by gender, with men choosing leaders and systems for managing what they defined as male affairs and women choosing parallel leaders to handle female matters. Tribal chiefs generally were men (although in some places there was a female counterpart), but the position customarily passed down not to the chief's son but to the son of the chief's eldest sister. African societies, in short, were characterized by a greater degree of sexual equality than those of most other parts of the world.

In those areas of west Africa where indigenous religions had survived the spread of Islam (which included most of the lands south of the empire of Mali), people worshiped many gods, whom they associated with various aspects of the natural world and whose spirits they believed lived in trees, rocks, forests, and streams. Most Africans also developed forms of ancestor worship and took great care in tracing family lineage; the most revered priests (who were often also important social and political leaders as well) were generally the oldest people.

(The I. N. Phelps Stokes Collection of American Historical Prints, Prints Division, The New York Public Library, Astor, Lenox and Tilden Foundations)

Europe acquired much of its early knowledge of electricity from experiments done in America. But the Enlightenment was only one part of the continuing intellectual connections within the Atlantic World, connections that spread artistic, scholarly, and political ideas widely through the lands bordering the ocean.

Instead of thinking of the early history of what became the United States simply as the story of the growth of thirteen small colonies along the Atlantic seaboard of North America, the idea of the "Atlantic World" encourages us to think of early American history as a vast pattern of exchanges and interactions—trade, migration, religious and intellectual exchange, and many other relationships—among all the societies bordering the Atlantic: western Europe, western Africa, the Caribbean, and North and South America. •

UNDERSTAND, ANALYZE, AND EVALUATE

1. What is the Atlantic World?
2. What has led historians to begin studying the idea of an Atlantic World?
3. Does studying American history in an Atlantic World context broaden or distort our understanding of American history?

African societies had elaborate systems of social ranks (or hierarchies). Small elites of priests and nobles stood at the top. Most people belonged to a large middle group of farmers, traders, crafts workers, and others. At the bottom of society were slaves—men and women who were put into bondage after being captured in wars or because of criminal behavior or unpaid debts. Slavery in Africa was not usually permanent; people were generally placed in bondage for a fixed period and in the meantime retained certain legal protections (including the right to marry). Their children, moreover, did not inherit their parents' condition of bondage.

The African slave trade began long before the European migration to the New World. As early as the eighth century A.D., west Africans began selling slaves to traders from the Mediterranean. They were responding to a demand from affluent families who wanted black men and women as domestic servants. They were also responding to more-general labor shortages in some areas of Europe and North Africa. When Portuguese sailors began exploring the coast of Africa in the fifteenth century, they too bought slaves—usually criminals and people captured in war—and took them back to Portugal, where there was a small but steady demand.

In the sixteenth century, however, the market for slaves grew dramatically as a result of the rising European demand for sugarcane. The small areas of sugar cultivation in the Mediterranean were proving inadequate, and production soon moved to the island of Madeira off the African coast, which became a Portuguese colony. Not long after that, it moved to the Caribbean islands and Brazil. Sugar was a labor-intensive crop, and the demand for workers in these new areas increased rapidly. European slave traders responded to that demand by increasing the recruitment of workers from along the coast of west Africa (and from some areas of east Africa as well). As the demand increased, African kingdoms warred with one another in an effort to capture potential slaves to exchange for European goods. At first the slave traders were overwhelmingly Portuguese and, to a lesser extent, Spanish. By the seventeenth century, the Dutch had won control of most of the slave market. In the eighteenth century, the English dominated it. (Despite some claims, Jews were never significantly involved in the slave trade.) By 1700, slavery had begun to spread well beyond its original locations in the Caribbean and South America and into the English colonies to the north.

GROWTH OF THE AFRICAN SLAVE TRADE

THE ARRIVAL OF THE ENGLISH

England's first documented contact with the New World came only five years after Spain's. In 1497, John Cabot (like Columbus, a native of Genoa) sailed to the northeastern coast of North America on an expedition sponsored by King Henry VII. Other English navigators continued Cabot's unsuccessful search for a northwest passage through the New World to the Orient. They explored other areas of North America during the sixteenth century. But even though England claimed dominion over the lands its explorers surveyed, nearly a century passed before the English made any serious efforts to establish colonies there. Like other European nations, England had to experience an internal transformation before it could begin settling new lands. That transformation occurred in the sixteenth century.

JOHN CABOT

THE COMMERCIAL INCENTIVE

Part of the attraction of the New World to the English was its newness, its contrast to their own troubled land. America seemed a place where human settlement could start anew, where a perfect society could be created without the flaws and inequities of the Old World. Such dreams began to emerge

EUROPE AND WEST AFRICA IN THE FIFTEENTH CENTURY Exploration of North and South America was in part an outgrowth of earlier European trade in the Eastern Hemisphere. Europeans delivered cloth and other manufactures to northern Africa; then camels carried the cargoes across the Sahara to cities such as Timbuktu, Gao, and Djenné. There they loaded gold, ivory, and kola nuts for return to the Mediterranean. Africans also traded with Asia to obtain cloth, porcelain, and spices.

• *What areas of trade were most important to the early interaction between Africa and the Americas?*

in England only a few years after Columbus's voyages. They found classic expression in Sir Thomas More's *Utopia* (published in Latin in 1516, translated into English thirty-five years later), which described a mythical and nearly perfect society on an imaginary island supposedly discovered by a companion of Amerigo Vespucci in the waters of the New World.

More's picture of an ideal community was, among other things, a comment on the social and economic ills of the England of his own time. The people of Tudor England suffered from frequent and costly European wars, from almost constant religious strife, and above all from a harsh economic transformation of the countryside. Because the worldwide demand for wool was growing rapidly, many landowners were finding it profitable to convert their land from fields for crops to pastures for sheep. The result was a significant growth in the wool trade. But that meant land worked at one time by agricultural serfs and later by rent-paying tenant farmers was steadily enclosed for sheep runs and taken away from the farmers. Thousands of evicted tenants roamed the countryside in gangs, begging from (and at times robbing) the more fortunate householders through whose communities they passed.

THE ENCLOSURE MOVEMENT

The government passed various laws designed to halt enclosures, relieve the worthy poor, and compel the able-bodied or "sturdy beggars" to work. Such laws had little effect. The enclosure movement continued unabated, and relatively few of the dislocated farmers could find reemployment in raising sheep or manufacturing wool. By removing land from cultivation, the enclosure movement also limited England's ability to feed its rising population, which grew from 3 million in 1485 to 4 million in 1603. Because of both the dislocation of farmers and the restriction of the food supply, therefore, the nation had a serious problem of surplus population.

Amid this growing distress, a rising class of merchant capitalists was prospering from the expansion of foreign trade. At first, England had exported little except raw wool; but new merchant capitalists helped create a domestic cloth industry that allowed them to begin marketing finished goods at home and abroad. At first, most exporters did business almost entirely as individuals. In time, however, some merchants joined forces and formed chartered companies. Each such enterprise operated on the basis of a charter acquired from the monarch, which gave the company a monopoly for trading in a particular region. Among the first of these were the Muscovy Company (1555), the Levant Company (1581), the Barbary Company (1585), the Guinea Company (1588), and the East India Company (1600). Investors in these companies often made fantastic profits from the exchange of English manufactures, especially woolens, for exotic goods; and they felt a powerful urge to continue the expansion of their profitable trade.

CHARTERED COMPANIES

MERCANTILISM RESTED ON THE ASSUMPTION THAT THE NATION AS A WHOLE, NOT THE INDIVIDUALS WITHIN IT, WAS THE PRINCIPAL ACTOR IN THE ECONOMY.

Central to this drive was the emergence of a new concept of economic life known as mercantilism, which was gaining favor throughout Europe. Mercantilism rested on the assumption that the nation as a whole, not the individuals within it, was the principal actor in the economy. The goal of economic activity should be to increase the nation's total wealth. Mercantilists believed that the world's wealth was finite. One person or nation could grow rich only at the expense of another. A nation's economic health depended, therefore, on extracting as much wealth as possible from foreign lands and exporting as little wealth as possible from home.

The principles of mercantilism guided the economic policies of virtually all the European nation-states in the sixteenth and seventeenth centuries. Mercantilism greatly enhanced the position of the new merchant capitalists, whose overseas ventures were thought to benefit the entire nation and to be worthy of government assistance. It also increased competition among nations. Every European state was trying to find markets for its exports while trying to limit its imports. One result was the increased attractiveness of acquiring colonies, which could become the source of goods that a country might otherwise have to buy from other nations.

MERCANTILISM

In England, the mercantilistic program thrived at first on the basis of the flourishing wool trade with the European continent and, particularly, with the great cloth market in Antwerp. Beginning in the 1550s, however, that glutted market collapsed, and English merchants found themselves obliged to look elsewhere for overseas trade. The establishment of colonies seemed to be a ready answer to that and other problems. Richard Hakluyt, an Oxford clergyman and the outstanding English propagandist for colonization, argued that colonies would not only create new markets for English goods but also help alleviate poverty and unemployment by siphoning off the surplus population. For the poor who remained in England "idly to the annoy of the whole state," there would be new work as a result of the prosperity the colonies would create. Perhaps most important, colonial commerce would allow England to acquire products from its own new territories for which the nation had previously been dependent on foreign rivals—products such as lumber, naval stores, and, above all, silver and gold.

RICHARD HAKLUYT'S ARGUMENT FOR COLONIES

THE RELIGIOUS INCENTIVE

In addition to these economic motives for colonization, there were religious ones, rooted in the events of the European and English Reformations. The Protestant Reformation began in Germany in 1517, when Martin Luther openly challenged some of the basic practices and beliefs of the Roman Catholic Church—until then, the supreme religious authority and also

MERCANTILISM AND COLONIAL COMMERCE

FOR more than two centuries, the economic life of Europe and its growing colonial possessions (the North American colonies among them) was shaped by a theory known as mercantilism. The actual application of mercantilism differed from country to country and empire to empire. But virtually all versions of mercantilism shared a belief in the economic importance of colonies to the health of the colonizing nations. As a result, mercantilism helped spur the growth of European empires around the world.

In one sense, mercantilism was a highly nationalist, as opposed to a global, theory. It rested on the conviction that the nation (not the individual) was at the center of economic life and that each nation should work to maximize its own share of the finite wealth for which all nations were competing. A gain for France, mercantilism taught, was in effect a loss for Britain or Spain. Thus, it encouraged each nation to work for itself and to attempt to weaken its rivals. But mercantilism was also a global force. What made it so was not the modern notion of the value of international economic growth but, rather, the belief that each nation must search for its own sources of trade and raw materials around the world. Every European state was trying to find markets for its exports, which

(© National Maritime Museum, London/The Image Works)

would bring wealth into the nation, while trying to limit imports, which would transfer wealth to others. (Most of these central mercantilist tenets would eventually be overturned in Adam Smith's 1776 tract *The Wealth of Nations,* which instead advocated free trade among nations and individual self-interest over national largesse as the route to increasing global—and thus national—wealth.)

In a mercantilist economy, colonies were critical to a nation's economic well-being. They served both as providers of raw materials and as markets for finished goods. Colonies, mercantilism taught, should trade only with their mother nation, and the direction of wealth should flow only in one direction, toward the center of the empire. Naval power became an integral part of the mercantilist idea. Only by controlling the sea lanes between the colonies and the homeland could a nation preserve its favorable balance of trade.

Despite the common assumptions underlying all forms of mercantilism, the system took many different forms, often depending on whether colonial merchants or state bureaucrats drove the economic discussion. In England, Spain, and the Netherlands, mercantilism was closely identified with the emerging middle class, who stood to profit personally from the increased trade. (Hence the term "mercantilism," from merchant.) In France and Germany, on the other hand, state officials rather than private citizens laid more of the groundwork for mercantilism principles. In France, mercantilism was often known as "Colbertism," after its primary proponent, Jean-Baptiste Colbert, foreign minister under Louis XIV. In Germany, the theory was known as "cameralism," for the *Kammer,* or royal treasury.

In its early years, mercantilism was closely associated with "bullionism," which is the theory that only gold and silver defined a nation's wealth. As

one of the strongest political authorities throughout western Europe. Luther, an Augustinian monk and ordained priest, challenged the Catholic belief that salvation could be achieved through good works or through loyalty (or payments) to the Church itself. He denied the Church's claim that God communicated to the world through the pope and the clergy. The Bible, not the church, was the authentic voice of God, Luther claimed, and salvation was to be found not through "works" or through the formal practice of religion, but through faith alone. Luther's

challenge quickly won him a wide following among ordinary men and women in northern Europe. He himself insisted that he was not revolting against the Church, that his purpose was to reform it from within. But when the pope excommunicated him in 1520, Luther defied him and began to lead his followers out of the Catholic Church entirely. A schism within European Christianity had begun that was never to be healed.

As the spirit of the Reformation spread rapidly throughout Europe, creating intellectual ferment and (in some places) such, the early Spanish colonies of the New World, in particular, emphasized the procurement of gold, silver, and other precious metals for the mother nation. (English colonies such as Jamestown were founded in part with the same intention, but they were much less successful at finding precious metals.) But even when gold and silver were scarce, colonies could still provide other important resources for the imperial capitals—for examples, fur, timber, sugar, tobacco, and slaves.

The theory of mercantilism taught that wealth creation was a zero-sum game: there was a fixed amount of wealth in the world, and any wealth a nation acquired was, in effect, taken away from some other nation. As a result, mercantilists believed that nations should heavily regulate the economic affairs of their colonies. One good example of this was England's passage of the Navigation Acts in the 1760s, laws that sharply restricted colonial trade with anyone else but England. But England was not alone in passing such restrictions. Spain took equally definitive control over its colonial economies, passing similarly intensive regulation and insisting until 1720 that all colonial trade pass through the port of Seville.

Still, naval vessels could not be everywhere at once. And despite the many laws restricting colonial economies to their home nations, many colonial merchants around the world struck up trade with their nonaffiliated neighbors when possible. The French, Spanish, and Dutch West Indies in particular became the site of a thriving intercolonial trade that was not, for all intent and purposes, legal according to mercantilist doctrine. Indeed, so many traders from so many countries violated mercantile laws in the eighteenth century, and so many of them amassed great profits in the process, the mercantilist system gradually began to unravel. By the time of the American Revolution, in part a result of the colonists' resistance to mercantilist policies, the patterns of global trade were already moving toward the freer, less-regulated trading patterns of the modern capitalist world. •

UNDERSTAND, ANALYZE, AND EVALUATE

1. What effect did mercantilism have on colonial economies? Did the effects differ according to which European nation owned the colony?
2. How did mercantilism contribute to power rivalries among the European nations?
3. Mercantilism as a nation's driving economic force has largely given way to economic globalization, that is, the increased interdependence of nations' economies. Why do you think this is so?

war, other dissidents began offering alternatives to orthodox Catholicism. The French theologian John Calvin was, after Luther, the most influential reformer and went even further than Luther had in rejecting the Catholic belief that human institutions could affect an individual's prospects for salvation. Calvin introduced the doctrine of predestination. God "elected" some people to be saved and condemned others to damnation; each person's destiny was determined before birth, and no one could change that predetermined fate. But while individuals could not

alter their destinies, they could strive to know them. Calvinists believed that the way people led their lives might reveal to

DOCTRINE OF PREDESTINATION

them their chances of salvation. A wicked or useless existence would be a sign of damnation; saintliness, diligence, and success could be signs of grace. Calvinism created anxieties among its followers, to be sure; but it also produced a strong incentive to lead virtuous, productive lives. The new creed spread rapidly throughout northern Europe and produced (among other groups) the Huguenots in France and the Puritans in England.

The English Reformation was very different. It occurred more because of a political dispute between the king and the

THE ENGLISH REFORMATION

pope than as a result of doctrinal revolts. In 1529 King Henry VIII became angered by the pope's refusal to grant him a divorce from his Spanish wife (who had failed to bear him the son he desperately wanted). In response, he broke England's ties with the Catholic Church and established himself as the head of the Christian faith in his country. He made relatively few other changes in English Christianity, however, and after his death the survival of Protestantism remained in doubt for a time. When Henry's Catholic daughter Mary ascended the throne, she quickly restored England's allegiance to Rome and harshly persecuted those who refused to return to the Catholic fold. Many Protestants were executed (the origin of the queen's enduring nickname, "Bloody Mary"); others fled to the European continent, where they came into contact with the most radical ideas of the Reformation. Mary died in 1558, and her half-sister, Elizabeth, became England's sovereign. Elizabeth once again severed the nation's connection with the Catholic Church (and, along with it, an alliance with Spain that Mary had forged).

The Church of England, as the official religion was now known, satisfied the political objectives of the queen, but it failed to satisfy the religious desires of many English Christians. Catholics continued to assert allegiance to the pope. More importantly, many Protestants believed that the "reformation" did not create enough changes in theology. The most ardent Protestants became known as "Puritans," because they hoped to "purify" the church.

Some Puritans took genuinely radical positions. They were known as Separatists, and they were determined to worship as

PURITAN SEPARATISTS

they pleased in their own independent congregations. That flew in the face of English law—which outlawed unauthorized religious meetings, required all subjects to attend regular Anglican services, and levied taxes to support the established church. The radicalism of the Separatists was visible in their rejection of prevailing assumptions about the proper religious roles of women. Many Separatist sects, perhaps most prominently the Quakers, permitted women to serve as preachers, which would have been impossible in the established church.

Most Puritans resisted separatism. Still, their demands were by no means modest. They wanted to simplify Anglican forms of worship. They wanted to reduce the power of the

THE DOCKS OF BRISTOL, ENGLAND By the eighteenth century, when this scene was painted, Bristol had become one of the principal English ports serving the so-called triangular trade among the American colonies, the West Indies, and Africa. The lucrativeness of that trade is evident in the bustle and obvious prosperity of the town. Even earlier, however, Bristol was an important port of embarkation for the thousands of English settlers migrating to the New World. (*Docks and Quay*. English School (18th Century). City of Bristol Museum and Art Gallery/The Bridgeman Art Library, London)

bishops, who were appointed by the crown and who were, in many cases, openly corrupt and highly extravagant. Perhaps above all they wanted to reform the local clergy, many of them greedy, uneducated men with little interest in (or knowledge of) theology.

Puritan discontent, already festering, grew rapidly after the death of Elizabeth, the last of the Tudors, and the accession to

PURITAN DISCONTENT

the throne of James I, a Scotsman and the first of the Stuarts, in 1603. James believed kings ruled by divine right, and he felt no obligation to compromise with his opponents. He quickly antagonized the Puritans, a group that included most of the rising businessmen, by resorting to arbitrary taxation, by favoring English Catholics in the granting of charters and other favors, and by supporting "high church" forms of ceremony. By the early seventeenth century, some religious nonconformists were beginning to look for places of refuge outside the kingdom.

Along with the other economic and social incentives for colonization, such religious discontent helped turn England's gaze to distant lands.

THE ENGLISH IN IRELAND

England's first experience with colonization came not in the New World, but in a land separated from Britain only by a narrow stretch of sea: Ireland. The English had long laid claim to the island and had for many years maintained small settlements in the area around Dublin. Only in the second half of the sixteenth century, however, did serious efforts at large-scale colonization begin. Through the 1560s and 1570s, would-be colonists moved through Ireland, capturing territory and attempting to subdue the native population. In the process they developed many of the assumptions that would guide later English colonists in America.

JOHN CALVIN Next to Martin Luther, John Calvin was the most important figure of the European Reformation. His belief in predestination was central to the Puritan faith of early New England. (Bettmann/Corbis)

ELIZABETH I The flemish artist Marcus Gheeraerts the Younger moved to England in 1568 (along with his father, also a painter) as a Protestant refugee from his homeland. In approximately 1593, he painted this portrait of the English queen, portraying her as she was seen by many of her contemporaries: a strong, confident ruler presiding over an ambitious, expansionist nation. She stands here on a map of England. (National Portrait Gallery, London)

The most important of these assumptions was that the native population of Ireland—approximately 1 million people,

SUBJUGATION OF IRELAND

loyal to the Catholic Church, with their own language (Gaelic) and their own culture— was a collection of wild, vicious, and ignorant "savages." The Irish lived in ways the English considered crude and wasteful ("like beasts"), and they fought back against the intruders with a ferocity that the English considered barbaric. Such people could not be tamed, the English concluded. They certainly could not be assimilated into English society. They must, therefore, be suppressed, isolated, and if necessary destroyed. Eventually, they might be "civilized," but only after they were thoroughly subordinated.

Whatever barbarities the Irish may have inflicted on the colonizers, the English more than matched them in return. Sir Humphrey Gilbert, who was later to establish the first British colony in the New World (an unsuccessful venture in Newfoundland), served for a time as governor of one Irish district and suppressed native rebellions with extraordinary viciousness. Gilbert was an educated and supposedly civilized man. But he considered the natives less than human and

therefore not entitled to whatever decencies civilized people reserved for their treatment of one another. As a result, he managed to justify, both to himself and to others, such atrocities as beheading Irish soldiers after they were killed in battle. Gilbert himself, Sir Walter Raleigh, Sir Richard Grenville, and others active in Ireland in the mid-sixteenth century derived from their experiences there an outlook they would take to America, where they made similarly vicious efforts to subdue and subjugate the natives.

The Irish experience led the English to another important (and related) assumption about colonization: that English settlements in distant lands must retain a rigid

THE PLANTATION MODEL

separation from the native populations. In Ireland, English colonizers established what they called "plantations," transplantations of English society in a foreign land. Unlike the Spanish in America, the English in Ireland did not try simply to rule a subdued native population; they tried to build a separate society, peopled with emigrants from England itself. The new society would exist within a "pale of settlement," an area physically separated from the natives. That concept, too, they would take with them to the New World, even though in Ireland, as later in America, the separation of peoples and the preservation of "pure" English culture proved impossible.

THE FRENCH AND THE DUTCH IN AMERICA

English settlers in North America, unlike those in Ireland, were to encounter not only natives but also other Europeans who were, like them, driven by mercantilist ideas to establish economic outposts abroad. To the south and southwest was the Spanish Empire. Spanish ships continued to threaten English settlements along the coast for years. But except for Mexico and scattered outposts such as those in Florida and New Mexico, the Spanish made little serious effort to colonize North America.

England's more formidable North American rivals in the early sixteenth century were the French. France founded its first permanent settlement in America at Quebec in 1608, less than a year after the English started their first colony at Jamestown. The French colony's population grew very slowly. Few French Catholics felt any inclination to leave their homeland, and French Protestants who might have wished to emigrate were excluded from the colony. The French, however, exercised an influ-

ence in the New World disproportionate to their numbers, largely because of their relationships with Native Americans. Unlike the English, who for many years hugged the coastline and traded with the Indians of the interior through intermediaries, the French forged close, direct ties with natives deep inside the continent. French Jesuit missionaries were among the first to penetrate Indian societies, and they established some of the first contacts between the two peoples. More important still were the *coureurs de bois*—adventurous fur traders and trappers—who also moved far into the wilderness and developed an extensive trade that became one of the underpinnings of the French colonial economy.

COUREURS DE BOIS

The fur trade was, in fact, more an Indian than a French enterprise. The *coureurs de bois* were, in many ways, little more than agents for the Algonquins and the Hurons, who were the principal fur traders among the Indians of the region and from whom the French purchased their pelts. The French traders were able to function only to the degree that they could form partnerships with the Indians. Successful partnerships often resulted from their ability to become virtually a part of native society, living among the Indians and at times marrying Indian women. The fur trade helped open the way for the other elements of the French presence in North America—the agricultural estates (or *seigneuries*) along the St. Lawrence River, the development of trade and military centers at Quebec and Montreal, and the creation of an alliance with the Algonquins and others—

> THE FRENCH FORGED CLOSE, DIRECT TIES WITH NATIVES DEEP INSIDE THE CONTINENT.

THE "RESTITUTION" OF NEW AMSTERDAM This is a detail from an elaborate engraving created to celebrate the "Restitutio" (or return) of New Amsterdam to the Dutch in 1673. England had captured New Amsterdam in 1664 and made claim to the entire province of New Netherland. But in 1672, war broke out between England and the Netherlands, and the Dutch recaptured their lost province. In celebration of that event, this heroic picture of the Dutch fleet in New York was created for sale in the Netherlands. Early in 1674, at the conclusion of the war, the Dutch returned the colony to England. (Museum of the City of New York)

that enabled the French to compete with the more numerous British in the contest for control of North America. That alliance also brought the French into conflict with the Iroquois, the Algonquins' ancient enemies, who assumed the central role in the English fur trade. An early result of these tensions was a 1609 attack led by Samuel de Champlain, the founder of Quebec, on a band of Mohawks, apparently at the instigation of his Algonquin trading partners.

The Dutch, too, were establishing a presence in North America. Holland had won its independence from Spain in the early seventeenth century and had become one of the leading trading nations of the world. Its merchant fleet was larger than England's, and its traders were active not only in Europe but also in Africa, Asia, and—increasingly—America. In 1609, an

HENRY HUDSON English explorer in the employ of the Dutch, Henry Hudson, sailed up the river that was to be named for him in what is now New York State. Because the river was so wide, he believed for a time that he had found the long-sought water route through the continent to the Pacific. He was wrong, of course, but his explorations led to a Dutch claim on territory in America and to the establishment of a permanent Dutch presence in the New World.

For more than a decade after Hudson's voyage, the Dutch maintained an active trade in furs in and around New York. In 1624, the Dutch West India Company established a series of per-

NEW AMSTERDAM manent trading posts on the Hudson, Delaware, and Connecticut Rivers. The company actively encouraged settlement of the region—not just from Holland itself, but also from such other parts of northern Europe as Germany, Sweden, and Finland. It transported whole families to the New World and granted vast feudal estates to landlords (known as "patroons") on condition that they bring still more immigrants to America. The result was the colony of New Netherland and its principal town, New Amsterdam, on Manhattan Island. Its population, diverse as it was, remained relatively small; the colony was only loosely united, with chronically weak leadership.

THE FIRST ENGLISH SETTLEMENTS

The first enduring English settlement in the New World was established at Jamestown, in Virginia, in 1607. But for nearly thirty years before that, English merchants and adventurers had been engaged in a series of failed efforts to create colonies in America. Through much of the sixteenth century, the English had mixed feelings about the New World. They knew of its existence and were intrigued by its possibilities. Under the leadership of Elizabeth I, they were developing a powerful sense of nationalism that encouraged dreams of expansion. At the same time, however, England was leery of Spain, which remained the dominant force in America and, it seemed, the dominant naval power in Europe.

But much changed in the 1570s and 1580s. English "sea dogs" such as Sir Francis Drake staged successful raids on Spanish merchant ships and built confidence in England's abil-

ity to challenge Spanish sea power. More important was the attempted invasion of England in 1588. Philip II, the powerful

THE SPANISH ARMADA Spanish king, had recently united his nation with Portugal. He was now determined to end England's challenges to Spanish commercial supremacy and to bring the English back into the Catholic Church. He assembled one of the largest military fleets in the history of warfare—known to history as the "Spanish Armada"—to carry his troops across the English Channel and into England itself. Philip's bold venture turned into a fiasco when the smaller English fleet dispersed the Armada and, in a single stroke, ended Spain's domination of the Atlantic. The English now felt much freer to establish themselves in the New World.

The pioneers of English colonization were Sir Humphrey Gilbert and his half-brother Sir Walter Raleigh—both friends of Queen Elizabeth and both veterans of the earlier colonial efforts in Ireland. In 1578, Gilbert obtained from Elizabeth a patent granting him the exclusive right for six years "to inhabit and possess at his choice all remote and heathen lands not in the actual possession of any Christian prince."

After numerous setbacks, Gilbert led an expedition to

GILBERT'S EXPEDITION TO NEWFOUNDLAND Newfoundland in 1583 and took possession of it in the queen's name. He proceeded southward along the coast, looking for a good place to build a military outpost that might eventually grow into a profitable colony. But a storm sank his ship, and he was lost at sea.

ROANOKE

Raleigh was undeterred by Gilbert's misfortune. The next year, he secured from Elizabeth a six-year grant similar to Gilbert's and sent a small group of men on an expedition to explore the North American coast. They returned with two captive Indians and glowing reports of what they had seen. They were particularly enthusiastic about an island the natives called Roanoke and about the area of the mainland just beyond it (in what is now North Carolina). Raleigh asked the queen for permission to name the entire region "Virginia" in honor of Elizabeth, "the Virgin Queen." But while Elizabeth granted the permission, she did not offer the financial assistance Raleigh had hoped his flattery would produce. So he turned to private investors to finance another expedition.

In 1585 Raleigh recruited his cousin, Sir Richard Grenville, to lead a group of men (most of them from the English plantations in Ireland) to Roanoke to establish a colony. Grenville deposited

THE FIRST ROANOKE COLONY the settlers on the island, remained long enough to antagonize the natives by razing an Indian village as retaliation for a minor theft, and returned to England. The following spring, Sir Francis Drake unexpectedly arrived in Roanoke. With supplies and reinforcements from England long overdue, the beleaguered colonists boarded Drake's ships and left.

Raleigh tried again in 1587, sending an expedition carrying ninety-one men, seventeen women (two of them pregnant), and

ROANOKE A drawing by one of the English colonists in the ill-fated Roanoke expedition of 1585 became the basis for this engraving by Theodore DeBry, published in England in 1590. A small European ship carrying settlers approaches the island of Roanoke, at left. The wreckage of several larger vessels farther out to sea and the presence of Indian settlements on the mainland and on Roanoke itself suggest some of the perils the settlers encountered. (New York Public Library, Astor, Lenox and Tilden Foundations)

nine children—the nucleus, he hoped, of a viable "plantation." The settlers landed on Roanoke and attempted to take up where the first group of colonists had left off. (Shortly after arriving, one of the women—the daughter of the commander of the expedition, John White—gave birth to a daughter, Virginia Dare, the first American-born child of English parents.) White returned to England after several weeks (leaving his daughter and granddaughter behind) in search of supplies and additional settlers; he hoped to return in a few months. But the hostilities with Spain intervened, and White did not return to the island for three years. When he did, in 1590, he found the island utterly deserted, with no clue to the settlers' fate other than the cryptic inscription "Croatoan" carved on a post. Some historians have argued that the colonists were slaughtered by the Indians in retaliation for Grenville's (and perhaps their own) hostilities. Others have contended that they left their settlement and joined native society, ultimately becoming entirely assimilated. But no conclusive solution to the mystery of the "Lost Colony" has ever been found.

The Roanoke disaster marked the end of Sir Walter Raleigh's involvement in English colonization of the New World. In 1603, when James I succeeded Elizabeth to the throne, Raleigh was accused of plotting against the king, stripped of his monopoly, and imprisoned for more than a decade. Finally (after being released for one last ill-fated maritime expedition), he was executed by the king in 1618. No later colonizer would receive grants of land in the New World as vast or undefined as those Raleigh and Gilbert had acquired. But despite the discouraging example of these early experiences, the colonizing impulse remained alive.

In the first years of the seventeenth century, a group of London merchants to whom Raleigh had assigned his charter rights decided to renew the attempt at colonization in Virginia. A rival group of merchants, from Plymouth and other West Country towns, were also interested in American ventures and were sponsoring voyages of exploration farther north, up to Newfoundland, where West Country fishermen had been going for many years. In 1606 James I issued a new charter, which divided America between the two groups. The London group got the exclusive right to colonize in the south, and the Plymouth merchants received the same right in the north. Through their efforts, the first enduring English colonies were planted in America.

NEW COLONIAL CHARTERS

LOOKING BACK

The lands that Europeans eventually named the Americas were the home of many millions of people before the arrival of Columbus. Having migrated from Asia thousands of years earlier, the pre-Columbian Americans spread throughout the Western Hemisphere and eventually created great civilizations. Among the most notable of them were the Incas in Peru, and the Mayas and Aztecs in Mexico. In the regions north of what was later named the Rio Grande, the human population was smaller and the civilizations less advanced than they were farther south. Even so, North American natives created a cluster of civilizations that thrived and expanded. There were several million people living north of Mexico by the time Columbus arrived.

In the century after European contact, these native populations suffered a series of catastrophes that all but destroyed the civilizations they had built: brutal invasions by Spanish and Portuguese conquistadores and, even more devastating, a series of plagues inadvertently imported by Europeans that decimated native populations. By the middle of the sixteenth century, the Spanish and Portuguese—no longer faced with effective resistance from the native populations—had established colonial control over all of South America and much of North America, creating one of the largest empires in the world.

In the parts of North America that would eventually become the United States, the European presence was for a time much less powerful. The Spanish established an important northern outpost in what is now New Mexico, a society in which Europeans and Indians lived together intimately, if unequally. They created a fort at St. Augustine, Florida. On the whole, however, the North American Indians remained largely undisturbed by Europeans until the English, French, and Dutch migrations began in the early seventeenth century. •

SIGNIFICANT EVENTS

Asians begin migrating to North America across the Bering Strait

Columbus sails west from Spain in search of Asia, reaches Bahama Islands in the Atlantic

First African slaves arrive in Spanish America

Magellan expedition circumnavigates globe

Pizarro conquers Incas in Peru

14,000B.C.–
12,000B.C.   **1480s**   **1492**   **1497**   **1502**   **1518–1530**   **1519–1522**   **1521**   **1532–1538**   **1558**

Portuguese explorers travel down west coast of Africa in search of sea route to Asia

John Cabot establishes first English claim in North America

Smallpox epidemic ravages Indian societies of Central and South America

Cortés captures Tenochtitlán and conquers Aztec Empire in Mexico

Elizabeth I ascends English throne

KEY TERMS/PEOPLE/PLACES/EVENTS

RECALL AND REFLECT

1. How did contact between the European arrivals and the native peoples of the Americas affect both groups?

2. How did Spanish settlement in America differ from that of the English, Dutch, and French?

3. What were the effects of the importation of African slaves into the Americas?

4. What is mercantilism and what did it have to do with the European colonization of North America?

5. How did the English experience at colonization in Ireland affect English colonization in America?

| | | | Don Juan de Oñate establishes Spanish colony in present-day New Mexico | | French establish Quebec, their first permanent settlement in America | | Dutch establish permanent settlements in what is now New York | | Spanish crush last Pueblo revolt in New Mexico |

English conquest of Ireland begins

1565 — **1566** — **1587** — **1598** — **1603** — **1608** — **1609** — **1624** — **1680** — **1696**

St. Augustine founded in Florida

"Lost Colony" established on Roanoke Island

James I succeeds Elizabeth I in England

Spanish colonists found Santa Fe

Pueblos revolt and drive Spanish colonists from present-day New Mexico

THE FORT AT JAMESTOWN The Jamestown settlement was beset with difficulties from its first days, and it was many decades before it became a stable and successful town. In its early years, the colonists suffered from the climate, the lack of food, and the spread of disease. They also struggled with the growing hostility of the neighboring Indians, illustrated in this map by the figure of their chief, Powhatan, in the upper right-hand corner. (Art Resource, NY)

2 TRANSPLANTATIONS AND BORDERLANDS

THE FIRST PERMANENT ENGLISH settlements in North America were mostly business enterprises—small, fragile communities, generally unprepared for the hardships they were to face. The Europeans attempted, as best they could, to isolate themselves from the Indians and create enclosed societies that would be wholly their own—"transplantations" of the English world they had left behind. This proved an impossible task. The English immigrants to America found a world populated by Native American tribes; by colonists, explorers, and traders from Spain, France, and the Netherlands; and by immigrants from other parts of Europe and, soon, Africa. American society was from the beginning a fusion of many cultures—what historians have come to call a "middle ground," in which disparate people and cultures coexist.

All of British North America was, in effect, a "middle ground" during the early years of colonization. Through much of the seventeenth century, European colonies both relied upon and did battle with the Indian tribes and struggled with challenges from other Europeans in their midst. Eventually, however, some areas of English settlement—especially the growing communities along the eastern seaboard—managed to dominate their own regions, marginalizing or expelling Indians and other challengers. In these eastern colonies, the English created significant towns and cities; built political, religious, and educational institutions; and created agricultural systems of great productivity. They also developed substantial differences from one another—perhaps most notably in the growth of a slave-driven agricultural economy in the south.

SETTING THE STAGE

"Middle grounds" survived well into the nineteenth century in much of North America, but mostly in the interior of the continent. In these communities Europeans had not yet established full control, and both Indians and Europeans exercised influence and power and lived intimately, if often uneasily, with one another.

LOOKING AHEAD

1. How did the English colonies in the Chesapeake, New England, and mid-Atlantic differ from one another in purpose and administration?
2. How "English" were the colonies in the decades after the British settlements?
3. What did the English want from the colonies in the first century of English settlement in North America?

THE EARLY CHESAPEAKE

After James I issued his 1606 charters to the London and Plymouth Companies, the principal obstacle to founding new American colonies was, as usual, money. The Plymouth group made an early, unsuccessful attempt to establish a colony at Sagadoahoc, on the coast of Maine; but in the aftermath of that failure, it largely abandoned its colonizing efforts. The London Company, by contrast, moved quickly and decisively. Only a few months after receiving its charter, it launched a colonizing expedition headed for Virginia—a party of 144 men aboard three ships: the *Godspeed,* the *Discovery,* and the *Susan Constant.*

THE FOUNDING OF JAMESTOWN

Only 104 men survived the journey. They reached the American coast in the spring of 1607, sailed into the Chesapeake Bay and up a river they named the James, and established their colony on a peninsula extending from the river's northern bank. They called it Jamestown. The colonists had chosen their site poorly. In an effort to avoid the mistakes of Roanoke (whose residents were assumed to have been killed by Indians), they selected what they thought to be an easily defended location—an inland setting that they believed would offer them security. But the site was low and swampy, hot and humid in the summer, and prey to outbreaks of malaria. It was surrounded by thick woods, which were difficult to clear for cultivation. And it lay within the territories of powerful local Indians, a confederation led by the imperial chief Powhatan. The result could hardly have been more disastrous.

The initial colonists, too many of whom were adventurous gentlemen and too few of whom were willing laborers, ran into

EARLY PROBLEMS serious difficulties from the moment they landed. Much like the Indians to the south who had succumbed quickly to European diseases when first exposed to them, these English settlers had had no prior exposure, and thus no immunity, to the infections of the new land. Malaria, in particular, debilitated the colony, killing some and weakening others so that they could do virtually no work. Because the promoters in London demanded a quick return on their investment, the colonists spent much of their limited and dwindling energy on futile searches for gold. They made only slightly more successful efforts to pile up lumber, tar, pitch, and iron for export. Agriculture was a low priority, in part because they wrongly assumed that they could rely on the Indians to provide them with food.

The London Company promoters had little interest in creating a family-centered community, and at first they sent no women to Jamestown. The absence of English women made it difficult for the settlers to establish any semblance of a "society." The colonists were seldom able (and also seldom willing) to intermarry with native women, although some native women are thought to have lived in the settlements with the English men. With so few women, settlers could not establish real households, could not order their domestic lives, and had difficulty feeling any sense of a permanent stake in the community.

Greed and rootlessness contributed to the failure to grow sufficient food; inadequate diets contributed to the colonists' vulnerability to disease; the ravages of disease made it difficult for the settlers to recover from their early mistakes. The result was a community without the means to sustain itself. By January

JOHN SMITH 1608, when ships appeared with additional men and supplies, all but 38 of the first 104 colonists were dead. Jamestown, now facing extinction, survived the crisis largely because of the efforts of twenty-seven-year-old Captain John Smith. He was already a famous world traveler, the hero of implausible travel narratives he had written and published. But he was also a capable organizer. Leadership in the colony had been divided among the several members of a council who quarreled continually. In the fall of 1608, however, Smith became council president and asserted his will. He imposed work and order on the community. He also organized raids on neighboring Indian villages to steal food. During the colony's second winter, fewer than a dozen (in a population of about 200) died. By the summer of 1609, when Smith was deposed from the council and returned to England, the colony was showing promise of survival.

REORGANIZATION

The London Company (now calling itself the Virginia Company) was, in the meantime, dreaming of bigger things. In 1609 it obtained a new charter from the king, which increased the company's power over the colony and enlarged the area of land to which it had title. The company raised additional capital by selling stock to "adventurers" who would remain in England but share in future profits. It attracted new settlers by offering shares of stock to "planters" who were willing to migrate at their own expense. And it provided free passage to Virginia for poorer people who would agree to serve the company for seven years. In the spring of 1609, confident that it was now poised to transform Jamestown into a vibrant, successful venture, the company launched a "great fleet" of nine vessels with about 600 people (including some women and children) aboard—headed for Virginia.

THE WINTER OF 1609–1610 BECAME KNOWN AS THE "STARVING TIME," A PERIOD WORSE THAN ANYTHING THE COLONISTS HAD SUFFERED BEFORE.

More disaster followed. One of the Virginia-bound ships was lost at sea in a hurricane. Another ran aground on one of the

THE STARVING TIME Bermuda islands and was unable to free itself for months. Many of those who reached Jamestown, still weak from their long and stormy voyage, succumbed to fevers before the cold weather came. The winter of 1609–1610 became known as the "starving time," a period worse than anything they had suffered before. The local Indians, antagonized by John Smith's raids and other hostile actions by the early English settlers, killed off the live-stock in the woods and kept the colonists barricaded within their palisade. The Europeans lived on what they could find: "dogs, cats, rats, snakes, toadstools, horsehides," and even the "corpses of dead men," as one survivor recalled. The following May, the migrants who had run aground and been stranded on Bermuda finally arrived in Jamestown. They found only about 60 people (out of 500 residents the previous summer) still alive—and those so weakened by the ordeal that they seemed scarcely human. There seemed no point in staying on. The new arrivals took the survivors onto their ship, abandoned the settlement, and sailed downriver for home.

That might have been the end of Jamestown had it not been for an extraordinary twist of fate. As the refugees proceeded down the James River toward the Chesapeake Bay, they met an English ship coming up the river—part of a fleet bringing supplies and the colony's first governor, Lord De La Warr. The departing settlers agreed to turn around and return to Jamestown. New relief expeditions with hundreds of colonists soon began to arrive, and the effort to turn a profit in Jamestown resumed.

De La Warr and his successors (Sir Thomas Dale and Sir Thomas Gates) imposed a harsh and rigid discipline on the colony. They organized settlers into work gangs. They sentenced offenders to be flogged, hanged, or broken on the wheel. But this communal system of labor did not function effectively for long. Settlers often evaded work. Governor Dale soon concluded that the colony would fare better if the colonists had personal incentives to work. He began to permit the private ownership and cultivation of land. Landowners would repay the company with part-time work and contributions of grain to its storehouses.

DE LA WARR'S HARSH DISCIPLINE

Under the leadership of these first, harsh governors, Virginia was not always a happy place. But it survived and even expanded. New settlements began lining the river above and below Jamestown. The expansion was partly a result of the order and discipline the governors at times managed to impose. It was partly a product of increased military assaults on the local Indian tribes, which provided protection for the new settlements. But it also occurred because the colonists had at last discovered a marketable crop: tobacco.

TOBACCO

Europeans had become aware of tobacco soon after Columbus's first return from the West Indies, where he had seen the Cuban natives smoking small cigars *(tabacos)*, which they inserted in the nostril. By the early seventeenth century, tobacco from the Spanish colonies was already in wide use in Europe. Some critics denounced it as a poisonous weed, the cause of many diseases. King James I himself led the attack with "A Counterblaste to Tobacco" (1604), in which he urged his people not to imitate "the barbarous and beastly manners of the wild, godless, and slavish Indians, especially in so vile and stinking a custom." Other critics were concerned because England's tobacco purchases from the Spanish colonies meant a drain of English

gold to the Spanish importers. Still, the demand for tobacco soared.

Then in 1612, the Jamestown planter John Rolfe began to experiment in Virginia with a harsh strain of tobacco that local Indians had been growing for years. He produced crops of high quality and found ready buyers in England. Tobacco cultivation quickly spread up and down the James. The character of this tobacco economy—its profitability, its uncertainty, its land and labor demands—transformed Chesapeake society in fundamental ways.

EMERGENCE OF THE TOBACCO ECONOMY

Of most immediate importance, perhaps, was that tobacco cultivation required territorial expansion. Tobacco growers needed large areas of farmland to grow their crops; and because tobacco exhausted the soil after only a few years, the demand for land increased even more. English farmers began establishing plantations deeper and deeper in the interior, isolating them-

THE GROWTH OF THE CHESAPEAKE, 1607–1750 This map shows the political forms of European settlement in the region of the Chesapeake Bay in the seventeenth and early eighteenth centuries. Note the several different kinds of colonial enterprises: the royal colony of Virginia, controlled directly by the English crown after the failure of the early commercial enterprises there; and the proprietary regions of Maryland, northern Virginia, and North Carolina, which were under the control of powerful English aristocrats.

• *Did these political differences have any significant effect on the economic activities of the various Chesapeake colonies?*

TOBACCO PLANT This 1622 woodcut, later hand-colored, represents the tobacco plant cultivated by English settlers in Virginia in the early seventeenth century after John Rolfe introduced it to the colonists. On the right is an image of a man smoking the plant through a very large pipe. (Getty Images)

selves from the center of European settlement at Jamestown and encroaching on territory the natives considered their own.

EXPANSION

Even the discovery of tobacco cultivation was not enough to help the Virginia Company. By 1616, there were still no profits, only land and debts. Nevertheless, the promoters continued to hope that the tobacco trade would allow them finally to turn the corner. In 1618, they launched a last great campaign to attract settlers and make the colony profitable.

Part of that campaign was an effort to recruit new settlers and workers to the colony. The company called it the "head-right" system. Headrights were fifty-acre grants of land, which new settlers could acquire in a variety of ways. Those who already lived in the colony received 100 acres apiece. Each new settler received a single headright for himself or herself. This system encouraged family groups to migrate together, since the more family members traveled to America, the larger the landholding the family would receive. In addition, anyone (new settler or old) who paid for the passage of other immigrants to Virginia would receive an additional headright for each new arrival—thus, the company hoped, inducing the prosperous to import new laborers to America. Some colonists were able to assemble sizable plantations with the combined headrights they received for their families and their servants. In

THE HEADRIGHT SYSTEM

return, they contributed a small quitrent (one shilling a year for each headright) to the company.

The company added other incentives as well. To diversify the colonial economy, it transported ironworkers and other skilled craftsmen to Virginia. In 1619, it sent 100 Englishwomen to the colony (which was still overwhelmingly male) to become the wives of male colonists. (The women were purchased for 120 pounds of tobacco. Their status was somewhere between indentured servants and free people, depending on the goodwill—or lack of it—of their husbands.) The company promised the colonists the full rights of Englishmen (as provided in the original charter of 1606), an end to the strict and arbitrary rule of the communal years, and even a share in self-government. On July 30, 1619, in the Jamestown church, delegates from the various communities met as the House of Burgesses. It was the first meeting of an elected legislature within what was to become the United States.

A month later, another event in Virginia established a very different but no less momentous precedent. As John Rolfe recorded, "about the latter end of August" a Dutch ship brought in "20 and odd Negroes." The status and fate of these first Africans in the English colonies remains obscure. There is some reason to believe that the colonists did not consider them slaves, that they thought of them as servants to be held for a term of years and then freed, like the white servants with whom the planters were already familiar. For a time, moreover, the use of black labor remained limited. Although Africans continued to trickle steadily into the colony, planters continued to prefer European indentured servants until at least the 1670s, when white servants began to become scarce and expensive. But whether or not anyone realized it at the time, the small group of black people who arrived in 1619 marked a first step toward the enslavement of Africans within what was to be the American republic.

The expansion of the colony was able to proceed only because of effective suppression of local Indians who resisted the expanding English presence. For two years, Sir Thomas Dale led unrelenting assaults against the Powhatan Indians and in the process kidnapped the great chief Powhatan's daughter Pocahontas. When Powhatan refused to ransom her, she converted to Christianity and in 1614 married John Rolfe. (Pocahontas accompanied her husband back to England, where, as a Christian convert and a gracious woman, she stirred interest in projects to "civilize" the Indians. She died while abroad.) At that point, Powhatan ceased his attacks on the English in the face of overwhelming odds. But after his death several years later, his brother, Opechancanough, became head of the native confederacy. Recognizing that the position of his tribe was rapidly deteriorating, he resumed the effort to defend tribal lands from European encroachments. On a March morning in 1622, tribesmen called on the white settlements as if to offer goods for sale, then suddenly attacked. Not until 347 whites of both sexes and all ages lay dead or dying were the Indian warriors finally forced to retreat. The surviving English struck back mercilessly at the Indians and turned back the threat for a time. Only after Opechancanough failed in

SUPPRESSION OF THE POWHATAN INDIANS

another uprising in 1644 did the Powhatans finally cease to challenge the eastern regions of the colony.

By then the Virginia Company in London was defunct. The company had poured virtually all its funds into its profitless Demise of the Virginia Company Jamestown venture and, in the aftermath of the 1622 Indian uprising, faced imminent bankruptcy. In 1624, James I revoked the company's charter, and the colony came under the control of the crown. It would remain so until 1776.

EXCHANGES OF AGRICULTURAL TECHNOLOGY

The hostility of the early English settlers toward their Indian neighbors was in part a result of their conviction that their own civilization was greatly superior to that of the natives—and perhaps above all that they were more technologically advanced. The English, after all, had great oceangoing vessels, muskets and other advanced implements of weaponry, and many other tools that the Indians had not developed. Indeed, when John Smith and other early Jamestown residents grew frustrated at their inability to find gold and other precious commodities, they often blamed their failure on the backwardness of the natives.

Yet the survival of Jamestown was, in the end, largely a result of agricultural technologies developed by Indians and borrowed from them by the English. Native agriculture was far better adapted to the soil and climate of Virginia than were the agricultural traditions the English settlers brought with them. The Indians of Virginia had built successful farms with neatly ordered fields in which grew a variety of crops, some of which had been previously unknown to the English. Some of the Indian farmlands stretched over hundreds of acres and supported substantial populations.

The English settlers did not adopt all the Indian agricultural techniques. Natives cleared fields not, as the English did, by cutting down and uprooting all the trees. Instead, they killed trees in place by "girdling" them (that is, making deep incisions around the base) in the areas in which they planted or by setting fire to their roots; and they planted crops not in long, straight rows, but in curving patterns around the dead tree trunks. But in other respects, the English learned a great deal from the Indians about how to grow food in the New World. In particular, they quickly recognized the great value of corn, which proved to be easier to cultivate and to produce much greater yields than any of the European grains the English had known at home. Corn was also attractive to the settlers because its stalks could be a source of sugar and because it spoiled less easily than other grains. The English also learned the advantages of growing beans alongside corn to enrich the soil.

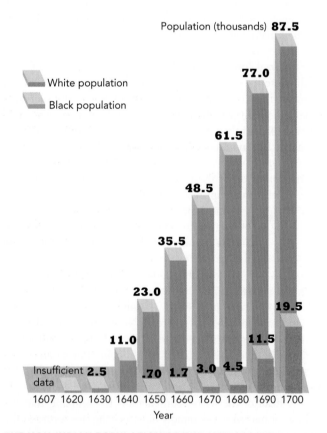

THE NON-INDIAN POPULATION OF THE CHESAPEAKE, 1607–1700 This graph shows the rapid growth of the population of the Chesapeake during its first century of European settlement. Note the dramatic increases in the first half of the century and the somewhat slower increase in the later decades. If the forcibly imported slave population were not counted in the last two decades of the century, the non-Indian population would have grown virtually not at all.

• *What impact would the growth of African slavery have had on the rate of immigration by Europeans?*

MARYLAND AND THE CALVERTS

Maryland was founded under circumstances very different from those of Virginia, but it nonetheless developed in ways markedly similar to those of its neighbor to the south. The new colony was the dream of George Calvert, the first Lord Baltimore, a recent convert to Catholicism and a shrewd businessman. Calvert envisioned establishing a colony both as a great speculative venture in real estate and as a retreat for English Catholics, many of whom felt oppressed by the Anglican establishment at home. He died before he could receive a charter from the king. But in 1632, his son Cecilius, the second Lord Baltimore, received a charter remarkable not only for the extent of the territory it granted him—an area that encompassed parts of what are now Pennsylvania, Delaware, and Virginia, in addition to present-day Maryland—but also for the powers it bestowed on him. He and Proprietary Rule his heirs were to hold their province as "true and absolute lords and proprietaries," and were to acknowledge the sovereignty of the king only by paying an annual fee to the crown.

Lord Baltimore named his brother, Leonard Calvert, governor and sent him with another brother to oversee the settlement of the province. In March 1634, two ships—the *Ark* and the *Dove*—bearing 200 to 300 passengers entered the Potomac River and turned into one of its eastern tributaries. On a high and dry bluff, these first arrivals laid out the village of St. Mary's

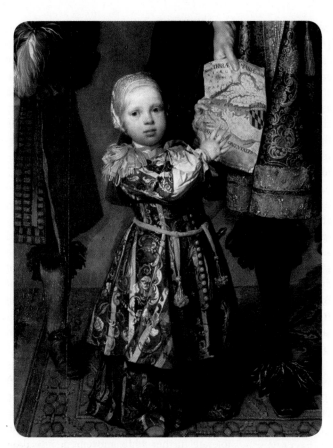

THE MARYLAND PROPRIETOR, C. 1670 In a detail of a portrait by the court painter to King Charles II, the young Cecilius Calvert reaches for a map of Maryland. His grandfather and namesake, the second Lord Baltimore (1606–1675), holds it out to him. George Calvert, the father of the elder Cecilius, began negotiations to win a royal charter for Maryland; his son completed them in 1632 and became the first proprietor of the colony. He published the map shown here in 1635 as part of an effort to attract settlers to the colony. By the time this portrait was painted, Lord Baltimore's son, Charles, was governor of Maryland. The boy Cecilius, the heir apparent, died in 1681 before he could assume his title. (Enoch Pratt Free Library, Baltimore)

(named, diplomatically, for the queen). The neighboring Indians, who were more worried about rival tribes in the region than they were about the new arrivals, befriended the settlers, provided them with temporary shelter, sold them land, and supplied them with corn. Unlike the Virginians, the early Marylanders experienced no Indian assaults, no plagues, no starving time.

The Calverts had invested heavily in their American possessions, and they needed to attract many settlers to make the effort profitable. As a result, they had to encourage

RELIGIOUS TOLERATION

the immigration of Protestants as well as their fellow English Catholics, who were both relatively few in number (about 2 percent of the population of England) and generally reluctant to emigrate. The Protestant settlers (mostly Anglicans) outnumbered the Catholics from the start, and the Calverts quickly realized that

Catholics would always be a minority in the colony. They prudently adopted a policy of religious toleration. To appease the non-Catholic majority, Calvert appointed a Protestant as governor in 1648. A year later, he sent from England the draft of an "Act Concerning Religion," which assured freedom of worship to all Christians.

Nevertheless, politics in Maryland remained plagued for years by tensions between the Catholic minority (which included the proprietor) and the Protestant majority. Zealous Jesuits and crusading Puritans frightened and antagonized their opponents with their efforts to establish the dominance of their own religion. At one point, the Protestant majority barred Catholics from voting and repealed the Toleration Act. There was frequent violence, and in 1655 a civil war temporarily unseated the proprietary government and replaced it with one dominated by Protestants.

By 1640, a severe labor shortage in the colony had forced a change in the land grant procedure; and Maryland, like Virginia, adopted a "headright" system—a grant of 100 acres to each male settler, another 100 for his wife and each servant, and 50 for each of his children. Like Virginia, Maryland became a center of tobacco cultivation; and as in Virginia, planters worked their land with the aid, first, of indentured servants imported from England and then, beginning late in the seventeenth century, with slaves imported from Africa.

TURBULENT VIRGINIA

By the mid-seventeenth century, the Virginia colony had survived its early disasters. Both its population and the complexity and profitability of its economy were increasing. It was also growing

VIRGINIA'S WESTWARD EXPANSION

more politically contentious, as emerging factions within the province began to compete for the favor of the government. Perhaps the most important dispute involved policy toward the natives. As settlement moved west, farther into Indian lands, border conflicts grew increasingly frequent. Much of the tension within English Virginia in the late seventeenth century revolved around how to respond to those conflicts.

Sir William Berkeley arrived in Virginia in 1642 at the age of thirty-six, having been appointed governor by King Charles I. With but one interruption, he remained in control of the government until the 1670s. Berkeley was a popular governor at first as he sent explorers across the Blue Ridge Mountains to open up the western interior of Virginia. He organized the force that put down the 1644 Indian uprising. The defeated Indians ceded a large area of land to the English. In return, Berkeley agreed to prohibit white settlement west of a line he negotiated with the tribes.

This attempt to protect Indian territory—like many such attempts later in American history—was a failure from the start, largely because of the rapid growth of the Virginia population. Oliver Cromwell's victory in

AS SETTLEMENT MOVED WEST, FARTHER INTO INDIAN LANDS, BORDER CONFLICTS GREW INCREASINGLY FREQUENT.

1649 in the English Civil War (see p. 50) and the flight of many of his defeated opponents to the colony contributed to what was already a substantial population increase. Between 1640 and 1650, Virginia's population doubled from 8,000 to 16,000. By 1660, it had more than doubled again, to 40,000. As the choice lands along the tidewater became scarce, new arrivals and indentured servants completing their terms or escaping from their masters pressed westward into the piedmont. By 1652, English settlers had established three counties in the territory promised to the Indians. Unsurprisingly, there were frequent clashes between natives and whites.

By the 1660s, Berkeley had gradually become a virtual autocrat in the colony. When the first burgesses were elected in 1619, all men aged seventeen or older were entitled to vote. By 1670, the vote was restricted to landowners, and elections were rare. The same burgesses, loyal and subservient to the governor, remained in office year after year. Each county continued to have only two representatives, even though some of the new counties of the interior contained many more people than the older ones of the tidewater area. Thus the more recent settlers in the "backcountry" were underrepresented or (if living in areas not yet formally organized as counties) not represented at all.

BERKELEY'S AUTOCRATIC RULE

BACON'S REBELLION

In 1676, backcountry unrest and political rivalries combined to create a major conflict. Nathaniel Bacon, a wealthy young graduate of Cambridge University, arrived in Virginia in 1673. He purchased a substantial farm in the west and won a seat on the governor's council. He established himself, in other words, as a member of the backcountry gentry.

But the new and influential western landowners were soon squabbling with the leaders of the tidewater region in the east. They disagreed on many issues but, above all, on policies toward the natives. The backcountry settlements were in constant danger of attack from Indians, because many of them had been established on lands reserved for the tribes by treaty. White settlers in western Virginia had long resented the governor's attempts to hold the line of settlement steady so as to avoid antagonizing the natives.

BACKCOUNTRY GRIEVANCES

Bacon, an aristocratic man with great political ambitions, had additional reasons for unhappiness with Berkeley. He resented his exclusion from the inner circle of the governor's council (the so-called Green Spring group, whose members enjoyed special access to patronage). Bacon also fumed about Berkeley's refusal to allow him a piece of the Indian fur trade. He was developing grievances that made him a natural leader of an opposing faction.

Bloody events thrust him into that role. In 1675, some Doeg Indians—angry about the European intrusions into their lands—raided a western plantation and killed a white servant. Bands of local whites struck back angrily and haphazardly, attacking not only the small Doeg tribe but the powerful Susquehannock as well. The Indians responded with more raids on plantations and

killed many more white settlers. As the fighting escalated, Bacon and other concerned landholders—unhappy with the governor's cautious response to their demand for help—defied Berkeley and struck out on their own against the Indians. Berkeley proclaimed him and his men rebels. At that point, what had started as an unauthorized assault on the Indians became a military challenge to the colonial government, a conflict known as Bacon's Rebellion. It was the largest and most powerful insurrection against established authority in the history of the colonies, one that would not be surpassed until the Revolution.

Twice, Bacon led his army east to Jamestown. The first time he won a temporary pardon from the governor; the second time, after the governor reneged on the agreement, he burned the city and drove the governor into exile. In the midst of widespread social turmoil throughout the colony, Bacon stood on the verge of taking command of Virginia. Instead, he died suddenly of dysentery; and Berkeley, his position bolstered by the arrival of British troops, soon managed to regain control. In 1677, the Indians (aware of their inability to defeat the white forces militarily) reluctantly signed a new treaty that opened additional lands to white settlement.

Bacon's Rebellion was significant for several reasons. It was part of the continuing struggle to define the boundary between Indian and white lands in Virginia; it showed how unwilling the English settlers were to abide by earlier agreements with the natives, and how unwilling the Indians were to tolerate further white movement into their territory. It revealed the bitterness of the competition between eastern and western landowners. But it also revealed something that Bacon himself had never intended to unleash: the potential for instability in the colony's large population of free, landless men. These men—most of them former indentured servants, propertyless, unemployed, with no real prospects—had formed the bulk of Bacon's constituency during the rebellion. They had become a large, unstable, floating population eager above all for access to land. Bacon had for a time maintained his popularity among them by exploiting their hatred of Indians. Gradually, however, he found himself unintentionally leading a movement that reflected the animosity of these landless men toward the landed gentry of which Bacon himself was a part.

SIGNIFICANCE OF BACON'S REBELLION

One result was that landed people in both eastern and western Virginia began to recognize a common interest in preventing social unrest from the former indentures. That was one of several reasons that they turned increasingly to the African slave trade to fulfill their need for labor. Enslaved blacks might pose dangers too, but the events of 1676 persuaded many colonists that the perils of importing a large white subordinate class were even greater.

THE GROWTH OF NEW ENGLAND

The first enduring settlement in New England—the second in English America—resulted from the discontent of a congregation of Puritan Separatists in England. For years, Separatists had been periodically imprisoned and even executed for defying the government and the Church of England; some of them, as a result, began to contemplate leaving England permanently in search of freedom to worship as they wished—even though Puritans did not believe in religious freedom for all others.

RELIGIOUS REPRESSION

PLYMOUTH PLANTATION

It was illegal to leave England without the consent of the king. In 1608, however, a congregation of Separatists from the hamlet of Scrooby began emigrating quietly, a few at a time, to Leyden, Holland, where they could worship without interference. They were, however, barred from the Dutch craft guilds and had to work at unskilled and poorly paid jobs. They were also troubled by the effects of the tolerant atmosphere of Dutch society, which threatened their dream of a close-knit Christian community. As a result, some of the Separatists decided to move again, this time across the Atlantic, where they hoped to create the kind of community they wanted and where they could spread "the gospel of the Kingdom of Christ in those remote parts of the world."

Leaders of the Scrooby group obtained permission from the Virginia Company to settle in British America. From the king, they received informal assurances that he would "not molest them, provided they carried themselves peaceably." (This was a historic concession by the crown, for it opened English America to settlement not only by the Scrooby group but by other dissenting Protestants as well.) Several English merchants agreed to advance the necessary funds in exchange for a share in the profits of the settlement at the end of seven years.

The migrating Puritans "knew they were pilgrims" even before they left Holland, their leader and historian, William Bradford, later wrote. In September 1620 they left the port of Plymouth, on the English coast, in the *Mayflower* with thirty-five "saints" (Puritan Separatists) and sixty-seven "strangers" (people who were not full members of the church) aboard. By the time they sighted land in November, it was too late in the year to go on. Their original destination was probably the mouth of the Hudson River, in what is now New York. But they found themselves instead on Cape Cod. After exploring the region for a while, they chose a site for their settlement just north of the cape, an area Captain John Smith had named "Plymouth" (after the English port from which the Puritans had sailed) during an exploratory journey some years before. Plymouth lay outside the London Company's territory, and the settlers realized they had no legal basis for settling there. As a result, forty-one male passengers signed a document, the Mayflower Compact, which established a civil government and proclaimed their allegiance to the king. Then, on December 21, 1620, the Pilgrims stepped ashore at Plymouth Rock.

THE MAYFLOWER COMPACT

They settled on cleared land that had once been an Indian village until, three years earlier, a mysterious epidemic—known as "the plague" and probably brought to the region by earlier European explorers—had swept through the region and substantially depopulated it. The Pilgrims' first winter was a diffi-cult one; half the colonists perished from malnutrition, disease, and exposure. Still, the colony survived.

Like the Spanish and Portuguese colonists in the southern regions of the Americas, the Pilgrims (and other future English colonists) brought more to the New World than people and ideas. They also made profound changes in the natural landscape of New England. A smallpox epidemic caused by English carriers almost eliminated the Indian population in the areas around Plymouth in the early 1630s. The English demand for furs, animal skins, and meat greatly depleted the number of wild animals in the areas around Plymouth, one reason colonists worked so hard to develop stocks of domestic animals such as horses, cattle, sheep, and hogs. The Pilgrims and later English settlers also introduced new crops (wheat, barley, oats, and others), while incorporating many native foods (among them corn, potatoes, and peas) into their own diets—and eventually exporting them back to England and the rest of Europe. Gradually, colonial society imposed a European pattern onto the American landscape, as the settlers fenced in pastures, meadows, orchards, and fields for cultivation.

The Pilgrims' experience with the Indians was, for a time at least, very different from the experiences of the early English settlers farther south. That was in part because the remaining natives in the region—their numbers thinned by disease—were significantly weaker than their southern neighbors and realized they had to get along with the Europeans. In the end, the survival and growth of the colony depended crucially on the assistance they received from natives. Important Indian friends—Squanto and Samoset, among others—showed them how to gather seafood, cultivate corn, and hunt local animals. Squanto, a Pawtuxet who had earlier been captured by an English explorer and taken to Europe, spoke English and was of particular help to the settlers in forming an alliance with the local Wampanoags, under Chief Massasoit. After the first harvest, in 1621, the settlers marked the alliance by inviting the Indians to join them in an October festival, the first Thanksgiving.

RELATIONS WITH THE INDIANS

But the good relationship between the settlers and the local Indians did not last. Thirteen years after the Pilgrims' arrival, a devastating smallpox epidemic—a result of contact with English settlers—wiped out much of the Indian population around Plymouth.

The Pilgrims could not hope to create rich farms on the sandy, marshy soil, and their early fishing efforts produced no profits. In 1622 the military officer Miles Standish, one of the leaders of the colony, established a semi-military regime to impose discipline on the settlers. Eventually the Pilgrims began to grow enough corn and other crops to provide them with a modest trading surplus. They also developed a small fur trade with the Abenaki Indians of Maine. From time to time new colonists arrived from England, and in a decade the population reached 300.

The people of "Plymouth Plantation," as they called their settlement, chose William Bradford again and again to be their governor. As early as 1621, he persuaded the Council for New England (the successor to the old Plymouth Company, which

WILLIAM BRADFORD

had charter rights to the territory) to give them legal permission to live there. He ended the communal labor plan Standish had helped create, distributed land among the families, and thus, as he explained it, made "all hands very industrious." He and a group of fellow "undertakers" took over the colony's debt to its original financiers in England and, with earnings from the fur trade, finally paid it off—even though the financiers had repeatedly cheated them and had failed to send them promised supplies.

> ## AS ONE SMALL CANDLE MAY LIGHT A THOUSAND, SO THE LIGHT HERE KINDLED HATH SHONE TO MANY, YEA IN SOME SORT TO OUR WHOLE NATION.
>
> **WILLIAM BRADFORD**

The Pilgrims were always a poor community. As late as the 1640s, they had only one plow among them. But they clung to the belief that God had put them in the New World to live as a truly Christian community; and they were, on the whole, content to live their lives in what they considered godly ways.

At times, they spoke of serving as a model for other Christians. Governor Bradford wrote in retrospect: "As one small candle may light a thousand, so the light here kindled hath shone to many, yea in some sort to our whole nation." But the Pilgrims were less committed to grand designs, less concerned about how they were viewed by others, than were the Puritans who settled the larger and more ambitious English colonies to their north.

THE PURITAN EXPERIMENT

Turbulent events in England in the 1620s (combined with the example of the Plymouth colony) created strong interest in colonization among other groups of Puritans. King James I had been creating serious tensions for years between himself and Parliament through his effort to claim the divine right of kings and by his harsh, repressive policies toward the Puritans. The situation worsened after his death in 1625, when he was succeeded by his son, Charles I. By favoring Roman Catholicism and trying to destroy religious nonconformity, Charles I started the nation down the road that in the 1640s would lead to civil war. The Puritans were particular targets of Charles's policies. Some were imprisoned for their beliefs, and many began to consider the climate of England intolerable. The king's disbanding of Parliament in 1629 (it was not to be recalled until 1640) ensured that there would be no political solution to the Puritans' problems.

In the midst of this political and social turmoil, a group of Puritan merchants began organizing a new enterprise designed MASSACHUSETTS BAY COMPANY to take advantage of opportunities in America. At first their interest was largely an economic one. They obtained a grant of land in New England for most of the area now comprising Massachusetts and New Hampshire; they acquired a charter from Charles I (who was evidently unaware that they were Puritans) allowing them to create the Massachusetts Bay Company and to establish a colony in the New World; and they bought equipment and supplies from a defunct fishing and trading company that had attempted (and failed) to establish a profitable enterprise in North America earlier. In 1629, they were ready to dispatch a substantial group of settlers to New England.

Among the members of the Massachusetts Bay Company, however, were a number of Puritans who saw the enterprise as something more than a business venture. They began to consider emigrating themselves and creating a haven for Puritans in New England. Members of this faction met secretly in Cambridge in the summer of 1629 and agreed to buy out the other investors and move en masse to America.

As governor, the new owners of the company chose John JOHN WINTHROP Winthrop, an affluent, university-educated gentleman with a deep piety and a forceful character. Winthrop had been instrumental in organizing the migration, and he commanded the expedition that sailed for New England in 1630: seventeen ships and 1,000 people (who were, unlike the earlier migrants to Virginia,

COLONIAL CURRENCY This seal was created in 1690 by the Massachusetts Bay Company to validate the paper "bills of credit" with which colonists conducted many financial transactions. Paper money met considerable resistance at first. Many people doubted its value and would not accept it, preferring instead the Spanish silver coins that were in wide circulation at the time. Gradually, however, a shortage of silver required increasing reliance on this and other paper devices. The seal shows an Indian saying "Come over and help us," which represents the English belief in the superiority of white European society. (Courtesy of the Massachusetts Historical Society)

PORTRAIT OF A BOSTON WOMAN Anne Pollard, a member of the original Winthrop expedition to Boston, was 100 years old when this portrait was painted in 1721. In 1643, thirteen years after her arrival in Massachusetts, she married a Boston innkeeper with whom she had 13 children. After her husband's death in 1679, she continued to manage the tavern on her own. When she died in 1725, at the age of 104, she left 130 direct descendants. The artist who painted this early portrait is unknown, but is assumed to be an American working in the relatively primitive style common in New England before the arrival in 1729 of the first academically trained portraitists from England. (Courtesy of the Massachusetts Historical Society)

clude all male citizens, not just the stockholders. John Winthrop dominated colonial politics just as he had dominated the original corporation, but after 1634 he and most other officers of the colony had to face election each year.

Unlike the Separatist founders of Plymouth, the founders of Massachusetts had no intention of breaking from the Church of England. Yet, if they continued to feel any real attachment to the Anglican establishment, they gave little sign of it. In every town, the community church had (in the words of the prominent minister John Cotton) "complete liberty to stand alone," unlike churches in the highly centralized Anglican structure in England. Each congregation chose its own minister and regulated its own affairs. In both Plymouth and Massachusetts, this form of parish organization eventually became known as the Congregational Church.

THE CONGREGATIONAL CHURCH

The Puritans, although nominally members of the Anglican Church, were in fact worshipers of a very different faith. They did not accept the authority of either the Roman Catholic hierarchy or the Church of England. They did not follow traditional ceremonial worship and did not receive sacraments from priests. They learned, instead, from reading the Bible and from listening to ministers who spoke from their own knowledge and belief, not from the orthodoxies of traditional institutional faith. They accepted the doctrines of John Calvin's vision that everyone was destined at birth for either salvation or damnation—that nothing in people's earthly life could change their fate after death. But living a good and productive life might be a sign of salvation. Puritans not only sought salvation. They also sought freedom—not the kind of freedom Americans understand today, but the right to worship without interference from England or from established churches. That did not mean that they were free to behave as they liked; the community expected obedience to authority. But authority was based largely within the community itself and monitored by its members. It did not come from England or from centralized institutions in America.

The Massachusetts Puritans were not grim or joyless, as many observers would later portray them. They were, however, serious and pious people. They strove to lead useful, conscientious lives of thrift and hard work, and they honored material success as evidence of God's favor. "We here enjoy God and Jesus Christ," Winthrop wrote to his wife soon after his arrival; "is this not enough?" He and the other Massachusetts founders believed they were founding a holy commonwealth—a "city upon a hill"—that could serve as a model for the rest of the world.

If Massachusetts was to become a beacon to other emigrants, it had first to maintain its own "holiness." Ministers had no formal political power, but they exerted great influence on church members, who were the only people who could vote or hold office. The government in turn protected the ministers, taxed the people (members and nonmembers alike) to support the church, and enforced the law requiring attendance at services. Dissidents had no more freedom of worship in America than the Puritans themselves had had in England. Colonial

A THEOCRATIC SOCIETY

mostly family groups). It was the largest single migration of its kind in the seventeenth century. Winthrop carried with him the charter of the Massachusetts Bay Company, which meant that the colonists would be responsible to no company officials in England, only to themselves.

The Massachusetts migration quickly produced several different new settlements. The port of Boston, at the mouth of the Charles River, became the company's headquarters and the colony's capital. But in the course of the next decade, colonists moved into a number of other new towns in eastern Massachusetts: Charlestown, Newtown (later renamed Cambridge), Roxbury, Dorchester, Watertown, Ipswich, Concord, Sudbury, and others.

The Massachusetts Bay Company soon transformed itself into a colonial government. According to the original company charter, the eight stockholders (or "freemen") were to meet as a general court to choose officers and adopt rules for the corporation. But eventually the definition of "freemen" changed to in-

Massachusetts was in many ways a "theocracy," a society in which the line between the church and the state was hard to see.

Like other new settlements, the Massachusetts Bay colony had early difficulties. During their first winter, an unusually severe one, nearly a third of the colonists died; others left in the spring. But more rapidly than Jamestown or Plymouth, the colony grew and prospered. The Pilgrims and neighboring Indians helped with food and advice. Affluent incoming settlers brought needed tools and other goods, which they exchanged for the cattle, corn, and other produce of the established colonists and the natives. The large number of family groups in the colony (in sharp contrast to the early years at Jamestown) helped ensure a feeling of commitment to the community and a sense of order among the settlers. It also allowed the population to reproduce itself more rapidly. The strong religious and political hierarchy ensured a measure of social stability.

THE EXPANSION OF NEW ENGLAND

As the population grew, more and more people arrived in Massachusetts who were not Puritan "saints" and hence could not vote. Newcomers had a choice of con-

GROWING RELIGIOUS DISSENT

forming to the religious practices of the colony or leaving. Many left, helping to begin a process that would spread settlement throughout present-day New England and beyond.

The Connecticut Valley, about 100 miles west of the edge of European settlement around Boston, began attracting English families as early as the 1630s. The valley appealed in particular to Thomas Hooker, a minister of Newtown (Cambridge), who defied the Massachusetts government in 1635 and led his congregation through the wilds to establish the town of Hartford. Four years later, the people of Hartford and of two other towns established a colonial government of their own and adopted a constitution known as the Fundamental Orders of Connecticut.

Another Connecticut colony, the project of a Puritan minister and a wealthy merchant from England, grew up around New Haven on the Connecticut coast. It reflected impatience with what its founders considered increasing religious laxity in Massachusetts. The Fundamental Articles of New Haven (1639) established a religious government even stricter than that in Boston. New Haven remained independent until 1662, when a royal charter combined it with Hartford to create the colony of Connecticut.

Rhode Island had its origins in the religious and political dissent of Roger Williams, an engaging but controversial young minister who lived for a time in Salem, Massachusetts. Even John Winthrop, who considered Williams a heretic, called him

ROGER WILLIAMS

a "sweet and amiable" man, and William Bradford described him as "a man godly and zealous." But he was, Bradford added, "very unsettled in judgment." Williams, a confirmed Separatist,

argued that the Massachusetts church should abandon all allegiance to the Church of England. More disturbing to the clergy, he called for a complete separation of church and state—to protect the church from the corruption of the secular world. The colonial government, alarmed at this challenge to its spiritual authority, banished him. During the bitter winter of 1635–1636, Williams took refuge with Narragansett tribesmen; the following spring he bought a tract of land from them and, with a few followers, created the town of Providence on it. Other communities of dissidents followed him to what became Rhode Island, and in 1644 Williams obtained a charter from Parliament permitting him to establish a government. Rhode Island's government gave no support to the church and allowed "liberty in religious concernments." For a time, it was the only colony in which members of all faiths (including Jews) could worship without interference.

An even greater challenge to the established order in Massachusetts Bay emerged in the person of Anne Hutchinson, an intelligent and charismatic woman from a substantial Boston family. Hutchinson had come to Massachusetts with her husband in 1634. She antagonized the leaders of the colony by arguing vehemently that the members of the Massachusetts clergy who were not among the "elect"—that is, had not undergone a conversion experience—had no right to spiritual office. Over time, she claimed that many clergy—among them her own uninspiring minister—were among the non-elect and had no right to exercise authority over their congregations. She eventually charged that all the ministers in Massachusetts—save community leader John Cotton and her own bother-in-law—were not among the elect. Alongside such teachings (which her critics called

ANNE HUTCHINSON

"Antinomianism," from the Greek word meaning "hostile to the law"), Hutchinson also created alarm by affronting prevailing assumptions about the proper role of women in Puritan society. She was not a retiring, deferential wife and mother, but a powerful religious figure in her own right.

Hutchinson developed a large following among women, to whom she offered an active role in religious affairs. She also attracted support from merchants, young men, and dissidents of many sorts who resented the oppressive character of the colonial government. As her influence grew, the Massachusetts leadership mobilized to stop her. Hutchinson's followers were numerous and influential enough to prevent Winthrop's reelection as governor in 1636, but the next year he returned to office and put her on trial for heresy. Hutchinson embarrassed her accusers by displaying a remarkable knowledge of theology; but because she continued to defy clerical authority (and because she claimed she had herself communicated directly with the Holy Spirit—a violation of the Puritan belief that the age of such revelations had passed), she was convicted of sedition and banished as "a woman not fit for our society." Her unorthodox views had challenged both religious belief and social order in Puritan Massachusetts.

NEWCOMERS HAD A CHOICE OF CONFORMING TO THE RELIGIOUS PRACTICES OF THE COLONY OR LEAVING.

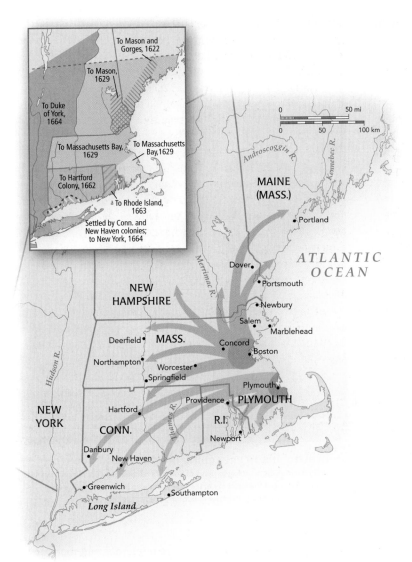

THE GROWTH OF NEW ENGLAND, 1620–1750 The European settlement of New England, as this map reveals, traces its origins primarily to two small settlements on the Atlantic coast. The first was the Pilgrim settlement at Plymouth, which began in 1620 and spread out through Cape Cod, southern Massachusetts, and the islands of Martha's Vineyard and Nantucket. The second, much larger settlement began in Boston in 1630 and spread rapidly through western Massachusetts, north into New Hampshire and Maine, and south into Connecticut.

• *Why would the settlers of Massachusetts Bay have expanded more rapidly and expansively than those of Plymouth?*

With her family and some of her followers, she moved to Rhode Island and then into New Netherland (later New York), where in 1643 she died during an Indian uprising.

Alarmed by Hutchinson's heresy, male clergy began to restrict further the already limited public activities of women within congregations. As a result, many of Hutchinson's followers began to migrate out of Massachusetts Bay, especially to New Hampshire and Maine.

Colonies had been established there in 1629 when two English proprietors, Captain John Mason and Sir Ferdinando Gorges, had received a grant from the Council for New England and divided it along the Piscataqua River to create two separate provinces. But despite their lavish promotional efforts, few settlers had moved into these northern regions until the religious disruptions in Massachusetts Bay. In 1639, John Wheelwright, a disciple of Anne Hutchinson, led some of his fellow dissenters to Exeter, New Hampshire. Other groups—of both dissenting and orthodox Puritans—soon followed. New

NEW HAMPSHIRE AND MAINE

Hampshire became a separate colony in 1679. Maine remained a part of Massachusetts until 1820.

SETTLERS AND NATIVES

Indians were less powerful rivals to the early New England immigrants than natives were to the English settlers farther south. By the mid-1630s, the native population, small to begin with, had been almost extinguished by the epidemics. The surviving Indians sold much of their land to the English (a great boost to settlement, since much of it had already been cleared). Some natives—known as "praying Indians"—even converted to Christianity and joined Puritan communities.

Indians provided crucial assistance to the early settlers as they tried to adapt to the new land. Whites learned from the natives about vital local food crops: corn, beans, pumpkins, and potatoes. They also learned such crucial agricultural techniques as annual burning for fertilization and

IMPORTANCE OF INDIAN ASSISTANCE

Population (thousands) **93.0**

87.0

68.5

32.0

33.0

23.0

13.5

2.0

1620 1630 1640 1650 1660 1670 1680 1690 1700
Year

THE NON-INDIAN POPULATION OF NEW ENGLAND, 1620–1700
As in the Chesapeake colonies, the European population of New England grew very rapidly after settlement began in 1620. The most rapid rate of growth, unsurprisingly, came in the first thirty years, when even a modest wave of immigraton could double or triple the small existing population. But the largest numbers of new immigrants arrived between 1650 and 1680.

• *What events in England in those years might have led to increased emigration to America in that period?*

ANNE HUTCHINSON PREACHING IN HER HOUSE IN BOSTON
Anne Hutchinson was alarming to many of Boston's religious leaders not only because she openly challenged the authority of the clergy, but also because she implicitly challenged norms of female behavior in Puritan society. (Bettmann/Corbis)

planting beans to replenish exhausted soil. Natives also served as important trading partners to European immigrants, particularly in the creation of the thriving North American fur trade. They were an important market for such manufactured goods as iron pots, blankets, metal-tipped arrows, eventually guns and rifles, and (often tragically) alcohol. Indeed, commerce with the Indians was responsible for the creation of some of the first great fortunes in British North America and for the emergence of wealthy families who would exercise influence in the colonies (and later the nation) for many generations.

But as in other areas of white settlement, there were also conflicts; and the early peaceful relations between whites and Indians did not last. Tensions soon developed as a result of the white colonists' continuing appetite for land. The expanding white demand for land was also a result of a change in the colonists' agrarian economy. As wild animals began to disappear from overhunting, colonists began to concentrate more and more on raising domesticated animals: cattle, sheep, hogs, horses, and others. As the herds expanded, so did the colonists' need for new land. As a result, the colonists moved steadily into territories such as the Connecticut Valley where they came into conflict with natives who were more numerous and more powerful than those along the Massachusetts coast.

The character of those conflicts—and the brutality with which whites assaulted their Indian foes—emerged in part out of changing Puritan attitudes toward the natives. At first, many white New Englanders had looked at the Indians with a slightly condescending admiration. Before long, however, they came to view them primarily as "heathens" and "savages," and hence as a constant threat to the existence of a godly community in the New World. Some Puritans believed the solution to the Indian "problem" was to "civilize" the natives by converting them to Christianity and European ways, and some English missionaries had modest success in producing converts. One such missionary, John Eliot, even translated the Bible into an Algonquian language. Other Puritans, however, envisioned a harsher "solution": displacing or, if that failed, exterminating the natives.

To the natives, the threat from the English was very direct. European settlers were penetrating deeper and deeper into the interior, seizing land, clearing forests, driving away much of the wild game on which the tribes depended for food. English farmers often let their livestock run wild, and the animals frequently

SHIFTING
ATTITUDES

A PEQUOT VILLAGE DESTROYED An English artist drew this view of a fortified Pequot village in Connecticut surrounded by English soldiers and their allies from other tribes during the Pequot War in 1637. The invaders massacred more than 600 residents of the settlement. (Rare Books Division, New York Public Library, Astor, Lenox and Tilden Foundations)

destroyed natives' crops. Land and food shortages exacerbated the drastic Indian population decline that had begun as a result of epidemic diseases. There had been more than 100,000 Indians in New England at the beginning of the seventeenth century; by 1675, only 10,000 remained. This decline created despair among New England natives. It drove some Indians to alcoholism and others to conversion to Christianity. But it drove others to war.

THE PEQUOT WAR, KING PHILIP'S WAR, AND THE TECHNOLOGY OF BATTLE

The first major conflict came in 1637, when hostilities broke out between English settlers in the Connecticut Valley and the

THE PEQUOT WAR

Pequot Indians of the region as a result of competition over trade with the Dutch in New Netherland and friction over land. In what became known as the Pequot War, English settlers allied with the Mohegan and Narragansett Indians (rivals of the Pequots). The greatest savagery in the conflict was the work of the English. In the bloodiest act of the war, white raiders under Captain John Mason marched against a palisaded Pequot stronghold and set it afire. Hundreds of Indians either burned to death in the flaming stockade or were killed as they attempted to escape. Those who survived were hunted down, captured, and sold as slaves. The Pequot tribe was almost wiped out.

The most prolonged and deadly encounter between whites and Indians in the seventeenth century began in 1675, a conflict

that the English would remember for generations as King Philip's War. As in the earlier Pequot War in Connecticut, an Indian tribe—in this case the Wampanoags, under the lead-

KING PHILIP'S WAR

ership of a chieftain known to the white settlers as King Philip and among his own people as Metacomet—rose up to resist the English. The Wampanoags had not always been hostile to the settlers; indeed, Metacomet's grandfather had once forged an alliance with the English, and Metacomet himself was well acquainted with the colonists. But by the 1670s, he had become convinced that only armed resistance could protect the Wampanoags from English incursions into their lands and, more immediately, from the efforts by the colonial governments to impose English law on them. (A court in Plymouth had recently tried and hanged several Wampanoags for murdering a member of their own tribe.)

For three years, the natives—well organized and armed with guns—terrorized a string of Massachusetts towns, destroying twenty of them and causing the deaths of as many as a thousand people (including at least one-sixteenth of the white males in the colony). The war greatly weakened both the society and economy of Massachusetts. But, in 1676, the white settlers fought back and gradually prevailed. They received critical aid from the Mohawks, longtime rivals of the Wampanoags, and guides, spies, and soldiers recruited from among the so-called praying Indians (Christian converts) of the region. While white militiamen attacked Indian villages and destroyed native food supplies, a group of Mohawks ambushed, shot, and killed Metacomet, then bore his severed head to Boston to present to the colonial leaders. After that, the fragile alliance that Metacomet had managed to forge among local tribes collapsed. Europeans were soon able to crush the uprising. Some Wampanoag leaders were executed; others were sold into slavery in the West Indies. The Wampanoags and their allies, their populations depleted and their natural resources reduced, were now powerless to resist the English.

Yet these victories by the white colonists did not end the danger to their settlements. Other Indians in other tribes survived and were still capable of attacking English settlements. The New England settlers also faced competition not only from the natives but also from the Dutch and the French, who claimed the territory on which some of the outlying settlements were established. The French, in particular, would pose a constant threat to the English through their alliance with the Algonquins. In later years, the French would join forces with Indians in their attacks on the New England frontier.

The character of the Pequot War, King Philip's War, and many other conflicts between natives and settlers in the years that followed was crucially affected by earlier exchanges of technology between the English and the tribes. In particular, the

Indians made effective use of a relatively new weapon intro-

FLINTLOCK
MUSKET

duced to New England by Miles Standish and others: the flintlock rifle. It replaced the earlier staple of colonial musketry, the matchlock rifle, which proved too heavy, cumbersome, and inaccurate to be useful in the kind of combat characteristic of Anglo-Indian struggles. The matchlock had to be steadied on a fixed object and ignited with a match before firing; the flintlock could be held up without support and fired without a match. (Indians using bows and arrows often outmatched settlers using the clumsy matchlocks.)

Many English settlers were slow to give up their cumbersome matchlocks for the lighter flintlocks. But the Indians recognized the advantages of the newer rifles right away and began purchasing them in large quantities as part of their regular trade with the colonists. Despite rules forbidding colonists to instruct natives on how to use and repair the weapons, the natives learned to handle the rifles, and even to repair them, very effectively on their own. They even built a substantial forge for shaping and repairing rifle parts. In King Philip's War, the very high casualties on both sides were a result of the use of these more advanced rifles.

Indians also used more traditional military technologies in their conflicts with the English—especially the construction of forts. The Narragansetts, allies of the Wampanoags in King Philip's War, built an enormous fort in the Great Swamp of Rhode Island in 1675, which became the site of one of the bloodiest battles of the war before English attackers burned it down. After that, a band of Narragansetts set out to build a large stone fort, with the help of a member of the tribe who had learned masonry while working with the English. When English soldiers discovered the stone fort in 1676, after the end of King Philip's War, they killed most of its occupants and destroyed it. In the end, the technological skills of the Indians (both those they borrowed from the English and those they drew from their own traditions) proved no match for the overwhelming advantages of the English settlers in both numbers and firepower.

THE RESTORATION COLONIES

By the end of the 1630s, English settlers had established six significant colonies in the New World: Virginia, Massachusetts, Maryland, Connecticut, Rhode Island, and New Hampshire. (Maine remained officially part of Massachusetts until after the American Revolution.) But for nearly thirty years after Lord Baltimore received the charter for Maryland in 1632, the English government launched no additional colonial ventures. It was preoccupied with troubles of its own at home.

THE ENGLISH CIVIL WAR

ORIGINS

England's problems had begun during the rule of James I, who attracted widespread opposition before he died in 1625. James, however, did not openly challenge Parliament. His son, Charles I, was not so prudent. He dissolved Parliament in 1629 and began ruling as an absolute monarch, steadily alienating a growing number of his subjects—and the members of the powerful Puritan community above all. Finally, desperately in need of money, Charles called Parliament back into session and asked it to levy new taxes. But he antagonized the members by dismissing them again twice in two years. In 1642, some of them organized a military challenge to the king, thus launching the English Civil War.

The conflict between the Cavaliers (the supporters of the king) and the Roundheads (the forces of Parliament, who were mostly Puritans) lasted seven years. Finally, in 1649, the Roundheads defeated the king's forces, captured Charles himself, and—in an action that horrified not only much of continental Europe at the time but also future generations of English men and women—beheaded the monarch. To replace him, they elevated the stern Roundhead leader Oliver Cromwell to the position of "protector," from which he ruled for the next nine years. When Cromwell died in 1658, his son and heir proved unable to maintain his authority. Two years later, King Charles II, son of the beheaded monarch, returned from exile and claimed the throne.

Among the many results of the Stuart Restoration—the

NEW
PROPRIETARY
COLONIES

return of Charles II, a member of the Stuart royal family—was the resumption of colonization in America. Charles II quickly began to reward faithful courtiers with grants of land in the New World; and in the twenty-five years of his reign, he issued charters for four additional colonies: Carolina, New York, New Jersey, and Pennsylvania. The new colonies were all proprietary ventures (modeled on Maryland rather than on Virginia and Massachusetts), thus exposing an important change in the nature of American settlement. No longer were private companies interested in launching colonies, realizing at last that there were no quick profits to be had in the New World. The goal of the new colonies was not so much quick commercial success as permanent settlements that would provide proprietors with land and power.

THE CAROLINAS

Carolina (a name derived from the Latinate form of "Charles") was, like Maryland, carved in part from the original Virginia grant. Charles II awarded the territory to a group of eight court favorites, all prominent politicians already active in colonial affairs. In successive charters issued in 1663 and 1665, the eight proprietors received joint title to a vast territory stretching south to the Florida peninsula and west to the Pacific Ocean. Like Lord Baltimore, they received almost kingly powers over their grant.

Also like Lord Baltimore, they expected to profit as landlords and land speculators. They reserved large estates for themselves, and they proposed to sell or give away the rest in smaller tracts (using a headright system similar to those in Virginia and Maryland) and to collect annual payments ("quitrents") from the settlers. Although committed Anglicans themselves, they welcomed any settlers they could get. The charter of the colony guaranteed religious freedom to everyone who would worship

INCENTIVES
FOR
SETTLEMENT

as a Christian. The proprietors also promised a measure of political freedom; laws were to be made by a representative assembly. With these incentives, they hoped to attract settlers from the existing American colonies and thus to avoid the expense of financing expeditions from England.

Their initial efforts failed dismally, and some of the original proprietors gave up. But one man—Anthony Ashley Cooper, soon to become the earl of Shaftesbury—persisted. Cooper convinced his partners to finance migrations to Carolina from England. In the spring of 1670, the first of these expeditions—a party of 300—set out from England. Only 100 people survived the difficult voyage; those who did established a settlement in the Port Royal area of the Carolina coast. Ten years later they founded a city at the junction of the Ashley and Cooper Rivers, which in 1690 became the colonial capital. They called it Charles Town. (It was later renamed Charleston.)

The earl of Shaftesbury, troubled by the instability in England, wanted a planned and well-ordered community. With

FUNDAMENTAL
CONSTITUTION
FOR CAROLINA

the aid of the English philosopher John Locke, he drew up the Fundamental Constitution for Carolina in 1669, which created an elaborate system of land distribution and an elaborately designed social order. In fact, however, Carolina developed along lines quite different from the almost utopian vision of Shaftesbury and Locke. For one thing, the colony was never really united in anything more than name. The northern and southern regions remained socially and economically distinct from one another. The northern settlers were mainly backwoods farmers, isolated from the outside world, scratching out a meager existence through subsistence agriculture. They developed no important aristocracy and for many years imported virtually no African slaves. In the south, fertile lands and the good harbor at Charles Town promoted a more prosperous economy and a more aristocratic society. Settlements grew up rapidly along the Ashley and Cooper Rivers, and

CHARLESTON, SOUTH CAROLINA This map, drawn on deerskin by an Indian chief around 1730, illustrates the close juxtaposition of the ordered English settlement in Charleston, South Carolina, seen on the left, and the more fluid Indian settlements near the town, on the right. It also illustrates the way in which southeastern Indians understood political relations as a series of linked circles. (Getty Images)

colonists established a flourishing trade in corn, lumber, cattle, pork, and (beginning in the 1690s) rice—which was to become the colony's principal commercial crop. Traders from the interior used Charles Town to market furs and hides they had acquired from Indian trading partners; some also marketed Indian slaves, generally natives captured by rival tribes and sold to the white traders.

Southern Carolina very early developed close ties to the large (and now overpopulated) English colony on the island of Barbados. For many years, Barbados was Carolina's most important trading partner. During the first ten years of settlement, most of the new settlers in Carolina were Barbadians, some of whom arrived with large groups of African workers and established themselves quickly as substantial landlords. African slavery had taken root on Barbados earlier than in any of the mainland colonies (see pp. 55–57); and the white Caribbean migrants—tough, uncompromising profit seekers—established a similar slave-based plantation society in Carolina. The proprietors, four of whom had a financial interest in the African slave trade, also encouraged the importation of Africans.

For several decades, Carolina remained one of the most unstable English colonies in America. There were tensions between the small farmers of the Albemarle region in the north and the wealthy planters in the south. There were conflicts between the rich Barbadians in southern Carolina and the smaller landowners around them. After Lord Shaftesbury's death, the proprietors proved unable to establish order, and in 1719 the colonists seized control of the colony from them. Ten years later, the king divided the region into two royal colonies, North and South Carolina.

NORTH AND SOUTH CAROLINA

NEW NETHERLAND, NEW YORK, AND NEW JERSEY

In 1664, one year after he issued the Carolina charter, Charles II granted to his brother James, the duke of York, all the territory lying between the Connecticut and Delaware Rivers. But much of the territory included in the grant was already claimed by the Dutch, who had established substantial settlements at New Amsterdam and other strategic points beginning in 1624.

The growing conflict between the English and the Dutch in America was part of a larger commercial rivalry between the two nations throughout the world. But the English particularly resented the Dutch presence in America, because it served as a wedge between the northern and southern English colonies and because it provided bases for Dutch smugglers evading English

NEW AMSTERDAM The small Dutch settlement on Manhattan Island, known before 1664 as New Amsterdam, fell to the English in 1664. This painting shows buildings clustered at the southern tip of the island, which remained the center of what became New York City until the nineteenth century. (Bettmann/Corbis)

customs laws. And so in 1664, an English fleet under the command of Richard Nicolls sailed into the lightly defended port of New Amsterdam and extracted a surrender from its unpopular

CAPTURE OF NEW AMSTERDAM

Dutch governor, Peter Stuyvesant, who had failed to mobilize resistance to the invasion. Under the Articles of Capitulation, the Dutch colony surrendered to the British in return for assurances that the Dutch settlers would not be displaced. In 1673, the Dutch briefly reconquered New Amsterdam. But they lost it for good in 1674.

James, the duke of York, his title to New Netherland now clear, renamed the colony New York and prepared to govern a colony of extraordinary diversity. New York contained not only Dutch and English, but Scandinavians, Germans, French, Africans (imported as slaves by the Dutch West India Company), and members of several different Indian tribes. There were, of course, many different religious faiths among these groups. James made no effort to impose his own Roman Catholicism on the colony. Like other proprietors before him, he remained in England and delegated powers to a governor and a council. But he provided for no representative assembly in New York perhaps because a parliament had executed his own father, Charles I. The laws did, however, establish local governments and guarantee religious toleration. Nevertheless, there were immediate tensions over the distribution of power in the colony. The great Dutch "patroons" (large landowners) survived with their economic and political power largely intact. James granted large estates as well to some of his own political supporters in an effort to create a class of influential landowners loyal to him. Power in the colony thus remained widely and unequally dispersed—among wealthy English landlords, Dutch patroons, fur traders (who forged important alliances with the Iroquois), and the duke's political appointees. Like Carolina, New York would for many years be a highly fractious society.

It was also a growing and generally prosperous colony. By 1685, when the duke of York ascended the English throne as James II, New York contained approximately 30,000 people, about four times as many as when James had received his grant twenty years before. Most of them still lived within the Hudson Valley, close to the river itself, with the largest settlement at its mouth, in the town of New York (formerly New Amsterdam).

Originally, James's claims in America extended south of the Hudson to the Delaware Valley and

ESTABLISHMENT OF NEW JERSEY

beyond. But shortly after receiving his charter, James gave a large portion of that land to a pair of political allies, Sir John Berkeley and Sir George Carteret, both of whom were also Carolina proprietors. Carteret named the territory New Jersey, after the island in the English Channel on which he had been born. In 1702, after nearly a decade of political squabbling and economic prof-

itlessness, the proprietors ceded control of the territory back to the crown and New Jersey became a royal colony.

Like New York (from which much of the population had come), New Jersey was a place of enormous ethnic and religious diversity. But unlike New York, New Jersey developed no important class of large landowners; most of its residents remained small farmers. Nor did New Jersey (which, unlike New York, had no natural harbor) produce any single major city.

THE QUAKER COLONIES

Pennsylvania, like Massachusetts, was born out of the efforts of dissenting English Protestants to find a home for their own

THE SOCIETY OF FRIENDS

religion and their own distinctive social order. The Society of Friends (also known as "Quakers") originated in mid-seventeenth-century England and grew into an important force as a result of the preachings of George Fox, a Nottingham shoemaker, and Margaret Fell. Their followers came to be known as Quakers because Fox urged them to "tremble at the name of the Lord." Unlike the Puritans, Quakers rejected the concepts of predestination and original sin. All people had divinity within themselves (an "Inner Light," which could guide them along the path of righteousness), and all who cultivated that divinity could attain salvation. Also unlike the Puritans, Quakers granted women a position within the church generally equal to that of men. Women and men alike could become preachers and define church doctrine, an equality symbolized by the longtime partnership between Fox and Fell.

A QUAKER MEETING An anonymous artist painted this view of a Quaker meeting in approximately 1790. Because the Society of Friends (or Quakers) believed that all people were equal in the eyes of God, they appointed no ministers and imposed no formal structure on their religious services. Members of the congregation stood up to speak at will. (©Museum of Fine Arts, Boston, Gift of Maxim Karolik, 64.456. Photograph © 2007 Museum of Fine Arts, Boston)

Of all the Protestant sectarians of the time, the Quakers were the most anarchistic and democratic. They had no church government, only periodic meetings of representatives from congregations. They had no paid clergy, and in their worship they spoke up one by one as the spirit moved them. Disregarding distinctions of gender and class, they addressed one another with the terms "thee" and "thou," words then commonly used in other parts of English society only in speaking to servants and social inferiors. And as confirmed pacifists, they refused to fight in wars. The Quakers were unpopular enough in England as a result of these beliefs and practices. They increased their unpopularity by occasionally breaking up other religious groups at worship. Many were jailed.

As a result, like the Puritans before them, the Quakers looked to America for asylum. A few went to New England. But except in Rhode Island, they were greeted there with fines, whippings, and banishment; three men and a woman who refused to leave were actually put to death. Others migrated to northern Carolina, and there they became the fastest-growing religious community in the region. They were soon influential in colonial politics. But many Quakers wanted a colony of their own. As a despised sect, they had little chance of getting the necessary royal grant without the aid of someone influential at court. But fortunately for Fox and his followers, a number of wealthy and prominent men had become attracted to the faith.

WILLIAM PENN One of them was William Penn—the son of an admiral in the Royal Navy who was a landlord of valuable Irish estates. He had received the gentleman's education expected of a person of his standing, but he resisted his father in moving to untraditional religions. Converted to the doctrine of the Inner Light, the younger Penn became an evangelist for Quakerism. With George Fox, he visited the European continent and found Quakers there who, like Quakers in England, longed to emigrate to the New World. He set out to find a place for them to go.

Penn turned his attention first to New Jersey and soon became an owner and proprietor of part of the colony. But in 1681, after the death of his father, Penn inherited his father's Irish lands and also his father's claim to a large debt from the king. Charles II, short of cash, paid the debt with a grant of territory between New York and Maryland—an area larger than England and Wales combined and which (unknown to him) contained more valuable soil and minerals than any other province of English America. Penn would have virtually total authority within the province. At the king's insistence, the territory was named Pennsylvania, after Penn's late father.

PENNSYLVANIA FOUNDED

Like most proprietors, Penn wanted Pennsylvania to be profitable for him and his family. And so he set out to attract settlers from throughout Europe through informative and honest advertising in several languages. Pennsylvania soon became the best known of all the colonies among ordinary people in England and on the European continent, and also the most cosmopolitan. Settlers flocked to the province from throughout Europe, joining several hundred Swedes and Finns who had been living in a small trading colony—New Sweden—established in 1638 at the mouth of the Delaware River. But the colony was never profitable for Penn and his descendants. Indeed, Penn himself, near the end of his life, was imprisoned in England for debt and died in poverty in 1718.

Penn was more than a mere real estate promoter, however, and he sought to create in Pennsylvania what he called a holy experiment. In 1682, he sailed to America and personally supervised the laying out of a city between the Delaware and the Schuylkill Rivers, which he named Philadelphia ("Brotherly Love"). With its rectangular streets, like those of Charles Town, Philadelphia helped set the pattern for most later cities in America. Penn believed, as had Roger Williams, that the land belonged to the Indians, and he was careful to see that they were reimbursed for it, as well as to see that they were not debauched by the fur traders' alcohol. Indians respected Penn as an honest white man, and during his lifetime the colony had no major conflicts with the natives. More than any other English colony, Pennsylvania prospered from the outset (even if its proprietor did not), because of Penn's successful recruitment of emigrants, his thoughtful planning, and the region's mild climate and fertile soil.

But the colony was not without conflict. By the late 1690s, some residents of Pennsylvania were beginning to resist the nearly absolute power of the proprietor. Southern residents in particular complained that the government in Philadelphia was unresponsive to their needs. As a result, a substantial opposition emerged to challenge Penn. Pressure from these groups grew to the point that in 1701, shortly before he departed for England for the last time, Penn agreed to a Charter of Liberties for the colony. The charter established a representative assembly (consisting, alone among the English colonies, of only one house), which greatly limited the authority of the proprietor. The charter also permitted "the lower counties" of the colony to establish their own representative assembly. The three counties did so in 1703 and as a result became, in effect, a separate colony: Delaware—although until the American Revolution, it had the same governor as Pennsylvania.

CHARTER OF LIBERTIES

> **PHILADELPHIA HELPED SET THE PATTERN FOR MOST LATER CITIES IN AMERICA.**

BORDERLANDS AND MIDDLE GROUNDS

The English colonies along the Atlantic seaboard of North America eventually united, expanded, and became the beginnings of a great nation. But in the seventeenth and early eighteenth

MAKING MOLASSES IN BARBADOS African slaves, who constituted the vast majority of the population of the flourishing sugar-producing island of Barbados, work here in a sugar mill grinding sugarcane and then boiling it to produce refined sugar, molasses, and—after a later distillation process not pictured here—rum. (Arents Collections, Rare Books Division, New York Public Library, Astor, Lenox and Tilden Foundations)

centuries, they were small, frail settlements surrounded by other, competing societies. The British Empire in North America was, in fact, a much smaller and weaker one than the great Spanish Empire to the south, and not, on the surface at least, clearly stronger than the enormous French Empire to the north.

The continuing contest for control of North America, and the complex interactions among the diverse peoples populating the continent, were most clearly visible in areas around the borders of English settlement—the Caribbean and along the northern, southern, and western borders of the coastal colonies.

THE CARIBBEAN ISLANDS

Throughout the first half of the seventeenth century, the most important destination for English immigrants was not the mainland, but rather the islands of the Caribbean and the northern way station of Bermuda. More than half the English migrants to the New World in those years settled on these islands. The island societies had close ties to English North America from the beginning and influenced the development of the mainland colonies in several ways. But they were also surrounded by, and sometimes imperiled by, outposts of the Spanish Empire.

THE ENGLISH CARIBBEAN

Before the arrival of Europeans, most of the Caribbean islands had substantial native populations—the Arawaks, the Caribs, and the Ciboney. But beginning with Christopher Columbus's first visit in 1492, and accelerating after the Spanish established their first colony on Hispaniola in 1496, the native population was all but wiped out by European epidemics. Indians were never a significant factor in European settlement of the Caribbean. Indeed, by the time significant European settlement of the islands began, many were almost entirely deserted.

IMPERIAL CONFLICT

The Spanish Empire claimed title to all the islands in the Caribbean, but there was substantial Spanish settlement only on the largest of them: Cuba, Hispaniola, and Puerto Rico. English, French, and Dutch traders began settling on some of the smaller islands early in the sixteenth century, although these weak colonies were always vulnerable to Spanish attack. After Spain and the Netherlands went to war in 1621 (distracting the Spanish navy and leaving the English in the Caribbean relatively unmolested), the pace of English colonization increased. By midcentury, there were several substantial English settlements on the islands, the most important of them on Antigua, St. Kitts, Jamaica, and Barbados. Even so, through the seventeenth century, the English settlements in the Caribbean were the targets of almost constant attacks and invasions by the

THE SEVENTEETH-CENTURY CARIBBEAN At the same time that European powers were expanding their colonial presence on the mainland of the American continents, they were also establishing colonies in the islands of the Caribbean. In some cases, these islands were even more important to the Atlantic economy than many of the mainland possessions, particularly the large, heavily populated sugar-growing islands (among them Jamaica and Barbados), in which the majority of the population consisted of African slaves.

• *What role did the Caribbean islands play in the spread of slavery in North America?*

Spanish, the Portuguese, the French, the Dutch, and the remaining Indians of the region. The world of the Caribbean was a violent and turbulent place.

The Caribbean colonies built their economies on raising crops for export. In the early years, English settlers experimented unsuccessfully with tobacco and cotton. But they soon discovered that the most lucrative crop was sugar, for which there was a substantial and growing market in Europe. Sugarcane could also be distilled into rum, for which there was also a booming market abroad. Within a decade of the introduction of sugar cultivation to the West Indies, planters were devoting almost all of their land to sugarcane. In their appetite for more land for sugarcane, they cut down forests and destroyed the natural habitats of many animals, and greatly reduced the amount of land available for growing food.

SUGAR AND SLAVERY

Because sugar was a labor-intensive crop, and because the remnant of the native population was too small to provide a workforce, English planters quickly found it necessary to import laborers. As in the Chesapeake, they began by bringing indentured servants from England. But the arduous work discouraged white laborers; many found it impossible to adapt to the harsh tropical climate so different from that of England. By midcentury, therefore, the English planters in the Caribbean (like the Spanish colonists who preceded them) were relying more and more heavily on an enslaved African workforce, which soon substantially outnumbered them.

On Barbados and other islands where a flourishing sugar economy developed, the English planters were a tough, aggressive, and ambitious breed. Some of them grew enormously wealthy; and since their livelihoods

> WITHIN A DECADE OF THE INTRODUCTION OF SUGAR CULTIVATION TO THE WEST INDIES, PLANTERS WERE DEVOTING ALMOST ALL OF THEIR LAND TO SUGARCANE.

depended on their workforces, they expanded and solidified the system of African slavery there remarkably quickly. By the late seventeenth century, there were four times as many African slaves as there were white settlers. By then the West Indies had ceased to be an attractive destination for ordinary English immigrants; most now went to the colonies on the North American mainland instead.

MASTERS AND SLAVES IN THE CARIBBEAN

A small, mostly wealthy white population and a large African population held in bondage made for a potentially explosive combination. As in other English colonies in the New World in which Africans came to outnumber Europeans, whites in the Caribbean grew fearful of slave revolts. They had good reason,

SLAVE REVOLTS

for there were at least seven major slave revolts in the islands, more than the English colonies of North America experienced in their entire history as slave societies. As a result, white planters monitored their labor forces closely and often harshly. Beginning in the 1660s, all the islands enacted legal codes to regulate relations between masters and slaves and to give white people virtually absolute authority over Africans. A master could even murder a slave with virtual impunity.

There was little either in the law or in the character of the economy to compel planters to pay much attention to the welfare of their workers. Many white slaveowners concluded that it was cheaper to buy new slaves periodically than to protect the well-being of those they already owned, and it was not uncommon for masters to work their slaves to death. Few African workers survived more than a decade in the brutal Caribbean working environment—they either were sold to planters in North America or died. Even whites, who worked far less hard than did the slaves, often succumbed to the harsh climate; most died before the age of forty—often from tropical diseases to which they had no immunity.

Establishing a stable society and culture was extremely difficult for people living in such harsh and even deadly conditions. Many of the whites were principally interested in getting rich and had no long-term commitment to the islands. Those who

UNSTABLE SOCIETIES

could returned to England with their fortunes and left their estates in the hands of overseers. A large proportion of the European settlers were single men, many of whom either died or left at a young age. Those who remained, many of them common white farmers and laborers living in desperate poverty, were too poor to contribute to the development of the society. With few white women on the islands and little intermarriage between blacks and whites, Europeans in the Caribbean lacked many of the institutions that gave stability to the North American settlements: church, family, community.

Africans in the Caribbean faced even greater difficulties, of course, but they managed to create a world of their own despite the hardships. They started families (although many of them were broken up by death or the slave trade); they sustained African religious and social traditions (and showed little interest in Christianity); and within the rigidly controlled world of the sugar plantations, they established patterns of resistance.

The Caribbean settlements were connected to the North American colonies in many ways. They were an important part

CONNECTION TO BRITISH NORTH AMERICA

of the Atlantic trading world in which many Americans became involved—a source of sugar and rum and a market for goods made in the mainland colonies and in England. They were the principal source of African slaves for the mainland colonies; well over half the slaves in North America came from the islands, not directly from Africa. And because Caribbean planters established an elaborate plantation system earlier than planters in North America, they provided models that many mainland people consciously or unconsciously copied. In the American South, too, planters grew wealthy at the expense of poor whites and, above all, of African slaves.

THE SOUTHWESTERN BORDERLANDS

By the end of the seventeenth century, the Spanish Empire had established only a small presence in the regions that became the United States. In Mexico and regions farther south, however, the Spanish had established a sophisticated and impressive empire. Their capital, Mexico City, was the most dazzling metropolis in the Americas. The Spanish residents, well over a million of them, enjoyed much greater prosperity than all but a few English settlers in North America.

The principal Spanish colonies north of Mexico—Florida, Texas, New Mexico, Arizona, and California—attracted reli-

SPAIN'S NORTHERN COLONIES

gious minorities, Catholic missionaries, independent ranchers fleeing the heavy hand of imperial authority, and Spanish troops defending the northern flank of the empire. These colonies remained weak and peripheral parts of the great empire to their south.

New Mexico was the most prosperous and populous of these Spanish outposts. Once the Spanish quelled the Pueblo revolt there in 1680 (see p. 18), they worked effectively with the natives of the region to develop a flourishing agriculture. By the early nineteenth century, New Mexico had a non-Indian population of over 10,000—the largest European settlement west of the Mississippi and north of Mexico—and it was steadily expanding through the region. But New Mexico was prosperous only when compared to other borderlands. Its residents were far less successful than the Spanish in Mexico and other more densely settled regions.

The Spanish began to colonize California once they realized that other Europeans—among them English merchants and French and Russian trappers—were beginning to establish a

CALIFORNIA

presence in the region. Formal Spanish settlement of California began in the 1760s, when the governor of Baja California was ordered to create outposts of the empire farther north. Soon a string of missions, forts (or *presidios*), and trading communities were springing up along the Pacific coast, beginning with San Diego and Monterey in 1769 and eventually San Francisco (1776), Los Angeles (1781), and Santa Barbara (1786). As in other areas of European settlement, the arrival of the Spanish in California (and the diseases they imported) had a devastating effect on the native population. Approximately 65,000 at the time of the first Spanish settlements, by 1820 it had declined by two-thirds. As the new settlements spread, however, the Spanish insisted that the remaining natives convert to Catholicism. That explains the centrality of missions in almost all the major Spanish outposts in California. But the Spanish colonists were also intent on creating a prosperous agricultural economy, and they enlisted Indian laborers to help them do so. California's Indians had no choice but to accede to the demands of the Spanish, although there were frequent revolts by natives against the harsh conditions imposed upon them. Already decimated by disease, the tribes now declined further as a result of malnutrition and overwork at the hands of the Spanish missions.

In the late seventeenth and early eighteenth centuries, the Spanish considered the greatest threat to the northern borders of their empire to be the growing ambitions of the French. In the 1680s, French explorers traveled down the Mississippi Valley to the mouth of the river and claimed the lands they had traversed for their king, Louis XIV. They called the territory Louisiana. Fearful of French incursions farther west, and unsettled by the nomadic Indians driven into the territory by the French, the Spanish began to fortify their claim to Texas by establishing new forts, missions, and settlements there, including San Fernando (later San Antonio) in 1731. The region that is now Arizona was also becoming increasingly tied to the Spanish Empire. Northern Arizona was a part of the New Mexico colony and was governed from Santa Fe. The rest of Arizona (from Phoenix south) was controlled by the Mexican region of Sonora. As in California, much of the impetus for these settlements came from Catholic missionaries (in this case Jesuits), eager to convert the natives to Catholicism. But the missionary project met with little success. Unlike the sedentary Pueblos around Santa Fe, the Arizona natives were nomadic peoples, unlikely to settle down or to Christianize, frequently at war with rival tribes, and—like natives elsewhere—tragically vulnerable to smallpox, measles, and other imported diseases. As in California, epidemics reduced the native population of Arizona by two-thirds in the early eighteenth century.

Although peripheral to the great Spanish Empire to the south, the Spanish colonies in the Southwest nevertheless helped create enduring societies very unlike those being established by the English along the Atlantic seaboard. The Spanish colonies were committed not to displacing the native populations but, rather, to enlisting them. They sought to convert them to Catholicism, to recruit them (sometimes forcibly) as agricultural workers, and to cultivate them as trading partners. The Spanish did not consider the natives to be their equals,

IMPORTANCE OF
THE SPANISH
BORDERLANDS

THE SPANISH COLONIES WERE COMMITTED NOT TO DISPLACING THE NATIVE POPULATIONS BUT TO ENLISTING THEM.

certainly, and they did not treat them very well. But neither did they consider them merely as obstacles to their own designs, as many English settlers in the East did.

THE SOUTHEASTERN BORDERLANDS

A more direct challenge to English ambitions in North America was the Spanish presence in the southeastern areas of what is now the United States. After the establishment of the Spanish claim to Florida in the 1560s (see p. 16), missionaries and traders began moving northward into Georgia and westward into what is now known as the panhandle, and some ambitious Spaniards began to dream of expanding their empire still farther north, into what became the Carolinas, and perhaps beyond. The founding of Jamestown in 1607 replaced those dreams with fears. The English colonies, they believed, could threaten their existing settlements in Florida and Georgia. As a result, the Spanish built forts in both regions to defend themselves against the slowly increasing English presence there. Throughout the eighteenth century, the area between the Carolinas and Florida was the site of continuing tension, and frequent conflict, between the Spanish and the English—and, to a lesser degree, between the Spanish and the French, who were threatening their northwestern borders with settlements in Louisiana and in what is now Alabama.

There was no formal war between England and Spain in these years, but that did not dampen the hostilities in the Southeast. English pirates continually harassed the Spanish settlements and, in 1668, actually sacked St. Augustine. Both sides in this conflict sought to make use of the native tribes. The English encouraged Indians in Florida to rise up against the Spanish missions. The Spanish, for their part, offered freedom to African slaves owned by Carolina settlers if they agreed to convert to Catholicism. About 100 Africans accepted the offer, and the Spanish later organized some of them into a military regiment to defend the northern border of New Spain. The English correctly viewed the Spanish recruitment of their slaves as an effort to undermine their economy. By the early eighteenth century, the constant fighting in the region had driven almost all the Spanish settlers out of Florida. The dwindling Spanish presence became almost entirely confined to St. Augustine on the Atlantic coast to Pensacola on the Gulf Coast, and to the modest colonies that surrounded the forts there. Because they were so few and so weak, they came to rely—far more than most British did—on natives and Africans and intermarried frequently with them.

HOSTILITIES IN
THE SOUTHEAST

Eventually, after more than a century of conflict in the southeastern borderlands, the English prevailed—acquiring Florida in the aftermath of the Seven Years' War (known in America as the French and Indian War; see pp. 107–109) and rapidly populating it with settlers from their colonies to the north. Before that point, however, protecting the southern boundary of the British Empire in North America was a continual concern to the English and contributed in crucial ways to the founding of the colony of Georgia.

THE FOUNDING OF GEORGIA

Georgia was unique in its origins. Its founders were a group of unpaid trustees led by General James Oglethorpe, a member of Parliament and military hero. They were interested in economic success, but they were driven primarily by military and philanthropic motives. They wanted to erect a military barrier against the Spanish lands on the southern border of English America, and they wanted to provide a refuge for the impoverished, a place where English men and women without prospects at home could begin anew.

JAMES OGLETHORPE'S VISION

The need for a military buffer between South Carolina and the Spanish settlements in Florida was particularly urgent in the first years of the eighteenth century. In a 1676 treaty, Spain had recognized England's title to lands already occupied by English settlers. But conflict between the two colonizing powers had continued. In 1686, a force of Indians and Creoles from Florida, directed by Spanish agents, attacked and destroyed an outlying South Carolina settlement south of the treaty line. And when hostilities broke out again between Spain and England in 1701 (known in England as Queen Anne's War and on the Continent as the War of the Spanish Succession), the fighting renewed in America as well.

Oglethorpe, himself a veteran of Queen Anne's War, was keenly aware of the military advantages of an English colony south of the Carolinas. Yet his interest in settlement rested even more on his philanthropic commitments. As head of a parliamentary committee investigating English prisons, he had grown appalled by the plight of honest debtors rotting in confinement. Such prisoners, and other poor people in danger of succumbing to a similar fate, could, he believed, become the farmer-soldiers of the new colony in America.

In 1732, King George II granted Oglethorpe and his fellow trustees control of the land between the Savannah and Altamaha Rivers. Their colonization policies reflected the vital military purposes of the colony. They limited the size of landholdings to make the settlement compact and easier to defend against Spanish and Indian attacks. They excluded Africans, free or slave; Oglethorpe feared slave labor would produce internal revolts and that disaffected slaves might turn to the Spanish as allies. The trustees prohibited rum (both because Oglethorpe disapproved of it on moral grounds and because the trustees feared its effects on the natives). They strictly regulated trade with the Indians, again to limit the possibility of wartime insurrection. They also excluded Catholics for fear they might collude with their coreligionists in the Spanish colonies to the south.

GEORGIA'S MILITARY RATIONALE

Oglethorpe himself led the first colonial expedition to Georgia, which built a fortified town at the mouth of the Savannah River in 1733 and later constructed additional forts south of the Altamaha. In the end, only a few debtors were released from jail and sent to Georgia. Instead, the trustees brought hundreds of impoverished tradesmen and artisans from England and Scotland and many religious refugees from Switzerland and Germany. Among the immigrants was a small group of Jews. English settlers made up a lower proportion of the European population of Georgia than of any other English colony.

The strict rules governing life in the new colony stifled its early development and ensured the failure of Oglethorpe's vision. Settlers in Georgia—many of whom were engaged in labor-intensive agriculture—needed a workforce as much as those in other southern colonies. Almost from the start they began demanding the right to buy slaves. Some opposed the restrictions on the size of individual property holdings. Many resented the nearly absolute political power of Oglethorpe and the trustees. As a result, newcomers to the region generally preferred to settle in South Carolina, where there were fewer restrictive laws.

Oglethorpe (whom some residents of Georgia began calling "our perpetual dictator") at first bitterly resisted the demands of the settlers for social and political reform. Over time, however, he wearied of the conflict in the colony and grew frustrated at its failure to grow. He also suffered military disappointments, such as a 1740 assault on the Spanish outpost at St. Augustine, Florida, which ended in failure. Oglethorpe, now disillusioned with his American venture, began to loosen his grip. Even before the 1740 defeat, the trustees had removed the limitation on individual landholdings. In 1750, they removed the ban on slavery. A year later they ended the prohibition of rum and returned control of the colony to the king, who immediately permitted the summoning of a representative assembly. Georgia continued to grow more slowly than the other southern colonies, but in other ways it now developed along lines roughly similar to those of South Carolina. By 1770, there were over 20,000 non-Indian residents of the colony, nearly half of them African slaves.

TRANSFORMATION OF GEORGIA

MIDDLE GROUNDS

The struggle for the North American continent was, of course, not just one among competing European empires. It was also a contest between the new European immigrants and the native populations.

In some parts of the British Empire—Virginia and New England, for example—English settlers quickly established their dominance, subjugating and displacing most natives until they had established societies that were dominated almost entirely by Europeans. But elsewhere the balance of power remained far more precarious. Along the western borders of English settlement, in particular,

ALONG THE WESTERN BORDERS OF ENGLISH SETTLEMENT, EUROPEANS AND INDIANS LIVED TOGETHER IN REGIONS IN WHICH NEITHER SIDE WAS ABLE TO ESTABLISH CLEAR DOMINANCE.

NATIVE AMERICANS AND THE "MIDDLE GROUND"

FOR many generations, historians chronicling the westward movement of European settlement in North America incorporated Native Americans into the story largely as weak and inconvenient obstacles swept aside by the inevitable progress of "civilization." Indians were presented either as murderous savages or as relatively docile allies of white people, but rarely as important actors of their own. Francis Parkman, the great nineteenth-century American historian, described Indians as a civilization "crushed" and "scorned" by the march of European powers in the New World. Many subsequent historians departed little from his assessment.

Challenges to this traditional view have come from many more recent historians—among them, Gary Nash in *Red, White, and Black* (1974) and Ramón Gutiérrez in *When Jesus Came, the Corn Mothers Went Away* (1991). They, and other scholars, rejected the optimistic, progressive view of white triumph over adversity and presented, instead, a picture of conquest that affected both the conqueror and the conquered and did not bring to an end their influence on one another.

A new, more recent view of the relationship between the peoples of the Old and New Worlds sees Native Americans and Euro-Americans as uneasy partners in the shaping of a new society in which, for a time at least, both were a vital part. In *The Middle Ground* (1991), Richard White examined the culture of the Great Lakes region in the eighteenth century, in which Algonquin Indians created complex trading and political relationships with French, English, and American settlers and travelers in the region. In this "borderland" between the growing European settlements in the East and the still largely intact Indian civilizations farther west, a new kind of hybrid society emerged in which many cultures intermingled. In his *Into the American Woods* (1999), James Merrell examined the world of negotiators and go-betweens along the western Pennsylvania frontier in the seventeenth and eighteenth centuries and, like White, emphasized the complicated blend of European and Native American diplomatic rituals that allowed both groups to conduct business, make treaties, and keep the peace.

Daniel Richter extended the idea of a "middle ground" further in *The Ordeal of the Longhouse* (1992) and *Facing East from Indian Country* (2001). Richter demonstrates that the Iroquois Confederacy was an active participant in the power relationships in the Hudson River basin. In his later book, he tells the story of European colonization from the Native American perspective, revealing how western myths of "first contact" such as the story of John Smith and Pocahontas look entirely different when seen through the eyes of Native Americans, who remained in many ways the more powerful of the two societies in the seventeenth century.

How did these important collaborations collapse? What happened to the "middle ground"? Over time, the delicate partnerships along the frontiers of white settlement gave way to the sheer numbers of Europeans (and, in some places, Africans) who moved westward. Joyce Chaplin in *Subject Matter* (2001) argues as well that Old World Americans at first admired the natives as a kind of natural nobility until European diseases ravaged the tribes, helping strengthen the Europeans' sense of superiority that had been a part of their view of Indians from the beginning. In *The Name of War* (1998), Jill Lepore describes how the violence of King Philip's War in seventeenth-century New England helped transform English views of the tribes both because of the white victory over the Indians and because of their success in turning this victory

Europeans and Indians lived together in regions in which neither side was able to establish clear dominance. In these "middle

CONFLICT AND ACCOMMODATION

grounds," as they have been called, the two populations—despite frequent conflicts—carved out ways of living together, with each side making concessions to the other. Here the Europeans found themselves obliged to adapt to tribal expectations at least as much as the Indians had to adapt to European ones.

To the Indians, the European migrants were both menacing and appealing. They feared the power of these strange people: their guns, their rifles, their forts. But they also wanted the French and British settlers to behave like "fathers"—to help them mediate their own internal disputes, to offer them gifts, to help them moderate their conflicts. Europeans came from a world in which the formal institutional and military power of a nation or empire governed relationships between societies. But the natives had no understanding of the modern notion of a "nation" and thought much more in terms of ceremony and kinship. Gradually, Europeans learned to fulfill at least some of their expectations.

In the seventeenth century, before many English settlers had entered the interior, the French were particularly adept at creating mutually beneficial relationships with the tribes. They welcomed the chance to form close relationships with—even to marry within—the tribes. They also recognized the importance of treating tribal chiefs with respect and channeling gifts and

MUTUALLY BENEFICIAL RELATIONS

tributes through them. But by the mid-eighteenth century, French influence in the interior was in decline, and British settlers gradually became the dominant European group in the "middle grounds." It took the British a considerable time to learn the lessons the French had long ago absorbed—that simple commands and raw force were much less

(Historical Society of Pennsylvania [AM 1702 CAM])

into a rationale for the moral superiority of Europeans by portraying the Indians as brutal, uncivilized people. (In reality, the Europeans had used as much "savagery" against the natives as the natives had used against them.) As the pressures of white settlement grew, as the Indian populations weakened as a result of disease and war, and as the relationship between the tribes and the European settlers grew more and more unequal, the cultural "middle ground" that for many decades characterized much of the contact between the Old and New Worlds gradually disappeared. By the time historians began seriously chronicling this story in the late nineteenth century, the Indian tribes had indeed become the defeated, helpless "obstacles" that they portrayed. But for generations before, the relationship between white Americans and Native Americans was a much less unequal one than it later became. •

UNDERSTAND, ANALYZE, AND EVALUATE

1. How have historians' views of Native Americans and their role in the European colonization of North America changed over time?
2. Why did the "middle ground" between Native Americans and European settlers disappear?
3. Is there a "middle ground" in the United States today? If so, where? How is this "middle ground" similar to and different from the middle ground between Native Americans and Euro-American settlers in the seventeenth and eighteenth centuries?

---

effective in creating a workable relationship with the tribes than were gifts and ceremonies and mediation. Eventually they did so, and in large western regions—especially those around the Great Lakes—they established a precarious peace with the tribes that lasted for several decades.

But as the British and (after 1776) American presence in the region grew, the balance of power between Europeans and natives shifted. Newer settlers had difficulty adapting to the complex rituals of gift-giving and mediation that the earlier migrants had developed. The stability of the relationship between the Indians and whites deteriorated. By the early nineteenth

THE SHIFTING BALANCE

BY THE EARLY NINETEENTH CENTURY, THE 'MIDDLE GROUNDS' HAD COLLAPSED, REPLACED BY A EUROPEAN WORLD IN WHICH INDIANS WERE MORE RUTHLESSLY SUBJUGATED AND EVENTUALLY REMOVED.

century, the "middle grounds" had collapsed, replaced by a European world in which Indians were more ruthlessly subjugated and eventually removed. Nevertheless, it is important to recognize that for a considerable period of early American history, the story of the relationship between whites and Indians was not simply a story of conquest and subjugation, but also—in some regions—a story of a difficult but stable accommodation and mutual adaptation. The Indians were not simply victims in the story of the growth of European settlement in North America. They were also important actors, sometimes obstructing and sometimes facilitating the development of the new societies.

THE EVOLUTION OF THE BRITISH EMPIRE

The English colonies in America had originated as quite separate projects, and for the most part they grew up independent of one another. But by the mid-seventeenth century, the growing commercial success of the colonial ventures was producing pressure in England for a more rational, uniform structure to the empire.

THE DRIVE FOR REORGANIZATION

Imperial reorganization, many people in England claimed, would increase the profitability of the colonies and the power of the English government to supervise them. Above all, it would contribute to the success of the mercantile system, the foundation of the English economy. Colonies would provide a market for England's manufactured goods and a source for raw materials it could not produce at home, thus increasing the total wealth of the nation. But for the new possessions truly to promote mercantilist goals, England would have to exclude foreigners (as Spain had done) from its colonial trade. According to mercantilist theory, any wealth flowing to another nation could come only at the expense of England itself. Hence the British government sought to monopolize trade relations with its colonies.

MERCANTILISM

In theory, the mercantile system offered benefits to the colonies as well by providing them with a ready market for the raw materials they produced and a source for the manufactured goods they did not. But some colonial goods were not suitable for export to England, which produced wheat, flour, and fish and had no interest in obtaining them from America. Colonists also found it more profitable at times to trade with the Spanish, French, or Dutch even in goods that England did import. Thus, a considerable trade soon developed between the English colonies and non-English markets.

For a time, the English government made no serious efforts to restrict this challenge to the principles of mercantilism. But gradually London began passing laws to regulate colonial trade. During Oliver Cromwell's "Protectorate," in 1650 and 1651, Parliament passed laws to keep Dutch ships out of the English colonies. After the Restoration, the government of Charles II adopted three Navigation Acts designed to regulate colonial commerce

THE NAVIGATION ACTS

SAVANNAH IN 1734 This early view of the English settlement at Savannah by an English artist shows the intensely orderly character of Georgia in the early moments of European settlement there. As the colony grew, its residents gradually abandoned the rigid plan created by Georgia's founders. (I. N. Phelps Stokes Collection of American Historical Prints, New York Public Library, Astor, Lenox and Tilden Foundations)

even more strictly. The first of them, in 1660, closed the colonies to all trade except that carried in English ships. This law also required the colonists to export certain items, among them tobacco, only to England or English possessions. The second act, in 1663, provided that all goods being shipped from Europe to the colonies had to pass through England on the way; that would make it possible for England to tax them. The third act, in 1673, was a response to the widespread evasion of the first two laws by the colonial shippers, who frequently left port claiming to be heading for another English colony but then sailed to a foreign port. It imposed duties on the coastal trade among the English colonies, and it provided for the appointment of customs officials to enforce the Navigation Acts. These acts formed the legal basis of England's mercantile system in America for a century.

The system created by the Navigation Acts had obvious advantages for England. But it had some advantages for the colonists as well. By restricting all trade to British ships, the laws encouraged the colonists (who were themselves legally British subjects) to create an important shipbuilding industry of their own. And because the English wanted to import as many goods as possible from their own colonies (as opposed to importing them from rival nations), they encouraged—and at times subsidized—the development of American production of goods they needed, among them iron, silk, and lumber. Despite the bitter complaints the laws provoked in America in the late seventeenth century, and the more bitter conflicts they would help to provoke decades later, the system of the Navigation Acts served the interests of the British and the Americans alike reasonably well through most of the eighteenth century.

THE DOMINION OF NEW ENGLAND

Enforcement of the Navigation Acts required not only the stationing of customs officials in America, but also the establishment of an agency in England to oversee colonial affairs. In 1679, Charles II attempted to increase his control over Massachusetts (which behaved at times as if its leaders considered it an independent nation) by stripping the colony of its authority over New Hampshire and chartering a separate, royal colony there whose governor he would himself appoint. Five years later, after the Massachusetts General Court defied instructions from Parliament to enforce the Navigation Acts, Charles revoked the Massachusetts corporate charter and made it a royal colony.

Charles II's brother and successor, James II, who came to the throne in 1685, went much further. In 1686, he created a single Dominion of New England, which combined the government of Massachusetts with the governments of the rest of the New England colonies and, in 1688, with those of New York and New Jersey as well. He eliminated the existing assemblies within the new Dominion and appointed a single governor, Sir Edmund Andros, to supervise the entire region from Boston.

SIR EDMUND ANDROS Andros was an able administrator but a stern and tactless man; his rigid enforcement of the Navigation Acts, his brusque dismissal of the colonists' claims to the "rights of Englishmen," and his crude and arbitrary tactics made him highly unpopular.

He was particularly despised in Massachusetts, where he tried to strengthen the Anglican Church.

THE "GLORIOUS REVOLUTION"

James II was not only losing friends in America; he was making powerful enemies in England by attempting to exercise autocratic control over Parliament and the courts. He was also appointing his fellow Catholics to high office, inspiring fears that he would try to reestablish Catholicism as England's official religion. By 1688, his popular support had all but vanished.

Until 1688, James's heirs were two daughters—Mary and Anne—both of whom were Protestant. But in that year the king had a son and made clear that the boy would be raised a Catholic. Some members of Parliament were so alarmed that they invited the king's daughter Mary and her husband, William of Orange, ruler of the Netherlands and Protestant champion of Europe, to assume the throne together. When William and Mary arrived in England with a small army, James II (perhaps remembering what had happened to his father, Charles I) offered no resistance and fled to France. As a result of this bloodless coup, which the English called "the Glorious Revolution," William and Mary became joint sovereigns.

When Bostonians heard of the overthrow of James II, they moved quickly to unseat his unpopular viceroy in New England. Andros managed to escape an angry mob, but he was arrested and imprisoned as he sought to flee the city dressed as a woman. The new sovereigns in England chose not to contest the toppling of Andros and quickly acquiesced in what the colonists had, in effect, already done: abolishing the Dominion of New England and restoring separate colonial governments. They did not, however, accede to all the colonists' desires. In 1691, they combined Massachusetts with Plymouth and made it a royal colony. The new charter restored the General Court, (Massachusetts's legislature), but it gave the crown the right to appoint the governor. It also replaced church membership with property ownership as the basis for voting and officeholding and required the Puritan leaders of the colony to tolerate Anglican worship.

END OF THE DOMINION

Andros had been governing New York through a lieutenant governor, Captain Francis Nicholson, who enjoyed the support of the wealthy merchants and fur traders of the province—the same groups who had dominated the colony for years. Other, less favored colonists—farmers, mechanics, small traders, and shopkeepers—had a long accumulation of grievances against both Nicholson and his allies. The leader of the New York dissidents was Jacob Leisler, a German immigrant and a prosperous merchant who had married into a prominent Dutch family but had never won acceptance as one of the colony's ruling class. Much like Nathaniel Bacon in Virginia, the ambitious Leisler resented his exclusion and eagerly grasped the opportunity to challenge the colonial elite. In May 1689, when news of the Glorious Revolution in England and the fall of Andros in Boston reached New York, Leisler raised a militia, captured the city fort, drove Nicholson into exile, and proclaimed himself the new head of government in New York. For two years, he tried in vain to stabilize his power in the colony amid fierce factional rivalry. In 1691, when William and Mary appointed a new governor, Leisler briefly resisted this challenge to his authority. Although he soon yielded, his hesitation allowed his many political enemies to charge him with treason. He and one of his sons-in-law were hanged, drawn, and quartered. Fierce rivalry between what became known as the "Leislerians" and the "anti-Leislerians" dominated the politics of New York for many years thereafter.

In Maryland, many people erroneously assumed when they heard news of the Glorious Revolution that their proprietor, the Catholic Lord Baltimore, who was living in England, had sided with the Catholic James II and opposed William and Mary. So in 1689, an old opponent of the proprietor's government, John Coode, started a new revolt, which drove out Lord Baltimore's

JOHN COODE'S
REBELLION

officials in the name of Protestantism. Through an elected convention, his supporters chose a committee to run the government and petitioned the crown for a charter as a royal colony. In 1691, William and Mary complied, stripping the proprietor of his authority. The colonial assembly established the Church of England as the colony's official religion and forbade Catholics to

hold public office, to vote, or even to practice their religion in public. Maryland became a proprietary colony again in 1715, but only after the fifth Lord Baltimore joined the Anglican Church.

As a result of the Glorious Revolution, the colonies revived their representative assemblies and successfully thwarted the plan for colonial unification. In the process, they legitimized the idea that the colonists had some rights within the empire, that the English government needed to consider their views in making policies that affected them. But the Glorious Revolution in America was not, as many Americans later came to believe, a clear demonstration of American resolve to govern itself or a clear victory for colonial self-rule. In New York and Maryland, in particular, the uprisings had more to do with local factional and religious divisions than with any larger vision of the nature of the empire. And while the insurgencies did succeed in eliminating the short-lived Dominion of New England, their ultimate results were governments that increased the crown's potential authority in many ways. As the first century of English settlement in America came to its end and as colonists celebrated their victories over arbitrary British rule, they were in fact becoming more a part of the imperial system than ever before.

LOOKING BACK

The English colonization of North America was part of a larger effort by several European nations to expand the reach of their increasingly commercial societies. Indeed, for many years, the British Empire in America was among the smallest and weakest of the imperial ventures there, overshadowed by the French to the north and the Spanish to the south.

In the British colonies along the Atlantic seaboard, new agricultural and commercial societies gradually emerged—in the South, centered on the cultivation of tobacco and cotton and reliant on slave labor; and in the northern colonies, centered on traditional food crops and based mostly on free labor. Substantial trading centers emerged in such cities as Boston, New York, Philadelphia, and Charleston, and a growing proportion of the population became prosperous and settled in these increasingly complex communities. By the early eighteenth century, English settlement had spread from northern New England (in what is now Maine) south into Georgia.

SIGNIFICANT EVENTS

1607	1619	1620	1624	1629	1630	1634	1635	1636	1637	1638

Jamestown founded

First African workers arrive in Virginia

Virginia House of Burgesses meets for first time

Pilgrims found Plymouth colony

Dutch establish settlement on Manhattan Island

New Hampshire and Maine established

Puritans establish Massachusetts Bay colony at Boston

First English settlements founded in Maryland

Hartford settled in Connecticut

Roger Williams founds settlement in Rhode Island

Anne Hutchinson expelled from Massachusetts Bay colony

Swedes and Finns establish New Sweden on the Delaware River

But this growing British Empire coexisted with, and often found itself in conflict with, the presence of other Europeans—most notably the Spanish and the French—in other areas of North America. In these borderlands, societies did not assume the settled, prosperous form they were taking in the Tidewater and New England. They were raw, sparsely populated settlements in which Europeans, including over time increasing numbers of English, had to learn to accommodate not only one another but also the still-substantial Indian tribes with whom they shared these interior lands. By the middle of the eighteenth century, there was a significant European presence across a broad swath of North America—from Florida to Maine, and from Texas to Mexico to California—only a relatively small part of it controlled by the British. But changes were underway within the British Empire that would soon lead to its dominance through a much larger area of North America. •

KEY TERMS/PEOPLE/PLACES/EVENTS

ANNE HUTCHINSON 46
ANTINOMIANISM 46
BACON'S REBELLION 42
DOMINION OF NEW ENGLAND 63
GEORGE AND CECILIUS CALVERT 40
GLORIOUS REVOLUTION 63
HEADRIGHT 39
JACOB LEISLER 63
JAMES OGLETHORPE 59
JOHN SMITH 37

JOHN WINTHROP 44
KING PHILIP'S WAR 49
MASSACHUSETTS BAY COMPANY 44
MAYFLOWER COMPACT 43
METACOMET 49
MIDDLE GROUND 59
NAVIGATION ACTS 62
PEQUOT WAR 49
PLYMOUTH PLANTATION 43
POWHATAN 39

QUAKERS 53
QUITRENT 50
ROGER WILLIAMS 46
SIR WILLIAM BERKELEY 41
THEOCRACY 45
VIRGINIA HOUSE OF BURGESSES 39
WILLIAM BRADFORD 43
WILLIAM PENN 54

RECALL AND REFLECT

1. Compare patterns of settlement and expansion in the Chesapeake with those in New England. What were the major differences? Were there any similarities?

2. What were the reasons for the revolts and rebellions that occurred in the colonies of Virginia, Maryland, Massachusetts, and New York between 1660 and 1700? How were these rebellions resolved?

3. How did the institution of slavery in England's Atlantic seaboard colonies differ from slavery in the Caribbean? What accounted for these differences?

4. What were the middle grounds, and how did conditions there differ from conditions in the colonies along the Atlantic seaboard?

5. How did the Glorious Revolution in England affect England's North American colonies?

				King Philip's War in New England		William Penn received charter for Pennsylvania		Glorious Revolution in England: William and Mary ascend throne	
	Charles I executed		Carolina colony chartered						

1642–1649 **1649** — **1660** — **1663** — **1664** — **1675–1676** — **1676** — **1681** — **1686** — **1688** — **1732**

English Civil War | | English Restoration: Charles II becomes king | | English capture New Netherland / New Jersey chartered | | Bacon's Rebellion in Virginia | | Dominion of New England established | | Georgia chartered

THE HUNTING PARTY This painting, by an anonymous artist, depicts an elegant hunting party in New Jersey in the early eighteenth century—an era in which affluent colonialists identified themselves as Englishmen and sought to replicate the lifestyle of British aristocrats. *(The Hunting Party*, © The Metropolitan Museum of Art/Art Resource, New York)

3 | SOCIETY AND CULTURE IN PROVINCIAL AMERICA

BY THE EARLY EIGHTEENTH CENTURY, the British colonies were, most people in both England and America believed, outposts of the British world. As the colonies grew and became more prosperous, they also became more English. The colonists adopted the tastes, styles, and customs of England, bought goods made in England, read books and pamphlets published in England, and modeled most of their political, cultural, and educational institutions on their English equivalents. Many, perhaps most, colonists considered themselves Englishmen just as much as the men and women in England itself did.

At the same time, however, life in the colonies was diverging in many ways from that in England. The physical environment was very different—vaster and less tamed. The population was more diverse as well. The area that would become the United States was a magnet for immigrants from many lands other than England: Scotland, Ireland, the European continent, as well as migrants from the Spanish and French Empires already established in America. And beginning with the first importation of slaves into Virginia, English North America became the destination for thousands of forcibly transplanted Africans. In addition, Europeans and Africans were interacting constantly with a native population. Despite the efforts of the colonists to isolate themselves from Indian society and create a culture all their own, the European, African, and Native American worlds could not remain entirely separate.

SETTING THE STAGE

To the degree that the colonists emulated English society, they were becoming more and more like one another. To the degree that they were shaped by the character of their own regions, they were becoming more and more diverse. Although Americans would ultimately discover that they had enough in common to join together to form a single nation, these regional differences continued to affect their society well beyond the colonial period.

LOOKING AHEAD

1. What accounted for the rapid increase in the colonial population in the seventeenth century?
2. Why did African slavery expand so rapidly in the late seventeenth century?
3. How did religion shape and influence colonial society?

THE COLONIAL POPULATION

Not until long after the beginning of European colonization did Europeans and Africans in North America outnumber the native population. But after uncertain beginnings at Jamestown and Plymouth, the nonnative population grew rapidly and substantially, through continued immigration and through natural increase, until by the late seventeenth century Europeans and Africans became the dominant population groups along the Atlantic coast.

IMMIGRATION AND NATURAL INCREASE

A few of the early English settlers were members of the upper classes—usually the younger sons of the lesser gentry, men who stood to inherit no land at home and aspired to establish estates for themselves in America. For the most part, however, the early English population was very unaristocratic. It included some members of the emerging middle class, businessmen who migrated to America for religious or commercial reasons, or (like John Winthrop) both. But the dominant element was English laborers. Some came to the New World independently. The religious dissenters who formed the bulk of the population of early New England, for example, were men and women of modest means who arranged their own passage, brought their families with them, and established themselves immediately on their own land. But in the Chesapeake, at least three-fourths of the immigrants in the seventeenth century arrived as indentured servants.

INDENTURED SERVITUDE

The system of temporary servitude in the New World developed out of existing practices in England. Young men and women bound themselves to masters for a fixed term of servitude (usually four to five years). In return they received passage to America, food, and shelter. Upon completion of their terms of service, male indentures were supposed to receive such benefits as clothing, tools, and occasionally land; in reality, however, many left service without anything at all, unprepared and unequipped to begin earning a living on their own. Roughly one-fourth of the indentures in the Chesapeake were women, most of whom worked as domestic servants. Because men greatly outnumbered women

ORIGINS

NORTH AMERICA IN 1700 This map reveals how tiny a proportion of North America was settled by Europeans in 1700, nearly a century after the first English settlements there. The largest area of settlement was the thin fringe of colonies along the northern Atlantic seaboard. There were additional scattered settlements, almost all of them tiny, in eastern Canada, along the southern Atlantic coast, in the Mississippi Valley, and in the Southwest.

• *What would account for the isolated colonies in noncoastal areas of North America?*

in the region in the seventeenth century, women could reasonably expect to marry when their terms of servitude expired. Male domestic servants, however, usually had no such options.

Most indentured servants came to the colonies voluntarily, but not all. Beginning as early as 1617, the English government occasionally dumped shiploads of convicts in America to be sold into servitude, although some criminals, according to Captain John Smith, "did chuse to be hanged ere they would go thither, and were." The government also sent prisoners taken in battles with the Scots and the Irish in the 1650s, as well as other groups deemed undesirable: orphans, vagrants, paupers, and those who were "lewd and dangerous." Other involuntary immigrants were neither dangerous nor indigent but were simply victims of kidnapping, or "impressment," by aggressive and unscrupulous investors and promoters.

It was not difficult to understand why the system of indentured servitude proved so appealing to colonial employers—particularly once it became clear, as it quickly did, that the Indian population could not easily be transformed into a servile workforce. The indenture system provided a means of coping with the severe labor shortage in the New World. In the Chesapeake, the headright system (by which masters received additional land grants for every servant they imported) offered another incentive. For the servants themselves, the attractions were not always so clear. Those who came voluntarily often did so to escape troubles in England; others came in the hope of establishing themselves on land or in trades of their own when their terms of service expired. Yet the reality often differed sharply from the hope.

Some former indentures managed to establish themselves successfully as farmers, tradespeople, or artisans. Others

REALITIES OF INDENTURED SERVITUDE

(mostly males) found themselves without land, without employment, without families, and without prospects. A large floating population of young single men traveled restlessly from place to place, often in groups, in search of work or land and were a potential (and at times actual) source of social unrest, particularly in the Chesapeake. Even free laborers who found employment or land and settled down with families often did not stay put for very long. The phenomenon of families simply pulling up stakes and moving to another, more promising location every several years was one of the most prominent characteristics of the colonial population.

Indentured servitude remained an important source of population growth well into the eighteenth century, but beginning in the 1670s the flow began to decline substantially. A decrease in the English birth rate and an increase in English prosperity reduced the pressures on many men and women who might otherwise have considered emigrating. After 1700, those who did travel to America as indentured servants generally avoided the southern colonies, where working conditions

> THE INDENTURE SYSTEM PROVIDED A MEANS OF COPING WITH THE SEVERE LABOR SHORTAGE IN THE NEW WORLD.

were arduous and prospects for advancement were slim, and took advantage of the better opportunities in the mid-Atlantic colonies, especially Pennsylvania and New York. In the Chesapeake, landowners themselves began to find the indenture system less attractive, in part because they were troubled by the instability that former servants created or threatened to create. That was one reason for the increasing centrality of African slavery in the southern agricultural economy.

BIRTH AND DEATH

At first, new arrivals in most colonies, whatever their background or status, could anticipate great hardship: inadequate food, frequent epidemics, and in an appalling number of cases, early death. Gradually, however, conditions improved enough to allow the non-Indian population to begin to expand. By the end of the seventeenth century, the non-Indian population in the English colonies of North America had grown to over a quarter of a million, of whom about 25 percent were Africans.

Population (thousands) **2,780**

2,148

1,594

1,171

906

629

466

332

251

1700 1710 1720 1730 1740 1750 1760 1770 1780

Year

THE NON-INDIAN POPULATION OF NORTH AMERICA, 1700–1780 The European population of North America grew much more dramatically in the eighteenth century than it had in the seventeenth, exceeding 2 million by 1770. But unlike in the seventeenth century, the most important reason for this expansion was natural increase (children born in America), replacing immigration from Europe.

• *Why would the natural increase have been so much larger than in the past?*

SERVANTS FOR SALE The *South Carolina Gazette* of Charles Town ran this advertisement in November 1749 to announce the arrival of a group of English "indentures"—men and women who had accepted passage to America in exchange for their agreement to sell themselves as servants for a fixed period of years once they arrived. Indentures were the most common form of labor in most of the colonies during much of the seventeenth century, but by 1749 the system was already beginning to die out—replaced in the South by the enslavement of Africans. (Charleston Library Society, Charleston, South Carolina)

Although immigration remained for a time the greatest source of population increase, marked improvement in the reproduction rate began in New England and the mid-Atlantic colonies in the second half of the seventeenth century. After the 1650s, natural increase became the most important source of population. The New England popula-

EXCEPTIONAL LONGEVITY IN NEW ENGLAND

tion more than quadrupled through reproduction alone in the second half of the seventeenth century. This was less a result of unusual fertility (families in New England and in other regions were probably equally fertile) than of exceptional longevity. Indeed, the average life spans of residents of some areas of New England were nearly equal to those of people in the twentieth century. In the first generation of American-born colonists, according to one study, men who survived infancy lived to an average age of seventy-one, women to seventy. The next generation's life expectancy declined somewhat—to sixty-five for men who survived infancy—but remained at least ten years higher than the English equivalent and approximately twenty years higher than life expectancy in the South. Scholars disagree on the reasons for these remarkable life spans, but contributing factors probably included the cool climate and the relatively disease-free environment it produced, clean water (a stark contrast to England in these

years), and the absence of large population centers that might breed epidemics.

Conditions improved much more slowly in the South. The mortality rates for whites in the Chesapeake region remained markedly higher than those elsewhere until the mid-eighteenth century (and the mortality rates for Africans higher still). Throughout the seventeenth century, the average life expectancy for white men in the region was just over forty years and, for white women, slightly less. One in four children died in infancy, and fully half died before the age of twenty. The high death rate among adults meant that only about a third of all marriages lasted more than ten years; thus those children who survived infancy often lost one or both of their parents before reaching maturity. Widows, widowers, and orphans formed a substantial proportion of the white population of the Chesapeake. The continuing ravages of disease (particularly malaria) and the prevalence of salt-contaminated water kept the death rate high in the South; only after the settlers developed immunity to the local diseases (a slow process known as "seasoning") did life expectancy increase significantly. Population growth was substantial in the region, but largely as a result of immigration.

Natural increases in the population, wherever they occurred, were largely a result of a steady improvement in the sex ratio through the seventeenth century. In the early years of settlement, more than three-quarters of the white population of the Chesapeake consisted of men. And even in New England, which from the beginning had attracted more families (and thus more

MORE-BALANCED SEX RATIO

women) than the southern colonies, 60 percent of the white inhabitants in 1650 were male. Gradually, however, more women began to arrive in the colonies; and increasing birth rates, which of course produced roughly equal numbers of males and females, contributed to shifting the sex ratio as well. Not until well into the eighteenth century did the ratio begin to match that in England (where women were a slight majority), but by the late seventeenth century, the proportion of males to females in all the colonies was becoming more balanced.

MEDICINE IN THE COLONIES

The very high death rates of women who bore children illustrate the primitive nature of medical knowledge and practice in the colonies. Seventeenth- and eighteenth-century physicians had little or no understanding of infection and sterilization. As a result, many people died from infections contracted during childbirth or surgery from dirty instruments or dirty hands. Because communities were unaware of bacteria, many were plagued with infectious diseases transmitted by garbage or unclean water.

One result of the limited extent of medical knowledge was that it was relatively easy for people to enter the medical field, even without professional training. The biggest beneficiaries of this ease of access were women, who established themselves in con-

MIDWIVES

siderable numbers as midwives. Midwives assisted women in childbirth, but they also dispensed other medical advice—usually urging their patients to use herbs or other natural remedies. Midwives were popular because they were usually friends and neighbors of the people they treated, unlike physicians, who were few and therefore not often well known to their patients. Male doctors felt threatened by the midwives and struggled continually to drive them from the field, although they did not make substantial progress in doing so until the nineteenth century.

Midwives and doctors alike practiced medicine on the basis of the prevailing assumptions of their time, most of them derived from the theory of "humoralism" popularized by the second-century Roman physician Galen. Galen argued that the human body was governed by four "humors" that were lodged in four bodily fluids: yellow bile (or "choler"), black bile ("melancholy"), blood, and phlegm. In a healthy body, the four humors existed in balance. Illness represented an imbalance and suggested the need for removing from the body the excesses of whatever fluid was causing the imbalance. That was the rationale that lay behind the principal medical techniques of the seventeenth century: purging, expulsion, and bleeding. Bleeding was the most extreme of the treatments (and the most destructive), and it was practiced mostly by male physicians. Midwives preferred more homeopathic treatments and favored "pukes" and laxatives. The great majority of early Americans, however, had little contact with physicians, or even midwives, and sought instead to deal with illness on their own, confident that their abilities were equal to those of educated physicians—which, given the state of medical knowledge, was often true.

That seventeenth-century medicine rested so much on ideas produced 1,400 years before is evidence of how little support there was for the scientific method—which rests on experimentation and observation rather than on inherited faiths—in England and America at the time. Bleeding, for example, had been in use for hundreds of years, during which time there had been no evidence that it helped people recover from illness; indeed, if anyone had chosen to look for it, there was considerable evidence that bleeding could do great harm. But what would seem in later eras to be the simple process of testing scientific assumptions was not yet a common part of Western thought. Only with the birth of the Enlightenment in the late seventeenth century—with its faith in human reason and its belief in the capacity of individuals and societies to create better lives— would the scientific method begin to find acceptance.

WOMEN AND FAMILIES IN THE CHESAPEAKE

The importance of reproduction in the labor-scarce society of seventeenth-century America had particularly significant effects on women. The high sex ratio meant that few women remained unmarried for long. The average European woman in America married for the first time at twenty or twenty-one years of age, MALE AUTHORITY considerably earlier than in England; in UNDERMINED some areas of the Chesapeake, the average bride was three to four years younger. In the Chesapeake, the most important factor affecting women

and families remained, until at least the mid-eighteenth century, the extraordinarily high mortality rate. Under those circumstances, the traditional male-centered family structure of England—by which husbands and fathers exercised firm, even dictatorial control over the lives of their wives and children— was difficult to maintain. Because so few families remained intact for long, rigid patterns of male authority were constantly undermined. Standards of sexual behavior were also more flexible in the South than they were in England or other parts of America. Because of the large numbers of indentured servants who were forbidden to marry until their terms of service expired, premarital sexual relationships were frequent. Female servants who became pregnant before the expiration of their terms could expect harsh treatment: heavy fines, whippings if no one could pay the fines, an extra year or two of service added to their contract, and the loss of their children after weaning. Bastard children were themselves bound out as indentures at a very early age. On the other hand, a pregnant woman whose term of service expired before the birth of her child or whose partner was able to buy her remaining time from her master might expect to marry quickly. Over a third of Chesapeake marriages occurred with the bride already pregnant.

Women in the Chesapeake could anticipate a life consumed with childbearing. The average wife became pregnant every two years. Those who lived long enough bore an average of eight children apiece (up to five of whom typically died in infancy or early childhood). Since childbirth was one of the most frequent causes of female death, relatively few women survived to see all their children grow to maturity.

For all the hardships women encountered in the seventeenth-century South, they also enjoyed more power and a greater level of freedom than women in other areas (or than southern women in later years). Because men were plentiful and women scarce, females had considerable latitude in choosing husbands. (They also often had no fathers or other male GREATER relatives nearby trying to control their INDEPENDENCE choices.) Because women generally married IN THE SOUTH at a much younger age than men, they often outlived their husbands (even though female life expectancy was somewhat shorter than male). Widows were often left with several children and with responsibility for managing a farm or plantation, a circumstance of enormous hardship but one that also gave them significant economic power.

Widows seldom remained unmarried for long, however. Those who had no grown sons to work the tobacco farms and plantations had particular need for male assistance, and marriage was the surest way to secure it. Since many widows married men who were themselves widowers, complex combinations of households were frequent. With numerous stepchildren, half brothers, and half sisters living together in a single household, women often had to play the role of peacemaker—a role that may have further enhanced their authority within the family.

By the early eighteenth century, the character of the Chesapeake population was beginning to change, and with it the nature of the typical family. Life expectancy was increasing;

indentured servitude was in decline; and natural reproduction was becoming the principal source of white population increase.

REVIVAL OF PATRIARCHY

The sex ratio was becoming more equal. One result of these changes was that life for white people in the region became less perilous and less arduous. Another result was that women lost some of the power that their small numbers had once given them. As families grew more stable, traditional patterns of male authority revived. By the mid-eighteenth century, southern families were becoming highly "patriarchal," that is, dominated by the male head of the family.

WOMEN AND FAMILIES IN NEW ENGLAND

In New England, where many more immigrants arrived with family members and where death rates declined quickly, family structure was much more stable than it was in the Chesapeake and hence much more traditional. Because the sex ratio was reasonably balanced, most men could expect to marry.

Women, however, remained in the minority; and as in the Chesapeake, they married young, began producing children early, and continued to do so well into their thirties. In contrast to the South, however, northern children were more likely to survive (the average family raised six to eight children to maturity), and families were more likely to remain intact. Fewer New England women became widows, and those who did generally lost their husbands later in life. Hence women were less often cast in roles independent of their husbands. Young women, moreover, had less control over the conditions of marriage, both because there were fewer unmarried men vying for them and because their fathers were more often alive and able to exercise control over their choice of husbands.

Among other things, increased longevity meant that, unlike in the Chesapeake (where three-fourths of all children lost at least one parent before the age of twenty-one), white parents in New England usually lived to see their children and even their grandchildren grow to maturity. Still, the lives of most New England women were nearly as consumed by child-

LIFE SPANS

bearing and child rearing as those of women in the Chesapeake. Even women who lived into their sixties spent the majority of their mature years with young children in the home. The longer lives in New England also meant that parents continued to control their children far longer than did parents in the South. Although they were less likely than parents in England to "arrange" marriages for their children, few sons and daughters could choose spouses entirely independent of their parents' wishes. Men usually depended on their fathers for land—generally a prerequisite for beginning families of their own. Women needed dowries from their parents if they were to attract desirable husbands. Stricter parental supervision of children meant, too, that fewer women became pregnant before marriage than in the South (although even in Puritan New England the premarital pregnancy rate was not insubstantial—as high as 20 percent in some communities).

Puritanism placed a high value on the family, which was the

THE PATRIARCHAL PURITAN FAMILY

principal economic and religious unit within every community. At the same time, however, Puritanism reinforced the

GUIDE TO THE SEASONS Among their many purposes, almanacs sought to help farmers predict weather and plan for the demands of changing seasons. This illustration, part of a "calendar" of farming images, shows a man and a woman tending fields in July, in preparation for the coming harvest. (American Antiquarian Society)

idea of nearly absolute male authority and the assumption of female weakness and inferiority. Women were expected to be modest and submissive. Such popular girls' names as Prudence, Patience, Chastity, and Comfort suggest something about Puritan expectations of female behavior. A wife was expected to devote herself to serving the needs of her husband and household.

> POPULAR GIRLS' NAMES SUCH AS PRUDENCE, PATIENCE, CHASTITY, AND COMFORT SUGGEST SOMETHING ABOUT PURITAN EXPECTATIONS OF FEMALE BEHAVIOR.

THE BEGINNINGS OF SLAVERY IN BRITISH AMERICA

Almost from the beginning of European settlement in North America, there was a demand for black servants to supplement the always scarce southern labor supply. The demand grew rapidly once tobacco cultivation became a staple of the Chesapeake economy. But the supply of African laborers was limited during much of the seventeenth century, because the Atlantic slave trade did not at first serve the English colonies in America. Portuguese slavers, who had dominated the trade since the sixteenth century, shipped captive men and women from the west coast of Africa to the new European colonies in South America and the Caribbean. Gradually, however, Dutch and French navigators joined the slave trade. A substantial commerce in slaves grew up within the Americas, particularly between the Caribbean islands and the southern colonies of British America. By the late seventeenth century, the supply of black workers in North America was becoming plentiful.

As the commerce in slaves grew more extensive and sophisticated, it also grew more horrible. Before it ended in the nineteenth century, it was responsible for the forced immigration of as many as 11 million Africans to the New World. (Until the late eighteenth century, the number of African immigrants to the Americas was higher than that of Europeans.) Native African chieftains captured members of enemy tribes in battle, tied them together in long lines, or "coffles," and sold them in the flourishing slave marts on the African coast. Then, after some haggling on the docks between the European traders and the African suppliers, the terrified victims were packed into the dark, filthy holds of ships for the horrors of the "middle passage"—the journey to America. For weeks, sometimes even months, the black prisoners remained chained in the bowels of the slave ships. Conditions varied from one ship to another. Some captains took care to see that their potentially valuable cargo remained reasonably healthy. Others accepted the deaths of numerous Africans as inevitable and tried to cram as many as possible into their ships to ensure that enough would survive to yield a profit at journey's end. On such ships, the African prisoners were sometimes packed together in such close quarters that they were unable to stand, hardly able to breathe. Some ships supplied them with only minimal food and water. Women were often victims of rape and other sexual abuse. Those who died en route were simply thrown overboard. Upon arrival in

THE MIDDLE PASSAGE

the New World, slaves were auctioned off to white landowners and transported, frightened and bewildered, to their new homes.

The first black laborers arrived in English North America before 1620, and as English seamen began to establish themselves in the slave trade, the flow of Africans to the colonies gradually increased. But North America was always a much less important market for Africans than were other parts of the New World, especially the Caribbean islands and Brazil, whose labor-intensive sugar economies created an especially large demand for slaves. Less than 5 percent of the Africans imported to the Americas went directly to the English colonies on the mainland. Most blacks who ended up in what became the United States spent time first in the West Indies. Not until the 1670s did traders start importing blacks directly from Africa to North America. Even then, however, the flow remained small for a time, mainly because a single group, the Royal African Company of England, maintained a monopoly on trade in the mainland colonies and managed as a result to keep prices high and supplies low.

A turning point in the history of the African population in North America came in the mid-1690s, when the Royal African Company's monopoly was finally broken. With the trade now opened to English and colonial merchants on a competitive basis, prices fell and the number of Africans arriving in North America rapidly increased. By the end of the seventeenth century, only about one in ten of the residents of the colonies was African (about 25,000 in all). But because Africans were so heavily concentrated in a few southern colonies, they were already beginning to outnumber Europeans in some areas. The high ratio of men to women among African immigrants (there were perhaps two males to one female in most areas) retarded the natural increase of the black population. But in the Chesapeake at least, more new slaves were being born by 1700 than were being imported from Africa. In South Carolina, by contrast, the difficult conditions of rice cultivation—and the high death rates of those who worked in the rice fields—ensured that the black population would barely be able to sustain itself through natural increase until much later.

GROWING SLAVE POPULATION

Between 1700 and 1760, the number of Africans in the colonies increased tenfold to about a quarter of a million. A relatively small number (16,000 in 1763) lived in New England; there were slightly more (29,000) in the middle colonies. The vast majority, however, continued to live in the South. By then the flow of free white laborers to that region had all but stopped, and Africans had become securely established as the basis of the southern work force.

It was not entirely clear at first that the status of black laborers in America would be fundamentally different from that of white indentured servants. In the rugged conditions of the seventeenth-century South, it was often difficult for Europeans and Africans to maintain strictly separate roles. In some areas—South Carolina,

UNCERTAIN STATUS

THE ORIGINS OF SLAVERY

THE debate among historians over how and why white Americans created a system of slave labor in the seventeenth century—and how and why they determined that people of African descent and no others should populate that system—has been a long and unusually heated one. At its center is the question of whether slavery was a result of white racism or whether slavery created racism.

In 1950, Oscar and Mary Handlin published an influential article, "Origins of the Southern Labor System," comparing slavery to other systems of "unfreedom" in the colonies. What differentiated slavery from other conditions of servitude, they argued, was that it was restricted to people of African descent, it was permanent, and it passed from one generation to the next. The unique characteristics of slavery, the Handlins maintained, were part of an effort by colonial legislatures to increase the available labor force. White laborers needed an incentive to come to America; black laborers, forcibly imported from Africa, did not. The distinction between the conditions of white workers and the conditions of black workers was, therefore, based on legal and economic motives, not on racism. Racism emerged to justify slavery; it did not cause slavery.

Winthrop D. Jordan was one of a number of historians who later challenged the Handlins' thesis and argued that white racism, more than economic interests, produced African slavery. In *White Over Black* (1968) and other works, Jordan argued that Europeans had long viewed people of color—and black Africans in particular—as inferior beings appropriate for serving whites. Those attitudes migrated with white Europeans to the New World, and white racism shaped the treatment of Africans in America—and the nature of the slave labor system—from the beginning.

George Fredrickson echoed Jordan's emphasis on the importance of racism as an independent factor reinforcing slavery; but unlike Jordan, he argued that racism did not precede slavery. "The treatment of blacks," he wrote, "engendered a cultural and psycho-social racism that after a certain point took on a life of its own. . . . Racism, although the child of slavery, not only outlived its parent but grew stronger and more independent after slavery's demise."

In *Black Majority* (1974), a study of seventeenth-century South Carolina, Peter Wood moved the debate away from racism and back toward social and economic conditions. Wood demonstrated that blacks and whites often worked together on relatively equal terms in the early years of settlement. But as rice cultivation expanded, finding white laborers willing to do the arduous work became more difficult. The forcible importation of African workers and the creation of a system of permanent bondage was a response to a growing demand for labor and to fears among whites that without slavery a black labor force would be difficult to control.

Edmund Morgan argued similarly in *American Slavery, American Freedom* (1975) that the southern labor system was at first relatively flexible and later grew more rigid. In colonial Virginia, he claimed, white settlers did not at first intend to create a system of permanent bondage. But as the tobacco economy grew and created a high demand for cheap labor, white landowners began to feel uneasy about their dependence on a large group of dependent white workers, since such workers were difficult to recruit and control. Thus slavery was less a result of racism than of the desire of white landowners to find a reliable and stable labor force.

for example, where the number of African arrivals swelled more quickly than anywhere else—whites and blacks lived and worked together for a time on terms of relative equality. Some blacks were treated much like white hired servants, and some were freed after a fixed term of servitude. A few Africans themselves became landowners, and some apparently owned slaves of their own.

By the early eighteenth century, however, a rigid distinction had become established between black and white. (See "Debating the Past," above.) Masters were contractually obliged to free white servants after a fixed term of servitude. There was no such necessity to free black workers, and the assumption slowly spread that blacks would remain in service permanently. Another incentive for making the status of Africans rigid was that the

> ## ONE FACTOR, AND ONE FACTOR ONLY, DETERMINED WHETHER A PERSON WAS SUBJECT TO THE SLAVE CODES: COLOR.

children of slaves provided white landowners with a self-perpetuating labor force.

White assumptions about the inferiority of people of color contributed to the growing rigidity of the system. Such assumptions came naturally to the English settlers. They had already defined themselves as a superior race in their relations with the native Indian population (and earlier in their relations with the Irish). The idea of subordinating a supposedly inferior race was, therefore, already established in the English imagination by the time substantial numbers of Africans appeared in America.

In the early eighteenth century, colonial assemblies began to pass "slave codes," limiting the rights of blacks in law and ensuring almost absolute authority to white masters. One factor,

LONDON'S VIRGINIA.

(The Granger Collection, New York)

In *The Making of New World Slavery* (1996), Robin Blackburn argues that while race was a factor in allowing whites to justify to themselves the enslavement of Africans, the real reasons for slavery were hardheaded economic decisions by ambitious entrepreneurs, who realized early on that a slave-labor system in the labor-intensive agricultural world of the American South and the Caribbean was more profitable than a free-labor system. Slavery served the interests of a powerful combination of groups: planters, merchants, governments, industrialists, and consumers. Race may have been a rationale for slavery, allowing planters and traders to justify to themselves the terrible human costs of the system. But the most important reason for the system was not racism, but the pursuit of profit—and the success of the system in producing it. Blackburn concludes that slavery was not an antiquated remnant of an older world but, rather, a recognizably modern labor system that, however horrible, served the needs of an emerging market economy. •

UNDERSTAND, ANALYZE, AND EVALUATE

1. What do historians say is the relationship between racism and slavery?
2. What are the economic arguments put forward by historians to explain the system of slave labor that developed in America? Do these arguments account fully for the development of slavery?
3. Why was slavery more successful than other labor systems in meeting the labor needs of colonial America's market economy?

and one factor only, determined whether a person was subject to the slave codes: color. In contrast to the colonial societies of

SLAVE CODES Spanish America, where people of mixed race had a different (and higher) status than pure Africans, English America recognized no such distinctions. Any African ancestry was enough to classify a person as black.

CHANGING SOURCES OF EUROPEAN IMMIGRATION

By the early eighteenth century, the flow of immigrants from England itself began to decline substantially—a result of better economic conditions there and of new government restrictions on emigration in the face of massive depopulation in some regions of the country. But as English immigration declined, French, German, Swiss, Irish, Welsh, Scottish, and Scandinavian immigration continued and increased.

The earliest, although not the most numerous, of these non-English European immigrants were the French Calvinists, or Huguenots. A royal proclamation, the Edict of Nantes of 1598, had allowed them to become practically a state within the state in Roman Catholic France. In 1685, however, the French government revoked the edict. Soon after that,

HUGUENOTS AND PENNSYLVANIA DUTCH
Huguenots began leaving the country. About 300,000 left France in the following decades. A small proportion of them traveled to the English colonies in North America. Many German Protestants suffered similarly from the arbitrary religious policies of their rulers; and all Germans, Catholics as well as Protestants, suffered from the devastating wars with King Louis XIV of France (the "Sun King"). The Rhineland of southwestern Germany, the area known as the Palatinate, experienced particular hardships. Because it was close to France, its people were particularly exposed to

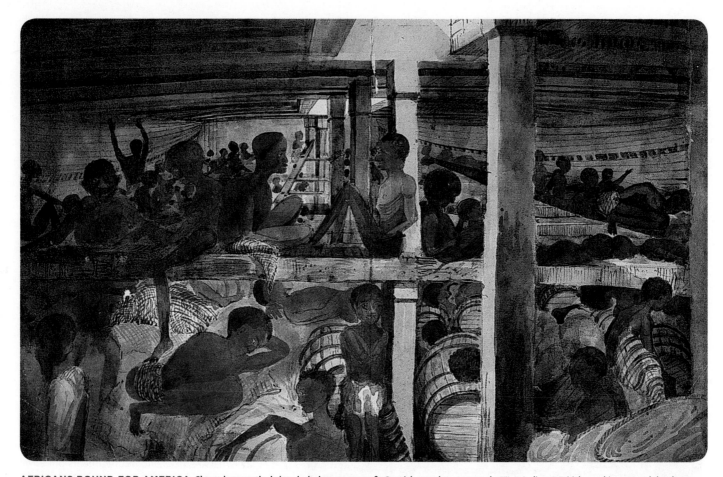

AFRICANS BOUND FOR AMERICA Shown here are the below-deck slave quarters of a Spanish vessel en route to the West Indies. A British warship captured the slaver, and a young English naval officer (Lt. Francis Meynell) made this watercolor sketch on the spot. The Africans seen in this picture appear somewhat more comfortable than prisoners on some other slave ships, who were often chained and packed together so tightly that they had no room to stand or even sit. (National Maritime Museum, London)

slaughter and ruin at the hands of invaders. The unusually cold winter of 1708–1709 dealt a final blow to the precarious economy of the region. More than 12,000 Palatinate Germans sought refuge in England, and approximately 3,000 of them soon found their way to America. They arrived in New York and tried at first to make homes in the Mohawk Valley, only to be ousted by the powerful landlords of the region. Some of the Germans moved farther up the Mohawk, out of reach of the patroons; but most made their way to Pennsylvania, where they received a warm welcome (and where they ultimately became known to English settlers as the "Pennsylvania Dutch," a corruption of their own word for "German": "Deutsch"). The Quaker colony became the most common destination for Germans, who came to America in growing numbers. (Among them were Moravians and Mennonites, with religious views similar in many ways to those of the Quakers.) Many German Protestants went to North Carolina as well, especially after the founding of New Bern in 1710 by a company of 600 German-speaking Swiss.

> PENNSYLVANIA BECAME THE MOST COMMON DESTINATION FOR GERMANS, WHO CAME TO AMERICA IN GROWING NUMBERS.

The most numerous of the newcomers were the Scots-Irish—Scottish Presbyterians who had settled in northern Ireland (in the province of Ulster) in the early seventeenth century. The Ulster colonists had prospered for a time despite the barren soil and the constant, never wholly successful, struggle to suppress the Catholic natives. But in the first years of the eighteenth century, Parliament prohibited Ulster from exporting to England the woolens and other products that had become the basis of the northern Irish economy; at the same time, the English government virtually outlawed the practice of the Presbyterian religion in Ulster and insisted on conformity with the Anglican Church. After 1710, moreover, the long-term leases of many Scots-Irish expired; English landlords doubled and even tripled the rents. Thousands of tenants embarked for America.

Often coldly received at the colonial ports, many of the Scots-Irish pushed out to the edges of European settlement. There they occupied land without much regard for who actually claimed to own it, whether

SCOTS-IRISH

THE SLAVE SHIP *BROOKES* The British slave ship *Brookes* provided this plan of its "stowage" of slaves to conform to 1798 legislation from Parliament. It illustrates vividly the terrible conditions under which slaves were shipped from Africa to the Americas—human beings squeezed into every available space like cargo for the long, dangerous passage during which many Africans died. (Library of Congress)

absentee whites, Indians, or the colonial governments. They were as ruthless in their displacement and suppression of the Indians as they had been with the native Irish Catholics.

Immigrants from Scotland and southern Ireland added other elements to the colonial population in the eighteenth century. Scottish Highlanders, some of them Roman Catholics who had been defeated in rebellions in 1715 and 1745, immigrated into several colonies, North Carolina above all. Presbyterian Lowlanders, faced in Scotland with high rents in the country and unemployment in the towns, left for America in large numbers shortly before the American Revolution, joining earlier groups of Scots, who had arrived in the late seventeenth century. They became a significant influence in New Jersey and Pennsylvania and helped establish Presbyterianism as an important religion in those colonies. The Catholic Irish migrated steadily over a long period, and by the time of the Revolution they were almost as numerous as the Scots, although less conspicuous. Many of them had by then abandoned their Roman Catholic religion and with it much of their ethnic identity.

Continuing immigration and natural increase contributed to a rapid population growth in the colonies in the eighteenth century. In 1700, the non-Indian population of the colonies totaled less than 250,000; by 1775, it was over 2 million—a nearly tenfold increase. Throughout the colonial period, the non-Indian population nearly doubled every twenty-five years.

THE COLONIAL ECONOMIES

To those who remained in Europe, and even to some who settled in North America, the English colonies often appeared so small and isolated as to seem virtually at the end of the world. But from the beginning, almost all the English colonies were commercial ventures and were tied in crucial ways to other economies. They developed substantial trade with the native population of North America, with the French settlers to the north and, to a lesser extent, with Spanish colonists to the south and west. And over time they developed an even more substantial trade within the growing Atlantic economy of the sixteenth

Population (thousands) **575**

325

150

69

28

.60 **3** **7**

1620 1640 1660 1680 1700 1720 1740 1760 1780

Year

**THE AFRICAN POPULATION OF THE BRITISH COLONIES,
1620-1780** From tiny beginnings in the seventeenth century, the African population of the British colonies grew rapidly in the eighteenth century. The growth of slavery was a result of both supply (a readily available population of African workers in the Caribbean islands) and demand (the growth of tobacco, rice, and cotton cultivation in larger areas of the South). The slave population in the colonies also increased naturally in this period at a far greater rate than in the past, largely because living conditions for African workers improved,

• *Why would slaveowners have invested in better conditions for their slaves?*

and seventeenth centuries, of which they became a critical part.

American colonists engaged in a wide range of economic pursuits. But except for a few areas in the West where the small white populations subsisted largely on the fur and skin trade with the Indians, farming dominated all areas of European and African settlement throughout the seventeenth and eighteenth

THE "PENNSYLVANIA DUTCH" This folk-art painted dish illustrates the traditional dress of the Pennsylvania Dutch. The Pennsylvania Dutch were, in fact, German immigrants, known to their neighbors as "Dutch" because that was how their native word for their nationality ("Deutsch") sounded to most English speakers. (Dish, Redware, lead glaze, slip and sgraffito decoration, 2¼ x 12⅛ inches (5.7 x 30.8 cm.), Gift of John T. Morris, 1900. The Philadelphia Museum of Art [#1900–19])

centuries. Some farmers engaged in simple subsistence agriculture; but whenever possible, American farmers attempted to grow crops for the local, intercolonial, and export markets.

THE SOUTHERN ECONOMY

In the Chesapeake region, tobacco quickly became the basis of the economy. A strong European demand for the crop enabled some planters to grow enormously wealthy and at times allowed the region as a whole to prosper.

TOBACCO

But production frequently exceeded demand, and as a result the price of tobacco periodically suffered severe declines. The first major bust in the tobacco economy occurred in 1640, and the boom-and-bust pattern continued throughout the colonial period and beyond. Growing more tobacco only made the problem of overproduction worse, but Chesapeake farmers never understood that. Those planters who could afford to do so expanded their landholdings, enlarged their fields, and acquired additional laborers. After 1700, tobacco plantations employing several dozen slaves or more were common.

The staple of the economies of South Carolina and Georgia was rice. By building dams and dikes along the many tidal rivers, farmers managed to create rice paddies that could be flooded and then drained. Rice cultivation was arduous work, performed standing knee-deep in the mud of malarial swamps under a blazing sun, surrounded by insects. It was a task so difficult and unhealthful that white laborers generally refused to perform it. As a result, planters in South Carolina and Georgia were even more dependent than those elsewhere on African slaves. It was not only because Africans could be compelled to perform difficult work that whites found them so valuable. It was also because they were much better at it. They showed from the beginning a greater resistance to malaria and other local diseases (although the impact of disease on African workers was by no means inconsiderable). And they proved more adept at the basic agricultural tasks required, in part because some of them had come from rice-producing regions of west Africa.

In the early 1740s, another staple crop contributed to the South Carolina economy: indigo. Eliza Lucas, a young Antiguan woman who managed her family's North American plantations, experimented with cultivating the West Indian plant (which was the source of a blue dye in great demand in Europe) on the mainland. She discovered that it could grow on the high ground of South Carolina, which was unsuitable for rice planting, and that its harvest came while the rice was still growing. Indigo

Immigrant Groups
- English
- Scots-Irish
- German
- Dutch
- African

INDIGO became an important complement to rice and a popular import in England.

Because of the South's early dependence on large-scale cash crops, the southern colonies developed less of a commercial or industrial economy than the colonies of the North. The trading in tobacco and rice was handled largely by merchants based in London and, later, in the northern colonies. Few cities of more than modest size developed in the South.

NORTHERN ECONOMIC AND TECHNOLOGICAL LIFE

In the North, agriculture was the single most important part of the economy. But unlike in the South, the northern colonies were less dominated by farming. The northern economy was more diverse than the economy in the South in part because

MORE DIVERSE ECONOMY IN THE NORTH conditions for farming were less favorable there. In northern New England, in particular, colder weather and hard, rocky soil made it difficult for colonists to develop the kind of large-scale commercial farming system that southerners were creating. Conditions for agriculture were better in southern New England and the middle colonies, where the soil was fertile and the weather more temperate. New York, Pennsylvania, and the Connecticut River valley were the chief suppliers of wheat to much of New England and to parts of the South. Even there, however, a substantial commercial economy emerged alongside the agricultural one.

PREPARING TOBACCO This 1790 engraving is designed to illustrate the African origins of the enslaved workers who processed tobacco in Virginia. Their "primitive" costumes seemed to the artist, a French visitor to America, to be in keeping with the crude processes they had created for drying, rolling, and sorting tobacco. (The Stapleton Collection/Bridgeman Art Library)

Almost every colonist engaged in a certain amount of industry at home. Occasionally these home industries provided families with surplus goods they could trade or sell. Beyond these domestic efforts, craftsmen and artisans established themselves in colonial towns as cobblers, blacksmiths, riflemakers, cabinetmakers, silversmiths, and printers. In some areas, entrepreneurs harnessed water power to run small mills for grinding grain, processing cloth, or milling lumber. And in several places, large-scale shipbuilding operations began to flourish.

The first effort to establish a significant metals industry in the colonies was an ironworks established in Saugus, Massachusetts, in the 1640s after iron ore deposits had been discovered in the region. Iron technology was already advancing rapidly in England, and the colonists attempted to transfer those skills to America. The Saugus works used water power to drive a bellows, which controlled the heat in a charcoal furnace. As the ore melted, it trickled down into molds or was taken in the form of simple "sow bars" to a forge to be shaped into such marketable objects as plows, hoes, axes, pots, and other tools. The Saugus works was a technological success; indeed, it could boast technological capabilities equal to those of any ironworks in Europe at the time. But it was a financial failure. It began operations in 1646; in 1668, its financial problems forced it to close its doors.

SAUGUS
IRONWORKS

Metalworks, however, gradually became an important part of the colonial economy. The largest industrial enterprise anywhere in English North America was the ironworks of the German ironmaster Peter Hasenclever in northern New Jersey. Founded in 1764 with British capital, it employed several hundred laborers, many of them imported from ironworks in Germany. There were other, smaller ironmaking enterprises in every northern colony (with particular concentrations in Massachusetts, New Jersey, and Pennsylvania), and there were ironworks as well in several of the southern colonies. Even so, these and other growing industries did not become the basis for the kind of explosive industrial growth that Great Britain experienced in the late eighteenth century—in part because English parliamentary regulations such as the Iron Act of 1750 restricted metal processing in the colonies. Similar prohibitions limited the manufacture of woolens, hats, and other goods. But the biggest obstacles to industrialization in America were an inadequate labor supply, a small domestic market, and inadequate transportation facilities and energy supplies.

More important than manufacturing were industries that exploited the natural resources of the continent. By the mid-seventeenth century, the flourishing fur trade of earlier years was in decline. Taking its place were lumbering, mining, and

EXTRACTIVE
INDUSTRIES

COMMERCE IN NEW ENGLAND This late-eighteenth-century painting of the home, wharves, countinghouse, and fleet of a prosperous New England fisherman gives some indication of how commerce was expanding even in such relatively small places as Duxbury, Massachusetts. The owner, Joshua Winsor, was active in the mackerel and cod fishing industry. The painting—evidently an effort to celebrate Winsor's great material success and record it for posterity—was by his son-in-law, Dr. Rufus Hathaway. (*A View of Mr. Joshua Winsor's House, 1793–95.* By Rufus Hathaway. Museum of American Folk Art, New York. Promised anonymous gift.)

fishing, particularly in the waters off the New England coast. These industries provided commodities that could be exported to England in exchange for manufactured goods. And they helped produce the most distinctive feature of the northern economy: a thriving commercial class.

THE EXTENT AND LIMITS OF TECHNOLOGY

Despite the technological progress that was occurring in some parts of America in the seventeenth and eighteenth centuries, much of colonial society was conspicuously lacking in even very basic technologies. Up to half the farmers in the colonies were so primitively equipped that they did not even own a plow. Substantial numbers of house-

holds owned no pots or kettles for cooking. And only about half the households in the colonies owned guns or rifles—with rural people almost as unlikely to have firearms as urban people. The relatively low levels of ownership of these and other elementary tools was not because such things were difficult to make, but because most Americans remained too poor or too isolated to be able to afford them. Many households had few if any candles, because they were unable to afford candle molds or tallow (wax), or because they had no access to commercially produced candles. In the early eighteenth century, very few farmers owned wagons. Most made do with two-wheeled carts, which could be hauled by hand (or by horse) around the farm but which were not very efficient for transporting crops to market. The most commonly owned tool on American farms was the axe, which suggests how much time most

> **UP TO HALF THE FARMERS IN THE COLONIES WERE SO PRIMITIVELY EQUIPPED THAT THEY DID NOT EVEN OWN A PLOW.**

farmers had to spend clearing land. But throughout the colonies, the ability of people to acquire manufactured implements lagged far behind the capacity to produce them.

Even so, few colonists were self-sufficient in the late seventeenth and early eighteenth centuries. The popular image of early American households is of people who had little connection to the market, who grew their own food, made their own clothes, and bought little from anyone else. In fact, relatively few colonial families owned spinning wheels or looms, which suggests that most people purchased whatever yarn and cloth they

MYTH OF SELF-SUFFICIENCY

needed, or could afford, from merchants. Most farmers who grew grain took it to centralized facilities for processing.

THE RISE OF COLONIAL COMMERCE

Perhaps the most remarkable feature of colonial commerce in the seventeenth century was that it was able to survive at all. American merchants faced such bewildering and intimidating obstacles, and lacked so many of the basic institutions of trade, they managed to stay afloat only with great difficulty. There was, first, no commonly accepted medium of exchange. The colonies

THE "TRIANGULAR TRADE" This map illustrates the complex pattern of trade that fueled the colonial American economy in the seventeenth and eighteenth centuries. A simple explanation of this trade is that the American colonies exported raw materials (agricultural products, furs, and others) to Britain and Europe and imported manufactured goods in return. But while that explanation is accurate, it is not complete, largely because the Atlantic trade was not a simple exchange between America and Europe, but a complex network of exchanges involving the Caribbean, Africa, and the Mediterranean. Note the important exchanges between the North American mainland and the Caribbean islands; the important trade between the American colonies and Africa; and the wide range of European and Mediterranean markets in which Americans were active. Not shown on this map, but also very important to colonial commerce, was a large coastal trade among the various regions of British North America.

• Why did the major ports of trade emerge almost entirely in the northern colonies?

had almost no specie (gold or silver coins). They experimented at times with different forms of paper currency—tobacco certifi-
SHORTAGE OF CURRENCY
cates, for example, which were secured by tobacco stored in warehouses; or land cer-tificates, secured by property. Such paper was not, however, acceptable as payment for any goods from abroad, and it was in any case ultimately outlawed by Parliament. For many years, colonial merchants had to rely on a haphazard barter system or on crude money substitutes such as beaver skins.

A second obstacle was the near impossibility of imposing order on their trade. In the fragmented, jerry-built commercial world of colonial America, no merchants could be certain that the goods they sold would be produced in sufficient quantity; nor could they be certain of finding adequate markets for them. Few channels of information existed to inform traders of what they could expect in foreign ports; vessels sometimes stayed at sea for several years, journeying from one market to another, trading one commodity for another, attempting to find some way to turn a profit. Engaged in this chaotic commerce, more-over, were an enormous number of small, fiercely competitive companies, which made the problem of stabilizing the system even more acute.

Despite these and other problems, commerce in the colo-nies not only survived but grew. There was an elaborate coastal trade, through which the colonies did business with one an-other and sold goods to the West Indies—among them rum, agricultural products, meat, and fish. The mainland colonies
TRIANGULAR TRADE
bought sugar, molasses, and slaves from the Caribbean markets in return. There was also an expanding transatlantic trade, which linked the North American colonies in an intricate net-work of commerce with England, continental Europe, and the west coast of Africa. This commerce has often been described, somewhat inaccurately, as the "triangular trade," suggesting a neat process: merchants carried rum and other goods from New England to Africa; exchanged their merchandise for slaves, whom they then transported to the West Indies (hence the term "middle passage" for the dreaded journey—it was the second of the three legs of the voyage); and then exchanged the slaves for sugar and molasses, which they shipped back to New England to be distilled into rum. In fact, the system was almost never so simple. The "triangular" trade in rum, slaves, and sugar was in fact part of a maze of highly diverse trade routes: between the northern and southern colonies, America and England, America and Africa, the West Indies and Europe, and other combinations.

Out of this complex and highly risky trade emerged a group of adventurous entrepreneurs who by the mid-eighteenth century were beginning to constitute a distinct merchant class. Concentrated in the port cities of the North (above all, Boston, New York, and Philadelphia), they enjoyed
EMERGING MERCHANT CLASS
protection from foreign competition within the English colonies—the British Navigation Acts had excluded all non-Brit-ish ships from the colonial carrying trade.

They had access to a market in England for such American products as furs, timber, and ships. That did not, however, satisfy all their commercial needs. Many colonial products—fish, flour, wheat, and meat, all of which England could pro-duce for itself—needed markets outside the British Empire. Ignoring laws restricting colonial trade to England and its possessions, many merchants developed markets in the French, Spanish, and Dutch West Indies, where prices were often higher than in the British colonies. The profits from this illegal commerce enabled the colonies to import the man-ufactured goods they needed from Europe.

THE RISE OF CONSUMERISM

Among relatively affluent residents of the colonies, the growing prosperity and commercialism of British America created both new appetites and new opportunities. The result was a growing preoccupation with the consumption of material goods—and of the association of possessions with social status.

The growth of eighteenth-century consumerism was partly a result of the increasing division of American societies by class. As the difference between the upper and lower classes became more glaring, people of means became more intent on demonstrating their own membership in the upper ranks of society. The ability to purchase and display consumer goods was an important way of doing so, particularly for affluent people in cities and towns. But the growth of consumerism
GROWING CONSUMERISM
was also a product of the early stages of the industrial revolution. Although there was relatively little industry in America in the eighteenth century, England and Europe were making rapid advances and producing more and more affordable goods for affluent Americans to buy. The new manufacturing was de-pendent, of course, on customers for its products. In an in-creasingly commercial society, therefore, there were many people committed to promoting the purchase of consumer goods as a positive social good. Consumption also grew be-cause of an increasing tendency among colonists to take on debt to finance purchases and because of the willingness of some merchants to offer credit.

To facilitate the new consumer appetites, merchants and traders began advertising their goods in journals and newspa-pers. Agents of urban merchants—the first traveling salesman—fanned out through the countryside, attempting to interest wealthy landowners and planters in luxury goods. George and Martha Washington, for example, spent considerable time and money ordering elegant furnishings for their home at Mount Vernon, goods that were shipped to them mostly from England and Europe.

Things that had once been considered expensive luxuries gradually became commonplace necessities—among them tea, household linens, glassware, manufactured cutlery, crockery,
SOCIAL CONSEQUENCES
and furniture, and many others. Another result of consumerism was the association of material goods—of the quality of a per-son's home and possessions and clothing, for example—with

TEA PARTY IN THE TIME OF GEORGE I This painting by an unknown artist dates from the 1720s and shows a prosperous Virginian posing with a fashionable and expensive tea service, some of it from China. His eagerness to display his possessions in this way is a sign of the growing interest in the badges of refinement among colonial Americans of means in the eighteenth century. (Colonial Williamsburg Foundation)

virtue and "refinement." The ideal of the cultivated "gentleman" and the gracious "lady" became increasingly powerful throughout the colonies in the eighteenth century. That meant striving to become educated and "refined"—"gentlemanly" or "ladylike" in speech and behavior. Americans read books on manners and fashion. They bought magazines about London society. They also commissioned portraits of themselves and their families, devoted large portions of their homes to entertainment, built shelves and cases in which they could display fashionable possessions, constructed formal gardens, and lavished attention on their wardrobes and hairstyles.

The growing importance of consumption and refinement was visible in public spaces as well. Eighteenth-century cities—in America as in England and Europe—began to plan their growth to ensure that there would be elegant and gracious public squares, parks, and boulevards. In the past, social interaction in American communities had largely been between neighbors and relatives, or at most among members of church congregations. Now that a wider "society" was emerging within cities, it

> THERE WERE OPPORTUNITIES IN AMERICA FOR SOCIAL MOBILITY—BOTH UP AND DOWN.

became important to create not just private but also public stages for social display.

PATTERNS OF SOCIETY

Although there were sharp social distinctions in the colonies, the deeply entrenched class system of England failed to reproduce itself in America. In England, where land was scarce and the population large, the relatively small number of people who owned property had enormous power over the great majority who did not; the imbalance between land and population became a foundation of the English economy and the cornerstone of its class system. In early America, the opposite was true. Land was abundant, and people were scarce. Aristocracies emerged in America, to be sure. But they tended to rely less on landownership than on control of a substantial workforce, and they were generally less secure and less powerful than their English counterparts. Far more than in England, there were opportunities in America for social mobility—both up and down.

SOCIAL MOBILITY

New forms of community reflected less the British model than the realities of the American environment. These forms varied greatly from one region to another, but several basic—and distinctly American—types emerged.

THE PLANTATION

The plantation defined a distinctive way of life for many white and black southerners that would survive, in varying forms, until the Civil War. The first plantations emerged in the early settlements of Virginia and Maryland, once tobacco became the economic basis of the Chesapeake.

Some plantations were enormous—much like some of the great estates of England. The Maryland plantation of Charles Carroll of Carrollton, reputedly the wealthiest man in the colonies, covered 40,000 acres and contained 285 slaves. On the whole, however, seventeenth-century colonial plantations were rough and relatively small estates. In the early days in Virginia, most plantations were little more than crude clearings where landowners and indentured servants worked side by side in conditions so rugged that death was an everyday occurrence. Even in later years, when the death rate declined and the landholdings became more established, plantation workforces seldom exceeded thirty people.

The economy of the plantation, like all agricultural economies, was precarious. In good years, successful growers could earn great profits and expand their operations. But since they could not control their markets, even the largest planters were

VAGARIES OF THE PLANTATION ECONOMY

AFRICAN POPULATION AS A PROPORTION OF TOTAL POPULATION, C. 1775 This map illustrates the parts of the colonies in which slaves made up a large proportion of the population—in some areas, a majority. The densest African population was in Tidewater Virginia, but there were black majorities as well in South Carolina and parts of North Carolina. The slave population was smallest in the western regions of the southern colonies and in the area north of the Chesapeake, although there remained a significant African population in parts of New Jersey and New York (some slave, some free).

• *What explains the dense concentrations of slaves in certain areas of the South?*

constantly at risk. When prices for their crops fell—as tobacco prices did, for example, in the 1660s—they faced ruin.

Because plantations were sometimes far from cities and towns—which were relatively few in the South—they tended to become self-contained communities. Residents lived in close proximity to one another in a cluster of buildings that included the "great house" of the planter (a house that was usually, although not always, far from great), the service buildings, the

barns, and the cabins of the slaves. Wealthier planters often created something approaching a full town on their plantations, with a school (for white children only), a chapel, and a large population. Smaller planters lived more modestly, but still in a relatively self-sufficient world. In some parts of the South, for example, the region around Charleston, South Carolina, planters often divided their time between the city and their nearby plantations.

On the larger plantations, the presence of a substantial slave workforce altered not only the economic but also the family lives of the planter class. The wives of plantation owners, unlike the wives of small farmers, could rely on servants to perform ordinary household chores. They could thus devote more time to their husbands and children than people in poorer parts of colonial society. But there were also frequent sexual liaisons between their husbands or sons and black women of the slave community. Southern white women generally learned to pretend not to notice these relationships, but they were almost certainly a source of anxiety and resentment. Black women, naturally, had even greater cause to resent such liaisons.

Southern society was highly stratified. Within given areas, great landowners controlled not only the lives of those who worked on their own plantations. Wealthy planters also shaped the livelihoods of small farmers, who could not effectively compete with the wealthy planters and thus depended on them to market crops and receive credit. Small farmers, working modest plots of land with few or no slaves to help them, formed the majority of the southern agrarian population, but it was the planters who dominated the southern agrarian economy. Most landowners lived in rough cabins or houses, with their servants or slaves nearby. Relatively few landowners lived in anything resembling aristocratic splendor.

STRATIFIED SOUTHERN SOCIETY

PLANTATION SLAVERY

African slaves, of course, lived very differently than white planters. On the smaller farms with only a handful of slaves, there was not always a rigid social separation between whites and blacks. But by the mid-eighteenth century, over three-fourths of all blacks lived on plantations of at least ten slaves; nearly half lived in communities of fifty slaves or more. In these larger establishments, Africans developed a society and culture of their own—influenced by their white masters, to be sure, but also partly independent of them.

Although whites seldom encouraged formal marriages among slaves, Africans themselves developed an elaborate family structure. This became possible beginning in the eighteenth century as a result of the increased life expectancy of slaves, the gradual equalization of the sex ratio, and the growth of the population through natural increase. Slaves attempted to construct nuclear families, and they managed at times to build stable households, even to work together growing their own food in gardens provided by their masters. But such efforts were in constant jeopardy. Any family member could be sold at any time to another planter, even to one in another colony. As

MULBERRY PLANTATION, 1770 This painting of a rice plantation in South Carolina is unusual in placing the slave quarters in the forefront of the picture. The steep roofs of the slave cabins, which were built by the slaves themselves, reflected African architectural styles. The high roofs helped keep the cabins cool by allowing the heat to rise into the rafters. The master's house and adjacent chapel, built in conventional European style, are in the background. *(View of Mulberry (House and Street)* by Thomas Coram, Gibbes Museum of Art/Carolina Art Association)

a result, the black family developed in ways different from its white counterpart. Africans placed special emphasis on extended kinship networks, even creating surrogate "relatives" for those who were separated from their own families. They adapted themselves, in short, to difficult conditions over which they had limited control.

African workers also developed languages of their own. In South Carolina, for example, the early slaves communicated with one another in Gullah, a hybrid of English and African SLAVE CULTURE tongues, which enabled them to engage in conversations their white masters could not understand. There emerged, too, a distinctive slave religion, which blended Christianity with African folklore.

Nevertheless, slave society was heavily tied to white society. African house servants, for example, at times lived in what was, by the standards of slavery, great luxury; but they were also isolated from their own community and under constant surveillance from whites. Black women were often subjected to unwanted sexual advances from owners and overseers and hence to bearing mulatto children, who were rarely recognized by their white fathers but generally accepted as members of the slave community. On some plantations, African workers received kindness and even affection from their masters and mistresses and displayed genuine devotion in return. On others, they encountered physical brutality and occasionally even sadism, against which they were powerless.

There were occasional acts of individual resistance by slaves against harsh masters, and at least twice during the colonial period there were actual slave rebellions. In the most important STONO REBELLION such revolt, the so-called Stono Rebellion in South Carolina in 1739, about 100 Africans rose up, seized weapons, killed several whites, and attempted to escape south to Florida. Whites quickly crushed the uprising and executed most participants. The most frequent form of resistance was simply running away, but for most slaves that provided no real solution either. There was nowhere to go.

Most slaves, male and female, worked as field hands (with women also shouldering the additional burdens of cooking and child rearing). On the larger plantations that aspired to genuine self-sufficiency, some slaves learned trades and crafts: blacksmithing, carpentry, shoemaking, spinning, weaving, sewing, midwifery, and others. These skilled craftsmen and craftswomen were at times hired out to other planters. Some set up their own establishments in towns or cities and shared their profits with their owners. On occasion, they were able to buy their freedom. There was a small free black population living in southern cities by the time of the Revolution.

THE PURITAN COMMUNITY

A very different form of community emerged in Puritan New England, but one that was also distinctively American. The characteristic social unit in New England was not the isolated farm, but the town. Each new settlement drew up a "covenant" among

PATTERNS OF SETTLEMENT

its members, binding all residents in a religious and social commitment to unity and harmony. Some such settlements consisted of people who had immigrated to America together (occasionally entire Puritan congregations who had traveled to the New World as a group).

The structure of the towns reflected the spirit of the covenant. Colonists laid out a village, with houses and a meetinghouse arranged around a central pasture, or "common." They also divided up the outlying fields and woodlands of the town among the residents; the size and

> THE CHARACTERISTIC SOCIAL UNIT IN NEW ENGLAND WAS NOT THE ISOLATED FARM, BUT THE TOWN.

location of a family's field depended on the family's numbers, wealth, and social station. But wherever their lands might lie, families generally lived in the village with their neighbors close by, reinforcing the strong sense of community.

Once established, a town was generally able to run its own affairs with little interference from the colonial government.

PURITAN DEMOCRACY

Residents held a yearly "town meeting" to decide important questions and to choose a group of "selectmen," who governed until the next meeting. Only adult males were permitted to participate in the meeting. But even among them, important social distinctions remained, the most crucial of which was membership in the church. Only those residents who could give evidence of grace, of being among the elect (the "visible saints") confident of salvation as a result of a conversion experience, were admitted to full membership. Residents who had not

THE NEW ENGLAND TOWN: SUDBURY, MASSACHUSETTS, 17TH CENTURY Just as the plantation was a characteristic social form in the southern colonies, the town was the most common social unit in New England. This map shows the organization of Sudbury, Massachusetts, a town west of Boston, in the early years in the seventeenth century. Note the location of the houses, which are grouped mostly together around a shared pasture (or "commons") and near the church. Note, too, the outlying fields, which were divided among residents of the town, even though they were often not connected to the land on which they lived. The gray areas of the map illustrate the holdings of a single resident of Sudbury, John Goodnow, whose house was on the common, but whose lands were scattered over a number of areas of Sudbury. (From Sumner Chilton Powell, *Puritan Village: The Formation of a New England Town.* Copyright ©1963 by Wesleyan University. Reprinted by permission from Wesleyan University Press)

• *What aspects of New England life might help explain the clustering of residences at the center of the town?*

experienced "conversion" could participate in the church through what was known as the "halfway covenant."

The English system of primogeniture—the passing of all inherited property to the firstborn son—did not take root in New England. Instead, a father divided his lands among all his sons. His control of this inheritance was one of the most effective means of exercising power over the male members of his family. Often a son would reach his late twenties before his father would allow him to move into his own household and work his own land. Even then, sons would usually continue to live in close proximity to their fathers. Young women were generally more mobile than their brothers, since they did not stand to inherit land; their dowries and their inheritances consisted instead of movable objects (furniture, household goods, occasionally money or precious objects) and thus did not tie them to a particular place.

As the years passed and the communities grew, the tight-knit social structure of the Puritans experienced strains. This was partly because of the increasing commercialization of New England society. But it was also a result of other pressures that developed even within purely agricultural communities, pressures that were a result primarily of population growth.

As towns grew larger, residents tended to cultivate lands farther and farther from the community center. Some farmers moved out of the town center to be nearer their lands and thus began to find themselves far away from the church. Outlying residents would

POPULATION PRESSURE

often apply for permission to build a church of their own, which was usually the first step toward creation of a new town. Such applications were frequently the occasion for bitter quarrels between the original townspeople and those who proposed to break away.

The dispersion of communities was a result of the practice of distributing land through the patriarchal family structure. In the first generations, fathers generally controlled enough land to satisfy the needs of all their sons. After several generations, however, when such lands were being subdivided for the third or fourth time, there was often too little to go around, particularly in communities surrounded by other towns, with no room to expand outward, forcing younger residents to break off and move elsewhere—at times far away—to form towns of their own where land was more plentiful.

Even within the family, economic necessity often undermined the patriarchal model to which most Puritans, in theory at least, subscribed. It was not only the sons who needed their

GENERATIONAL CONFLICT

fathers (as a source of land and wealth); fathers needed their sons, as well as their wives and daughters, as a source of labor to keep the farm and the household functioning. Thus, while in theory men had nearly dictatorial control over their wives and children, in reality relationships were more contractual, with the authority of husbands and fathers limited by economic necessity (and, of course, bonds of affection).

THE WITCHCRAFT PHENOMENON

By the late seventeenth century, growth and diversity had begun to undermine the cohesiveness of many New England communities. At times, such tensions could produce bizarre and disastrous events. One example was the widespread hysteria in the 1680s and 1690s over supposed witchcraft in New England.

The most famous outbreak (although by no means the only

SALEM WITCH TRIALS

one) was in Salem, Massachusetts, where adolescent girls began to exhibit strange behavior and leveled accusations of witchcraft against several West Indian servants steeped in voodoo lore.

IMAGES OF WITCHCRAFT In the late seventeenth century, Americans and Europeans alike believed that many people in their midst were witches. These illustrations of what witches might do are from a 1681 book, *Full and Plain Evidence Concerning Witches and Apparitions,* and depict the various ways in which witches could fly and hover. (Houghton Library, Harvard University)

The hysteria they produced spread throughout the town, and before it was over, hundreds of people (most of them women) were accused of witchcraft. As the crisis in Salem grew, accusations shifted from marginal women like the West Indians to more prominent and substantial people. Nineteen residents of Salem were put to death before the trials ended in 1692; the girls who had been the original accusers later recanted and admitted that they had made up the story.

The Salem experience was only one of many. Accusations of witchcraft spread through many New England towns in the early 1690s (and indeed had emerged periodically in Puritan society for many years before). Research into the background of accused witches reveals that most were middle-aged women, often widowed, with few or no children. Many accused witches were of low social position, were often involved in domestic conflicts, had frequently been accused of other crimes, and were considered abrasive by their neighbors. Others were women who, through inheritance or enterprise, had come into possession of substantial land and property on their own and hence also challenged the gender norms of the community. Puritan society had little tolerance for "independent" women. That so many "witches" were women who were not securely lodged within a male-dominated family structure (and that many seemed openly to defy the passive, submissive norms society had created for them) suggests that tensions over gender roles played a substantial role in generating the crisis.

Above all, however, the witchcraft controversies were a reflection of the highly religious character of these societies. New Englanders believed in the power of Satan and his ability to assert his power in the world. Belief in witchcraft was not a marginal superstition, rejected by the mainstream. It was a common feature of Puritan religious conviction.

CITIES

To call the commercial centers that emerged along the Atlantic coast in the eighteenth century "cities" would be to strain the modern definition of that word. Even the largest colonial community was scarcely bigger than a modern small town. Yet, by the standards of the eighteenth century, cities did indeed exist in America. By the 1770s the two largest ports—Philadelphia and New York—had populations of 28,000 and 25,000, respectively, which made them larger than most English urban centers.

GROWTH OF COLONIAL CITIES

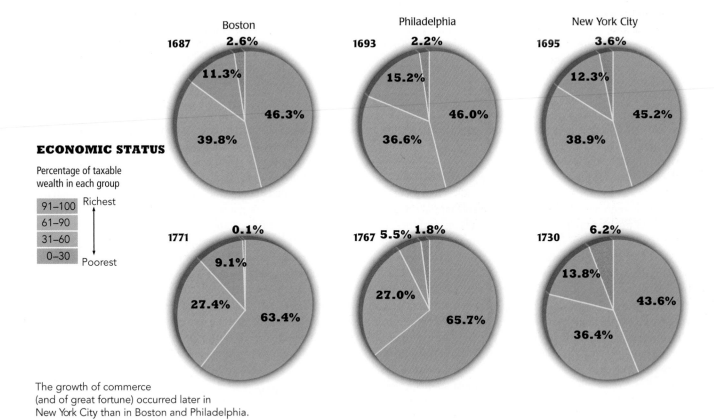

The growth of commerce (and of great fortune) occurred later in New York City than in Boston and Philadelphia.

WEALTH DISTRIBUTION IN COLONIAL CITIES, 1687–1771 Although the gap between rich and poor in colonial America was not as large as it would become in the nineteenth and twentieth centuries, the rise of commerce in the early eighteenth century did produce increasing inequality. This chart shows the distribution of wealth in three important commercial cities—Boston, Philadelphia, and New York. The upper pie charts show the distribution of wealth in the late seventeenth century, and the lower charts show how that distribution had changed by the mid- or late eighteenth century. Note the heavy concentration of wealth in the top 10 percent of the population in the seventeenth century, and the even heavier concentration of wealth in Boston and Philadelphia in the eighteenth century. In New York, by contrast, wealth distribution became slightly more equal between 1695 and 1730, because of the breaking up of the great Dutch estates once the colony came under the control of the British. In later years, New York would show the same pattern of growing inequality that Boston and Philadelphia experienced.

• *What aspects of colonial commerce helped concentrate so much wealth in the hands of a relatively small group?*

THE WITCHCRAFT TRIALS

THE witchcraft trials of the 1690s—which began in Salem, Massachusetts, and spread to other areas of New England—have been the stuff of popular legend for centuries. They have also engaged the interest of generations of historians, who have tried to explain why these seventeenth-century Americans became so committed to the belief that some of their own neighbors were agents of Satan. Although there have been many explanations of the witchcraft phenomenon, some of the most important in recent decades have focused on the central place of women in the story.

Through the first half of the twentieth century, most historians dismissed the witchcraft trials as "hysteria," prompted by the intolerance and rigidity of Puritan society. This interpretation informed perhaps the most prominent popular portrayal of witchcraft in the twentieth century: Arthur Miller's play *The Crucible,* first produced in 1953, which was clearly an effort to use the Salem trials as a comment on the great anticommunist frenzy of his own time. But at almost the same time, the renowned scholar of Puritanism Perry Miller argued in a series of important studies that belief in witchcraft was not a product of hysteria or intolerance but, rather, a widely shared part of the religious worldview of the seventeenth century. To the Puritans, witchcraft seemed not only plausible, but scientifically rational as well.

A new wave of interpretation of witchcraft began in the 1970s, with the publication of *Salem Possessed* (1976), by Paul Boyer and Stephen Nissenbaum. Their examination of the town records of Salem in the 1690s led them to conclude that the witchcraft controversy there was a product of class tensions between the poorer, more marginal residents of one part of Salem and the wealthier, more privileged residents of another. These social tensions, which could not find easy expression on their own terms, led some poorer Salemites to lash out at their richer neighbors by charging them, or their servants, with witchcraft. A few years later, John Demos, in *Entertaining Satan* (1983), examined witchcraft accusations in a larger area of New England and similarly portrayed them as products of displaced anger about social and economic grievances that could not be expressed otherwise. Demos provided a far more complex picture of the nature of these grievances than had Boyer and Nissenbaum but, like them, saw witchcraft as

---

Boston (16,000), Charles Town (later Charleston), South Carolina (12,000), and Newport, Rhode Island (11,000), were also substantial communities by the standards of the day.

Colonial cities served as trading centers for the farmers of their regions and as marts for international trade. Their leaders were generally merchants who had acquired substantial estates. Disparities of wealth were features of almost all communities in America, but in cities they seemed particularly glaring. Moving beside the wealthy merchants were numerous minor tradesmen, workers, and indigents who lived in crowded and often filthy conditions. More than in any other area of colonial life (except, of course, in the relationship between masters and slaves), social distinctions were real and visible in urban areas.

Cities were also the centers of much of what industry there was in the colonies, such as ironworks and distilleries for turning imported molasses into exportable rum. And they were the locations of the most advanced schools, the most sophisticated cultural activities, and shops where imported goods could be

COMMERCIAL AND CULTURAL IMPORTANCE bought. In addition, they were communities with peculiarly urban social problems: crime, vice, pollution, epidemics, traffic. Unlike smaller towns, cities were required to establish elaborate governments. They set up constables' offices and fire departments. They developed systems for supporting the urban poor, whose numbers grew steadily and became especially large in times of economic crisis.

Cities were also particularly vulnerable to fluctuations in trade. When a market for a particular product became glutted and prices fell, the effects on merchants and other residents could be severe. In the countryside, the impact of economic instability was generally more muted than in cities. Farmers were still somewhat independent from the larger world of the markets.

Of particular importance for the political future of the colonies, cities became places where new ideas could circulate and be discussed. Because there were printers, it was possible to have regular newspapers. Books and other publications from abroad introduced new intellectual influences. And the taverns and coffeehouses of cities provided forums in which people could gather and debate the issues of the day. It was not surprising that when the revolutionary crisis began to build in the 1760s and 1770s, it was first visible in the cities.

INEQUALITY

New England, for all its belief in community and liberty, was far from an egalitarian society. "Some must be rich and some poor," John Winthrop wrote early in the seventeenth century, and his prediction perhaps exceeded his expectations. Wealthy families and socially distinguished ones (which were usually the same people) had privileges and rights that were not available to poor citizens. Elites were called "ladies" and "gentleman," while people in the lower levels of society were known as "goodman" a symptom of a persistent set of social and psychological tensions.

At about the same time, however, a number of scholars were beginning to look at witchcraft through the scholarly lens of gender. Carol Karlsen's *The Devil in the Shape of a Woman* (1987) demonstrated through intensive scrutiny of records across New England that a disproportionate number of those accused of witchcraft were property-owning widows or unmarried women—in other words, women who did not fit comfortably into the normal pattern of male-dominated families. Karlsen concluded that such women were vulnerable to these accusations because they seemed threatening to people (including many women) who were accustomed to women as subordinate members of the community.

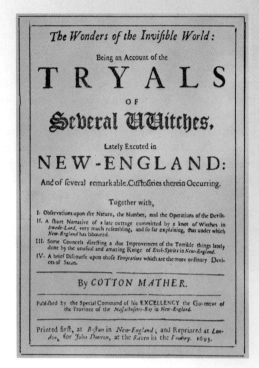

(The Granger Collection, New York)

Mary Beth Norton's *In the Devil's Snare* (2002) placed the witchcraft trials in the context of other events of their time—particularly in the terrifying upheavals and disloca-tions that the Indian wars of the late seventeenth century created in Puritan communities. In the face of this crisis, in which refugees from King William's War were fleeing towns destroyed by the Indians and flooding Salem and other eastern towns, fear and social instability helped create a more-than-normal readiness to connect aberrant behavior (such as the actions of unusually independent or eccentric women) to supernatural causes. The result was a wave of witchcraft accusations that ultimately led to the execution of at least twenty people, mostly women. •

UNDERSTAND, ANALYZE, AND EVALUATE

1. How did the Salem witchcraft trials reflect attitudes toward women and the status of women in colonial New England?
2. Why were colonial New Englanders willing to believe accusations of witchcraft about their fellow colonists?
3. What contemporary parallels are there to the Salem witchcraft trials?

or "goodwife." Elites were given the best seats in their churches and had the most influence over the parish. Men had more power than women. Servants had few rights. The church itself taught that inequality reflected God's intention.

In cities, such economic stratification was significant—although, unlike in later eras, the ranks of the richest were the largest group in the population and, in Boston in the eighteenth century, the majority. That was partly because wealthy people were more likely to move to cities and participate in commerce. In the agricultural countryside, many fewer people accumulated significant wealth.

AWAKENINGS AND ENLIGHTENMENTS

Two powerful forces were competing in American intellectual life in the eighteenth century. One was the traditional outlook of the sixteenth and seventeenth centuries, with its emphasis on a personal God, intimately involved with the world, keeping watch over individual lives. The other was the new spirit of the Enlightenment, a movement sweeping both Europe and America, which stressed the importance of science and human reason. The old views supported such phenomena as the belief in witchcraft, and they placed great value on a stern moral code in which intellect was less important than faith. The Enlightenment, by contrast, suggested that people had substantial control over their own lives and the course of their societies, that the world could be explained and therefore could be structured along rational scientific lines. Much of the intellectual climate of colonial America (and long after) was shaped by the tension between these two impulses.

THE PATTERN OF RELIGIONS

Religious toleration flourished in many parts of America to a degree unmatched in any European nation, not because

ROOTS OF RELIGIOUS TOLERATION

Americans deliberately sought to produce it but because conditions virtually required it. Settlers in America brought with them so many different religious practices that it proved difficult to impose a single religious code on any large area.

The Church of England was established as the official faith in Virginia, Maryland, New York, the Carolinas, and Georgia. But with few exceptions, the laws establishing the Church of England as the official colonial religion were largely ignored. Even in New England, where the Puritans had originally believed that they were all part of a single faith, there was a growing tendency in the eighteenth century for different congregations to affiliate with different denominations, especially Congregationalism and

Presbyterianism. In parts of New York and New Jersey, Dutch settlers had established their own Calvinist denomination, Dutch Reformed, which survived after the colonies became part of the British Empire. American Baptists (considered to have been introduced to Americans by Roger Williams) developed a great variety of sects. All Baptists shared the belief that rebaptism, usually by total immersion, was necessary when believers reached maturity. But while some Baptists remained Calvinists (believers in predestination), others came to believe in salvation by free will.

Protestants extended toleration to one another more readily than they did to Roman Catholics. Many Protestants in America, like many in England, feared and hated the pope. New Englanders, in particular, viewed their Catholic neighbors in New France (Canada) not only as commercial and military rivals but also as dangerous agents of Rome. In most of the English colonies, however, Roman Catholics were too few to cause serious conflict. They were most numerous in Maryland, and even there they numbered no more than 3,000. Perhaps for that reason they suffered their worst persecution in that colony. After the overthrow of the original proprietors in 1691, Catholics in Maryland not only lost their political rights but also were forbidden to hold religious services except in private houses.

ANTI-CATHOLICISM

Jews in provincial America totaled no more than about 2,000 at any time. The largest community lived in New York City. Smaller groups settled in Newport and Charleston, and there were scattered Jewish families in all the colonies. Nowhere could they vote or hold office. Only in Rhode Island could they practice their religion openly.

By the beginning of the eighteenth century, some Americans were growing troubled by the apparent decline in religious piety in their society. The movement of the population westward and the wide scattering of settlements had caused many communities to lose touch with organized religion. The rise of commercial prosperity created a secular outlook in urban areas. The progress of science and free thought in Europe—and the importation of Enlightenment ideas to America—caused at least some colonists to doubt traditional religious beliefs.

Concerns about weakening piety surfaced as early as the 1660s in New England, where the Puritan oligarchy warned of a decline in the power of the church. Sabbath after Sabbath, ministers preached sermons of despair (known as "jeremiads"), deploring the signs of waning piety. By the standards of other societies or other eras, the Puritan faith remained remarkably strong. But New Englanders measured their faith by their own standards, and to them the "declension" of religious piety seemed a serious problem.

JEREMIADS

SINNERS IN HELL, 1744 This mid-eighteenth-century religious image illustrates both the fears and prejudices of many colonial Christians. The idyllic city of Sion, in the center of the drawing, is threatened on all sides by forces of evil, which include images not just of Satan and sin, but also of some of the perceived enemies of Protestants—the Catholic Church (symbolized by the image of the pope) and Islam (symbolized by Turks). (The Granger Collection, New York)

THE GREAT AWAKENING

By the early eighteenth century, concerns about declining piety and growing secularism were emerging in other regions and among members of other faiths. The result was the first major American revival: the Great Awakening.

The Great Awakening began in earnest in the 1730s, reached its climax in the 1740s, and brought a new spirit of religious fervor to the colonies. The revival had particular appeal to women (who constituted the majority of converts) and to younger sons of the third or fourth generation of settlers—those who stood to inherit the least land and who faced the most uncertain futures. The rhetoric of the revival emphasized the potential for every person to break away from the constraints of the past and start anew in his or her relationship with God. Such beliefs may have reflected the desires of many people to break away from their families or communities and start a new life.

Powerful evangelists from England helped spread the revival. John and Charles Wesley, the founders of Methodism, visited Georgia and other colonies in the 1730s. George Whitefield, a powerful open-air preacher and for a time an

GEORGE WHITEFIELD Whitefield succeeded John Wesley as leader of the Calvinist Methodists in Oxford, England. Like Wesley, he was a major force in promoting religious revivalism in both England and America. He made his first missionary journey to the New World in 1738 and returned in the mid-1740s for a celebrated journey through the colonies that helped spark the Great Awakening. (National Portrait Gallery, London)

associate of the Wesleys, made several evangelizing tours through the colonies and drew tremendous crowds. But the outstanding preacher of the Great Awakening was the New England Congregationalist Jonathan Edwards, a deeply orthodox Puritan but a highly original theologian. From his pulpit in Northampton, Massachusetts, Edwards attacked the new doctrines of easy salvation for all. He preached anew the traditional Puritan ideas of the absolute sovereignty of God, predestination, and salvation by God's grace alone. His vivid descriptions of hell could terrify his listeners.

The Great Awakening led to the division of congregations between "New Light" revivalists and "Old Light" traditionalists.

OLD LIGHTS AND NEW LIGHTS It also affected areas of society outside the churches. Some of the revivalists denounced book learning as a hindrance to salvation, and some communities repudiated secular education altogether. But other evangelists saw education as a

means of furthering religion, and they founded or led schools for the training of New Light ministers.

THE ENLIGHTENMENT

The Great Awakening caused one great upheaval in the culture of the colonies. The Enlightenment, a very different—and in many ways competing—phenomenon, caused another.

The Enlightenment was largely the product of some of the great scientific and intellectual discoveries in seventeenth-century Europe. As scientists and other thinkers discovered natural laws that they believed regulated the workings of nature, they came to celebrate the power of human reason and scientific inquiry. Enlightenment thinkers argued that reason, not just faith, could create progress and advance knowledge. They argued that humans had a moral sense on which they could rely to tell the difference between right and wrong—that they did not need always to turn to God for guidance in making decisions. They insisted that men and women could, through the power of their own reason, move civilization to ever greater heights.

In celebrating reason, the Enlightenment slowly helped undermine the power of traditional authority—something the Great Awakening did as well. But unlike the Great Awakening, the Enlightenment encouraged men and women to look to themselves—not to God—for guidance as to how to live their

TRADITIONAL AUTHORITY CHALLENGED lives and to shape society. Enlightenment thought, with its emphasis on human rationality, encouraged a new emphasis on education and a heightened interest in politics

and government (for through governments, the believers in reason argued, society had its best chance of bettering itself). Most Enlightenment figures did not challenge religion and insisted that rational inquiry would support, not undermine, Christianity. But they challenged the notion of some religious groups that the answer to all questions about human society should, or could, come directly from God.

In the early seventeenth century, Enlightenment ideas in America were largely borrowed from abroad—from such earlier giants as Francis Bacon and John Locke, and from more contemporary Enlightenment thinkers in England and Scotland. Few Americans had yet made important contributions of their own to the new age of science and reason. Later, however, such Americans as Benjamin Franklin, Thomas Jefferson, Thomas Paine, and James Madison made their own contributions to the Enlightenment tradition.

EDUCATION

Even before Enlightenment ideas became common in America, colonists had placed a high value on education, despite the difficulties they confronted in gaining access to it. Some families tried to teach their children to read and write at home, although the heavy burden of work in most agricultural households limited the time available for schooling. In Massachusetts, a 1647 law required every town to support a public school, and while many communities failed to comply, a modest network of

COLONIAL ALMANACS

BOOKS were scarce and expensive in colonial America, and many families owned only one: the Bible. But starting very early in the life of the English colonies, men and women had another important source of information: almanacs, the most popular nonreligious literature in early America.

Almanacs first appeared in America in 1638 or 1639 when printers in Cambridge, Massachusetts, began publishing the *Philomath Almanac,* which combined an elaborate calendar of religious holidays with information about astronomy, astrology, and other popular interests. By the 1680s, the *Farmer's Almanac,* a heavily illustrated publication that added medical advice, practical wisdom, navigational information, and humor, began to rival the *Philomath.* Through a combination of superstition, popular folklore, and astronomical (and astrological) devices, the *Farmer's Almanac* also predicted weather patterns throughout the year, crop yields, and many other things. Almanac predictions were notoriously unreliable, but many people relied on them nevertheless.

By 1700, there were dozens, perhaps hundreds, of almanacs circulating throughout the colonies and even in the sparsely settled lands to the west and north. The most popular almanacs sold tens of thousands of copies every year. Most families had at least one, and many had several. "It is easy to prove," one almanac writer claimed in the mid-eighteenth century, "that no book we read (except the Bible) is so much valued and so serviceable to the community." America was a multilingual society, and although most almanacs were in English, some appeared in French, Dutch, Hebrew, Norwegian, Spanish, German, and various Indian languages. For five years just after the Revolution, Benjamin Banneker of Maryland was the only African American almanac writer, publishing a book that occasionally included harsh commentary on slavery and the slave trade.

The best-known almanac in the colonies in the years before the American Revolution was *Poor Richard's Almanack,* published in Philadelphia by Benjamin Franklin under the pseudonym Richard Saunders. "I endeavor'd to make it both entertaining and useful," Franklin later wrote in his autobiography. "And observing that it was generally read, . . . I consider'd it as a proper vehicle for conveying instruction among the common people, who bought scarcely any other books." In issue after issue, Franklin accompanied his calendars, astronomical information, and other standard almanac fare with "proverbial sentences, chiefly such as inculcated industry and frugality." Poor Richard's many sayings became among the most familiar passages in America. Franklin was among many writers who used the almanac to promote the new scientific discoveries of his time and to try to discredit what he considered the backward superstitions standing in the way of knowledge.

Almanacs were virtually the only widely read publications in America that contained popular humor, and they are one of the best sources today for understanding what early Americans considered funny. Not unlike later generations, they delighted in humor that ridiculed the high and mighty (aristocrats, lawyers, clergymen, politicians), made fun of relationships between men and women, and expressed stereotypes about racial and ethnic groups. In the 1760s and 1770s, almanac humor was often used to disguise political ideas, in the way it ridiculed British officials and American Tories. During the war itself, humorous anecdotes about military officers and political leaders reflected the uneasy views of Americans about the long and difficult struggle.

During and after the Revolution, much almanac humor consisted of admiring anecdotes

---

educational establishments emerged as a result. Elsewhere, the Quakers and other sects operated church schools. And in some communities, widows or unmarried women conducted "dame schools" by holding private classes in their homes. In cities, master craftsmen set up evening schools for their apprentices; at least a hundred such schools appeared between 1723 and 1770.

Only a relatively small number of children received education beyond the primary level; but white male Americans, at least, achieved a high degree of literacy. By the time of the Revolution, well over half of all white men could read and write, a rate substantially higher than in most European countries. The large number of colonists who could read helped create a market for the first widely circulated publications in America other than the Bible: almanacs (see "Colonial Almanacs," above). The literacy rate of women lagged behind that of men until the nineteenth century; and while opportunities for education beyond

HIGH WHITE LITERACY RATES

primary school were scarce for males, they were almost nonexistent for females. Nevertheless, in their early years colonial girls often received the same home-based education as boys, and their literacy rate too was substantially higher than that of their European counterparts. African slaves had virtually no access to education. Occasionally a master or mistress would teach slave children to read and write, but they had few real incentives to do so. Indeed, as the slave system became firmly entrenched, strong social (and ultimately legal) sanctions developed to discourage any efforts to promote black literacy, lest it encourage slaves to question their station. Indians, too, remained largely outside the white educational system—to a large degree by choice; most tribes preferred to educate their children in their own way. But some white missionaries and philanthropists established schools for Native Americans and helped create a small but significant population of Indians literate in spoken and written English.

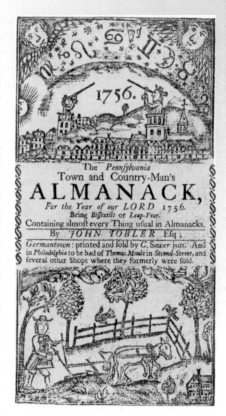

II Mon.	April hath xxx days.

Kind Katharine to her husband kiss'd these words,
' Mine own sweet *Will*, how dearly I love thee!
'If true (quoth Will) the World no such affords.
And that its true I durst his warrant be ;
For ne'er heard I of Woman good or ill,
But always loved best, her own sweet Will.

POOR RICHARD'S ALMANACK This page
from a 1757 edition of *Poor Richard's Almanack*
illustrates the wide range of material that almanacs
presented to their readers—an uplifting poem, a
calendar of holidays and weather predictions, and
such scattered pieces of advice and wisdom as "A
rich rogue is like a fat hog, who does good till
as dead as a log." (New York Public Library, Astor,
Lenox and Tilden Foundations)

The *Pennsylvania*
Town and Country-Man's
ALMANACK,
For the Year of our LORD 1756.
Being Bissextile or Leap-Year.
Containing almost every Thing usual in Almanacks.
By *JOHN TOBLER* Esq ;

Germantown : printed and sold by *C. Sower* jun. And
in *Philadelphia* to be had of *Thomas Maule* in *Second-Street*, and
several other Shops where they formerly were sold.

**TOWN AND COUNTRY-MAN'S
ALMANACK** As the population of colonial cities
and towns grew, almanacs—originally targeted
mainly at farmers—began to make explicit appeal to
townspeople as well. (Princeton University Library.
Sinclair Hamilton Collection, Graphic Arts Division,
Department of Rare Books and Special Collections)

about the man who was by then perhaps the
most famous and beloved man in America—
Poor Richard himself, Benjamin Franklin. Much
less reverential, and probably funnier to readers,
was the often ribald ethnic and racial humor in
almanacs. In *Beer's Almanac* of 1801, an Irishman
boasted that he had owned a large estate in
Ireland before leaving for America. Why, he was
asked, had he left it to come to the United States?
"Ah," he replied, "It was indeed under a small
encumbrance; for another man's land lay right a
top of it."

Almanacs remained enormously popular
throughout the nineteenth century, and some
are still published today. But they had their greatest influence in the early years of European settlement when, for thousands of Americans, they
were virtually the only source of printed information available. "A good Almanac," the printer
Isaac Briggs wrote in 1798, in a preface to one of
his own, "is, like iron, far more valuable (although much less valued) than gold, if we estimate its value by its absolute usefulness to the
common purposes of life." •

UNDERSTAND, ANALYZE, AND EVALUATE

1. Why were almanacs so popular in colonial
   America?
2. What can almanacs tell us about life in colonial America?
3. The *Farmer's Almanac* is still popular today,
   distributing more than 4 million copies a
   year. Why do you think it continues to be
   popular?

Nowhere was the intermingling of the influences of traditional religiosity and the new spirit of the Enlightenment clearer
than in the colleges and universities that grew up in colonial
America. Of the six colleges in operation by 1763, all but two
were founded by religious groups primarily for the training of
preachers. Yet in almost all, the influences of the new scientific,
rational approach to knowledge could be felt. Harvard, the first
American college, was established in 1636 by the General Court
(legislature) of Massachusetts at the behest of Puritan theologians, who wanted to create a training center for ministers. The
college was named for a Charlestown minister, John Harvard,
who had died and left his library and half his estate to the
college. Decades later, in 1693, William and Mary College
(named for the English king and queen) was established in
Williamsburg, Virginia, by Anglicans; like Harvard, it was con-
ceived as an academy to train clergymen. In 1701, conservative
Congregationalists, dissatisfied with what they considered the
growing religious liberalism of Harvard, founded Yale (named
for one of its first benefactors, Elihu Yale) in New Haven,
Connecticut. Out of the Great Awakening emerged the College
of New Jersey, founded in 1746 and known later as Princeton
(after the town in which it is located). One of its first presidents
was Jonathan Edwards.

Despite the religious basis of these colleges, students at most
of them could derive something of a secular education from the
curricula, which included not only theology, but logic, ethics,
physics, geometry, astronomy, rhetoric, Latin, Hebrew, and
Greek as well. From the beginning, Harvard attempted not only

**LIBERAL
CURRICULA**

to provide an educated ministry but also to
"advance learning and perpetuate it to posterity." Members of the Harvard faculty
made strenuous efforts to desseminate new scientific ideas—
particularly the ideas of Copernican astronomy—to a larger
public, often publishing their ideas in popular almanacs. By

A "DAME SCHOOL" PRIMER More than the residents of any other region of North America (and far more than those of most of Europe), the New England colonists strove to educate their children and achieved perhaps the highest level of literacy in the world. Throughout the region, young children attended institutions known as "dame schools" (because the teachers were almost always women) and learned from primers like this one. Puritan education emphasized both basic skills (the alphabet and reading) and moral and religious precepts, as this sample page suggests. (American Antiquarian Society)

theory that lightning and electricity were the same was widely celebrated in the colonies.

The high value that influential Americans were beginning to place on scientific knowledge was clearly demonstrated by the most daring and controversial scientific experiment of the eighteenth century: inoculation against smallpox. The Puritan theologian Cotton Mather heard, reportedly from his own slave, of the practice of deliberately infecting people with mild cases of smallpox in order to immunize them against the deadly disease. He learned, too, that experiments in inoculation were being conducted, with some success, in England. Mather was not, certainly, a wholly committed scientist. He continued to believe that disease was a punishment for sin. Yet, despite strong opposition from many of his neighbors, he urged inoculation on his fellow Bostonians during an epidemic in the 1720s. The results confirmed the effectiveness of the technique. Other theologians (including Jonathan Edwards) took up the cause, along with many physicians. By the mid-eighteenth century, inoculation had become a common medical procedure in America.

SMALLPOX INOCULATION

doing so, they hoped to stamp out popular belief in astrology, which they considered pagan superstition.

King's College, founded in New York in 1754 and later renamed Columbia, was even more devoted to the spread of secular knowledge. Although it was founded in part by the Anglican Trinity Church in New York, it had no theological faculty and was interdenominational from the start. The Academy and College of Philadelphia, which became the University of Pennsylvania, was a completely secular institution, founded in 1755 by a group of laymen under the inspiration of Benjamin Franklin. It offered courses in utilitarian subjects—mechanics, chemistry, agriculture, government, commerce, and modern languages—as well as in the liberal arts. It also became the site of the first medical school in British America, founded in 1765.

THE SPREAD OF SCIENCE

The clearest indication of the spreading influence of the Enlightenment in America was an increasing interest in scientific knowledge. Most of the early colleges established chairs in the natural sciences and introduced some of the advanced scientific theories of Europe, including Copernican astronomy and Newtonian physics, to their students. But the most vigorous promotion of science in these years occurred outside the colleges, through the private efforts of amateurs and the activities of scientific societies. Leading merchants, planters, and even theologians became corresponding members of the Royal Society of London, the leading English scientific organization. Benjamin Franklin, the most celebrated amateur scientist in America, won international fame through his experimental proof of the nature of lightning and electricity and his invention of the lightning rod. His 1752 demonstration, using a kite, of his

CONCEPTS OF LAW AND POLITICS

In seventeenth- and eighteenth-century law and politics, as in other parts of their lives, Americans of European descent believed that they were re-creating in the New World the practices and institutions of the Old. But as in other areas, they managed, without meaning to or even realizing it, to create something very different.

Changes in the law in America resulted in part from the scarcity of English-trained lawyers, who were almost unknown in the colonies until after 1700. Not until well into the eighteenth century did authorities in England try to impose the common law and the statutes of the realm upon the provinces. By then, it was already too late. Although the American legal system adopted most of the essential elements of the English system, including such ancient rights as trial by jury, significant differences had already become well established. Pleading and court procedures were simpler in America than in England, and punishments were different. Instead of the gallows or prison, colonists more commonly resorted to the whipping post, the branding iron, the stocks, and (for "gossipy" women) the ducking stool. In a labor-scarce society, it was not in the interests of communities to execute or incarcerate potential workers. Crimes were redefined. In England, a printed attack on a public official, whether true or false, was considered libelous. In the 1734–1735 trial of the New York publisher John Peter Zenger, who was powerfully defended by the Philadelphia lawyer Andrew Hamilton, the courts ruled that criticisms of the government were not libelous if factually true—a verdict that removed some restrictions on the freedom of the press. There was a subtle but decisive transformation in legal philosophy. Some colonists came to think of law as a reflection of the divine will; others saw it as a result of the natural

BENJAMIN FRANKLIN ON ELECTRICITY The discovery of electricity was one of the great scientific events of the eighteenth century, even though large-scale practical use of electrical energy emerged much later. Benjamin Franklin was one of the first Americans, and certainly the most famous one, to experiment with electricity. This is the frontispiece for a book, originally published in 1750 in Philadelphia, that describes his "experiments and observations." The pages shown here are from the London edition, which appeared in 1774. (Getty Images)

order. In neither case did they consider it an expression of the power of an earthly sovereign.

Even more significant for the future of the relationship between the colonies and England were important differences between the American and British political systems. Because the royal government was so far away, **COLONIAL GOVERNMENTS** Americans created a group of institutions of their own that gave them—in reality, if not in theory—a large measure of self-government. In most colonies, local communities grew accustomed to running their own affairs with minimal interference from higher authorities. Communities also expected to maintain strict control over their delegates to the colonial assemblies, and those assemblies came to exercise many of the powers that Parliament exercised in England (even though in theory Parliament remained the ultimate authority in America). Provincial governors appointed by the crown had broad powers on paper, but in fact their influence was sharply limited. They lacked control over appointments and contracts; such influence resided largely in England or with local colonial leaders. They could never be certain of their tenure in office; because

PUNISHMENT IN NEW ENGLAND New England communities prescribed a wide range of punishments for misconduct and crime in the seventeenth and eighteenth centuries. Among the more common punishments were public humiliations—placing offenders in stocks, forcing them to wear badges of shame, or, as in this woodcut, publicly ducking them in a stream or pond to create both discomfort and embarrassment. (British Museum)

governorships were patronage appointments, a governor could be removed any time his patron in England lost favor. And in many cases, governors were not even familiar with the colonies they were meant to govern. Some governors were native-born Americans, but most were Englishmen who came to the colonies for the first time to assume their offices. The result of all this was that the focus of politics in the colonies became a local one. The provincial governments became accustomed to acting more or less independently of Parliament, and a set of assumptions and expectations about the rights of the colonists began to take hold in America that policymakers in England did not share. These differences caused few problems before the 1760s, because the British did little to exert the authority they believed they possessed. But when, beginning in 1763, the English government began attempting to tighten its control over the American colonies, a great imperial crisis developed.

LOOKING BACK

What began as a few small, isolated, precarious settlements in the wilderness had evolved by the mid-eighteenth century into a large and complex society. The English colonies in America grew steadily between the 1650s and the 1750s: in population, in the size of their economies, and in the sophistication—and diversity—of their cultures. In many ways the colonies had become more like England by the mid-eighteenth century than they had been during their frail early years. In other ways, life in America and life in Britain had begun to diverge.

Many distinct societies developed in the colonies, but the greatest distinction was between the colonies of the North and those of the South. In the North, society was dominated by relatively small family farms and by towns and cities of growing size. A thriving commercial class was developing and, with it, an increasingly elaborate urban culture. In the South, there were many family farms as well. But there were also large plantations cultivating tobacco, rice, indigo, and cotton for export.

REGIONAL DIFFERENCES

By the late seventeenth century, these plantations were relying heavily on African workers who had been brought to the colonies forcibly as slaves. There were few significant towns and cities in the South, and little commerce other than the marketing of crops.

The colonies did, however, also have much in common. Most white Americans accepted common assumptions about racial inequality. That enabled them to accept (and at times celebrate) the enslavement of African men and women and to justify a campaign of displacement and often violence against Native Americans that would continue for two centuries. Most white Americans (and, in different ways, most nonwhite Americans as well) were deeply religious. The Great Awakening, therefore, had a powerful impact throughout the colonies, North and South. And most white colonists shared a belief in certain basic principles of law and politics, which they considered embedded in the English constitution, and which in the years after the 1750s would lead to a great imperial crisis. •

SIGNIFICANT EVENTS

Massachusetts law requires a public school in every town

Slave traders begin importing slaves directly from Africa to North America

Official toleration of Catholics ends in Maryland

Slave importations increase

1636
Harvard College founded in Massachusetts

1647

1662
Halfway Covenant established in New England

1670s

1685
Edict of Nantes revoked in France; Huguenots begin migrating to North America

1691

1692
Witchcraft trials begin in Salem

1693
College of William and Mary founded in Virginia

1697

KEY TERMS/PEOPLE/PLACES/EVENTS

COTTON MATHER 96
COVENANT 87
GEORGE WHITEFIELD 93
GREAT AWAKENING 92
GULLAH 86
HUGUENOTS 75
INDENTURED SERVITUDE 68

INDIGO 79
JEREMIAD 92
JOHN AND CHARLES WESLEY 92
JOHN PETER ZENGER 96
JONATHAN EDWARDS 93
MIDDLE PASSAGE 73
PRIMOGENITURE 88

SAUGUS IRONWORKS 80
SCOTS-IRISH 76
SLAVE CODES 74
STONO REBELLION 86
TRIANGULAR TRADE 83
THE ENLIGHTENMENT 93

RECALL AND REFLECT

1. How did patterns of family life and attitudes toward women differ in the northern and southern colonies?

2. How did the lives of African slaves change over the course of the first century of slavery?

3. Who emigrated to North America in the seventeenth century, and why did they come?

4. What was the intellectual culture of colonial America, as expressed in literature, philosophy, science, education, and law?

5. How and why did life in the English colonies diverge from life in England?

Cotton Mather initiates smallpox inoculations in Massachusetts

George Whitefield arrives in North America

Stono slave rebellion in South Carolina

College of New Jersey founded at Princeton

Academy and College of Philadelphia (later University of Pennsylvania) founded

1701   **1720**   **1734**   **1739**   **1740s**   **1746**   **1754**   **1755**

Yale College founded in Connecticut

Great Awakening begins in Massachusetts

Peter Zenger tried in New York

Indigo production begins in South Carolina

King's College (later Columbia University) founded in New York

TOPPLING GEORGE III In the immediate aftermath of the Declaration of Independence, patriots in New York pulled down a statue of King George III from its pedestal in the center of the city. Among those pulling down the statue were a number of African Americans—both free blacks and slaves. This print was a French illustration of the event, with captions in both French and German. (Library of Congress [LC-USZC4–1476])

4 | THE EMPIRE IN TRANSITION

AS LATE AS THE 1750S, few Americans objected to their membership in the British Empire. The imperial system provided them with many benefits: opportunities for trade and commerce, military protection, political stability. And for the most part, the English government left the colonies alone. Beginning in 1763, however, the British government embarked on a series of new policies toward its colonies—policies dictated by changing international realities and new political

SETTING THE STAGE

circumstances within England itself. In the beginning, most Americans reacted to the changes with relative restraint. Gradually, however, as crisis followed crisis, a large group of Americans found themselves fundamentally disillusioned with the imperial relationship.

By the mid-1770s, the relationship between the American colonies and their British rulers had become so strained, so poisoned, so characterized by suspicion and resentment, the once seemingly unbreakable bonds of empire were ready to snap. And in the spring of 1775, the first shots were fired in a war that would ultimately win America its independence.

LOOKING AHEAD

1. How did the Seven Years' War change the balance of power in North America and throughout the world?
2. What policies did Parliament implement with regard to the colonies in the 1760s and 1770s, and why did Britain adopt these policies?
3. How did the colonists respond to Parliament's actions?

LOOSENING TIES

After the Glorious Revolution of 1688 in England and the collapse of the Dominion of New England in America, the English government (which became the British government after 1707, when a union of England and Scotland created Great Britain) made no serious or sustained effort to tighten its control over the colonies for over seventy years. During those years, an increasing number of colonies were brought under the direct control of the king. New Jersey in 1702, North and South Carolina in 1729, Georgia in 1754—all became royal colonies, bringing the total to eight; in all of them, the king had the power to appoint the governors and other colonial officials. During those years, Parliament also passed new laws supplementing the original Navigation Acts and strengthening the mercantilist program—laws restricting colonial manufactures, prohibiting paper currency, and regulating trade. On the whole, however, the British government remained uncertain and divided about the extent to which it ought to interfere in colonial affairs. The colonies were left, within broad limits, to go their separate ways.

A Tradition of Neglect

In the fifty years after the Glorious Revolution, the British Parliament established a growing supremacy over the king.

GROWING POWER OF PARLIAMENT

During the reigns of George I (1714–1727) and George II (1727–1760), both of whom were German born and unaccustomed to English ways, the prime minister and his fellow cabinet ministers began to become the nation's real executives. They held their positions not by the king's favor but by their ability to control a majority in Parliament.

These parliamentary leaders were less inclined than the seventeenth-century monarchs had been to try to tighten imperial organization. They depended heavily on the support of the great merchants and landholders, most of whom feared that any such experiments would require large expenditures, would increase taxes, and would diminish the profits they were earning from the colonial trade. The first of the modern prime ministers, Robert Walpole, deliberately refrained from strict enforcement of the Navigation Acts, believing that relaxed trading restrictions would stimulate commerce.

Meanwhile, the day-to-day administration of colonial affairs remained decentralized and inefficient. There was no colonial office in London. The nearest equivalent was the Board of Trade

DECENTRALIZED COLONIAL ADMINISTRATION

and Plantations, established in 1696—a mere advisory body that had little role in any actual decisions. Real authority rested in the Privy Council (the central administrative agency for the government as a whole), the admiralty, and the treasury. But those agencies were responsible for administering laws at home as well as overseas; none could concentrate on colonial affairs. To complicate matters further, there was considerable overlapping and confusion of authority among the departments.

Few of the London officials, moreover, had ever visited America; few knew very much about conditions there. What information they did gather came in large part from agents sent to England by the colonial assemblies to lobby for American interests. These agents, naturally, did nothing to encourage interference with colonial affairs. (The best known of them, Benjamin Franklin, represented not only his own colony, Pennsylvania, but also Georgia, New Jersey, and Massachusetts.)

It was not only the weakness of administrative authority in London and the policy of neglect that weakened England's hold on the colonies. It was also the character of the royal officials in America—among them the governors, the collectors of customs, and naval officers. Some of these officeholders were able and intelligent men; most were not. Appointments generally came as the result of bribery or favoritism, not as a reward for merit. Many appointees remained in England and, with part of their salaries, hired substitutes to take their places in America. Such deputies received paltry wages and thus faced great temptations to augment their incomes with bribes. Few resisted the temptation. Customs collectors, for example, routinely waived duties on goods when merchants paid them to do so. Even honest and well-paid officials usually found it expedient, if they wanted to get along with their neighbors, to yield to the colonists' resistance to trade restrictions.

Resistance to imperial authority centered in the colonial legislatures. By the 1750s, the American assemblies had claimed the right to levy taxes, make appropriations, approve appointments, and pass laws for their respective colonies. Their legislation was subject to veto by the governor or the Privy Council. But the assemblies had leverage over the governor through their control of the colonial budget, and they could circumvent the Privy Council by repassing disallowed laws in slightly altered form. The assemblies came to look upon themselves as little parliaments, each practically as sovereign within its colony as Parliament itself was in England.

POWERFUL COLONIAL LEGISLATURES

The Colonies Divided

Despite their frequent resistance to the authority of London, the colonists continued to think of themselves as loyal English subjects. In many respects, in fact, they felt stronger ties to England than they did to one another. "Fire and water," an English traveler wrote, "are not more heterogeneous than the different colonies in North America." New Englanders and Virginians viewed each other as something close to foreigners. A Connecticut man denounced the merchants of New York for their "frauds and unfair practices," while a New Yorker condemned Connecticut because of the "low craft and cunning so incident to the people of that country." Only an accident of geography, it seemed, connected these disparate societies to one another.

Yet, for all their differences, the colonies could scarcely avoid forging connections with one another. The growth of the colonial population produced an almost continuous line of settlement along the seacoast and led to the gradual

AN APPEAL FOR COLONIAL UNITY This sketch, one of the first American editorial cartoons, appeared in Benjamin Franklin's Philadelphia newspaper, the *Pennsylvania Gazette*, on May 9, 1754. It was meant to illustrate the need for intercolonial unity and, in particular, for the adoption of Franklin's Albany Plan. (Library Company of Philadelphia)

THE STRUGGLE FOR THE CONTINENT

In the late 1750s and early 1760s, a great war raged through North America, changing forever the balance of power both on the continent and throughout much of the world. The war in America was part of a titanic struggle between England and France for dominance in world trade and naval power. The British victory in that struggle, known in Europe as the Seven Years' War, rearranged global power and cemented England's role as the world's great commercial and imperial nation. It also cemented its control of most of the settled regions of North America.

In America, however, the conflict was the final stage in a long battle among the three principal powers in northeastern North America: the English, the French, and the Iroquois. For more than a century prior to the conflict known in America as the French and Indian War, these three groups had maintained an uneasy balance of power. The events of the 1750s upset that balance, produced a prolonged and open conflict, and established a precarious dominance for the English societies throughout the region.

AN UNEASY
BALANCE OF
POWER

The French and Indian War was important to the English colonists in America for another reason as well. By bringing the Americans into closer contact with British authority than ever before, it raised to the surface some of the underlying tensions in the colonial relationship.

NEW FRANCE AND THE IROQUOIS NATION

The French and the English had coexisted relatively peacefully in North America for nearly a century. But by the 1750s, religious and commercial tensions began to produce new conflicts. The crisis began in part because of the expansion of the French presence in America in the late seventeenth century—a result of Louis XIV's search for national unity and increased world power. The lucrative fur trade drew immigrant French peasants deeper into the wilderness, while missionary zeal drew large numbers of French Jesuits into the interior in search of potential converts. The bottomlands of the Mississippi River valley attracted French farmers discouraged by the short growing season in Canada.

NEW SOURCES
OF CONFLICT

By the mid-seventeenth century, the French Empire in America comprised a vast territory. Louis Joliet and Father Jacques Marquette, French explorers of the 1670s, journeyed together by canoe from Green Bay on Lake Michigan as far south as the junction of the Arkansas and Mississippi Rivers. A year later, René Robert Cavelier, Sieur

construction of roads and the rise of intercolonial trade. The colonial postal service helped increase communication. In 1691, it had operated only from Massachusetts to New York and Pennsylvania. In 1711, it extended to New Hampshire in the North; in 1732, to Virginia in the South; and ultimately, all the way to Georgia.

Still, the colonists were loath to cooperate even when, in 1754, they faced a common threat from their old rivals, the French, and France's Indian allies. A conference of colonial leaders—with delegates from Pennsylvania, Maryland, New York, and New England—was meeting in Albany in that year to negotiate a treaty with the Iroquois, as the British government had advised the colonists to do. The delegates stayed on to talk about forming a colonial federation for defense against the Indians. Benjamin Franklin proposed, and the delegates tentatively approved, a plan by which Parliament would set up in America "one general government" for all the colonies (except Georgia and Nova Scotia). Each colony would "retain its present constitution," but would grant to the new general government such powers as the authority to govern all relations with the Indians. The central government would have a "president general" appointed and paid by the king (just as colonial governors were) and a legislature (a "grand council") elected by the colonial assemblies.

ALBANY PLAN

War with the French and Indians was already beginning when this Albany Plan was presented to the colonial assemblies. None approved it. "Everyone cries, a union is necessary," Franklin wrote to the Massachusetts governor, "but when they come to the manner and form of the union, their weak noodles are perfectly distracted."

> **66** EVERYONE CRIES, A UNION IS NECESSARY, BUT WHEN THEY COME TO THE MANNER AND FORM OF THE UNION, THEIR WEAK NOODLES ARE PERFECTLY DISTRACTED. **99**
>
> **BENJAMIN FRANKLIN**

de La Salle, began the explorations that in 1682 took him to the delta of the Mississippi, where he claimed the surrounding country for France and named it Louisiana in the king's honor. Subsequent traders and missionaries wandered to the southwest as far as the Rio Grande; and the explorer Pierre Gaultier de Varennes, Sieur de La Verendrye, pushed westward in 1743 from Lake Superior to a point within sight of the Rocky Mountains. The French had by then revealed the outlines of, and laid claim to, almost the whole continental interior.

To secure their hold on these enormous claims, they founded a string of widely separated communities, fortresses, missions,

FRANCE'S NORTH AMERICAN EMPIRE

and trading posts. Fort Louisbourg, on Cape Breton Island, guarded the approach to the Gulf of St. Lawrence. Would-be feudal lords established large estates (*seigneuries*) along the banks of the St. Lawrence River; and on a high bluff above the river stood the fortified city of Quebec, the center of the French Empire in America. To the south was Montreal, and to the west Sault Sainte Marie and Detroit. On the lower Mississippi emerged plantations much like those in the southern colonies of English America, worked by black slaves and owned by "Creoles" (white immigrants of French descent). New Orleans, founded in 1718 to service the French plantation economy, soon was as big as some of the larger cities of the Atlantic seaboard; Biloxi and Mobile to the east completed the string of French settlement.

But the French were not, of course, alone in the continental interior. They shared their territories with a large and powerful Indian population—in regions now often labeled the "middle grounds" (see pp. 59–61)—and their relations with the natives were crucial to the shaping of their empire. They also shared the interior with a growing number of English traders and settlers, who had been moving beyond the confines of the colonial boundaries in the East. Both the French and the English were aware that the battle for control of North America would be determined in part by which group could best win the allegiance of native tribes—as trading partners and, at times, as military allies. The Indians, for their part, were principally concerned with protecting their independence. Whatever alignments they formed with the European societies growing up around them were generally marriages of convenience, determined by which group offered the most attractive terms.

The English—with their more advanced commercial economy—could usually offer the Indians better and more plentiful goods. But the French offered something that was often more important: tolerance. Unlike the English settlers, most of whom tried to impose their own social norms on the Native Americans they encountered, the French settlers in the interior generally adjusted their own behavior to Indian patterns. French fur traders frequently married Indian women and adopted tribal ways. Jesuit missionaries interacted comfortably with the natives and converted them to Catholicism by the thousands without challenging most of their social customs. By the mid-eighteenth century, therefore, the French had better and closer relations with most of the tribes of the interior than did the English.

The most powerful native group, however, had a different relationship with the French. The Iroquois Confederacy—the

THE IROQUOIS CONFEDERACY

five Indian nations (Mohawk, Seneca, Cayuga, Onondaga, and Oneida) that had formed a defensive alliance in the fifteenth century—had been the most powerful tribal presence in the Northeast since the 1640s, when they had fought—and won—a bitter war against the Hurons. Once their major competitors were largely gone from the region, the Iroquois forged an important commercial relationship with the English and Dutch along the eastern seaboard—although they continued to trade with the French as well. Indeed, the key to the success of the Iroquois in maintaining their independence was that they avoided too close a relationship with either group and astutely played the French and the English against each other. As a result, they managed to maintain an uneasy balance of power in the Great Lakes region and beyond.

The principal area of conflict among these many groups was the Ohio Valley. The French claimed it. Several competing Indian tribes (many of them refugees from lands farther east, driven into the valley by the English expansion) lived there. English settlement was expanding into it. And the Iroquois were trying to establish a presence there as traders. With so many competing groups jostling for influence, the Ohio Valley quickly became a potential battleground.

ANGLO-FRENCH CONFLICTS

As long as England and France remained at peace in Europe, and as long as the precarious balance in the North American interior survived, the tensions among the English, French, and Iroquois remained relatively mild. But after the Glorious Revolution in England, the English throne passed to one of

EUROPEAN SEEDS OF CONFLICT

Louis XIV's principal enemies, William III, who was also the stadholder (chief magistrate) of the Netherlands and who had long opposed French expansionism. William's successor, Queen Anne (the daughter of James II), ascended the throne in 1702 and carried on the struggle against France and its new ally, Spain. The result was a series of Anglo-French wars that continued intermittently in Europe for nearly eighty years.

The wars had important repercussions in America. King William's War (1689–1697) produced a few, indecisive clashes between the English and French in northern New England. Queen Anne's War, which began in 1701 and continued for nearly twelve years, generated substantial conflicts: border fighting with the Spaniards in the South as well as with the French and their Indian allies in the North. The Treaty of Utrecht, which brought the conflict to a close in 1713, transferred substantial areas of French territory in North America to the English, including Acadia (Nova Scotia) and Newfoundland. Two decades later, European rivalries led to still more conflicts in America. Disputes over British trading rights in the Spanish colonies produced a war between England and Spain and led to clashes between the British in Georgia and the Spaniards in

THE SIEGE OF LOUISBOURG, 1758 The fortress of Louisbourg, on Cape Breton Island in Nova Scotia, was one of the principal French outposts in eastern Canada during the French and Indian War. It took a British fleet of 157 ships nearly two months to force the French garrison to surrender. "We had not had our Batteries against the Town above a Week," wrote a British soldier after the victory, "tho we were ashore Seven Weeks; the Badness of the Country prevented our Approaches. It was necessary to make Roads for the Cannon, which was a great Labour, and some Loss of Men; but the spirits the Army was in is capable of doing any Thing." (The New Brunswick Museum, Saint John, NB)

Florida. (It was in the context of this conflict that the last English colony in America, Georgia, was founded in 1733; see p. 59.) The Anglo-Spanish conflict soon merged with a much larger European war, in which England and France lined up on opposite sides of a territorial dispute between Frederick the Great of Prussia and Maria Theresa of Austria. The English colonists in America were soon drawn into the struggle, which they called King George's War; and between 1744 and 1748, they engaged in a series of conflicts with the French. New Englanders captured the French bastion at Louisbourg on Cape Breton Island; but the peace treaty that finally ended the conflict forced them (in bitter disappointment) to abandon it.

In the aftermath of King George's War, relations among the English, French, and Iroquois in North America quickly deteriorated. The Iroquois (in what in retrospect appears a major blunder) began to grant trading concessions in the interior to English merchants. In the context of the already tense Anglo-French relationship in America, the decision to side with the British set in motion a chain of events disastrous for the Iroquois Confederacy. The French feared that the English were using the concessions as a first step toward expansion into French lands (which to some extent they were). They began in 1749 to construct new fortresses in the Ohio Valley. The English interpreted the French activity as a threat to their western settlements. They protested and began making military preparations and building fortresses of their own. The balance of power that the Iroquois had striven to maintain for so long rapidly disintegrated, and the five Indian nations allied themselves with the British and assumed an essentially passive role in the conflict that followed.

For the next five years, tensions between the English and the French increased. In the summer of 1754, the governor of Virginia sent a militia force (under the command of an inexperienced young colonel, George Washington) into the Ohio Valley to challenge French expansion. Washington built a crude stockade (Fort Necessity) not far from the larger French outpost, Fort Duquesne, on the site of what is now Pittsburgh. After the Virginians staged an unsuccessful attack on a French detachment, the French countered with an assault on Fort Necessity, trapping Washington and his soldiers inside. After a third of them died in the fighting, Washington surrendered.

That clash marked the beginning of what became the French and Indian War, the American part of the much larger

FORT NECESSITY

THE FIRST GLOBAL WAR

THE French and Indian War in North America was only a small part of a much larger conflict. Known in Europe as the Seven Years' War it was one of the longest, most widespread, and most important wars in modern history. "Ministers in this country, where every part of the World affects us, in some way or another, should consider the whole Globe," the duke of Newcastle wrote in Britain in 1758, reflecting the international achievements and war aims of the British in the mid-eighteenth century. Two centuries later, Winston Churchill, the former British prime minister, wrote of the Seven Years' War as the first "World War."

In North America, the war was a result of tensions along the frontiers of the British Empire, but in larger part the war resulted from conflicts among the great powers in Europe. It began in the 1750s with what historians have called a "diplomatic revolution." Well-established alliances between Britain and the Austro-Hungarian Empire, and between France and Prussia, collapsed, replaced by new alliances that set Britain and Prussia against France and Austria. The instability that these changing alliances produced helped speed the European nations toward war. The one thing that did not change was the continuing rivalry between Britain and France.

The Austrian-British alliance collapsed because Austria suffered a series of significant defeats at the hands of the Prussians. To the British government, these failures suggested that the Austro-Hungarian Empire was now too weak to help Britain balance French power. As a result, Britain sought new partnerships with the rising powers of northern Germany, Austria's enemies. Seeking protection from the power of their former British allies, the Austrians allied with France. Russia, concerned about the Austro-Hungarian Empire's possible dominance in central Europe, allied with Britain and Prussia.

The tensions that these complicated realignments created eventually led to war (just as the complicated alliances in Europe in the early

(The Granger Collection, New York)

twentieth century helped produce World War I). The European part of the war was a result of the continuing conflict between Prussia and Austria and the effect of those wars on the allies of both. The Seven Years' War soon spread across much of the world, engaging not only most of the great powers in Europe, from England to Russia, but also the emerging colonial world—India, West Africa, the Caribbean, and the Philippines—as the powerful British Navy worked to strip France, and eventually Spain, of their valuable colonial holdings.

Like most modern conflicts, the Seven Years' War was a struggle for economic power. Colonial possessions, many European nations believed, were critical to their future wealth, well worth fighting for. The war's outcome affected not only the future of America, but also the distribution of power through much of the world. It destroyed the French navy and much of the French Empire, and it elevated Great Britain to undisputed preeminence among colonial powers—especially when, at the conclusion of the war, India and all of eastern North America fell firmly under English control. The war also reorganized the balance of power in Europe, with Britain now preeminent among the great powers and Prussia (later to become the core of modern Germany) rapidly rising in wealth and military power.

The Seven Years' War was not only one of the first great colonial wars; it was also one of the last great wars of religion. It extended the dominance of Protestantism in Europe. In what is now Canada, the war replaced French with British rule and thus Catholic with Protestant rule. The Vatican, no longer a military power itself, had relied on the great Catholic empires—Spain, France, and Austria-Hungary—as bulwarks of the Vatican's power and influence. The shift of power toward Protestant governments in Europe and North America weakened the Catholic Church and reduced its geopolitical influence.

The conclusion of the Seven Years' War strengthened Britain and Germany and weakened France. But it did not provide any lasting solution to the rivalries among the great colonial powers. In North America, a dozen years after the end of the war, the American Revolution—the origins of which were in many ways a direct result of the Seven Years' War—stripped the British Empire of one of its most important and valuable colonial appendages. By the time the American Revolution came to an end, the French Revolution had sparked another lengthy period of war, culminating in the Napoleonic Wars of the early nineteenth century, which once again redrew the map of Europe and, for a while, the world. •

UNDERSTAND, ANALYZE, AND EVALUATE

1. How did the Seven Years' War change the balance of power among the nations of Europe? Who gained and who lost in the war?
2. What effect did the war's outcome have on the European colonies in North America?
3. Why is the Seven Years' War described as one of the "most important wars in modern history"?

Seven Years' War that spread through Europe at the same time. It was the climactic event in the long Anglo-French struggle for empire.

THE GREAT WAR FOR THE EMPIRE

The French and Indian War lasted nearly nine years, and it proceeded in three distinct phases. The first of these phases lasted from the Fort Necessity debacle in 1754 until the expansion of the war to Europe in 1756. It was primarily a local, North American conflict, which the English colonists managed largely on their own.

The British provided modest assistance during this period, but they provided it so ineptly that it had little impact on the

BRADDOCK
DEFEATED

struggle. The British fleet failed to prevent the landing of large French reinforcements in Canada; and the newly appointed commander in chief of the British army in America, General Edward Braddock, failed miserably in a major effort in the summer of 1755 to retake the crucial site at the forks of the Ohio River where Washington had lost the battle at Fort Necessity. A French and Indian ambush a few miles from the fort left Braddock dead and what remained of his forces in disarray.

The local colonial forces, meanwhile, were preoccupied with defending themselves against raids on their western settlements by the Indians of the Ohio Valley. Virtually all of the tribes (except the Iroquois) were now allied with the French, having interpreted the defeat of the Virginians at Fort Duquesne as evidence of British weakness. Even the Iroquois, who were nominally allied with the British, remained fearful of antagonizing the French. They engaged in few hostilities and launched no offensive into Canada, even though they had, under heavy English pressure, declared war on the French. By late 1755, many English settlers along the frontier had withdrawn to the east of the Allegheny Mountains to escape the hostilities.

The second phase of the struggle began in 1756, when the governments of France and England formally opened hostilities and a truly international conflict (the Seven Years' War) began. In Europe, the war was marked by a realignment within the complex system of alliances. France allied itself with its former enemy, Austria; England joined France's former ally, Prussia. The fighting now spread to the West Indies, India, and Europe itself. But the principal struggle remained the one in North America, where so far England had suffered nothing but frustration and defeat.

Beginning in 1757, William Pitt, the English secretary of state (and future prime minister), began to transform the war effort

WILLIAM PITT
TAKES CHARGE

in America by bringing it for the first time fully under British control. Pitt himself began planning military strategy for the North American conflict, appointing military commanders, and issuing orders to the colonists. Military recruitment had slowed dramatically in America after the defeat of Braddock. To replenish the army, British commanders began forcibly enlisting colonists (a practice known as "impressment"). Officers also began to seize supplies and equipment from local farmers and tradesmen and compelled colonists to offer shelter to British troops—all generally without compensation. The Americans had long ago become accustomed to running their own affairs and had been fighting for over two years without much assistance or direction from the British. They resented these new impositions and firmly resisted them—at times, as in a 1757 riot in New York City, violently. By early 1758, the friction between the British authorities and the colonists was threatening to bring the war effort to a halt.

Beginning in 1758, therefore, Pitt initiated the third and final phase of the war by relaxing many of the policies that Americans found obnoxious. He agreed to reimburse the colonists for all supplies requisitioned by the army. He returned control over military recruitment to the colonial assemblies (which resulted in an immediate and dramatic increase in enlistments). And he dispatched large numbers of additional troops to America.

Finally, the tide of battle began to turn in England's favor. The French had always been outnumbered by the British colonists; after 1756, the French colonies suffered as well from a series of poor harvests. As a result, they were unable to sustain their early military successes. By mid-1758, the British regulars (who did the bulk of the actual fighting) and the colonial militias were seizing one French stronghold after another. Two brilliant English generals, Jeffrey Amherst and James Wolfe, captured the fortress at Louisbourg in July 1758; a few months later Fort Duquesne fell without a fight. The next year, at the end of a siege of

SIEGE OF QUEBEC Quebec, supposedly impregnable atop its towering cliff, the army of General James Wolfe struggled up a hidden ravine under cover of darkness, surprised the larger forces of the Marquis de Montcalm, and defeated them in a battle in which both commanders died. The dramatic fall of Quebec on September 13, 1759, marked the beginning of the end of the American phase of the war. A year later, in September 1760, the French army formally surrendered to Amherst in Montreal.

Not all aspects of the struggle were as romantic as Wolfe's dramatic assault on Quebec. The British resorted at times to such brutal military expedients as population dispersal. In Nova Scotia, for example, they uprooted several thousand French inhabitants, whom they suspected of disloyalty, and scattered them throughout the English colonies. (Some of these Acadians eventually made their way to Louisiana, where they became the ancestors of the present-day Cajuns.) Elsewhere, English and colonial troops inflicted even worse atrocities on the Indian allies of the French—for example, offering "scalp bounties" to those who could bring back evidence of having killed a native. The French and their Indian allies retaliated, and hundreds of families along the English frontier perished in brutal raids on their settlements.

Peace finally came after the accession of George III to the British throne and the resignation of Pitt, who, unlike the new king, wanted to continue hostilities. The British achieved most of Pitt's aims nevertheless in the Peace of Paris, signed in 1763.

PEACE OF PARIS Under its terms, the French ceded to Great Britain some of their West Indian islands and most of their colonies in India. They also transferred Canada and all other French territory east of the Mississippi, except New Orleans, to Great Britain. They ceded New Orleans and their claims west of the Mississippi to Spain, thus surrendering all title to the mainland of North America.

The French and Indian War had profound effects on the British Empire and the American colonies. It greatly expanded England's territorial claims in the New World. At the same time, it greatly enlarged Britain's debt; financing the vast war had been a major drain on the treasury. It also generated substantial resentment toward the Americans among British leaders, many of whom were contemptuous of the colonists for what they considered American military ineptitude during the war. They were angry as well that the colonists had made so few financial contributions to a struggle waged largely for American benefit; they were particularly bitter that some colonial merchants had been selling food and other goods to the French in the West Indies throughout the conflict. All these factors combined to persuade many English leaders that a major reorganization of the empire, giving London increased authority over the colonies, would be necessary in the aftermath of the war.

The war had an equally profound but very different effect on the American colonists. It forced them, for the first time, to act in concert against a common foe. The friction of 1756–1757 over British requisition and impressment policies, and the 1758 return of authority to the colonial assemblies, established an important precedent in the minds of the colonists: it seemed to confirm the illegitimacy of English interference in local affairs.

CONSEQUENCES OF THE SEVEN YEARS' WAR For thousands of Americans—the men who served in the colonial armed forces—the war was an important socializing experience. The colonial troops, unlike the British regiments, generally viewed themselves as part of a "people's army." The relationship of soldiers to their units was, the soldiers believed, in some measure voluntary; their army was a communal, not a coercive or hierarchical, organization. The contrast with the British regulars, whom the colonists widely resented for their arrogance and arbitrary use of power, was striking; and in later years, the memory of that contrast helped to shape the American response to British imperial policies.

For the Indians of the Ohio Valley, the third major party in the French and Indian War, the British victory was disastrous. Those tribes that had allied themselves with the French had earned the enmity of the victorious English. The Iroquois Confederacy, which had allied itself with Britain, fared only slightly better. English officials saw the passivity of the Iroquois during the war (a result of their effort to hedge their bets and avoid antagonizing the French) as evidence of duplicity. In the aftermath of the peace settlement, the Iroquois alliance with the

> FOR THE THOUSANDS OF AMERICANS WHO SERVED IN THE COLONIAL ARMED FORCES, THE WAR WAS AN IMPORTANT SOCIALIZING EXPERIENCE.

THE SEVEN YEARS' WAR After Washington's surrender and Braddock's defeat in the Pennsylvania backcountry, the British and French waged their final contest for supremacy in North America in northern New York and Canada. But the rivalry for empire between France and Britain was worldwide, with naval superiority providing the needed edge to Britain.

British quickly unraveled, and the Iroquois Confederacy itself began to crumble from within. The Iroquois nations would continue to contest the English for control of the Ohio Valley for another fifty years; but increasingly divided and increasingly outnumbered, they would seldom again be in a position to deal with their white rivals on terms of military or political equality.

THE NEW IMPERIALISM

With the treaty of 1763, England found itself at peace for the first time in more than fifty years. But saddled with enormous debts and responsible for vast new lands in the New World, the imperial government could not long avoid expanding its involvement in its colonies.

BURDENS OF EMPIRE

The experience of the French and Indian War suggested that such increased involvement would not be easy to achieve. Not only had the colonists proved so resistant to British control that Pitt had been forced to relax his policies in 1758, but the colonial assemblies had continued after that to respond to British needs slowly and grudgingly. Unwilling to be taxed by Parliament to support the war effort, the colonists were generally reluctant to tax themselves as well. Defiance of imperial trade regulations and other British demands continued, and even increased, through the last years of the war.

The problems of managing the empire became more difficult after 1763 because of a basic shift in Britain's imperial design. In the past, the English had viewed their colonial empire

THE THIRTEEN COLONIES IN 1763 This map is a close-up of the thirteen colonies at the end of the Seven Years' War. It shows the line of settlement established by the Proclamation of 1763 (the red line), as well as the extent of actual settlement in that year (the blue line). Note that in the middle colonies (North Carolina, Virginia, Maryland, and southern Pennsylvania), settlement had already reached the red line—and in one small area of western Pennsylvania moved beyond it—by the time of the Proclamation of 1763. Note also the string of forts established beyond the Proclamation line.

• *How do the forts help to explain the efforts of the British to restrict settlement? And how does the extent of actual settlement help explain why it was so difficult for the British to enforce their restrictions?*

COMMERCIAL
VERSUS
TERRITORIAL
IMPERIALISTS

primarily in terms of trade; they had opposed acquisition of territory for its own sake. But by the mid-eighteenth century, a growing number of English and American leaders (including both William Pitt and Benjamin Franklin) were beginning to argue that land itself was

of value to the empire—because of the population it could support, the taxes it could produce, and the imperial splendor it would confer. The debate between the old commercial imperialists and the new territorial ones came to a head at the conclusion of the French and Indian War. The mercantilists wanted England to return Canada to France in exchange for Guadeloupe, the most commercially valuable of the French "sugar islands" in the West Indies. The territorialists, however, prevailed. The acquisition of the French territories in North America was a victory for, among others, Benjamin Franklin, who had long argued that the American people would need these vast spaces to accommodate their rapid and, he believed, limitless growth.

With the territorial annexations of 1763, the area of the British Empire was suddenly twice as great as it had been, and the problems of governing it were thus considerably more complex. Some British officials argued that the empire should restrain rapid settlement in the western territories. To allow Europeans to move into the new lands too quickly, they warned, would run the risk of stirring up costly conflicts with the Indians. Restricting settlement would also keep the land available for hunting and trapping.

Many colonists wanted to see the new territories opened for immediate development, but they disagreed among themselves about who should control the western lands. Colonial governments made fervent, and often conflicting, claims of jurisdiction. Other colonists argued that control should remain in England, and that the territories should be considered entirely new colonies, unlinked to the existing settlements. There were, in short, a host of problems and pressures that the British could not ignore.

At the same time, the government in London was running out of options in its effort to find a way to deal with its staggering war debt. Landlords and merchants in **BRITAIN'S STAGGERING WAR DEBT** England itself were objecting strenuously to increases in what they already considered excessively high taxes. The necessity of stationing significant numbers of British troops on the Indian border after 1763 was adding even more to the cost of defending the American settlements. And the halfhearted response of the colonial assemblies to the war effort had suggested that in its search for revenue, England could not rely on any cooperation from the colonial governments. Only a system of taxation administered by London, the leaders of the empire believed, could effectively meet England's needs.

At this crucial moment in Anglo-American relations, with the imperial system in desperate need of redefinition, George III became king in 1760 on the death of his grandfather. He brought two particularly unfortunate qualities to the office. First, he was determined, unlike his two predecessors, to be an active and responsible monarch. In part because of pressure from his ambitious mother, he removed from power the long-standing and relatively stable coalition of Whigs, who had (under Pitt and others) governed the empire for much of the century and whom the new king mistrusted. In their place, he created a new coalition of his own through patronage and bribes and gained an uneasy control of Parliament. The new ministries that emerged as a result of these changes were unstable, each lasting in office only about two years.

The king had serious intellectual and psychological limitations that compounded his political difficulties. He suffered, apparently, from a rare disease that produced intermittent bouts of insanity. (Indeed, in the last years of his long reign he was,

according to most accounts, deranged, confined to the palace **GEORGE III'S SHORTCOMINGS** and unable to perform any official functions.) Yet even when George III was lucid and rational, which in the 1760s and 1770s was most of the time, he was painfully immature (he was only twenty-two when he ascended the throne) and insecure—striving constantly to prove his fitness for his position but time and again finding himself ill equipped to handle the challenges he seized for himself. The king's personality, therefore, contributed to both the instability and the intransigence of the British government during these critical years.

More immediately responsible for the problems that soon emerged with the colonies, however, was George Grenville, whom the king made prime minister in 1763. Grenville did not share his brother-in-law William Pitt's sympathy with the American point of view. He agreed instead with the prevailing opinion within Britain that the colonists had been too long indulged and that they should be compelled to obey the laws and to pay a part of the cost of defending and administering the empire. He promptly began trying to impose a new system of control upon what had been a loose collection of colonial possessions in America.

GEORGE III George III was twenty-two years old when he ascended the throne in 1760, and for many years almost all portraits of him were highly formal, with the king dressed in elaborate ceremonial robes. This more informal painting dates from much later in his reign, after he had begun to suffer from the mental disorders that eventually consumed him. After 1810, he was blind and permanently deranged, barred from all official business by the Regency Act of 1811. His son (later King George IV) served as regent in those years until he became king himself after the death of his father in 1820. (The Granger Collection, New York)

THE BRITISH AND THE TRIBES

The western problem was the most urgent. With the departure of the French, settlers and traders from the English colonies moved immediately into the upper Ohio Valley. The Indians of the region objected to this intrusion, and an alliance of tribes, under the Ottawa chieftain Pontiac, struck back. To prevent an escalation of the fighting that might threaten western trade, the British government issued a ruling—the Proclamation of 1763—forbidding settlers to advance beyond a line drawn along the Appalachian Mountains.

PROCLAMATION OF 1763   The Proclamation of 1763 was appealing to the British for several reasons. It would allow London, rather than the provincial governments and their land-hungry constituents, to control the westward movement of the white population. Hence, westward expansion would proceed in an orderly manner, and conflicts with the tribes, which were both militarily costly and dangerous to trade, might be limited. Slower western settlement would also slow the population exodus from the coastal colonies, where England's most important markets and investments were. And it would reserve opportunities for land speculation and fur trading for English rather than colonial entrepreneurs.

Although the tribes were not enthusiastic about the Proclamation, which required them to cede still more land to the white settlers, many tribal groups supported the agreement as the best bargain available to them. The Cherokee, in particular, worked actively to hasten the drawing of the boundary, hoping to put an end to white encroachments. Relations between the western tribes and the British improved in at least some areas after the Proclamation, partly as a result of the work of the Indian superintendents the British appointed. John Stuart was in charge of Indian affairs in the southern colonies, and Sir William Johnson in the northern ones. Both were sympathetic to Native American needs and lived among the tribes; Johnson married a Mohawk woman, Mary Brant, who was later to play an important role in the American Revolution.

In the end, however, the Proclamation of 1763 failed to meet even the modest expectations of the Native Americans. It had some effect in limiting colonial land speculation in the West and in controlling the fur trade, but on the crucial point of the line of settlement it was almost completely ineffective. White settlers continued to swarm across the boundary and to claim lands farther and farther into the Ohio Valley. The British authorities tried repeatedly to establish limits to the expansion but continually failed to prevent the white colonists from pushing the line of settlement still farther west.

WHITE ENCROACHMENT

THE COLONIAL RESPONSE

The Grenville ministry soon moved to increase its authority in the colonies in more direct ways. Regular British troops, London announced, would now be stationed permanently in America; and under the Mutiny Act of 1765 the colonists were required to assist in provisioning and maintaining the army. Ships of the British navy were assigned to patrol American waters and search for smugglers. The customs service was reorganized and enlarged. Royal officials were ordered to take up their colonial posts in person instead of sending substitutes. Colonial manufacturing was to be restricted so that it would not compete with the rapidly expanding industry of Great Britain.

SUGAR, CURRENCY, AND STAMP ACTS   The Sugar Act of 1764, designed in part to eliminate the illegal sugar trade between the continental colonies and the French and Spanish West Indies, strengthened enforcement of the duty on sugar (while lowering the duty on molasses, further damaging the market for sugar grown in the colonies). It also established new vice-admiralty courts in America to try accused smugglers—thus depriving them of the benefit of sympathetic local juries. The Currency Act of 1764 required the colonial assemblies to stop issuing paper money (a widespread practice during the war) and to retire on schedule all the paper money already in circulation. Most momentous of all, the Stamp Act of 1765 imposed a tax on most printed documents in the colonies: newspapers, almanacs, pamphlets, deeds, wills, licenses.

The new imperial program was an effort to reapply to the colonies the old principles of mercantilism. And in some ways, it proved highly effective. British officials were soon collecting more than ten times as much annual revenue from America as before 1763. But the new policies created many more problems than they solved.

The colonists may have resented the new imperial regulations, but at first they found it difficult to resist them effectively. Americans continued to harbor as many grievances against one another as against the authorities in London. Often, the conflicts centered around tensions between the established societies of the Atlantic coast and the "backcountry" farther west, whose residents often felt isolated from, and underrepresented in, the colonial governments. These western settlers sometimes felt resentful because they lived closer to the worlds of the Indian tribes than the societies of the East. In 1763, for example, a band of people from western Pennsylvania known as the Paxton Boys descended on Philadelphia with demands for relief from colonial (not British) taxes and for money to help them defend themselves against Indians; the colonial government averted bloodshed only by making concessions to them.

PAXTON BOYS

In 1771, a small-scale civil war broke out as a result of the so-called Regulator movement in North Carolina. The Regulators were farmers of the Carolina upcountry who organized in opposition to the high taxes that local sheriffs (appointed by the colonial governor) collected. The western counties were badly underrepresented in the colonial assembly, and the Regulators failed to win redress of their grievances there. Finally, they armed themselves and began resisting tax collections by force. To suppress the revolt, Governor William Tryon raised an army of militiamen, mostly from the eastern counties, who defeated a band of 2,000 Regulators in the Battle of Alamance. Nine on each side were killed, and many others were wounded. Afterward, six Regulators were hanged for treason.

REGULATOR MOVEMENT

NORTH AMERICA IN 1763 The victory of the English over the French in the Seven Years' War (or, as it was known in America, the French and Indian War) reshaped the map of colonial North America. Britain gained a vast new territory, formerly controlled by France—Canada, and a large area west of the Mississippi River—thus more than doubling the size of the British Empire in America. French possessions in the New World dwindled to a few islands in the Caribbean. Spain continued to control a substantial empire in the North American interior. The red line along the western borders of the English colonies represents the line of settlement established by Britain in 1763. White settlers were not permitted to move beyond that line.

• Why did the British wish to restrict settlement of the western lands?

The bloodshed was exceptional, but bitter conflicts within the colonies were not. After 1763, however, the new policies of the British government began to create common grievances among virtually all colo-

THERE WAS SOMETHING IN THE GRENVILLE PROGRAM TO ANTAGONIZE EVERYONE.

nists that to some degree counterbalanced these internal divisions.

Indeed, there was something in the Grenville program to antagonize everyone. Northern merchants believed they would suffer from restraints on commerce, closing

PREPARING TO MEET THE PAXTON BOYS The "Paxton Boys" were residents of western Pennsylvania who were declared outlaws by the assembly in Philadelphia after they launched an unauthorized attack on neighboring Conestoga Indians. Instead of surrendering, they armed themselves and marched on Philadelphia. This engraving satirizes the haphazard military preparations in the city for the expected invasion. An accompanying poem, expressing the contempt some colonists felt toward the urbanized, pacifist Quakers of Philadelphia, commented: "To kill the Paxtonians, they then did Advance, With Guns on their Shoulders, but how did they Prance." Benjamin Franklin finally persuaded the Paxton rebels not to attack in return for greater representation in the legislature. (Library Company of Philadelphia)

opportunities for manufacturing, and increased taxes. Settlers in the northern backcountry resented the closing of the West to land speculation and fur trading. Southern planters, in debt to English merchants, feared having to pay additional taxes and losing their ability to ease their debts by speculating in western land. Professionals—ministers, lawyers, professors, and others—depended on merchants and planters for their livelihood and thus shared their concerns about the effects of English law. Small farmers, the largest group in the colonies, believed they would suffer from increased taxes and from the abolition of paper money, which had enabled them to pay their loans. Workers in towns opposed the restraints on manufacturing.

The new restrictions came, moreover, at the beginning of an economic depression. The British government, by pouring

POSTWAR
DEPRESSION

money into the colonies to finance the fighting, had stimulated a wartime boom. When the flow of funds stopped after the peace in 1763, an economic bust followed. The imperial policies would, many colonists feared, doom them to permanent economic stagnation and a declining standard of living.

In reality, most Americans soon found ways to live with (or circumvent) the new British policies. The American economy was not, in fact, being destroyed. But economic anxieties were rising in the colonies nevertheless, and they created a growing sense of unease.

Whatever the economic consequences of the British government's programs, the political consequences were—in the eyes of the colonists, at least—far worse. Perhaps nowhere else in the late-eighteenth-century world did so large a

POLITICAL
CONSEQUENCES
OF THE
GRENVILLE
PROGRAM

proportion of the people take an active interest in public affairs. That was partly because Anglo-Americans were deeply attached to broad powers of self-government; and the colonists were determined to protect those powers. The keys to self-government, they believed, were the provincial assemblies; and the key to the power of the provincial assemblies was their long-established right to give or withhold appropriations for the colonial governments, a right the British were now challenging. Home rule, therefore, was not something new and different that the colonists were striving to attain, but something old and familiar that they desired to keep. The movement to resist the new imperial policies, a movement for which many would ultimately fight and die, was at the same time democratic and conservative. It was a movement to conserve liberties Americans believed they already possessed.

STIRRINGS OF REVOLT

By the mid-1760s, a hardening of positions had begun in both England and America that would bring the colonies into increasing conflict with the mother country. The victorious war for empire had given the colonists a heightened sense of their own importance and a renewed commitment to protecting their political autonomy. But it had also given the British a strengthened belief in the need to tighten administration of the empire and use the colonies as a source of revenue. The result was a series of events that, more rapidly than anyone had imagined, shattered the British Empire in America.

THE STAMP ACT CRISIS

Even if he had tried, Prime Minister Grenville could not have devised a better method for antagonizing and unifying the colonies than the Stamp Act of 1765. The Sugar Act of a year earlier had affected few people other than the New England merchants. But the new tax fell on all Americans, and it evoked particular opposition from some of the most powerful members of the population. Merchants and lawyers were obliged to buy stamps for ships' papers and legal documents. Tavern owners, often the political leaders of their neighborhoods, were required to buy stamps for their licenses. Printers—the most influential group in distributing information and ideas in colonial society—had to buy stamps for their newspapers and other publications.

EFFECTS OF THE STAMP ACT

The actual economic burdens of the Stamp Act were, in the end, relatively light; the stamps were not expensive. What made the law obnoxious to the colonists was the precedent it seemed to set. In the past, Americans had rationalized the taxes and duties on colonial trade as measures to regulate commerce, not raise money. Some Americans had even managed to persuade themselves that the Sugar Act, which was in fact designed primarily to raise money, was not fundamentally different from the traditional imperial duties. The Stamp Act, however, they could interpret in only one way: it was a direct attempt by England to raise revenue in the colonies without the consent of the colonial assemblies. If this new tax passed without resistance, the door would be open for more burdensome taxation in the future.

Few colonists believed that they could do anything more than grumble and buy the stamps—until the Virginia House of Burgesses sounded what one colonist called a "trumpet of sedition" that aroused Americans to action almost everywhere. The "trumpet" was the collective voice of a group of young Virginia aristocrats. They hoped, among other things, to challenge the power of tidewater planters who (in alliance with the royal governor) dominated Virginia politics. Foremost among the malcontents was Patrick Henry, who had already achieved fame for his fiery oratory and his occasional defiance of British authority. Henry made a dramatic speech to the House of Burgesses in May 1765, concluding with a vague prediction that if present

THE ALTERNATIVES OF WILLIAM BURG In the aftermath of the Boston Tea Party and in response to the Coercive Acts Great Britain enacted to punish the colonists, the First Continental Congress called on Americans to boycott British goods until the acts were repealed. In this drawing, a prosperous Virginia merchant is seen signing a pledge to honor the nonimportation agreement—unsurprisingly given the alternative, visible in the background of the picture: tar and feathers hanging from a post labeled "A Cure for the Refractory." (Colonial Williamsburg Foundation)

policies were not revised, George III, like earlier tyrants, might lose his head. There were shocked cries of "Treason!" and, according to one witness, an immediate apology from Henry (although many years later he was quoted as having made the defiant reply: "If this be treason, make the most of it").

Henry introduced a set of resolutions declaring that Americans possessed the same rights as the English, especially the right to

VIRGINIA RESOLVES

be taxed only by their own representatives; that Virginians should pay no taxes except those voted by the Virginia assembly; and that anyone advocating the right of Parliament to tax Virginians should be deemed an enemy of the colony. The House of Burgesses defeated the most extreme of Henry's resolutions. All of them, however, were printed and circulated as the "Virginia Resolves" (creating an impression in other colonies that the people of Virginia were more militant than they actually were).

In Massachusetts at about the same time, James Otis persuaded his fellow members of the colonial assembly to call an intercolonial congress for action against the new tax. In October 1765, the Stamp Act Congress met in New York with delegates from nine colonies and decided to petition the king and the two houses of Parliament. Their petition conceded that Americans owed to Parliament "all due subordination," but it denied that the colonies could rightfully be taxed except through their own provincial assemblies.

Meanwhile, in several colonial cities, crowds began taking the law into their own hands. During the summer of 1765, serious riots broke out up and down the coast, the largest of them in Boston. Men belonging to the newly organized Sons of Liberty terrorized stamp agents and burned the stamps. The agents, themselves Americans, hastily resigned; and the sale of stamps in the continental colonies virtually ceased. In Boston, a crowd also attacked such pro-British "aristocrats" as the lieutenant governor, Thomas Hutchinson (who had privately opposed passage of the Stamp Act but who, as an officer of the crown, felt obliged to support it once it became law). The protesters pillaged Hutchinson's elegant house and virtually destroyed it.

SONS OF LIBERTY

The Stamp Act crisis was a dangerous moment in the relationship between the colonies and the British government. But the crisis subsided, largely because England backed down. The authorities in London changed their attitude not because of the colonists' defiance but because of economic pressure. Even before the Stamp Act, many New Englanders had stopped buying English goods to protest the Sugar Act of 1764. Now the colonial boycott spread, and the Sons of Liberty intimidated colonists who were reluctant to participate in it. The merchants of England, feeling the loss of much of their colonial market, begged Parliament to repeal the Stamp Act; and stories of unemployment, poverty, and discontent arose from English seaports and manufacturing towns.

The marquis of Rockingham, who succeeded Grenville as prime minister in July 1765, tried to appease both the English merchants and the American colonists, and he finally convinced the king to kill the Stamp Act. On March 18, 1766, Parliament repealed it. Rockingham's opponents were strong and vociferous, and they insisted that unless England compelled the colonists to obey the Stamp Act, they would soon cease to obey any laws of Parliament. So, on the same day, to satisfy such critics, Parliament passed the Declaratory Act, asserting Parliament's authority over the colonies "in all cases whatsoever." In their rejoicing over the repeal of the Stamp Act, most Americans paid little attention to this sweeping declaration of power.

PARLIAMENT RETREATS

INTERNAL REBELLIONS

The conflicts with Britain were not the only uprisings emerging in the turbulent years of the 1760s. In addition to the Stamp Act crisis and other challenges to London, there were internal rebellions that had their roots in the class system in New York and New England. In the Hudson Valley in New York, great estates had grown up, whose owners had rented out their land to small farmers. The revolutionary fervor of the time led many of these tenants to demand ownership of the land they worked. To emphasize their determination, they stopped paying rents. The challenge to landownership soon failed. But other challenges to

"THE TORY'S DAY OF JUDGMENT" A mob of American Patriots hoists a Loyalist neighbor up a flagpole in this woodcut, which is obviously sympathetic to the victim. The crowd is shown as fat, rowdy, and drunken. Public humiliations of Tories were not infrequent during the war. More common, however, was seizure of their property. (Library of Congress)

landownership continued in other colonies. In Vermont, which still was governed by New York, insurgent farmers challenged landowners (many of them the same owners whom tenants had challenged on the Hudson) by taking up arms and demanding ownership of the land they worked. Ethan Allen (later a hero of the Revolutionary War and himself a land speculator) took up the cause of the Green Mountain farmers and accused the landowners of trying to "enslave a free people." Allen eventually succeeded in making Vermont into a separate state, which broke up some of the large estates.

THE TOWNSHEND PROGRAM

The reaction in England to the Rockingham government's policy of appeasement was less enthusiastic than it was in America. English landlords, a powerful political force, angrily protested that the government had "sacrificed the landed gentlemen to the interests of traders and colonists." They feared that backing down from taxing the colonies would lead the government to increase taxes on them. The king finally bowed to their pressure and dismissed the Rockingham ministry. To replace it, he called upon the aging but still powerful William Pitt to form a government. Pitt had been a strong critic of the Stamp Act and had a reputation in America as a friend of the colonists. Once in office, however, Pitt (now Lord Chatham) was so hobbled by gout and at times so incapacitated by mental illness that the actual leadership of his administration fell to the chancellor of the exchequer, Charles Townshend—a brilliant, flamboyant, and at times reckless politician known to his contemporaries variously as "the Weathercock" and "Champagne Charlie."

Among Townshend's first challenges was dealing with the continuing American grievances against Parliament, now most notably the Mutiny (or Quartering) Act of 1765, which required the colonists to provide quarters and supplies for the British troops in America. The British considered this a reasonable requirement. The troops were stationed in North America to protect the colonists from Indian or French attack and to defend the frontiers; lodging the troops in coastal cities was simply a way to reduce the costs to England of supplying them. To the colonists, however, the law was another assault on their liberties.

MUTINY ACT

They did not so much object to quartering the troops or providing them with supplies; they had been doing that voluntarily ever since the last years of the French and Indian War. They resented that these contributions were now mandatory, and they considered it another form of taxation without consent. The Massachusetts Assembly refused to vote the mandated supplies to the troops. The New York Assembly soon did likewise, posing an even greater challenge to imperial authority, since the army headquarters were in New York City.

To enforce the law and to try again to raise revenues in the colonies, Townshend steered two inflammatory measures through Parliament in 1767. The first disbanded the New York Assembly until the colonists agreed to obey the Mutiny Act. (By singling out New York, Townshend thought he would avoid Grenville's mistake of arousing all the colonies at once.) The second levied new taxes (known as the Townshend Duties) on various goods imported to the colonies from England—lead, paint, paper, and tea. The colonists could not logically object to taxation of this kind, Townshend reasoned, because it met standards they themselves had accepted. Benjamin Franklin, as a colonial agent in London trying to prevent the passage of the Stamp Act, had long ago argued for the distinction between "internal" and "external" taxes and had denounced the stamp duties as internal taxation. Townshend himself had considered the distinction laughable; but he was nevertheless imposing duties on what he believed were clearly external transactions.

INTERNAL AND EXTERNAL TAXES

Yet Townshend's efforts to satisfy colonial grievances were to no avail. He might call them external taxes, but they were no more acceptable to colonial merchants than the Stamp Act. Their purpose, Americans believed, was the same as that of the Stamp Act: to raise revenue from the colonists without their consent. And the suspension of the New York Assembly, far from isolating New York, aroused the resentment of all the colonies. They considered this assault on the rights of one provincial government a precedent for the annihilation of the rights of all of them.

The Massachusetts Assembly took the lead in opposing the new measures by circulating a letter to all the colonial governments urging them to stand up against every tax, external or internal, imposed by Parliament. At first, the circular evoked little response in some of the legislatures (and ran into strong opposition in Pennsylvania's). Then Lord Hillsborough, secretary of state for the colonies, issued a circular letter of his own from London in which he warned that assemblies endorsing the Massachusetts letter would be dissolved. Massachusetts defiantly reaffirmed its support for the circular. (The vote in the Assembly was 92 to 17, and for a time "ninety-two" became a patriotic rallying cry throughout British America.) The other colonies, including Pennsylvania, promptly rallied to the support of Massachusetts.

In addition to his other unpopular measures, Townshend tried to strengthen enforcement of commercial regulations in the colonies by, among other things, establishing a new board of customs commissioners in America. Townshend hoped the new board would stop the rampant corruption in the colonial customs houses, and to some extent his hopes were fulfilled. The new commissioners virtually ended smuggling in Boston, their headquarters, although smugglers continued to carry on a busy trade in other colonial seaports.

The Boston merchants—accustomed to loose enforcement of the Navigation Acts and doubly aggrieved now that the new commission was diverting the lucrative smuggling trade—were indignant and took the lead in organizing another boycott. In 1768, the merchants of Philadelphia and New York joined them in a nonimportation agreement, and later some southern merchants and planters also agreed to cooperate. Colonists boycotted British goods subject to the Townshend Duties; and throughout the colonies, American homespun and other domestic products became suddenly fashionable, while English luxuries fell from favor.

COLONIAL BOYCOTTS

Late in 1767, Charles Townshend suddenly died—before the consequences of his ill-conceived program had become fully apparent. The question of dealing with colonial resistance to the Townshend Duties fell, therefore, to the new prime minister, Lord North. Hoping to break the nonimportation agreement and divide the colonists, Lord North secured the repeal of all the Townshend Duties except the tax on tea in March 1770.

THE BOSTON MASSACRE

The withdrawal of the Townshend Duties never had a chance to pacify colonial opinion. Before news of the repeal reached America, an event in Massachusetts raised colonial resentment to a new level of intensity. The colonists' harassment of the new customs commissioners in Boston had grown so intense that the British government had placed four regiments of regular troops inside the city. The presence of the

COMPETITION FOR SCARCE EMPLOYMENT

THE BOSTON MASSACRE (1770), BY PAUL REVERE This is one of many sensationalized engravings, by Revere and others, of the conflict between British troops and Boston laborers that became important propaganda documents for the Patriot cause in the 1770s. Among the victims of the massacre listed by Revere was Crispus Attucks, probably the first black man to die in the struggle for American independence. (Library of Congress)

"redcoats" was a constant affront to the colonists' sense of their independence and a constant reminder of what they considered British oppression. In addition, British soldiers, poorly paid and poorly treated by the army, wanted jobs in their off-duty hours; and they competed with local workers in an already tight market. Clashes between them were frequent.

On the night of March 5, 1770, a few days after a particularly intense skirmish between workers at a ship-rigging factory and British soldiers who were trying to find work there, a crowd of dockworkers, "liberty boys," and others began pelting the sentries at the customs house with rocks and snowballs. Hastily, Captain Thomas Preston of the British regiment lined up several of his men in front of the building to protect it. There was some scuffling; one of the soldiers was knocked down; and in the midst of it all, apparently, several British soldiers fired into the crowd, killing five people (among them a mulatto sailor, Crispus Attucks).

This murky incident, almost certainly the result of panic and confusion, was quickly transformed by local resistance leaders into the "Boston Massacre"—a graphic symbol of British oppression and brutality. The victims became popular martyrs; the event became the subject of many lurid (and inaccurate) accounts. A famous engraving by Paul Revere, widely reproduced and circulated, falsely portrayed the "massacre" as a carefully organized, calculated assault on a peaceful crowd. A jury of Massachusetts colonists found two British soldiers guilty of manslaughter and acquitted six others. Colonial pamphlets and newspapers, however, convinced many Americans that all of the soldiers were guilty of official murder. Year after year, resistance leaders marked the anniversary of the massacre with demonstrations and speeches.

The leading figure in fomenting public outrage over the Boston Massacre was Samuel Adams, the most effective radical

SAMUEL ADAMS in the colonies. Adams (a distant cousin of John Adams, second president of the United States) was born in 1722 and was thus somewhat older than other leaders of colonial protest. As a member of an earlier generation with strong ties to New England's Puritan past, he was particularly inclined to view public events in stern moral terms. A failure in business, he became an unflagging voice expressing outrage at British oppression. England, he argued, had become a morass of sin and corruption; only in America did public virtue survive. He spoke frequently at Boston town meetings; and as one unpopular English policy followed another—the Townshend Duties, the placement of customs commissioners in Boston, the stationing of British troops in the city (with its violent results)—his message attracted increasing support. In 1772, he proposed the creation of a committee of correspondence" in Boston to publicize the grievances against England throughout the colony. He became its first head. Other colonies followed Massachusetts's lead, and a loose network of political organizations grew up that kept the spirit of dissent alive through the 1770s.

THE PHILOSOPHY OF REVOLT

A superficial calm settled on the colonies for approximately three years after the Boston Massacre. But the crises of the 1760s had helped arouse enduring ideological challenges to England and had produced powerful instruments for publicizing colonial grievances. Gradually a political outlook gained a following in America that would ultimately serve to justify revolt.

The ideas that would support the Revolution emerged from many sources. Some were drawn from religious (particularly Puritan) sources or from the political experiences of the colonies. Others came from abroad. Most important, perhaps, were the "radical" ideas of those in Great Britain who stood in opposition to their government. Some were Scots, who considered the English state tyrannical. Others were embittered "country Whigs," who felt excluded from power and considered the existing political system corrupt and oppressive. Drawing from some of the great philosophical minds of earlier generations—most notably John Locke—these English dissidents framed a powerful argument against their government.

Central to this emerging ideology was a new concept of what government

"THE CRUEL FATE OF THE LOYALISTS" This British cartoon, published near the end of the American Revolution, shows three Indians, representing American revolutionaries, murdering six Loyalists: four by hanging, one by scalping, and one—appealing to Fate—about to be killed by an axe-wielding native. By using Indians to represent Anglo-American soldiers, the British were trying to equate the presumed savagery of Native Americans with the behavior of the revolutionaries. (Library of Congress)

should be. Because humans were inherently corrupt and selfish, government was necessary to protect individuals from the evil in one another. But because any government was run by corruptible people, the people needed safeguards against its possible abuses of power. Most people in both England and America had long considered the English constitution the best system ever devised to meet these necessities. By distributing

ENGLAND'S power among the three elements of soci-
BALANCED ety—the monarchy, the aristocracy, and the
CONSTITUTION common people—the English political system ensured that no individual or group could exercise authority unchecked by another. Yet, by the mid-seventeenth century, dissidents in both England and America had become convinced that the constitution was in danger. A single center of power—the king and his ministers—was becoming so powerful that it could not be effectively checked. The system, they believed, was becoming a corrupt and dangerous tyranny.

Such arguments found little sympathy in most of England. The English constitution was not a written document or a fixed set of unchangeable rules. It was a general sense of the "way things are done," and most people in England were willing to accept changes in it. Americans, by contrast, drew from their experience with colonial charters, in which the shape and powers of government were permanently inscribed on paper. They resisted the idea of a flexible, changing set of basic principles.

One basic principle, Americans believed, was the right of people to be taxed only with their own consent—a belief that gradually took shape in the widely repeated slogan, "No taxation without representation." This clamor about "representation" made little sense to the English. According to English

❝ NO TAXATION WITHOUT REPRESENTATION. ❞

constitutional theory, members of Parliament did not represent individuals or particular geographic areas. Instead, each member represented the interests of the whole nation and indeed the whole empire, no matter where the member happened to come from. The many boroughs of England that had no representative in Parliament, the whole of Ireland, and the colonies thousands of miles away—all were thus represented in the Parliament at London, even though they elected no representatives of their own. This was the theory of "virtual" representation. But Americans, drawing from their experiences with their town meetings and their colonial assemblies, believed in "actual" representation: every community was entitled to its own representative, elected by the people of that community and directly responsible to them. Since the colonists had none of their own representatives in Parliament, it followed that they were not represented there. Instead, Americans believed that the colonial assemblies played the same role within the colonies that Parliament did within England. The empire, the Americans began to argue, was a sort of federation of commonwealths, each with its own legislative body, all tied together by common loyalty to the king.

Such ideas illustrated a fundamental difference of opinion between England and America over the nature of sovereignty—over the question of where ultimate power lay. By arguing that Parliament had the right to legislate for England and for the empire as a whole, but that only the provincial assemblies could legislate for the individual colonies, Americans were in effect arguing for a division of sovereignty. Parliament would be sovereign in some matters; the assemblies

VIRTUAL VERSUS ACTUAL REPRESENTATION

would be sovereign in others. To the British, such an argument was absurd. In any system of government there must be a single, ultimate authority. And since the empire was, in their view, a single, undivided unit, there could be only one authority within it: the English government of king and Parliament.

THE TEA EXCITEMENT

The relatively calm first years of the 1770s disguised a growing sense of resentment at the increasingly heavy-handed British enforcement of the Navigation Acts. The customs commissioners, who remained in the colonies despite the repeal of the Townshend Duties, were mostly clumsy, intrusive, and arrogant officials. They harassed colonial merchants and seamen constantly with petty restrictions, and they also enriched themselves through graft and illegal seizures of merchandise.

Colonists also kept revolutionary sentiment alive through writing and talking. Dissenting leaflets, pamphlets, and books circulated widely through the colonies. In towns and cities, men gathered in churches, schools, town squares, and above all in taverns to discuss politics and express their growing disenchantment with English policy. The rise of revolutionary ideology was not simply a result of the ideas of intellectuals. It was also a product of a social process by which ordinary people heard, discussed, and absorbed new ideas.

REVOLUTIONARY DISCOURSE

The popular anger lying just beneath the surface was also visible in occasional acts of rebellion. At one point, colonists seized a British revenue ship on the lower Delaware River. And in 1772, angry residents of Rhode Island boarded the

Monday Morning, December 27, 1773.
THE Tea-Ship being arrived, every Inhabitant who will to preserve the Liberty of America, is desired to meet the STATE-HOUSE, This Morning, precisely at TEN o'Clock, advise what is best to be done on this alarming Crisis.

To the PUBLIC.

THE Sense of the City relative to the Landing the India Company's Tea, being signified to Captain Lockyer, by the Committee, nevertheless, it is the Desire of a Number of the Citizens, that at his Departure from hence, he should see, with his own Eyes, their Detestation of the Measures pursued by the Ministry and the India Company, to enslave this Country. This will be declared by the Convention of the People at his Departure from this City; which will be on next Saturday Morning, about nine o'Clock, when no Doubt, every Friend to this Country will attend. The Bells will give the Notice about an Hour before he embarks from Murray's Wharf.

By Order of the COMMITTEE.

NEW YORK, APRIL 21ſt, 1774.

THE BOSTON TEA PARTY The artist Ramberg produced this wash drawing of the Boston Tea Party in 1773. A handbill in a Philadelphia newspaper ten days later and another distributed in New York the following April illustrate how quickly the spirit of resistance spread to other colonies. (*Left*, The Metropolitan Museum of Art, Bequest of Charles Allen Munn, 1924. (24.90.1865); *Upper Right*, Chicago Historical Society; *Bottom Right*, Bettmann/Corbis)

British schooner *Gaspée,* set it afire, and sank it in Narragansett Bay. The British response to the *Gaspée* affair further inflamed American opinion. Instead of putting the accused attackers on trial in colonial courts, the British sent a special commission to America with power to send the defendants back to England for trial.

What finally revived the revolutionary fervor of the 1760s, however, was a new act of Parliament—one that the English government had expected to be relatively uncontroversial. It involved the business of selling tea. In 1773, Britain's East India Company (which had an official monopoly on trade with the Far East) was on the verge of bankruptcy and sitting on large stocks of tea that it could not sell in England. In an effort to save the company, the government passed the Tea Act of 1773, which gave the company the right to export its merchandise directly to the colonies without paying any of the navigation taxes that were imposed on the colonial merchants, who had traditionally served as the middlemen in such transactions. With these privileges, the East India Company could undersell American merchants and monopolize the colonial tea trade.

The Tea Act angered many colonists for several reasons. First, it enraged influential colonial merchants, who feared being replaced and bankrupted by a powerful monopoly. The East India Company's decision to grant franchises to certain American merchants for the sale of its tea created further resentments among those excluded from this lucrative trade. More important, however, the Tea Act revived American passions about the issue of taxation without representation. The law provided no new tax on tea. But it exempted the East India Company from having to pay the normal customs duties. That put colonial merchants at a grave competitive disadvantage. Lord North assumed that most colonists would welcome the new law because it would reduce the price of tea to consumers by removing the middlemen. But resistance leaders in America argued that it was another insidious example of the results of an unconstitutional tax. Many colonists responded by boycotting tea.

The boycott was an important event in the history of colonial resistance. Unlike earlier protests, most of which had involved relatively small numbers of people, the boycott mobilized large segments of the population. It also helped link the colonies in a common experience of mass popular protest. Particularly important to the movement were the activities of colonial women, who were among the principal consumers of tea and now became leaders of the effort to boycott it.

Women had played a significant role in resistance activities from the beginning. Several women (most prominently Mercy Otis Warren) had been important in writing the dissident literature—in Warren's case, satirical plays—that did much to fan colonial resentments in the 1760s. Women had participated actively in anti-British riots and crowd activities in the 1760s; they had formed an informal organization—the Daughters of Liberty—that occasionally mocked their male counterparts as

THE TEA ACT

> ❝ RATHER THAN FREEDOM, WE'LL PART WITH OUR TEA. ❞
>
> **THE DAUGHTERS OF LIBERTY**

insufficiently militant. Now, as the sentiment for a boycott grew, some women mobilized as never before, determined (as the Daughters of Liberty had written) "that rather than Freedom, we'll part with our Tea."

In the last weeks of 1773, with strong popular support, leaders in various colonies made plans to prevent the East India Company from landing its cargoes in colonial ports. In Philadelphia and New York, determined colonists kept the tea from leaving the company's ships. In Charleston, they stored it in a public warehouse. In Boston, after failing to turn back the three ships in the harbor, local Patriots staged a spectacular drama. On the evening of December 16, 1773, three companies of fifty men each, masquerading as Mohawks, passed through a tremendous crowd of spectators (which served to protect them from official interference), went aboard the three ships, broke open the tea chests, and heaved them into the harbor. As the electrifying news of the Boston "tea party" spread, other seaports followed the example and staged similar acts of resistance.

BOSTON TEA PARTY

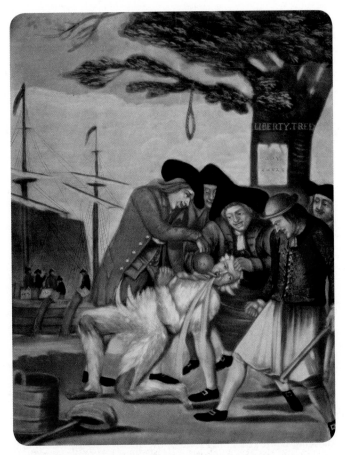

PAYING THE EXCISEMAN This eighteenth-century satirical drawing by a British artist depicts Bostonians forcing tea down the throat of a customs official, whom they have tarred and feathered. In the background, colonists are dumping tea into the harbor (presumably a representation of the 1773 Boston Tea Party); and on the tree at right is a symbol of the Stamp Act, which the colonists had defied eight years earlier. (Art Resource, NY)

TEA PARTIES

THE BOSTON Tea Party of 1773 was a revolt against "taxation without representation." The poem "Ye glorious sons of freedom" celebrates the action of the Boston Tea Party, expresses the colonists' resentments and complaints against the distant London government, and calls upon Boston patriots to continue to resist British actions.

The twenty-first century Tea Party movement became prominent in 2009. Although not an official political party, members tend to endorse Republican candidates. The modern Tea Party movement has borrowed its name from the Boston event that took place more than two hundred years ago, and has picked up some (although not all) of the ideas of the 1773 Boston Tea Party: hostility to distant authority (London then, Washington now) and resentment of taxes (imposed by Britain then, and by Washington now). Although taxation in our time does not really take place "without representation," today's Tea Partiers certainly feel that contemporary taxation is as illegitimate as the Bostonians felt it was in 1773.

BOSTON TEA PARTY—1773

Poem honoring the Boston Tea Party, Dec. 1773

CHORUS:

Bostonian's SONS keep up your Courage good,
Or Dye, like Martyrs, in fair Free-born Blood.

YE GLORIOUS SONS OF FREEDOM, brave and bold,
That has flood forth—fair LIBERTY to hold;
Though you were INDIANS, come from distant shores,
Like MEN you acted—not like savage Moors.

CHORUS

Our LIBERTY, and LIFE is now invaded,
And FREEDOM's brightest Charms are darkly shaded;
But, we will STAND—and think it noble mirth,
To DART the man that dare oppress the Earth.

CHORUS

How grand the Scene!—(No Tyrant shall oppose)
The TEA is sunk in spite of all our foes.
A NOBLE SIGHT—to see th' accursed TEA
Mingled with MUD—and ever for to be;
For KING and PRINCE shall know that we are FREE.

CHORUS

Must we be still— and live on Blood-bought Ground,
And not oppose the Tyrants cursed found?
We Scorn the thought—our views are well refin'd
We scorn those slavish shackles of the Mind,
"We've Souls that were not made to be confin'd."

CHORUS

Could our Fore-fathers rise from their cold Graves,
And view their Land, with all their Children SLAVES;
What would they say! how would their Spirits rend,
And, Thunder-strucken, to their Graves descend.

CHORUS

Let us with hearts of steel now stand the task,
Throw off all darksome ways, nor wear a Mask.
Oh! may our noble Zeal support our frame,
And brand all Tyrants with eternal SHAME.

CHORUS

UNDERSTAND, ANALYZE, AND EVALUATE

1. What is the prevailing tone of the document? To whom is the poem addressed? What specific complaints or resentments against the British government are expressed in the poem?

2. How does the style of the document contribute to the sentiments it expresses? Why might this style have been more effective in arousing the colonists' feelings about the Tea Party than an objective account of the event?

TEA PARTY MOVEMENT—2010

Although the Tea Party movement has no centralized leadership, one organization that claims to be the "official" home of the American Tea Party movement is TeaParty.org. A description and set of core beliefs provided by this organization appear below.

TEAPARTY.ORG DESCRIPTION AND CORE BELIEFS

What Is the Tea Party?

The Tea Party is a grassroots movement that calls awareness to any issue that challenges the security, sovereignty, or domestic tranquility of our beloved nation, the United States of America.

From our founding, the Tea Party is the voice of the true owners of the United States, WE THE PEOPLE.

Many claim to be the founders of this movement—however, it was the brave souls of the men and women in 1773, known today as the Boston Tea Party, who dared defy the greatest military might on earth.

We are the beneficiaries of their courage. By joining the Tea Party, you are taking a stand for our nation. You will be upholding the grand principles set forth in the U.S. Constitution and Bill of Rights.

Non-negotiable core beliefs

Illegal Aliens Are Here Illegally.
Pro-Domestic Employment Is Indispensable.
Stronger Military Is Essential.
Special Interests Eliminated.
Gun Ownership Is Sacred.
Government Must Be Downsized.
National Budget Must Be Balanced.
Deficit Spending Will End.
Bail-Out and Stimulus Plans Are Illegal.
Reduce Personal Income Taxes A Must.
Reduce Business Income Taxes Is Mandatory.
Political Offices Available To Average Citizens.
Intrusive Government Stopped.
English As Core Language Is Required.
Traditional Family Values Are Encouraged.
Common Sense Constitutional.
Conservative Self-Governance.

(Reprinted by permission of Tea Party/1776 Tea Party)

MAKE CONNECTIONS

1. How does the statement from TeaParty.org echo the sentiments expressed in the broadside about the Boston Tea Party of 1773?
2. The message from TeaParty.org makes a specific connection to the Boston Tea Party of 1773. Do you think TeaParty.org is justified in claiming a connection to the original Tea Party?

TAVERNS IN REVOLUTIONARY MASSACHUSETTS

IN colonial Massachusetts, as in many other American colonies in the 1760s and 1770s, taverns (or "public houses," or "pubs," as they came to be known) were crucial to the development of popular resistance to British rule. The Puritan culture of New England created some resistance to taverns, and there were continuing efforts by reformers to regulate or close them to reduce the problems caused by "public drunkenness," "lewd behavior," and anarchy. But as the commercial life of the colonies expanded, and as increasing numbers of people began living in towns and cities, taverns became a central institution in American social life—and eventually in its political life as well.

Taverns were appealing, of course, because they provided alcoholic drinks in a culture where the craving for alcohol—and the extent of drunkenness—was very high. But taverns had other attractions as well. There were few other places where people could meet and talk openly in public, and to many colonists the life of the tavern came to seem the most democratic experience available to them. Gradually, many came to see the attacks on the public houses as efforts to increase the power of existing elites and suppress the freedoms of ordinary people. The tavern was a mostly male institution, just as politics was considered a mostly male concern. And so the fusion of male camaraderie and political discourse emerged naturally out of the tavern culture.

As the revolutionary crisis deepened, taverns and pubs became the central meeting places for discussions of the ideas that fueled resistance to British polices. Educated and uneducated men alike joined in animated discussions of events. Those who could not read—and there were many—could learn about the contents of revolutionary pamphlets from listening to tavern discussions. They could join in the discussion of the new republican ideas emerging in the Americas by participating in tavern celebrations of, for example, the anniversaries of resistance to the Stamp Act. Those anniversaries inspired elaborate toasts in public houses throughout the colonies. Such toasts were the equivalents of political speeches, and illiterate men could learn much from them about the political concepts that were circulating through the colonies.

When the Bostonians refused to pay for the property they had destroyed, George III and Lord North decided on a policy of coercion, to be applied only against Massachusetts—the chief center of resistance. In four acts of 1774, Parliament closed the port of Boston, drastically reduced colonial self-government, permitted royal officers to be tried in other colonies or in England when accused of crimes, and provided for the quartering of troops in the colonists' barns and empty houses.

Parliament followed these Coercive Acts—or, as they were more widely known in America, Intolerable Acts—with the

COERCIVE ACTS   Quebec Act, which was separate from them in origin and quite different in purpose. Its object was to provide a civil government for the French-speaking Roman Catholic inhabitants of Canada and the Illinois country. The law extended the boundaries of Quebec to include the French communities between the Ohio and Mississippi Rivers. It also granted political rights to Roman Catholics and recognized the legality of the Roman Catholic Church within the enlarged province. In many ways it was a tolerant and long overdue piece of legislation. But in the inflamed atmosphere of the time, many people in the thirteen English-speaking colonies considered it a threat. They were already alarmed by rumors that the Church of England was scheming to appoint a bishop for America who would impose Anglican authority on all the various sects. Since the line between the Church of England and the Church of Rome had always seemed to many Americans dangerously thin, the passage of the Quebec Act convinced some of them that a plot

was afoot in London to subject Americans to the tyranny of the pope. Those interested in western lands, moreover, believed that the act would hinder westward expansion.

The Coercive Acts, far from isolating Massachusetts, made it a martyr to residents of other colonies and sparked new resistance up and down the coast. Colonial legislatures passed a series of resolves supporting Massachusetts. Women's groups throughout the colonies mobilized to extend the boycotts of British goods and to create substitutes for the tea, textiles, and other commodities they were shunning.

CONSEQUENCES

COOPERATION AND WAR

Revolutions do not simply happen. They need organizers and leaders. Beginning in 1765, colonial leaders developed a variety of organizations for converting popular discontent into direct action—organizations that in time formed the basis for an independent government.

NEW SOURCES OF AUTHORITY

The passage of authority from the royal government to the colonists themselves began on the local level, where the tradition of autonomy was already strong. In colony after colony, local institutions responded to the resistance movement by simply

THE SCALES OF JUSTICE This sign for a Hartford tavern promises hospitality (from "the charming Patroness") and "entertainment" as well as food and drink. (The Connecticut Historical Society, gift of Mrs. Morgan Brainard)

Taverns were important sources of information in an age before any wide distribution of newspapers. Tavernkeepers were often trusted informants and confidants to the Sons of Liberty and other activists, and they were fountains of information about the political and social turmoil of the time. Taverns were also the settings for political events. In 1770, for example, a report circulated through the taverns of Danvers, Massachusetts, about a local man who was continuing to sell tea despite the colonial boycott. The Sons of Liberty brought the seller to the Bell Tavern and persuaded him to sign a confession and apology before a crowd of defiant men.

Almost all politicians found it necessary to visit taverns in colonial Massachusetts if they wanted any real contact with the public. Samuel Adams spent considerable time in the public houses of Boston, where he sought to encourage resistance to British rule while taking care to drink moderately so as not to erode his stature as a leader. His cousin John Adams was somewhat more skeptical of taverns, more sensitive to the vices they encouraged. But he, too, recognized their political value. In taverns, he once said, "bastards, and legislatores are frequently begotten." •

TAVERN BILLIARDS Gentlemen in Hanover Town, Virginia, gather for a game of billiards in a local tavern in this 1797 drawing by Benjamin Henry Latrobe. (Maryland Historical Society, Baltimore)

UNDERSTAND, ANALYZE, AND EVALUATE

1. Why were taverns so important in educating colonists about the relationship with Britain?
2. The tavern is described as a "mostly male institution" yet women often participated in political activities. Where might women have gathered and discussed political ideas (if not in the tavern)?
3. What gathering places today serve the same purposes that taverns did in colonial America?

---

seizing authority on their own. At times, entirely new, extralegal bodies emerged semispontaneously and began to perform some of the functions of government. In Massachusetts in 1768, for example, Samuel Adams called a convention of delegates from the towns of the colony to sit in place of the General Court, which the governor had dissolved. The Sons of Liberty, which Adams had helped organize in Massachusetts and which sprang up elsewhere as well, became another source of power. Its members at times formed disciplined bands of vigilantes who made certain that all colonists respected the boycotts and other forms of popular resistance. And in most colonies, committees of prominent citizens began meeting to perform additional political functions.

The most effective of these new groups were the committees of correspondence, which Adams had inaugurated in Massachusetts in 1772. Virginia later established the first intercolonial committees of correspondence, which made possible continuous cooperation among the colonies. Virginia also took the greatest step of all toward united action in 1774 when, after the royal governor dissolved the assembly, a special session met in the Raleigh Tavern at Williamsburg, declared that the Intolerable Acts menaced the liberties of every colony, and issued a call for a Continental Congress. Variously elected by the assemblies

FIRST CONTINENTAL CONGRESS

TO ALL BRAVE, HEALTHY, ABLE BODIED, AND WELL DISPOSED YOUNG MEN, IN THIS NEIGHBOURHOOD, WHO HAVE ANY INCLINATION TO JOIN THE TROOPS, NOW RAISING UNDER GENERAL WASHINGTON, FOR THE DEFENCE OF THE LIBERTIES AND INDEPENDENCE OF THE UNITED STATES, Against the hostile designs of foreign enemies,

TAKE NOTICE,

RECRUITING PATRIOTS This Revolutionary War recruiting poster attracted recruits by appealing to their patriotism (asking them to defend "the liberties and independence of the United States"), their vanity (by showing the "handsome clothing" and impressive bearing of soldiers), and their greed (by offering them "a bounty of twelve dollars" and "sixty dollars a year"). (Library of Congress) and by extralegal meetings, delegates from all the thirteen colonies except Georgia were present when, in September 1774, the First Continental Congress convened in Carpenter's Hall in Philadelphia. They made five major decisions. First, in a very close vote, they rejected a plan (proposed by Joseph Galloway of Pennsylvania) for a colonial union under British authority (much like the earlier Albany Plan). Second, they endorsed a statement of grievances, whose tortured language reflected the conflicts among the delegates between moderates and extremists. The statement seemed to concede Parliament's right to regulate colonial trade and addressed the king as "Most Gracious Sovereign"; but it also included a more extreme demand for the repeal of all the oppressive legislation passed since 1763. Third, they approved a series of resolutions, recommending, among other things, that the colonists make military preparations for defense against possible attack by the

> **❝ I EXPECT NO REDRESS, BUT, ON THE CONTRARY, INCREASED RESENTMENT AND DOUBLE VENGEANCE; WE MUST FIGHT. ❞**
>
> **JOHN ADAMS**

British troops in Boston. Fourth, they agreed to nonimportation, nonexportation, and nonconsumption as means of stopping all trade with Great Britain, and they formed a "Continental Association" to enforce the agreements. And fifth, when the delegates adjourned, they agreed to meet again the next spring, thus indicating that they considered the Continental Congress a continuing organization.

Through their representatives in Philadelphia the colonies had, in effect, reaffirmed their autonomous status within the empire and declared something close to economic war to maintain that position. The more optimistic of the Americans hoped that this economic warfare alone would win a quick and bloodless victory, but the more pessimistic had their doubts. "I expect no redress, but, on the contrary, increased resentment and double vengeance," John Adams wrote to Patrick Henry; "we must fight." And Henry replied, "By God, I am of your opinion."

THE BATTLES OF LEXINGTON AND CONCORD, 1775 This map shows the fabled series of events that led to the first battle of the American Revolution. On the night of April 18, 1775, Paul Revere and William Dawes rode out from Boston to warn the outlying towns of the approach of British troops. Revere was captured just west of Lexington, but Dawes escaped and returned to Boston. The next morning, British forces moved out of Boston toward Lexington, where they met armed American minutemen on the Lexington common and exchanged fire. The British dispersed the Americans in Lexington. But they next moved on to Concord, where they encountered more armed minutemen, clashed again, and were driven back toward Boston. All along their line of march, they were harassed by riflemen.

• *What impact did the battles of Lexington and Concord (and the later battle of Bunker Hill, also shown on this map) have on colonial sentiment toward the British?*

During the winter, the Parliament in London debated proposals for conciliating the colonists. Lord Chatham (William Pitt), the former prime minister, urged the withdrawal of troops from America. Edmund Burke called for the repeal of the Coercive Acts. But their efforts were in vain. Lord North finally won approval early in 1775 for a series of measures known as the Conciliatory Propositions, but they were in fact far less conciliatory than the approaches Burke or Chatham had urged. Parliament now proposed that the colonies, instead of being taxed directly by Parliament, would tax themselves at Parliament's demand. With this offer, Lord North hoped to divide the American moderates, who he believed represented the views of the majority, from the extremist minority. But his offer was too little and, in any case, too late. It did not reach America until after the first shots of war had been fired.

THE CONCILIATORY PROPOSITIONS

LEXINGTON AND CONCORD

For months, the farmers and townspeople of Massachusetts had been gathering arms and ammunition and training as "minutemen," preparing to fight on a minute's notice. The Continental Congress had approved preparations for a defensive war, and the citizen-soldiers awaited an aggressive move by the British regulars in Boston.

In Boston, General Thomas Gage, commanding the British garrison, knew of the military preparations in the countryside but considered his army too small to do anything until reinforcements arrived. He resisted the advice of less cautious officers, who assured him that the Americans would never dare actually to fight, that they would back down quickly before any show of British force. Major John Pitcairn, for example, insisted that a single "small action," such as the burning of a few towns, would "set everything to rights."

General Gage still hesitated when he received orders from England to arrest the rebel leaders Sam Adams and John Hancock, known to be in the vicinity of Lexington. But when he heard that the minutemen had stored a large supply of gunpowder in Concord (eighteen miles from Boston), he at last decided to act. On the night of April 18, 1775, he sent a detachment of about 1,000 soldiers out from Boston on the road to Lexington and Concord. He intended to surprise the colonials and seize the illegal supplies without bloodshed.

GENERAL THOMAS GAGE

But Patriots in Boston were watching the British movements closely, and during the night two horsemen, William Dawes

The Retreat

From Concord to Lexington of the Army of Wild Irish Asses Defeated by the Brave American Militia

W⁰ Deacon M⁰ Loeings M⁰ Mulikens M⁰ Bonds Houses and Barn all Plundert and Burnt on April 19⁰

THE BRITISH RETREAT FROM CONCORD, 1775 This American cartoon satirizes the retreat of British forces from Concord after the battle there on April 19, 1775. Patriot forces are lined up on the left, and the retreating British forces (portrayed with dog heads, perhaps because many of the soldiers were "wild" Irish) straggle off at right—some fleeing in panic, others gloating over the booty they have plundered from the burning homes above. In its crude and exaggerated way, the cartoon depicts the success of Patriot forces at the Old North Bridge in Concord in repulsing a British contingent under the command of Lord Percy. As the redcoats retreated to Lexington and then to Boston, they continued to encounter fire from colonial forces, not arrayed in battle lines as shown here, but hidden along the road. One British soldier described the nightmarish withdrawal: "We were fired on from Houses and behind Trees . . . the Country was . . . full of Hills, Woods, stone Walls . . . which the Rebels did not fail to take advantage of." (Anne S. K. Brown Military Collection, Brown University Library) and Paul Revere, rode out to warn the villages and farms. When the British troops arrived in Lexington the next day, several dozen minutemen awaited them on the town common. Shots were fired and minutemen fell; eight of them were killed and ten more wounded. Advancing to Concord, the British discovered that the Americans had hastily removed most of the powder supply, but the British burned what was left of it. All along the road from Concord back to Boston, farmers hiding behind trees, rocks, and stone fences harassed the British with continual gunfire. By the end of the day, the British had lost almost three times as many men as the Americans.

The first shots—the "shots heard round the world," as Americans later called them—had been fired. But who had fired them? According to one of the minutemen at Lexington, Major Pitcairn had shouted to the colonists on his arrival, "Disperse, ye rebels!" When the Americans ignored the command, he had given the order to fire. British officers and soldiers told a different story. They claimed that the minutemen had fired first, that only after seeing the flash of American guns had the British begun to shoot. Whatever the truth, the rebels succeeded in circulating their account well ahead of the British version, adorning it with lurid tales of British atrocities. The effect was to rally to the rebel cause thousands of colonists, north and south, who previously had had little enthusiasm for war.

It was not immediately clear to the British, and even to many Americans, that the skirmishes at Lexington and Concord were

THE REVOLUTION BEGINS

the first battles of a war. Many saw them as simply another example of the tensions that had been afflicting Anglo-American relations for years. But whether they recognized it at the time or not, the British and the Americans had taken a decisive step. The War for Independence had begun.

LOOKING BACK

When the French and Indian War ended in 1763, it might have seemed reasonable to expect that relations between the English colonists in America and Great Britain itself would have been cemented more firmly than ever. America and Britain had fought together in a great war against the French and their Indian allies. They had won impressive victories. They had vastly expanded the size of the British Empire.

But in fact the end of the French and Indian War altered the imperial relationship forever, in ways that ultimately drove Americans to rebel against English rule and begin a war for independence. To the British, the lesson of the war was that the colonies in America needed firmer control from London. The empire was now much bigger, and it needed better administration. The war had produced great debts, and the Americans—among the principal beneficiaries of the war—should help pay them. And so for more than a decade after the end of the fighting, the British tried one strategy after another to tighten control over and extract money from the colonies, all of them in the end failures.

To the colonists, this effort to tighten imperial rule was both a betrayal of the sacrifices they had made in the war and a challenge to their long-developing assumptions about the

SIGNIFICANT EVENTS

Albany Plan for intercolonial cooperation rejected

French and Indian War begins in North America

George III becomes king

French army surrenders to Amherst at Montreal

Stamp Act crisis

Mutiny Act passed

1754 | **1756** | **1760** | **1764** | **1765** | **1766**

Seven Years' War begins in Europe

Sugar Act passed

Currency Act passed

Stamp Act repealed

Declaratory Act passed

rights of English people to rule themselves. Gradually, white Americans came to see in the British policies evidence of a conspiracy to establish tyranny in the New World. And so throughout the 1760s and 1770s, the colonists developed ever more overt and effective forms of resistance. By the time the first shots were fired in the American Revolution in 1775, Britain and America—once bonded so closely to one another that most white Americans considered themselves just as English as any resident of London—had come to view each other as two very different societies. Their differences, which came to seem irreconcilable, propelled them into a war that would change the course of history. •

KEY TERMS/PEOPLE/PLACES/EVENTS

ALBANY PLAN 103
BENJAMIN FRANKLIN 103
BOSTON MASSACRE 117
BOSTON TEA PARTY 121
CHARLES TOWNSHEND 117
COERCIVE ACTS 124
COMMITTEES OF
  CORRESPONDENCE 125
CREOLES 104
CURRENCY ACT 112

DAUGHTERS OF LIBERTY 121
FIRST CONTINENTAL
  CONGRESS 125
GEORGE GRENVILLE 111
IMPRESSMENT 107
IROQUOIS CONFEDERACY 104
LORD NORTH 117
MUTINY ACT 117
PATRICK HENRY 115
PROCLAMATION OF 1763 112

QUEBEC ACT 124
SAMUEL ADAMS 119
SONS OF LIBERTY 116
STAMP ACT 112
STAMP ACT CONGRESS 115
SUGAR ACT 112
TEA ACT 121
TOWNSHEND DUTIES 117
VIRGINIA RESOLVES 115
WILLIAM PITT 107

RECALL AND REFLECT

1. How did the Seven Years' War and its outcome affect Britain's attitude and policies toward its North American colonies?

2. What Native Americans fought in the French and Indian War, and how did the war's outcome affect them? What about Native Americans who did not participate in the war?

3. How and why did the colonists' attitude toward Britain change from the time of the Seven Years' War to the beginning of the American Revolution?

4. What were the philosophical underpinnings of the colonists' revolt against Britain?

5. What did the slogan "No taxation without representation" mean, and why was it a rallying cry for the colonists?

Townshend
Duties imposed

Regulator
movement quelled
in North Carolina

Tea Act passed
Bostonians stage
tea party

Clashes at
Lexington and
Concord begin
American
Revolution

1767　　**1770**　　**1771**　　**1772**　　**1773**　　**1774**　　**1775**

Boston Massacre
Most Townshend
Duties repealed

Committees of
correspondence
established in Boston
Gaspée incident in
Rhode Island

Intolerable Acts
passed
First Continental
Congress meets at
Philadelphia

THE BRITISH SURRENDER This contemporary drawing depicted the formal surrender of British troops at Yorktown on October 19, 1781. Columns of American troops and a large French fleet flank the surrender ceremony, suggesting part of the reason for the British defeat. General Cornwallis, the commander of British forces in Virginia, did not himself attend the surrender. He sent a deputy in his place. (Getty Images)

5 | THE AMERICAN REVOLUTION

TWO STRUGGLES OCCURRED SIMULTANEOUSLY during the seven years of war that began in April 1775. One was the military conflict with Great Britain. The second was a political battle within America.

The military conflict was, by the standards of later wars, a relatively modest one. By the standards of its own day, however, it was an unusually savage conflict, pitting not only army against army, but also the civilian population against a powerful external force. The shift of the war from a traditional, conventional struggle to a new kind of conflict—a revolutionary war for liberation—made it possible for the American army finally to defeat the vastly more powerful British.

At the same time, Americans were wrestling with the great political questions the conflict necessarily produced: first, whether to demand independence from Britain; second, how to structure the new nation they had proclaimed; and third, how to deal with questions the Revolution had raised about slavery, the rights of Indians, the role of women, and limits of religious tolerance in the new American

SETTING THE STAGE

society. Only the first of these questions had been resolved when the British surrendered at Yorktown in 1781. But by then the United States had already established itself as a new kind of nation, one with a special mission dedicated to enlightened ideals.

Neither at the time nor later did the United States always follow those ideals. At the same time that revolutionaries were celebrating the "rights of man," they were consolidating the enslavement of African Americans, depriving loyalists (those who supported the British during the Revolution) of rights and property, barring women from participation in public life, and denying Indian tribes the limited rights the British had accorded them. Yet despite these contradictions, the belief that the nation should try to live up to the ideals proclaimed in the Revolution exercised a continuing influence on the future history of the United States.

LOOKING AHEAD

1. What were the military strategies (both British and American) of each of the three phases of the American Revolution? How successful were these strategies during each phase?
2. How did the American Revolution become an international conflict, not just a colonial war against the British?
3. How did the new national government of the United States reflect the assumptions of republicanism?

THE STATES UNITED

Although many Americans had been anticipating a military conflict with Britain for months, even years, the actual beginning of hostilities in 1775 found the colonies generally unprepared for the enormous challenges awaiting them. America was an unformed nation, with a population less than a third as large as the 9 million of Great Britain, and with vastly inferior economic and military resources. It faced the task of mobilizing for war against the world's greatest armed power at the same time Americans were deeply divided about what they were fighting for.

DEFINING AMERICAN WAR AIMS

Three weeks after the battles of Lexington and Concord, the Second Continental Congress met in the State House in Philadelphia, with delegates from every colony except Georgia, which sent no representative until the following autumn. The members agreed to support the war, but they disagreed, at times profoundly, about its purpose.

At one pole was a group led by the Adams cousins (John and Samuel), Richard Henry Lee of Virginia, and others, who favored complete independence from Great Britain. At the other pole was a group led by such moderates as John Dickinson of Pennsylvania, who hoped for modest reforms in the imperial relationship that would permit an early reconciliation with Great Britain. Most of the delegates tried to find some middle ground between these positions. They demonstrated their uncertainty in two very different declarations, which they adopted in quick succession. They approved one last, conciliatory appeal to the king,

OLIVE BRANCH PETITION
the "Olive Branch Petition," which the British government rejected. Then, on July 6, 1775, they adopted a more antagonistic "Declaration of the Causes and Necessity of Taking Up Arms." It proclaimed that the British government had left the American people with only two alternatives, "unconditional submission to the tyranny of irritated ministers or resistance by force."

The attitude of much of the public mirrored that of the Congress. At first, most Americans believed they were fighting not for independence but for a redress of grievances within the British Empire. During the first year of fighting, however, many of them began to change their minds, for several reasons. First, the costs of the war—human and financial—were so high that the original war aims began to seem too modest to justify them. Second, what lingering affection American Patriots retained for England greatly diminished when the British began trying to recruit Indians, African slaves, and foreign mercenaries (the hated Hessians) against them. Third, and most important, colonists came to believe that the British government was forcing them toward independence by rejecting the Olive Branch Petition and instead enacting a "Prohibitory Act." It closed the colonies to all overseas trade and made no concessions to American demands except an offer to pardon repentant rebels. The British enforced the Prohibitory Act with a naval blockade of colonial ports.

THOMAS PAINE Paine emigrated to America in 1774 and quickly became involved in the revolutionary circles in Philadelphia. Early in 1776, he published an anonymous pamphlet entitled *Common Sense*, which called for an end to British rule. He served in the American army during the Revolution in New Jersey, while also writing additional tracts promoting independence. In later years, he joined the French Revolution and published *The Rights of Man* in 1791—1792. The portrait above was painted by A. Easton in 1800. (Labour Society, London, UK/Bridgeman Art Library International)

But the growing support for independence remained to a large degree unspoken until January 1776, when an impassioned pamphlet appeared that galvanized many Americans. It was called, simply, *Common Sense*. Its author, unmentioned on the title page, was thirty-eight-year-old Thomas Paine, who had emigrated from England to America fifteen months before.

COMMON SENSE
Long a failure in various trades, Paine now proved a brilliant success as a Revolutionary propagandist. His pamphlet helped change the American outlook toward the war. Paine wanted to turn the anger of Americans away from the specific parliamentary measures they were resisting and toward what he considered the root of the problem—the English constitution itself. It was not enough, he argued, for Americans to continue blaming their problems on particular ministers, or even on Parliament. It was the king, and the system that permitted him to rule, that was to blame. It was, he argued, simple common sense for Americans to break completely with a government that could produce so corrupt a monarch as George III, a government that could inflict such brutality on its own people, a government that could drag Americans into wars in which America had no interest. The island kingdom of England was no more fit to rule the

American continent, Paine claimed, than a satellite was fit to rule the sun.

THE DECISION FOR INDEPENDENCE

Common Sense sold more than 100,000 copies in its first few months. To many of its readers it was a revelation. Although sentiment for independence remained far from unanimous, support for the idea grew rapidly in the first months of 1776.

At the same time, the Continental Congress was moving slowly and tentatively toward a final break with England. It declared American ports open to the ships of all nations except Great Britain. It entered into communication with foreign pow-

THE DECLARATION OF INDEPENDENCE

ers. It recommended to the various colonies that they establish new governments independent of the British Empire, as in fact most already were doing. Congress also appointed a committee to draft a formal declaration of independence. On July 2, 1776, it adopted a resolution: "That these United Colonies are, and, of right, ought to be, free and independent states; that they are absolved from all allegiance to the British crown, and that all political connexion between them and the state of Great Britain is, and ought to be, totally dissolved." Two days later, on July 4, Congress approved the Declaration of Independence itself, which provided the formal justifications for the actions the delegates had in fact taken two days earlier.

Thomas Jefferson, a thirty-three-year-old delegate from Virginia, wrote most of the Declaration, with help from Benjamin Franklin and John Adams. As Adams later observed, Jefferson said little in the document that was new. Its power lay in the eloquence with which it expressed beliefs already widespread in America. In particular, it repeated ideas that had been voiced throughout the colonies in the preceding months in the form of at least ninety local "declarations of independence"—declarations drafted up and down the coast by town meetings, artisan and militia organizations, county officials, grand juries, Sons of Liberty, and colonial assemblies. Jefferson borrowed heavily from these texts, both for the ideas he expressed and, to some extent, for the precise language he used.

The document was in two parts. In the first, the Declaration restated the familiar contract theory of John Locke: that governments were formed to protect the rights of life, liberty, and property; Jefferson gave the theory a more idealistic tone by replacing "property" with "the pursuit of happiness." In the second part, the Declaration listed the alleged crimes of the king, who, with the backing of Parliament, had violated his "contract" with the colonists and thus had forfeited all claim to their loyalty.

The Declaration's ringing endorsement of the idea that "all men are created equal"—a phrase borrowed from an earlier document by Jefferson's fellow Virginian George Mason—later helped inspire movements of liberation and reform of many kinds in the United States and abroad, among them the French Revolution's own Declaration of the Rights of Man. More immediately, the Declaration—and its bold claim that the American colonies were now a sovereign nation, "The United States of America"—led to increased foreign aid for the struggling rebels and prepared the way for France's intervention on their side. The Declaration also encouraged American Patriots, as those opposing the British called themselves, to fight on and to reject the idea of a peace that stopped short of winning independence. At the same time, it created deep divisions within American society.

RESPONSES TO INDEPENDENCE

At the news of the Declaration of Independence, crowds in Philadelphia, Boston, and other places gathered to cheer, fire guns and cannons, and ring church bells. But there were many in America who did not rejoice. Some had disapproved of the war from the beginning. Others had been willing to support it only so long as its aims did not conflict with their basic loyalty to the king. Such people were a minority, but a substantial one. They called themselves Loyalists; supporters of independence called them Tories.

In the aftermath of the Declaration of Independence, the colonies began to call themselves states—a reflection of their

DIVIDED AMERICANS

belief that each province was now in some respects a separate and sovereign entity. Even before the Declaration, colonies were beginning to operate independently of royal authority. The Parliament in London had suspended representative government in America. That suspension did not end colonial self-government. It increased it, since the colonial assemblies continued to meet, now independent of imperial law. After the Declaration of 1776, the former colonies marked their independence by writing formal constitutions for themselves. By 1781, most of the new states had produced such constitutions, which established republican governments. Some of these constitutions survived for many decades without significant change.

At the national level, however, the process of forming a government was more halting and less successful. For a time, Americans were uncertain whether they even wanted a real national government; the Continental Congress had not been much more than a coordinating mechanism, and virtually everyone considered the individual colonies (now states) the real centers of authority. Yet fighting a war required a certain amount of central direction. Americans began almost immediately to do something they would continue to do for more than two centuries: balance the commitment to state and local autonomy against the need for some centralized authority.

In November 1777, Congress adopted the Articles of Confederation (which were not finally ratified until 1781). They

ARTICLES OF CONFEDERATION

did little more than confirm the weak, decentralized system already in operation. The Continental Congress would survive as the chief coordinating agency of the war effort. Its powers over the individual states would be very limited. Indeed, the Articles did not make it entirely clear that the Congress was to be a real government. As a result, the new nation had to fight a

THE AMERICAN REVOLUTION

THE long-standing debate over the origins of the American Revolution has tended to reflect two broad schools of interpretation. One sees the Revolution largely as a political and intellectual event and argues that the revolt against Britain was part of a defense of ideals and principles. The other views the Revolution as a social and economic phenomenon and contends that material interests were at its heart.

The Revolutionary generation itself portrayed the conflict as a struggle over ideals, and their interpretation prevailed through most of the nineteenth century. But in the early twentieth century, historians influenced by the reform currents of the progressive era began to identify social and economic forces that they believed had contributed to the rebellion. In a 1909 study of New York, Carl Becker wrote that two questions had shaped the Revolution: "The first was the question of home rule; the second was the question . . . of who should rule at home." Not only were the colonists fighting the British, they were also engaged in a kind of civil war, a contest for power between radicals and conservatives that led to the "democratization of American politics and society."

Other "progressive" historians elaborated on Becker's thesis. In *The American Revolution Considered as a Social Movement* (1926), J. Franklin Jameson argued that "many economic desires, many social aspirations, were set free by the political struggle, many aspects of society profoundly altered by the forces thus let loose." In a 1917 book, Arthur M. Schlesinger maintained that colonial merchants, motivated by their own interest in escaping the restrictive policies of British mercantilism, aroused American resistance in the 1760s and 1770s.

Beginning in the 1950s, a new generation of scholars began to re-emphasize the role of ideology and to de-emphasize the role of economic interests. Robert E. Brown (in 1955) and Edmund S. Morgan (in 1956) both argued that most eighteenth-century white Americans shared basic political principles and that the social and economic conflicts the progressives had identified were not severe. The rhetoric of the Revolution, they suggested, was not propaganda but, rather, a real reflection of the colonists' ideas. Bernard Bailyn, in *The Ideological Origins of the American Revolution* (1967), demonstrated the complex roots of the ideas behind the Revolution and argued that this carefully constructed political stance was not a disguise for economic interests but a genuine ideology, rooted in deeply held convictions about rights and power.

By the late 1960s, however, a group of younger historians were challenging the ideological interpretation again by illuminating social and

---

war for its own survival with a weak and uncertain central government, never sure of its own legitimacy.

MOBILIZING FOR WAR

The new governments of the states and the nation faced a series of overwhelming challenges: raising and organizing armies, providing them with supplies and equipment, and finding a way to pay for it all. Without access to the British markets on which the colonies had come to depend, finding necessary supplies was exceptionally difficult.

America had many gunsmiths, but they could not come close to meeting the wartime demand for guns and ammunition, let alone the demand for heavy arms. Although Congress created a government arsenal at Springfield, Massachusetts, in 1777, the Americans managed to manufacture only a small fraction of the equipment they needed. Instead, they relied heavily on weapons and matériel they were able to capture from the British. But they got most of their war supplies from European nations, mainly from France.

Financing the war proved in many ways the most nettlesome problem. Congress had no authority to levy taxes directly on the people; it had to requisition funds from the state governments.

But hard money was scarce in America, and the states were little better equipped to raise it than Congress was. None of them contributed more than a small part of their expected share. Congress tried to raise money by selling long-term bonds, but few Americans could afford them and those who could generally preferred to invest in more profitable ventures, such as privateering. In the end, the government had no choice but to issue paper money. Continental currency came from the printing presses in large and repeated batches. The states printed sizable amounts of paper currency of their own.

The result, predictably, was inflation. Prices rose to fantastic heights, and the value of paper money plummeted. Many American farmers and merchants began to prefer doing business with the British, who could pay for goods in gold or silver coin. (That was one reason why George Washington's troops suffered from severe food shortages at Valley Forge in the winter of 1777–1778; many Philadelphia merchants would not sell to them.) Congress tried and failed repeatedly to stem the inflationary spiral. In the end, the new American government was able to finance the war effort only by borrowing heavily from other nations.

After the first great surge of patriotism faded in 1775, few Americans volunteered for military service. As a result, the

FINANCING THE WAR

The Farmer and his Son's return from a visit to the CAMP.

FATHER and I went down to camp,
  Along with Captain Gooding,
And there we see the men and boys
  As thick as hasty pudding.
Yankey doodle keep it up, yankey doodle
  dandy,
M'ind the music and the step,
And with the girls be handy.

And there we see a thousand men,
  As rich as 'Squire David,
And what they wasted every day,
  I wish it had been saved.
  Yankey doodle, &c.

The 'lasses they eat every day,
  Would keep an house a winter;
They have as much that I'll be bound,
  They eat it when they're mind to.
  Yankey doodle, &c.

And there we see a swamping gun,
  Large as a log of maple,
Upon a ducid little cart,
  A load for father's cattle.
  Yankey doodle, &c.

And every time they shoot it off,
  It takes a horn of powder,
And makes a noise like father's gun,
  Only a nation louder.
  Yankey doodle, &c.

I went as nigh to one myself,
  As 'Siah's underpinning;
And father went as nigh again,
  I thought the duce was in him.
  Yankey doodle, &c.

Captain Simon grew so bold,
  I thought he would have cock'd it;
It scar'd me so I shrink'd it off,
  And hung by father's pocket.
  Yankey doodle, &c.

And captain Davis had a gun,
  He kind of clapt his hand on't,

And stuck a crooked stabbing iron
  Upon the little end on't.
  Yankey doodle, &c.

And there I see a pumpkin shell,
  As big as mother's bason,
And every time they touch'd it off,
  They scamper'd like the nation.
  Yankey doodle, &c.

I see a little barrel too,
  The heads were made of leather,
They knock'd upon't with little clubs,
  And call'd the folks together.
  Yankey doodle, &c.

And there was captain Washington,
  And gentlefolks about him,
They say he's grown so tarnal proud,
  He will not ride without them.
  Yankey doodle, &c.

He got him on his meeting clothes,
  Upon a slapping stallion,
He set the world along in rows,
  In hundreds and in millions.
  Yankey doodle, &c.

The flaming ribbons in his hat,
  They look'd so taring fine ah,
I wanted pockily to get,
  To give to my Jemima.
  Yankey doodle, &c.

I see another snarl of men,
  A digging graves they told me,
So tarnal long, so tarnal deep,
  They tended they should hold me.
  Yankey doodle, &c.

It scar'd me so I hook'd it off,
  Nor stopt as I remember,
Nor turn'd about till I got home,
  Lock'd up in mother's chamber.
  Yankey doodle, &c.

(The Granger Collection, New York)

Kerber has written, newer interpretations have "reinvigorated the Progressive focus on social conflict between classes and extended it to include the experience not only of rich

economic tensions within colonial society that they claimed helped shape the Revolutionary struggle. Jesse Lemisch and Dirk Hoerder pointed to the actions of mobs in colonial cities as evidence of popular resentment of both American and British elites. Joseph Ernst reemphasized the significance of economic pressures on colonial merchants and tradesmen. Gary Nash, in *The Urban Crucible* (1979), emphasized the role of growing economic distress in colonial cities in creating a climate in which Revolutionary sentiment could flourish.

Some newer social interpretations of the Revolution attempt to break free of the old debate pitting ideas against interests. The two things are not in competition with but, rather, reinforce each other, more recent scholars argue. "Everyone has economic interests," Gary Nash has written, "and everyone . . . has an ideology." Only by exploring the relationships between the two can historians hope fully to understand either. Also, as Linda

and poor but of a wide variety of interest groups, marginal communities, and social outsiders." That extension of focus to previously little-studied groups includes work by Mary Beth Norton on women, Silvia Frey on slaves, and Colin Calloway on Native Americans.

Gordon Wood, in *The Radicalism of the American Revolution* (1992) and *Empire of Liberty* (2009), helped revive a once-popular interpretation of the Revolution that had fallen out of fashion: that it was a genuinely radical event, which led to the breakdown of such long-standing patterns of society as deference, patriarchy, and traditional gender relations. Class conflict and radical goals may not have caused the Revolution; but the Revolution had a profound, even radical, ideological impact on society nevertheless. •

UNDERSTAND, ANALYZE, AND EVALUATE

1. How has the debate over the origins of the American Revolution shifted over time? What are some reasons for the changing interpretations?
2. In what way was the American Revolution an ideological struggle?
3. In what way was the American Revolution a social and economic conflict?
4. Was the American Revolution a radical event? Why or why not?

---

states had to resort to persuasion and force: to paying bounties to attract new recruits and to drafting them. Even when it was possible to recruit substantial numbers of militiamen, they remained under the control of their respective states. Congress quickly recognized the disadvantages of this decentralized system and tried, with some success, to correct it. In the spring of 1775, it created a Continental army with a single

GENERAL GEORGE WASHINGTON

commander in chief. George Washington, the forty-three-year-old Virginia planter-aristocrat who had commanded colonial forces during the French and Indian War, and—despite his defeat at the battle at Fort Necessity in 1754—possessed more experience than any other American-born officer available. He had also been an early advocate of independence. Above all, he was admired, respected, and trusted by nearly all Patriots. He was the unanimous choice of the delegates, and he took command in June 1775.

Congress had chosen well. Throughout the war, Washington never flagged, despite difficulties and discouragements that

WASHINGTON PROVIDED THE ARMY—AND THE PEOPLE—WITH A SYMBOL OF STABILITY AROUND WHICH THEY COULD RALLY.

would have daunted a lesser man. There were serious problems of morale among soldiers who consistently received short rations and low pay. Open mutinies broke out in 1781 among the Pennsylvania and New Jersey troops. The Continental Congress always seemed too little interested in supplying him with manpower and equipment and too much interested in interfering with his conduct of military operations.

Washington had some shortcomings as a military commander. But he was, in the end, a great war leader. With the aid

FOREIGN ASSISTANCE

of foreign military experts such as the marquis de Lafayette from France and Baron von Steuben from Prussia, he succeeded in building and holding together an army of fewer than 10,000 men that, along with state militias, ultimately prevailed against the greatest military power in the world. Even more important, perhaps, in a new nation still unsure of either its purposes or its structure, with a central government both weak and divided, Washington provided the army—and the people—with a symbol of stability around which they could rally. He may not have been the most brilliant of the

VOTING FOR INDEPENDENCE The Continental Congress actually voted in favor of independence from Great Britain on July 2, 1776. July 4, the date Americans now celebrate as Independence Day, is when the Congress formally ratified the Declaration of Independence. This painting by Edgar Pine-Savage re-creates the scene in Philadelphia as delegates from the various colonies made their momentous decision. (Courtesy of The Historical Society of Pennsylvania Collection, Atwater Kent Museum of Philadelphia)

country's early leaders, but in the crucial years of the war, at least, he was the most successful in holding the new nation together.

THE WAR FOR INDEPENDENCE

On the surface, at least, all the advantages in the military struggle between America and Great Britain appeared to lie with the British. They possessed the greatest navy and the best-equipped army in the world. They had access to the resources of an empire. They had a coherent structure of command. The Americans, by contrast, were struggling to create a new army and a new government at the same time that they were trying to fight a war.

> **THEY CANNOT DEFEAT AN IDEA WITH AN ARMY.**
> **THOMAS PAINE**

Yet the United States had advantages that were not at first apparent. Americans were fighting on their own ground, while the English were far from home (and from their own resources). The American Patriots were, on the whole, deeply committed to the conflict; the British people only halfheartedly supported the war. As Thomas Paine said at the time, "They cannot defeat an idea with an army." Beginning in 1777, moreover, the Americans had the benefit of substantial aid from abroad, when the American war became part of a larger world contest in which Great Britain faced the strongest powers of Europe—most notably France—in a struggle for imperial supremacy.

The American victory was not, however, simply the result of these advantages—nor even of the remarkable spirit and resourcefulness of the people and the army. It was a result,

AMERICAN ADVANTAGES

REVOLUTIONARY SOLDIERS Jean Baptiste de Verger, a nineteen-year-old French officer serving in America during the Revolution, kept a journal of his experiences illustrated with watercolors. Here he portrays four American soldiers carrying different kinds of arms: a black infantryman with a light rifle, a musketman, a rifleman, and an artilleryman. (Anne S. K. Brown Military Collection, Brown University Library)

too, of a series of egregious blunders and miscalculations by the British in the early stages of the fighting, when England could (and probably should) have won. And it was, finally, a result of the transformation of the war—which proceeded in three different phases—into a new kind of conflict that the British military, for all its strength, could not win.

THE FIRST PHASE: NEW ENGLAND

For the first year of the fighting, the British remained uncertain about whether or not they were actually engaged in a war. Many English authorities continued to believe that British forces were simply attempting to quell pockets of rebellion in the contentious area around Boston. Gradually, however, colonial forces took the offensive and made almost the entire territory of the American colonies a battleground.

After the British withdrawal from Concord and Lexington in April 1775, American forces besieged the army of General

BUNKER HILL Thomas Gage in Boston. The Patriots suffered severe casualties in the Battle of Bunker Hill (actually fought on Breed's Hill) on June 17, 1775, and were ultimately driven from their position there. But they inflicted much greater losses on the enemy than the enemy in-

flicted on them. Indeed, the British suffered their heaviest casualties of the entire war at Bunker Hill. After the battle, the Patriots continued to tighten the siege.

By the first months of 1776, the British had concluded that Boston was not the best place from which to wage war. Not only was it in the center of the most fervently anti-British region of the colonies, it was also tactically indefensible—a narrow neck of land, easily isolated and besieged. By late winter, in fact, Patriot forces had surrounded the city and occupied strategic positions on the heights. On March 17, 1776 (a date still celebrated in Boston as Evacuation Day), the British departed Boston for Halifax in Nova Scotia with hundreds of Loyalist refugees. Less than a year after the firing of the first shots, the Massachusetts colonists had driven the British—temporarily—from American soil.

Elsewhere, the war proceeded fitfully and inconclusively. To the south, at Moore's Creek Bridge in North Carolina, a band of Patriots crushed an uprising of Loyalists on February 27, 1776, and in the process discouraged a British plan to invade the southern states. The British had expected substantial aid from local Tories in the South; they realized now that such aid might not be as effective as they had hoped. To the north, Americans launched an invasion of Canada—hoping to remove the British threat and win the Canadians to their cause. Benedict Arnold, the commander of a small American force, threatened Quebec in late 1775 and early 1776 after a winter march of incredible hardship. Richard Montgomery, coming to his assistance, combined his forces with Arnold's and took command of both. Montgomery died in the assault on the city; and although a wounded Arnold kept up the siege for a time, the Quebec campaign ended in frustration. Congress sent a civilian commission to Canada, headed by the seventy-year-old Benjamin Franklin. But Franklin also failed to win the allegiance of the northern colonists. Canada did not become part of the new nation.

INVASION OF
CANADA

The British evacuation of Boston in 1776 was not, therefore, so much a victory for the Americans as a reflection of changing English assumptions about the war. By the spring of 1776, it had become clear to the British that England must be prepared to fight a much larger and longer conflict. The departure of the British, therefore, signaled the beginning of a new phase in the war.

THE SECOND PHASE: THE MID-ATLANTIC REGION

The next phase of the war, which lasted from 1776 until early 1778, was when the British were in the best position to win. Indeed, had it not been for a series of blunders and misfortunes, they probably would have crushed the rebellion then. During this period the struggle became, for the most part, a traditional, conventional war. And in that, the Americans were woefully overmatched.

The British regrouped quickly after their retreat from Boston. During the summer of 1776, in the weeks immediately following the Declaration of Independence, the waters around New York City grew crowded with the most formidable military force Great Britain had ever sent abroad. Hundreds of man-of-war vessels and troopships and 32,000 disciplined soldiers arrived, under the command of the affable William Howe. Howe felt no particular hostility toward the Americans. He hoped to awe them into submission rather than fight them, and he believed that most of them, if given a chance, would show their loyalty to the king. In a meeting with commissioners from Congress, he offered them a choice between submission with royal pardon and a battle against overwhelming odds.

To oppose Howe's impressive array, Washington could muster only about 19,000 poorly armed and lightly trained soldiers, even after combining the Continental army with state militias; he had no navy at all. Even so, the Americans quickly rejected

BRITISH TAKE
NEW YORK

BATTLE OF GERMANTOWN On October 4, 1777, Washington launched an attack on General Howe's camp at Germantown, near Philadelphia. Although the Patriots were successful in the first hours of the battle, a heavy fog confused them and allowed the British finally to force them to retreat. This 1782 painting re-creates a part of the battle: an attack by American forces led by "Mad Anthony" Wayne. (National Center for the American Revolution/Valley Forge Historical Society)

THE REVOLUTION IN THE NORTH, 1775–1776 After initial battles in and around Boston, the British forces left Massachusetts and (after a brief stay in Halifax, Canada) moved south to New York. In the meantime, American forces moved north in an effort to capture British strongholds in Montreal and Quebec, with little success.

• *Why would the British have considered New York a better base than Boston?*

Howe's offer and chose to continue the war—a decision that led inevitably to a succession of rapid defeats. The British pushed the defenders off Long Island, compelled them to abandon Manhattan, and then drove them in slow retreat over the plains of New Jersey, across the Delaware River, and into Pennsylvania.

For eighteenth-century Europeans, warfare was a seasonal activity. Fighting generally stopped in cold weather. The British settled down for the winter at various points in New Jersey, leaving an outpost of Hessians (German mercenaries) at Trenton on the Delaware River. But Washington did not sit still. On Christmas night 1776, he boldly recrossed the icy river, surprised and scattered the Hessians, and occupied the town. Then he advanced to Princeton and drove a British force from their base in the college there. But Washington was unable to hold either Princeton or Trenton, and he finally took refuge for the rest of the winter in the hills around Morristown, New Jersey.

For their campaigns of 1777, the British devised a strategy to cut the United States in two. Howe would move north from **BRITAIN'S STRATEGY** New York City up the Hudson to Albany, while another British force would come south from Canada to meet him. One of the younger British officers, the dashing John Burgoyne, secured command of this northern force and planned a two-pronged attack along both the Mohawk and the upper Hudson approaches to Albany.

But after setting this plan in motion, Howe himself abandoned it. He decided instead to launch an assault on the rebel capital Philadelphia—an assault that would, he hoped, discourage the Patriots, rally the Loyalists, and bring the war to a speedy conclusion. He removed the bulk of his forces from New York by sea, landed at the head of the Chesapeake Bay, brushed Washington aside at the Battle of Brandywine Creek on September 11, and proceeded north to Philadelphia, which he was able to occupy with little resistance. Meanwhile, Washington, after an unsuccessful October 4 attack at Germantown (just outside Philadelphia), went into winter quarters at Valley Forge. The Continental Congress, now dislodged from its capital, reassembled at York, Pennsylvania.

Howe's move to Philadelphia left Burgoyne to carry out the campaign in the north alone. Burgoyne sent Colonel Barry St. Leger up the St. Lawrence River toward Lake Ontario and the headwaters of the Mohawk, while Burgoyne himself advanced

THE BATTLE OF BUNKER HILL, 1775 British troops face Patriot forces outside Boston on June 17, 1775, in the first great battle of the American Revolution. The British ultimately drove the Americans from their positions on Breed's Hill and Bunker Hill, but only after suffering enormous casualties. General Gage, the British commander, reported to his superiors in London after the battle: "These people show a spirit and conduct against us they never showed against the French." This anonymous painting reveals the array of British troops and naval support and also shows the bombardment and burning of Charlestown from artillery in Boston. (Gift of Edgar William and Bernice Chrysler Garbisch, © 1998 Board of Trustees, National Gallery of Art, Washington)

directly down the upper Hudson Valley. He got off to a flying start. He seized Fort Ticonderoga easily and with it an enormous store of powder and supplies; this caused such dismay in Congress that the delegates removed General Philip Schuyler from command of American forces in the north and replaced him with Horatio Gates.

By the time Gates took command, Burgoyne had already experienced two staggering defeats. In one of them—at Oriskany, New York, on August 6—a Patriot band of German farmers led by Nicholas Herkimer held off a force of Indians and Tories commanded by St. Leger. That gave Benedict Arnold time to go to the relief of Fort Stanwix and close off the Mohawk Valley to St. Leger's advance.

In the other battle—at Bennington, Vermont, on August 16—New England militiamen under the Bunker Hill veteran John Stark severely mauled a British detachment that Burgoyne had sent out to seek supplies. Short of materials, with all help cut off, Burgoyne fought several costly engagements and then withdrew to Saratoga, where Gates surrounded him. On October 17, 1777, Burgoyne ordered what was left of his army, nearly 5,000 men, to surrender to the Americans.

To the Patriots and peoples watching from around the world,

PATRIOT VICTORY AT SARATOGA the New York campaign was a remarkable victory. The British surrender at Saratoga became a major turning point in the war— above all, perhaps, because it led directly to an alliance between the United States and France.

The British failure to win the war during this period, a period in which they had overwhelming advantages, was in large

BRITISH BLUNDERS part a result of their own mistakes. And in assessing them, the role of William Howe looms large. He abandoned his own most important strategic initiative—the northern campaign— leaving Burgoyne to fight alone. And even in Pennsylvania, where he chose to engage the enemy, he refrained from moving in for a final attack on the weakened Continental army, even though he had several opportunities. Instead, he repeatedly allowed Washington to retreat and regroup; and he permitted the American army to spend a long winter unmolested in Valley Forge, where—weak and hungry—they might have been easy prey for a British attack. Some British critics believed that Howe did not want to win the war, that he was

THE REVOLUTION IN THE MIDDLE COLONIES, 1776–1778 These maps illustrate the major campaigns of the Revolution in the middle colonies—New York, New Jersey, and Pennsylvania—between 1776 and 1778. The large map on the left shows the two prongs of the British strategy: first, a movement of British forces south from Canada into the Hudson Valley; and second, a movement of other British forces, under General William Howe, out from New York and south into New Jersey and Pennsylvania. The strategy was designed to trap the American army between the two British movements. The two smaller maps on the right show detailed pictures of some of the major battles. The upper one reveals the surprising American victory at Saratoga. The lower one shows a series of inconclusive battles between New York and Philadelphia in 1777 and 1778.

• *What movements of Howe helped thwart that plan?*

secretly in sympathy with the American cause. His family had close ties to the colonies, and he himself was linked politically to those forces within the British government that opposed the war. Others pointed to personal weaknesses: Howe's apparent alcoholism, his romantic attachment (he spent the winter of 1777–1778 in Philadelphia with his mistress when many of his advisers were urging him to move elsewhere). But the most important problem, it seems clear, was his failure to understand the nature of the war that he was fighting—or even to understand that it was truly a war.

THE IROQUOIS AND THE BRITISH

The campaign in upstate New York was not just a British defeat. It was a setback for the ambitious efforts of several Iroquois leaders, who had hoped to involve Indian forces in the English military effort, believing that a British victory would help stem white movement onto tribal lands. The Iroquois Confederacy

had declared itself neutral in the war in 1776, but not all its members were content to remain passive in the northern campaign. Among those who worked to expand the Native American role in the war were a Mohawk brother and sister, Joseph and Mary Brant. Both were people of stature within the Mohawk nation: Joseph was a celebrated warrior; Mary was a magnetic woman and the widow of Sir William Johnson, the British superintendent of Indians, who had achieved wide popularity among the tribes. The Brants persuaded their own tribe to contribute to the British cause and attracted the support of the Seneca and Cayuga as well. They played an important role in Burgoyne's unsuccessful campaigns in the north.

But the alliance was also a sign of the growing divisions within the Iroquois Confederacy. Only three of the six nations of the Confederacy supported the British. The Oneida and the Tuscarora backed the Americans; the Onondaga split into several factions. The three-century-old Confederacy,

DIVISIONS IN
THE IROQUOIS
CONFEDERACY

weakened by the aftermath of the French and Indian War, continued to unravel.

The alliance had other unhappy consequences for the Iroquois. A year after Oriskany, Indians joined British troops in a series of raids on outlying white settlements in upstate New York. Months later, Patriot forces under the command of General John Sullivan harshly retaliated, wreaking such destruction on tribal settlements that large groups of Iroquois fled north into Canada to seek refuge. Many never returned.

SECURING AID FROM ABROAD

The failure of the British to crush the Continental army in the mid-Atlantic states, combined with the stunning American victory at Saratoga, was a turning point in the war. It transformed the conflict and ushered it into a new and final phase.

Central to this transformation of the war was American success in winning support from abroad—indirectly from several European nations and directly from France. Even before the Declaration of Independence, Congress dispatched representatives to the capitals of Europe to negotiate commercial treaties with the governments there; if America was to leave the British Empire, it would need to cultivate new trading partners. Such treaties would, of course, require European governments to recognize the United States as an independent nation. John Adams called the early American representatives abroad "militia diplomats." Unlike the diplomatic regulars of Europe, they had little experience with the formal art and etiquette of Old World diplomacy. Since transatlantic communication was slow and uncertain (it took from one to three months for a message to cross the Atlantic), they had to interpret the instructions of Congress very freely and make crucial decisions entirely on their own.

MILITIA DIPLOMATS

The most promising potential ally for the United States was France. King Louis XVI, who had come to the throne in 1774, and his astute foreign minister, the count de Vergennes, were eager to see Britain lose a crucial part of its empire. Through a series of secret bargains, facilitated by the creation of a fictional trading firm and the use of secret agents on both sides (among them the famed French dramatist Caron de Beaumarchais), France began supplying the Americans large quantities of much-needed supplies. But the French government remained reluctant to provide the United States with what it most wanted: diplomatic recognition.

Finally, Benjamin Franklin himself went to France to represent the United States. A natural diplomat, Franklin became a popular hero among the French—aristocrats and common people alike. His popularity there greatly helped the American cause. Of even greater help was the news of the American victory at Saratoga, which arrived in London on December 2, 1777, and in Paris two days later. On February 6, 1778—in part to forestall a British peace offensive that Vergennes feared might persuade the Americans to abandon the war—France formally recognized the United States as a sovereign nation and laid the groundwork for greatly expanded assistance to the American war effort.

France's intervention made the war an international conflict. In the course of the next two years, France, Spain, and the Netherlands all drifted into another general war with Great Britain in Europe, and all contributed both directly and indirectly to the ultimate American victory. But France was America's truly indispensable ally. Not only did it furnish the new nation with most of its money and munitions; it also provided a navy and an expeditionary force that proved invaluable in the decisive phase of the Revolutionary conflict.

PIVOTAL FRENCH AID

THE FINAL PHASE: THE SOUTH

The last phase of the military struggle in America was very different from either of the first two. The British government had never been fully united behind the war; after the defeat at Saratoga and the intervention of the French, it imposed new limits on its commitment to the conflict. Instead of a full-scale military struggle against the American army, therefore, the British decided to try to enlist the support of those elements of the American population—a majority, they continued to believe—who were still loyal to the crown; in other words, they would work to undermine the Revolution from within. Since the British believed Loyalist sentiment was strongest in the southern colonies (despite their earlier failure to enlist Loyalist support in North Carolina), the main focus of their effort shifted there; and so it was in the South, for the most part, that the final stages of the war occurred.

The new British strategy was a dismal failure. British forces spent three years (from 1778 to 1781) moving through the South, fighting small battles and large, and attempting to neutralize the territory through which they traveled. All such efforts ended in frustration. The British badly overestimated the extent of Loyalist sentiment. There were many Tories in Georgia and the Carolinas, some of them disgruntled members of the Regulator movement. But there were also many more Patriots than the British had believed. In Virginia, support for independence was as fervent as in Massachusetts. And even in the lower South, Loyalists often refused to aid the British because they feared reprisals from the Patriots around them. The British also harmed their own cause by encouraging southern slaves to desert their owners in return for promises of emancipation. Many slaves (perhaps 5 percent of the total) took advantage of this offer, despite the great difficulty of doing so. But white southerners were aghast; and even many who might otherwise have been inclined to support the crown now joined the Patriot side, which posed no such threat to slavery. The British also faced severe logistical problems in the South. Patriot forces could move at will throughout the region, living off the resources of the countryside, blending in with the civilian population and leaving the British unable to distinguish friend from foe. The British, by contrast, suffered all the disadvantages of an army in hostile territory.

THE REVOLUTION IN THE SOUTH, 1778–1781 The final phase of the American Revolution occurred largely in the South, which the British thought would be a more receptive region for their troops. This map reveals the many, scattered military efforts of the British and the Americans in those years, none of them conclusive. It also shows the final chapter of the Revolution around the Chesapeake Bay and the James River.

• *What errors led the British to their surrender at Yorktown?*

It was this phase of the conflict that made the war truly "revolutionary"—not only because it introduced a new kind of combat, but also because it had the effect of mobilizing and politicizing large groups of the population who had previously remained aloof from the struggle. With the war expanding into previously isolated communities, with many civilians forced to involve themselves whether they liked it or not, the political climate of the United States grew more heated than ever. And support for independence, far from being crushed as the British had hoped, greatly increased.

That was the context in which the important military encounters of the last years of the war occurred. In the North,

REVOLUTIONARY CONSEQUENCES OF THE SOUTHERN CAMPAIGN

where significant numbers of British troops remained, the fighting settled into a relatively quiet stalemate. Sir Henry Clinton replaced the hapless William Howe in 1778 and moved what had been Howe's army from Philadelphia back to New York. There the British troops stayed for more than a year, with Washington using his army to keep watch around them. The American forces in New York did so little fighting in this period that Washington sent some troops west to fight hostile Indians who had been attacking white settlers. In that same winter, George Rogers Clark, under orders from the state of

Virginia—not from either Washington or Congress—led a daring expedition over the mountains and captured settlements in the Illinois country from the British and their Indian allies.

During this period of relative calm, General Benedict Arnold shocked the American forces—and Washington in particular—by becoming a traitor. Arnold had been one of the early heroes of the war, but now, convinced that the American cause was hopeless, he conspired with British agents to betray the Patriot stronghold at West Point on the Hudson River. The scheme unraveled before Arnold could complete it, and he fled to the safety of the British camp, where he spent the rest of the war.

In the meantime, decisive fighting was in progress in the South. The British did have some significant military successes during this period. On December 29, 1778, they captured Savannah, on the coast of Georgia; and on May 12, 1780, they took the port of Charleston, South Carolina. They also inspired some Loyalists to take up arms and advance with them into the interior. But although the British were able to win conventional battles, they were constantly harassed as they moved through the countryside by Patriot guerrillas led by such resourceful fighters as Thomas Sumter, Andrew Pickens, and Francis Marion, the "Swamp Fox."

Moving inland to Camden, South Carolina, Lord Cornwallis (Clinton's choice as British commander in the South) met and crushed a Patriot force under Horatio Gates on August 16, 1780. Congress recalled Gates, and Washington gave the southern command to Nathanael Greene, a Quaker and a former blacksmith from Rhode Island and probably the ablest of all the American generals of the time next to Washington himself.

NATHANAEL GREENE

Even before Greene joined the southern army, the tide of battle began to turn against Cornwallis. At King's Mountain (near the North Carolina–South Carolina border) on October 7, 1780, a band of Patriot riflemen from the backwoods killed, wounded, or captured an entire force of 1,100 New York and South Carolina Tories that Cornwallis was using as auxiliaries. Once Greene arrived, he confused and exasperated Cornwallis further by dividing the American forces into small, fast-moving contingents and refraining from a showdown in open battle. One of the contingents inflicted what Cornwallis admitted was "a very unexpected and severe blow" at Cowpens on January 17, 1781. Finally, after receiving reinforcements, Greene combined all his forces and maneuvered to meet the British on ground of his own choosing, at Guilford Court House, North Carolina. After a hard-fought battle there on March 15, 1781, Greene

THE BRITISH ON THE HUDSON, 1776 In one of the largest troop movements of the Revolution, English commanders sent 13,000 British and Hessian troops up the Hudson River to drive George Washington and his Patriot army from strongholds in the palisades above the river. The British took nearly 3,000 prisoners when the Patriots surrendered on November 16, 1776. Thomas Davies painted this watercolor of the British landing at the time. (Emmet Collection. Miriam & Ira D. Wallach Division of Art, Prints & Photographs, The New York Public Library, Astor, Lenox and Tilden Foundations)

withdrew from the field; but Cornwallis had lost so many men that he decided at last to abandon the Carolina campaign.

Cornwallis withdrew to the port town of Wilmington, North Carolina, to receive supplies being sent to him by sea; later he moved north to launch raids in the interior of Virginia. But Clinton, concerned for the army's safety, ordered him to take up a position on the peninsula between the York and James Rivers and wait for ships to carry his troops to New York or Charleston. So Cornwallis retreated to Yorktown and began to build fortifications there.

George Washington—along with count Jean Baptiste de Rochambeau, commander of the French expeditionary force in America, and Admiral François Joseph Paul de Grasse, commander of the French fleet in American waters—set out to trap

YORKTOWN Cornwallis at Yorktown. Washington and Rochambeau marched a French-American army from New York to join other French forces under Lafayette in Virginia, while de Grasse sailed with additional troops for Chesapeake Bay and the York River. These joint operations, perfectly timed and executed, caught Cornwallis between land and sea. After a few shows of resistance, he capitulated on October 17, 1781 (four years to the day after the surrender of Burgoyne at Saratoga). Two days later, as a military band played the old tune "The World Turn'd Upside Down," Cornwallis, claiming to be ill, sent a deputy who formally surrendered the British army of more than 7,000 men.

Except for a few skirmishes, the fighting was now over; but the United States had not yet won the war. British forces continued to hold the seaports of Savannah, Charleston, Wilmington, and New York. Before long, a British fleet met and defeated Admiral de Grasse's fleet in the West Indies, ending Washington's hopes for further French naval assistance. For more than a year, although there was no significant further combat between British and American forces, it remained possible that the war might resume and the struggle for independence might still be lost.

WINNING THE PEACE

Cornwallis's defeat provoked outcries in England against continuing the war. Lord North resigned as prime minister; Lord Shelburne emerged from the political wreckage to succeed him; and British emissaries appeared in France to talk informally with the American diplomats in Paris. The three American principals were Benjamin Franklin, John Adams, and John Jay.

The Americans were under instructions to cooperate fully with France in their negotiations with England. But Vergennes insisted that France could not agree to any settlement of the war with England until its ally Spain had achieved its principal war aim: winning back Gibraltar from the British. There was no real prospect of that happening soon, and the Americans began to fear that the alliance with France might keep them at war indefinitely. As a result, Franklin, Jay, and Adams began proceeding on their own, without informing Vergennes, and signed a preliminary treaty with Great Britain on November 30, 1782.

Franklin, in the meantime, skillfully pacified Vergennes and avoided an immediate rift in the French-American alliance.

The British and Americans reached a final settlement—the Treaty of Paris—on September 3, 1783, when both Spain and France agreed to end hostilities. It was, on the whole, remarkably

TREATY OF PARIS favorable to the United States in granting a clear-cut recognition of its independence and a generous, though ambiguous, cession of territory—from the southern boundary of Canada to the northern boundary of Florida and from the Atlantic to the Mississippi. With good reason, Americans celebrated in the fall of 1783 as the last of the British occupation forces embarked from New York and General Washington, at the head of his troops, rode triumphantly into the city.

WAR AND SOCIETY

Historians have long debated whether the American Revolution was a social as well as a political revolution. Some have argued that the colonists were struggling not only over the question of home rule, but also over "who should rule at home." Others claim that domestic social and economic concerns had little to do with the conflict. (See "Debating the Past," pp. 134–135.) Whatever the motivations of Americans, however, there can be little doubt that the War for Independence had important effects on the nature of American society.

LOYALISTS AND MINORITIES

The losers in the American Revolution included not only the British but also American Loyalists. There is no way to be sure how many Americans remained loyal to England during the Revolution, but it is clear that there were many—at least a fifth (and some historians estimate as much as a third) of the white population. Their motivations were varied. Some were office-holders in the imperial government, who stood to lose their positions as a result of the Revolution. Others were merchants engaged in trade closely tied to the imperial system. (Most merchants, however, supported the Revolution.) Still others were people who lived in relative isolation and had not been exposed to the wave of discontent that had turned so many Americans against Britain. There were cultural and ethnic minorities who feared that an independent America would not offer them sufficient protection. There were settled, cautious people who feared social instability. And there were those who, expecting the British to win the war, were simply currying favor with the anticipated victors.

What happened to these men and women during the war was a turbulent and at times tragic story. Hounded by Patriots in their communities, harassed by legislative and judicial

THE LOYALISTS' PLIGHT actions, the position of many Loyalists became intolerable. Up to 100,000 fled the country. Those who could afford to—for example, the hated Tory governor of Massachusetts, Thomas Hutchinson—moved to England, where many lived in difficult

THE AGE OF REVOLUTIONS

THE American Revolution was a result of specific tensions and conflicts between Britain and its North American colonies. But it was also a part, and a cause, of what historians have come to call an "age of revolutions" that spread through much of the Western world in the late eighteenth and early nineteenth centuries.

The modern idea of revolution—the overturning of old systems and regimes and the creation of new ones—was largely a product of the ideas of the Enlightenment. Among those ideas was the notion of popular sovereignty, articulated by the English philosopher John Locke and others. Locke argued that political authority did not derive from the divine right of kings or the inherited authority of aristocracies but, rather,

STORMING THE BASTILLE This painting portrays the storming of the great Parisian fortress and prison, the Bastille, on July 14, 1789. The Bastille was a despised symbol of royal tyranny to many of the French, because of the arbitrarily arrested and imprisoned people who were sent there. The July assault was designed to release the prisoners, but in fact the revolutionaries found only seven people in the vast fortress. Even so, the capture of the Bastille—which marked one of the first moments in which ordinary Frenchmen joined the Revolution—became one of the great moments in modern French history. The anniversary of the event, "Bastille Day," remains the French national holiday. (Bridgeman–Giraudon/Art Resource, NY)

from the consent of the governed. A related Enlightenment idea was the concept of individual freedom, which challenged the traditional belief that governments had the right to prescribe the way people act, speak, and even think. Champions of individual freedom in the eighteenth century—among them the French philosopher Voltaire—advocated religious toleration and freedom of thought and expression. The Swiss-French Enlightenment theorist Jean-Jacques Rousseau helped spread the idea of political and legal equality for all people—the end of special privileges for aristocrats and elites, the right of all citizens to participate in the formation of policies and laws.

The American Revolution was the first and in many ways the most influential of the Enlightenment-derived uprisings against established orders. It served as an inspiration to people in other lands who were trying to find a way to oppose unpopular regimes. In 1789, a little over a decade after the beginning of the American Revolution, revolution began in France. The monarchy was abolished (and the king and queen publicly executed in 1793), the authority of the Catholic Church was challenged and greatly weakened, and at the peak of revolutionary chaos during the Jacobin period (1793–1794), more than 40,000 suspected enemies of the revolution were executed and hundreds of thousands of others imprisoned. The most radical phase of the revolution came to an end in 1799, when Napoleon Bonaparte, a young general, seized power and began to build a new French empire. But France's *ancien régime* of king and aristocracy never wholly revived.

The American and French Revolutions helped inspire uprisings in many other parts of the Atlantic world. In 1791, a major slave uprising began in Haiti and soon attracted more than 100,000 rebels. The slave army defeated

and lonely exile. Others of more modest means moved to Canada, establishing the first English-speaking community in the province of Quebec. Some returned to America after the war and, as the earlier passions and resentments faded, managed to reenter the life of the nation. Others remained abroad for the rest of their lives.

Most Loyalists were people of average means, but a substantial minority consisted of men and women of wealth. They left

behind large estates and vacated important positions of social and economic leadership. Even some who remained in the country saw their property confiscated and their positions forfeited. The result was new opportunities for Patriots to acquire land and influence, a situation that produced significant social changes in many communities.

It would be an exaggeration, however, to claim that the departure of the Loyalists was responsible for anything approaching a both the white settlers of the island and the French colonial armies sent to quell their rebellion. Under the leadership of General Toussaint L'Ouverture, they began to agitate for independence, which they obtained on January 1, 1804, a few months after Toussaint's death.

Revolution spread next into the Spanish and Portuguese colonies in the Americas, particularly among the so-called Creoles, people of European ancestry born in the Americas. In the late eighteenth century, they began to resist the authority of colonial officials sent from Spain and Portugal and to demand a greater say in governing their own lands. Napoleon's invasion of Spain and Portugal in 1807 weakened the ability of the European regimes to sustain authority over their American colonies. In the years that followed, revolutions swept through much of Latin America. Mexico became an independent nation in 1821, and provinces of Central America that had once been part of Mexico (Guatemala, El Salvador, Honduras, Nicaragua, and Costa Rica) established their independence three years later. Simón Bolívar, modeling his efforts on those of George Washington, led a great revolutionary movement that won independence for Brazil in 1822 and also helped lead revolutionary campaigns in Venezuela, Ecuador, and Peru—all of which won their independence in the 1820s. Across the Atlantic, Greek patriots—drawing from the examples of other revolutionary nations—launched a movement to win their independence from the Ottoman Empire, which finally succeeded in 1830.

The age of revolutions left many new, independent nations in its wake. It did not, however, succeed in establishing the ideals of popular sovereignty, individual freedom, and political equality in all the nations it affected. Slavery survived in the United States and in many areas of Latin America. New forms of aristocracy and even monarchy emerged in France, Mexico, Brazil, and elsewhere. Women—many of whom had hoped the revolutionary age would win new rights for them—made few legal or political gains in this era. But the ideals that the revolutionary era introduced to the Western world continued to shape the histories of nations throughout the nineteenth century and beyond. •

UNDERSTAND, ANALYZE, AND EVALUATE

1. How did the American Revolution influence the French Revolution?
2. What other nations were affected by the example of the American Revolution?
3. What was the significance of the revolution in Haiti, and how much attention did it get in other nations?

social revolution or that the Revolution created a general assault on the wealthy and powerful in America. When the war ended, those who had been wealthy at its beginning were, for the most part, still wealthy at the end. Most of those who had wielded social and political influence continued to wield it.

The war had a significant effect on other minorities as well, and on certain religious groups in particular. No sect suffered more than the Anglicans, many of whom were Loyalists. In Virginia and Maryland, where the colonial governments had recognized Anglicanism as the official religion and had imposed a tax for its maintenance, the new Revolutionary regimes disestablished the church and eliminated the subsidy. By the time the fighting ended, many Anglican parishes no longer had clergymen, for there were few ministers to take the place of those who had died or who had left the country as Loyalist refugees. Anglicanism survived in America, but the losses during the Revolution permanently weakened it. The Revolution weakened the Quakers in Pennsylvania and elsewhere. They incurred widespread unpopularity because of their pacifism, which destroyed much of the social and political prestige they had once enjoyed.

WEAKENING OF THE ANGLICAN CHURCH

While the war was weakening the Anglicans and the Quakers, it was strengthening the position of the Roman Catholic Church. On the advice of Charles Carroll of Carrollton, a Maryland statesman and Catholic lay leader, most American Catholics supported the Patriot cause during the war. The French alliance brought Catholic troops and chaplains to the country, and the gratitude with which most Americans greeted them did much to erode old and bitter hostilities toward Catholics. The Church did not greatly increase its numbers as a result of the Revolution, but it did gain considerable strength as an institution. Not long after the end of the war, the Vatican provided the United States with its own Catholic hierarchy. (Until then, Catholic bishops in Europe had controlled the American church.) Father John Carroll (also of Maryland) was named head of Catholic missions in America in 1784 and, in 1789, the first American bishop. In 1808 he became archbishop of Baltimore.

STRENGTHENING OF THE CATHOLIC CHURCH

THE WAR AND SLAVERY

For the largest of America's minorities—the African American population—the war had limited, but nevertheless profound, significance. For some, it meant freedom, because many slaves took advantage of the British presence in the South in the final years of the war to escape. The British enabled many of them to leave the country—not so much as any principled commitment to emancipation, but more as a way of disrupting the American war effort. In South Carolina, for example, nearly a third of all slaves defected during the war. Africans had constituted over 60 percent of the population in 1770; by 1790, that figure had declined to about 44 percent.

For other African Americans, the Revolution meant an increased exposure to the concept, although seldom to the reality, of liberty. Most black Americans could not read, but few could avoid the new and exciting ideas circulating through the towns and cities and even at times on the plantations. The results included incidents in several communities in which African Americans engaged in open resistance to white control. In Charleston, South Carolina, for example, Thomas Jeremiah, a free black, was executed in 1775

AFRICAN AMERICAN DESIRE FOR FREEDOM

after Patriot leaders accused him of conspiring to smuggle British guns to South Carolina slaves. The Revolution also produced some eloquent efforts by black writers (mostly in the North) to articulate its lessons for their people. "Liberty is a jewel which was handed Down to man from the cabinet of heaven." the black New Englander Lemuel Hayes wrote in 1776. "Even an African has Equally good a right to his Liberty in common with Englishmen. . . . Shall a man's Couler Be the Decisive Criterion wherby to Judg of his natural right?"

> 66 LIBERTY IS A JEWEL WHICH WAS HANDED DOWN TO MAN FROM THE CABINET OF HEAVEN. 99
>
> **LEMUEL HAYES**

That was one reason why in South Carolina and Georgia—where slaves constituted half or more of the population—there was great ambivalence about the Revolution. Slaveowners opposed British efforts to emancipate their slaves, but they also feared that the Revolution itself would foment slave rebellions. The same fears helped prevent English colonists in the Caribbean islands (who were far more greatly outnumbered by African slaves) from joining with the continental Americans in the revolt against Britain. In much of the North, the combination of Revolutionary sentiment and evangelical Christian fervor helped spread antislavery sentiments widely through society. But in the South, white support for slavery survived. Southern churches rejected the antislavery ideas of the North and worked instead to develop a rationale for slavery—in part by reinforcing ideas about white superiority, in part by encouraging slaveowners to make slavery more humane.

As in so many other periods of American history, the Revolution exposed the continuing tension between the nation's commitment to liberty and its commitment to slavery. To people in our time, and even to some people in Revolutionary times, it seems obvious that liberty and slavery are incompatible. But to many white Americans in the eighteenth century, especially in the South, that did not seem obvious. Many white southerners believed, in fact, that enslaving Africans—whom they considered inferior and unfit for citizenship—was the best way to ensure liberty for white people. They feared the impact of

TENSION BETWEEN LIBERTY AND SLAVERY

free black people living alongside whites. They also feared that without slaves, it would be necessary to recruit a servile white workforce in the South, and that the resulting inequalities would jeopardize the survival of liberty. One of the ironies of the American Revolution, therefore, was that white Americans were fighting both to secure freedom for themselves and to preserve slavery for others.

NATIVE AMERICANS AND THE REVOLUTION

Most Indians viewed the American Revolution with considerable uncertainty. The American Patriots tried to persuade them to remain neutral in the conflict, which they described as a "family quarrel" between the colonists and Britain that had nothing to do with the tribes.

But in fact a great deal was at stake for Native Americans in the American Revolution. During the colonial period, the British government struggled for many years to restrain the growth of white migration into the Indian lands west of the Appalachian Mountains. Such efforts were mostly unsuccessful. The white colonists, the royal governor of Virginia wrote, "do not conceive that the government has any right to forbid taking possession of a vast tract of country." But the British believed that the government did have a right to protect the lands of the Indians—not because of benevolence, but because of their desire to avoid further battles with the tribes, especially on land that had been promised to the Indians.

Once the Revolutionary War began, the role of the Indians became of critical significance to both sides of the conflict. For the American patriots, among the goals of battle for independence was their right to expand into the western lands, at the expense of the Indians. Some of the most eminent figures in the new nation were themselves land speculators in the west, among them George Washington, and many such men had long complained about the Proclamation of 1763, which had forbidden white movement into tribal lands. Other colonial grievances against the British included the recruitment of Indians to join the royal army. In fact, both sides tried to recruit Indians to help them.

In the western Carolinas and Virginia, a Cherokee faction led by Dragging Canoe attacked outlying white settlements in the summer of 1776. Patriot militias responded with overwhelming force, ravaging Cherokee lands and forcing Dragging Canoe and many of his followers to flee west across the Tennessee River. Those Cherokees who remained behind agreed to a new treaty by which they gave up still more land. Not all Native American military efforts were so unsuccessful. Some Iroquois, despite the setbacks at Oriskany, continued to wage war against white Americans in the West and caused widespread destruction in large agricultural areas of New York and Pennsylvania—areas whose crops were of crucial importance to the Patriot cause. And although the retaliating United States armies inflicted heavy losses on the Indians, the attacks continued throughout the war.

In the end, however, the Revolution generally weakened the position of Native Americans in several ways. The Patriot victory increased the white demand for western lands; many American whites associated restrictions on settlement with British oppression and expected the new nation to remove the obstacles. At the same time, white attitudes toward the tribes, seldom friendly in the best of times, took a turn for the worse.

TAKING SIDES

Many whites deeply resented the assistance the Mohawk and other Indian nations had given the British and insisted on treating them as conquered people. Others adopted a paternalistic view of the tribes that was only slightly less dangerous to them. Thomas Jefferson, for example, came to view the Native Americans as "noble savages" uncivilized in their present state but redeemable if they were willing to adapt to the norms of white society.

Among the tribes themselves, the Revolution both revealed and increased the deep divisions that made it difficult for them to form a common front to resist the growing power of whites. In 1774, for example, the Shawnee Indians in western Virginia

GROWING DIVISIONS AMONG THE INDIANS

had attempted to lead an uprising against white settlers moving into the lands that would later become Kentucky. They attracted virtually no allies and (in a conflict known as Lord Dunmore's War) were defeated by the colonial militia and forced to cede more land to white settlers. And the Iroquois, whose power had been eroding since the end of the French and Indian War, were similarly unable to act in unison in the Revolution.

Bands of Native Americans continued to launch raids against white settlers on the frontier. White militias, often using such raids as pretexts, continued to attack Indian tribes who stood in the way of expansion. Perhaps the most vicious massacre of the era occurred in 1782, after the British surrender, when white militias slaughtered a peaceful band of Delaware Indians at Gnadenhuetten in Ohio. They claimed to be retaliating for the killing of a white family several days before, but few white settlers believed this band of Delaware (who were both Christian converts and pacifists) had played any role in the earlier attack. The white soldiers killed ninety-six people, including many women and children. Such massacres did not become the norm of Indian-white relations. But they did reveal how little the Revolution had done to settle the basic conflict between the two peoples.

The triumph of the American patriots in the Revolution contributed to the ultimate defeat of the Indian tribes. To white Americans, independence meant, among other things, their right to move aggressively into the western lands, despite the opposition of the Indians. To the Indians, American independence was "the greatest blow that could have been dealt us," one tribal leader warned.

WOMEN'S RIGHTS AND WOMEN'S ROLES

The long Revolutionary War, which touched the lives of people in almost every region, naturally had a significant effect on American women. The departure of so many men to fight in the Patriot armies left wives, mothers, sisters, and daughters in charge of farms and businesses. Other women whose husbands or fathers went off to war did not have even a farm or shop to fall back on. Many cities and towns developed significant populations of impoverished women, who on occasion led popular protests against price increases. On a few occasions, hungry women rioted and looted for food. Elsewhere (in New Jersey and Staten Island), women launched attacks on occupying British troops, whom they were required to house and feed at considerable expense.

> **❝ I DESIRE YOU WOULD REMEMBER THE LADIES AND BE MORE GENEROUS AND FAVORABLE TO THEM THAN YOUR ANCESTORS. ❞**
>
> **ABIGAIL ADAMS**

Not all women, however, stayed behind when the men went off to war. Sometimes by choice, but more often out of economic necessity or because they had been

WOMEN OF THE ARMY

driven from their homes by the enemy (and by the smallpox and dysentery the British army carried with it), women flocked in increasing numbers to the camps of the Patriot armies to join their male relatives. George Washington looked askance at these female "camp followers," convinced that they were disruptive and distracting (even though his own wife, Martha, spent the winter of 1778–1779 with him at Valley Forge). Other officers were even more hostile, voicing complaints that reflected a high level of anxiety over this seeming violation of traditional gender roles (and also, perhaps, over the generally lower-class backgrounds of the camp women). One described them in decidedly hostile terms: "their hair falling, their brows beady with the heat, their belongings slung over one shoulder, chattering and yelling in sluttish shrills as they went." In fact, however, the women were of significant value to the new army. It had not yet developed an adequate system of supply and auxiliary services, and it profited greatly from the presence of women, who increased army morale and performed such necessary tasks as cooking, laundry, and nursing.

But female activity did not always remain restricted to "women's" tasks. In the rough environment of the camps, traditional gender distinctions proved difficult to maintain. Considerable numbers of women became involved, at least intermittently, in combat—including the legendary Molly Pitcher (so named because she carried pitchers of water to soldiers on the battlefield). She watched her husband fall during one encounter and immediately took his place at a field gun. A few women even disguised themselves as men so as to be able to fight.

After the war, of course, the soldiers and the female camp followers returned home. The experience of combat had little visible impact on how society (or on how women themselves) defined female roles in peacetime. The Revolution did, however, call certain assumptions about women into question in other ways. The emphasis on liberty and the "rights of man" led some women to begin to question their position in society as well. "By the way," Abigail Adams wrote to her husband, John Adams, in 1776, "in the new code of laws which I suppose it will be necessary for you to make, I desire you would remember the ladies and be more generous and favorable to them than your ancestors."

Adams was calling for a very modest expansion of women's rights. She wanted new protections against abusive and tyrannical men. A few women, however, went further. Judith Sargent Murray, one of the leading essayists of the late eighteenth century, wrote in 1779 that women's minds were as good as men's and that girls as well as boys therefore deserved access to education.

Some political leaders—among them Benjamin Franklin and Benjamin Rush—also voiced support for the education of women and for other feminist reforms. Yale students in the 1780s debated the question "Whether women ought to be admitted into the magistracy and government of empires and republics." And there was for a time wide discussion of the future role of women in a new republic that had broken with so many other traditions already. But few concrete reforms became either law or common social practice.

CALLS FOR
WOMEN'S
RIGHTS

In colonial society, under the doctrines of English common law, an unmarried woman had some legal rights (to own property, to enter contracts, and others), but a married woman had virtually no rights at all. She could own no property and earn no independent wages; everything she owned and everything she earned belonged to her husband. She had no legal authority over her children; the father was, in the eyes of the law, the autocrat of the family. Because a married woman had no property rights, she could not engage in any legal transactions (buying or selling, suing or being sued, writing wills). She could not vote. Nor could she obtain a divorce in most states; that, too, was a right reserved mostly for men, although in much of the South men could not obtain divorces either. These restrictions were what Abigail Adams (who herself enjoyed a successful marriage) was describing when she appealed to her husband not to put "such unlimited power into the hands of the Husbands."

The Revolution did little to change any of these legal customs. In some states, it did become easier for women to obtain divorces. And in New Jersey, women obtained the right to vote (although that right was repealed in 1807). Otherwise, there were few advances and some setbacks—including widows' loss of the right to regain their dowries from their husbands' estates. That change left many widows without any means of support and was one of the reasons for the increased agitation for female education: such women needed a way to support themselves.

The Revolution, in other words, far from challenging the patriarchal structure of American society, actually confirmed and strengthened it. Few American women challenged the belief that they occupied a special sphere distinct from that of men. Most accepted that their place remained in the family. Nevertheless, the revolutionary experience did contribute to a subtle but important alteration of women's roles. In the past, they had often been little better than servants in their husbands' homes. But the Revolution encouraged people of both genders to reevaluate the contribution of women to the family and the society.

A STRENGTHENED
PATRIARCHAL
STRUCTURE

One reason for this was a reevaluation of American life during and after the Revolutionary struggle. As the republic searched for a cultural identity for itself, it began to place additional value on the role of women as mothers. The new nation was, many Americans liked to believe, producing a new kind of citizen, steeped in the principles of liberty. Mothers had a particularly important task, therefore, in instructing their children in the virtues the republican citizenry was expected now to possess. Wives were still far from equal partners in marriage, but their ideas, interests, and domestic roles received increased respect from many men.

THE WAR ECONOMY

Inevitably, the Revolution produced important changes in the structure of the American economy. After more than a century

THE BRITISH INFANTRY The world's greatest military power raised its armies in almost haphazard fashion. Command of a British regiment was a favor to well-positioned gentlemen, who received a cash reward for every man they enlisted. With that incentive, they were hardly picky, and the foot soldiers of the British army were mostly men who could be persuaded (or tricked) into enlisting through a combination of liquor and cash. Even so, the rough-and-ready quality of the British infantry made them good soldiers on the whole. This drawing portrays a British encampment during the American Revolution. As with the colonial armies, the British troops attracted women, seen at left, some of whom served as "camp followers," doing chores to help the soldiers. The soldiers themselves wore highly ornamental uniforms that were in many ways very impractical. To keep himself properly groomed and attired could take a soldier up to three hours a day. (Anne S. K. Brown Military Collection, Brown University Library)

of dependence on the British imperial system, American trade suddenly found itself on its own. No longer did it have the protection of the great British navy; on the contrary, English ships now attempted to drive American vessels from the seas. No longer did American merchants have access to the markets of the empire; those markets were now hostile ports—including, of course, the most important source of American trade: England itself.

Yet, while the Revolution disrupted traditional economic patterns, in the long run it strengthened the American economy. Well before the war was over, American ships had learned to evade the British navy with light, fast, easily maneuverable vessels. Indeed, the Yankees began to prey on British commerce with hundreds of privateers. For many shipowners, privateering proved to be more profitable than ordinary peacetime trade. More important in the long run, the end of imperial restrictions on American shipping opened up enormous new areas of trade to the nation. Enterprising merchants in New England and elsewhere began to develop new commerce in the Caribbean and in South America. By the mid-1780s, American merchants were developing an important new pattern of trade with Asia; and by the end of that decade, Yankee ships were regularly sailing from the eastern seaboard around Cape Horn to the Pacific coast of North America, there exchanging manufactured goods for hides and furs, and then proceeding across the Pacific to barter for goods in China. There was also a substantial increase in trade among the American states.

When English imports to America were cut off—first by the prewar boycott, then by the war itself—there were desperate efforts throughout the states to stimulate domestic manufacturing of certain necessities. No great industrial expansion resulted, but there were several signs of the economic growth that was to come

NEW PATTERNS OF TRADE

in the next century. Americans began to make their own cloth—"homespun," which became both patriotic and fashionable—to replace now unobtainable British fabrics. It would be some time before a large domestic textile industry would emerge, but the nation was never again to rely exclusively on foreign sources for its cloth. There was, of course, pressure to build factories for the manufacture of guns and ammunition. And there was a growing general awareness that America need not forever be dependent on other nations for manufactured goods.

The war stopped well short of revolutionizing the American economy; not until the nineteenth century would that begin to occur. But it did serve to release a wide range of entrepreneurial energies that, despite the temporary dislocations, encouraged growth and diversification.

THE CREATION OF STATE GOVERNMENTS

At the same time that Americans were struggling to win their independence on the battlefield, they were also struggling to create new institutions of government to replace the British system they had repudiated. That struggle continued for more than fifteen years, but its most important phase occurred during the war itself, at the state level.

THE ASSUMPTIONS OF REPUBLICANISM

If Americans agreed on nothing else when they began to build new governments for themselves, they agreed that those governments would be republican. To them, that meant a political system in which all power came from the people, rather than from some supreme authority (such as a king). The success of such a government depended on the nature of its citizenry. If the population consisted of sturdy, independent property owners imbued with civic virtue, then the republic could survive. If it consisted of a few powerful aristocrats and a great mass of dependent workers, then it would be in danger. From the beginning, therefore, the ideal of the small freeholder (the independent landowner) was basic to American political ideology.

IMPORTANCE OF CIVIC VIRTUE

Another crucial part of that ideology was the concept of equality. The Declaration of Independence had given voice to that idea in its most ringing phrase: "All men are created equal." It was a belief that stood in direct contrast to the old European assumption of an inherited aristocracy. The innate talents and energies of individuals, not their positions at birth, would determine their roles in society. Some people would inevitably be wealthier and more powerful than others. But all people would have to earn their success. There would be no equality of condition, but there would be equality of opportunity.

In reality, of course, the United States was never a nation in which all citizens were independent property holders. From the beginning, there was a sizable dependent labor force. White laborers enjoyed some of the privileges of citizenship. Black workers were allowed virtually none. American women remained both politically and economically subordinate. Native Americans were systematically exploited and displaced. Nor was there ever full equality of opportunity. American society was more open and more fluid than that of most European nations, but the condition of a person's birth was almost always a crucial determinant of success.

PERSISTENT INEQUALITY

Nevertheless, in embracing the assumptions of republicanism, Americans were adopting a powerful, even revolutionary, ideology, and their experiment in statecraft became a model for many other countries. It made the United States for a time the most admired and studied nation on earth.

THE FIRST STATE CONSTITUTIONS

The first and perhaps most basic decision about the character of government was that the constitutions were to be written down, because Americans believed the vagueness of England's unwritten constitution had produced corruption. The second decision was that the power of the executive, which Americans believed had grown too great in England, must be limited. Pennsylvania eliminated the executive altogether. Most other states inserted provisions that limited the power of governors to make appointments and veto legislation. Most states also prevented governors from dismissing the legislature. Most important, every state forbade the governor or any other executive officer from holding a seat in the legislature, thus ensuring that, unlike in England, the executive and legislative branches of government would remain wholly separate.

WRITTEN CONSTITUTIONS AND STRONG LEGISLATURES

But the new constitutions did not embrace direct popular rule. In Georgia and Pennsylvania, the legislature consisted of one popularly elected house. But in every other state, there was an upper and a lower chamber, and in most cases, the upper chamber was designed to represent the "higher orders" of society. There were property requirements for voters—some modest, some substantial—in all states.

REVISING STATE GOVERNMENTS

By the late 1770s, many Americans were growing concerned about the apparent divisiveness and instability of their new state governments. Most states were having trouble accomplishing anything. Many believed the problem was one of too much democracy. As a result, most of the states began to revise their constitutions to limit popular power. Massachusetts, which waited until 1780 to ratify its first constitution, was the first to act on the new concerns.

Two changes in particular differentiated the Massachusetts and later constitutions from the earlier ones. The first was a change in the process of constitution writing itself. Most of the first documents had been written by state legislatures and thus could easily be amended (or violated) by them. Massachusetts and, later, other states sought a way to protect the constitutions from ordinary politics and created the constitutional convention: a special assembly of the people that would meet only for the purpose of writing the constitution and that would never (except under extraordinary circumstances) meet again.

The second change was a significant strengthening of the executive, a reaction to what many Americans believed was the instability of the original state governments that had weak governors. The 1780 Massachusetts constitution made the governor one of the strongest in any state. He was to be elected directly by the people; he was to have a fixed salary (in other words, he would not be dependent on the goodwill of the legislature each year for his wages); he would have significant appointment powers and a veto over legislation. Other states followed. Those with weak or nonexistent upper houses strengthened or created them. Most increased the powers of the governor. Pennsylvania, which had no executive at all at first, now produced a strong one. By the late 1780s, almost every state had either revised its constitution or drawn up a new one in an effort to produce stability in government.

SHIFT TO STRONG EXECUTIVES

TOLERATION AND SLAVERY

The states moved far in the direction of complete religious freedom. Most Americans continued to believe that religion should play some role in government, but they did not wish to give special powers to any particular denomination. The privileges that churches had once enjoyed were now largely stripped away. In 1786, Virginia enacted the Statute of Religious Liberty, written by Thomas Jefferson, which called for the complete separation of church and state.

STATUTE OF RELIGIOUS LIBERTY

A FREE BLACK MAN John Singleton Copley, the great American portraitist of the Revolutionary age, painted this picture of a young African American in 1777–78. He was probably a worker on New England fishing boats who appeared in another Copley painting (*Watson and the Shark*). It is one of a relatively small number of portrayals of the free blacks in the North in this era, and one of even a smaller number that portrays them realistically and seriously. (*Head of a Negro, 1777–1778.* By John Singleton Copley. Oil on canvas, 53.3 × 41.3 cm. Founders Society Purchase, Gibbs-Williams Fund. Photograph © 1986 The Detroit Institute of Arts)

More difficult to resolve was the question of slavery. In areas where slavery was already weak—in New England, where there had never been many slaves, and in Pennsylvania, where the Quakers opposed slavery—it was abolished relatively early. Even in the South, there were some pressures to amend or even eliminate the institution; every state but South Carolina and Georgia prohibited further importation of slaves from abroad, and South Carolina banned the slave trade during the war. Virginia passed a law encouraging manumission (the freeing of slaves).

Nevertheless, slavery survived in all the southern and border states. There were several reasons: racist assumptions among whites about the inferiority of blacks; the enormous economic investments many white southerners had in their slaves; and the inability of even such men as Washington and Jefferson, who had moral misgivings about slavery, to envision any alternative to it. If slavery were abolished, what would happen to the black people in America? Few whites believed blacks could be integrated into American society as equals. In maintaining slavery, Jefferson once remarked, Americans were holding a "wolf by the ears." However unappealing it was to hold on to it, letting go would be even worse.

THE SEARCH FOR A NATIONAL GOVERNMENT

Americans were much quicker to agree on state institutions than they were on the structure of their national government. At first, most believed that the central government should remain a relatively weak and unimportant force and that each state would be virtually a sovereign nation. It was in response to such ideas that the Articles of Confederation emerged.

THE CONFEDERATION

The Articles of Confederation, which the Continental Congress had adopted in 1777, provided for a national government much like the one already in place. Congress remained the central—indeed the only—institution of national authority. Its powers expanded to give it authority to conduct wars and foreign relations and to appropriate, borrow, and issue money. But it did not have power to regulate trade, draft troops, or levy taxes directly on the people. For troops and taxes, it had to make formal requests to the state legislatures, which could—and often did—refuse them. There was no separate executive; the "president of the United States" was merely the presiding officer at the sessions of Congress. Each state had a single vote in Congress, and at least nine of the states had to approve the admission of a new state. All thirteen state legislatures had to approve any amendment of the Articles.

LIMITED POWER OF THE NATIONAL GOVERNMENT

During the process of ratifying the Articles of Confederation (which required approval by all thirteen states), broad disagreements over the plan became evident. The small states had insisted on equal state representation, but the larger states wanted representation to be based on population. The smaller states prevailed on that issue. More important, the states claiming western lands wished to keep them, but the rest of the states demanded that all such territory be turned over to the national government. New York and Virginia had to give up their western claims before the Articles were finally approved. They went into effect in 1781.

The Confederation, which existed from 1781 until 1789, was not a complete failure, but it was far from a success. It lacked adequate powers to deal with interstate issues or to enforce its will on the states, and it had little stature in the eyes of the world.

DIPLOMATIC FAILURES

POSTWAR DISPUTES WITH BRITAIN AND SPAIN

Evidence of the low esteem in which the rest of the world held the Confederation was its difficulty in persuading Great Britain (and to a lesser extent Spain) to live up to the terms of the peace treaty of 1783.

THE CONFLICT OVER WESTERN LANDS The American victory in the Revolution transformed the colonies into "states" within a new nation whose central government claimed at least some sovereignty over the individual units. An early conflict between national and state power took place over the state claims to western lands—claims established during the colonial period. This map shows the extensive western lands claimed by most of the original thirteen colonies to land in the West, and it illustrates the shifting nature of those claims over time—as colonies and then states transferred land to one another. The new national government gradually persuaded the states to give it control of the western lands, and in 1784 and 1785 it issued ordinances governing the process of settling those lands.

• *Why did the national government consider it important for the states to give up their claim to these territories?*

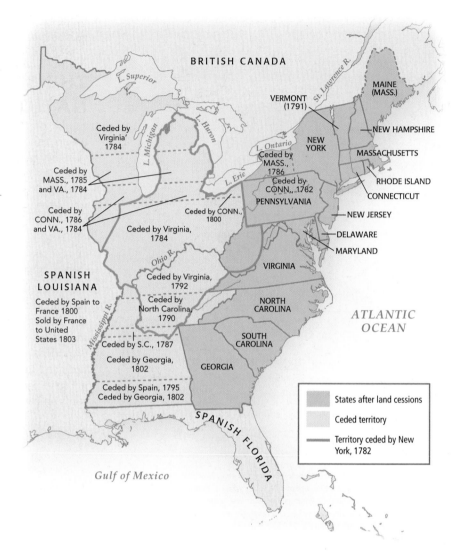

The British had promised to evacuate American territory, but British forces continued to occupy a string of frontier posts along the Great Lakes within the United States. Nor did the British honor their agreement to make restitution to slaveowners whose slaves the British army had confiscated. There were also disputes over the boundaries of the new nation. Americans wanted full access to British markets; England, however, placed sharp restrictions on that access.

In 1784, Congress sent John Adams as minister to London to resolve these differences, but Adams made no headway with the English, who were never sure whether he represented a single nation or thirteen different ones. Throughout the 1780s, the British government refused even to send a diplomatic minister to the American capital.

THE CONFEDERATION AND THE NORTHWEST

The Confederation's most important accomplishment was its resolution of controversies over the western lands. When the Revolution began, only a few thousand whites lived west of the Appalachian mountains; but by 1790 their numbers had increased to 120,000. The Confederation had to find a way to include these new settlements in the political structure of the nation. The landed states began to yield their western claims to the national government in 1781, and by 1784 the Confederation controlled enough land to permit Congress to begin making policy for the western lands.

The Ordinance of 1784, based on a proposal by Thomas Jefferson, divided the western territory into ten self-governing districts, each of which could petition Congress for statehood when its population equaled the number of free inhabitants of the smallest existing state. The provision reflected the desire of the Revolutionary generation to avoid creating second-class citizens in subordinate territories. Then, in the Ordinance of 1785, Congress created a system for surveying and selling the western lands. The territory north of the Ohio River was to be surveyed and marked off into neat rectangular townships, each divided into thirty-six identical sections. In every township, four sections were to be set aside for the United States; the revenue from the sale of one

THE ORDINANCES OF 1784 AND 1785

THE TREATY OF GREENVILLE These two documents represent the Treaty of Greenville of 1795, which settled a conflict between Native Americans and U.S. frontiersmen in the aftermath of the Indian defeat in the Battle of Fallen Timbers. The treaty ensured that much of the Northwestern Territory, once dominated by Indians, would now become territory for U.S. settlement. The document on the left contains signature marks of the Native American chiefs and warriors; on the right is a document that includes the signatures of General Anthony Wayne and several Wyandot Native American leaders. (The Granger Collection, NY)

(The Granger Collection, NY)

of the other sections was to support creation of a public school. Sections were to be sold at auction for no less than one dollar an acre.

Among the many important results of the Ordinance of 1785 was the establishment of an enduring pattern of dividing

THE GRID

up land for human use. Many such systems have emerged throughout history. Some have relied on natural boundaries (rivers, mountains, and other topographical features). Some have reflected informal claims of landlords over vast but vaguely defined territories. Some have rested on random allocations of acres, to be determined by individual landholders. But many Enlightenment thinkers began in the eighteenth century to imagine more precise, even mathematical, forms of land distribution, which required both careful surveying and a clear method for defining boundaries. The result was the method applied in 1785 in the Northwest Territory, which came to be known as the grid—the division of land into carefully measured and evenly divided squares or rectangles. This pattern of land distribution eventually became the norm for much of the land west of the Appalachians. It also became a model for the organization of many towns and cities, which distributed land in geometrical patterns within rectangular grids defined by streets. Although older land-distribution systems survive within the United States, the grid has become the most com-

mon form by which Americans impose human ownership and use on the landscape.

The original ordinances were highly favorable to land specu-

NORTHWEST ORDINANCE

lators and less so to ordinary settlers, many of whom could not afford the price of the land. Congress compounded the problem by selling much of the best land to the Ohio and Scioto land companies before making it available to anyone else. Criticism of these policies led to the passage in 1787 of another law governing western settlement—legislation that became known as the "Northwest Ordinance." The 1787 Ordinance abandoned the ten districts established in 1784 and created a single Northwest Territory out of the lands north of the Ohio; the territory could eventually be divided into between three and five territories. It also specified a population of 60,000 as a minimum for statehood, guaranteed freedom of religion and the right to trial by jury to residents of the Northwest, and prohibited slavery throughout the territory.

The western lands south of the Ohio River received less attention from Congress, and development was more chaotic there. The region that became Kentucky and Tennessee developed rapidly in the late 1770s, and in the 1780s speculators and settlers began setting up governments and asking for recognition as states. The Confederation Congress was never able to successfully resolve the conflicting claims in that region.

LAND SURVEY: ORDINANCE OF 1785 In the Ordinance of 1785, the Congress established a new system for surveying and selling western lands. These maps illustrate the way in which the lands were divided in an area of Ohio. Note the highly geometrical grid pattern that the ordinance imposed on these lands. Each of the squares in the map on the left was subdivided into 36 sections, as illustrated in the map at the lower right.

• *Why was this grid pattern so appealing to the planners of the western lands?*

The Seven Ranges First Area Survey
GEOGRAPHER'S LINE (BASE LINE)

* Four sections reserved for subsequent sales

Section 16 reserved for school funds

One Section = 640 acres (1 mile square)
A Half section = 320 acres
B Quarter section = 160 acres
C Half-quarter section = 80 acres
D & E Quarter-quarter section = 40 acres

One township (six miles square)

36	30	24	18	12	6
35	29*	23	17	11*	5
34	28	22	16	10	4
33	27	21	15	9	3
32	26*	20	14	8*	2
31	25	19	13	7	1

INDIANS AND THE WESTERN LANDS

On paper at least, the western land policies of the Confederation created a system that brought order and stability to the process of white settlement in the Northwest. But in reality, order and stability came slowly and at great cost, because much of the land the Confederation was neatly subdividing and offering for sale consisted of territory claimed by the Indians of the region. Congress tried to resolve that problem in 1784, 1785, and 1786 by persuading Iroquois, Choctaw, Chickasaw, and Cherokee leaders to sign treaties ceding substantial western lands in the North and South to the United States. But those agreements proved ineffective. In 1786, the leadership of the Iroquois Confederacy repudiated the treaty it had signed two years earlier and threatened to attack white settlements in the disputed lands. Other tribes had never accepted the treaties affecting them and continued to resist white movement into their lands.

Violence between whites and Indians on the Northwest frontier reached a crescendo in the early 1790s. In 1790 and again in 1791, a group of tribes led by the famed Miami warrior Little

BATTLE OF FALLEN TIMBERS Turtle defeated United States forces in two major battles near what is now the western border of Ohio; in the second of those battles, on November 4, 1791, 630 white Americans died in fighting at the Wabash River (the greatest military victory Indians had ever or would ever again achieve in their battles with whites). Efforts to negotiate a settlement failed

because of the Miami's insistence that no treaty was possible unless it forbade white settlement west of the Ohio River. Negotiations did not resume until after General Anthony Wayne led 4,000 soldiers into the Ohio Valley in 1794 and defeated the Indians in the Battle of Fallen Timbers.

A year later, the Miami signed the Treaty of Greenville, ceding substantial new lands to the United States (which was now operating under the Constitution of 1789) in exchange for a formal acknowledgment of their claim to the territory they had managed to retain. In doing so, the United States was affirming that Indian lands could be ceded only by the tribes themselves. That hard-won assurance, however, proved a frail protection against the pressure of white expansion westward in later years.

DEBTS, TAXES, AND DANIEL SHAYS

The postwar depression, which lasted from 1784 to 1787, increased the perennial American problem of **POSTWAR DEPRESSION** an inadequate money supply, a problem that weighed particularly heavily on debtors. In dealing with this problem, Congress most clearly demonstrated its weakness.

The Confederation itself had an enormous outstanding debt that it had accumulated at home and abroad during the Revolutionary War. It had few means with which to pay it, having no power to tax. It could only make requisitions of the states, and it received only about one-sixth of the money it requisitioned.

The fragile new nation was faced with the grim prospect of defaulting on its obligations.

This alarming possibility brought to the fore a group of leaders who would play a crucial role in the shaping of the republic for several decades. Committed nationalists, they sought ways to increase the powers of the central government and to meet its financial obligations. Robert Morris, the head of the Confederation's treasury; Alexander Hamilton, his young protégé; James Madison of Virginia; and others called for a

POLITICAL DISPUTES OVER ECONOMIC ISSUES

"continental impost"—a 5 percent duty on imported goods to be levied by Congress and used to fund the debt. Many Americans, however, feared that the impost plan would concentrate too much financial power in the hands of Morris and his allies in Philadelphia. Congress failed to approve the impost in 1781 and again in 1783. Angry and discouraged, the nationalists largely withdrew from any active involvement in the Confederation.

The states had war debts, too, and they generally relied on increased taxation to pay them. But poor farmers, already bur-

DANIEL SHAYS AND JOB SHATTUCK Shays and Shattuck were the principal leaders of the 1786 uprising by poor farmers in Massachusetts demanding relief from their indebtedness. Shattuck led an insurrection in the east, which collapsed when he was captured on November 30. Shays organized the rebellion in the west, which continued until the state militia dispersed the rebels in late February 1787. The following year, state authorities pardoned Shays; even before that, the legislature responded to the rebellion by providing some relief to the impoverished farmers. These drawings are part of a hostile account of the rebellion published in 1787 in a Boston almanac. (National Portrait Gallery, Smithsonian Institution/Art Resource, NY)

dened by debt and now burdened again by new taxes, considered such policies unfair, even tyrannical. They demanded that the state governments issue paper currency to increase the money supply and make it easier for them to meet their obligations. Resentment was especially high among farmers in New England, who felt that the states were squeezing them to enrich already wealthy bondholders in Boston and other towns.

Throughout the late 1780s, therefore, mobs of distressed farmers rioted periodically in various parts of New England. Dissidents in the Connecticut Valley and the Berkshire Hills of Massachusetts, many of them Revolutionary veterans, rallied

SHAYS'S REBELLION

behind Daniel Shays, a former captain in the Continental army. Shays issued a set of demands that included paper money, tax relief, a moratorium on debts, the relocation of the state capital from Boston to the interior, and the abolition of imprisonment for debt. During the summer of 1786, the Shaysites concentrated on preventing the collection of debts, private or public, and used force to keep courts from sitting and sheriffs from selling confiscated property. In Boston, members of the legislature, including Samuel Adams, denounced Shays and his men as rebels and traitors. When winter came, the rebels advanced on Springfield, hoping to seize weapons from the arsenal there. An army of state militiamen, financed by a loan from wealthy merchants, set out from Boston to confront them. In January 1787, this army met Shays's band and dispersed his ragged troops.

As a military enterprise, Shays's Rebellion was a failure, although it produced some concessions to the aggrieved farmers. Shays and his lieutenants, at first sentenced to death, were later pardoned, and Massachusetts offered the protesters some tax relief and a postponement of debt payments. The rebellion had more important consequences for the future of the United States, however, for it added urgency to a movement already gathering support throughout the new nation—the movement to produce a new, national constitution.

LITTLE TURTLE Little Turtle led the Miami confederacy in its wars with the United States in what is now Ohio and Indiana in the early 1790s. For a time he seemed almost invincible, but in 1794 Little Turtle was defeated in the Battle of Fallen Timbers. In this sketch (a rough copy of a painting attributed to Gilbert Stuart), Little Turtle wears a medal bearing the likeness of George Washington, awarded him by the United States after the signing of the Treaty of Greenville. (Bettmann/Corbis)

LOOKING BACK

Between a small, inconclusive battle on a village green in New England in 1775 and a momentous surrender at Yorktown in 1781, the American people fought a great and terrible war against the mightiest military nation in the world. No one outside America, and few within it, would have predicted in 1775 that the makeshift armies of the colonies could withstand the armies and navies of the British Empire. But a combination of luck, brilliance, determination, and timely aid from abroad allowed the Patriots, as they began to call themselves, to make full use of the advantages of fighting on their home soil and to frustrate British designs time and again.

The war was not just a historic military event. It was also a great political one, for it propelled the colonies to unite, to organize, and—in July 1776—to declare their independence. Having done so, they fought with even greater determination, defending now not just a set of principles, but an actual, fledgling nation. By the end of the war, they had created new governments at both the state and national level and had begun experimenting with new political forms that would distinguish the United States from any previous nation in history.

The war was also important for its effects on American society—for the way it shook (although never overturned) the existing social order; for the way it caused women to question (although seldom openly to challenge) their place in society; and for the way it spread notions of liberty and freedom throughout a society that in the past had often been rigidly hierarchical and highly deferential. Even African American slaves absorbed some of the ideas of the Revolution, although it would be many years before they would be in any position to make very much use of them.

Victory in the American Revolution solved many of the problems of the new nation, but it also produced others. What should the United States do about its relations with the Indians and with its neighbors to the north and south? What should it do about the distribution of western lands? What should it do about slavery? How should it balance its commitment to liberty with its need for order? These questions bedeviled the new national government in its first years of existence and ultimately led Americans to create a new political order. •

SIGNIFICANT EVENTS

	Thomas Paine's *Common Sense* published		French-American alliance established	Patriots defeat Tories at King's Mountain, South Carolina	Cornwallis surrenders at Yorktown
	Declaration of Independence debated and signed (July 2–4)		War shifts to the South		Articles of Confederation ratified
1775	**1776**	**1777**	**1778**	**1780**	**1781**
Second Continental Congress meets	Battle of Trenton	Articles of Confederation adopted		Cornwallis defeats Gates at Camden, South Carolina	
George Washington appointed to command American forces	First state constitutions written	Washington camps at Valley Forge for winter		Massachusetts state constitution ratified	
Battle of Bunker Hill		Burgoyne surrenders to Gates at Saratoga		Slavery abolished in Pennsylvania	

PEOPLE/PLACES/EVENTS

RECALL AND REFLECT

1. What questions did the Second Continental Congress debate, and how did it answer them?

2. What was the impact of Thomas Paine's *Common Sense* on Americans' view of the war with Britain?

3. How and why were the Americans able to prevail in their War for Independence?

4. What were the ideological ideals of the new state and national governments, and how did those ideals compare with the realities of American society?

5. What was the purpose of the Articles of Confederation?

6. How did the Revolution affect the role of religion and the position of churches in American society?

Treaty of Paris with Great Britain recognizes American independence

Slavery abolished in Massachusetts

Northwest Ordinance enacted

1781-1784	1783	1784-1785	1786-1787	1787	1794
States cede western lands to Confederation		First ordinances establishing procedures for settling western lands enacted	Shays's Rebellion in Massachusetts		Anthony Wayne defeats Indians in Ohio

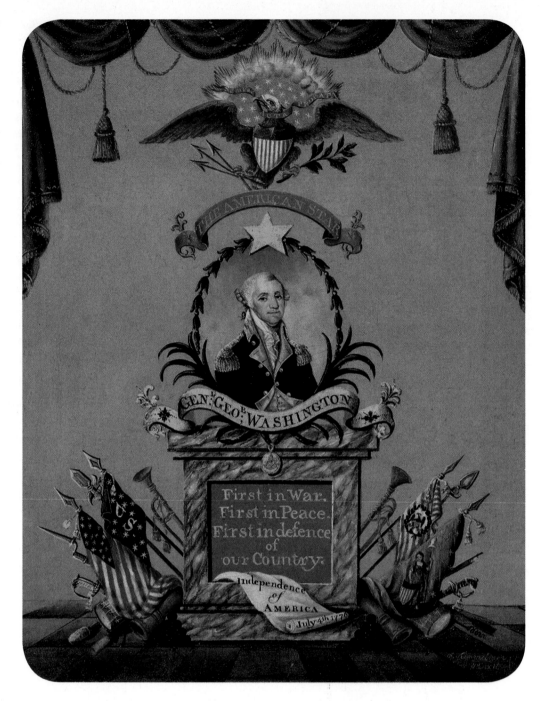

THE AMERICAN STAR Frederick Kemmelmeyer painted this tribute to George Washington sometime in the 1790s. It was one of many efforts by artists and others to create an iconography for the new republic. (The Metropolitan Museum of Art, Gift of Edgar William and Bernice Chrysler Garbisch, 1962. (62.256.7) Photograph © 1981 The Metropolitan Museum of Art)

6 | THE CONSTITUTION AND THE NEW REPUBLIC

BY THE LATE 1780s, most Americans had grown deeply dissatisfied with the Confederation government: with its inability to deal with factions and instability, its powerlessness (as shown in dealing with Shays's Rebellion), and its failure to handle economic problems effectively. A decade earlier, Americans had deliberately avoided creating a strong national government, fearing that it would encroach on the sovereignty of the individual states. Now they reconsidered. In 1787, they produced a new constitution that created a new, powerful national government.

The new government created in 1787 has survived for more than two centuries as one of the stablest and most successful in the world. Many Americans have described the Constitution's provisions as unassailable "fundamental law," from which all public policies, all political principles, all solutions of controversies must spring. Yet the adoption of the Constitution did not complete the creation of the republic; it only defined the terms in which debate over the future of government would continue. Americans may have agreed that the

SETTING THE STAGE

Constitution was a nearly perfect document, but they disagreed—at times fundamentally—on what that document meant. They still do. Out of such disagreements emerged the first great political battles of the new nation.

LOOKING AHEAD

1. What were the most important questions debated at the Constitutional Convention of 1787, and how were they resolved?
2. What were the main tenets of the Federalist and Antifederalist arguments on ratification of the Constitution?
3. What were the origins of America's "first party system"?

FRAMING A NEW GOVERNMENT

So unpopular and ineffectual had the Confederation Congress become by the mid-1780s that it began to lead an almost waiflike existence. In 1783, its members timidly withdrew from Philadelphia to escape from the clamor of army veterans demanding back pay. They took refuge for a while in Princeton, New Jersey, then moved to Annapolis, and in 1785 settled in New York. Through all of this, the delegates were often conspicuous largely by their absence. Only with great difficulty did Congress secure a quorum to ratify the treaty with Great Britain ending the Revolutionary War. Eighteen members, representing only eight states, voted on the Confederation's most important piece of legislation, the Northwest Ordinance. In the meantime, a major public debate was beginning over the future of the Confederation.

A Weak Central Government

ADVOCATES OF CENTRALIZATION

Weak and unpopular though the Confederation was, it had for a time satisfied a great many—probably a majority—of the people. They believed they had fought the Revolutionary War to avert the danger of what they considered remote and tyrannical authority; now they wanted to keep political power centered in the states, where they could carefully and closely control it.

But during the 1780s, some of the wealthiest and most powerful groups in the country began to clamor for a more genuinely national government capable of dealing with the nation's problems—particularly the economic problems that most directly afflicted them. Some military men, many of them members of the exclusive and hereditary Society of the Cincinnati (formed by Revolutionary army officers in 1783), were disgruntled at the refusal of Congress to fund their pensions. They began aspiring to influence and invigorate the national government; some even envisioned a form of military dictatorship and flirted briefly (in 1783, in the so-called Newburgh Conspiracy) with a direct challenge to Congress, until George Washington intervened and blocked the potential rebellion.

Supporters of a Strong National Government

American manufacturers—the artisans and "mechanics" of the nation's cities and towns—wanted to replace the various state tariffs with a uniformly high national duty. Merchants and shippers wanted to replace the thirteen different (and largely

GEORGE WASHINGTON AT MOUNT VERNON Washington was in his first term as president in 1790 when an anonymous folk artist painted this view of his home at Mount Vernon, Virginia. Washington appears in uniform, along with members of his family, on the lawn. After he retired from office in 1797, Washington returned happily to his plantation and spent the two years before his death in 1799 "amusing myself in agricultural and rural pursuits." He also played host to an endless stream of visitors from throughout the country and Europe. (Gift of Edgar William and Bernice Chrysler Garbisch, © 1998 Board of Trustees, National Gallery of Art, Washington)

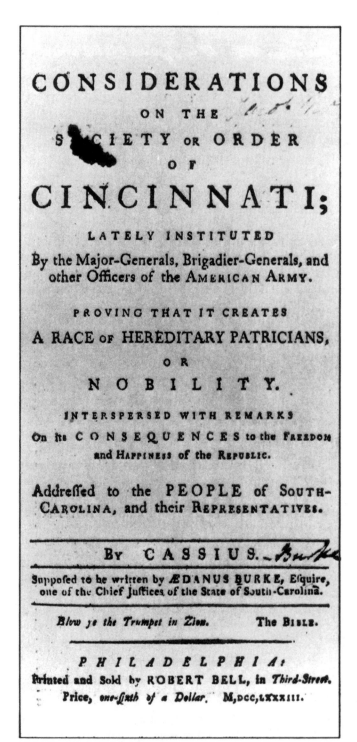

A BROADSIDE AGAINST "NOBILITY" This 1783 pamphlet was one of many expressions of the broad democratic sentiment that the Revolution unleashed in American society. The Society of the Cincinnati was an organization created shortly after the Revolution by men who had served as high-ranking officers in the Patriot army. To many Americans, however, the society—membership in which was to be hereditary—looked suspiciously like the inherited aristocracies of England. This pamphlet, printed in Philadelphia but intended for South Carolinians, warns of the dangers the society supposedly posed to the "Freedom and Happiness of the Republic." (New York Public Library)

ineffective) state commercial policies with a single, national one. Land speculators wanted the "Indian menace" finally removed from their western tracts. People who were owed money wanted to stop the states from issuing paper money, which would lower the value of what they received in payment. Investors in Confederation securities wanted the government to fund the debt and thus enhance the value of their securities. Large property owners looked for protection from the threat of mobs, a threat that seemed particularly menacing in light of such episodes as Shays's Rebellion. This fear of disorder and violence expressed a tension between the resolute defense of individual rights, which was a core principle of the Revolution and found reflection in the Bill of Rights, and the public concern for safety and security, which the occasional chaos of the Confederation period had reinforced. Frequent conflicts between liberty and order became, and remain, a central feature of American democracy.

By 1786, these diverse demands had grown so powerful that the issue was no longer whether the Confederation should be changed but how drastic the changes should be. Even the defenders of the existing system reluctantly came to agree that the government needed strengthening at its weakest point—its lack of power to tax.

The most resourceful of the reformers was Alexander Hamilton, political genius, New York lawyer, onetime military aide to General Washington, and illegitimate son of a Scottish merchant in the West Indies. From the beginning, Hamilton had been unhappy with the Articles of Confederation and the weak central government they had created. He now called for a national convention to overhaul the entire document. He found an important ally in James Madison of Virginia, who persuaded the Virginia legislature to convene an interstate conference on commercial questions. Only five states sent delegates to the meeting, held in Annapolis, Maryland, in 1786; but the delegates approved a proposal drafted by Hamilton (who was representing New York) recommending that Congress call a convention of special delegates from all the states to gather in Philadelphia the next year and consider ways to "render the constitution of the Federal government adequate to the exigencies of the union."

ALEXANDER HAMILTON

At that moment, in 1786, there seemed little possibility that the Philadelphia convention would attract any more interest than the meeting at Annapolis had attracted. Only by winning the support of George Washington, the centralizers believed, could they hope to prevail. But Washington at first showed little interest in joining the cause. Then, early in 1787, the news of Shays's Rebellion spread throughout the nation. Thomas Jefferson, then the American minister in Paris, was not alarmed. "I hold," he confided in a letter to James Madison, "that a little rebellion, now and then, is a good thing, and as necessary in the political world as storms in the physical." But Washington took the news less calmly. In May, he left his home at Mount Vernon in Virginia for the Constitutional Convention in Philadelphia. His support gave the meeting immediate credibility.

A Divided Convention

Fifty-five men, representing all the states except Rhode Island, attended one or more sessions of the convention that sat in the Philadelphia State House from May to September 1787. These "Founding Fathers," as they would later become known, were relatively young men; their average age was forty-four, and only one delegate (Benjamin Franklin, then eighty-one) was of advanced age. They were well educated by the

THE FOUNDING FATHERS

standards of their time. Most represented the great propertied interests of the country, and many feared what one of them called the "turbulence and follies" of democracy. Yet all were also products of the American Revolution and retained the Revolutionary suspicion of concentrated power.

The convention unanimously chose Washington to preside over its sessions and then closed its business to the public and the press. The members then ruled that each state delegation would have a single vote. Major decisions would not require unanimity, as they did in Congress, but only a simple majority. Virginia, the most populous state, sent the best-prepared delegation to Philadelphia. James Madison (thirty-six years old) was its intellectual leader. He had devised a detailed plan for a new "national" government, and the Virginians used it to control the agenda from the moment the convention began.

Edmund Randolph of Virginia began the discussion by proposing that "a national government ought to be established, consisting of a supreme Legislative, Executive, and Judiciary." Despite its vagueness, it was a drastic proposal. It called for the creation of a government very different from the existing

THE VIRGINIA PLAN

Confederation, which, among other things, had no executive branch. But so committed were the delegates to fundamental reform that they approved this resolution after only perfunctory debate. Then Randolph introduced the details of Madison's plan. The Virginia Plan (as it came to be known) called for a new national legislature consisting of two houses. In the lower house, the states would be represented in proportion to their population; thus the largest state (Virginia) would have about ten times as many representatives as the smallest (Delaware). Members of the upper house were to be elected by the lower house under no rigid system of representation; thus some of the smaller states might at times have no members at all in the upper house.

The proposal aroused immediate opposition among delegates from Delaware, New Jersey, and other small states. Some responded by arguing that Congress had called the convention "for the sole and express purpose of revising the Articles of

> 66 A LITTLE REBELLION, NOW AND THEN, IS A GOOD THING, AND AS NECESSARY IN THE POLITICAL WORLD AS STORMS IN THE PHYSICAL. 99
>
> **THOMAS JEFFERSON**

> 66 MANKIND MAY HEREAFTER, FROM THIS UNFORTUNATE INSTANCE, DESPAIR OF ESTABLISHING GOVERNMENTS BY HUMAN WISDOM, AND LEAVE IT TO CHANCE, WAR AND CONQUEST. 99
>
> **BENJAMIN FRANKLIN**

Confederation" and had no authority to do more than that. Eventually, however, William Paterson of New Jersey submitted a substantive alternative to the Virginia Plan, a proposal for a "federal" as opposed to a "national" government. The New Jersey Plan would preserve the existing one-house legislature, in which each state had equal representation, but it gave Congress expanded powers to tax and to regulate commerce. The delegates voted to table Paterson's proposal, but not without taking note of the substantial support for it among small-state representatives.

The Virginia Plan remained the basis for discussion. But its supporters realized they would have to make concessions to the small states if the convention was ever to reach a general agreement. They soon conceded an important point by agreeing to permit the members of the upper house to be elected by the state legislatures rather than by the lower house of the national legislature. Thus each state would be sure of always having at least one member in the upper house.

But many questions remained. Would the states be equally represented in the upper house, or would the large states have

SMALL STATES VERSUS LARGE STATES

more members than the small ones? Would slaves (who could not vote) be counted as part of the population in determining the size of a state's representation in Congress, or were they to be considered simple property? Delegates from states with large and apparently permanent slave populations—especially those from South Carolina—wanted to have it both ways. They argued that slaves should be considered persons in determining representation. But they wanted slaves to be considered property if the new government were to levy taxes on each state on the basis of population. Representatives from states where slavery had disappeared or was expected soon to disappear argued that slaves should be included in calculating taxation but not representation. No one argued seriously for giving slaves citizenship or the right to vote.

Compromise

The delegates bickered for weeks. By the end of June, as both temperature and tempers rose to uncomfortable heights, the convention seemed in danger of collapsing. Benjamin Franklin, who remained a calm voice of conciliation through the summer, warned that if they failed, the delegates would "become a reproach and by-word down to future ages. And what is worse, mankind may hereafter, from this unfortunate instance, despair of establishing governments by human wisdom, and leave it to chance, war and conquest." Partly because of Franklin's soothing presence, the delegates refused to give up.

Finally, on July 2, the convention agreed to create a "grand committee," with a single delegate from each state (and with Franklin as chairman), to resolve the disagreements. The committee produced a proposal that became the basis of the "Great Compromise." Its most important achievement was resolving the difficult problem of representation. The proposal called for a legislature in which the states would be represented in the lower house on the basis of population. Each slave would count as three-fifths of a free person in determining the basis for both representation and direct taxation. (The three-fifths formula was based on the false assumption that a slave was three-fifths as productive as a free worker and thus contributed only three-fifths as much wealth to the state.) The committee proposed that in the upper house, the states should be represented equally with two members apiece. The proposal broke the deadlock. On July 16, 1787, the convention voted to accept the compromise.

THE GREAT COMPROMISE

"THE GRAND CONVENTION" The engraver John Norman created this imagined view of the Constitutional Convention in 1787 for the *Weatherwise's Federal Almanack*, whose title suggested its pro-Constitution political leanings. Norman was familiar with the interior of the hall in Philadelphia where the convention took place, which gave this engraving a sense of reality—even though Norman never attended a session of the convention. (Hall of Representatives, Washington, D.C./Bridgeman Art Library International)

Over the next few weeks, the convention as a whole agreed to another important compromise on the explosive issue of slavery. The representatives of the southern states feared that the power to regulate trade might interfere with their agrarian economy, which relied heavily on sales abroad, and with slavery. In response, the convention agreed that the new legislature would not be permitted to tax exports; Congress would also be forbidden to impose a duty of more than $10 a head on imported slaves, and it would have no authority to stop the slave trade for twenty years. To those delegates who viewed the continued existence of slavery as an affront to the principles of the new nation, this was a large and difficult concession. They agreed to it because they feared that without it the Constitution would fail.

The convention chose to ignore differences of opinion it was unable to resolve, leaving important questions alive that would surface again in later years. The Constitution provided no definition of citizenship. Most important was the absence of a list of individual rights, which would restrain the powers of the national government in the way that bills of rights restrained the state governments. Madison opposed the idea, arguing that specifying rights that were reserved to the people would, in effect, limit those rights. Other delegates, however, feared that without such protections the national government might abuse its new authority.

THE CONSTITUTION OF 1787

Many people contributed to the creation of the American Constitution, but the single most important of them was James Madison—the most creative political thinker of his generation. Perhaps Madison's most important achievement was in helping

JAMES MADISON

resolve two important philosophical questions that had served as obstacles to the creation of an effective national government: the question of sovereignty and the question of limiting power.

The question of sovereignty had been one of the chief sources of friction between the colonies and Great Britain, and it continued to trouble Americans as they attempted to create their own government. How could both the national government and the state governments exercise sovereignty at the same time? Where did ultimate sovereignty lie? The answer, Madison and his contemporaries decided, was that all power, at all levels of government, flowed ultimately from the people. Thus neither the federal government nor the state governments were truly sovereign. All of them derived their authority from below. The opening phrase of the Constitution (devised by Gouverneur Morris) was "We the people of the United States"—an expression of the belief that the new government derived its power not from the states but from its citizens.

THE QUESTION OF SOVEREIGNTY

Resolving the problem of sovereignty made possible one of the distinctive features of the Constitution—its distribution of powers between the national and state governments. It was, Madison wrote at the time, "in strictness, neither a national nor a federal Constitution, but a composition of both." The Constitution and the government it created were to be the "supreme law" of the land; no state would have the authority to defy it. The federal government was to have broad powers, including the power to tax, to regulate commerce, to control the currency, and to pass such laws as would be "necessary and proper" for carrying out its other responsibilities. Gone was the stipulation of the Articles that "each State shall retain every power, jurisdiction, and right not expressly delegated to the United States in Congress assembled." On the other hand, the Constitution

THE MEANING OF THE CONSTITUTION

THE Constitution has inspired debate from the moment it was drafted. Some people argue that the Constitution is a flexible document intended to evolve in response to society's evolution. Others argue that it has a fixed meaning, rooted in the "original intent" of the framers, and that to move beyond that is to deny its value.

Historians, too, disagree about why the Constitution was written and what it meant. To some scholars, the creation of the federal system was an effort to preserve the ideals of the Revolution and to create a strong national government capable of exercising real authority. To others, the Constitution was an effort to protect the economic interests of existing elites, even at the cost of betraying the principles of the Revolution. To still others, the Constitution was designed to protect individual freedom and to limit the power of the federal government.

The first influential exponent of the heroic view of the Constitution as the culmination of the Revolution was John Fiske. In *The Critical Period of American History* (1888), Fiske described the many problems that beset the nation under the Articles of Confederation: economic difficulties, the weakness and ineptitude of the new national government, threats from abroad, interstate jealousies, and widespread lawlessness. Only the timely adoption of the Constitution, Fiske claimed, saved the young republic from disaster.

In *An Economic Interpretation of the Constitution of the United States (1913)*, Charles A. Beard challenged Fiske's view. According to Beard, the 1780s had been a "critical period" primarily for conservative businessmen who feared that the decentralized political structure of the republic imperiled their financial position. Such men, he claimed, wanted a government able to promote industry and trade, protect private property, and make good the public debt—much of which was owed to them. The Constitution was,

Beard claimed, "an economic document drawn with superb skill by men whose property interests were immediately at stake" and who won its ratification over the opposition of a majority of the people.

A series of powerful challenges to Beard's thesis emerged in the 1950s, as many scholars began to argue that the Constitution was not an effort to preserve property but, rather, an enlightened effort to ensure stability and order. Examining the debate between the Federalists and the Antifederalists, Forrest McDonald, in *We the People* (1958), concluded that there was no consistent relationship between wealth and property and support for the Constitution. Instead, opinion on the new system was far more likely to reflect local and regional interests. The cumulative effect of these challenges greatly weakened Beard's argument; few historians any longer accepted his thesis without reservation.

In the 1960s, a new group of scholars began to revive an economic interpretation of the

accepted the existence of separate states and left important powers in their hands.

In addition to solving the question of sovereignty, the Constitution produced a solution to a problem that was particularly troubling to Americans: the problem of concentrated authority. Nothing so frightened the leaders of the new nation as the prospect of creating a tyrannical government. Indeed, that fear had been one of the chief obstacles to the creation of a national government at all. Drawing from the ideas of the French philosopher Baron de Montesquieu, most Americans had long believed that the best way, perhaps the only way, to avoid tyranny was to keep government close to the people. A republic, they thought, must remain confined to a relatively small area; a large nation would breed corruption and despotism because the rulers would be so distant from most of the people that there would be no way to control them. In the first years of the new American nation, these assumptions had led to the belief that the individual states must remain sovereign and that a strong national government would be dangerous.

Madison, however, helped break the grip of these assumptions by arguing that a large republic would be less, not more, likely to produce tyranny, because it would contain so many different factions that no single group would ever be able to

dominate it. (In this, he drew from—among other sources—the Scottish philosopher David Hume.) This idea of many centers of power "checking each other" and preventing any single, despotic authority from emerging not only made possible the idea of a large republic, but also helped shape the internal structure of the federal government. The Constitution's most distinctive feature was its "separation of powers" within the government, its creation of "checks and balances" among the legislative, executive, and judicial branches. The array of forces within the government would constantly compete with (and often frustrate) one another. Congress would have two chambers, the Senate and the House of Representatives, each with members elected in a different way and for different terms, and each checking the other, since both would have to agree before any law could be passed. The president would have the power to veto acts of Congress. The federal courts would have protection from both the executive and the legislature because judges and justices, once appointed by the president and confirmed by the Senate, would serve for life.

SEPARATION OF POWERS

The "federal" structure of the government, which divided power between the states and the nation, and the system of "checks and balances," which divided power among various

(National Archives)

Constitution—one that differed from Beard's in important ways but that nevertheless emphasized social and economic factors as motives for supporting the federal system. Jackson Turner Main argued, in *The Anti-federalists* (1961), that supporters of the Constitution were "cosmopolitan commercialists," eager to advance the economic development of the nation; the Antifederalists, by contrast, were "agrarian localists," fearful of centralization. Gordon Wood, in *The Creation of the American Republic* (1969), suggested that the debate over the state constitutions in the 1770s and 1780s reflected profound social divisions and that those same divisions helped shape the argument over the federal Constitution. The Federalists, Wood suggested, were largely traditional aristocrats deeply concerned over the instability of life under the Articles of Confederation and particularly alarmed by the decline in popular deference toward social elites. The creation of the Constitution, Wood argued, was part of a larger search to create a legitimate political leadership based on the existing social hierarchy.

Historians have continued to examine the question of "intent." Did the framers intend a strong, centralized political system; or did they intend to create a decentralized system with a heavy emphasis on individual rights? The answer, according to Jack Rakove in *Original Meanings* (1996) and *Revolutionaries* (2010), is both—and many other things as well. The Constitution, Rakove argues, was the result of a long and vigorous debate through which the views of many different groups found their way into the document. James Madison, a strong nationalist, believed that only a powerful central government could preserve stability in a large nation. Alexander Hamilton also saw the Constitution as a way to protect order and property and to defend the nation against the dangers of too much liberty. But if Madison and Hamilton feared too much liberty, they also feared too little. And that made them receptive to the vigorous demands of the "Antifederalists" for protections of individual rights, which culminated in the Bill of Rights. The Constitution is not, Rakove argues, "infinitely malleable." But neither does it have a fixed meaning that can be a reliable guide to how we interpret it today. •

UNDERSTAND, ANALYZE, AND EVALUATE

1. Is the Constitution a conservative, liberal, or radical document? Did the framers consider the Constitution something "finished" (with the exception of constitutional amendments), or did they consider it a document that would evolve in response to changes in society over time?

2. Which parts of the Constitution suggest that the framers' intent was to create a strong, centralized political system? Which parts suggest that the framers' intent was to create a decentralized system with heavy emphasis on individual rights?

3. Although many amendments have been proposed, only twenty-seven amendments have been added to the Constitution. Why do you think so few have been added?

elements within the national government itself, were designed to protect the United States from the kind of despotism Americans believed had emerged in England. But they were also designed to protect the nation from another kind of despotism, perhaps equally menacing: the tyranny of the people. Fear of the "mob," of an "excess of democracy," was at least as important to the framers as fear of a single tyrant. Shays's Rebellion had been only one example, they believed, of what could happen if a nation did not defend itself against the unchecked exercise of popular will. Thus, in the new government, only the members of the House of Representatives would be elected directly by the people. Senators, the president, and federal judges would be insulated in varying degrees from the public.

On September 17, 1787, thirty-nine delegates signed the Constitution, doubtless sharing the feelings that Benjamin Franklin expressed at the end: "Thus I consent, Sir, to this Constitution, because I expect no better, and because I am not sure it is not the best."

> 66 THUS I CONSENT, SIR, TO THIS CONSTITUTION, BECAUSE I EXPECT NO BETTER, AND BECAUSE I AM NOT SURE IT IS NOT THE BEST. 99
>
> **BENJAMIN FRANKLIN**

THE LIMITS OF THE CONSTITUTION

The Constitution of 1789 was a document that established a democratic republic for white people, mostly white men. Indians and African Americans, the two largest population groups sharing the lands of the United States with Anglo-Americans, enjoyed virtually none of the rights and privileges provided to the white population. Native Americans had at least the semblance of a legal status within the nation, through treaties that assured them lands that would be theirs forever. But most of these treaties did not survive for long, and the Indians found themselves driven farther and farther west with little of the protection that the government had promised them.

Among the white leaders of the United States, there were eminent figures who believed Indians could in fact join the republic as citizens. Jefferson was among them, believing that Indians could be taught the ways of "civilization." Jefferson, and other Americans with good intentions, sought to teach the Indians to live as white

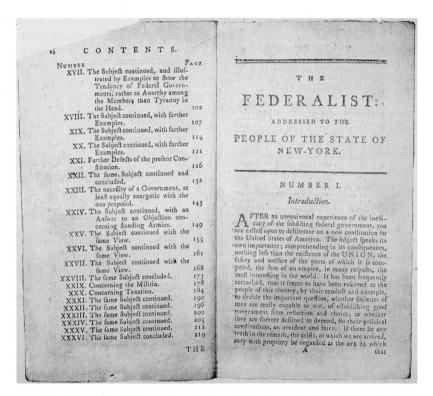

FEDERALIST #1 The Federalist Papers, gathered together here in a book distributed to the people of New York, began as essays, letters, and articles published in newspapers throughout America during the debate over the Constitution. Its authors—James Madison, Alexander Hamilton, and John Jay—were defenders of the new Constitution and wrote these essays to explain its value and importance. They remain today one of the most important American contributions to political theory. (The Granger Collection, New York)

African Americans. He was an uneasy defender of slavery, worrying about excluding "a whole race of men" from the natural rights that Jefferson himself had done so much to promote. But he could never accept the idea that black men and black women could attain the level of knowledge and intelligence of white people. Jefferson's long romantic relationship with a black woman, Sally Hemmings, did nothing to change his mind. Hemmings was a light-skinned woman who was a slave on Jefferson's plantation in Virginia. Jefferson lived with her after the death of his wife and fathered several of her children. But his intimate relationship with the Hemmings family did not ultimately change his postion on slavery. Unlike George Washington, who freed his slaves after his death, Jefferson (deeply in debt) required his heirs to sell his slaves after he died (after liberating the Hemmings family). Not until the end of the Civil War were black men and black women eligible to live as citizens in the United States, and even then with only partial rights until a century later.

FEDERALISTS AND ANTIFEDERALISTS

The delegates at Philadelphia had greatly exceeded their instructions from Congress and the states. Instead of making simple revisions to the Articles of Confederation, they had produced a plan for a completely different form of government. They feared, therefore, that the Constitution might never be ratified under the rules of the Articles of Confederation, which required unanimous approval by the state legislatures. So the convention changed the rules. The Constitution specified that the new government would come into existence among the ratifying states when any nine of the thirteen had ratified it. The delegates recommended to Congress that special state conventions, not state legislatures, consider the document. They were required to vote "yes" or "no" on the document. They could make no changes until after the Constitution was ratified by the required number of states, at which point the Constitution's amendment process could be used (as it was for the Bill of Rights).

The old Confederation Congress, now overshadowed by the events in Philadelphia, passively accepted the convention's work and submitted it to the states for approval. All the state legislatures except Rhode Island's elected delegates to ratifying conventions, most of which began meeting by early 1788. Even before the ratifying conventions convened, however, a great national debate on the new Constitution had begun—in the state legislatures, in mass meetings, in the columns of newspapers, and in ordinary conversations. Occasionally, passions rose to the point that opposing factions came to blows. In at least one place—Albany, New York—such clashes resulted in injuries and death.

Americans did. Efforts to teach them Anglo farming methods were based on sedentary farms that relied on men doing the farming and women caring for the home. Indians had no interest in such ways and preferred to retain their own traditional cultures. Their repudiation of white civilization contributed to the erosion of support among white Americans. Indians were not granted citizenship of the United States until the 1920s.

Far more removed from the guarantees of the Constitution were African American slaves, who were given virtually none of the rights and protections that the new government provided to white people. They were, one southern official noted, not "constituent members of our society." The French-Canadian writer Hector St. John de Crèvecoeur, who after the Revolution settled in the United States, wrote a famous book, *Letters from an American Farmer*, in 1782. In it, he posed what became a famous question: "What then is the American, this new man?" Crèvecoeur answered his own question by noting that "individuals of all nations" would become "melted" into a common citizenry. But he too saw no room for African Americans in the community of the "new man." Indeed, among the first laws passed by the new United States under the Constitution was the Naturalization Act of 1790, which helped legalize the stream of immigrants coming into the country and allowed them to become citizens. But it defined citizenry as a status available only to white people. Even free black people were barred from citizenship.

Jefferson, who had briefly tried without result to give Indians a legal status within the new nation, had no such aspirations for

Supporters of the Constitution had a number of advantages. They were better organized than their opponents, and they had the support of the two most eminent men in America, Franklin and Washington. And they seized an appealing label for them-

THE FEDERALIST PAPERS

selves: "Federalists"—the term that opponents of centralization had once used to describe themselves—thus implying that they were less committed to a "nationalist" government than in fact they were. The Federalists also had the support of the ablest political philosophers of their time: Alexander Hamilton, James Madison, and John Jay. Those three men, under the joint pseudonym "Publius," wrote a series of essays—widely published in newspapers throughout the nation—explaining the meaning and virtues of the Constitution. They did so in an effort to counter the powerful arguments that those opposed to the Constitution—those who became known as the Antifederalists—were making. Without a powerful defense of the new Constitution, they feared, the Antifederalists might succeed in several crucial states, most notably in New York. The essays were later issued as a book, and they are known today as *The Federalist Papers*. They are among the most important American contributions to political theory.

The Federalists called their critics "Antifederalists," implying that their rivals had nothing to offer except opposition and

THE ANTIFEDERALISTS

chaos. But the Antifederalists had serious and intelligent arguments of their own. They presented themselves as the defend-

ers of the true principles of the Revolution. The Constitution, they believed, would betray those principles by establishing a strong, potentially tyrannical, center of power in the new national government. The "federal" government, they claimed, would increase taxes, obliterate the states, wield dictatorial powers, favor the "well born" over the common people, and put an end to individual liberty. But their biggest complaint was that the Constitution lacked a bill of rights, a concern that revealed one of the most important sources of their opposition: a basic mistrust of human nature and of the capacity of human beings to wield power. The Antifederalists argued that any government that centralized authority would inevitably produce despotism. Their demand for a bill of rights was a product of this belief: no government could be trusted to protect the liberties of its citizens; only by enumerating the natural rights of the people could there be any assurance that those rights would be preserved.

At its heart, then, the debate between the Federalists and the Antifederalists was a battle between two fears. The Federalists were afraid, above all, of disorder, anarchy, chaos; they feared the unchecked power of the masses, and they sought in the Constitution to create a government that would function at some distance from popular passions. The Antifederalists were

DEBATING THE CONSTITUTION

not anarchists; they too recognized the need for an effective government. But they were much more concerned about the dangers of

concentrated power than about the dangers of popular will. They opposed the Constitution for some of the same reasons the Federalists supported it: because it placed obstacles between the people and the exercise of power.

Despite the Antifederalist efforts, ratification proceeded quickly (although not without occasional difficulty) during the winter of 1787–1788. The Delaware convention was the first to act, when it ratified the Constitution unanimously. The New Jersey and Georgia conventions did the same. In the larger states of Pennsylvania and Massachusetts, the Antifederalists put up a more determined struggle but lost in the final vote. New Hampshire ratified the document in June 1788—the ninth state to do so. It was now theoretically possible for the Constitution to go into effect.

A new government could not hope to flourish, however, without the participation of Virginia and New York, the two most populous states, whose conventions remained closely divided. By the end of June, first Virginia and then New York had consented to the Constitution by narrow margins. The New York convention yielded to expediency—even some of the most staunchly Antifederalist delegates feared that the state's commercial interests would suffer if, once the other states gathered under the "New Roof," New York were to remain outside. Massachusetts, Virginia, and New York all ratified, on the assumption that a bill of rights would be added to the Constitution. The North Carolina convention adjourned without taking action, waiting to see what happened to the amendments. Rhode Island, whose leaders had opposed the Constitution almost from the start, did not even call a convention to consider ratification.

COMPLETING THE STRUCTURE

The first elections under the Constitution took place in the early months of 1789. Almost all the newly elected congressmen and senators had favored ratification, and many had served as delegates to the Philadelphia convention. There was never any real doubt about who would be the first president. George Washington had presided at the Constitutional Convention, and many delegates who had favored ratification did so only because they expected him to preside over the new government as well. Washington received the votes of all the presidential electors. John Adams, a leading Federalist, became vice president. After a journey from Mount Vernon marked by elaborate celebrations along the way, Washington was inaugurated in New York—the national capital for the time being—on April 30, 1789.

The first Congress served in many ways almost as a continuation of the Constitutional Convention, because its principal responsibility was filling in the various gaps in the Constitution. Its

THE BILL OF RIGHTS

most important task was drafting a bill of rights. By early 1789, even Madison had come to agree that some sort of bill of rights was

essential to legitimize the new government in the eyes of its opponents. Congress approved twelve amendments on September 25, 1789; ten of them were ratified by the states by the end of 1791. What we know as the Bill of Rights is these first ten amendments to the Constitution. Nine of them placed limitations on Congress by forbidding it to infringe on certain basic rights: freedom of religion, speech, and the press; immunity from arbitrary arrest; trial by jury; and others. The Tenth Amendment reserved to the states all powers except those specifically withheld from them or dele-gated to the federal government.

On the subject of the federal courts, the Constitution said only: "The judicial power of the United States shall be vested in one Supreme Court, and in such inferior courts as the Congress may from time to time ordain and establish." It was left to Congress to determine the number of Supreme Court judges to be appointed and the kinds of lower courts to be organized. In the Judiciary Act of 1789, Congress provided for a Supreme Court of six members, with a chief justice and five associate justices; thirteen district courts with one judge apiece; and three circuit courts of appeal, each to consist of one of the district judges sitting with two of the Supreme Court justices. In the same act, Congress gave the Supreme Court the power to make the final decision in cases involving the constitutionality of state laws.

The Constitution referred indirectly to executive departments but did not specify what or how many there should be. The first Congress created three such departments—state, treasury, and THE CABINET war—and also established the offices of the attorney general and the postmaster general. To the office of secretary of the treasury, Washington appointed Alexander Hamilton of New York, who at age thirty-two was an acknowledged expert in public finance. For secretary of war he chose a Massachusetts Federalist, General Henry Knox. As attorney general he named Edmund Randolph of Virginia, sponsor of the plan on which the Constitution had been based. As secretary of state he chose another Virginian, Thomas Jefferson, who had recently served as minister to France.

FEDERALISTS AND REPUBLICANS

The resolution of these initial issues, however, did not resolve the deep disagreements about the nature of the new government. On the contrary, for the first twelve years under the Constitution, American politics was characterized by a level of acrimony seldom matched in any period since. The framers of the Constitution had dealt with many disagreements not by solving them but by papering them over with a series of vague compromises; as a result, the conflicts survived to plague the new government.

At the heart of the controversies of the 1790s was the same basic difference in philosophy that had been at the heart of the debate over the Constitution. On one side stood a powerful group that believed America required a strong, national govern-COMPETING ment: that the country's mission was to be-VISIONS come a genuine nation-state, with centralized authority, a complex commercial economy, and a proud standing in world affairs. On the other side stood another group—a minority at first, but one that gained strength during the decade—that envisioned a far weaker central government. American society should not, this group believed, aspire to be highly commercial or urban. It should remain predominantly rural and agrarian, and it should have a central govern-

ment of modest size and powers that would leave most power in the hands of the states and the people. The centralizers became known as the Federalists and gravitated to the leadership of Alexander Hamilton. Their opponents took the name Republicans and gathered under the leadership of James Madison and Thomas Jefferson.

HAMILTON AND THE FEDERALISTS

For twelve years, control of the new government remained firmly in the hands of the Federalists. That was in part because George Washington had always envisioned a strong national government and as president had quietly supported those who were attempting to create one. His enormous prestige throughout the nation was one of the Federalists' greatest assets. But Washington also believed that the presidency should remain above political controversies, and so he avoided any personal involvement in the deliberations of Congress. As a result, the dominant figure in his administration became his talented secretary of the treasury, Alexander Hamilton, who exerted more influence on domestic and foreign policy than anyone else both during his term of office and, to an almost equal extent, after his resignation in 1794.

Of all the national leaders of his time, Hamilton was one of the most aristocratic in personal tastes and political philosophy—ironically, perhaps, since his own origins as an illegitimate child in the Caribbean had been so humble. Far from embracing the republican ideals of the virtue of the people, he believed that a stable and effective government required an enlightened ruling class. Thus the new government needed the support of the wealthy and powerful; and to get that support it needed to give those elites a stake in its success. Hamilton proposed, therefore, ASSUMING THE that the new government take responsibility DEBT for the existing public debt. Many of the miscellaneous, uncertain, depreciated certificates of indebtedness that the old Congress had issued during and after the Revolution were now in the hands of wealthy speculators; the government should call them in and exchange them for uniform, interest-bearing bonds, payable at definite dates. (This policy was known as "funding" the debt.) He also recommended that the federal government "assume" (or take over) the debts the states had accumulated during the Revolution; this assumption policy would encourage state as well as federal bondholders to look to the central government for eventual payment. Hamilton did not, in other words, envision paying off and thus eliminating the debt. He wanted instead to create a large and permanent national debt, with new bonds being issued as old ones were paid off. The result, he believed, would be that creditors—the wealthy classes most likely to lend money to the government—would have a permanent stake in seeing the government survive.

Hamilton also wanted to create a national bank. At the time, there were only a few banks in the country, located principally in Boston, Philadelphia, and New York. A new, national bank would help fill the void that the absence of a well-developed

BANK NOTE How to create a stable currency was one of the greatest challenges facing the new American nation. This fifty-dollar bank note illustrates the principal form paper money assumed in the early republic. It was issued in 1797 by a bank in Philadelphia, and its value was directly tied to the stability of the bank itself. Only many years later did the national government assume control of printing and distributing currency. (Newman Money Museum, Mildred Lane Kemper Art Museum)

banking system had created. It would provide loans and currency to businesses. It would give the government a safe place to deposit federal funds. It would help collect taxes and disburse the government's expenditures. The bank would be chartered by the federal government, would have a monopoly of the government's own banking business, and would be controlled by directors, of whom one-fifth would be appointed by the government. It would provide a stable center to the nation's small and feeble banking system.

The funding and assumption of debts would require new sources of revenue, since the government would now have to pay interest on the loans it was accepting. Up to now, most government revenues had come from the sale of public lands in the West. Hamilton proposed two new kinds of taxes. One was an excise to be paid by distillers of alcoholic liquors, a tax that would fall most heavily on the whiskey distillers of the backcountry, especially in Pennsylvania, Virginia, and North Carolina—small farmers who converted part of their corn and rye crop into whiskey. The other was a tariff on imports, which not only would raise revenue but also would protect American manufacturing from foreign competition. In his famous "Report on Manufactures" of 1791, Hamilton laid out a grand scheme for stimulating the growth of industry in the United States and wrote glowingly of the advantages to the nation of a healthy manufacturing base.

HAMILTON'S REPORT ON MANUFACTURING

The Federalists, in short, offered more than a vision of how to stabilize the new government. They offered a vision of the sort of nation America should become—a nation with a wealthy, enlightened ruling class, a vigorous, independent commercial economy, and a thriving industrial sector; a nation able to play a prominent role in world economic affairs.

ENACTING THE FEDERALIST PROGRAM

Few members of Congress objected to Hamilton's plan for funding the national debt, but many did oppose his proposal to accept the debt "at par," that is, at face value. The old certificates had been issued to merchants and farmers in payment for war supplies during the Revolution, or to officers and soldiers of the Revolutionary army in payment for their services. But many of these original holders had sold their bonds during the hard times of the 1780s to speculators, who had bought them at a fraction of their face value. Many members of Congress believed that if the federal government was to assume responsibility for these bonds, some of them should be returned to the original purchasers. James Madison, now a representative from Virginia, proposed dividing the federally funded bonds between the original purchasers and the speculators. But Hamilton's allies insisted that such a plan was impractical and that the honor of the government required that it pay the bondholders themselves, not the original lenders who had sold their bonds of their own accord. Congress finally passed the funding bill Hamilton wanted.

DEBATING HAMILTON'S PROGRAM

Hamilton's proposal that the federal government assume the state debts encountered greater difficulty. His opponents argued that if the federal government took over the state debts, the people of states with few debts would have to pay taxes to service the larger debts of other states. Hamilton and his supporters struck a bargain with the Virginians to win passage of the bill.

The deal involved the location of the national capital. The capital had moved from New York back to Philadelphia in 1790. But the Virginians wanted a new capital near them in the South. Hamiton met with Thomas Jefferson and agreed over dinner to provide northern support for placing the capital in the South in exchange for Virginia's votes for the assumption bill. The bargain called for the construction of a new capital city on the banks of the Potomac River, which divided Virginia and Maryland, on land to be selected by Washington himself. The government would move there by the beginning of the new century.

LOCATION OF THE CAPITAL

Hamilton argued that creation of a national bank was compatible with the intent of the Constitution, even though the document did not explicitly authorize it. But Madison, Jefferson, Randolph, and others argued that Congress should exercise no powers that the Constitution had not clearly assigned it.

BANK OF THE UNITED STATES

Nevertheless, both the House and the Senate finally agreed to Hamilton's bill. Washington displayed some uncertainty about its legality at first, but he finally signed it. The Bank of the United States began operations in 1791, under a charter that granted it the right to continue for twenty years.

Once enacted, Hamilton's program had many of the effects he had intended and won the support of influential segments of the population. It quickly restored public credit; the bonds of the United States were soon selling at home and abroad at prices even above their face value. Speculators (among them many members of Congress) reaped large profits as a result. Manufacturers profited from the tariffs, and merchants in the seaports benefited from the new banking system.

Small farmers, who formed the vast majority of the population, complained that they had to bear a disproportionate tax burden. Not only did they have to pay property taxes to their state governments, but they bore the brunt of the excise tax on distilleries that Hamilton had initiated. They also opposed a 1792 tariff, also promoted by Hamilton. Many Americans came to believe that the Federalist program served the interests not of the people but of small, wealthy elites. Partly as a result, an organized political opposition arose.

> 66 THE PUBLIC GOOD IS DISREGARDED IN THE CONFLICTS OF RIVAL PARTIES, AND . . . MEASURES ARE TOO OFTEN DECIDED, NOT ACCORDING TO THE RULES OF JUSTICE AND THE RIGHTS OF THE MINOR PARTY, BUT BY THE SUPERIOR FORCE OF AN INTERESTED AND OVERBEARING MAJORITY. 99
>
> **JAMES MADISON**

THE REPUBLICAN OPPOSITION

The Constitution had made no reference to political parties, and the omission was not an oversight. Most of the framers—George Washington in particular—believed that organized parties were dangerous and should be avoided. Disagreement on particular issues was inevitable, but most of the founders believed that such disagreements need not and should not lead to the formation of permanent factions. "The public good is disregarded in the conflicts of rival parties," Madison wrote in *The Federalist Papers*, Number 10, perhaps the most influential of all the essays, "and . . . measures are too often decided, not according to the rules of justice and the rights of the minor party, but by the superior force of an interested and overbearing majority."

Yet, within just a few years after ratification of the Constitution, Madison and others became convinced that Hamilton and his followers had become just such an "interested and overbearing majority." The Hamiltonians, Madison and others agreed, had worked to establish a national network of influence that embodied all the worst features of a party. The Federalists had used their

THE JEFFERSONIAN IDYLL American artists in the early nineteenth century were drawn to tranquil rural scenes, symbolic of the Jeffersonian vision of a nation of small, independent farmers. By 1822, when Francis Alexander painted this pastoral landscape of "Ralph Wheelock's Farm," the simple agrarian republic it depicts was already being transformed by rapid economic growth. (Gift of Edgar William and Bernice Cbrysler Garbisch, © 1998 Board of Trustees, National Gallery of Art, Washington)

ESTABLISHMENT OF THE FEDERALIST PARTY

control over appointments and the awarding of government franchises to reward their supporters and win additional allies. They had encouraged the formation of local associations—largely aristocratic in nature—to strengthen their standing in local communities. They were doing many of the same things, their opponents believed, that the corrupt British governments of the early eighteenth century had done.

Because the Federalists appeared to be creating a menacing and tyrannical structure of power, their opponents believed that there was no alternative but to organize a vigorous opposition. The result was the emergence of an alternative political

FORMATION OF THE REPUBLICAN PARTY

organization, which called itself the Republican Party. (This first "Republican" Party is not an ancestor of the modern Republican Party, which was born in the 1850s.) By the late 1790s, the Republicans were going to even greater lengths than the Federalists to create an apparatus of partisan influence. In every state they formed committees, societies, and caucuses. Republican groups corresponded with one another across state lines. They banded together to influence state and local elections. And they justified their actions by claiming that they and they alone represented the true interests of the nation—that they were fighting to defend the people against a corrupt conspiracy by the Federalists. Just as Hamilton believed that the network of supporters he was creating represented the only legitimate interest group in the nation, so the Republicans believed that their party organization represented the best interests of the people. Neither side was willing to admit that it was acting as a party; neither would concede the right of the other to exist. This institutionalized factionalism is known to scholars as the "first party system."

From the beginning, the preeminent figures among the Republicans were Thomas Jefferson and James Madison. Indeed, the two men were such intimate collaborators with such similar political philosophies that it is sometimes difficult to distinguish the contributions of one from those of the other. But Jefferson, the more charismatic personality of the two, gradually emerged as the most prominent spokesman for the Republicans. Jefferson considered himself a farmer. (He was, in fact, a substantial planter; but he had spent relatively little time in recent years at his estate in Virginia.) He believed in an agrarian republic, most of whose citizens would be sturdy, independent farmer-citizens tilling their own soil.

Jefferson did not scorn commercial activity; he assumed farmers would market their crops in the national and even international markets. Nor did he oppose industry; he believed the United States should develop some manufacturing capacity. But he was suspicious of large cities, feared urban mobs as "sores upon the body politic," and opposed the development of an advanced industrial economy because it would, he feared, increase the number of propertyless workers packed in cities. In short, Jefferson envisioned a decentralized society, dominated by small property owners engaged largely in agrarian activities.

The difference between the Federalist and Republican social philosophies was visible in, among other things, reactions to

DIFFERENCES OVER THE FRENCH REVOLUTION

the French Revolution. As that revolution grew increasingly radical in the 1790s, with its attacks on organized religion, the overthrow of the monarchy, and eventually the execution of the king and queen, the Federalists expressed horror. But the Republicans generally applauded the democratic, antiaristocratic spirit they believed the French Revolution embodied. Some even imitated the French radicals (the Jacobins) by cutting their hair short, wearing pantaloons, and addressing one another as "Citizen" and "Citizeness."

Although both parties had supporters in all parts of the country and among all classes, there were regional and economic differences. The Federalists were most numerous in the commercial centers of the Northeast and in such southern seaports as Charleston; the Republicans were most numerous in the rural areas of the South and the West.

As the 1792 presidential election—the nation's second—approached, both Jefferson and Hamilton urged Washington to run for another term. The president reluctantly agreed. But while most Americans considered Washington above the partisan battle, he was actually much more in sympathy with the Federalists than with the Republicans. And during his presidency, Hamilton remained the dominant figure in government.

ESTABLISHING NATIONAL SOVEREIGNTY

The Federalists consolidated their position—and for a time attracted wide public support for the new national government—by dealing effectively with two problems the old Confederation had been unable fully to resolve. They helped stabilize the nation's western lands, and they strengthened America's international position.

SECURING THE FRONTIER

Despite the Northwest Ordinance, the Confederation Congress had largely failed to tie the outlying western areas of the country firmly to the government. Farmers in western Massachusetts had risen in revolt; settlers in Vermont, Kentucky, and Tennessee had toyed with the idea of separating from the Union. The new government under the Constitution inherited these problems.

In 1794, farmers in western Pennsylvania raised a major challenge to federal authority when they refused to pay a whiskey excise tax and began terrorizing the tax collectors (much as colonists had done at the time of the Stamp Act). But the federal government did not leave settlement of the so-called

Whiskey Rebellion to Pennsylvania, as the Confederation
Congress had left Shays's Rebellion to
Massachusetts. At Hamilton's urging,
Washington called out the militias of three
states, raised an army of nearly 15,000 (a larger force than he
had commanded against the British during most of the
Revolution), and personally led the troops into Pennsylvania.
As the militiamen approached Pittsburgh, the center of the re-
sistance, the rebellion quickly collapsed.

WHISKEY
REBELLION

The federal government won the allegiance of the whiskey
rebels by intimidating them. It won the loyalties of other frontier people by accepting their territories as new states in the
Union. The last of the original thirteen colonies joined the
Union once the Bill of Rights had been appended to the
Constitution—North Carolina in 1789 and Rhode Island in 1790.
Then Vermont, which had had its own state government since
the Revolution, became the fourteenth state in 1791 after New
York and New Hampshire finally agreed to give up their claims
to it. Next came Kentucky, in 1792, when Virginia gave up its
claim to that region. After North Carolina finally ceded its western lands to the Union, Tennessee became first a territory and,
in 1796, a state.

NATIVE AMERICANS AND THE NEW NATION

The new government faced a greater challenge, also inherited
from the Confederation, in the more distant areas of the
Northwest and the Southwest, where Indians (occasionally in
alliance with the British and Spanish) fought to retain tribal
lands that the U.S. government claimed for itself. The ordinances of 1784–1787 had produced a series of border conflicts
with Indian tribes resisting white settlement in what they considered their lands. Although the United States eventually defeated virtually every Indian challenge (if often at great cost), it
was clear that the larger question of who was to control the
lands of the West—the United States or the Indian nations—remained unanswered.

These clashes revealed another issue the Constitution had
done little to resolve: the place of the Indian nations within the
new federal structure. The Constitution barely mentioned Native
Americans. Article I excluded "Indians not
taxed" from being counted in the population
totals that determined the number of seats
states would receive in the House of
Representatives; and it gave Congress the power to "regulate
Commerce with foreign Nations, and among the several States,
and with the Indian tribes." Article VI bound the new government to respect treaties negotiated by the Confederation, most of
which had been with the tribes. But none of this did very much
to clarify the precise legal standing of Indians or Indian nations
within the United States.

INDIANS
AND THE
CONSTITUTION

On the one hand, the Constitution seemed to recognize the
existence of the tribes as legal entities. On the other hand, it
made clear that they were not "foreign Nations" (in the same
sense that European countries were); nor were their members
citizens of the United States. The tribes received no direct representation in the new government. Above all, the Constitution
did not address the major issue that would govern relations
between whites and Indians: land. Indian nations lived within
the boundaries of the United States, yet they claimed (and the
white government at times agreed) that they had some measure of sovereignty within their own lands. But neither the
Constitution nor common law offered any clear guide to the
rights of a "nation within a nation" or to the precise nature of
tribal sovereignty, which ultimately depended on control of
land. Thus, the relationship between the tribes and the United
States remained to be determined by a series of treaties, agreements, and judicial decisions in a process that has continued
for more than 200 years.

MAINTAINING NEUTRALITY

Not until 1791—eight years after the end of the Revolution—
did Great Britain send a minister to the United States, and
then only because Madison and the Republicans were threatening to place special trade restrictions on British ships. That
was one of many symbols of the difficulty the new government
had in establishing its legitimacy in the eyes of the British.
Another crisis in Anglo-American relations emerged in 1793
when the new French government, created by the revolution
of 1789, went to war with Great Britain and its allies. Both the
president and Congress took steps to establish American neutrality in that conflict. But the neutrality quickly encountered
severe tests.

The first challenge to American neutrality came from revolutionary France and its first diplomatic representative to
America, the brash and youthful Edmond Genet. Instead of
landing at Philadelphia and presenting himself immediately to
the president, Genet disembarked at Charleston. There he
made plans to use American ports to outfit French warships,
encouraged American shipowners to serve
as French privateers, and commissioned
the aging George Rogers Clark to lead a military expedition
against Spanish lands to the south. (Spain was at the time an
ally of Great Britain and an enemy of France.) In all of this,
Genet was brazenly ignoring Washington's policies and fla-
grantly violating the Neutrality Act. His conduct infuriated
Washington (who provided "Citizen Genet," as he was known,
with an icy reception in Philadelphia) and the Federalists; it
also embarrassed all but the most ardent admirers of the
French Revolution among the Republicans. Washington eventually demanded that the French government recall him, but by
then Genet's party was out of power in France. (The president
granted him political asylum in the United States, and he settled with his American wife on a Long Island farm.) The neutrality policy had survived its first serious test.

CITIZEN GENET

A second and even greater challenge came from Great
Britain. Early in 1794, the Royal Navy began seizing hundreds of
American ships engaged in trade in the French West Indies,

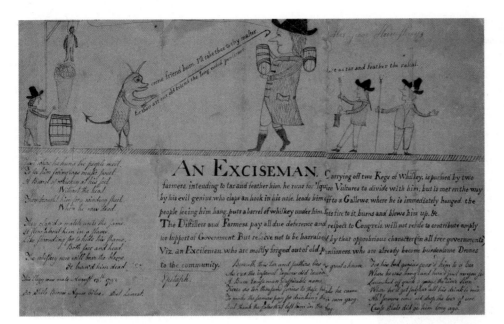

outraging public opinion in the United States. Anti-British feeling rose still higher at the report that the governor general of Canada had delivered a warlike speech to the Indians on the northwestern frontier encouraging them to challenge U.S. dominance there. Hamilton was deeply concerned. War would mean an end to imports from England, and most of the revenue for maintaining his financial system came from duties on those imports.

JAY'S TREATY AND PINCKNEY'S TREATY

This was, Hamilton believed, no time for ordinary diplomacy. He did not trust the State Department to reach a settlement with Britain. Jefferson had resigned as secretary of state in 1793 to devote more time to his political activities, but his successor, Edmund Randolph, was even more ardently pro-French than Jefferson had been. So Hamilton persuaded Washington to name a special commissioner to England: John Jay, chief justice of the United States Supreme Court and a staunch New York Federalist. Jay was instructed to secure compensation for the recent British assaults on American shipping, to demand withdrawal of British forces from the frontier posts, and to negotiate a new commercial treaty.

The long and complex treaty Jay negotiated in 1794 failed to achieve these goals. But it was not without merit. It settled the conflict with Britain and helped prevent what had seemed likely to become a war between the two nations. It established undisputed American sovereignty over the entire Northwest. And it produced a reasonably satisfactory commercial relationship with Britain, whose trade was important to the United States. Nevertheless, when the terms became public in America, there were bitter public denunciations of it for having failed to extract enough promises from the British. Jay himself was

Jay's Treaty

burned in effigy in various parts of the country. Opponents of the treaty—nearly all the Republicans and even some Federalists, encouraged by agents of France—went to extraordinary lengths to defeat it in the Senate. The American minister to France, James Monroe, and even the secretary of state, Edmund Randolph, joined the desperate attempt to prevent ratification. But in the end the Senate ratified what was by then known as Jay's Treaty.

Among other things, the treaty made possible a settlement of America's conflict with the Spanish, because it raised fears in Spain that the British and the Americans might now join together to challenge Spanish possessions in North America. When Thomas Pinckney arrived in Spain as a special negotiator, he had no difficulty in gaining nearly everything the United States had sought from the Spaniards for more than a decade. Under Pinckney's Treaty (signed in 1795), Spain recognized the right of Americans to navigate the Mississippi to its mouth and to deposit goods at New Orleans for reloading on oceangoing ships; agreed to fix the northern boundary of Florida where Americans always had insisted it should be, along the 31st parallel; and required Spanish authorities to prevent the Indians in Florida from launching raids across the border.

Pinckney's Treaty

THE DOWNFALL OF THE FEDERALISTS

The Federalists' impressive triumphs did not ensure their continued dominance in the national government. On the contrary, success seemed to produce problems of its own—problems that led to their downfall.

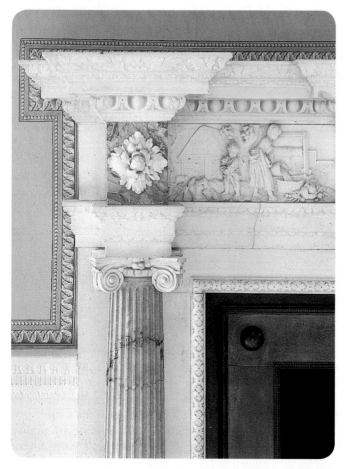

MOUNT VERNON George and Martha Washington lavished enormous attention on their home at Mount Vernon, importing materials and workmen from Europe to create a house that they hoped would rival some of the elegant country homes of England. This detail from a mantle suggests the degree to which they—like many wealthy planters and merchants of their time—strove to bring refinement and gentility to their lives. (Paul Rocheleau/Rebus, Inc.)

Since almost all Americans in the 1790s agreed that there was no place in a stable republic for an organized opposition, the emergence of the Republicans as powerful contenders for popular favor seemed to the Federalists a grave threat to national stability. Beginning in the late 1790s, when international perils confronted the government as well, the Federalists could not resist the temptation to move forcefully against the opposition. Facing what they believed was a stark choice between respecting individual liberties and preserving stability, the Federalists chose stability. The result was political disaster. After 1796, the Federalists never won another election. The popular respect for the institutions of the federal government, which they had worked so hard to produce among the people, survived. But the Federalists themselves gradually vanished as an effective political force.

THE ELECTION OF 1796

Despite strong pressure from his many admirers to run for a third term as president, George Washington insisted on retiring from office in 1797. In a "Farewell Address" to the American

people (actually a long letter, composed in part by Hamilton and published in a Philadelphia newsletter), he reacted sharply to the Republicans. His reference to the "insidious wiles of foreign influence" was not just an abstract warning against international entanglements; it was also a specific denunciation of those Republicans who had been conspiring with the French to frustrate the Federalist diplomatic program.

WASHINGTON'S FAREWELL ADDRESS

With Washington out of the running, no obstacle remained to an open expression of the partisan rivalries that had been building over the previous eight years. Jefferson was the uncontested candidate of the Republicans in 1796. The Federalists faced a more difficult choice. Hamilton, the personification of Federalism, had created too many enemies to be a credible candidate. So Vice President John Adams, who had been directly associated with none of the unpopular Federalist measures, became his party's nominee for president.

The Federalists were still clearly the dominant party, and there was little doubt of their ability to win a majority of the presidential electors. But without Washington to mediate, they fell victim to fierce factional rivalries that almost led to their

JOHN ADAMS Adams's illustrious career as Revolutionary leader, diplomat, and president marked the beginning of four generations of public distinction among members of his family. His son, John Quincy Adams, served as secretary of state and president. His grandson, Charles Francis Adams, was one of the great diplomats of the Civil War era. His great-grandson, Henry Adams, was one of America's most distinguished historians and writers. (Adams National Historic Site, Quincy, Massachusetts)

undoing. Hamilton and many other Federalists (especially in the South) were not reconciled to Adams's candidacy and favored his running mate, Thomas Pinckney, instead. And when, as expected, the Federalists elected a majority of the presidential electors, some of these Pinckney supporters declined to vote for Adams; he managed to defeat Jefferson by only three electoral votes. Because a still larger number of Adams's supporters declined to vote for Pinckney, Jefferson finished second in the balloting and became vice president. (Until the Twelfth Amendment was adopted in 1804, the Constitution provided for the candidate receiving the second highest number of electoral votes to become vice president—hence the awkward result of men from different parties serving in the nation's two highest elected offices.)

Adams thus assumed the presidency under unhappy circumstances. He presided over a divided party, which faced a

DIVIDED FEDERALISTS

strong and resourceful Republican opposition committed to its extinction. Adams himself was not even the dominant figure in his own party; Hamilton remained the most influential Federalist, and Adams was never able to challenge him effectively. The new president was one of the country's most accomplished and talented diplomats, but he had few skills as a politician. Austere, rigid, aloof, he had little talent at conciliating differences, soliciting support, or inspiring enthusiasm. He was a man of enormous, indeed intimidating, rectitude, and he seemed to assume that his own virtue and the correctness of his positions would alone be enough to sustain him.

THE QUASI WAR WITH FRANCE

American relations with Great Britain and Spain improved as a result of Jay's and Pinckney's Treaties. But the nation's relations with revolutionary France quickly deteriorated. French vessels captured American ships on the high seas and at times imprisoned the crews. When the South Carolina Federalist Charles Cotesworth Pinckney, brother of Thomas Pinckney, arrived in France, the government refused to receive him as the official representative of the United States.

Some of President Adams's advisers favored war, most notably Secretary of State Thomas Pickering, a stern New Englander who detested France. But Hamilton recommended conciliation, and Adams agreed. In an effort to stabilize relations, Adams appointed a bipartisan commission—consisting of Charles Cotesworth Pinckney, the recently rejected minister; John Marshall, a Virginia Federalist, later chief justice of the Supreme Court; and Elbridge Gerry, a Massachusetts Republican but a friend of the president—to negotiate with France. When the Americans arrived in Paris in 1797, three agents of the French foreign minister, Prince Talleyrand, demanded a loan for France and a bribe for French officials before any negotiations could begin. Pinckney responded: "No! No! Not a sixpence!"

When Adams heard of the incident, he sent a message to Congress denouncing the French insults and urging prepara-

tions for war. He then turned the report of the American commissioners over to Congress, after deleting the names of the three French agents and designating them only as "Messrs. X, Y, and Z." When the report was published, it created widespread popular outrage at France's actions and strong support for the Federalists' response. For nearly two years after the "XYZ Affair," as it became known, the United States found itself engaged in an undeclared war with France.

THE XYZ AFFAIR

Adams persuaded Congress to cut off all trade with France and to authorize American vessels to capture French armed

THE QUASI WAR

ships on the high seas. In 1798, Congress created a Department of the Navy and appropriated money for the construction of new warships. The navy soon won a number of duels with French vessels and captured a total of eighty-five ships, including armed merchantmen. The United States also began cooperating closely with the British and became virtually an ally of Britain in the war with France.

In the end, France chose to conciliate the United States before the conflict grew. Adams sent another commission to Paris in 1800, and the new French government (headed now by "first consul" Napoleon Bonaparte) agreed to a treaty with the United States that canceled the old agreement of 1778 and established new commercial arrangements. As a result, the "quasi war" came to a reasonably peaceful end.

REPRESSION AND PROTEST

The conflict with France helped the Federalists increase their majorities in Congress in 1798. Armed with this new strength,

ALIEN AND SEDITION ACTS

they began to consider ways to silence the Republican opposition. The result was some of the most controversial legislation in American history: the Alien and Sedition Acts.

The Alien Act placed new obstacles in the way of foreigners who wished to become American citizens, and it strengthened the president's hand in dealing with aliens. The Sedition Act allowed the government to prosecute those who engaged in "sedition" against the government. In theory, only libelous or treasonous activities were subject to prosecution; but since such activities were open to widely varying definitions, the law made it possible for the federal government to stifle almost any opposition. The Republicans interpreted the new laws as part of a Federalist campaign to destroy them and fought back.

President Adams signed the new laws but was cautious in implementing them. He did not deport any aliens, and he prevented the government from launching a major crusade against the Republicans. But the legislation had a significant repressive effect nevertheless. The Alien Act helped discourage immigration and encouraged some foreigners already in the country to leave. And the administration made use of the Sedition Act to arrest and convict ten men, most of them Republican newspaper editors whose only crime had been to criticize the Federalists in government.

THE XYZ AFFAIR The sensational "XYZ Affair" of 1798 is the subject of this American political cartoon. The five-headed figure in the center represents the Directory of the French government; he is demanding "money, money, money" from the three diplomats at left who were in Paris representing the United States. The monster at the top right is operating a guillotine—a symbol of the violence and terror of the later stages of the French Revolution. (The Granger Collection, New York)

Republican leaders pinned their hopes for a reversal of the Alien and Sedition Acts on the state legislatures. (The Supreme

VIRGINIA AND KENTUCKY RESOLUTIONS

Court had not yet established its sole right to nullify congressional legislation, and there were many Republican leaders who believed that the states had that power too.) The Republicans laid out a theory for state action in two sets of resolutions in 1798–1799, one written (anonymously) by Jefferson and adopted by the Kentucky legislature and the other drafted by Madison and approved by the Virginia legislature. The Virginia and Kentucky Resolutions, as they were known, used the ideas of John Locke to argue that the federal government had been formed by a "compact" or contract among the states and possessed only certain delegated powers. Whenever the federal government exercised any undelegated powers, its acts were "unauthoritative, void, and of no force." If the parties to the contract, the states, decided that the central government had exceeded those powers, the Kentucky Resolution claimed, they had the right to "nullify" the appropriate laws. (Such claims emerged again in the South in the decades before the Civil War.)

The Republicans did not win wide support for nullification; only Virginia and Kentucky declared the congressional statutes void. The Republicans did, however, succeed in elevating their

dispute with the Federalists to the level of a national crisis. By the late 1790s, the entire nation was deeply and bitterly divided politically. State legislatures at times resembled battlegrounds. Even the United States Congress was plagued with violent disagreements. In one celebrated incident in the chamber of the House of Representatives, Matthew Lyon, a Republican from Vermont, responded to an insult from Roger Griswold, a Federalist from Connecticut, by spitting in Griswold's face. Griswold attacked Lyon with his cane. Lyon fought back with a pair of fire tongs, and the two men ended up wrestling on the floor.

THE "REVOLUTION" OF 1800

These bitter controversies shaped the 1800 presidential election. Adams and Jefferson were again the opposing candidates. But

THE ELECTION OF 1800

the campaign of 1800 was very different from the one preceding it. Indeed, it may have been the ugliest in American history. Adams and Jefferson themselves displayed reasonable dignity, but their supporters showed no such restraint. The Federalists accused Jefferson of being a dangerous radical and his followers of being wild men who, if they should come to power, would bring on a reign of terror comparable to that of the French

CONGRESSIONAL BRAWLERS This cartoon lampoons a celebrated fight on the floor of the House of Representatives in 1798 between Matthew Lyon, a Republican from Vermont, and Roger Griswold, a Federalist from Connecticut. The conflict began when Griswold insulted Lyon by attacking his military record in the Revolutionary War. Lyon replied by spitting in Griswold's face. Two weeks later, Griswold attacked Lyon with his cane, and Lyon seized a pair of fire tongs and fought back. That later scene is depicted (and ridiculed) here. Other members of Congress are portrayed as enjoying the spectacle. On the wall is a picture entitled "Royal Sport," showing animals fighting. (New York Public Library)

Revolution. The Republicans portrayed Adams as a tyrant conspiring to become king, and they accused the Federalists of plotting to subvert human liberty and impose slavery on the people. There was considerable personal invective as well. For example, it was during this campaign that the story of Jefferson's romantic involvement with a slave woman on his plantation was first widely aired. (Recent DNA evidence has proven that the story was true.)

The election was close, and the crucial contest was in New York. There, Aaron Burr had mobilized an organization of Revolutionary War veterans, the Tammany Society, to serve as a Republican political machine. And through Tammany's efforts, the Republicans carried the city by a large majority and, with it, the state. Jefferson was, apparently, elected.

But an unexpected complication soon jeopardized the Republican victory. The Constitution called for each elector to "vote by ballot for two persons." The normal practice was for an elector to cast one vote for his party's presidential candidate and another for the vice presidential candidate. To avoid a tie between Jefferson and Aaron Burr (the Republican vice presidential candidate), the Republicans had intended for one elector to refrain from voting for Burr. But the plan went awry. When the votes were counted, Jefferson and Burr each had 73. No candidate had a majority. According to the Constitution, the House of Representatives had to choose between the two leading candidates when no one had a majority; in this case, that meant deciding between Jefferson and Burr. Each state delegation would cast a single vote.

The new Congress, elected in 1800 with a Republican majority, was not to convene until after the inauguration of the president, so it was the Federalist Congress that had to decide the question. Some Federalists hoped to use the situation to salvage the election for their party; others wanted to strike a bargain with Burr and elect him. But after a long deadlock, several leading Federalists, most prominent among them Alexander Hamilton, concluded that Burr (whom many suspected of having engineered the deadlock in the first place) was too unreliable to trust with the presidency. On the thirty-sixth ballot, Jefferson was elected.

After the election of 1800, the only branch of the federal government left in Federalist hands was the judiciary. The Adams administration spent its last months in office taking steps to make the party's hold on the courts secure. By the Judiciary Act of 1801, passed by the lame duck Congress, the Federalists reduced the number of Supreme Court justiceships by one but greatly increased the number of federal judgeships as a whole. Adams quickly appointed Federalists to the newly created positions. Indeed, there were charges that he stayed up until midnight on his last day in office to finish signing the new judges' commissions. These officeholders became known as the "midnight appointments."

THE JUDICIARY ACT OF 1801

Even so, the Republicans viewed their victory, incorrectly, as almost complete. The nation, they believed, had been saved from tyranny. A new era could now begin, one in which the true principles on which America had been founded would once again govern the land. The exuberance with which the victors viewed the future—and the importance they attributed to the Federalists' defeat—was evident in the phrase Jefferson himself later used to describe his election. He called it the "Revolution of 1800." It remained to be seen how revolutionary it would really be.

LOOKING BACK

The writing of the Constitution of 1787 was the single most important political event in the history of the United States, and a notable event in the political history of the modern world. In creating a "federal" system of dispersed and divided authority—authority divided among national and state governments, authority divided among an executive, a legislature, and a judiciary—the young nation sought to balance its need for an effective central government against its fear of concentrated and despotic power. The ability of the delegates to the Constitutional Convention to compromise again and again to produce the ultimate structure gave evidence of the deep yearning among them for a stable political system. The same willingness to compromise allowed the greatest challenge to the ideals of the new democracy—slavery—to survive intact.

The writing and ratifying of the Constitution settled some questions about the shape of the new nation. The first twelve years under the government created by the Constitution solved others. And yet by the year 1800, a basic disagreement about the future of the nation—a disagreement personified by the differences between committed nationalist Alexander Hamilton and the self-proclaimed champion of democracy Thomas Jefferson—remained unresolved and was creating bitter divisions and conflicts within the political world. The election of Thomas Jefferson to the presidency that year opened a new chapter in the nation's public history. It also brought to a close, at least temporarily, savage political conflicts that had seemed to threaten the nation's future. •

KEY TERMS/PEOPLE/PLACES/EVENTS

ALEXANDER HAMILTON 163
ALIEN AND SEDITION ACTS 177
ANTIFEDERALISTS 169
BILL OF RIGHTS 170
CHECKS AND BALANCES 167
CITIZEN GENET AFFAIR 174
FEDERALISTS 168
FEDERAL STRUCTURE 174
GREAT COMPROMISE 165

JAMES MADISON 165
JAY'S TREATY 175
JOHN ADAMS 176
NEW JERSEY PLAN 164
PINCKNEY'S TREATY 175
QUASI WAR 177
REPUBLICANS 170
REVOLUTION OF 1800 178
SEPARATION OF POWERS 166

SOVEREIGNTY 165
THE FEDERALIST PAPERS 169
VIRGINIA AND KENTUCKY
  RESOLUTIONS 178
VIRGINIA PLAN 164
WHISKEY REBELLION 174
XYZ AFFAIR 177

SIGNIFICANT EVENTS

Constitutional Convention in Philadelphia meets

Washington becomes first president
Bill of Rights adopted by Congress
Judiciary Act of 1789 passed
French Revolution begins

Washington reelected without opposition

1786
Annapolis Conference meets

1787
Constitution adopted (September 17)

1787-1788
States ratify Constitution

1789

1791
Hamilton issues "Report on Manufactures"
First Bank of the United States chartered

1792

RECALL AND REFLECT

1. How did the Constitution of 1787 attempt to resolve the weaknesses of the Articles of Confederation?

2. What role did *The Federalist Papers* play in the battle over ratification of the Constitution?

3. What were the main tenets of Alexander Hamilton's financial program?

4. What diplomatic crises did the United States face in the first decade of its existence, and how did the new government respond to these crises?

5. What was the "Revolution of 1800" and in what way was it a revolution?

Whiskey Rebellion
quelled in Pennsylvania

Jay's Treaty signed

John Adams
elected president

Jefferson and Burr
tie vote in electoral
college

1793

Citizen Genet
affair challenges
American neutrality

1794

1795

Pinckney's
Treaty signed

1796

1798

XYZ Affair precipitates
state of quasi war with
France

Alien and Sedition Acts
passed

Virginia and Kentucky
Resolutions passed

1800

1801

Jefferson becomes
president after
Congress confirms
election

Judiciary Act of 1801
passed

THE BURNING OF WASHINGTON This dramatic engraving somewhat exaggerates the extent of the blazes in Washington when the British occupied the city in August 1814. But the invaders did set fire to the Capitol, the White House, and other public buildings in retaliation for the American burning and looting of the Canadian capital at York. (The Granger Collection, New York)

7 | THE JEFFERSONIAN ERA

THOMAS JEFFERSON AND HIS FOLLOWERS assumed control of the national government in 1801 as the champions of a distinctive vision of America—a vision sharply different from that of Andrew Hamilton and other Federalists. They envisioned a society of sturdy, independent farmers, happily free from the workshops, industrial towns, and city mobs of Europe. They promoted a cultural outlook that emphasized localism and republican simplicity. And they proposed a federal government of sharply limited power, with most authority remaining at the state level.

Almost nothing worked out as they planned, for during their years in power the young republic was

THE JEFFERSONIAN VISION

developing in ways that made much of their vision obsolete. The American economy became steadily more diversified and complex. Growing cities, surging commerce, and expanding industrialism made the ideal of a simple, agrarian society impossible to maintain. American cultural life, far from reflecting localism and simplicity, reflected a vigorous and ambitious nationalism.

SETTING THE STAGE

The Republicans did manage to translate some of their political ideals into reality. Jefferson dismantled much of the bureaucratic

power structure the Federalists had erected in the 1790s, and he helped ensure that in many respects the federal government would remain a relatively unimportant force in American life. Yet he also frequently encountered situations that required him to exercise strong national authority, as, for example, when he arranged the greatest single increase in the size of the United States in its history. The Republicans did not always like these nationalizing and modernizing trends, but for the most part, they adjusted to them and, in doing so, became agents of the transformation of American life they had once resisted.

LOOKING AHEAD

1. How successful was Jefferson's effort to create a "republican" society dominated by sturdy, independent farmers?
2. How did the Napoleonic wars affect the United States?
3. What events and issues led to the War of 1812?

THE RISE OF CULTURAL NATIONALISM

In many respects, American cultural life in the early nineteenth century seemed to reflect the Republican vision of the nation's future. Opportunities for education increased; the nation's literary and artistic life began to free itself from European influences; and American religion began to confront and adjust to the spread of Enlightenment rationalism. In other respects, however, the new culture was posing a serious challenge to Republican ideals.

PATTERNS OF EDUCATION

Central to the Republican vision of America was the concept of a virtuous and enlightened citizenry. Jefferson himself called emphatically for a national "crusade against ignorance."

IMPORTANCE OF A VIRTUOUS CITIZENRY

Republicans believed, therefore, in the establishment of a nationwide system of public schools to create the educated electorate they believed a republic required. All white male citizens (the nation's prospective voters) should, they argued, receive free education.

Some states endorsed the principle of public education for all in the early years of the republic, but none actually created a working system of free schools. A Massachusetts law of 1789 reaffirmed the colonial laws by which each town was obligated to support a school, but there was little enforcement. In Virginia, the state legislature ignored Jefferson's call for universal elementary education and for advanced education for the gifted. As late as 1815, not a single state had a comprehensive public school system.

A SEMINARY FOR WOMEN Educational opportunities for women were scarce in the early nineteenth century, but by the 1820s a number of seminaries were created for young ladies, mostly affluent students. The watercolor on silk is by an unknown artist and portrays two women studying geography. (The Granger Collection, New York)

Instead, schooling became primarily the responsibility of private institutions, most of which were open only to those who could afford to pay for them. In the South and in the mid-Atlantic states, religious groups ran most of the schools. In New

PRIVATE SCHOOLING

England and elsewhere, private academies were usually more secular, many of them modeled on schools founded by the Phillips family at Andover, Massachusetts, in 1778, and at Exeter, New Hampshire, three years later. By 1815, there were thirty such private secondary schools in Massachusetts, thirty-seven in New York, and several dozen more scattered throughout the country. Many were frankly aristocratic in outlook, training their students to become members of the nation's elite. There were a few schools open to the poor offering education that was clearly inferior to that provided at exclusive schools.

Private secondary schools such as those in New England, and even many public schools, accepted only male students. Yet the early nineteenth century did see some important advances in female education.

In the eighteenth century, women received very little education of any kind, and the female illiteracy rate at the time of the

NEW EDUCATIONAL OPPORTUNITIES FOR WOMEN

Revolution was very high—at least 50 percent. At the same time, however, Americans had begun to place a new value on the contribution of the "republican mother" to the training of the new generation. That raised an important question: If mothers remained ignorant, how could they raise their children to be enlightened? Beginning as early as the 1770s and accelerating thereafter, such concerns led to the creation of a network of female academies throughout the nation (usually for the daughters of affluent families). In 1789, Massachusetts required that its public schools serve females as well as males. Other states, although not all, soon followed.

Most white men, at least, assumed that female education should serve only to make women better wives and mothers. Women therefore had no need for advanced or professional training; there was no reason for colleges and universities to make space for female students. Some women, however, aspired to more. In 1784, Judith Sargent Murray published an essay defending women's rights to education, a defense set in terms very different from those used by most men. Men and women were equal in intellect and potential, Murray argued. Women, therefore, should have precisely the same educational opportunities as men. Moreover, they should have opportunities to earn their own living, to establish a role for themselves in society apart from their husbands and families. Murray's ideas became an inspiration to later generations of women, but during most of her own lifetime (1751–1820) they attracted relatively little support.

Reformers who believed in the power of education to reform and redeem ignorant and "backward" people spurred a growing interest in Indian education. Because Jefferson and his followers liked to

think of Native Americans as "noble savages" (uncivilized but, unlike their view of African Americans, not necessarily in-
INDIAN EDUCATION
nately inferior), they hoped that schooling the Indians in white culture would tame and "uplift" the tribes. Although white governments did little to promote Indian education, missionaries and mission schools proliferated among the tribes.

Almost no white people in the early nineteenth century believed that there was a need to educate African Americans, almost all of whom were still slaves. In a few northern states, some free black children attended segregated schools. In the South, slaveowners generally tried to prevent their black workers from learning to read or write, fearful that knowledge would make them unhappy with their condition. Some African Americans managed to acquire some education despite these obstacles, by teaching themselves and their own children. But the numbers of literate slaves remained very small.

Higher education was much less widely available than education at lower levels, despite Republican hopes for a wide dis-
HIGHER EDUCATION
persion of advanced knowledge. (Jefferson himself founded the University of Virginia to promote that ideal.) The number of colleges and universities in America grew from nine at the start of the Revolution to twenty-two by 1800 and continued to increase thereafter. None of the new schools, however, was truly public. Even those established by state legislatures (in Georgia, North Carolina, Vermont, Ohio, and South Carolina, for example) relied on private contributions and on tuition fees. Scarcely more than one white man in a thousand (and no women, blacks, or Indians at all) had access to any college education, and those few who did attend universities were almost without exception members of prosperous, propertied families.

The education that the colleges provided was exceedingly limited—narrow training in the classics and a few other areas and intensive work in theology. Indeed, the clergy was the only profession for which college training was generally a prerequisite. A few institutions attempted to provide their students advanced education in other fields. The College of William and Mary in Virginia, the University of Pennsylvania, and Columbia College in New York all created law schools before 1800, but most lawyers continued to train for their profession simply by apprenticing themselves to practicing attorneys.

MEDICINE AND SCIENCE

The University of Pennsylvania created the first American medical school in the eighteenth century. In the early nineteenth century, however, most doctors studied medicine by working with an established practitioner. Some American physicians believed in applying new scientific methods to medicine and struggled against age-old prejudices and superstitions. Efforts to teach anatomy, for example, encountered strong public hostility because of the dissection of cadavers that the study required. Municipal authorities had virtually no understanding of medical science and almost no idea of what to do

in the face of the severe epidemics that so often swept their populations; only slowly did they respond to the warnings of, among others, Benjamin Rush, a pioneering Philadelphia physician, that lack of adequate sanitation programs was to blame for disease.

Individual patients often had more to fear from their doctors than from their illnesses. Even the leading advocates of scien-
BENJAMIN RUSH
tific medicine often embraced useless and dangerous treatments. Benjamin Rush, for example, was an advocate of the new and supposedly scientific techniques of bleeding and purging, and many of his patients died. George Washington's death in 1799 was probably less a result of the minor throat infection that had afflicted him than of his physicians' efforts to cure him by bleeding and purging.

The medical profession also used its newfound commitment to the "scientific" method to justify expanding its own role to
DECLINE OF MIDWIFERY
kinds of care that had traditionally been outside its domain. Most childbirths, for example, had been attended by female midwives. In the early nineteenth century, physicians began to handle deliveries themselves and to demand restrictions on the role of midwives. Among the results of that change was a narrowing of opportunities for women (midwifery was an important female occupation) and a restriction of access to childbirth care for poor mothers (who could have afforded midwives, but who could not pay the higher physicians' fees).

Education and professional training in the early republic—in medicine and in many other fields—thus fell far short of the Jeffersonian vision. Indeed, efforts to promote education and increase professionalism often had the effect of strengthening existing elites rather than eroding them.

CULTURAL ASPIRATIONS IN THE NEW NATION

Many Americans in the Jeffersonian era may have repudiated the Federalist belief in political and economic centralization,
ESTABLISHMENT OF A NATIONAL CULTURE
but most embraced another form of nationalism with great fervor. Having won political independence from Europe, they aspired now to a form of cultural independence. In the process, they dreamed of an American literary and artistic life that would rival the greatest achievements of Europe. As a popular "Poem on the Rising Glory of America" had predicted as early as 1772, Americans believed that their "happy land" was destined to become the "seat of empire" and the "final stage" of civilization, with "glorious works of high invention and of wond'rous art." The United States, another eighteenth-century writer had proclaimed, would serve as "the last and greatest theatre for the improvement of mankind."

Such nationalism found expression, among other places, in early American schoolbooks. The Massachusetts geographer Jedidiah Morse, author of *Geography Made Easy* (1784), said the country must have its own textbooks to prevent the aristocratic

THE PENNSYLVANIA HOSPITAL The ideas of the Enlightenment spread through American culture in the eighteenth and nineteenth centuries and strengthened the belief that every individual was a divine being and could be redeemed from even the most miserable condition. Hospitals and asylums—such as this institution in Pennsylvania—began to emerge to provide settings for the redemption of the poor, the ill, and the deviant. (Library Company of Philadelphia)

ideas of England from infecting the people. The Connecticut schoolmaster and lawyer Noah Webster argued similarly that American students should be educated as patriots, their minds filled with nationalistic, American thoughts.

To encourage a distinctive American culture and help unify the new nation, Webster insisted on a simplified and Americanized system of spelling—"honor" instead of "honour," for example. His *American Spelling Book,* first published in 1783 and commonly known as the "blue-backed speller," eventually sold over 100 million copies, to become the best-selling book (except for the Bible) in the history of American publishing. In addition, his school dictionary, issued in 1806, was republished in many editions and was eventually enlarged to become (in 1828) *An American Dictionary of the English Language.* His speller and his dictionary established a national standard of words and usages.

NOAH WEBSTER

Those Americans who aspired to create a more elevated national literary life faced a number of obstacles. There was, to be sure, a large potential audience for a national literature—a substantial reading public, created in part by the wide circulation of newspapers and political pamphlets during the Revolution. But there were few opportunities for would-be American authors to get their work before the public. Printers preferred to publish popular works by English writers (for which they had to pay no royalties); magazine publishers filled their pages largely with items clipped from British periodicals. Only those American writers willing to pay the cost and bear the risk of publishing their own works could compete for public attention.

> AMERICANS BELIEVED THAT THEIR "HAPPY LAND" WAS DESTINED TO BECOME THE "SEAT OF EMPIRE" AND THE "FINAL STAGE" OF CIVILIZATION, WITH "GLORIOUS WORKS OF HIGH INVENTION AND OF WOND'ROUS ART."

Even so, a growing number of American authors struggled to create a strong native literature so that, as the poet Joel Barlow wrote, "true ideas of glory may be implanted in the minds of men here, to take the place of the false and destructive ones that have degraded the species in other countries." Barlow himself, one of a group of Connecticut writers known as the "Hartford Wits," published an epic poem, *The Columbiad,* in 1807, in an effort to convey the special character of American civilization. The acclaim it received helped to encourage other native writers.

Among the most ambitious was the Philadelphian Charles Brockden Brown. Like many Americans, he was attracted to the relatively new literary form of the novel, which had become popular in England in the late eighteenth century and had been successfully imported to America. But Brown sought to do more than simply imitate the English forms; he tried to use his novels to give voice to distinctively American themes, to convey the "soaring passions and intellectual energy" of the new nation. His obsession with originality led him to produce a body of work characterized by a fascination with horror and deviant behavior. Perhaps as a result, his novels failed to develop a large popular following.

Much more successful was Washington Irving, a resident of New York State who won wide acclaim for his satirical histories of early American life and his powerful fables of society in the New World. His popular folktales, recounting the adventures of such American rustics as Ichabod Crane and Rip Van Winkle,

WASHINGTON IRVING

made him the widely acknowledged leader of American literary life in his era and one of the few writers of that time whose works would continue to be read by later generations.

Perhaps the most influential works by American authors in the early republic were not poems, novels, or stories, but works of history that glorified the nation's past. Mercy Otis Warren, who had been an influential playwright and agitator during the 1770s, continued her literary efforts with a three-volume *History of the Revolution,* published in 1805 and emphasizing the heroism of the American struggle. Mason Weems, an Anglican clergyman, published a eulogistic *Life of Washington* in 1806, which became one of the best-selling books of the era. Weems had little interest in historical accuracy. He portrayed the aristocratic former president as a homespun man possessing simple republican virtues. (He also invented, among other things, the famous story of Washington and the cherry tree.) History, like literature, was serving as a vehicle for instilling a sense of nationalism in the American people.

RELIGIOUS SKEPTICISM

The American Revolution weakened traditional forms of religious practice by detaching churches from government and by elevating ideas of individual liberty and reason. By the 1790s, only a small proportion of white Americans (perhaps as few as 10 percent) were members of formal churches, and ministers were complaining often about the "decay of vital piety." Religious traditionalists were particularly alarmed about the emergence of new, "rational" theologies that reflected modern, scientific attitudes and de-emphasized the role of God in the world.

Some Americans, including Jefferson and Franklin, embraced "deism," which had originated among Enlightenment philosophers in France. Deists accepted the existence of God, but considered Him a remote being who, after having

DEISM created the universe, had withdrawn from direct involvement with the human race and its sins. Books and articles attacking religious "superstitions" attracted wide readerships and provoked much discussion, among them Thomas Paine's *The Age of Reason,* published in parts between 1794 and 1796. Paine once declared that Christianity was the "strangest religion ever set up," for "it committed a murder upon Jesus in order to redeem mankind from the sin of eating an apple."

Religious skepticism also produced the philosophies of "universalism" and "unitarianism," which emerged at first as dissenting views within the New England Congregational Church. Disciples of these new ideas rejected the Calvinist belief in predestination, arguing that salvation was available to all. They rejected, too, the idea of the Trinity. Jesus was only a great religious teacher, they claimed, not the Son of God. So wide was the gulf

> BY THE 1790S, ONLY A SMALL PROPORTION OF WHITE AMERICANS (PERHAPS AS FEW AS 10 PERCENT) WERE MEMBERS OF FORMAL CHURCHES, AND MINISTERS WERE COMPLAINING OFTEN ABOUT THE "DECAY OF VITAL PIETY."

between these dissenters and the Congregationalist establishment that it finally became a permanent schism. James Murray (who later married Judith Sargent Murray) founded the Universalist Church as a separate denomination in Gloucester, Massachusetts, in 1779; the Unitarian Church was established in Boston three years later.

Some Americans believed that the spread of rationalism marked the end of traditional, evangelistic religion in the new nation. But quite the contrary was true. In fact, most Americans continued to hold strong religious beliefs. What had declined was their commitment to organized churches and denominations, which many considered too formal and traditional for their own zealous religious faith. Deism, Universalism, Unitarianism, and other "rational" religions seemed more powerful than they actually were because for a time traditional evangelicals were confused and disorganized. But beginning in 1801, traditional religion staged a dramatic comeback in the form of a wave of revivalism known as the Second Great Awakening.

THE SECOND GREAT AWAKENING

The origins of the Second Awakening lay in the efforts of conservative theologians of the 1790s to fight the spread of religious rationalism, and to encourage church establishments to revitalize their organizations.

Leaders of several different denominations participated in the evangelizing efforts that drove the revival. Presbyterians tried to arouse the faithful on the western fringe of white settlement, and conservatives in the church denounced New Light dissenters (people who had altered their religious views to make them more compatible with the world of scientific rationalism). Methodism, which John Wesley had founded in England, spread to America in the 1770s and became a formal denomination in 1784 under the leadership of Francis Asbury. Authoritarian and hierarchical in structure, the Methodist Church sent itinerant preachers throughout the nation to win recruits; it soon became the fastest-growing denomination in America. Almost as successful were the Baptists, who were themselves relatively new to America; they found an especially fervent following in the South.

By 1800, the revivalist energies of all these denominations were combining to create the greatest surge of evangelical fervor since the first Great Awakening sixty

CANE RIDGE years before. Beginning among Presbyterians in several eastern colleges (most notably at Yale, under the leadership of President Timothy Dwight), the new awakening soon spread rapidly throughout the country, reaching its greatest heights in the western regions. In only a few years, a large proportion of the American people were mobilized by the

RELIGIOUS REVIVALS

Camp (or revival) meetings were popular among some evangelical Christians in America as early as 1800. By the 1820s, there were approximately 1,000 meetings a year, most of them in the South and West. Estimated attendance at some of the larger meetings was as large as 25,000 people.

Today, there are many large "megachurches" throughout the United States. Although opinions vary on what constitutes a "megachurch," the Hartford Institute on Religious Research lists these characteristics: 1) 2,000 or more persons in attendance at weekly worship; 2) A charismatic, authoritative senior minister; 3) A very active seven-day-a-week congregational community; 4) A multitude of social and outreach ministries; and 5) A complex differentiated organizational structure. By this definition, there are over 1,200 megachurches in the United States, most of them located in Sunbelt states, especially California, Texas, Georgia, and Florida.

The two images below, the first a lithograph dated 1837 and the second a photograph of a modern megachurch, suggest both comparisons and contrasts between the two religious movements.

CAMP MEETINGS—1837

METHODIST CAMP MEETING, 1837. (The Granger Collection, New York)

UNDERSTAND, ANALYZE, AND EVALUATE

1. What does the illustration reveal about the type of people who attended camp or religious revival meetings? In what types of activities are the people of this image engaged?
2. How would you characterize the setting in which this meeting is taking place? What does the setting tell us about the places where people gathered and the ways in which they practiced their religion?

MEGACHURCHES—2010

LOCATED IN GARDEN GROVE, CALIFORNIA, THE CRYSTAL CATHEDRAL IS THE HOME BASE FOR THE INTERNATIONAL CRYSTAL CATHEDRAL MINISTRIES, INCLUDING A CONGREGATION OF OVER 10,000 MEMBERS AND THE INTERNATIONALLY TELEVISED "HOUR OF POWER." (Source: http://www.nationalchristianchoir.org/PhotoGallery/1990's/Large/19961013CrystalCath.jpg)

MAKE CONNECTIONS

1. How would you characterize this setting? How does it differ from the setting of the revival meeting? What does it have in common with the first setting?
2. List the various things that people are doing in this photograph. How does that differ from the activities portrayed in the 1837 lithograph?
3. What do these images suggest about the connections between today's megachurches and the camp meetings of the Second Great Awakening?

movement, and membership in those churches embracing the revival—most prominently the Methodists, the Baptists, and the Presbyterians—was mushrooming. At Cane Ridge, Kentucky, in the summer of 1801, a group of evangelical ministers presided over the nation's first "camp meeting"—an extraordinary revival that lasted several days and impressed all who saw it with its size (some estimated that 25,000 people attended) and its fervor. Such events became common in subsequent years, as the Methodists in particular came to rely on them as a way to "harvest" new members. The Methodist circuit-riding preacher Peter Cartwright won national fame as he traveled from region to region exhorting his listeners to embrace the church. Even Cartwright, however, was often unprepared for the results of his efforts—a religious frenzy that at times produced convulsions, fits, rolling in the dirt, and twitching "holy jerks."

The message of the Second Great Awakening was not entirely consistent, but its basic thrust was clear. Individuals must readmit God and Christ into their daily lives, must embrace a fervent, active piety, and must reject the skeptical rationalism that threatened traditional beliefs. Even so, the wave of revivalism did not serve to restore the religious ideas of the past. Few of the revivalist denominations any longer accepted the idea of predestination; and the belief that a person could affect his or her own destiny added intensity to the individual's search for salvation. The Awakening, in short, combined a more active piety with a belief in God as an active force in the world whose grace could be attained through faith and good works.

The Second Awakening also accelerated the growth of different sects and denominations. It helped create a broad popular

MESSAGE OF THE GREAT AWAKENING acceptance of the idea that men and women could belong to different Protestant churches and still be committed to essentially the same Christian faith. Finally, the new evangelicalism—by spreading religious fervor into virtually every area of the nation—provided a vehicle for establishing a sense of order and social stability in communities still searching for an identity.

One of the most striking features of the Second Great Awakening was the preponderance of women (particularly young women) within it. One reason for this was that women were more numerous in certain regions than men. Adventurous young men often struck out on their own and moved west; women, for the most part, had no such options. Their marriage prospects thus diminished and their futures plagued with uncertainty, some women discovered in religion a foundation on which to build their lives. But even where there was no shortage of men, women flocked to the revivals in enormous numbers, which suggests that they were responding to their changing economic roles as well. The movement of industrial work out of the home (where women had often contributed to the family economy through spinning and weaving) and into the factory— a process making rapid strides in the early nineteenth century (see pp. 188–189)—robbed older women, in particular, of one of their most important social roles. Religious enthusiasm helped compensate for the losses and adjustments these transitions

produced; it also provided access to a new range of activities associated with the churches—charitable societies ministering to orphans and the poor, missionary organizations, and others— in which women came to play important roles.

Although revivalism was most widespread within white society, it penetrated other cultures as well. In some areas of the

AFRICAN AMERICANS AND THE REVIVALS country, revivals were open to people of all races, and many African Americans not only attended but eagerly embraced the new religious fervor as well. Out of these revivals, in fact, emerged a substantial group of black preachers, who became important figures within the slave community. Some of them translated the apparently egalitarian religious message of the Second Awakening—that salvation was available to all—into a similarly egalitarian message for blacks in the present world. Out of black revival meetings in Virginia arose an elaborate plan in 1800 (devised by Gabriel Prosser, the brother of an African American preacher) for a slave rebellion and attack on Richmond. The plan was discovered and the rebellion forestalled by whites, but revivalism continued to stir racial unrest in the South.

The spirit of revivalism was also particularly strong in these years among Native Americans, although very different from revivalism in white or black society. It drew heavily from earlier tribal experiences. In the 1760s, the Delaware prophet Neolin had sparked a widespread revival in the Old Northwest with a message combining Christian and Indian imagery and bringing to Native American religion a vision of a personal God, intimately involved in the affairs of man. Neolin had also called for Indians to rise up in defense of their lands and had denounced the growth of trade and other relationships with white civilization. His vehement statements had helped stimulate the Indian military efforts of 1763 and beyond.

The dislocations and military defeats Indians suffered in the aftermath of the American Revolution created a sense of crisis

INDIANS AND THE SECOND GREAT AWAKENING among many of the eastern tribes in particular; as a result, the 1790s and early 1800s became another era of Indian religious fervor and prophecy. Presbyterian and Baptist missionaries were active among the southern tribes and sparked a great wave of conversions. The most important revivalism came from the efforts of another great prophet: Handsome Lake, a Seneca whose seemingly miraculous "rebirth" after years of alcoholism helped give him a special stature within his tribe. Handsome Lake, like Neolin before him, called for a revival of traditional Indian ways. (He claimed to have met Jesus, who instructed him to "tell your people they will become lost when they follow the ways of the white man.") Handsome Lake's message spread through the scattered Iroquois communities and inspired many Indians to give up whiskey, gambling, and other destructive customs derived from white society.

But the revival did not, in fact, lead to a true restoration of traditional Iroquois culture. Instead, Handsome Lake encouraged Christian missionaries to become active within the tribes, and he urged Iroquois men to abandon their roles as hunters (partly because so much of their hunting land had been seized by whites) and become sedentary farmers instead. Iroquois women, who had traditionally done the farming, were to move into more domestic roles. When some women resisted the change, Handsome Lake denounced them as witches. He demanded confessions from them and killed some of those who refused.

The Second Great Awakening also had important effects on those Americans who did not accept its teachings. The rational FREETHINKERS "freethinkers," whose skeptical philosophies had helped produce the revivals, were in many ways victims of the new religious fervor. They did not disappear after 1800, but their influence rapidly declined, and for many years they remained a small and defensive minority within American Christianity. Instead, the dominant religious characteristic of the new nation became a fervent evangelicalism, which would survive into the mid-nineteenth century and beyond.

STIRRINGS OF INDUSTRIALISM

Despite the hopes of Jefferson and his followers that the United States would remain a simple agrarian republic, the nation took its first, tentative steps in these years toward its transformation into an urban, industrial society.

TECHNOLOGY IN AMERICA

Americans imported some of these technological advances from England. (See "America in the World," pp. 194–195.) The British government attempted to protect the nation's manufacturing preeminence by preventing the export of textile machinery or the emigration of skilled mechanics. Despite such efforts, immigrants arrived in the United States with advanced knowledge of English technology, eager to introduce the new machines to America. Samuel Slater, for example, used the knowledge he had acquired before leaving England to build a spinning mill for the Quaker merchant Moses Brown in Pawtucket, Rhode Island, in 1790. It was the first modern factory in America.

America in the early nineteenth century also produced several important inventors of its own. Among them was Oliver Evans of Delaware, who devised a number of ingenious new machines: an automated flour mill, a card-making machine, and others. He made several important improvements in the steam engine, and in 1795 he published America's first textbook of mechanical engineering: *The Young Mill-Wright's and Miller's Guide*. His own flour mill, which began operations in 1787, required only two men to operate: one of them emptying a bag of wheat into the machinery, another putting the lid on the barrels of flour and rolling them away.

Even more influential for the future of the nation were the inventions of the Massachusetts-born, Yale-educated Eli Whitney, who revolutionized both cotton production and weap-

THE COTTON GIN Eli Whitney's cotton gin revolutionized the cotton economy of the South by making the processing of short-staple cotton simple and economical. These 1794 drawings are part of Whitney's application for a federal patent on his device. (National Archives)

ons manufacturing. The growth of the textile industry in England had created an enormous demand for cotton, a demand that planters in the American South were finding impossible to meet. Their greatest obstacle was separating the seeds from cotton fiber—a difficult and time-consuming process that was essential before cotton could be sold. Long-staple, or Sea Island, cotton, with its smooth black seeds and long fibers, was easy to clean, but it grew successfully only along the Atlantic coast or on the offshore islands of Georgia and South Carolina. There was not nearly enough of it to satisfy the demand. Short-staple cotton, by contrast, could grow inland through vast areas of the South. But its sticky green seeds were extremely difficult to remove. A skilled worker could clean no more than a few pounds a day by hand. Then, in 1793, Whitney, who was working at the time as a tutor on the Georgia plantation of General ELI WHITNEY'S Nathanael Greene's widow, invented a machine that performed the arduous task COTTON GIN quickly and efficiently. It was dubbed the cotton gin ("gin" was an abbreviation for "engine"), and it transformed the life of the South.

Mechanically, the gin was very simple. A toothed roller caught the fibers of the cotton boll and pulled them between the wires of a grating. The grating caught the seeds while a revolving brush removed the lint from the roller's teeth. With the device, a single operator could clean as much cotton in a few hours as a group of workers had once needed a whole day to do. The results were profound. Soon cotton growing spread into the upland South and beyond, and within a decade the total crop increased eightfold. African American slavery, which with the decline of tobacco production some had considered a dwindling institution, regained its importance, expanded, and became more firmly fixed upon the South.

The cotton gin not only changed the economy of the South, it also helped transform the North. The large supply of domestically produced fiber was a strong incentive to entrepreneurs in New England and elsewhere to develop an American textile industry. Few northern states could hope to thrive on the basis of agriculture alone; by learning to turn cotton into yarn and thread, plantation owners could become industrially prosperous instead. The manufacturing preeminence of the North, which emerged with the development of the textile industry in the 1820s and 1830s, helped drive a wedge between the nation's two most populous regions—one becoming increasingly industrial, the other more firmly wedded to agriculture.

THE COTTON GIN'S IMPACT ON THE NORTH

Whitney also made a major contribution to the development of modern warfare and in the process made a contribution to other industrial techniques. During the two years of undeclared war with France (1798 and 1799), Americans were deeply troubled by their lack of sufficient armaments for the expected hostilities. Production of muskets—each carefully handcrafted by a skilled gunsmith—was discouragingly slow. Whitney devised a machine to make each part of a gun according to an exact pattern. Tasks could thus be divided among several workers, and one laborer could quickly assemble a weapon out of parts made by several others. Before long, manufacturers of sewing machines, clocks, and many other complicated products were using the same system.

The new technological advances were relatively isolated phenomena during the early years of the nineteenth century. Not until at least the 1840s did the nation begin to develop a true manufacturing economy. But the inventions of this period were crucial in making the eventual transformation possible.

TRANSPORTATION INNOVATIONS

One of the prerequisites for industrialization is an efficient system for transporting raw materials to factories and finished

PAWTUCKET BRIDGE AND FALLS One reason for the growth of the textile industry in New England in the early nineteenth century was that there were many sources of water power in the region to run the machinery in the factories. That was certainly the case with Slater's Mill, one of the first American textile factories. It was located in Pawtucket, Rhode Island, alongside a powerful waterfall, demonstrating the critical importance of water power to early American industry. This view was painted by an anonymous artist in the 1810s. (Rhode Island Historical Society)

goods to markets. The United States had no such system in the early years of the republic. But work was under way that would ultimately remove the transportation obstacle.

There were several ways to solve the problem of the small American market. One was to look for customers overseas, and American merchants continued their efforts to do that. Among the first acts of the new Congress when it met in 1789 were two tariff bills giving preference to American ships in American ports, helping to stimulate an expansion of domestic shipping. More important—indeed the principal reason for the growth of American trade in this period—was the outbreak of war in Europe in the 1790s, allowing Yankee merchant vessels to take over most of the carrying trade between Europe and the Western Hemisphere. As early as 1793, the young republic had a merchant marine and a foreign trade larger than those of any country except England. In proportion to its population, the United States had more ships and international commerce than any country in the world. Between 1789 and 1810, the total tonnage of American vessels engaged in overseas traffic rose from less than 125,000 to nearly 1 million. American ships had carried only 30 percent of the country's exports in

RAPID GROWTH OF AMERICAN SHIPPING

1789; they were carrying over 90 percent in 1810. The figures for American ships carrying imports increased even more dramatically, from 17.5 percent to 90 percent in the same period.

Another solution to the problem of limited markets was to develop new markets at home, by improving transportation between the states and into the interior of the continent. In river transportation, a new era began with the development of the steamboat. A number of inventors began experimenting with steam-powered craft in the late eighteenth century; John Fitch exhibited a forty-five-foot vessel with paddles operated by steam to some of the delegates at the Constitutional Convention in 1787. But the real breakthrough was Oliver Evans's development of a high-pressure engine, lighter and more efficient than James Watt's, which made steam more feasible for powering boats (and, eventually, locomotives) as well as mill machinery.

The inventor Robert Fulton and the promoter Robert R. Livingston were principally responsible for perfecting the steamboat and bringing it to the attention of the nation. Their *Clermont,* equipped with paddle wheels and an English-built engine, sailed up the Hudson in the summer of 1807, demonstrating the practicability of steam navigation

ROBERT FULTON'S STEAMBOAT

A SCENE OF THE ROAD The watercolorist George Tattersall painted this image of a stagecoach negotiating the rough roads and bridges that were beginning to link the disparate regions of early-nineteenth-century America. (Museum of Fine Arts, Boston, Gift of Maxim Karolik, 56.400.11. Photograph © 2007 Museum of Fine Arts, Boston)

THE GLOBAL INDUSTRIAL REVOLUTION

THE tentative stirrings of industrial activity in the United States in the early nineteenth century were part of a vast movement that over the course of the century transformed much of the globe. Historians differ over precisely when the industrial revolution began, but it is clear that by the end of the eighteenth century it was well under way in many parts of the world. By the beginning of the twentieth century, industrialization had transformed the societies of Britain, most of continental Europe, Japan, and the United States.

For Americans, the industrial revolution was largely a result of the rapid changes in Great Britain, the nation with which they had the closest relations. Britain was the first nation to develop significant industrial capacity. The factory system took root in England in the late eighteenth century, revolutionizing the manufacture of cotton thread and cloth. One invention followed another in quick succession. Improvements in weaving drove improvements in spinning, and these changes created a demand for new devices for carding (combing and straightening the fibers for the spinner). Water, wind, and animal power continued to be important in the textile industry; but more important was the emergence of steam power—which began to proliferate after the appearance of James Watt's advanced steam engine (patented in 1769). England's textile industry quickly became the most profitable in the world, and it helped encourage comparable advances in other fields of manufacturing as well. Despite the efforts of the British government to prevent the export of English industrial technology, knowledge of the new machines reached other nations quickly, usually through the emigration of people who had learned the technology in British factories.

America benefited the most from English technology, because it received more immigrants from Great Britain than from any other country. But English technology also spread quickly to the nations of continental Europe as well. In Japan, the sudden intrusion of American and European traders helped cause the so-called Meiji reforms of the 1880s and 1890s, which launched a period of rapid industrialization there as well.

Industrialization changed not just the world's economies, but also its societies. First in England, and then in Europe, America, and Japan, social systems underwent wrenching changes. Hundreds of thousands, and eventually millions, of men and women moved from rural areas into cities to work in factories, where they experienced both the benefits and the costs of industrialization. Many of those who moved from farm to factory experienced some improvement in nutrition and other material circumstances, even in their health. But there were psychological costs to being suddenly uprooted from one way of life and thrust into another, fundamentally different one.

THE ENGLISH CANAL AGE Industrialization in England contributed, as it did in America, to the building of new transportation facilities to serve the growing commercial markets of the new economy. Among the most popular such facilities were canals, among them the Regent's Canal in London, pictured here in the 1820s. (Guildhall Library, Corporation of London/The Bridgeman Art Library)

(even though it took the ship thirty hours to go 150 miles). In 1811, a partner of Living-ston's, Nicholas J. Roosevelt (a remote ancestor of Theodore Roosevelt), introduced the steamboat to the West by sending the *New Orleans* from Pittsburgh down the Ohio and Mississippi. The next year, this vessel began a profitable career of service between New Orleans and Natchez.

Meanwhile, what was to become known as the "turnpike era" THE TURNPIKE ERA had begun. In 1792, a corporation constructed a toll road running the sixty miles from Philadelphia to Lancaster, Pennsylvania, with a hard-packed surface of crushed rock. This venture proved so successful that several other companies laid out

Little in most workers' prior experience had prepared them for the nature of industrial labor. The routinized, rigidly scheduled work of the urban factory contrasted sharply with the varying, seasonal work pattern of the rural economy. Industrial workers experienced, too, a fundamental change in their relationship with their employers. Unlike rural landlords and local aristocrats, factory owners and managers—the new class of industrial capitalists, many of them accumulating unprecedented wealth—were usually remote and inaccessible figures. They dealt with their workers impersonally, and the result was a growing schism between the two classes—each lacking access to or understanding of the other. Working men and women throughout the globe began thinking of themselves as a distinct class, with common goals and interests. Their efforts simultaneously to adjust to their new way of life and to resist its most damaging aspects sometimes created great social turbulence. Battles between workers and employers became a characteristic feature of industrial life throughout the world.

Life in industrial nations changed at every level. Populations in industrial countries grew rapidly, and people began to live longer. At the same time, industrial cities began to produce great increases in pollution, crime, and—until modern sanitation systems emerged—infectious disease. Around the industrial world, middle classes expanded and came, in varying degrees, to dominate the economy (although not always the culture or the politics) of their nations.

Not since the agrarian revolution thousands of years earlier, when many humans had turned from hunting to farming for sustenance, had there been an economic change of a magnitude comparable to that of the industrial revolution. Centuries of traditions, social patterns, and cultural and religious assumptions were challenged and often shattered. The social and economic consequences of industrialism were complex and profound, and they continue today to shape the nature of global society. •

UNDERSTAND, ANALYZE, AND EVALUATE

1. Why did the British government attempt to prevent the export of Britain's industrial technology?
2. Was the industrial revolution truly a global revolution? Why or why not?
3. Some observers have compared the information technology developments of the late twentieth century to those of the industrial revolution. Are the changes that have resulted from the high-tech developments of the late twentieth century as profound as those resulting from the industrial revolution? In what way might the high-tech advances be considered a "revolution"? What have been the social and economic consequences of these advances?

similar turnpikes (so named from the kind of tollgate frequently used) from other cities to neighboring towns. Since the turnpikes had to produce profits for the companies that built them, construction costs had to be low enough and the prospective traffic heavy enough to ensure an early and ample return. As a result, these roads, radiating from eastern cities, ran

comparatively short distances and through densely settled areas. No private operators were willing to build similar highways over the mountains and into the less populated interior. State governments and the federal government eventually had to finance them.

THE RISING CITIES

Despite all the changes and all the advances, America in the early nineteenth century remained an overwhelmingly rural and agrarian nation. Only 3 percent of the non-Indian population lived in towns of more than 8,000 at the time of the second census, in 1800. Ten percent lived west of the Appalachian Mountains, far from what urban centers there were. Much of the country remained a wilderness. Even the nation's largest cities could not begin to compare, either in size or in cultural sophistication, with such European capitals as London and Paris.

Yet here too there were signs of change. The leading American cities might not yet have become world capitals, but they were large and complex enough to rival the important secondary cities of Europe. Philadelphia, with 70,000 residents, and New York, with 60,000, were becoming major centers of commerce and learning. The cities were also developing a distinctively urban culture. So too were the next-largest cities of the new nation: Baltimore (26,000 in 1800), Boston (24,000), and Charleston (20,000).

People living in towns and cities lived differently than the vast majority of Americans who continued to work as farmers. Among other things, urban life produced affluence, and affluent people sought amenities that would not have entered the imaginings of any but the wealthiest farmers. They sought increasing elegance and refinement in their homes, their grounds, and their dress. They also looked for diversions—music, theater, dancing, and, for many people, one of the most popular entertainments of all, horse racing. (See "Patterns of Popular Culture," pp. 198–199.)

URBAN LIFE

Much remained to be done before this small and still half-formed nation would become a complex modern society. It was still possible in the early nineteenth century to believe that those changes might not ever occur. But forces were already at work that, in time, would lastingly transform the United States.

JEFFERSON THE PRESIDENT

Privately, Thomas Jefferson may well have considered his victory over John Adams in 1800 to be what he later termed it: a revolution "as real . . . as that of 1776." Publicly, however, he was restrained and conciliatory as he assumed office, attempting to minimize the differences between the two parties and to calm the passions that the bitter campaign had aroused. "We are all republicans, we are all federalists," he said in his inaugural address. And during his eight years in office, he did much to prove those words correct. There was no complete repudiation of Federalist policies, no true "revolution." Indeed, at times

NORTH AMERICA IN 1800 This map illustrates how substantially the non-Indian settlement of British North America (much of it by 1800 the United States) had expanded since 1700. On p. 68, a similar map shows a tiny fringe of settlement along the Atlantic seaboard. Note the new areas of settlement here: west of the original thirteen colonies— including, in Kentucky, an area that reaches almost to the Mississippi River. Significant settlements are also now visible along the Gulf Coast, especially in the territory around New Orleans. Scattered non-Indian settlements are visible in the Southwest and along the coast of California, as well as in southern Canada (where the settlements were largely forts).

• *How does this map help explain the spread of settlement south from Pittsburgh into western Virginia and Kentucky?*

Jefferson seemed to outdo the Federalists at their own work— most notably in overseeing a remarkable expansion of the territory of the United States.

THE FEDERAL CITY AND THE "PEOPLE'S PRESIDENT"

Symbolic of the relative unimportance of the federal government during the Jeffersonian era was the character of the newly

THE NEW CAPITAL CITY

founded national capital, the city of Washington. The French architect Pierre L'Enfant had designed the capital on a grand scale, with broad avenues radiating out from the uncompleted Capitol building, set on one of the area's highest hills. Washington was, many Americans believed, to become the Paris of the United States.

In reality, however, throughout Jefferson's presidency—and indeed through most of the nineteenth century—Washington remained little more than a straggling, provincial village. Although the population increased steadily from the 3,200 counted in the 1800 census, it never rivaled that of New York,

Philadelphia, or the other major cities of the nation. The city remained a raw, inhospitable community with few public buildings of any consequence. Members of Congress viewed Washington not as a home but as a place to visit briefly during sessions of the legislature and leave as quickly as possible. Most lived in a cluster of simple boardinghouses in the vicinity of the Capitol. It was not unusual for a member of Congress to resign his seat in the midst of a session to return home if he had an opportunity to accept the more prestigious post of member of his state legislature.

Jefferson set out as president to act in a spirit of democratic simplicity in keeping with the frontierlike character of the unfinished federal city. He was a wealthy and aristocratic planter by background, the owner of more than 100 slaves, and a man of rare cultivation and sophistication; but he conveyed to the public an image of plain, almost crude disdain for pretension. He walked like an ordinary citizen to and from his inauguration at the Capitol. In the presidential mansion, which had not yet acquired the name "White House," he disregarded the courtly etiquette of his predecessors (in part, no doubt, because as a widower he had no first lady to take charge of social affairs). At

Major government buildings
Legislators' residences in 1807
Executives' residences, 1800–1828

Capitol

Marine Camp

White House

PENNSYLVANIA AVENUE

Treasury

Tiber River

Navy Yard

Anacostia River (Eastern Branch)

Additional residences to the west, in Georgetown

Potomac River

0   1/2 mi
0   1/2   1 km

WASHINGTON, D.C., IN THE EARLY NINETEENTH CENTURY The nation's capital moved from New York to Washington in 1800, into a new city designed on a grand scale by the French planner Pierre L'Enfant. But in the early eighteenth century, it remained little more than a village on a marshy tract of land, with hot, humid summers. This map shows the location of the principal government buildings in the early republic, and also the sites of the homes of members of the executive and legislative branches. Note how the homes of executive officials mostly clustered around the White House and the Treasury, while those of legislators mainly clustered around the Capitol.

• *How did the geography of the city help shape the relationship between the executive and legislative branches?*

state dinners, he let his guests scramble pell-mell for places at the table. He did not always bother to dress up, once prompting the fastidious British ambassador to complain of being received by the president in coat and pantaloons that were "indicative of utter slovenliness and indifference to appearances."

Yet Jefferson managed nevertheless to impress most of those who knew him. He was a brilliant conversationalist, a gifted writer, and one of the nation's most intelligent and creative men, with perhaps a wider range of interests and accomplishments than any public figure in American history. In addition to politics and diplomacy, he was an active architect, educator, inventor, scientific farmer, and philosopher-scientist.

Jefferson was, above all, a shrewd and practical politician. On the one hand, he went to great lengths to eliminate the aura of majesty surrounding the presidency that he believed his predecessors had created. At the same time, however, Jefferson worked hard to exert influence as the leader of his party, giving direction to Republicans in Congress by quiet and sometimes even devious means. Although the Republicans had objected strenuously to the efforts of their Federalist predecessors to build a network of influence through patronage, Jefferson, too, used his powers of appointment as an effective political weapon. By the end of his first term about half the government jobs, and by the end of his second term practically all of them, were in the hands of loyal Republicans.

JEFFERSON THE POLITICIAN

When Jefferson ran for reelection in 1804, he won overwhelmingly. The Federalist presidential nominee, Charles C. Pinckney, could not even carry most of the party's New England strongholds. Jefferson won 162 electoral votes to Pinckney's 14, and the Republican majorities in both houses of Congress increased.

DOLLARS AND SHIPS

Under Washington and Adams, the Republicans believed, the government had been needlessly extravagant. Yearly federal ex-

penditures had almost tripled between 1793 and 1800. Hamilton had, as he had intended, increased the public debt and created an extensive system of internal taxation, including the hated whiskey excise tax.

The Jefferson administration moved deliberately to reverse the trend. In 1802, it persuaded Congress to abolish all internal taxes, leaving customs duties and the sale of western lands as the only sources of revenue for the government. Meanwhile, Secretary of the Treasury Albert Gallatin drastically reduced government spending, cutting the already small staffs of the executive departments to minuscule levels. Although Jefferson was unable to retire the entire national debt, as he had hoped, he did cut it almost in half (from $83 million to $45 million) during his presidency.

LIMITING THE FEDERAL GOVERNMENT

Jefferson also scaled down the armed forces. He reduced the army of 4,000 men to 2,500. He cut the navy from twenty-five ships to seven and reduced the number of officers and sailors accordingly. Anything but the smallest of standing armies, he argued, might menace civil liberties and civilian control of government. And a large navy, he feared, might promote overseas commerce, which Jefferson believed should remain secondary to agriculture. Yet Jefferson was not a pacifist. At the same time that he was reducing the size of the army and navy, he was helping to establish the United States Military Academy at West Point, founded in 1802. And when trouble began brewing overseas, he began again to build up the fleet.

Such trouble appeared first in the Mediterranean, off the coast of northern Africa. For years the Barbary states of North Africa—Morocco, Algiers, Tunis, and Tripoli (now part of Libya)—had been demanding protection money from all nations whose ships sailed the Mediterranean. Even Great Britain gave regular contributions to the pirates. During the 1780s and 1790s the United States agreed to treaties providing for annual tribute to the Barbary states, but Jefferson

CHALLENGING THE BARBARY PIRATES

PATTERNS OF POPULAR CULTURE

HORSE RACING IN EARLY AMERICA

INFORMAL horse racing began in North America almost as soon as Europeans settled the English colonies. Formal racing followed quickly. The first race track in North America—New Market (named for a popular race course in England)—was established in 1665 near the site of present-day Garden City, on Long Island in New York. Tracks quickly developed wide appeal, and soon horse racing had spread up and down the Atlantic coast. By the time of the American Revolution, it

OAKLAND HOUSE AND RACE COURSE This 1840 painting by Robert Brammer and August A. Von Smith portrays men and women flocking to an early race course in Louisville, Kentucky, which provided entertainment to affluent white southerners. (*Oakland House and Race Course, Louisville, 1840.* By Robert Brammer and August A. Von Smith. Collection of The Speed Art Museum, Louisville, Kentucky. Purchase, Museum Art Fund, 56.19)

had become popular in almost every colony and was moving as well into the newly settled areas of the Southwest. Andrew Jackson was a founder of the first racing track in Nashville, Tennessee, in the early nineteenth century. Kentucky—whose native bluegrass was early recognized as ideal for grazing horses—had eight tracks by 1800.

Like almost everything else in the life of early America, the world of horse racing was bounded by lines of class and race. For many years, it was considered the exclusive preserve of "gentlemen," so much so that in 1674 a court in Virginia fined James Bullocke, a tailor, for proposing a race, "it being contrary to Law for a Labourer to make a race, being a sport only for Gentlemen." But while white aristocrats retained control of racing, they were not the only people who participated in it. Southern aristocrats often trained young male slaves as jockeys for their horses, just as northern horse owners employed the services of free blacks as riders. In the North and the South, African Americans eventually emerged as some of the most talented and experienced trainers of racing horses. And despite social and legal pressures, free blacks and poor whites often staged their own informal races.

Racing also began early to reflect the growing sectional rivalry between the North and the South. In 1824, the Union Race Course on Long

was reluctant to continue this policy of appeasement. "Tribute or war is the usual alternative of these Barbary pirates," he said. "Why not build a navy and decide on war?"

In 1801, the pasha (leader) of Tripoli forced Jefferson's hand. Unsatisfied by the American response to his extortionate demands, he ordered the flagpole of the American consulate chopped down—a symbolic declaration of war. Jefferson responded cautiously, building up the American fleet in the region over the next several years. Finally, in 1805, the United States reached an agreement with the pasha that ended American payments of tribute to Tripoli but required the United States to pay a substantial (and humiliating) ransom of $60,000 for the release of American prisoners seized by Barbary pirates.

CONFLICT WITH THE COURTS

Having won control of the executive and legislative branches of government, the Republicans looked with suspicion on the judi-

ciary, which remained largely in the hands of Federalist judges. Soon after Jefferson's first inauguration, his followers in Congress launched an attack on this last preserve of the opposition. Their first step was the repeal of the Judiciary Act of 1801, thus eliminating the judgeships to which Adams had made his "midnight appointments."

The debate over the courts led to one of the most important
judicial decisions in the history of the nation. Federalists had long maintained that the Supreme Court had the authority to nullify acts of Congress (although the Constitution said nothing specifically to support the claim), and the Court itself had actually exercised the power of judicial review in 1796 when it upheld the validity of a law passed by the legislature. But the Court's authority in this area would not be secure, it was clear, until it actually declared a congressional act unconstitutional.

In 1803, in the case of *Marbury v. Madison,* it did so. William Marbury, one of Adams's "midnight appointments," had been

JUDICIAL REVIEW

THE ECLIPSE-HENRY MATCH RACE "Match races" between famous horses were a popular feature of early-nineteenth-century horse racing. This famous 1823 race on Long Island, New York, pitted prize-winning horses from the North and the South against one another. American Eclipse, the northern entry, won. (Private collection)

Island established an astounding $24,000 purse for a race between two famous thoroughbreds: American Eclipse (from the North) and Sir Henry (from the South). American Eclipse won two of the three heats, but a southern racehorse prevailed in another such celebrated contest in 1836. These intersectional races, which drew enormous crowds and created tremendous publicity, continued into the 1850s, until the North-South rivalry began to take a deadly form.

Horse racing remained popular after the Civil War, but two developments changed its character considerably. One was the successful effort to drive African Americans out of the sport. At least until the 1890s, black jockeys and trainers remained central to racing. At the first Kentucky Derby, in 1875, fourteen of the fifteen horses had African American riders. One black man, Isaac Murphy, won a remarkable 44 percent of all races in which he rode, including three Kentucky Derbys. Gradually, however, the same social dynamics that enforced racial segregation in so many other areas of American life penetrated racing as well. By the beginning of the twentieth century, white jockeys and organized jockey clubs had driven almost all black riders and many black trainers out of the sport.

The second change was the introduction of formalized betting to the sport. In the late nineteenth century, race tracks began creating betting systems to lure customers to the races. At the same time that the breeding of racehorses was moving into the hands of enormously wealthy families, the audience for racing was becoming increasingly working class

and lower middle class. The people who now came to tracks were mostly white men, and some white women, lured to the races not by a love of horses—which were coming to play a less central role in their everyday lives—but by the usually futile hope of quick and easy riches through gambling. •

UNDERSTAND, ANALYZE, AND EVALUATE

1. Why do you think horse racing was such a popular spectator sport in early America? Why has it continued to be popular?
2. How did changes in the sport of horse racing reflect similar changes in American society at large?
3. Is horse racing still a sport "bounded by lines of class and race"? What other spectator sports were or are similarly bounded?

named a justice of the peace in the District of Columbia. But his commission, although signed and sealed, had not been delivered to him before Adams left office. Once Jefferson became president, the new secretary of state, James Madison, was responsible for transmitting appointments. He had refused to hand over the commission to Marbury. Marbury appealed to the Supreme Court for an order directing Madison to perform his official duty. In its historic ruling, the Court found that Marbury had a right to his commission but that the Court had no authority to order Madison to deliver it. On the surface, therefore, the decision was a victory for the administration. But of much greater importance than the relatively insignificant matter of Marbury's commission was the Court's reasoning in the decision.

MARBURY V. MADISON

The original Judiciary Act of 1789 had given the Court the power to compel executive officials to act in such matters as the delivery of commissions, and it was on that basis that Marbury had filed his suit. But the Court ruled that Congress had ex-

ceeded its authority in creating that statute: that the Constitution had defined the powers of the judiciary and that the legislature had no right to expand them. The relevant section of the 1789 act was therefore void. In seeming to deny its own authority, the Court was in fact radically enlarging it. The justices had repudiated a relatively minor power (the power to force the delivery of a commission) by asserting a vastly greater one (the power to nullify an act of Congress).

The chief justice of the United States at the time of the ruling was John Marshall, one of the towering figures in the history of American law. A leading Federalist and prominent Virginia lawyer, he had served John Adams as secretary of state. (It had been Marshall, ironically, who had neglected to deliver Marbury's commission in the closing hours of the administration.) In 1801, just before leaving office, Adams had appointed him chief justice, and almost immediately Marshall established himself as the dominant figure on the Court, shaping virtually all its

JOHN MARSHALL

THOMAS JEFFERSON This 1805 portrait by the noted American painter Rembrandt Peale shows Jefferson at the beginning of his second term as president. It also conveys (through the simplicity of dress and the slightly unkempt hair) the image of democratic simplicity that Jefferson liked to project. (New-York Historical Society)

JEFFERSON THE ARCHITECT Among his many accomplishments, Thomas Jefferson was a gifted architect. This rotunda is the centerpiece of the central campus of the University of Virginia, which Jefferson designed near the end of his life. Earlier, he designed his own home near Charlottesville, Monticello; and his proposal for a president's mansion in Washington placed second in a blind competition. (University of Virginia Library)

most important rulings—including, of course, *Marbury v. Madison*. Through a succession of Republican administrations, he established the judiciary as a branch of government coequal with the executive and the legislature—a position that the founders of the republic had never clearly indicated it should occupy.

Jefferson recognized the threat that an assertive judiciary could pose to his policies. Even while the *Marbury* case was still pending, he was preparing for a renewed assault on this last Federalist stronghold. He urged Congress to impeach obstructive judges, and Congress attempted to oblige him. The Republicans successfully removed from office a district judge, John Pickering of New Hampshire (on the perhaps specious grounds that he was insane and thus unfit for office). They later

IMPEACHMENT OF SAMUEL CHASE targeted a justice of the Supreme Court itself: Justice Samuel Chase, a highly partisan Federalist. Chase had certainly been injudicious; he had, for example, delivered stridently partisan speeches from the bench. But he had committed no crime. Some Republicans argued, however, that impeachment was not merely a criminal proceeding. Congress could properly impeach a judge for political reasons—for obstructing the other branches of the government and disregarding the will of the people.

At Jefferson's urging, the House impeached Chase and sent him to trial before the Senate early in 1805. But Republican leaders were unable to get the necessary two-thirds vote for conviction in the Senate. Chase's acquittal helped establish that impeachment would not become a routine political weapon, that something more than partisan disagreement should have to underlie the process, a precedent that Congress only occasionally violated in future years. Marshall remained secure in his position as chief justice. And the judiciary survived as a powerful force within the government—more often than not ruling on behalf of the centralizing, expansionary policies that the Republicans had hoped to reverse.

DOUBLING THE NATIONAL DOMAIN

In the same year that Jefferson became president of the United States, Napoleon Bonaparte made himself ruler of France with the title of first consul. In the year that Jefferson was reelected, Napoleon named himself emperor. The two men had little in common. Yet for a time they were of great help to each other in international politics—until Napoleon's ambitions moved from Europe to America and created conflict and estrangement.

JEFFERSON AND NAPOLEON

Having failed in a grandiose plan to seize India from the British Empire, Napoleon turned his imperial ambitions in a new direction: he began to dream of restoring French power in the New World. The territory east of the Mississippi, which France had ceded to Great Britain in 1763, was now mostly part of the

WEST POINT Creating a professional military was an important task for the leaders of the early republic. Without an army, they realized, it would be difficult for the United States to win respect in the world. The establishment in 1802 of the United States Military Academy at West Point (whose parade ground is pictured here) was, therefore, an important event in the early history of the republic. (U.S. Military Academy, West Point)

United States and lost to France forever. But Napoleon wanted to regain the lands west of the Mississippi, which now belonged to Spain, over which Napoleon now exercised strong influence. Under the secret Treaty of San Ildefonso of 1800 between the French and the Spanish, France regained title to Louisiana, which included almost the whole of the Mississippi Valley to the west of the river, plus New Orleans near its mouth. The Louisiana Territory would, Napoleon hoped, become the heart of a great French empire in America.

Also part of Napoleon's empire in the New World were the sugar-rich and strategically valuable West Indian islands that still belonged to France—Guadeloupe, Martinique, and above all Santo Domingo. But unrest among the Caribbean slaves posed a threat to Napoleon's hopes for the islands. Africans in Santo Domingo (inspired by the French Revolution) revolted and created a republic of their own, under the remarkable black leader Toussaint L'Ouverture. Taking

TOUSSAINT L'OUVERTURE

advantage of a truce in his war with England, Napoleon sent an army to the West Indies. It temporarily crushed the insurrection and restored French authority; but the incident was an early sign of the problems Napoleon would have in realizing his ambitions in America.

Jefferson was unaware at first of Napoleon's imperial ambitions in America, and for a time he pursued a foreign policy that reflected his well-known admiration for France. He appointed as American minister to Paris the ardently pro-French Robert R. Livingston. He worked to secure ratification of the Franco-American settlement of 1800 and began observing the terms of the treaty even before it was ratified. The Adams administration had joined with the British in recognizing and supporting the rebel regime of Toussaint L'Ouverture in Santo Domingo; Jefferson assured the French minister in Washington that the American people, especially those of the slaveholding states, did not approve of the black revolutionary, who was setting a bad example for their own slaves. He even implied that the United States might join with France in putting down the rebellion (although nothing ever came of the suggestion). Jefferson began to reconsider his position toward France, however, when he heard rumors of the secret transfer of Louisiana.

Jefferson was even more alarmed when, in the fall of 1802, he learned that the Spanish intendant at New Orleans (who still governed the city, since the French had not yet taken formal possession of the region) had announced a disturbing new regulation. American ships sailing the Mississippi River had for many years been accustomed to depositing their cargoes in New

Orleans for transfer to oceangoing vessels. The intendant now forbade the practice—even though Spain had guaranteed Americans that right in the Pinckney Treaty of 1795—thus effectively closing the lower Mississippi to American shippers.

Westerners demanded that the federal government do something to reopen the river. The president faced a dilemma. If he yielded to the frontier clamor and tried to change the policy by force, he would run the risk of a major war with France. If he ignored the westerners' demands, he might lose political support. But Jefferson saw another solution. He instructed Robert Livingston, the American ambassador in Paris, to negotiate the purchase of New Orleans. Livingston, on his own authority, proposed that the French sell the United States the vast western part of Louisiana as well.

In the meantime, Jefferson persuaded Congress to appropriate funds for an expansion of the army and the construction of a river fleet, and he deliberately gave the impression that American forces might soon descend on New Orleans and that the United States might form an alliance with Great Britain if the problems with France were not resolved.

NAPOLEON'S OFFER

Perhaps that was why Napoleon suddenly decided to accept Livingston's proposal and offer the United States the entire Louisiana Territory.

Napoleon had good reasons for the decision. His plans for an American empire had already gone seriously awry. That was partly because a yellow fever epidemic had wiped out much of the French army in the New World. But it was also because the expeditionary force Napoleon sent to take possession of

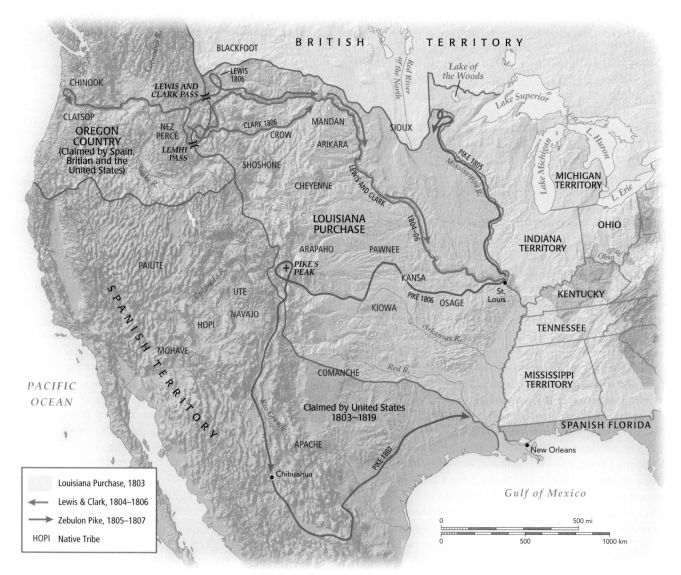

EXPLORING THE LOUISIANA PURCHASE, 1804–1807 When Jefferson purchased the Louisiana Territory from France in 1803, he doubled the size of the nation. But few Americans knew what they had bought. The Lewis and Clark expedition set out in 1804 to investigate the new territories, and this map shows their route, along with that of another inveterate explorer, Zebulon Pike. Note the vast distances the two parties covered (including, in both cases, a great deal of land outside the Louisiana Purchase). Note, too, how much of this enormous territory lay outside the orbit of even these ambitious explorations.

• *How did the American public react to the addition of these new territories?*

Louisiana had been frozen into a Dutch harbor through the winter of 1802–1803. By the time the harbor thawed in the spring of 1803, Napoleon was preparing for a renewed war in Europe. He would not, he realized, have the resources now to secure an American empire.

IN THE SPRING OF 1804, LEWIS AND CLARK, WITH A COMPANY OF FOUR DOZEN MEN, STARTED UP THE MISSOURI RIVER FROM ST. LOUIS.

River. In 1803, even before Napoleon's offer to sell Louisiana, Jefferson helped plan an expedition that was to cross the continent to the Pacific Ocean, gather geographic facts, and investigate prospects for trade with the Indians. He named as its leader his private secretary and Virginia neighbor, the thirty-three-year-old Meriwether Lewis, a veteran of Indian wars skilled in the ways of the wilderness. Lewis chose as a colleague the twenty-nine-year-old William Clark, who—like George Rogers Clark, his older brother—was an experienced frontiersman and Indian fighter. In the spring of 1804, Lewis and Clark, with a company of four dozen men, started up the Missouri River from St. Louis. With a Shoshone woman, Sacajawea, as their guide, they eventually crossed the Rocky Mountains, descended the Snake and Columbia Rivers, and in the late autumn of 1805

THE LOUISIANA PURCHASE

Faced with Napoleon's startling proposal, Livingston and James Monroe, whom Jefferson had sent to Paris to assist in the negotiations, had to decide first whether they should even consider making a treaty for the purchase of the entire Louisiana Territory, since they had not been authorized by their government to do so. But fearful that Napoleon might withdraw the offer, they decided to proceed without further instructions from home. After some haggling over the price, Livingston and Monroe signed the agreement on April 30, 1803.

By the terms of the treaty, the United States was to pay a total of 80 million francs ($15 million) to the French government. The United States was also to grant certain exclusive commercial privileges to France in the port of New Orleans and was to incorporate the residents of Louisiana into the Union with the same rights and privileges as other citizens. The boundaries of the purchase were not clearly defined; the treaty simply specified that Louisiana would occupy the "same extent" as it had when France and Spain had owned it.

In Washington, the president was both pleased and embarrassed when he received the treaty. He was pleased with the terms of the bargain but uncertain whether the United States had authority to accept it, since he had always insisted that the federal government could rightfully exercise only those powers explicitly assigned to it. Nowhere did the Constitution say anything about the acquisition of new territory. But Jefferson's advisers persuaded him that his treaty-making power under the Constitution would justify the purchase of Louisiana. The president finally agreed, trusting, as he said, "that the good sense of our country will correct the evil of loose construction when it shall produce ill effects." The Republican Congress promptly approved the treaty and appropriated money to implement its provisions. Finally, late in 1803, the French assumed formal control of Louisiana from Spain just long enough to turn the territory over to General James Wilkinson, the commissioner of the United States.

JEFFERSON'S QUANDARY

The government organized the Louisiana Territory much as it had organized the Northwest Territory, with the assumption that its various territories would eventually become states. The first of these was admitted to the Union as the state of Louisiana in 1812.

LEWIS AND CLARK EXPLORE THE WEST

Meanwhile, several ambitious explorations were revealing the geography of the far-flung new territory to white Americans, few of whom had ever ventured much beyond the Mississippi

THE JOURNAL OF LEWIS AND CLARK This page is from the journal the explorers Meriwether Lewis and William Clark kept on their famous journey through the territory the United States had acquired in the Louisiana Purchase—and beyond. Shown here is one of the rough maps they drew to describe the lands they had seen. (British Museum)

camped on the Pacific coast. In September 1806, they were back in St. Louis with elaborate records of the geography and the Indian civilizations they had observed along the way, and a lengthy diary recounting their experiences.

While Lewis and Clark were still on their journey, Jefferson dispatched other explorers to other parts of the Louisiana Territory. Lieutenant Zebulon Montgomery Pike, twenty-six

ZEBULON PIKE years old, led an expedition in the fall of 1805 from St. Louis into the upper Mississippi valley. In the summer of 1806, he set out again up the valley of the Arkansas River and into what later became Colorado, where he encountered (but failed in his attempt to climb) the peak that now bears his name. His account of his western travels created an enduring (and inaccurate) impression among many Americans in the East that the land between the Missouri River and the Rockies was an uninhabitable, uncultivable desert.

THE BURR CONSPIRACY

Jefferson's triumphant reelection in 1804 suggested that most of the nation approved the new territorial acquisition. But some New England Federalists raged against it. They realized that the more the West grew and the more new states joined the Union, the less power the Federalists and their region would retain. In

ESSEX JUNTO Massachusetts, a group of the most extreme Federalists, known as the Essex Junto, concluded that the only recourse for New England was to secede from the Union and form a separate "Northern Confederacy." If this confederacy was to have any hope for lasting success, the Federalists believed, it would have to include New York and New Jersey as well. But the leading Federalist in New York, Alexander Hamilton, refused to support the secessionist scheme. "Dismemberment of our empire," he wrote, "will be a clear sacrifice of great positive advantages without any counterbalancing good, administering no relief to our real disease, which is democracy."

Federalists in New York then turned to Hamilton's greatest political rival: Vice President Aaron Burr. He was a politician without prospects in his own party. Jefferson had never forgiven him for the 1800 election deadlock. Burr accepted a Federalist proposal that he become their candidate for governor of New York in 1804, and there were rumors (unsupported by any

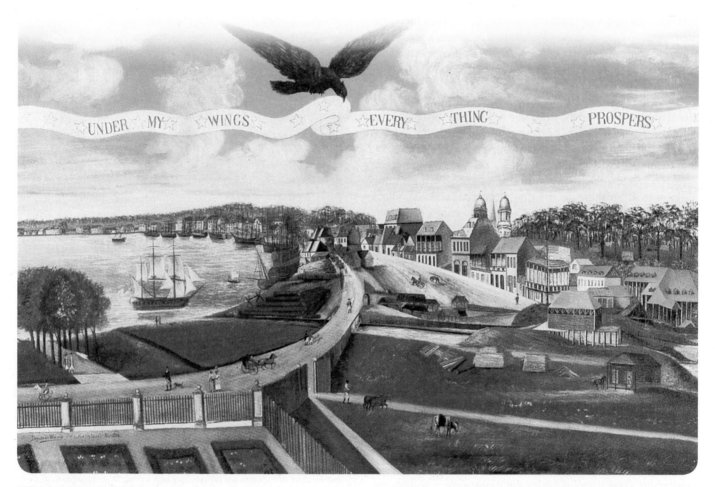

UNDER MY WINGS EVERY THING PROSPERS

NEW ORLEANS IN 1803 Because of its location near the mouth of the Mississippi River, New Orleans was the principal port of western North America in the early nineteenth century. Through it, western farmers shipped their produce to markets in the East and Europe. This 1803 painting celebrates the American acquisition of the city from France as part of the Louisiana Purchase. (Chicago Historical Society)

HAMILTON AND BURR

evidence) that he had also agreed to support the Federalist plans for secession. Hamilton accused Burr of plotting treason and made numerous private remarks, widely reported in the press, about Burr's "despicable" character. When Burr lost the New York election, he blamed his defeat on Hamilton's malevolence. "These things must have an end," Burr wrote. He challenged Hamilton to a duel.

Dueling had by then already fallen into some disrepute in America, but many people still considered it a legitimate institution for settling matters of "honor." Hamilton feared that refusing Burr's challenge would brand him a coward. And so, on a July morning in 1804, the two men met at Weehawken, New Jersey. Hamilton was mortally wounded; he died the next day.

The resourceful and charismatic Burr was now a political outcast who had to flee New York to avoid an indictment for murder. But he found new outlets for his ambitions in the West. Even before the duel, he had begun corresponding with prominent white settlers in the Southwest, especially with General James Wilkinson, now governor of the Louisiana Territory. Burr and Wilkinson hoped to lead an expedition that would capture Mexico from the Spanish. "Mexico glitters in all our eyes," Burr wrote; "the word is all we wait for." But there were also rumors that they wanted to separate the Southwest from the United States and create a western empire that Burr would rule. There is little evidence to support them.

Whether the rumors were true or not, many of Burr's opponents—including, ultimately, Jefferson himself—chose to believe them. When Burr led a group of armed followers down the Ohio River by boat in 1806, disturbing reports flowed into Washington. The most alarming was from Wilkinson. He had suddenly turned against Burr and now informed the president that treason was afoot and that an attack on New Orleans was imminent. Jefferson ordered Burr and his men arrested as traitors. Burr was brought to Richmond for trial. Determined to win a conviction, Jefferson carefully managed the government's case from Washington. But Chief Justice Marshall, presiding over the trial on circuit duty, limited the evidence the government could present and defined the charge in such a way that the jury had little choice but to acquit Burr.

The Burr "conspiracy" was in part the story of a single man's soaring ambitions and flamboyant personality. But it was also a symbol of the larger perils still facing the new nation. With a central government that remained deliberately weak, with vast tracts of land only nominally controlled by the United States, with ambitious political leaders willing, if necessary, to circumvent normal channels in their search for power, the legitimacy of the federal government, and indeed the existence of the United States as a stable and united nation, remained to be fully established.

THE BURR "CONSPIRACY" WAS IN PART THE STORY OF A SINGLE MAN'S SOARING AMBITIONS AND FLAMBOYANT PERSONALITY. BUT IT WAS ALSO A SYMBOL OF THE LARGER PERILS STILL FACING THE NEW NATION.

EXPANSION AND WAR

Two very different conflicts were taking shape in the later years of Thomas Jefferson's presidency that would, together, draw the United States into a difficult and frustrating war. One was the continuing tension in Europe, which in 1803 escalated once again into a full-scale conflict (the Napoleonic Wars). As the fighting escalated, both the British and the French took steps to prevent the United States from trading with (and thus assisting) the other.

THE NAPOLEONIC WARS

The other conflict was in North America itself, a result of the ceaseless westward expansion of white settlement, which was now stretching to the Mississippi River and beyond, colliding again with Native American populations committed to protecting their lands and their trade from intruders. In both the North and the South, the threatened tribes mobilized to resist white encroachments. They began as well to forge connections with British forces in Canada and Spanish forces in Florida. The Indian conflict on land therefore became intertwined with the European conflict on the seas and ultimately helped cause the War of 1812, an unpopular conflict with ambiguous results.

CONFLICT ON THE SEAS

The early nineteenth century saw a dramatic expansion of American shipping in the Atlantic. Britain retained significant naval superiority, but the British merchant marine was preoccupied with commerce in Europe and Asia and devoted little energy to trade with America. Thus the United States stepped effectively into the void and developed one of the most important merchant marines in the world, which soon controlled a large proportion of the trade between Europe and the West Indies.

In 1805, at the Battle of Trafalgar, a British fleet virtually destroyed what was left of the French navy. Because France could no longer challenge the British at sea, Napoleon now chose to pressure England through economic rather than naval means. He announced the creation of what he called the Continental System. It was designed to close the European continent to British trade. The British government replied to Napoleon's decrees by establishing—through a series of "orders in council"—a blockade of the European coast. It required that any goods being shipped to Napoleon's Europe be carried either in British vessels or in neutral vessels stopping at British ports—precisely what Napoleon's policies forbade.

American ships were caught between Napoleon's decrees and Britain's orders in council. If they sailed directly for the European continent, they risked being captured by the British navy; if they sailed by way of a British port, they risked seizure by the French. Both of the warring powers were violating America's rights as a neutral nation. But most Americans considered the British, with their greater sea power, the worse offender. British ships pounced on Yankee merchantmen all over the ocean. Particularly infuriating to Americans, British vessels stopped United States ships on the high seas and seized sailors off the decks, making them victims of "impressment."

AMERICA'S
PREDICAMENT

IMPRESSMENT

The British navy—with its floggings, low pay, and terrible shipboard conditions—was known as a "floating hell" to its sailors. Few volunteered. Most had to be "impressed" (forced) into the service. At every opportunity they deserted. By 1807, many of these deserters had joined the American merchant marine or the American navy. To check this loss of vital manpower, the British claimed the right to stop and search American merchant ships (although at first not naval vessels) and reimpress deserters.

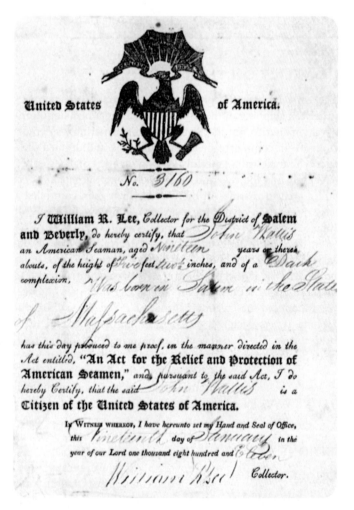

PROTECTION FROM IMPRESSMENT To protect American sailors from British impressment, the federal government issued official certificates of United States citizenship—known as "protection papers." But British naval officers, aware that such documents were often forged, frequently ignored them. (Peabody Essex Museum, Salem, Massachusetts)

They did not claim the right to take native-born Americans, but they did claim the right to seize naturalized Americans born on British soil. In practice, the British navy often made no such distinctions, impressing British deserters and native-born Americans alike into service.

In the summer of 1807, the British went to more provocative extremes in an incident involving a vessel of the American navy. Sailing from Norfolk, with several alleged deserters from the British navy among the crew, the American naval frigate *Chesapeake* encountered the British ship *Leopard*. When the American commander, James Barron, refused to allow the British to search the *Chesapeake*, the *Leopard* opened fire. Barron had no choice but to surrender, and a boarding party from the *Leopard* dragged four men off the American frigate.

CHESAPEAKE-
LEOPARD
INCIDENT

When news of the *Chesapeake-Leopard* incident reached the United States, there was great popular clamor for revenge. If Congress had been in session, it might have declared war. But Jefferson and Madison tried to maintain the peace. Jefferson expelled all British warships from American waters to lessen the likelihood of future incidents. Then he sent instructions to his minister in England, James Monroe, to demand that the British government renounce impressment. The British government disavowed the action of the officer responsible for the *Chesapeake-Leopard* affair and recalled him; it offered compensation for those killed and wounded in the incident; and it promised to return three of the captured sailors (one of the original four had been hanged). But the British refused to renounce impressment.

"PEACEABLE COERCION"

In an effort to prevent future incidents that might bring the nation again to the brink of war, Congress enacted a drastic measure known as the Embargo. It became one of the most controversial political issues of its time. The Embargo prohibited American ships from leaving the United States for any foreign port anywhere in the world. The law was widely evaded, but it was effective enough to create a serious depression through most of the nation. Hardest hit were the merchants and shipowners of the Northeast, most of them Federalists.

THE EMBARGO

The election of 1808 came in the midst of the Embargo-induced depression. James Madison, Jefferson's secretary of state and political ally, won the presidency. But the Embargo was clearly a growing political liability, and Jefferson decided to back down. A few days before leaving office, he approved a bill ending his experiment with what he called "peaceable coercion."

To replace the Embargo, Congress passed the Non-Intercourse Act just before Madison took office. The new law reopened trade with all nations but Great Britain and France. A year later, in 1810, Congress allowed the Non-Intercourse Act to expire and replaced it with Macon's Bill No. 2, which conditionally reopened free commercial relations with Britain and France. Napoleon announced that France would no

NON-
INTERCOURSE
ACT

longer interfere with American shipping, and Madison announced that an embargo against Great Britain alone would automatically go into effect early in 1811 unless Britain renounced its restrictions on American shipping. The British government repealed its blockade of Europe. But the repeal came too late to prevent war.

THE "INDIAN PROBLEM" AND THE BRITISH

The 1807 war crisis following the *Chesapeake-Leopard* incident

WILLIAM HENRY HARRISON

revived the conflict between Indians and white Americans. Two important (and very different) leaders emerged to oppose one another in the conflict: William Henry Harrison and Tecumseh.

The Virginia-born Harrison, already a veteran Indian fighter at age twenty-six, became a congressional delegate from the

Northwest Territory in 1799. He was a committed advocate of growth and development in the western lands, and he was largely responsible for the passage in 1800 of the so-called Harrison Land Law, which enabled white settlers to acquire farms from the public domain on much easier terms than before.

In 1801, Jefferson appointed Harrison governor of the Indiana Territory to administer the president's proposed solution to the

JEFFERSON'S OFFER

"Indian problem." Jefferson offered the Native Americans a choice: they could convert themselves into settled farmers and assimilate—become a part of white society; or they could migrate to the west of the Mississippi. In either case, they would have to give up their claims to tribal lands in the Northwest.

Jefferson considered the assimilation policy a benign alternative to continuing conflict between Indians and white settlers, a conflict he assumed the tribes were destined to lose. But to the tribes, the new policy seemed far from benign, especially given the bludgeonlike efficiency with which Harrison set out to

STRUGGLING WITH THE EMBARGO This cartoon lampoons the US Embargo against Britain in 1807, a decision that created much economic hardship for many people. The word "Ograbme" (a common nickname for a snapping turtle) is "embargo" spelled backwards. It shows a struggling merchant wrestling with the results of the Embargo. It was an effort to prevent the United States from being drawn into the wars between Britain and France. But the Embargo, which continued until 1812, not only hurt the American economy but helped draw the nation into the War of 1812. (The Granger Collection, New York)

implement it. He played one tribe against another and used threats, bribes, trickery, and whatever other tactics he felt would help him conclude treaties. In the first decade of the nineteenth century, the number of western Americans who had settled east of the Appalachians had grown to more than 500,000—a population far larger than that of the Native Americans. It was becoming almost inevitable, as a result, that the tribes would face ever-growing pressure to move out of the way of the rapidly growing white settlements.

By 1807, the United States had extracted from reluctant tribal leaders treaty rights to eastern Michigan, southern Indiana, and most of Illinois. Meanwhile, in the Southwest, white Americans were taking millions of acres from other tribes in Georgia, Tennessee, and Mississippi. The Indians wanted to resist, but the separate tribes were helpless by themselves against the power of the United States. They might have accepted their fate passively but for the emergence of two new factors.

One factor was the policy of the British authorities in Canada. After the *Chesapeake* incident and the surge of anti-British feeling throughout the United States, the British colonial authorities began to expect an American invasion of Canada and took measures for their own defense. Among those measures were

THE INDIAN RESPONSE TO WHITE ENCROACHMENT With land cessions and white western migration placing increased pressure on Indian cultures after 1790, news of the Prophet's revival fell on eager ears. It spread especially quickly northward along the shores of Lake Michigan and westward along Lake Superior and the interior of Wisconsin. Following the Battle of Tippecanoe, Tecumseh eclipsed the Prophet as the major leader of Indian resistance, but his trips south to forge political alliance met with less success.

efforts to renew friendship with the Indians and provide them with increased supplies.

TECUMSEH AND THE PROPHET

The second, and more important, factor intensifying the border conflict was the rise of two remarkable Native American leaders,

THE PROPHET'S MESSAGE

who together helped create an age of religious fervor and prophecy. One was Tenskwatawa, a charismatic religious leader and orator known as the Prophet. He had experienced a mystical awakening in the process of recovering from alcoholism. Having freed himself from what he considered the evil effects of white culture, he began to speak to his people of the superior virtues of Indian civilization and the sinfulness and corruption of the white world. In the process, he inspired a religious revival that spread through numerous tribes and helped unite them. Like Neolin before him, and like his contemporary to the east, Handsome Lake, Tenskwatawa demonstrated the power of religious leaders to mobilize Indians behind political and military objectives. The Prophet's headquarters at the confluence of Tippecanoe Creek and the Wabash River (known as Prophetstown) became a sacred place for people of many tribes and attracted thousands of Indians from throughout the Midwest. Out of their common religious experiences, they began to consider joint political and military efforts as well. Tenskwatawa advocated an Indian society entirely separate from that of white Americans and a culture rooted in tribal tradition. The effort to trade with the Anglos and to borrow from their culture would, he argued, lead to the death of Indian ways.

Tecumseh—the chief of the Shawness called by his tribe "the Shooting Star"—was in many ways even more militant than his brother. "Where today are the Pequot?" he thundered. "Where are . . . the other powerful tribes of our people? They have vanished before the avarice and oppression of the white man." And he warned of his tribe's extermination if they did not take action against the white Americans moving into their lands.

Tecumseh understood, as few other Indian leaders had, that only through united action could the tribes hope to resist the

TECUMSEH'S STRATEGY

advance of white civilization. Beginning in 1809, after tribes in Indiana had ceded vast lands to the United States, he set out to unite all the Indians of the Mississippi Valley, north and south. Together, he promised, they would halt white expansion, recover the whole Northwest, and make the Ohio River the boundary between the United States and the Indian country. He maintained that Harrison and others, by negotiating treaties with individual tribes, had obtained no real title to land. The land belonged to all the tribes; none of them could rightfully cede any of it without the consent of the others.

In 1811, Tecumseh left Prophetstown and traveled down the Mississippi to visit the tribes of the South, hoping to

BATTLE OF TIPPECANOE

persuade them to join the alliance. During his absence, Harrison camped near Prophetstown with 1,000 soldiers. On November 7, 1811, he provoked a battle. The white

> **❝ WHERE TODAY ARE THE PEQUOT? WHERE ARE . . . THE OTHER POWERFUL TRIBES OF OUR PEOPLE? THEY HAVE VANISHED BEFORE THE AVARICE AND OPPRESSION OF THE WHITE MAN. ❞**
>
> **TECUMSEH**

TECUMSEH Tecumseh's efforts to unite the tribes of the Mississippi valley against further white encroachments on their lands led him ultimately into an alliance with the British after the Battle of Tippecanoe in 1811. In the War of 1812, he was commissioned a brigadier general by the British and fought against the United States in the Battle of the Thames. He is shown in this painting (by the daughter of an English officer stationed near Detroit) wearing British military trousers. (Fort Malden National Historical Park)

JAMES AND DOLLEY MADISON James Madison may have been the most brilliant of the early leaders of the republic, but he was also one of the most serious and humorless, as this grim portrait suggests. His wife (born Dolley Payne in North Carolina and raised a Quaker in Virginia) was twenty-six when she married the forty-three-year-old Madison in 1794. Her charm and social grace made her one of her husband's greatest political assets. She acted as hostess for Thomas Jefferson, a widower, while her husband was secretary of state. And she presided over a lively social life during her eight years in the White House as first lady. (New-York Historical Society)

forces suffered losses as heavy as those of the natives, but Harrison drove off the Indians and burned the town. The Battle of Tippecanoe (named for the creek near the fighting) disillusioned many of the Prophet's followers, who had believed that his magic would protect them. Tecumseh returned to find the confederacy in disarray. But there were still many warriors eager for combat, and by the spring of 1812 they were raiding white settlements and terrifying white settlers.

The bloodshed along the western borders was largely a result of the Indians' own initiative, but Britain's agents in Canada had encouraged and helped supply the uprising. To Harrison and most white residents of the regions, there seemed only one way to make the West safe for Americans: drive the British out of Canada and annex that province to the United States.

FLORIDA AND WAR FEVER

While white "frontiersmen" in the North demanded the conquest of Canada, those in the South wanted the United States to acquire Spanish Florida, a territory that included the present state of Florida and the southern areas of what are now Alabama, Mississippi, and Louisiana. The territory was a continuing threat to whites in the southern United States. Slaves escaped across the Florida border; Indians launched frequent raids north into white settlements from Florida. But white southerners also coveted Florida because through it ran rivers that could provide residents of the Southwest with access to valuable ports on the Gulf of Mexico.

In 1810, American settlers in West Florida (an area that is part of Mississippi and Louisiana today) seized the Spanish fort at Baton Rouge and asked the federal government to annex the captured territory to the United States. President Madison happily agreed and then began planning to get the rest of Florida, too. The desire for Florida became yet another motivation for war with Britain. Spain was Britain's ally, and a war with Britain might provide a pretext for taking Spanish territory.

By 1812, war fever was growing on both the northern and southern borders of the United States. In the congressional elections of 1810, voters from these regions elected a large number of representatives of both parties eager for war with Britain. WAR HAWKS They became known as the "war hawks." Some of them were ardent nationalists fired by passion for territorial expansion—among them two men who would play a great role in national politics for much of the next four decades: Henry Clay of Kentucky and John C. Calhoun of South Carolina. Others were men impassioned in their defense of Republican values. Together, they formed a powerful coalition in favor of war.

Clay became Speaker of the House in 1811, and he filled committees with those who shared his eagerness for war. He appointed Calhoun to the crucial Committee on Foreign Affairs, and both men began agitating for the conquest of Canada. Madison still hoped for peace. But he shared the concerns of other Republicans about the dangers to American trade, and he was losing control of Congress. On June 18, 1812, he gave in to the pressure and approved a declaration of war against Britain.

THE WAR OF 1812

Preoccupied with their struggle against Napoleon in Europe, the British were not eager for a conflict with the United States. Even after the Americans declared war, Britain largely ignored them for a time. But in the fall of 1812, Napoleon launched a catastrophic campaign against Russia that left his army in disarray and his power in Europe diminished. By late 1813, with the French Empire on its way to final defeat, Britain was able to turn its military attention to America.

BATTLES WITH THE TRIBES

Americans entered the War of 1812 with great enthusiasm, but events on the battlefield soon cooled their ardor. In the summer of 1812, American forces invaded Canada through Detroit. They soon had to retreat back to Detroit and in August surrendered the fort there. Other invasion efforts also failed. In the meantime, Fort Dearborn (Chicago) fell before an Indian attack.

Things went only slightly better for the United States on the

EARLY DEFEATS seas. At first, American frigates won some spectacular victories over British warships, and American privateers destroyed or captured many British merchant ships, occasionally braving the coastal waters of the British Isles themselves and burning vessels within sight of the shore. But by 1813, the British navy—now less preoccupied with Napoleon—was counterattacking effectively, driving the American frigates to cover and imposing a blockade on the United States.

The United States did, however, achieve significant early military successes on the Great Lakes. First, the Americans took command of Lake Ontario, which permitted them to raid and burn York (now Toronto), the capital of Canada. American forces then

seized control of Lake Erie, mainly through the work of the

PUT-IN-BAY youthful Oliver Hazard Perry, who engaged and dispersed a British fleet at Put-In-Bay on September 10, 1813. This made possible another invasion of Canada by way of Detroit, which Americans could now reach easily by water. William Henry Harrison, the American commander in the West, pushed up the river Thames into upper Canada and, on October 5, 1813, won a victory notable for the death of Tecumseh, who was serving as a brigadier general in the British army. The Battle of the Thames weakened and disheartened the Native Americans of the Northwest and greatly diminished their ability to defend their claims to the region.

In the meantime, another white military leader was striking an even harder blow at the tribes of the Southwest. The Creeks, whom Tecumseh had aroused on a visit to the South and whom the Spanish had supplied with weapons, had been attacking white settlers near the Florida border. Andrew Jackson, a wealthy Tennessee planter and a general in the state militia, temporarily abandoned plans for an invasion of Florida and set off in pursuit of them. On March 27, 1814, in the Battle of Horseshoe Bend, Jackson's men took terrible revenge on the Indians—slaughtering women and children along with warriors—and broke the resistance of the Creeks. The tribe agreed to cede most of its lands to the United States and retreated westward, farther into the interior. The battle also won Jackson a commission as a major general in the United States Army. In that capacity he led his men farther south into Florida and, on November 7, 1814, seized the Spanish fort at Pensacola.

BATTLES WITH THE BRITISH

The victories over the tribes were not enough for the United

THE BRITISH INVASION States to win the war. After the surrender of Napoleon in 1814, England prepared to invade the United States. A British armada sailed up the Patuxent River from Chesapeake Bay and landed an army that marched a short distance overland to Bladensburg, on the outskirts of Washington, where it dispersed a poorly trained force of American militiamen. On August 24, 1814, the British troops entered Washington and set fire to several public buildings, including the White House, in retaliation for the earlier American burning of the Canadian capital at York. This was the low point of American fortunes in the war.

Leaving Washington in partial ruins, the British army proceeded up the bay toward Baltimore. But Baltimore harbor, guarded by Fort McHenry, was prepared. To block the approaching fleet, the American garrison had sunk several ships to clog the entry to the harbor, thus forcing the British to bombard the fort from a distance.

FRANCIS SCOTT KEY, A WASHINGTON LAWYER WHO WAS ON BOARD ONE OF THE BRITISH SHIPS, WATCHED THE BOMBARDMENT. THE NEXT MORNING, "BY THE DAWN'S EARLY LIGHT," HE COULD SEE THE FLAG ON THE FORT STILL FLYING.

THE WAR OF 1812 This map illustrates the military maneuvers of the British and the Americans during the War of 1812. It shows all the theaters of the war, from New Orleans to southern Canada, the extended land and water battle along the Canadian border and in the Great Lakes, and the fighting around Washington and Baltimore. Note how in all these theaters there are about the same number of British and American victories.

• *What finally brought this inconclusive war to an end?*

Through the night of September 13, Francis Scott Key, a Washington lawyer who was on board one of the British ships trying to secure the release of an American prisoner, watched the bombardment. The next morning, "by the dawn's early light," he could see the flag on the fort still flying; he recorded his pride in the moment by scribbling a poem—"The Star-Spangled Banner"—on the back of an envelope. The British withdrew from Baltimore, and Key's words were soon set to the tune of an old English drinking song. In 1931, "The Star-Spangled Banner" became the official national anthem.

Meanwhile, American forces repelled another British invasion in northern New York at the Battle of Plattsburgh, on September 11, 1814, which turned back a much larger British naval and land force and secured the northern border of the United States. In the South, a formidable array of battle-hardened British veterans, fresh from the campaign against the French in Spain, landed below New Orleans and prepared to advance north up the Mississippi. Awaiting the British was Andrew Jackson with a motley collection of Tennesseans, Kentuckians, Creoles, blacks, pirates, and regular army troops behind earthen fortifications. On

BATTLE OF NEW ORLEANS

January 8, 1815, the British advanced, but their exposed forces were no match for Jackson's well-protected men. After the Americans had repulsed several waves of attackers, the British finally retreated, leaving behind 700 dead (including their commander, Sir Edward Pakenham), 1,400 wounded, and 500 prisoners. Jackson's losses were 8 killed and 13 wounded. Only later did news reach North America that the United States and Britain had signed a peace treaty several weeks before the Battle of New Orleans.

THE REVOLT OF NEW ENGLAND

With a few notable exceptions, such as the Battles of Put-In-Bay and New Orleans, the military operations of the United States between 1812 and 1815 consisted of a series of humiliating failures. As a result, the American government faced increasing popular opposition as the contest dragged on. In New England, opposition both to the war and to the Republican government that was waging it was so extreme that some Federalists celebrated British victories. In Congress, in the meantime, the Republicans had persistent trouble with the Federalist opposition, led by a young congressman from New Hampshire, Daniel Webster, who missed no opportunity to embarrass the administration.

By now the Federalists were a minority in the country as a whole, but they were still the majority party in New England. Some of them began to dream again of creating a separate nation in that region, which they could dominate and in which they could escape what they saw as the tyranny of slaveholders and backwoodsmen. Talk of secession revived and reached a climax in the winter of 1814–1815.

On December 15, 1814, delegates from the New England states met in Hartford, Connecticut, to discuss their grievances. Those who favored secession at the

HARTFORD CONVENTION

Hartford Convention were outnumbered by a comparatively moderate majority. But while the convention's report only hinted at secession, it reasserted the right of nullification and proposed seven amendments to the Constitution (presumably as the condition of New England's remaining in the Union)—amendments designed to protect New England from the growing influence of the South and the West.

Because the war was going badly and the government was becoming desperate, the New Englanders assumed that the Republicans would have to agree to their demands. Soon after the convention adjourned, however, the news of Jackson's smashing victory at New Orleans reached the cities of the Northeast. A day or two later, reports arrived from abroad of a negotiated peace. In the euphoria of this apparent triumph, the Hartford Convention and the Federalists came to seem futile, irrelevant, even treasonable. The failure of the secession effort was a virtual death blow to the Federalist Party.

THE PEACE SETTLEMENT

Peace talks between the United States and Britain had begun even before fighting in the War of 1812 began. John Quincy Adams, Henry Clay, and Albert Gallatin led the American delegation.

In the negotiations, the Americans gave up their demand for a British renunciation of impressment and for the cession of

TREATY OF GHENT

Canada to the United States. The British abandoned their call for the creation of an Indian buffer state in the Northwest. The negotiators referred other disputes to arbitration. Hastily drawn up, a treaty was signed on Christmas Eve 1814. It was named the Treaty of Ghent after the Dutch city in which it was signed.

Other settlements followed the Treaty of Ghent and contributed to a long-term improvement in Anglo-American relations. A commercial treaty in 1815 gave Americans the right to trade

RUSH-BAGOT AGREEMENT

freely with England and much of the British Empire. The Rush-Bagot agreement of 1817 provided for mutual disarmament on the Great Lakes; eventually (although not until 1872) the Canadian-American boundary became the longest "unguarded frontier" in the world.

THE BOMBARDMENT OF FORT McHENRY The British bombardment of Fort McHenry in Baltimore harbor in September 1814 was of modest importance to the outcome of the War of 1812. It is remembered as the occasion for Francis Scott Key to write his poem "The Star-Spangled Banner," which recorded his sentiments at seeing an American flag still flying over the fort "by the dawn's early light." (I. N. Pbelps Stokes Collection of American Historical Prints, New York Public Library)

ATTACKING THE FEDERALISTS A Republican cartoonist derided the secession efforts of New England Federalists at the Hartford Convention in this cartoon. It portrays timid men representing Massachusetts, Connecticut, and Rhode Island preparing to leap into the arms of George III. (Library of Congress [LC–USZC4–12748])

For the other parties to the War of 1812, the Indian tribes east of the Mississippi, the Treaty of Ghent was of no lasting value. It required the United States to restore to the tribes lands seized by white Americans in the fighting, but those provisions were never enforced. Ultimately, the war was another disastrous blow to the capacity of Native Americans to resist white expansion.

Tecumseh, their most important leader, was dead. The British, their most important allies, were gone from the Northwest. The alliance that Tecumseh and the Prophet had forged was in disarray. And the end of the war spurred a great new drive by white settlers deeper into the West, into land the Indians were less than ever able to defend.

LOOKING BACK

Thomas Jefferson called his election to the presidency the "Revolution of 1800," and his supporters believed that his victory would bring a dramatic change in the character of the nation—a retreat from Hamilton's dreams of a powerful, developing nation with great stature in the world; a return to an ideal of a simple agrarian republic happily isolated from the corruption and intrigue of Europe.

But American society was changing rapidly in the early nineteenth century, making it virtually impossible for the

Jeffersonian dream to prevail. The nation's population was expanding and diversifying. Its cities were growing, and its commercial life was becoming ever more important. In 1803, Jefferson himself made one of the most important contributions to the growth of the United States: the Louisiana Purchase, which dramatically expanded the physical boundaries of the nation—and which began extending white settlement deeper into the continent. In the process, it greatly widened the battles between Europeans and Native Americans.

The growing national pride and commercial ambitions of the United States gradually created another serious conflict with Great Britain: the War of 1812, a war that went badly for the Americans on the whole, but that was settled finally in 1814 on terms at least mildly favorable to the United States. By then, the bitter party rivalries that had characterized the first years of the republic had to some degree subsided, and the nation was poised to enter what became known as the "era of good feelings." It was to be an era in which good feelings did not last for very long. •

KEY TERMS/PEOPLE/PLACES/EVENTS

SIGNIFICANT EVENTS

Eli Whitney invents cotton gin

Second Great Awakening begins

John Marshall appointed chief justice

Louisiana Territory purchased from French

Supreme Court establishes power of judicial review in *Marbury v. Madison*

1790
Samuel Slater builds textile mill, first modern factory in America, in Pawtucket, Rhode Island

1793

1800
United States capital moves to Washington, D.C.

Gabriel Prosser's plans for slave rebellion foiled

1801

1801–1805
Conflict with Tripoli

1803

1804
Thomas Jefferson reelected president

RECALL AND REFLECT

1. What was the impact of the Second Great Awakening on women, African Americans, and Native Americans?

2. What was the long-term significance of the *Marbury v. Madison* ruling?

3. How did Americans respond to the Louisiana Purchase?

4. What foreign entanglements and questions of foreign policy did Jefferson have to deal with during his presidency? How did these issues affect his political philosophy?

5. What were the consequences of the War of 1812?

Lewis and Clark, and Zebulon Pike, explore Louisiana Territory

Embargo Act repealed

Tecumseh establishes tribal confederacy

United States declares war on Great Britain (June 18)

Jackson wins Battle of New Orleans

1804–1805   **1807**   **1808**   **1809**   **1810**   **1812**   **1814**   **1815**

Embargo begins

Madison elected president

Macon's Bill No. 2 reopens trade with Britain and France

Madison reelected president

Hartford Convention meets

Treaty of Ghent signed

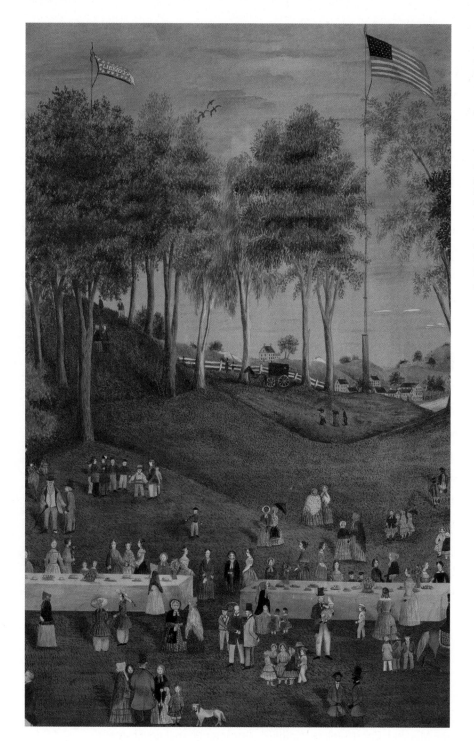

FOURTH OF JULY PICNIC AT WEYMOUTH LANDING (C. 1845), BY SUSAN MERRITT Celebrations of Independence Day, like this one in eastern Massachusetts, became major festive events throughout the United States in the early nineteenth century, a sign of rising American nationalism. (*Fourth of July picnic at Weymouth Landing*, c. 1845 Susan Torrey Merritt, American, 1826–1879 (Detail) Anti-Slavery Picnic at Weymouth Landing, Massachusetts, c. 1845, watercolor, gouache, and collage on paper, 660 × 914 mm, Gift of Elizabeth R. Vaughan, 1950.1846, The Art Institute of Chicago. Photography © The Art Institute of Chicago.)

8 | VARIETIES OF AMERICAN NATIONALISM

LIKE A "FIRE BELL IN THE NIGHT," as Thomas Jefferson put it, the issue of slavery arose after the War of 1812 to threaten the unity of the nation. The debate began when the territory of Missouri applied for admission to the Union, raising the question of whether it would be a free or a slaveholding state. But the larger issue, one that would arise again and again to plague the republic, was whether the vast new western regions of the United States would ultimately move into the orbit of the North or the South.

The Missouri crisis, which Congress settled by compromise in 1820, was significant at the time not only because it was a sign of the sectional crises to come but also because it stood in such sharp contrast to the rising American nationalism of the years following the war. Whatever forces might be working to pull the nation apart, stronger ones were acting for the moment to draw it together. A set of widely (although never universally) shared sentiments and ideals worked to bind the nation together: the memory of the Revolution, the veneration of

SETTING THE STAGE

the Constitution and its framers, the belief that America had a special destiny in the world.

On July 4, 1826—the fiftieth anniversary of the adoption of the Declaration of Independence—an event occurred that to many seemed to confirm that the United States was a nation specially chosen by God. On that remarkable day, two of the greatest of the country's founders and former presidents—Thomas Jefferson, author of the Declaration, and John Adams, whom Jefferson had called "its ablest advocate and defender"— died within hours of each other. Jefferson's last words, those at his bedside reported, were "Is it the Fourth?" And Adams comforted those around him moments before his death by saying, "Thomas Jefferson still survives."

LOOKING AHEAD

1. How did the economic developments and territorial expansion of this era affect American nationalism?
2. What was the "era of good feelings," and why was it given that name?
3. How did the Marshall Court seek to establish a strong national government?

BUILDING A NATIONAL MARKET

The end of the War of 1812 allowed the United States to resume the economic growth and territorial expansion that had characterized the first decade of the nineteenth century. A vigorous postwar boom led to a disastrous bust in 1819. Brief though it was, the collapse was evidence that the United States continued to lack some of the basic institutions necessary to sustain long-term growth. In the years to follow, there were strenuous efforts to introduce stability to the expanding economy.

BANKING, CURRENCY, AND PROTECTION

The War of 1812 may have stimulated the growth of manufacturing by cutting off imports, but it also produced chaos in shipping and banking, and it exposed dramatically the inadequacy of the existing transportation and financial systems. The aftermath of the war, therefore, saw the emergence of a series of political issues connected with national economic development.

POSTWAR ISSUES

The wartime experience underlined the need for another national bank. After the expiration of the first Bank of the United States's charter in 1811, a large number of state banks had begun operations. They issued vast quantities of bank notes but did not always bother to retain enough reserves of gold or silver to redeem the notes on demand. The notes passed from hand to hand more or less as money, but their actual value depended on the reputation of the bank that issued them. Thus there was a wide variety of notes, of widely differing value, in circulation at the same time. The result was a confusion that made honest business difficult and counterfeiting easy.

Congress dealt with the currency problem by chartering a second Bank of the United States in 1816. It was essentially the same institution Hamilton had founded in 1791 except that it had more capital than its predecessor. The national bank could not forbid state banks to issue currency, but its size and power enabled it to dominate the state banks. It could compel them to issue only sound notes or risk being forced out of business.

SECOND BANK OF THE UNITED STATES

Congress also acted to promote the already burgeoning manufacturing sector of the nation's economy. Manufactured goods had been so scarce during the conflict that, even with comparatively unskilled labor and inexperienced management, new factories could start operations virtually assured of quick profits.

The American textile industry experienced a particularly dramatic growth. Between 1807 and 1815, the total number of cotton spindles increased more than fifteenfold, from 8,000 to 130,000. Until 1814, the textile factories—most of them in New England—produced only yarn and thread; families operating hand-looms at home did the actual weaving of cloth. Then the Boston merchant Francis Cabot Lowell, after examining textile machinery in England, developed a power loom that was better than its English counterpart. In 1813, Lowell organized the Boston Manufacturing Company and, at Waltham, Massachusetts, founded the first mill in America to carry on the processes of spinning and weaving under a single roof. Lowell's company was an important step in revolutionizing American manufacturing and in shaping the character of the early industrial work force. (See pp. 277–283.)

GROWTH OF THE TEXTILE INDUSTRY

But the end of the war suddenly dimmed the prospects for American industry. British ships—determined to recapture their lost markets—swarmed into American ports and unloaded cargoes of manufactured goods, many priced below cost. As one English leader explained to Parliament, it was "well worth while to incur a loss upon the first exportation, in order, by the glut, to stifle in the cradle those rising manufactures in the United

AN EARLY MILL IN NEW ENGLAND This early folk painting of about 1814 shows the small town of East Chelmsford, Massachusetts—still primarily agrarian, with its rural houses, open fields, and grazing livestock, but with a small textile mill already operating along the stream, at right. A little more than a decade later, the town had been transformed into a major manufacturing center and renamed for the family that owned the mills: Lowell. (*Part of the Town of Chelmsford.* By Miss Warren. Abby Aldrich Rockefeller Folk Art Museum, Colonial Williamsburg Foundation, Williamsburg, VA)

Embargo Act Passed
(in effect 1808-1809)

Nonintercourse
Law (in effect)

War of 1812

Panic of 1819
(followed by
business
depression)

AMERICAN IMPORTS AND EXPORTS, 1790–1820 This chart shows the pattern of goods imported to and exported from the United States—the level of foreign trade, and the balance between goods bought and goods sold. Americans were heavily dependent on Britain and Europe for "finished" or "manufactured" goods in these years; and as you can see, imports grew as rapidly as, and often even more rapidly than, exports. Note how the nation's disputes with European powers depressed both exports and imports from about 1808 to 1814.

• *How does this chart help explain Congress's passage of a protective tariff law in 1816?*

States." The "infant industries" cried out for protection against these tactics, arguing that they needed time to grow strong enough to withstand the foreign competition.

In 1816, protectionists in Congress won passage of a tariff law that effectively limited competition from abroad on a wide range of items, among the most important of which was cotton cloth. There were objections from agricultural interests, who would have to pay higher prices for manufactured goods as a result. But the nationalist dream of creating an important American industrial economy prevailed.

A PROTECTIVE
TARIFF

TRANSPORTATION

The nation's most pressing economic need in the aftermath of the war was for a better transportation system. Without one, manufacturers would not have access to the raw materials they needed or to domestic markets. So an old debate resumed: Should the federal government help to finance roads and other "internal improvements"?

The idea of using government funds to finance road building was not a new one. When Ohio entered the Union in 1803, the federal government agreed that part of the proceeds from the government's sale of public lands should

AN OLD DEBATE RESUMED:
SHOULD THE FEDERAL
GOVERNMENT HELP TO FINANCE
ROADS AND OTHER "INTERNAL
IMPROVEMENTS"?

finance road construction. In 1807, Jefferson's secretary of the treasury, Albert Gallatin, proposed that revenues from the Ohio land sales should help finance a National Road from the Potomac River to the Ohio River. Both Congress and the president approved. After many delays, construction of the National Road finally began in 1811 at Cumberland, Maryland, on the Potomac; and by 1818, this highway—with a crushed stone surface and massive stone bridges—ran as far as Wheeling, Virginia, on the Ohio River. Meanwhile, the state of Pennsylvania gave $100,000 to a private company to extend the Lancaster pike westward to Pittsburgh. Over both of these roads a heavy traffic soon moved: stagecoaches, Conestoga wagons, private carriages, and other vehicles, as well as droves of cattle. Despite high tolls, the roads made transportation costs across the mountains lower than ever before. Manufactures, particularly textiles, moved from the Atlantic seaboard to the Ohio Valley in unprecedented quantities.

GOVERNMENT-
FUNDED ROADS

At the same time, on the rivers and the Great Lakes, steam-powered shipping was expanding rapidly. The development of steamboat lines was already well under way before the War of 1812, thanks to the technological advances introduced by Robert Fulton and others. The war had retarded expansion for a time, but by 1816, river steamers were beginning to journey up and down the Mississippi to the Ohio River, and up the Ohio as far as Pittsburgh. Within a few years, steamboats were carrying far more cargo on the Mississippi than all the earlier forms of river transport—flatboats, barges, and others—combined. They stimulated the agricultural economy of the West and the South, by providing much readier access to markets at greatly reduced cost. They enabled eastern manufacturers to send their finished goods west.

STEAMBOATS

Despite the progress with steamboats and turnpikes, there remained serious gaps in the nation's transportation network, as the War of 1812 had shown. Once the British blockade cut off Atlantic shipping, the coastal roads became choked by the unaccustomed volume of north-south traffic. Long lines of wagons waited for a chance to use the ferries that were still the only means of crossing most rivers. Oxcarts, pressed into emergency service, took six or seven weeks to go from Philadelphia to Charleston. In some areas there were serious shortages of goods that normally traveled by sea, and prices rose to new heights. Rice cost three times as much in New York as in Charleston, flour three times as much in Boston as in Richmond—all because

DECK LIFE ON THE *PARAGON*, 1811–1812 The *North River Steamboat Clermont*, launched in 1806 by the inventor Robert Fulton and propelled by an engine he had developed, traveled from Manhattan to Albany (about 150 miles) in thirty-two hours. That was neither the longest nor the fastest steam voyage to date, but the *Clermont* proved to be the first steam-powered vessel large enough and reliable enough to be commercially valuable. Within a few years, Fulton and his partner Robert R. Livingston had several steamboats operating profitably around New York. The third vessel in their fleet, the *Paragon*, shown here in a painting by the Russian diplomat and artist Pavel Petrovich Svinin, could carry 150 people and contained an elegant dining salon fitted with bronze, mahogany, and mirrors. Svinin called it "a whole floating town," and Fulton told a friend that the *Paragon* "beats everything on the globe, for made as you and I are we cannot tell what is in the moon." (Metropolitan Museum of Art/Art Resource, New York)

of the difficulty of transportation. There were military consequences, too. On the northern and western frontiers, the absence of good roads had frustrated American campaigns.

In 1815, with this wartime experience in mind, President Madison called the attention of Congress to the "great importance of establishing throughout our country the roads and canals which can be best executed under the national authority," and suggested that a constitutional amendment would resolve any doubts about Congress's authority to provide for their construction. Representative John C. Calhoun promptly introduced a bill that would have used the funds owed the government by the Bank of the United States to finance internal improvements. "Let us, then, bind the republic together with a perfect system of roads and canals," Calhoun urged. "Let us conquer space."

Congress passed Calhoun's internal improvements bill, but President Madison, on his last day in office (March 3, 1817), vetoed it. He supported the purpose of the bill, he explained,

VETOING INTERNAL IMPROVEMENTS

but he still believed that Congress lacked authority to fund the improvements without a constitutional amendment. It remained for state governments and private enterprise to undertake the tremendous task of building the transportation network necessary for the growing American economy.

EXPANDING WESTWARD

One reason for the growing interest in internal improvements was the sudden and dramatic surge in westward expansion in the years following the War of 1812. "Old America seems to be breaking up and moving westward," wrote an English observer at the time. By the time of the census of 1820, white settlers had pushed well beyond the Mississippi River, and the population of the western regions was increasing more rapidly than that of the nation as a

> 66 **OLD AMERICA SEEMS TO BE BREAKING UP AND MOVING WESTWARD.** 99

whole. Almost one of every four white Americans lived west of the Appalachians in 1820; ten years before, only one in seven had resided there.

THE GREAT MIGRATIONS

The westward movement of the white American population was one of the most important developments of the nineteenth century. It had a profound effect on the nation's economy, bringing vast new regions into the emerging capitalist system. It had great political ramifications, which ultimately became a major factor in the coming of the Civil War. And like earlier movements west, it thrust peoples of different cultures and traditions into intimate (and often disastrous) association with one another.

REASONS FOR WESTWARD EXPANSION

There were several important reasons for this expansion. The pressures driving white Americans out of the East came in part from the continued growth of the nation's population—both through natural increase and through immigration. Between 1800 and 1820, the population nearly doubled—from 5.3 million to 9.6 million. The growth of cities absorbed some of that increase, but most Americans were still farmers. The agricultural lands of the East were by now largely occupied, and some of them were exhausted. In the South, the spread of the plantation system, and of a slave labor force, limited opportunities for new settlers.

At the same time, the West itself was becoming increasingly attractive to white settlers. The War of 1812 had helped diminish (although it did not wholly eliminate) one of the traditional deterrents to western expansion: Native American opposition. And in the aftermath of the war, the federal government continued its policy of pushing the remaining tribes farther and farther west. A series of treaties in 1815 wrested more land from the Indians. In the meantime, the government was erecting a chain of stockaded forts along the Great Lakes and the Mississippi to protect the frontier. It also created a "factor" system, by which government factors (or agents) supplied the tribes with goods at cost. This not only worked to drive Canadian traders out of the region; it also helped create a situation of dependency on the factors that made Native Americans themselves easier to control.

THE FACTOR SYSTEM

Now that fertile lands were secure for white settlement, migrants from throughout the East flocked to what was then known as the Old Northwest (now called the Midwest). The Ohio and Monongahela Rivers were the main routes westward, until the completion of the Erie Canal in 1825. Once on the Ohio, they floated downstream on flatboats bearing all their possessions, then left the river (often at Cincinnati, which was becoming one of the region's—and the nation's—principal cities) and pressed on overland with wagons, handcarts, packhorses, cattle, and hogs.

THE PLANTATION SYSTEM IN THE SOUTHWEST

In the Southwest, the new agricultural economy emerged along different lines. The principal attraction was cotton. The

FORT SNELLING This is an 1838 sketch of Fort Snelling (at the juncture of the Minnesota and Mississippi Rivers), containing instructions for reaching it from St. Louis. It was one of a string of fortifications built along the western edge of European settlement along the Great Lakes and the upper Mississippi in the first three decades of the nineteenth century. The forts were designed to protect the new white communities from hostile Indians. Fort Snelling stands today in Minnesota as a "living history" site. ("Fort Snelling from the East." Smithsonian Institution Archives. Record Unit 7290, Carl Andreas Geyer Journal, 1838. Negative # SA–861)

cotton lands in the uplands of the Old South had lost much of their fertility through overplanting and erosion. But the market for cotton continued to grow, so there was no lack of ambitious farmers seeking fresh soil in a climate suitable for the crop. In the Southwest, there were vast tracts of land appropriate for growing cotton. They included what was to become known as the Black Belt of central Alabama and Mississippi, a large region with a dark, productive soil of rotted limestone.

The growth of southern settlement spread cotton, plantations, and slavery. The first arrivals in an uncultivated region were usually small farmers who made rough clearings in the forest. But wealthier planters soon followed. They bought up cleared or partially cleared land, and the original settlers moved farther west and started over again.

COTTON AND THE EXPANSION OF SLAVERY

The large planters made the westward journey in a style quite different from that of the first pioneers. Over the alternately dusty and muddy roads came great caravans consisting of herds of livestock, wagonloads of household goods, long lines of slaves, and—at the rear—the planter's family riding in carriages. Success in the wilderness was by no means ensured, even for the wealthiest settlers. But many planters soon expanded small clearings into vast cotton fields. They replaced the cabins of the early pioneers with sumptuous log dwellings and ultimately with imposing mansions that symbolized the emergence of a newly wealthy class. In later years, these western planters would assume the airs of a longstanding aristocracy. But by the time of the Civil War, few planter families in the Southwest had been there for more than one or two generations.

The rapid growth of the Northwest and Southwest resulted in the admission of four new states to the Union in the immediate aftermath of the War of 1812: Indiana in 1816, Mississippi in 1817, Illinois in 1818, and Alabama in 1819.

TRADE AND TRAPPING IN THE FAR WEST

Not many Anglo-Americans had much knowledge of or interest in the far western areas of the continent. But a significant trade nevertheless began to develop between these far western regions and the United States beginning early in the nineteenth century and growing steadily for decades.

Mexico, which controlled Texas, California, and much of the rest of the Southwest, won its independence from Spain in 1821. Almost immediately, it opened its northern territories to trade with the United States. American traders poured into the

region—overland into Texas and New Mexico, by sea into California. Merchants from the United States quickly displaced both Indian and Mexican traders who had previously dominated trade. A steady traffic of commercial wagon trains was moving back and forth along the Santa Fe Trail between Missouri and New Mexico.

Fur traders created a wholly new commerce with the West. Before the War of 1812, John Jacob Astor's American Fur Company had established Astoria as a trading post at the mouth of the Columbia River in Oregon. But when the war came, Astor sold his suddenly imperiled interests to the Northwestern Fur Company, a British concern operating out of Canada. After the war, Astor centered his operations in the Great Lakes area and eventually extended them westward to the Rockies. Other companies carried on operations up the Missouri and its tributaries and into the Rocky Mountains.

ASTOR'S AMERICAN FUR COMPANY

At first, fur traders did most of their business by purchasing pelts from the Indians. But increasingly, white trappers entered the region and began to hunt beaver on their own. Substantial numbers of Anglo-Americans and French Canadians moved deep into the Great Lakes region and beyond to join the Iroquois and other Indians in pursuit of furs.

As the trappers, or "mountain men," moved west from the Great Lakes region, they began to establish themselves in what

GREEN RIVER RENDEZVOUS, BY WILLIAM HENRY JACKSON The annual gathering of fur trappers and traders was a major event in the lives of the lonely men who made their livelihoods gathering furs. It was also a meeting of representatives of the many cultures that mingled in the Far West, among them Anglo-Americans, French Canadians, Indians, and Hispanics. (Denver Public Library)

is now Utah and in parts of New Mexico. In 1822, Andrew Henry and William Ashley founded the Rocky Mountain Fur Company and recruited white trappers to move permanently into the Rockies in search of furs, which were becoming increasingly scarce farther east. Henry and Ashley dispatched supplies annually to their trappers in exchange for furs and skins. The arrival of the supply train became the occasion for a gathering of scores of mountain men, some of whom lived much of the year in considerable isolation.

But however isolated their daily lives, these mountain men were closely bound up with the expanding market economy of the United States. Some were employees of the Rocky Mountain Fur Company (or some other, similar enterprise), earning a salary in return for providing a steady supply of furs. Others were nominally independent but relied on the companies for credit; they were almost always in debt and hence economically bound to the companies. Some trapped entirely on their own and simply sold their furs for cash, but they too depended on merchants from the East for their livelihoods. And it was to those merchants that the bulk of the profits from the trade flowed.

THE FUR TRADE AND THE MARKET ECONOMY

Many trappers and mountain men lived peacefully and successfully with the Native Americans and Mexicans whose lands they shared. Perhaps two-thirds of the white trappers married Indian or Hispanic women while living in the West. But white-Indian relations were not always friendly or peaceful. Jedediah S. Smith, a trapper who became an Ashley partner, led a series of forays deep into Mexican territory that ended in disastrous battles with the Mojaves and other tribes. Four years after an 1827 expedition to Oregon in which sixteen members of his party of twenty had died, Smith set out for New Mexico and was killed by Comanches, who took the weapons he was carrying and sold them to Mexican settlers.

EASTERN IMAGES OF THE WEST

Americans in the East were only dimly aware of the world the trappers were entering and helping to reshape. Smith and others became the source of dramatic (and often exaggerated) popular stories. But few trappers themselves wrote of their lives.

More important in increasing eastern awareness of the West were explorers, many of them dispatched by the United States government with instructions to chart the territories they visited. In 1819 and 1820, Stephen H. Long led nineteen soldiers on a journey up the Platte and South Platte Rivers through what is now Nebraska and eastern Colorado, and then returned eastward along the Arkansas River through what is now Kansas. He

STEPHEN LONG'S EXPEDITION

wrote an influential report on his trip, including an assessment of the region's potential for future settlement and development that echoed the dismissive conclusions of Zebulon Pike fifteen years before. On the published map of his expedition, he labeled the Great Plains the "Great American Desert."

THE "ERA OF GOOD FEELINGS"

The expansion of the economy, the growth of white settlement and trade in the West, the creation of new states—all reflected the rising spirit of nationalism that was permeating the United States in the years following the War of 1812. That spirit found reflection for a time in the character of national politics.

THE END OF THE FIRST PARTY SYSTEM

Ever since 1800, the presidency seemed to have been the special possession of Virginians. After two terms in office, Jefferson

THE TRIUMPHANT TOUR OF JAMES MONROE After James Monroe's enormously successful tour of the northern and eastern states in 1818, midway through his first term as president, there was widespread self-congratulation through much of the United States for the apparent political unity that had gripped the nation. Only a few years earlier, the Northeast had been the bastion of Federalist Party opposition to the Republican governments of the early nineteenth century. At one point, some Federalist leaders had even proposed secession from the United States. But now a Virginia Republican president had been greeted as a hero in the former Federalist strongholds. This book, published in 1820 (when Monroe ran virtually unopposed for reelection), is an account of the president's triumphant tour and a short account of his life—an early version of the now-familiar campaign biography. (Collection of David J. and Janice L. Frent)

chose his secretary of state, James Madison of Virginia, to succeed him, and after two more terms, Madison secured the presidential nomination for his secretary of state, James Monroe, also of Virginia. Many in the North were expressing impatience with the so-called Virginia Dynasty, but the Republicans had no difficulty electing their candidate in the listless campaign of 1816. Monroe received 183 ballots in the electoral college; his Federalist opponent, Rufus King of New York, received only 34—from Massachusetts, Connecticut, and Delaware.

THE VIRGINIA DYNASTY

Monroe was sixty-one years old when he became president. In the course of his long career, he had served as a soldier in the Revolution, as a diplomat, and most recently as a cabinet officer. He entered office under what seemed to be remarkably favorable circumstances. With the decline of the Federalists, his party faced no serious opposition. With the conclusion of the War of 1812, the nation faced no important international threats. American politicians had dreamed since the first days of the republic of a time in which partisan divisions and factional disputes might come to an end. In the prosperous postwar years, Monroe attempted to use his office to realize that dream.

He made that clear, above all, in the selection of his cabinet. For secretary of state, he chose the New Englander and former Federalist John Quincy Adams. Jefferson, Madison, and Monroe had all served as secretary of state before becoming president; Adams, therefore, immediately became the heir apparent, suggesting that the "Virginia Dynasty" would soon come to an end. Speaker of the House Henry Clay declined an offer to be secretary of war, so Monroe named John C. Calhoun instead. In his other appointments, too, Monroe took pains to include both northerners and southerners, easterners and westerners, Federalists and Republicans.

Soon after his inauguration, Monroe did what no president since Washington had done: he made a goodwill tour through the country. In New England, so recently the scene of rabid Federalist discontent, he was greeted everywhere with enthusiastic demonstrations. The *Columbian Centinel,* a Federalist newspaper in Boston, commenting on the "Presidential Jubilee" in that city, observed that an "era of good feelings" had arrived. And on the surface, at least, the years of Monroe's presidency did appear to be an "era of good feelings." In 1820, Monroe was reelected without opposition. For all practical purposes, the Federalist Party had now ceased to exist.

MONROE'S GOODWILL TOUR

JOHN QUINCY ADAMS AND FLORIDA

Like his father, the second president, John Quincy Adams had spent much of his life in diplomatic service. Even before becoming secretary of state, he had become one of the great diplomats in American history. He was also a committed nationalist, and he considered his most important task to be the promotion of American expansion.

SEMINOLE DANCE This 1838 drawing by a U.S. military officer portrays a dance by Seminole Indians near Fort Butler in Florida. It was made in the midst of the prolonged Second Seminole War, which ended in 1842 with the removal of most of the tribe from Florida to reservations west of the Mississippi. (© Huntington Library/SuperStock)

His first challenge as secretary of state was Florida. The United States had already annexed West Florida, but that claim remained in dispute. Most Americans believed the nation should gain possession of the entire peninsula. In 1817, Adams began negotiations with the Spanish minister, Luis de Onís, in hopes of resolving the dispute and gaining the entire territory for the United States.

In the meantime, events were taking their own course in Florida itself. Andrew Jackson, now in command of American troops along the Florida frontier, had orders from Secretary of War Calhoun to "adopt the necessary measures" to stop continuing raids on American territory by Seminole Indians south of the Florida border. Jackson used those orders as an excuse to invade Florida, seize the Spanish forts at St. Marks and Pensacola, and order the hanging of two British subjects on the charge of supplying and inciting the Indians. The operation became known as the Seminole War.

THE SEMINOLE WAR

Instead of condemning Jackson's raid, Adams urged the government to assume responsibility for it. The United States, he told the Spanish, had the right under international law to defend itself against threats from across its borders. Since Spain was unwilling or unable to curb those threats, America had simply done what was necessary. Jackson's raid demonstrated to the Spanish that the United States could easily take Florida by force. Adams implied that the nation might consider doing so.

Onís realized, therefore, that he had little choice but to come to terms with the Americans. Under the provisions of the

ADAMS-ONÍS TREATY

Adams-Onís Treaty of 1819, Spain ceded all of Florida to the United States and gave up as well its claim to territory north of the 42nd parallel in the Pacific Northwest. In return, the American government gave up its claims to Texas.

THE PANIC OF 1819

But the Monroe administration had little time to revel in its diplomatic successes, for the nation was falling victim to a serious economic crisis: the Panic of 1819. It followed a period of high foreign demand for American farm goods and thus of exceptionally high prices for American farmers (all as a result of the disruption of European agriculture caused by the Napoleonic Wars). The rising prices for farm goods had stimulated a land boom in the western United States. Fueled by speculative investments, land prices soared.

The availability of easy credit to settlers and speculators—from the government (under the land acts of 1800 and 1804), from state banks and wildcat banks, even for a time from the

BOOM AND BUST

rechartered Bank of the United States—fueled the land boom. Beginning in 1819, however, new management at the national bank began tightening credit, calling in loans, and foreclosing mortgages. This precipitated a series of failures by state banks. The result was a financial panic, which many Americans, particularly those in the West, blamed on the national bank. Six

years of depression followed and began a process that would eventually make the Bank's existence one of the nation's most burning political issues.

SECTIONALISM AND NATIONALISM

For a brief but alarming moment in 1819–1820, the increasing differences between the North and the South threatened the unity of the United States—until the Missouri Compromise temporarily averted a sectional crisis.

THE MISSOURI COMPROMISE

When Missouri applied for admission to the Union as a state in 1819, slavery was already well established there. Even so, Representative James Tallmadge Jr. of New York proposed an

TALLMADGE AMENDMENT

amendment to the Missouri statehood bill that would prohibit the further introduction of slaves into Missouri and provide for the gradual emancipation of those already there. The Tallmadge Amendment provoked a controversy that raged for the next two years.

Since the beginning of the republic, partly by chance and partly by design, new states had come into the Union more or less in pairs, one from the North, another from the South. In 1819, there were eleven free states and eleven slave states; the admission of Missouri as a "free state" would upset that balance and increase the political power of the North over the South. Hence the controversy over slavery and freedom in Missouri.

THE MISSOURI COMPROMISE, 1820 This map illustrates the way the Missouri Compromise proposed to settle the controversy over slavery in the new western territories of the United States. The compromise rested on the virtually simultaneous admission of Missouri and Maine to the Union, one a slave state and the other a free one. Note the red line extending beyond the southern border of Missouri, which in theory established a permanent boundary between areas in which slavery could be established and areas where it was banned.

• *What precipitated the Missouri Compromise?*

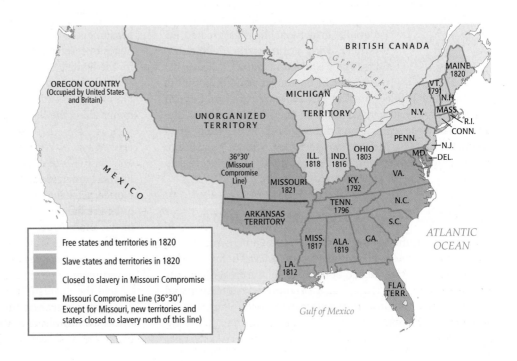

Complicating the Missouri question was the application of Maine (previously the northern part of Massachusetts) for admission as a new (and free) state. Speaker of the House Henry Clay informed northern members that if they blocked Missouri from entering the Union as a slave state, southerners would block the admission of Maine. But Maine ultimately offered a way out of the impasse, as the Senate agreed to combine the Maine and Missouri proposals into a single bill. Maine would be admitted as a free state, Missouri as a slave state. Then Senator Jesse B. Thomas of Illinois proposed an amendment prohibiting slavery in the rest of the Louisiana Purchase territory north of the southern boundary of Missouri (the 36°30′ parallel) Congress adopted the Thomas Amendment.

MISSOURI COMPROMISE

Nationalists in both North and South hailed this settlement—which became known as the Missouri Compromise—as a happy resolution of a danger to the Union. But the debate over the bill had revealed a strong undercurrent of sectionalism that was competing with—although at the moment failing to derail—the powerful tides of nationalism.

MARSHALL AND THE COURT

John Marshall served as chief justice of the United States from 1801 to 1835, and he dominated the Court more fully than anyone else before or since. More than anyone but the framers themselves, he molded the development of the Constitution: strengthening the judicial branch at the expense of the executive and legislative branches, increasing the power of the federal government at the expense of the states, and advancing the interests of the propertied and commercial classes.

Committed to promoting commerce, the Marshall Court staunchly defended the inviolability of contracts. In *Fletcher v. Peck* (1810), which arose out of a series of notorious land frauds in Georgia, Marshall held that a land grant was a valid contract and could not be repealed even if corruption was involved.

Dartmouth College v. Woodward (1819) further expanded the meaning of the contract clause of the Constitution. Having gained control of the New Hampshire state government, Republicans tried to revise Dartmouth College's charter (granted by King George III in 1769) to convert the private college into a state university. Daniel Webster, a Dartmouth graduate and brilliant orator, argued the college's case. The Dartmouth charter, he insisted, was a contract, protected by the same doctrine that the Court had already upheld in *Fletcher v. Peck*. Then, according to legend, he brought some of the justices to tears with an irrelevant passage that concluded: "It is, sir, . . . a small college. And yet there are those who love it." The Court ruled for Dartmouth. The decision placed important restrictions on the ability of state governments to control corporations.

DARTMOUTH COLLEGE V. WOODWARD

In overturning the act of the legislature and the decisions of the New Hampshire courts, the justices also implicitly claimed for themselves the right to override the decisions of state courts. But advocates of states' rights, especially in the South, continued to challenge its right to do so. In *Cohens v. Virginia* (1821),

JOHN MARSHALL The imposing figure in this image is John Marshall, the most important chief justice of the Supreme Court in American history. A former secretary of state, Marshall served as chief justice from 1801 until his death in 1835 at the age of eighty. Such was the power of his intellect and personality that he dominated his fellow justices throughout that period, regardless of their previous party affiliations or legal ideologies. Marshall established the independence of the Court, gave it a reputation for nonpartisan integrity, and established its powers, which were only vaguely described by the Constitution. (National Archives)

Marshall explicitly affirmed the constitutionality of federal review of state court decisions. The states had given up part of their sovereignty in ratifying the Constitution, he explained, and their courts must submit to federal jurisdiction; otherwise, the federal government would be powerless "at the feet of every state in the Union."

Meanwhile, in *McCulloch v. Maryland* (1819), Marshall confirmed the "implied powers" of Congress by upholding the constitutionality of the Bank of the United States. The Bank had become so unpopular in the South and the West that several of the states tried to drive branches out of business by outright prohibition or by confiscatory taxes. This case presented two constitutional questions: Could Congress charter a bank? And if so, could individual states ban it or tax it? Daniel

CONFIRMING IMPLIED POWERS

Webster, one of the Bank's attorneys, argued that establishing such an institution came within the "necessary and proper" clause of the Constitution and that the power to tax involved a "power to destroy." If the states could tax the Bank at all, Webster said, they could "tax it to death." Marshall adopted Webster's words in deciding for the Bank.

In the case of *Gibbons v. Ogden* (1824), the Court strengthened Congress's power to regulate interstate commerce. The state of New York had indirectly granted Aaron Ogden the business of carrying passengers across the river between New York and New Jersey. But Thomas Gibbons, with a license granted under an act of Congress, began competing with Ogden for the ferry traffic. Ogden brought suit against him and won in the New York courts. Gibbons appealed to the Supreme Court. The most important question facing the justices was whether Congress's power to give Gibbons a license to operate his ferry superseded the state of New York's power to grant Ogden a monopoly. Marshall claimed that the power of Congress to regulate interstate commerce (which, he said, included navigation) was "complete in itself" and might be "exercised to its utmost extent." Ogden's state-granted monopoly, therefore, was void.

The decisions of the Marshall Court established the primacy of the federal government over the states in regulating the econ-

ESTABLISHING
FEDERAL
PRIMACY

omy and opened the way for an increased federal role in promoting economic growth. They protected corporations and other private economic institutions from local government interference. They were, in short, highly nationalistic decisions, designed to promote the growth of a strong, unified, and economically developed United States.

THE COURT AND THE TRIBES

The nationalist inclinations of the Marshall Court were visible as well in a series of decisions concerning the legal status of Indian tribes within the United States. But these decisions did not simply affirm the supremacy of the United States; they also carved out a distinctive position for Native Americans within the constitutional structure.

The first of the crucial Indian decisions was in the case of *Johnson v. McIntosh* (1823). Leaders of the Illinois and Pinakeshaw tribes had sold parcels of their land to a group of white settlers (including Johnson) but later signed a treaty with the federal government ceding territory that included those same parcels to the United States. The government proceeded to grant homestead rights to new white settlers (among them McIntosh) on the land claimed by Johnson. The Court was asked to decide which claim had precedence. Marshall's ruling, not surprisingly, favored the United States. But in explaining it, he offered a preliminary definition of the place of Indians within the nation. The tribes had a basic right to their tribal lands, he said, that preceded all other American law. Individual American citizens could not buy or take land from the tribes; only the federal government—the supreme authority—could do that.

Even more important was the Court's 1832 decision in *Worcester v. Georgia,* in which the Court invalidated Georgia

WORCESTER
v. GEORGIA

laws that attempted to regulate access by U.S. citizens to Cherokee country. Only the federal government could do that, Marshall claimed, thus taking another important step in consolidating federal authority over the states (and over the tribes). In doing so, he further defined the nature of the Indian nations. The tribes, he explained, were sovereign entities in much the same way Georgia was a sovereign entity—"distinct political communities, having territorial boundaries within which their authority is exclusive." In defending the power of the federal government, he was also affirming, indeed expanding, the rights of the tribes to remain free from the authority of state governments.

The Marshall decisions, therefore, did what the Constitution itself had not done: they defined a place for Indian tribes within the American political system. The tribes had basic property rights. They were sovereign entities not subject to the authority of state governments. But the federal government, like a "guardian" governing its "ward," had ultimate authority over tribal affairs—even if that authority was, according to the Court, limited by the government's obligation to protect Indian welfare. These provisions were seldom enough to defend Indians from the steady westward march of white civilization, but they formed the basis of what few legal protections they had.

THE LATIN AMERICAN REVOLUTION AND THE MONROE DOCTRINE

Americans looking southward in the years following the War of 1812 beheld a gigantic spectacle: the Spanish Empire in its death

REVOLUTION IN
LATIN AMERICA

throes, a whole continent in revolt, new nations in the making. Already the United States had developed a profitable trade with Latin America and was rivaling Great Britain as the principal trading nation there. Many Americans believed the success of the anti-Spanish revolutions would further strengthen America's position in the region.

In 1815, the United States proclaimed neutrality in the wars between Spain and its rebellious colonies, implying a partial recognition of the rebels' status as nations. Moreover, the United States sold ships and supplies to the revolutionaries, a clear indication that it was not genuinely neutral but was trying to help the insurgents. Finally, in 1822, President Monroe established diplomatic relations with five new nations—La Plata (later Argentina), Chile, Peru, Colombia, and Mexico—making the United States the first country to recognize them.

In 1823, Monroe went further and announced a policy that

THE MONROE
DOCTRINE

would ultimately be known (beginning some thirty years later) as the "Monroe Doctrine," even though it was primarily the work of John Quincy Adams. "The American continents,"

CHEROKEE LEADERS Sequoyah, left (who also used the name George Guess), was a mixed-blood Cherokee who translated his tribe's language into writing through an elaborate syllabary (equivalent to an alphabet) of his own invention, pictured here. He opposed Indian assimilation into white society and saw the preservation of the Cherokee language as a way to protect the culture of his tribe. He moved to Arkansas in the 1820s and became a chief of the western Cherokee tribes. Major George Lowery, shown on the right, was also a mixed-blood Cherokee and served as assistant principal chief of the Cherokees from 1828 to 1838. He supported acculturation but remained a Cherokee nationalist. He wears a U.S. presidential medal around his neck. (*Left,* National Portrait Gallery, Smithsonian Institute/Art Resource, NY. *Right,* From the collection of the Gilcrease Museum, Tulsa, Oklahoma)

Monroe declared, ". . . are henceforth not to be considered as subjects for future colonization by any European powers." The United States would consider any foreign challenge to the sovereignty of existing American nations an unfriendly act. At the same time, he proclaimed, "Our policy in regard to Europe . . . is not to interfere in the internal concerns of any of its powers."

The Monroe Doctrine emerged directly out of America's relations with Europe in the 1820s. Many Americans feared that

AMERICAN FEARS

Spain's European allies (notably France) would assist Spain in an effort to retake its lost empire. Even more troubling to Adams (and many other Americans) was the fear that Great Britain had designs on Cuba. Adams wanted to keep Cuba in Spanish hands until it fell (as he believed it ultimately would) to the Americans.

The Monroe Doctrine had few immediate effects, but it was important as an expression of the growing spirit of nationalism in the United States in the 1820s. And it established the idea of the United States as the dominant power in the Western Hemisphere.

THE REVIVAL OF OPPOSITION

After 1816, the Federalist Party offered no presidential candidate and soon ceased to exist as a national political force. The Republican Party (which considered itself not a party but an organization representing the whole of the population) was the only organized force in national politics.

By the late 1820s, however, partisan divisions were emerging once again. In some respects, the division mirrored the schism that had produced the first party system in

NEW POLITICAL DIVISIONS

the 1790s. The Republicans had in many ways come to resemble the early Federalist regimes in their promotion of economic growth and centralization. And the opposition, like the opposition in the 1790s, objected to the federal government's expanding role in the economy. There was, however, a crucial difference. At the beginning of the century, the opponents of centralization had also often been opponents of economic growth. Now, in the 1820s, the controversy involved not whether but how the nation should continue to expand.

THE "CORRUPT BARGAIN"

Until 1820, when the Federalist Party effectively ceased operations and James Monroe ran for reelection unopposed, presidential candidates were nominated by caucuses of the two parties in Congress. But in the presidential election of 1824, "King Caucus" was overthrown. The Republican caucus nominated William H. Crawford of Georgia, the secretary of the treasury and the favorite of the extreme states' rights faction of the party. But other candidates received nominations from state legislatures and won endorsements from irregular mass meetings throughout the country.

END OF THE
CAUCUS
SYSTEM

One of them was Secretary of State John Quincy Adams, who held the office that was the traditional stepping-stone to the presidency. But as he himself ruefully understood, he was a man of cold and forbidding manners, with little popular appeal. Another contender was Henry Clay, the Speaker of the House. He had a devoted personal following and a definite and coherent program: the "American System," which proposed creating a great home market for factory and farm producers by raising the protective tariff, strengthening the national bank, and financing internal improvements. Andrew Jackson, the fourth major candidate, had no significant political record—even though he had served briefly as a representative in Congress and was now a new member of the United States Senate. But he was a military hero and had the help of shrewd political allies from his home state of Tennessee.

Jackson received more popular and electoral votes than any other candidate, but not a majority. He had 99 electoral votes to Adams's 84, Crawford's 41, and Clay's 37. The Twelfth Amendment to the Constitution (passed in the aftermath of the contested 1800 election) required the House of Representatives to choose among the three candidates with the largest numbers of electoral votes. Crawford was by then seriously ill and not a plausible candidate. Clay was out of the running, but he was in a strong position to influence the result. Jackson was Clay's most formidable political rival in the West, so Clay supported Adams, in part because, alone among the candidates, Adams was an ardent nationalist and a likely supporter of the American System. With Clay's endorsement, Adams won election in the House.

ELECTION OF
1824

The Jacksonians believed their large popular and electoral pluralities entitled their candidate to the presidency, and they were enraged when he lost. But they grew angrier still when Adams named Clay his secre-

JOHN QUINCY ADAMS This photograph of the former president was taken shortly before his death in 1848 at the age of eighty—almost twenty years after he had left the White House—when he was serving as a congressman from Massachusetts. During his years as president, he was—as he had been throughout his life—an intensely disciplined and hardworking man. He rose at four in the morning and made a long entry in his diary for the previous day. He wrote so much that his right hand at times became paralyzed with writer's cramp, so he taught himself to write with his left hand as well. (Brown Brothers)

tary of state. The State Department was the well-established route to the presidency, and Adams thus appeared to be naming Clay as his own successor. The outrage the Jacksonians expressed at what they called a "corrupt bargain" haunted Adams throughout his presidency.

> THE OUTRAGE THE JACKSONIANS EXPRESSED AT WHAT THEY CALLED A "CORRUPT BARGAIN" HAUNTED ADAMS THROUGHOUT HIS PRESIDENCY.

THE SECOND PRESIDENT ADAMS

Throughout Adams's term in the White House, the political bitterness arising from the "corrupt bargain" charges thoroughly frustrated his policies. Adams proposed an ambitiously nationalist program reminiscent of Clay's American System. But Jacksonians in Congress blocked most of it.

Adams also experienced diplomatic frustrations. He appointed delegates to an international conference that the Venezuelan liberator, Simón Bolívar, had called in Panama in 1826. But Haiti was one of the participating nations, and southerners in Congress opposed the idea of white Americans mingling with the black delegates. Congress delayed approving the Panama mission so long that the American delegation did not arrive until after the conference was over.

Adams also lost a contest with the state of Georgia, which wished to remove the remaining Creek and Cherokee Indians from the state to gain additional soil for cotton planters. The United States government, in a 1791 treaty, had guaranteed that land to the Creeks; but in 1825, white Georgians had extracted a new treaty from William McIntosh, the leader of one faction in the tribe and a longtime advocate of Indian cooperation with the United States. Adams believed the new treaty had no legal force, since McIntosh clearly did not represent the wishes of the tribe; and he refused to enforce the treaty, setting up a direct conflict between the president and the state. The governor of Georgia defied the president and proceeded with plans for Indian removal. Adams found no way to stop him.

Even more damaging to the administration was its support for a new tariff on imported goods in 1828. This measure originated with the demands of Massachusetts and Rhode Island woolen manufacturers, who complained that the British were dumping textiles on the American market at artificially low prices. But to win support from middle and western states, the administration had to accept duties on other items. In the process, it antagonized the original New England supporters of the bill; the benefits of protecting their manufactured goods from foreign competition now had to be weighed against the prospects of having to pay more for raw materials. Adams signed the bill, earning the animosity of southerners, who cursed it as the "tariff of abominations."

TARIFF OF ABOMINATIONS

JACKSON TRIUMPHANT

By the time of the 1828 presidential election, a new two-party system had begun to emerge out of the divisions among the Republicans. On one side stood the supporters of John Quincy Adams, who called themselves the National Republicans and who supported the economic nationalism of the preceding years. Opposing them were the followers of Andrew Jackson, who took the name Democratic Republicans and who called for an assault on privilege and a widening of opportunity. Adams attracted the support of most of the remaining Federalists; Jackson appealed to a broad coalition that opposed the "economic aristocracy."

But issues seemed to count for little in the end, as the campaign degenerated into a war of personal invective. The Jacksonians charged that Adams as president had been guilty

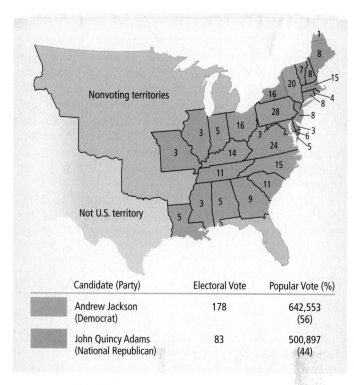

Candidate (Party)	Electoral Vote	Popular Vote (%)
Andrew Jackson (Democrat)	178	642,553 (56)
John Quincy Adams (National Republican)	83	500,897 (44)

THE ELECTION OF 1828 As this map shows, Andrew Jackson's victory over John Quincy Adams was one of the most decisive in American history for a challenger facing an incumbent president.

• *What accounts for this decisive repudiation of President Adams?*

of gross waste and extravagance and had used public funds to buy gambling devices (a chess set and a billiard table) for the White House. Adams's supporters hurled even worse accusations at Jackson. They called him a murderer and distributed a "coffin handbill," which listed, within coffin-shaped outlines, the names of militiamen whom Jackson was said to have shot in cold blood during the War of 1812. (The men had been deserters who were legally executed after sentence by a court-martial.) And they called his wife a bigamist. Jackson had married his beloved Rachel at a time when the pair incorrectly believed her first husband had divorced her. (When Jackson's wife first read of the accusations against her shortly after the election, she collapsed and, a few weeks later, died; not without reason, Jackson blamed his opponents for her death.)

Jackson's victory was decisive, but sectional. He won 56 percent of the popular vote and an electoral majority of 178 votes to 83. Adams swept virtually all of New England and showed significant strength in the mid-Atlantic region. Nevertheless, the Jacksonians considered their victory as complete and as important as Jefferson's in 1800. Once again, the forces of privilege had been driven from Washington. Once again, a champion of democracy would occupy the White House and restore liberty to the people and to the economy. America had entered, some Jacksonians claimed, a new era of democracy, the "age of the common man."

JACKSON TRIUMPHANT

LOOKING BACK

In the aftermath of the War of 1812, a vigorous nationalism came increasingly to characterize the political and popular culture of the United States. In all regions of the country, white men and women celebrated the achievements of the early leaders of the republic, the genius of the Constitution, and the success of the nation in withstanding serious challenges from both without and within. Party divisions faded to the point that James Monroe, the fifth president, won reelection in 1820 without opposition.

But the broad nationalism of the so-called era of good feelings disguised some deep divisions within the United States. Indeed, the character of American nationalism differed sub-stantially from one region, and one group, to another. Battles continued between those who favored a strong central government committed to advancing the economic development of the nation and those who wanted a decentralization of power to open opportunity to more people. Battles continued as well over the role of slavery in American life—and in particular over the place of slavery in the new western territories that the United States was rapidly populating (and wresting from the tribes). The Missouri Compromise of 1820 postponed the day of reckoning on that issue—but only for a time, as Andrew Jackson would discover soon after becoming president in 1829. •

SIGNIFICANT EVENTS

Monroe elected
president

Commercial panic
destabilizes economy

1815

U.S. signs treaties with
tribes taking western lands
from Indians

1816

Second Bank of
the United States
chartered

1818

Jackson invades
Florida, ends first
Seminole War

1819

Spain cedes Florida to United
States in Adams-Onís Treaty

Supreme Court hears
Dartmouth College v. Woodward
and *McCulloch v. Maryland*

Terms/People/Places/Events

Adams-Onís Treaty 226
American System 230
Factor system 222
Francis Cabot Lowell 219
Gibbons v. Ogden 228

Henry Clay 227
John Quincy Adams 225
McCulloch v. Maryland 227
Missouri Compromise 226
Monroe Doctrine 228

Seminole War 225
Stephen H. Long 224
Tallmadge Amendment 226

RECALL AND REFLECT

1. How did the War of 1812 stimulate the national economy?

2. What were the reasons for the rise of sectional differences in this era? What attempts were made to resolve these differences? How successful were those attempts?

3. Why was the Monroe Doctrine proclaimed?

4. What was the significance of Andrew Jackson's victory in the election of 1828?

Missouri
Compromise
enacted

Supreme Court rules in
Gibbons v. Ogden

1820
Monroe reelected
president without
opposition

1821
Mexico achieves
independence
from Spain

1823
Monroe
Doctrine
proclaimed

1824
John Quincy Adams wins
disputed presidential
election

1828
"Tariff of
abominations"
passed

Andrew Jackson
elected president

THE VERDICT OF THE PEOPLE **(1855), BY GEORGE CALEB BINGHAM** This scene of an election-day gathering is peopled almost entirely by white men. Women and African Americans were barred from voting, but political rights expanded substantially in the 1830s and 1840s among white males. (Courtesy of the Saint Louis Art Museum, Gift of Bank of America)

9 | JACKSONIAN AMERICA

DURING THE YEARS OF ECONOMIC AND TERRITORIAL expansion in the early nineteenth century, Americans pondered the future of their democracy. Some feared that the nation's rapid growth would produce social chaos and insisted that the country's first priority must be to establish order and a clear system of authority. Others argued that the greatest danger facing the nation was privilege and that society's goal should be to eliminate the favored status of powerful elites and make opportunity more widely available. Advocates of this latter vision won control of the federal government in 1829 with the inauguration of Andrew Jackson.

The "democratization" of government over which Andrew Jackson presided was accompanied by a lofty rhetoric of equality and aroused the excitement of working people, but Jackson and his followers were not egalitarians. They accepted the necessity of economic inequality and social gradation. Jackson himself was a frontier aristocrat, and most of those who served him were people of wealth and standing. They were not, however, usually aristocrats by birth. They had, they believed, risen to prominence on the basis of their own talents and energies, and their goal in public life was to ensure that

SETTING THE STAGE

others like themselves would have the opportunity to do the same. For these national leaders the purpose of democratization was not primarily to aid farmers and laborers or to assist the truly disenfranchised: African Americans (both slave and free), women, and Native Americans. It was, rather, to challenge the power of eastern elites for the sake of the rising entrepreneurs of the South and the West.

LOOKING AHEAD

1. How did the electorate expand during the Jacksonian era, and what were the limits of that expansion?
2. What events fed the growing tension between nationalism and states' rights, and what were the arguments on both sides of that issue?
3. What was the Second Party System, and how did its emergence and rise change national politics?

THE RISE OF MASS POLITICS

On March 4, 1829, an unprecedented throng—thousands of Americans from all regions of the country, including farmers,

JACKSON'S INAUGURATION

laborers, and others of modest social rank—crowded before the Capitol in Washington, D.C., to witness the inauguration of Andrew Jackson. After the ceremonies, the boisterous crowd poured down Pennsylvania Avenue, following their hero to the White House. There, at a public reception open to all, they filled the state rooms to overflowing, trampling one another, soiling the carpets, ruining elegantly upholstered sofas and chairs in their eagerness to shake the new president's hand. "It was a proud day for the people," wrote Amos Kendall, one of Jackson's closest political associates. "General Jackson is their own President." To other observers, however, the scene was less appealing. Justice of the Supreme Court Joseph Story, a friend and colleague of John Marshall, looked on the inaugural levee, as it was called, and remarked with disgust: "The reign of King 'Mob' seems triumphant."

EXPANDING DEMOCRACY

What some have called the "age of Jackson" did not much advance the cause of economic equality. The distribution of wealth and property in America was little different at the end of the Jacksonian era than it had been at the start. But it did mark a transformation of American politics that widely extended to new groups the right to vote.

Until the 1820s, relatively few Americans had been permitted

BROADENING THE FRANCHISE

to vote. Most states restricted the franchise to white males who were property owners or taxpayers or both, effectively barring an enormous number of the less affluent from the voting rolls. But beginning even before Jackson's election, the rules governing voting began to expand. Changes came first in Ohio and other new states of the West, which, on joining the Union, adopted constitutions that guaranteed all adult white males the right to vote and gave all voters the right to hold public office. Older states, concerned about the loss of their population to the West and thinking that extending the franchise might encourage some residents to stay, began to grant similar political rights to their citizens, dropping or reducing their property ownership or taxpaying requirements. Eventually, every state democratized its electorate to some degree, although some much later and less fully than others.

Change provoked resistance, and at times the democratic trend fell short of the aims of the more radical reformers, as when Massachusetts held its constitutional convention in 1820. Reform-minded delegates complained that in the Massachusetts government the rich were better represented than the poor, both because of restrictions on voting and officeholding and because of a peculiar system by which members of the state senate represented property rather than simply people. But Daniel Webster, one of the conservative delegates, opposed democratic changes on the grounds that "power naturally and necessarily follows property" and that "property as such should have its

ANDREW JACKSON This stern portrait suggests something of the fierce determination that characterized Andrew Jackson's military and political careers. Shattered by the death of his wife a few weeks after his election as president—a death he blamed (not without reason) on the attacks his political opponents had leveled at her—he entered office with a steely determination to live by his own principles and give no quarter to his adversaries. (New-York Historical Society)

weight and influence in political arrangement." Webster and the rest of the conservatives could not prevent the reform of the rules for representation in the state senate; nor could they prevent elimination of the property requirement for voting. But, to the dismay of the radicals, the new constitution required that every voter be a taxpayer and that the governor be the owner of considerable real estate.

More often, however, the forces of democratization prevailed in the states. In the New York convention of 1821, for example, conservatives led by James Kent insisted that a taxpaying requirement for suffrage was not enough and that, at least in the election of state senators, the property qualification should survive. But reformers, citing the Declaration of Independence, maintained that life, liberty, and the pursuit of happiness, not property, were the main concerns of society and government. The property qualification was abolished.

The wave of state reforms was generally peaceful, but in Rhode Island democratization efforts created considerable instability. The Rhode Island constitution (which was still basically the old colonial charter) barred more than half the adult males of the state from voting. The conservative legislature, chosen by this restricted electorate, consistently blocked all efforts at reform. In 1840, the lawyer and activist Thomas W. Dorr and

Percentage

26.9 | 57.6 | 55.4 | 57.8 | 80.2 | 78.9 | 72.7 | 69.6 | 78.9 | 81.2

1824 1828 1832 1836 1840 1844 1848 1852 1856 1860
Year

PARTICIPATION IN PRESIDENTIAL ELECTIONS, 1824–1860 This chart reveals the remarkable increase in popular participation in presidential elections in the years after 1824. Participation almost doubled between 1824 and 1828, and it increased substantially again beginning in 1840 and continuing through and beyond the Civil War.

• *What accounts for this dramatic expansion of the electorate? Who remained outside the voting population in these years?*

The democratization process was far from complete. In much of the South, election laws continued to favor the planters and politicians of the older counties and to limit the influence of newly settled western areas. Slaves, of course, were disenfranchised by definition; they were not considered citizens and were believed to have no legal or political rights. Free blacks could vote nowhere in the South and hardly anywhere in the North. Pennsylvania, in fact, amended its state constitution in 1838 to strip African Americans of the right to vote they had previously enjoyed. In no state could women vote. Nowhere was the ballot secret, and often voters had to cast a spoken vote rather than a written one, which meant that political bosses could, and often did, bribe and intimidate them.

DEMOCRATIC REFORMS

Despite the persisting limitations, however, the number of voters increased far more rapidly than did the population as a whole. Indeed, one of the most striking political trends of the early nineteenth century was the change in the method of choosing presidential electors and the dramatic increase in popular participation in the process. In 1800, the legislature had chosen the presidential electors in ten of the states, and the people in only six. By 1828, electors were chosen by popular vote in every state but South Carolina. In the presidential election of 1824, less than 27 percent of adult white males had voted. In the election of 1828, the figure rose to 58 percent, and in 1840 to 80 percent.

THE DORR REBELLION

a group of his followers formed a "People's party," held a convention, drafted a new constitution, and submitted it to a popular vote. It was overwhelmingly approved. The existing legislature, however, refused to accept the Dorr document and submitted a new constitution of its own to the voters. It was narrowly defeated. The Dorrites, in the meantime, had begun to set up a new government, under their own constitution, with Dorr as governor; and so, in 1842, two governments were claiming legitimacy in Rhode Island. The old state government proclaimed that Dorr and his followers were rebels and began to imprison them. Meanwhile, the Dorrites made a brief and ineffectual effort to capture the state arsenal. The Dorr Rebellion, as it was known, quickly failed. Dorr himself surrendered and was briefly imprisoned. But the episode helped pressure the old guard to draft a new constitution, which greatly expanded the suffrage.

THE DORR REBELLION The democratic sentiments that swept much of the nation in the 1830s and 1840s produced, among many other things, the Dorr Rebellion (as its opponents termed it) in Rhode Island. Thomas Dorr was one of many Rhode Islanders who denounced the state's constitution, which limited voting rights to a small group of property owners known as "freeholders." This "ticket" was what Dorr's supporters placed in ballot boxes as they cast their votes. (Courtesy of The Rhode Island Historical Society, RHi X5 304)

PEOPLE'S
Constitutional and State Rights'
TICKET.
[*Election Monday, April 18th, 1842.*]

FOR GOVERNOR,
THOMAS W. DORR,
OF PROVIDENCE.

FOR LIEUTENANT GOVERNOR,
AMASA EDDY, JR.
OF GLOCESTER.

WILLIAM H. SMITH, *Secretary of State.*
JOSEPH JOSLIN, *General Treasurer.*
JONAH TITUS, *Attorney General.*

For Sheriff of the County of Providence,
BURRINGTON ANTHONY.

THE "AGE OF JACKSON"

TO many Americans in the 1820s and 1830s, Andrew Jackson was a champion of democracy, a symbol of a spirit of anti-elitism and egalitarianism that was sweeping American life. In the twentieth and twenty-first centuries, however, historians have disagreed sharply not only in their assessments of Jackson himself, but also in their portrayal of American society in his era.

The "progressive" historians of the early twentieth century tended to see the politics of Jackson and his supporters as a forerunner of their own generation's battles against economic privilege and political corruption. Frederick Jackson Turner encouraged scholars to see Jacksonianism as the product of the democratic West: a protest by the people of the frontier against the conservative aristocracy of the East, which they believed restricted their own freedom and opportunity. Jackson represented those who wanted to make government responsive to the will of the people rather than to the power of special interests. The culmination of this progressive interpretation of Jacksonianism was the publication in 1945 of Arthur M. Schlesinger Jr.'s *The Age of Jackson*. Less interested in the regional basis of Jacksonianism than Turner's disciples had been, Schlesinger argued that Jacksonian democracy was an effort "to control the power of the capitalist groups, mainly Eastern, for the benefit of non-capitalist groups, farmers and laboring men, East, West, and South." He portrayed Jacksonianism as an early version of modern reform efforts to "restrain the power of the business community."

TOCQUEVILLE AND *DEMOCRACY IN AMERICA*

The rapid growth of the electorate—and the emergence of political parties—were among the most striking events of the early nineteenth century. As the right to vote spread widely in these years, it came to be the mark of freedom and democracy. One of the most important commentaries on this extraordinary moment in American life was a book by a French aristocrat, Alexis de Tocqueville. He spent two years in the United States in the 1830s watching the dramatic political changes in the age of Andrew Jackson. The French government had requested him to make a study of American prisons, which were thought to be more humane and effective institutions than prisons in Europe. But Tocqueville quickly went far beyond the study of prisons and wrote a classic study of American life, titled *Democracy in America*. Tocqueville examined not just the politics of the United States, but also the daily lives of many groups of Americans and their cultures, their associations, and their visions of democracy. In France in the early decades of the nineteenth century, the fruits of democracy were largely restricted to landowners and aristocrats. But Tocqueville recognized that traditional aristocracies were rapidly fading in America and that new elites could rise and fall no matter what their backgrounds.

Tocqueville also realized that the rising democracy of America had many limits. Democracy was a powerful, visible force in the lives of most white men. Few women could vote, although some shared the democratic ethos through their families. For many other Americans, democracy was a distant hope. Tocqueville wrote of the limits of equality and democracy:

> . . . he first who attracts the eye, the first in enlightenment, in power and in happiness, is the white man, the European, man par excellence; below him appear the Negro and the Indian. These two unfortunate races have neither birth, nor face, nor language, nor mores in common; only their misfortunes look alike. Both occupy an equally inferior position in the country that they inhabit; both experience the effects of tyranny; and if their miseries are different, they can accuse the same author for them.

Tocqueville's book helped spread the idea of American democracy into France and other European nations. Only later did it become widely read and studied in the United States as a remarkable portrait of the emerging democracy of the United States.

THE LEGITIMIZATION OF PARTY

The high level of voter participation was only partly the result of an expanded electorate. It was also the result of a growing interest

Richard Hofstadter, in an influential essay in his 1948 book *The American Political Tradition*, sharply disagreed. Jackson, he argued, was the spokesman of rising entrepreneurs—aspiring businessmen who saw the road to opportunity blocked by the monopolistic power of eastern aristocrats. The Jacksonian leaders were less sympathetic to the aspirations of those below them than they were to the destruction of obstacles to their own success. Bray Hammond, writing in 1957, argued similarly that the Jacksonian cause was "one of enterpriser against capitalist." Other historians saw Jacksonianism less as a democratic reform movement than as a nostalgic effort to restore a lost (and largely imagined) past. In *The Jacksonian Persuasion* (1957), Marvin Meyer argued that Jackson and his followers looked with misgivings on the new industrial society emerging around them and yearned instead for a restoration of the agrarian, republican virtues of an earlier time.

In the 1960s, historians examining the Jacksonian era began looking less at Jackson himself and more at the nature of American society in the early nineteenth century. Lee Benson's *The Concept of Jacksonian Democracy* (1961) used quantitative methods to demonstrate the role of religion and ethnicity in determining political divisions in the 1830s. Edward Pessen's *Jacksonian America* (1969) portrayed the Jacksonian era as an increasingly stratified society. This inclination to look more closely at society than at formal "Jacksonianism" continued into the late twentieth and early twenty-first centuries. Sean Wilentz, in *Chants Democratic* (1984) and in *The Rise of American Democracy* (2005), examined the rise in the 1820s of powerful movements among ordinary citizens, who were attracted less to Jackson himself than to the notion of popular democracy.

Gradually, this attention to Jacksonian-era society has led to reassessments of Jackson himself and the nature of his regime. In *Fathers and Children: Andrew Jackson and the Subjugation of the American Indian* (1975), Michael Rogin portrays Jackson as a leader of a new American revolution, not against British tyranny but against those who challenged the ability of white men to control the continent. Alexander Saxton, in *The Rise and Fall of the White Republic* (1990), makes the related point that "Jacksonian democracy" was ex-plicitly a white man's democracy that rested on the subjugation of women, slaves, and Indians. But the portrayal of Jackson as a champion of the common man has not vanished from scholarly life. The leading Jackson biographer of the postwar era, Robert V. Remini, has noted the flaws in Jackson's concept of democracy; but within the context of his time, Remini claims, Jackson was a genuine "man of the people." •

UNDERSTAND, ANALYZE, AND EVALUATE

1. What was Jacksonian democracy? Was it a reform movement against conservative special interests? Was it a regional movement designed to shift power to the West? Or was it a class-based movement to elevate workers and farmers?

2. Jackson was known as a "man of the people." Which people were attracted to him?

3. Can you think of a political movement today that is similar to Jacksonianism (a people's protest against restrictions on their freedom and opportunity, and the desire to make government responsive to the will of the people rather than to the power of special interests)?

---

in politics and a strengthening of party organization and, perhaps equally important, party loyalty. Although party competition was part of American politics almost from the beginning of the republic, acceptance of the idea of party was not. For more than thirty years, most Americans who had opinions about the nature of government considered parties evils to be avoided and thought the nation should seek a broad consensus in which permanent factional lines would not exist. But in the 1820s and 1830s, those assumptions gave way to a new view: that permanent, institutionalized parties were a desirable part of the political process, that indeed they were essential to democracy.

The elevation of the idea of party occurred first at the state level, most prominently in New York State. There Martin Van Buren led a dissident political faction (known as the "Bucktails" or the "Albany Regency"). In the years after the War of 1812, this group began to challenge the established political leadership—led by the aristocratic governor, De Witt Clinton—that had dominated the state for years. Factional rivalries were not new, of course. But the nature of Van Buren's challenge was. Refuting the traditional view of a political party as undemocratic, they argued that only an institutionalized party, based in the populace at large, could ensure genuine democracy. The alternative was the sort of closed elite that Clinton had created. In the new kind of party the Bucktails proposed, ideological commitments would be less important than loyalty to the party itself. Preservation of the party as an institution—through the use of favors, rewards, and patronage—would be the principal goal of the leadership. Above all, for a party to survive, it must have a permanent opposition. Competing parties would give each political faction a sense of purpose; they would force politicians to remain continually attuned to the will of the people; and they would check and balance each other in much the same way that the different branches of government checked and balanced one another.

By the late 1820s, this new idea of party was spreading beyond New York. The election of Jackson in 1828, the result of a popular movement that seemed to stand apart from the usual political elites, seemed further to legitimize the idea of party as a popular, democratic institution. "Parties of some sort must exist," said a New York newspaper. "'Tis in the nature and genius of our government."

THE SECOND PARTY SYSTEM

Finally, in the 1830s, a fully formed two-party system began to operate at the national level, with each party committed to its own existence as an institution and willing to accept the legitimacy of its opposition. The anti-Jackson forces began to call themselves Whigs. Jackson's followers called themselves Democrats (no longer Democratic Republicans), thus giving a permanent name to what is now the nation's oldest political party.

ELECTION POSTER, 1828 This poster shows how hotly contested the presidential race of 1828 was. John Quincy Adams, who had defeated Andrew Jackson narrowly (and, Jackson believed, dishonestly), was running against Jackson again. Jackson's campaign criticized Adams for his role in supporting the National Bank, which Jackson and his followers despised. (© Bettman/Corbis)

"PRESIDENT OF THE COMMON MAN"

Unlike Thomas Jefferson, Jackson was no democratic philosopher. The Democratic Party, much less than Jefferson's Republicans, embraced no clear or uniform ideological position. But Jackson himself did embrace a distinct, if simple, theory of democracy. It should offer "equal protection and equal benefits" to all its white male citizens and favor no region or class over another. In practice, that meant an assault on what Jackson and his associates considered the citadels of the eastern aristocracy and an effort to extend opportunities to the rising classes of the West and the South. It also meant a firm commitment to the continuing subjugation of African Americans and Indians (and, although for different reasons, women), for the Jacksonians believed that only by keeping these "dangerous" elements from the body politic could the white-male democracy they valued be preserved.

Jackson's first targets were the entrenched officeholders in the federal government, many of whom had been in place for a generation or more. Official duties, he believed, could be made "so plain and simple that men of intelligence may readily qualify themselves for their performance." Offices belonged to the people, he argued, not to the entrenched officeholders. Or, as one of his henchmen, William L. Marcy of New York, cynically put it, "To the victors belong the spoils."

In the end, Jackson removed a total of no more than one-fifth of the federal officeholders during his eight years in office,

THE SPOILS SYSTEM — many of them less for partisan reasons than because they had misused government funds or engaged in other corruption. Proportionally, Jackson dismissed no more jobholders than Jefferson had dismissed during his presidency. But by embracing the philosophy of the "spoils system," a system already well entrenched in a number of state governments, the Jackson administration helped make the right of elected officials to appoint their own followers to public office an established feature of American politics.

Jackson's supporters also worked to transform the process by which presidential candidates won their party's nomination. They had long resented the congressional caucus, a process they believed favored entrenched elites. Jackson himself had avoided the caucus process in 1828. In 1832, the president's followers staged a national party convention to renominate him for the presidency—one year after the Anti-Masons (see p. 251) became the first party to hold such a meeting. In later generations, some Americans would see the party convention as a source of corruption and political exclusivity. But those who created it in the 1830s considered it a great triumph for democracy. Through the convention, they believed, power would arise directly from the people, not from aristocratic political institutions such as the caucus.

The "spoils" system and the political convention did serve to limit the power of two entrenched elites—permanent officeholders and the exclusive party caucus. Yet neither really trans-

LIMITED NATURE OF DEMOCRATIC REFORM — ferred power to the people. Appointments to office almost always went to prominent political allies of the president and his associates. Delegates to national conventions were less often common men than members of local party organizations. Political opportunity within the party was expanding, but much less so than Jacksonian rhetoric suggested.

"OUR FEDERAL UNION"

Jackson's commitment to extending power beyond entrenched elites led him to want to reduce the functions of the federal government. The concentration of power in Washington, he believed, restricted opportunity to people with political connections. But Jackson also believed in forceful presidential leadership and was strongly committed to the preservation of the Union. Thus, at the same time that Jackson was promoting an economic program to reduce the power of the national government, he was asserting the supremacy of the Union in the face of a potent challenge. For no sooner had he entered office than his own vice president—John C. Calhoun—began to champion a controversial (and, in Jackson's view, dangerous) constitutional theory: nullification.

CALHOUN AND NULLIFICATION

Calhoun was forty-six years old in 1828, with a distinguished past and an apparently promising future. But the smoldering issue of the tariff created a dilemma for him. Once he had been an outspoken protectionist and had strongly supported the tariff of 1816. But by the late 1820s, many South Carolinians had come to believe that the "tariff of abominations" was responsible for the stagnation of the state's economy—even though the stagnation was largely a result of the exhaustion of South Carolina's farmland, which could no longer compete effectively with the newly opened fertile lands of the Southwest. Some exasperated Carolinians were ready to consider a drastic remedy—secession.

CALHOUN'S THEORY OF NULLIFICATION

Calhoun's future political hopes rested on how he met this challenge in his home state. He did so by developing a theory that he believed offered a moderate alternative to secession: the theory of nullification. Drawing from the ideas

JOHN C. CALHOUN This photograph, by Mathew Brady, captured Calhoun toward the end of his life, when he was torn between his real commitment to the ideals of the Union and his equally fervent commitment to the interests of the South. The younger generation of southern leaders, who would dominate the politics of the region in the 1850s, were less idealistic and more purely sectional in their views. (Library of Congress)

of Madison and Jefferson and their Virginia and Kentucky Resolutions of 1798–1799 and citing the Tenth Amendment to the Constitution, Calhoun argued that since the federal government was a creation of the states, the states—not the courts or Congress—were the final arbiters of the constitutionality of federal laws. If a state concluded that Congress had passed an unconstitutional law, then it could hold a special convention and declare the federal law null and void within the state. The nullification doctrine—and the idea of using it to nullify the 1828 tariff—quickly attracted broad support in South Carolina. But it did nothing to help Calhoun's standing within the new administration, in part because he had a powerful rival in Martin Van Buren.

THE RISE OF VAN BUREN

MARTIN VAN BUREN

Van Buren was about the same age as Calhoun and equally ambitious. He had won election to the governorship of New York in 1828 and then resigned in 1829 when Jackson appointed him secretary of state. Alone among the figures in the Jackson administration, Van Buren soon established himself as a member both of the official cabinet and of the president's unofficial circle of political allies, known as the "Kitchen Cabinet" (which included such Democratic newspaper editors as Isaac Hill of New Hampshire and Amos Kendall and Francis P. Blair of Kentucky). Van Buren's influence with the president was unmatched and grew stronger still as a result of a quarrel over etiquette that drove a wedge between the president and Calhoun.

Peggy O'Neale was the attractive daughter of a Washington tavernkeeper with whom both Andrew Jackson and his friend John H. Eaton had taken lodgings while serving as senators from Tennessee. O'Neale was married, but rumors circulated in Washington in the mid-1820s that she and the unmarried Senator Eaton were having an affair. O'Neale's husband died in 1828, and she and Eaton were soon married. A few weeks later, Jackson named Eaton secretary of war and thus made the new Mrs. Eaton a cabinet wife. The rest of the administration wives, led by Mrs. Calhoun, refused to receive her socially. Jackson (remembering the effects of public slander directed against his own late wife) was furious and demanded that the members of the cabinet accept her into their social world. Calhoun, under pressure from his wife, refused. Van Buren, a widower, befriended the Eatons and thus ingratiated himself with Jackson. By 1831, partly as a result of the Peggy Eaton affair, Jackson had chosen Van Buren to succeed him in the White House, apparently ending Calhoun's dreams of the presidency.

THE WEBSTER-HAYNE DEBATE

In January 1830, as the controversy over nullification grew more intense, a great debate occurred in the United States Senate over another sectional controversy. In the midst of a routine debate over federal policy toward western lands, a senator from Connecticut suggested that all land sales and surveys in the west be temporarily discontinued so as to slow the growth of

MARTIN VAN BUREN As leader of the so-called Albany Regency in New York in the 1820s, Van Buren helped create one of the first modern party organizations in the United States. Later, as Andrew Jackson's secretary of state and (after 1832) vice president, he helped bring party politics to the national level. In 1840, when he ran for reelection to the presidency, he lost to William Henry Harrison, whose Whig Party made effective use of many of the techniques of mass politics that Van Buren himself had pioneered. (Library of Congress)

DANIEL WEBSTER The great Civil War photographer Mathew Brady took this portrait of Daniel Webster shortly before Webster's death in 1852. It conveys something of Webster's intensity of purpose—an intensity that was perhaps most famously visible in his dramatic 1830 debate with South Carolina senator Robert Y. Hayne. In his response to Hayne, he spoke words that became a rallying cry in the North: "Liberty and Union, now and forever, one and inseparable." During his long political career, Webster was one of the giants of American politics, a man of much greater stature than many of the presidents who were his contemporaries. (Library of Congress)

slavery. Robert Y. Hayne, a young senator from South Carolina, responded, charging that slowing down the growth of the West was a way for the East to retain its political and economic power. Although he had no real interest in western lands, he hoped his stance would attract support from westerners in Congress for South Carolina's drive to lower the tariff. Both the South and the West, he argued, were victims of the tyranny of the Northeast. He hinted that the two regions might combine to defend themselves against that tyranny.

Daniel Webster, now a senator from Massachusetts and a nationalistic Whig, attacked Hayne the next day, and through him Calhoun, for what he considered

> ❝ LIBERTY AND UNION, NOW AND FOREVER, ONE AND INSEPARABLE! ❞
>
> **DANIEL WEBSTER**

> ❝ OUR FEDERAL UNION—IT MUST BE PRESERVED. ❞
>
> **PRESIDENT ANDREW JACKSON**

their challenge to the integrity of the Union. He was, in fact, challenging Hayne to a debate not on public lands and the tariff but on the issue of states' rights versus national power. Hayne, coached by Calhoun, responded with a defense of the theory of nullification. Webster then spent two full afternoons delivering what became known as his "Second Reply to Hayne," a speech that northerners quoted and revered for years to come. He concluded with the ringing appeal: "Liberty and Union, now and forever, one and inseparable!"

STATES' RIGHTS VERSUS NATIONAL POWER

Both sides now waited to hear what President Jackson thought of the argument. The answer became clear at the annual Democratic Party banquet in honor of Thomas Jefferson. After dinner, guests delivered a series of toasts. The president arrived with a written text in which he had underscored certain words: "Our Federal Union—It must be preserved." While he spoke,

CHARLESTON, 1831 The little-known South Carolina artist S. Bernard painted this view of Charleston's East Battery in 1831. Then, as now, residents and visitors liked to stroll along the battery and watch the activity in the city's busy harbor. But Charleston in the 1830s was a less important commercial center than it had been a few decades earlier. By then, overseas traders were increasingly avoiding southern ports and doing more and more business in New York. (Yale University Art Gallery/Art Resource)

he looked directly at Calhoun. The diminutive Van Buren, who stood on his chair to see better, thought he saw Calhoun's hand shake and a trickle of wine run down his glass as he responded to the president's toast with his own: "The Union, next to our liberty most dear." The two most important figures in government had drawn sharp lines between themselves.

THE NULLIFICATION CRISIS

In 1832, finally, the controversy over nullification produced a crisis. A congressional tariff bill was passed that offered South Carolinians no relief from the 1828 "tariff of abominations." Almost immediately, the legislature summoned a state convention, which voted to nullify the tariffs of 1828 and 1832 and to forbid the collection of duties within the state. At the same time, South Carolina elected Hayne to serve as governor and Calhoun (who resigned as vice president) to replace Hayne as senator.

Jackson insisted that nullification was treason and that those implementing it were traitors. He strengthened the federal forts in South Carolina and ordered a warship and several revenue ships to Charleston. When Congress convened early in 1833, Jackson proposed a force bill authorizing the president to use the military to see that acts of Congress were obeyed. Violence seemed a real possibility.

> **❝ THE UNION, NEXT TO OUR LIBERTY MOST DEAR. ❞**
>
> **JOHN C. CALHOUN**

Calhoun faced a predicament as he took his place in the Senate. Not a single state had come to South Carolina's support. Even South Carolina itself was divided and could not hope to prevail in a showdown with the federal government. But the timely intervention of Henry Clay, newly elected to the Senate, averted a crisis. Clay devised a compromise by which the tariff would be lowered gradually so that, by 1842, it would reach approximately the same

COMPROMISE level as in 1816. The compromise and the force bill were passed on the same day, March 1, 1833. Jackson signed them both. In South Carolina, the convention reassembled and repealed its nullification of the tariffs. Calhoun and his followers claimed a victory for nullification, which had, they insisted, forced the revision of the tariff. But the episode made clear that no state could defy the federal government alone.

THE REMOVAL OF THE INDIANS

There had never been any doubt about Andrew Jackson's attitude toward the Indian tribes that continued to live in the eastern states and territories of the United States. He wanted them to move west, beyond the Mississippi, out of the way of expanding white settlement. Jackson's antipathy toward the Native Americans had a special intensity because of his own earlier experiences leading military campaigns against tribes along the southern border. But in most respects, his views were little different from those of most other white Americans.

WHITE ATTITUDES TOWARD THE TRIBES

In the eighteenth century, many white Americans had considered the Indians "noble savages," peoples without real civilization but with an inherent dignity that made civilization possible among them. By the first decades of the nineteenth century, this vaguely paternalistic attitude (the attitude of Thomas Jefferson, among others) was giving way to a more hostile one, particularly among the whites in the western states and territories whom Jackson came to represent. Such whites were coming to view Native Americans simply as "savages," not only uncivilized but uncivilizable. Whites, they believed, should not be expected to live in close proximity to the tribes.

CHANGING ATTITUDES TOWARD THE INDIANS

White westerners favored removal as well because they feared that continued contact between the expanding white settlements and the Indians would produce endless conflict and violence. Most of all, however, they favored Indian removal because of their own insatiable desire for territory. The tribes possessed valuable land in the path of expanding white settlement. White Americans wanted it.

THE BLACK HAWK WAR

In the Old Northwest, the long process of expelling the woodland Indians culminated in a last battle in 1831–1832, between white settlers in Illinois and an alliance of Sauk (or Sac) and Fox Indians under the fabled and now aged warrior Black Hawk. An earlier treaty had ceded tribal lands in Illinois to the United States; but Black Hawk and his followers refused to recognize the legality of the agreement, which a rival tribal faction had signed. Hungry and resentful, a thousand of them crossed the river and reoccupied vacant lands in Illinois. White settlers in the region feared that the resettlement was the beginning of a substantial invasion, and they assembled the Illinois state militia and federal troops to repel the "invaders."

The Black Hawk War, as it became known, was notable chiefly for the viciousness of the white military efforts. White leaders in western Illinois vowed to exterminate the "bandit collection of Indians" and attacked them even when Black Hawk attempted to surrender. The Sauks and Foxes, defeated and starving, retreated across the Mississippi into Iowa. White troops (and some bands of Sioux whom they encouraged to join the chase) pursued them as they fled and slaughtered most of them. United States troops captured Black Hawk himself and sent him on a tour of the East, where Andrew Jackson was one of many curious whites who arranged to meet him. (Abraham Lincoln served as a captain of the militia, but saw no

SAUK AND FOX INDIANS DEFEATED

BLACK HAWK AND WHIRLING THUNDER After his defeat by white settlers in Illinois in 1832, the famed Sauk warrior Black Hawk and his son Whirling Thunder were captured and sent on a tour by Andrew Jackson, displayed to the public as trophies of war. They showed such dignity through the ordeal that much of the white public quickly began to sympathize with them. This portrait, by John Wesley Jarvis, was painted on the tour's final stop, in New York City. Black Hawk wears the European-style suit, while Whirling Thunder wears native costume to emphasize his commitment to his tribal roots. Soon thereafter, Black Hawk returned to his tribe, wrote a celebrated autobiography, and died in 1838. (Bettmann/Corbis)

action, in the Black Hawk War; Jefferson Davis was a lieutenant in the regular army.)

THE "FIVE CIVILIZED TRIBES"

More troubling to the government in the 1830s were the tribes remaining in the South. In western Georgia, Alabama, Mississippi, and Florida lived what were known as the "Five Civilized Tribes"—the Cherokee, Creek, Seminole, Chickasaw, and Choctaw—most of whom had established settled agricultural societies with successful economies. The Cherokees in Georgia had formed a particularly stable and sophisticated culture, with their own written language and a formal constitution (adopted in 1827) that created an independent Cherokee Nation. They were more closely tied to their lands than many of the nomadic tribes to the north.

AGRARIAN TRIBES OF THE SOUTH

Even some whites argued that the Cherokees, unlike other tribes, should be allowed to retain their eastern lands, since they had become such a "civilized" society and had, under pressure from missionaries and government agents, given up many of their traditional ways. Cherokee men had once been chiefly hunters and had left farming mainly to women. By now the men had given up most of their hunting and (like most white men) took over the farming themselves; Cherokee women, also like their white counterparts, restricted themselves largely to domestic tasks.

The federal government worked steadily to negotiate treaties with the southern Indians that would remove them to the West and open their lands for white settlement. But the negotiating process did not proceed

REMOVAL ACT

JACKSONIAN AMERICA • 245

fast enough to satisfy the region's whites. The state of Georgia's independent effort to dislodge the Creeks, over the objection of President Adams, was one example of this impatience. That same impatience became evident early in Jackson's administration, when the legislatures in Georgia, Alabama, and Mississippi began passing laws to regulate the tribes remaining in their states. They received assistance in these efforts from Congress, which in 1830 passed the Removal Act (with Jackson's approval), which appropriated money to finance federal negotiations with the southern tribes aimed at relocating them to the West. The president quickly dispatched federal officials to negotiate nearly a hundred new treaties with the remaining tribes. Thus the southern tribes faced a combination of pressures from both the state and federal governments. Most tribes were too weak to resist, and they ceded their lands in return for token payments. Some, however, balked.

In Georgia, the Cherokees tried to stop the white encroachments (which were actively encouraged by Jackson) by appealing to the Supreme Court. The Court's decisions in *Cherokee Nation v. Georgia* and *Worcester v. Georgia* in 1831 and 1832 (see p. 228) seemed at least partially to vindicate the tribe. But Jackson's longtime hostility toward Native Americans left him with little sympathy for the Cherokees and little patience with the Court. He was eager to retain the support of white southerners and westerners in the increasingly bitter partisan battles in which his administration was becoming engaged. When the chief justice announced the decision in *Worcester v. Georgia*, Jackson reportedly responded with contempt. "John Marshall has made his decision," he was reported to have said. "Now let him enforce it." The decision was not enforced.

CHEROKEE RESISTANCE

In 1835, the federal government extracted a treaty from a minority faction of the Cherokees, none of them a chosen representative of the Cherokee Nation. The treaty ceded the tribe's land to Georgia in return for $5 million and a reservation west of the Mississippi. The great majority of the 17,000 Cherokees did not recognize the treaty as legitimate and refused to leave their homes. But Jackson would not be thwarted. He sent an army of 7,000 under General Winfield Scott to round them up and drive them westward at bayonet point.

TRAILS OF TEARS

About 1,000 Cherokees fled across the state line to North Carolina, where the federal government

CHEROKEE REMOVAL

eventually provided a small reservation for them in the Smoky Mountains, which survives today. But most of the rest made the long, forced trek to

> **JOHN MARSHALL HAS MADE HIS DECISION. NOW LET HIM ENFORCE IT.**
>
> **PRESIDENT ANDREW JACKSON**

> **EVEN AGED FEMALES, APPARENTLY NEARLY READY TO DROP IN THE GRAVE, WERE TRAVELLING WITH HEAVY BURDENS ATTACHED TO THEIR BACKS, SOMETIMES ON FROZEN GROUND AND SOMETIMES ON MUDDY STREETS, WITH NO COVERING FOR THEIR FEET.**

"Indian Territory" (which later became Oklahoma) beginning in the winter of 1838. Along the way, a Kentuckian observed: "Even aged females, apparently nearly ready to drop in the grave, were travelling with heavy burdens attached to their backs, sometimes on frozen ground and sometimes on muddy streets, with no covering for their feet."

INDIAN REMOVAL

Thousands, perhaps an eighth or more of the emigrés, perished before or soon after reaching their unwanted destination. In the harsh new reservations in which they were now forced to live, the survivors never forgot the hard journey. They called their route "The Trail Where They Cried," the Trail of Tears. Jackson claimed that the "remnant of that ill-fated race" was now "beyond the reach of injury or oppression," apparently trying to convince himself or others that he had supported removal as a way to protect the tribes.

The Cherokees were not alone in experiencing the hardships of the Trail of Tears. Between 1830 and 1838, virtually all the "Five Civilized Tribes" were expelled from the southern states and forced to relocate in the new Indian Territory, which Congress had officially created by the Indian Intercourse Act of 1834. The Choctaws of Mississippi and western Alabama were the first to make the trek, beginning in 1830. The army moved out the Creeks of eastern Alabama and western Georgia in 1836. The Chickasaws in northern Mississippi began the long march westward a year later, and the Cherokees, finally, a year after that. The government thought the Indian Territory was safely distant from existing white settlements and consisted of land that most whites considered undesirable. It had the additional advantage, the government believed, of being on the eastern edge of what earlier white explorers had christened the "Great American Desert," land unfit for habitation. It seemed unlikely that whites would ever seek to settle along the western borders of the Indian Territory; and thus the prospect of whites surrounding the reservation and producing further conflict seemed remote.

Only the Seminoles in Florida managed to resist the pressures to relocate, and even their success was limited. Like other tribes, the Seminoles had agreed under pressure to a settlement (the 1832–1833 treaties of Payne's Landing), by which they ceded their lands to the government and agreed to move to Indian Territory within three years. Most did move west, but a substantial minority, under the leadership of the chieftain Osceola, refused to leave and staged an uprising beginning in 1835 to defend their lands. (Joining the Seminoles in their struggle was a group of runaway black slaves who had been living with the tribe.) The Seminole War dragged on for years. Jackson sent troops to Florida, but the

THE EXPULSION OF THE TRIBES, 1830–1835 Andrew Jackson was famous well before he became president for his military exploits against the tribes. Once in the White House, he ensured that few Indians would remain in the southern states of the nation, now that white settlement was increasing there. The result was a series of dramatic "removals" of Indian tribes out of their traditional lands and into new territories west of the Mississippi—mostly in Oklahoma. Note the very long distance many of these tribes had to travel.

• *Why was the route of the Cherokees, shown in the upper portion of the map, known as the "Trail of Tears"?*

Seminoles with their African American associates were mas-

THE SEMINOLE WAR

ters of guerrilla warfare in the jungly Everglades. Even after Osceola had been treacherously captured by white troops while under a flag of truce and had died in prison; even after white troops had engaged in a systematic campaign of extermination against the resisting Indians and their black allies; even after 1,500 white soldiers had died and the federal government had spent $20 million on the struggle—even then, followers of Osceola remained in Florida. Finally, in 1842, the government abandoned the war. By then, many of the Seminoles had been either killed or forced westward. But the relocation of the Seminoles, unlike the relocation of most of the other tribes, was never complete.

THE MEANING OF REMOVAL

By the end of the 1830s, almost all the important Indian societies east of the Mississippi had been removed to the West. The tribes had ceded over 100 million acres of eastern land to the federal government; they had received in return about $68 million and 32 million acres in the far less hospitable lands west of the Mississippi between the Missouri and Red Rivers. There

they lived, divided by tribe into a series of carefully defined reservations, in a territory surrounded by a string of United States forts to keep them in (and to keep most whites out), in a region whose climate and topography bore little relation to anything they had known before. Eventually, even this forlorn enclave would face incursions from white civilization.

What were the alternatives to the removal of the eastern Indians? There was probably never any realistic possibility that the government could stop white expansion westward. White people had already been penetrating the West for nearly two centuries, and such penetrations were certain to continue. But did that expansion really require removal?

There were, in theory at least, several alternatives to the bru-

ALTERNATIVES TO REMOVAL

tal removal policy. There were many examples in the West of white settlers and native tribes living side by side and creating a shared (if not necessarily equal) world. In the pueblos of New Mexico, in the fur trading posts of the Pacific Northwest, in parts of Texas and California, settlers from Mexico, Canada, and the United States had created societies in which Indians and whites were in intimate contact with each other. Even during the famous Lewis and Clark expedition, white explorers had lived with western Indians on terms of such intimacy that many

THE TRAIL OF TEARS The devastating Indian policies of the Jackson administration forced thousands of Native Americans to relocate from their traditional tribal lands to new "reservations" west of the Mississippi. The Cherokee Nation was among the first tribes forced to move. They called their long and tragic trek west the "Trail of Tears," both because of the loss of their ancestral homes and because of the terrible hardships (which left thousands dead) of the journey. Other tribes were soon forced to move west as well. (© Woolaroc Museum, Oklahoma, USA/Peter Newark Western Americana/The Bridgeman Art Library)

of them contracted venereal disease from Indian partners. Sometimes these close contacts between whites and Indians were beneficial to both sides, even reasonably equal. Sometimes they were cruel and exploitive. But the early multiracial societies of the West did not separate whites and Indians. They demonstrated ways in which the two cultures could interact, each shaping the other.

By the mid-nineteenth century, however, white Americans had adopted a different model as they contemplated westward expansion. Much as the early British settlers along the Atlantic coast had established "plantations," from which natives were, in theory, to be excluded, so the westward-moving whites of later years came to imagine the territories they were entering as virgin land, with no preexisting civilization. Native Americans, they believed, could not be partners—either equal or subordinate—in the creation of new societies in the West. They were obstacles, to be removed and, as far as possible, isolated. Indians, Andrew Jackson once said, had "neither the intelligence, the industry, the moral habits, nor the desire of improvement" to be fit partners in the project of extending white civilization westward. By dismissing Native American cultures in that way, white

Americans justified to themselves a series of harsh policies that they believed (incorrectly) would make the West theirs alone.

JACKSON AND THE BANK WAR

Jackson was quite willing to use federal power against rebellious states and Indian tribes. On economic issues, however, he was

JACKSON'S OPPOSITION TO CONCENTRATED POWER

consistently opposed to concentrating power either in the federal government or in powerful and, in his view, aristocratic institutions associated with it. An early example of his skeptical view of federal power was his 1830 veto of a congressional measure providing a subsidy to the proposed Maysville Road in Kentucky. The bill was unconstitutional, Jackson argued, because the road in question lay entirely within Kentucky and was not, therefore, a part of "interstate commerce." But the bill was also unwise, he believed, because it committed the government to what Jackson considered extravagant expenditures.

Jackson's opposition to federal power and aristocratic privilege lay behind the most celebrated episode of his presidency: the war against the Bank of the United States.

Biddle's Institution

The Bank of the United States in the 1830s was a mighty institution, and it is not surprising that it would attract Jackson's

NICHOLAS BIDDLE

wrath. Its stately headquarters in Philadelphia seemed to symbolize its haughty image of itself. It had branches in twenty-nine other cities, making it the most powerful and far-flung financial institution in the nation. By law, the Bank was the only place that the federal government could deposit its own funds; the government, in turn, owned one-fifth of the Bank's stock. The Bank did a tremendous business in general banking. It provided credit to growing enterprises; it issued bank notes, which served as a dependable medium of exchange throughout the country; and it exercised a restraining effect on the less well-managed state banks. Nicholas Biddle, who served as president of the Bank from 1823 on, had done much to put the institution on a sound and prosperous basis. Nevertheless, Andrew Jackson was determined to destroy it.

Opposition to the Bank came from two very different groups: the "soft-money" faction and the "hard-money" faction. Advocates of soft money—people who wanted more currency in circulation and believed that issuing bank notes unsupported by gold and silver was the best way to circulate more currency— consisted largely of state bankers and their allies. They objected

HARD AND SOFT MONEY

to the Bank of the United States because it restrained the state banks from issuing notes freely. The hard-money people believed that gold and silver were the only basis for money. They condemned all banks that issued bank notes, including the Bank of the United States. The soft-money advocates were believers in rapid economic growth and speculation; the hard-money forces embraced older ideas of "public virtue" and looked with suspicion on expansion and speculation.

Jackson himself supported the hard-money position. Many years before, he had been involved in some grandiose land and commercial speculations based on paper credit. His business had failed in the Panic of 1797, and he had fallen deeply into debt. After that, he was suspicious of all banks and all paper currency. But as president he was also sensitive to the complaints of his many soft-money supporters in the West and the South. He made it clear that he would not favor renewing the charter of the Bank of the United States, which was due to expire in 1836.

A Philadelphia aristocrat unaccustomed to politics, Biddle nevertheless began granting financial favors to influential men who he thought might help him preserve the Bank. In particular, he turned to Daniel Webster and cultivated a close personal friendship with him. He named Webster the Bank's

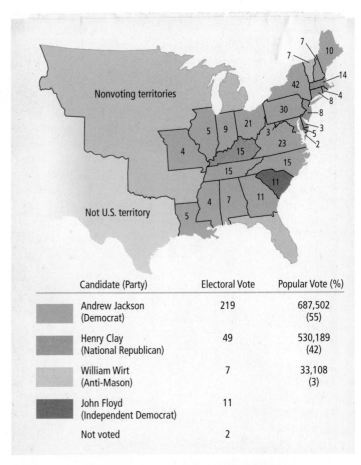

Candidate (Party)	Electoral Vote	Popular Vote (%)
Andrew Jackson (Democrat)	219	687,502 (55)
Henry Clay (National Republican)	49	530,189 (42)
William Wirt (Anti-Mason)	7	33,108 (3)
John Floyd (Independent Democrat)	11	
Not voted	2	

THE ELECTION OF 1832 Jackson's reelection victory in 1832 was almost as decisive as his earlier victory in 1828.

• What changes are visible in party loyalties since the previous election?

legal counsel and director of its Boston branch; Webster was also a frequent, heavy borrower from the Bank. He helped Biddle win the support of other important figures, among them Henry Clay.

Clay, Webster, and other advisers persuaded Biddle to apply to Congress in 1832 for a bill to renew the Bank's charter. That was four years ahead of the date the original charter was scheduled to expire. But forcing a vote now would allow the Bank to become a major issue in the 1832 national elections. Congress

JACKSON'S VETO

passed the recharter bill; Jackson, predictably, vetoed it; and the Bank's supporters in Congress failed to override the veto. Just as Clay had hoped, the 1832 campaign now centered on the future of the Bank.

Clay himself ran for president that year as the unanimous choice of the National Republicans, who held a nominating convention in Baltimore late in 1831. But the Bank War failed to provide him with the winning issue for which he had hoped. Jackson, with Van Buren as his running mate, overwhelmingly defeated Clay (and several minor party candidates) with 55 percent of the popular vote and 219 electoral votes (more than four times as many as Clay received). These results were a defeat not only for Clay, but also for Biddle.

THE "MONSTER" DESTROYED

Jackson was now more determined than ever to destroy the "monster" Bank as quickly as possible. He could not legally abolish the institution before the expiration of its charter.

REMOVAL OF GOVERNMENT DEPOSITS

Instead, he tried to weaken it. He decided to remove the government's deposits from the Bank. His secretary of the treasury believed that such an action would destabilize the financial system and refused to give the order. Jackson fired him and appointed a new one. When the new secretary similarly balked, Jackson fired him too and named a third, more compliant secretary: Attorney General Roger B. Taney, his close friend and loyal ally. Taney began placing the government's deposits not in the Bank of the United States, as it had in the past, but in a number of state banks (which Jackson's enemies called "pet banks").

Nicholas Biddle, whom Jacksonians derisively called "Czar Nicholas," did not give in without a fight. "This worthy President," he wrote sarcastically, "thinks that because he has scalped Indians and imprisoned Judges, he is to have his way with the Bank. He is mistaken." When the administration began to transfer funds directly from the Bank of the United States to the pet banks (as opposed to the initial practice of simply depositing new funds in those banks), Biddle called in loans and raised interest rates, explaining that without the government deposits the Bank's resources were stretched too thin. He realized his actions were likely to cause financial distress. He hoped a short recession would persuade Congress to recharter the Bank. "Nothing but the evidence of suffering," he told a colleague, would "produce any effect in Congress." By now, the struggle had become not just a conflict over policy and principle, but also a bitter personal battle between two proud men—both of them acting recklessly in an effort to humiliate and defeat the other.

As financial conditions worsened in the winter of 1833–1834, supporters of the Bank blamed Jackson's policies for the recession. They organized meetings around the country and sent petitions to Washington urging a rechartering of the Bank. But the Jacksonians blamed the recession on Biddle and refused to budge. When distressed citizens appealed to the president for help, he dismissively answered, "Go to Biddle."

Finally, Biddle contracted credit too far even for his own allies in the business community, who began to fear that in his effort to save his own bank he was threatening their interests. Some of them did "go to Biddle." A group of New York and Boston merchants protested. To appease the business community, Biddle at last reversed himself and began to grant credit in abundance and on reasonable terms. His vacillating and unpopular tactics ended his chances of winning a recharter of the Bank.

> **" THIS WORTHY PRESIDENT THINKS THAT BECAUSE HE HAS SCALPED INDIANS AND IMPRISONED JUDGES, HE IS TO HAVE HIS WAY WITH THE BANK. HE IS MISTAKEN. "**
>
> **NICHOLAS BIDDLE**

JACKSON VICTORIOUS

Jackson had won a considerable political victory. But when the Bank of the United States died in 1836, the country lost a valuable, albeit flawed, financial institution and was left with a fragmented and chronically unstable banking system that would plague the economy for more than a century.

THE TANEY COURT

In the aftermath of the Bank War, Jackson moved against the most powerful institution of economic nationalism of all: the Supreme Court. In 1835, when John Marshall died, the president appointed as the new chief justice his trusted ally Roger B. Taney. Taney did not bring a sharp break in constitutional interpretation, but he gradually helped modify Marshall's vigorous nationalism.

Perhaps the clearest indication of the new judicial mood was

CHARLES RIVER BRIDGE V. WARREN BRIDGE

the celebrated case of *Charles River Bridge v. Warren Bridge* of 1837. The case involved a dispute between two Massachusetts companies over the right to build a bridge across the Charles River between Boston and Cambridge. One company had a long-standing charter from the state to operate a toll bridge and claimed that this charter guaranteed it a monopoly of the bridge traffic. Another company had applied to the legislature for authorization to construct a second, competing bridge that would—since it would be toll free—greatly reduce the value of the first company's charter.

The first company contended that in granting the second charter the legislature was engaging in a breach of contract and noted that the Marshall Court, in the *Dartmouth College* case and other decisions, had ruled that states had no right to abrogate contracts. But now Taney, speaking for the Democratic majority on the Court, supported the right of Massachusetts to award the second charter. The object of government, Taney maintained, was to promote the general happiness, an object that took precedence over the rights of contract and property. A state, therefore, had the right to amend or abrogate a contract if such action was necessary to advance the well-being of the community. Such an abrogation was clearly necessary in the case of the Charles River Bridge, he argued, because the original bridge company, by exercising a monopoly, was benefiting from unjustifiable privilege. (It did not help the first company that its members were largely Boston aristocrats closely associated with Harvard College; the challenging company, by contrast, consisted largely of newer, aspiring entrepreneurs—the sort of people with whom Jackson and his allies instinctively identified.) The decision reflected one of the cornerstones of the Jacksonian ideal: that the key to democracy was an expansion of economic opportunity, which would not occur if older corporations could maintain monopolies and choke off competition from newer companies.

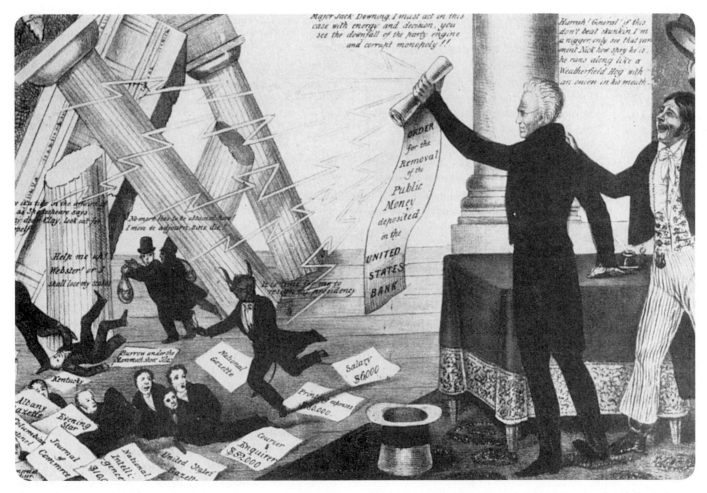

"THE DOWNFALL OF MOTHER BANK" This 1832 Democratic cartoon celebrates Andrew Jackson's destruction of the Bank of the United States. The president is shown here driving away the Bank's corrupt supporters by ordering the withdrawal of government deposits. (New-York Historical Society)

THE CHANGING FACE OF AMERICAN POLITICS

Jackson's forceful—some people claimed tyrannical—tactics in crushing first the nullification movement and then the Bank of the United States helped galvanize a growing opposition coalition that by the mid-1830s was ready to assert itself in national politics. Denouncing the president as "King Andrew I," they began to refer to themselves as Whigs, after the party in England that had traditionally worked to limit the power of the king. With the emergence of the Whigs, the nation once again had two competing political parties. What scholars now call the "second party system" began what turned out to be its relatively brief life.

BIRTH OF THE WHIG PARTY

DEMOCRATS AND WHIGS

The two parties were different from one another in their philosophies, in their constituencies, and in the character of their leaders. But they became increasingly alike in the way they approached the process of electing their followers to office.

Democrats in the 1830s envisioned a future of steadily expanding economic and political opportunities for white males. The role of government should be limited, they believed, but it should include efforts to remove obstacles to opportunity and to avoid creating new ones. That meant defending the Union, which Jacksonians believed was essential to the dynamic economic growth they favored. It also meant attacking centers of corrupt privilege. As Jackson himself said in his farewell address, the society of America should be one in which "the planter, the farmer, the mechanic, and the laborer, all know that their success depends on their own industry and economy," in which artificial privilege would stifle no one's opportunity. Among the most radical members of the party—the so-called Locofocos, mainly workingmen and

DEMOCRATS' EMPHASIS ON OPPORTUNITY

> ❝ THE PLANTER, THE FARMER, THE MECHANIC, AND THE LABORER, ALL KNOW THAT THEIR SUCCESS DEPENDS ON THEIR OWN INDUSTRY AND ECONOMY. ❞
>
> **ANDREW JACKSON**

small businessmen and professionals in the Northeast—sentiment was strong for a vigorous, perhaps even violent assault on monopoly and privilege far in advance of anything Jackson himself ever contemplated.

The political philosophy that became known as Whiggery was very different. It favored expanding the power of the federal

WHIGS' CALL FOR ECONOMIC UNION

government, encouraging industrial and commercial development, and knitting the country together into a consolidated economic system. Whigs embraced material progress enthusiastically; but unlike the Democrats, they were cautious about westward expansion, fearful that rapid territorial growth would produce instability. Their vision of America was of a nation embracing the industrial future and rising to world greatness as a commercial and manufacturing power. Thus, while Democrats were inclined to oppose legislation establishing banks, corporations, and other modernizing institutions, Whigs generally favored such measures.

The Whigs were strongest among the more substantial merchants and manufacturers of the Northeast; the wealthier planters of the South (those who favored commercial development and the strengthening of ties with the North); and the ambitious farmers and rising commercial class of the West—usually migrants from the Northeast—who advocated internal improvements, expanding trade, and rapid economic progress. The Democrats drew more support from smaller merchants and the workingmen of the Northeast; from southern planters suspicious of industrial growth; and from westerners—usually with southern roots—who favored a predominantly agrarian economy and opposed the development of powerful economic institutions in their region. Whigs tended to be wealthier than Democrats, to have more aristocratic backgrounds, and to be more commercially ambitious.

But Whig and Democratic politicians alike were more interested in winning elections than in maintaining philosophical purity. And both parties made frequent adjustments in their public postures to attract the largest possible number of voters. In New York, for example, the Whigs worked to develop a pop-

ANTI-MASONS

ular following by making a connection to a movement known as Anti-Masonry. The Anti-Mason movement had emerged in the 1820s in response to widespread resentment against the secret, exclusive, and hence supposedly undemocratic, Society of Freemasons. Such resentments greatly increased in 1826 when a former Mason, William Morgan, mysteriously disappeared (and was assumed to have been murdered) from his home in Batavia, New York, shortly before he was scheduled to publish a book exposing the supposed secrets of Freemasonry. Whigs seized on the Anti-Mason frenzy to launch harsh attacks on Jackson and Van Buren (both Freemasons), implying that the Democrats were part of the antidemocratic conspiracy. In the process, the Whigs presented themselves as opponents of aristocracy and exclusivity. They were attacking the Democrats with the Democrats' own issues.

Religious and ethnic divisions also played an important role in determining the constituencies of the two parties. Irish and

German Catholics, among the largest of the recent immigrant groups, tended to support the Democrats, who appeared to

CULTURAL ISSUES

share their own vague aversion to commercial development and entrepreneurial progress and who seemed to respect family- and community-centered values and habits. Evangelical Protestants gravitated toward the Whigs because they associated the party with constant development and improvement, goals their own faith embraced. These and other ethnic, religious, and cultural tensions were often more influential in determining party alignments than any concrete political or economic proposals.

The Whig Party was more successful at defining its positions and attracting a constituency than it was in uniting behind a national leader. No single person was ever able to command the loyalties of the party in the way Andrew Jackson did the Democrats. Instead, Whigs tended to divide their loyalties among three figures, each of whom was so substantial a figure that together they became known as the "Great Triumvirate": Henry Clay, Daniel Webster, and John Calhoun.

Clay won support from many of those who favored his program for internal improvements and economic development,

CLAY'S AMERICAN SYSTEM

what he called the "American System"; but his image as a devious operator and his identification with the West proved to be serious liabilities. He ran for president three times and never won. Daniel Webster, the greatest orator of his era, won broad support with his passionate speeches in defense of the Constitution and the Union; but his close connection with the Bank of the United States and the protective tariff, his reliance on rich men for financial support, and his excessive and often embarrassing fondness for brandy prevented him from developing enough of a national constituency to win him the office he so desperately wanted. John C. Calhoun, the third member of the Great Triumvirate, never considered himself a true Whig, and his identification with the nullification controversy in effect disqualified him from national leadership in any case. But he had tremendous strength in the South, supported a national bank, and shared with Clay and Webster a strong animosity toward Andrew Jackson.

The problems that emerged from this divided leadership

ELECTION OF 1836

became particularly clear in 1836. The Democrats were united behind Andrew Jackson's personal choice for president, Martin Van Buren. The Whigs could not agree on a single candidate. Instead, they ran several candidates, hoping to profit from the regional strength of each. Webster represented the party in New England; Hugh Lawson White of Tennessee ran in the South; and the former Indian fighter and hero of the War of 1812, William Henry Harrison, from Ohio, was the candidate in the middle states and the West. Party leaders hoped the three candidates together might draw enough votes from Van Buren to prevent his getting a majority and throw the election to the House of Representatives, where the Whigs might be able to elect one of their own leaders. In the end, however, Van Buren won easily, with 170 electoral votes to 124 for all his opponents combined.

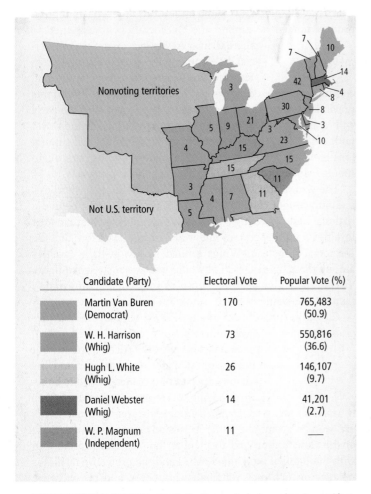

Candidate (Party)	Electoral Vote	Popular Vote (%)
Martin Van Buren (Democrat)	170	765,483 (50.9)
W. H. Harrison (Whig)	73	550,816 (36.6)
Hugh L. White (Whig)	26	146,107 (9.7)
Daniel Webster (Whig)	14	41,201 (2.7)
W. P. Magnum (Independent)	11	—

THE ELECTION OF 1836 Martin Van Buren, who had served as vice president and secretary of state for Andrew Jackson, was the Democratic candidate for president in 1836. His connection to the revered Jackson helped him easily defeat his Whig opponent, William Henry Harrison. Four years later, the same two men contested the presidency, but that time it was Harrison who won.

VAN BUREN AND THE PANIC OF 1837

Andrew Jackson retired from public life in 1837, beloved by most Americans. Martin Van Buren was very different from his predecessor and far less fortunate. He was never able to match Jackson's personal popularity, and his administration encountered economic difficulties that devastated the Democrats and helped the Whigs.

Van Buren's success in the 1836 election was a result in part of a nationwide economic boom that was reaching its height in that year. Canal and railroad builders were at a peak of activity. Prices were rising, money was plentiful, and credit was easy as banks increased their loans and notes with little regard to their reserves of cash. The land business, in particular, was booming. Between 1835 and 1837, the government sold nearly 40 million acres of public land, nearly three-fourths of it to speculators, who purchased large tracts in hopes of reselling them at a profit. These land sales, along with revenues the government received from the tariff of 1833, created a series of substantial federal budget surpluses and made possible a steady reduction of the

national debt (something Jackson had always advocated). From 1835 to 1837, the government for the first and only time in its history was out of debt, with a substantial surplus in the Treasury.

Congress and the administration now faced the question of what to do with the Treasury surplus. Reducing the tariff was not an option, since no one wanted to raise that thorny issue again. Instead, support grew for returning the federal surplus to the states. In 1836, Congress passed a "distribution" act requiring the federal government to pay its surplus funds to the states each year in four quarterly installments as interest-free, unsecured loans. No one expected the "loans" to be repaid. The states spent the money quickly, mainly to encourage construction of highways, railroads, and canals. The distribution of the surplus thus gave further stimulus to the economic boom.

DISTRIBUTION ACT

Congress did nothing to check the speculative fever, with which many congressmen themselves were badly infected. Webster, for one, was buying up thousands of acres in the West. But Jackson, always suspicious of paper currency, was unhappy that the government was selling good land and receiving in return various state bank notes worth no more than the credit of the issuing bank.

In 1836, not long before leaving office, he issued a presidential order, the "specie circular." It provided that in payment for public lands the government would accept only gold or silver coins or currency securely backed by gold or silver. Jackson was right to fear the speculative fever but wrong in thinking the specie circular would cure it. On the contrary, it produced a financial panic that began in the first months of Van Buren's presidency. Hundreds of banks and businesses failed. Unemployment grew. Bread riots broke out in some of the larger cities. Prices fell, especially the price of land. Many railroad and canal projects failed. Several of the debt-burdened state governments ceased to pay interest on their bonds, and a few repudiated their debts, at least temporarily. It was the worst depression in American history to that point, and it lasted for five years. It was a political catastrophe for Van Buren and the Democrats.

PANIC OF 1837

Both parties bore some responsibility for the panic. But the depression was only partly a result of American policies. England and western Europe were facing panics of their own, which caused European (and especially English) investors to withdraw funds from America, putting an added strain on American banks. A succession of crop failures on American farms reduced the purchasing power of farmers and required increased imports of food, which sent more money out of the country. But whatever its actual causes, the Panic of 1837 occurred during a Democratic administration, and the Democrats paid the political price for it. The Van Buren administration, which strongly opposed government intervention in the economy, did little to fight the depression. Some of the steps it took—borrowing money to pay government debts and accepting only specie for payment of taxes—may have made things worse. Van Buren did succeed in establishing a ten-hour workday on all federal projects, by presidential order, but he had only a few legislative achievements.

"THE TIMES," 1837 This savage caricature of the economic troubles besetting the United States in 1837 illustrates, among other things, popular resentment of the hard-money orthodoxies of the time. A sign on the Custom House reads: "All bonds must be paid in Specie." Next door, the bank announces: "No specie payments made here." Women and children are shown begging in the street, while unemployed workers stand shoeless in front of signs advertising loans and "grand schemes." (New-York Historical Society)

The most important and controversial of them was the creation of a new financial system to replace the Bank of the United States. Under Van Buren's plan, known as the "independent treasury" or "subtreasury" system, the government would place its funds in an independent treasury at Washington and in subtreasuries in other cities. No private banks would have the government's money or name to use as a basis for speculation; the government and the banks would be "divorced."

INDEPENDENT TREASURY

Van Buren called a special session of Congress in 1837 to consider the proposal, which failed in the House. In 1840, the last year of Van Buren's presidency, the administration finally succeeded in driving the measure through both houses of Congress.

THE LOG CABIN CAMPAIGN

As the campaign of 1840 approached, the Whigs realized that they would have to settle on one candidate for president this time if they were to have any hope of winning. As a result, they held their first national nominating convention in Harrisburg, Pennsylvania, in December 1839. Passing over the controversial Henry Clay, who had expected the nomination, the convention chose William Henry Harrison and, for vice president, John Tyler of Virginia. Harrison was a descendant of the Virginia aristocracy but had spent his adult life in the Northwest. He was a renowned soldier, a famous Indian fighter, and a popular national figure. The Democrats nominated Van Buren. But because they were not much more united than the Whigs, they failed to nominate a vice presidential candidate, leaving the choice of that office to the electors.

The 1840 campaign was the first in which the new popular "penny press" carried news of the candidates to a large audience of workers and tradespeople. It also illustrated how fully the concept of party competition, the subordination of ideology to immediate political needs, had established itself in America.

NEW TECHNIQUES OF POLITICAL CAMPAIGNING

The Whigs represented the more affluent elements of the population, and they favored government policies that would aid business. But they presented themselves in 1840 as the party of the common people. So, of course, did the Democrats. Both parties used the same techniques of mass voter appeal, the same evocation of simple, rustic values. What mattered now was not the philosophical purity of the party but its ability to win votes. The Whig campaign was

HARRISON AND REFORM This hand-colored engraving was made for a brass brooch during the 1840 presidential campaign and served the same purposes that modern campaign buttons do. It conveys Harrison's presumably humble beginnings in a log cabin. In reality, Harrison was a wealthy, aristocratic man; but the unpopularity of the aristocratic airs of his opponent, President Martin Van Buren, persuaded the Whig Party that it would be good political strategy to portray Harrison as a humble "man of the people." (Collection of David J. and Janice L. Frent)

particularly effective in portraying William Henry Harrison, a wealthy member of the frontier elite with a considerable estate, as a simple man of the people who loved log cabins and hard cider. They accused Van Buren of being an aloof aristocrat who used cologne, drank champagne, and ate from gold plates. The Democrats had no defense against the combination of these campaign techniques and the effects of the depression. Harrison won the election with 234 electoral votes to 60 for Van Buren and with a popular vote majority of 53 percent.

THE FRUSTRATION OF THE WHIGS

Despite their decisive victory, the Whigs found their four years in power frustrating and divisive ones. In large part, that was because their popular new president, "Old Tippecanoe," William Henry Harrison, died of pneumonia one month after taking office. Vice President Tyler succeeded him. Control of the administration thus fell to a man with whom the Whig party leadership had relatively weak ties. Harrison had generally deferred to Henry Clay and Daniel Webster, whom he named secretary of state. Under Tyler, things quickly changed.

Tyler was a former Democrat who had left the party in reaction to what he considered Jackson's excessively egalitarian program and imperious methods. But there were still signs of his Democratic past in his approach to public policy. The president did agree to bills abolishing Van Buren's independent treasury system and raising tariff rates. But he refused to support Clay's attempt to recharter a Bank of the United States. And he vetoed several internal improvement bills that Clay and other congressional Whigs sponsored.

WHIGS BREAK WITH TYLER

Finally, a conference of congressional Whigs read Tyler out of the party. Every cabinet member but Webster resigned; five former Democrats took their places. When Webster, too, left the cabinet, Tyler appointed Calhoun, who had rejoined the Democratic Party, to replace him.

A new political alignment was emerging. Tyler and a small band of conservative southern Whigs were preparing to rejoin the Democrats. Joining the "common man's party" of Jackson and Van Buren was a faction with decidedly aristocratic political ideas, who thought that government had an obligation to protect and even expand the institution of slavery, and who believed in states' rights with almost fanatical devotion.

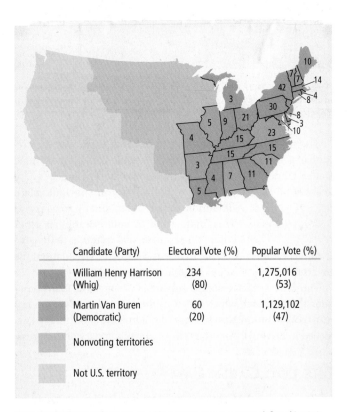

Candidate (Party)	Electoral Vote (%)	Popular Vote (%)
William Henry Harrison (Whig)	234 (80)	1,275,016 (53)
Martin Van Buren (Democratic)	60 (20)	1,129,102 (47)
Nonvoting territories		
Not U.S. territory		

THE ELECTION OF 1840 President Martin Van Buren was defeated in 1840 despite his close relationship to the popular former president, Andrew Jackson. Van Buren, unlike Jackson, was president during a sharp economic recession. And even though his opponent, William Henry Harrison, was a wealthy frontier aristocrat, the Whig Party effectively portrayed him as a humble man of the people, a contrast to what they claimed was Van Buren's extravagance and elitism.

A BEAUTIFUL GOBLET OF WHITE-HOUSE CHAMPAGNE.

AN UGLY *MUG* OF LOG-CABIN HARD CIDER.

AN ATTACK ON VAN BUREN This "pull card," made during the 1840 presidential campaign, which Van Buren lost to William Henry Harrison, satirizes the president as an aristocratic dandy. The card displays Van Buren grinning while he drinks champagne in the White House. Pulling a tab on the card changes his champagne glass to a mug of hard cider (with Harrison's initials on it) and changes his expression from delight to revulsion. (Division of Political History, American History Museum, Smithsonian Institution, Washington, D.C.)

WHIG DIPLOMACY

In the midst of these domestic controversies, a series of incidents in the late 1830s brought Great Britain and the United States once again to the brink of war. Residents of the eastern provinces of Canada launched a rebellion against the British colonial government in 1837, and some of the rebels chartered an American steamship, the *Caroline,* to ship supplies across the Niagara River to them from New York. British authorities in Canada seized the *Caroline* and burned it, killing one American in the process. The British government refused either to disavow the attack or to provide compensation for it, and resentment in the United States ran high. But the British soon had reasons for anger as well. Authorities THE CAROLINE in New York, attempting to exploit the AFFAIR *Caroline* affair, arrested a Canadian named Alexander McLeod and charged him with the murder of the American who had died in the incident. The British government, expressing majestic rage, insisted that McLeod could not be accused of murder because he had acted under official orders. The foreign secretary, the belli-

cose Lord Palmerston, demanded McLeod's release and threatened that his execution would bring "immediate and frightful" war.

Webster as secretary of state did not think McLeod was worth a war, but he was powerless to release him. The prisoner was under New York jurisdiction and had to be tried in the state courts, a peculiarity of American jurisprudence that the British did not seem to understand. A New York jury did what Webster could not: it defused the crisis by acquitting McLeod.

At the same time, tensions flared over the boundary between AROOSTOOK Canada and Maine, which had been in dis- WAR pute since the Treaty of 1783. In 1838, groups of Americans and Canadians, mostly lumberjacks, began moving into the Aroostook River region in the disputed area, precipitating a violent brawl between the two groups that became known as the "Aroostook War."

Several years later, there were yet more Anglo-American problems. In 1841, an American ship, the *Creole,* sailed from Virginia for New Orleans with more than 100 slaves aboard. En route the slaves mutinied, took possession of the ship, and took it to the Bahamas. British officials there declared the slaves free,

THE PENNY PRESS

On September 3, 1833, a small newspaper appeared in New York City for the first time: the *New York Sun*, published by a young former apprentice from Massachusetts named Benjamin Day. Four pages long, it contained mostly trivial local news, with particular emphasis on sex, crime, and violence. It sold for a penny, launching a new age in the history of American journalism, the age of the "penny press."

Before the advent of the penny press, newspapers in America were far too expensive for most ordinary citizens to buy. But several important changes in the business of journalism and the character of American society paved the way for Benjamin Day and others to challenge the established press. New technologies—the steam-powered cylinder printing press, new machines for making paper, railroads and canals for distributing issues to a larger market—made it possible to publish newspapers inexpensively and to sell them widely. A rising popular literacy rate, a result in part of the spread of public education, created a bigger reading public.

The penny press was also a response to the changing culture of the 1820s and 1830s. The spread of an urban, market economy contributed to the growth of the penny press by drawing a large population of workers, artisans, and clerks into large cities, where they became an important market for the new papers. The spirit of democracy—symbolized by the popularity of Andrew Jackson and the rising numbers of white male voters across the country—helped create an appetite for journalism that spoke to and for "the people." Hence Benjamin Day's slogan for his new paper: "It Shines for ALL." The *Sun* and papers like it were committed to feeding the appetites of the people of modest means, who constituted most of their readership. "Human interest stories" helped solidify their hold on the working public. Condescending stories about poor black men and women—ridiculing their subjects' illiteracy and their accents—were also popular among these papers' virtually all-white readership.

Within six months of its first issue, the *Sun* had the largest circulation in New York—8,000 readers, more than twice the number of its nearest competitors. James Gordon Bennett's *New York Herald*, which began publication in 1835, soon surpassed the *Sun* in popularity with its lively combination of sensationalism and local gossip and with its aggressive pursuit of national and international stories. The *Herald* pioneered a "letters to the editor" column, was the first paper

THE NEW YORK *SUN* This 1834 front page of *The Sun*, which had begun publication a year earlier, contains advertisements, human interest stories, a description of a slave auction in Charleston, S.C., and homespun advice: "Life is short. The poor pittance of several years is not worth being a villain for." (Collection of the New-York Historical Society)

---

and the English government refused to overrule them. Many Americans, especially southerners, were furious.

At this critical juncture, a new government eager to reduce the tensions with the United States came to power in Great Britain. In the spring of 1842, it sent Lord Ashburton, an admirer of America, to negotiate an agreement on the Maine boundary and other matters. The result of his negotiations with Secretary of State Webster and representatives from Maine and Massachusetts was the Webster-Ashburton Treaty of 1842. Its terms established a firm northern boundary between the United States and Canada along the Maine–New Brunswick border that survives to this day; the new border gave the United States a bit more than half of the previously disputed territory. Other, smaller provisions placated Maine and Massachusetts and protected critical trade routes in both the northern United States and southern Canada. In a separate

WEBSTER-ASHBURTON TREATY

exchange of notes, Ashburton eased the memory of the *Caroline* and *Creole* affairs by expressing regret and promising no future "officious interference" with American ships.

During the Tyler administration, the United States established its first diplomatic relations with China. In 1842, Britain forced China to open certain ports to foreign trade. Eager to share the new privileges, American mercantile interests persuaded Tyler and Congress to send a commissioner—Caleb Cushing—to China to negotiate a treaty giving the United States some part in the China trade. In the Treaty of Wang Hya, concluded in 1844, Cushing secured most-favored-nation provisions giving Americans the same privileges as the English. He also won for Americans the right of "extraterritoriality"—the right of Americans accused of crimes in China to be tried by American, not Chinese, officials. In the next ten years, American trade with China steadily increased.

TREATY OF WANG HYA

THE FIRST "EXTRA" This 1840 "special edition" of the *New York Sun* was innovative in two ways. It was probably the first "extra" edition of any daily newspaper in America. It was also one of the first examples of large and (in this case at least) lurid illustration in the daily press. This dramatic picture accompanies a story about the explosion of a ship. (Print Collection Miriam and Ira D. Wallach Division, New York Public Library, Astor, Lenox and Tilden Foundations)

"We do not mean to write as if we were in a passion—unless that shall really be the case," the *Times* huffily proclaimed in its first issue, in an obvious reference to Greeley and his impassioned reportage; "and we shall make it a point to get into a passion as rarely as possible."

The newspapers of the penny press initiated the process of turning journalism into a profession. They were the first to pay their reporters and the first to rely heavily on advertisements, often devoting up to half their space to paid advertising. They tended to be sensationalist and opinionated, but they were often also aggressive in uncovering serious and important news—in police stations, courts, jails, streets, and private homes as well as in city halls, state capitals, Washington, D.C., and the world. •

UNDERSTAND, ANALYZE, AND EVALUATE

1. How were the penny press newspapers a product of the Jacksonian era?
2. Before the advent of the penny press, newspapers in America were aimed at a much narrower audience. Some published mainly business news, and others worked to advance the aims of a political party. What nationally circulated newspapers and other media today continue this tradition?
3. What characteristics of penny press newspapers are still common in newspapers today? In what other contemporary news media do you see these same (or similar) elements?

to have regular reviews of books and the arts, and launched the first daily sports section. By 1860, its circulation of more than 77,000 was the largest of any daily newspaper in the world.

Not all the new penny papers were as sensationalist as the *Sun* and the *Herald*. Both the *Philadelphia Public Ledger* and the *Baltimore Sun*, founded in 1836 and 1837 respectively, strove to provide serious coverage of the news. The *Baltimore Sun* even developed a Washington bureau, the first of the penny papers to do so. The *New York Tribune*, founded in 1841 by Horace Greeley, prided itself on serious reporting and commentary, all of it tinged with a conspicuous sympathy for socialism and for the aspirations of working people. As serious as the *Tribune*, but more sober and self-consciously "objective" in its reportage, was the *New York Times*, which Henry Raymond founded in 1851.

In their diplomatic efforts, at least, the Whigs were able to secure some important successes. But by the end of the Tyler administration, the party could look back on few other victories. In the election of 1844, the Whigs lost the White House. They were to win only one more national election in their history.

LOOKING BACK

The election of Andrew Jackson to the presidency in 1828 marked not only the triumph of a particular vision of government and democracy. It represented as well the emergence

JACKSON'S LEGACY

of a new political world. Throughout the American nation, the laws governing political participation were loosening and the number of people permitted to vote (which eventually included most white males, but almost no one else) was increasing. Along with this expansion of the electorate was emerging a new spirit of party politics. Parties had once been reviled by American leaders as contributing to the spirit of faction. Now a new set of ideas was emerging that saw in institutionalized parties not a challenge, but a contribution to democracy. Party competition would be a way of containing and muting disagreements that might otherwise run amok. It would be another of the healthy restraints—another part of the system of checks and balances—that made American government work.

Andrew Jackson was a party man, and he set out as president to entrench his party, the Democrats, in power. He was also a fierce defender of his region, the West, and a sharp critic of what he considered the stranglehold of the aristocratic East on the nation's economic life. He sought to limit the role of the federal government in economic affairs, fearful that it would serve to entrench existing patterns of wealth and power. He worked to destroy the Bank of the United States, which he considered a corrupt vehicle of aristocratic influence. Jackson was, finally, a nationalist. And he confronted the greatest challenge to American unity yet to have emerged in the young nation—the nullification crisis of 1832–1833—with a strong assertion of the power and importance of the Union. These positions won him broad popularity and ensured his reelection in 1832 and the election of his designated successor, Martin Van Buren, in 1836.

But the Democrats were not the only ones to have learned the lessons of the age of parties. A new coalition of anti-Jacksonians, who called themselves the Whigs, launched a powerful new party that used much of the same anti-elitist rhetoric the Democrats had used to win support for their own much more nationalist program. Their emergence culminated in the campaign of 1840 with the election of the first Whig president. •

KEY TERMS/PEOPLE/PLACES/EVENTS

ANDREW JACKSON 236
ANTI-MASONRY 251
AROOSTOOK WAR 255
BANK WAR 247
CAROLINE AFFAIR 255
DANIEL WEBSTER 242
DORR REBELLION 237
"FIVE CIVILIZED TRIBES" 244
INDIAN TERRITORY 245

JOHN C. CALHOUN 241
JOHN TYLER 253
MARTIN VAN BUREN 241
NICHOLAS BIDDLE 248
NULLIFICATION 241
PANIC OF 1837 252
REMOVAL ACT 244
ROGER B. TANEY 249
SEMINOLE WAR 246

SPECIE CIRCULAR 252
SPOILS SYSTEM 240
TRAIL OF TEARS 245
WEBSTER-ASHBURTON TREATY 256
WEBSTER-HAYNE DEBATE 241
WHIGS 250
WILLIAM HENRY HARRISON 253

SIGNIFICANT EVENTS

Calhoun's South Carolina Exposition and Protest outlines nullification doctrine

Webster and Hayne debate

Indian Removal Act passed

Anti-Mason party established

Nullification crisis erupts

1828

1829
Andrew Jackson inaugurated

1830

1830-1838
Indians expelled from Southeast

1831

1832
Democrats hold first national party convention

Jackson vetoes bill to recharter Bank of the United States

Jackson reelected president

1832-1833

1835
Roger Taney succeeds Marshall as chief justice of the Supreme Court

RECALL AND REFLECT

1. What was Andrew Jackson's political philosophy, and how was it reflected in the policies and actions of his administration?

2. Who benefited under Jacksonian democracy? Who suffered?

3. How did Andrew Jackson change the office of the presidency?

4. Who supported and who opposed the Bank of the United States, and why? Who was right?

5. How and why did white attitudes toward Native Americans change, and how did these changes lead to the Indian Removal Act and the Trail of Tears?

Seminole War

1835-1842

1836
Jackson issues "specie circular"

Martin Van Buren elected president

Commercial panic and depression

1837-1842

1838
"Aroostook War" fought in Maine and Canada

Whigs hold their first national convention

1839

1840
William Henry Harrison elected president

Independent Treasury Act passed

Harrison dies
John Tyler becomes president

1841

Dorr Rebellion hastens reform in Rhode Island

1842
Webster-Ashburton Treaty signed

THE LOWELL MILLS Fifteen years earlier, Lowell, Massachusetts, had been a small farming village known as East Chelmsford. By the 1840s, when Fitzhugh Lane painted *The Middlesex Company Woolen Mills*, the town had become one of the most famous manufacturing centers in America and a magnet for visitors from around the world. Lane's painting shows female workers, who dominated the labor force in Lowell, entering the factory. (American Textile History Museum, Lowell, Massachusetts)

10 | AMERICA'S ECONOMIC REVOLUTION

WHEN THE UNITED STATES ENTERED THE WAR OF 1812, it was still an essentially agrarian nation. There were, to be sure, cities in America, several of substantial size, and there was modest but growing manufacturing activity. But the overwhelming majority of Americans were farmers and tradespeople, and the economy was largely a local one.

By the time the Civil War began in 1861, the United States had transformed itself. Most Americans were still rural people, but even most American farmers were now part of a national, and increasingly international, market economy. The United States had developed a major manufacturing sector and was beginning to challenge the industrial nations of Europe for supremacy. The nation had experienced the first stage of its industrial revolution.

The dramatic changes that resulted from the industrial revolution affected the nation's economy, society, culture, and politics, but the changes did not have the same impact everywhere. The Northeast and the Northwest were rapidly developing a complex, modern economy and society,

SETTING THE STAGE

increasingly dominated by large cities, important manufacturing, and profitable commercial farming. It was

in many ways an unequal society, but it was also a fluid one, firmly committed to the ideal of free labor.

In the South and Southwest, there were changes, too. Southern agriculture,

REGIONAL
DIVERGENCES

particularly cotton farming, flourished as never before in response to the growing demand from textile mills in New England and elsewhere. But the South remained much less economically developed than the North. As the North became ever more committed to the fluidity and mobility of its free-labor system, the South was becoming more and more resolute in its defense of slavery. The economic revolution was transforming the nation. It was also dividing it.

LOOKING AHEAD

1. What were the factors in the U.S. economic revolution of the mid-nineteenth century?
2. How did the U.S. population change between 1820 and 1840, and how did the population change affect the nation's economy, society, and politics?
3. Why did America's industrial revolution affect the northern economy and society differently than it did the southern economy and society?

THE CHANGING AMERICAN POPULATION

The American industrial revolution was a result of many factors. Before it could occur, the United States needed a population large enough both to grow its own food and to provide a surplus workforce for an industrial economy. It needed a transportation and communications system capable of sustaining commerce over a large geographic area. It needed the technology to permit manufacturing on a large scale. And it needed systems of business organization capable of managing large industrial enterprises. By 1860, the northern regions of the nation had acquired at least the beginnings of all those things.

THE AMERICAN POPULATION, 1820–1840

Three trends characterized the American population between 1820 and 1840, all of them contributing in various ways to economic growth. The population was increasing rapidly; much of it was moving from the countryside into the industrializing cities of the Northeast and Northwest; and much of it was migrating westward.

The American population had stood at only 4 million in 1790. By 1820, it had reached 10 million; by 1830, nearly 13 million; and by 1840, 17 million. The United States was growing much more rapidly in population than Britain or Europe. One reason for this

REASONS FOR POPULATION INCREASE

substantial population growth was improvements in public health. The number and ferocity of epidemics (such as the great cholera plague of 1832)—which had periodically decimated urban and even rural populations in America—slowly declined, as did the nation's mortality rate as a whole. The population increase was also a result of a high birth rate. In 1840, white women bore an average of 6.14 children each, a decline from the very high rates of the eighteenth century but still substantial enough to produce rapid population increases, particularly since a larger proportion of children could expect to grow to adulthood than had been the case a generation or two earlier.

Immigration, choked off by wars in Europe and economic crises in America, contributed little to the American population in the first three decades of the nineteenth century but rapidly revived beginning in the 1830s. Of the total 1830 population of nearly 13 million, the foreign-born numbered fewer than 500,000. But the number of immigrants climbed by 60,000 in

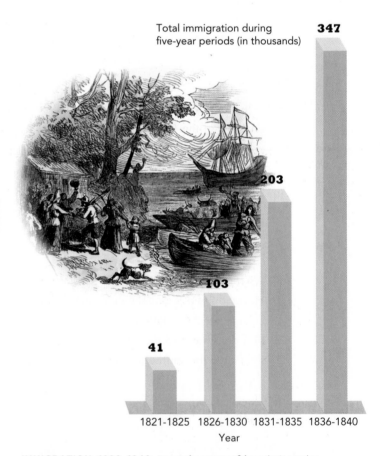

Population (millions)

.005	.05	.15	.35	.90	2.15	5.30	12.90	31.50
1620	1650	1680	1710	1740	1770	1800	1830	1860

Year

POPULATION GROWTH, 1620–1860 From its tiny beginnings in the seventeenth century, the American population grew rapidly and dramatically so that by 1860—with over 31 million people—the United States was one of the most populous countries in the world.

• How did this growing population contribute to the nation's economic transformation?

Total immigration during five-year periods (in thousands)

41	103	203	347
1821-1825	1826-1830	1831-1835	1836-1840

Year

IMMIGRATION, 1820–1840 Among the sources of the nation's growing population in the nineteenth century was rapidly increasing immigration. This graph shows how rapidly immigration to the United States increased in the 1820s and 1830s. The 347,000 immigrants in the last half of the 1830s were almost nine times the number in the first half of the 1820s.

• Where did most of these new immigrants settle?

1832 and nearly 80,000 in 1837. Reduced transportation costs and increasing economic opportunities helped stimulate the immigration boom, as did deteriorating economic conditions in some areas of Europe. The migrations introduced new groups to the United States. In particular, the number of immigrants arriving from the southern counties of Ireland began to grow, marking the beginning of a tremendous influx of Irish Catholics that was to continue through the three decades before the Civil War.

Much of this new European immigration flowed into the rapidly growing cities of the Northeast. But urban growth was a result of substantial internal migration as well. As the agricultural regions of New England and other areas grew less profitable, more and more people picked up stakes and moved—some to more promising agricultural regions in the West, but many to eastern cities. In 1790, one person in thirty had lived in a city (defined as a community of 8,000 or more); in 1820, one in twenty; and in 1840, one in twelve.

The rise of New York City was particularly dramatic. By 1810, it was the largest city in the United States. That was partly a result of its superior natural harbor. It was also a result of the Erie Canal (completed in 1825), which gave the city unrivaled access to the interior, and of liberal state laws that made the city attractive for both foreign and domestic commerce.

IMMIGRATION AND URBAN GROWTH, 1840–1860

RAPID URBANIZATION The growth of cities accelerated even more dramatically between 1840 and 1860. The population of New York, for example, rose from 312,000 to 805,000. (New York's population would

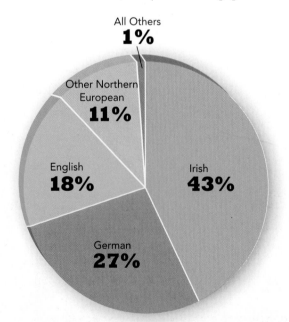

All Others
1%

Other Northern European
11%

English
18%

Irish
43%

German
27%

SOURCES OF IMMIGRATION, 1820–1840 This pie chart shows where the large numbers of immigrants portrayed in the previous chart came from. Note the very large number of Irish immigrants.

• Why were the Irish among the most likely immigrant groups to become part of the industrial workforce?

have numbered 1.2 million in 1860 if Brooklyn, which was then a separate municipality, had been included in the total.) Philadelphia's population grew over the same twenty-year period from 220,000 to 565,000; Boston's from 93,000 to 177,000. By 1860, 26 percent of the population of the free states was living in towns (places of 2,500 people or more) or cities (8,000 people or more), up from 14 percent in 1840. That percentage was even higher for the industrializing states of the Northeast. (In the South, by contrast, the increase of urban residents was only from 6 percent in 1840 to 10 percent in 1860.)

The booming agricultural economy of the western regions of the nation produced significant urban growth as well. Between 1820 and 1840, communities that had once been small western villages or trading posts became major cities: St. Louis, Pittsburgh, Cincinnati, Louisville. All of them benefited from strategic positions on the Mississippi River or one of its major tributaries. All of them became centers of the growing carrying trade that connected the farmers of the Midwest with New Orleans and, through it, the cities of the Northeast. After 1830, however, substantial shipping began from the Mississippi River to the Great Lakes, creating major new urban centers that gradually superseded the river ports. Among them were Buffalo, Detroit, Milwaukee, Cleveland, and—most important in the end—Chicago.

The enlarged urban population was in part a reflection of the growth of the national population as a whole, which rose by more than a third—from 23 million to over 31 million—in the decade of the 1850s alone. By 1860, the American population was larger than Britain's and quickly approaching that of France and Germany. Urban growth was also a result of the increasing flow of people into cities from the farms of the Northeast.

SURGING IMMIGRATION Immigration from abroad continued to increase as well. Between 1840 and 1850, more than 1.5 million Europeans moved to America, three times the number of arrivals in the 1830s. Still greater numbers arrived in the 1850s—over 2.5 million. Almost half the residents of New York City in the 1850s were recent immigrants. In St. Louis, Chicago, and Milwaukee, the foreign-born outnumbered those of native birth. Few immigrants settled in the South. Only 500,000 lived in the slave states in 1860, and a third of these were concentrated in Missouri, mostly in St. Louis.

GERMAN AND IRISH IMMIGRANTS The newcomers came from many different countries and regions: England, France, Italy, Scandinavia, Poland, and Holland. But the overwhelming majority came from Ireland and Germany. In 1850, the Irish constituted approximately 45 percent and the Germans over 20 percent of the foreign-born in America. By 1860, there were more than 1.5 million Irish-born and approximately 1 million German-born people in the United States. In Germany, the economic dislocations of the industrial revolution had caused widespread poverty, and the collapse of the liberal revolution there in 1848 also persuaded many Germans to emigrate. In Ireland, the oppressiveness and unpopularity of English rule drove many people out. But even more important was the greatest disaster in Ireland's history: a

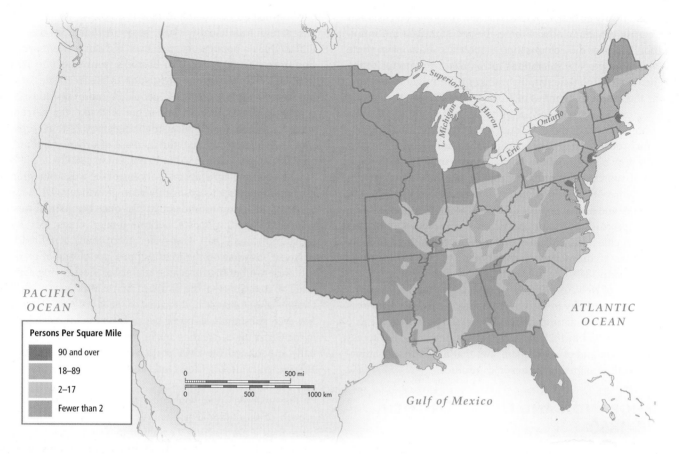

Persons Per Square Mile

■ 90 and over

□ 18–89

□ 2–17

□ Fewer than 2

AMERICAN POPULATION DENSITY, 1820 The population of the United States in 1820 was still overwhelmingly rural and agrarian and was still concentrated largely in the original thirteen states, although settlement was growing in the Ohio River valley to the west. Note how few areas of the country were populated really densely: a small area in northeastern Massachusetts, the area around New York City, and the area in Maryland adjoining Baltimore.

• *What accounts for the density in these areas?*

BROADWAY IN 1836 This image of the area of New York City's Broadway in what is now lower Manhattan suggests the way in which New York was becoming an increasingly important center of trade and commerce—and a densely urban place—in the 1830s. (New York Public Library/Art Resource, NY)

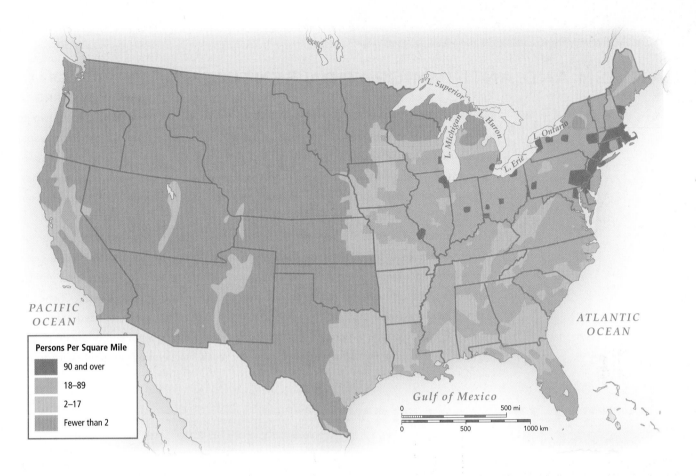

AMERICAN POPULATION DENSITY, 1860 By 1860, the population of the United States had spread much more evenly across the entire country. Communities that had once been small trading posts emerged as major cities. Among them were St. Louis, Pittsburgh, Cincinnati, and Louisville. In the meantime, the Erie Canal had opened up a large and prosperous market area for New York City. Note the larger and more numerous areas of dense population, including many in the Midwest.

• *What accounts for the growing population density in some areas of the Deep South?*

catastrophic failure of the potato crop (and other food crops) that caused the devastating "potato famine" of 1845–1849. Nearly a million people died of starvation and disease. Well over a million more emigrated to the United States.

The great majority of the Irish settled in the eastern cities, where they swelled the ranks of unskilled labor. Most Germans moved on to the Northwest, where they became farmers or went into business in the western towns. One reason for the difference was wealth: German immigrants generally arrived with at least some money; the Irish had practically none. Another important reason was gender. Most German immigrants were members of family groups or were single men, for whom movement to the agricultural frontier was both possible and attractive. Many Irish immigrants were young, single women, for whom movement west was much less plausible. They were more likely to stay in the eastern cities, where factory and domestic work was available.

THE RISE OF NATIVISM

Some native-born Americans welcomed the new immigration, which provided a large supply of cheap labor that they believed would help keep wage rates low. Land speculators and others with investments in the sparsely populated West hoped that immigrants would move into the region and help expand the population, and thus the market for land and goods, there. Political leaders in western states and territories wanted the immigrants to swell their population, also increase the political influence of the region. Wisconsin, for example, permitted foreign-born residents to become voters as soon as they had declared their intention of seeking citizenship and had resided in the state for a year; other western states soon followed its lead. In eastern cities, too, urban political organizations eagerly courted immigrant voters, hoping to enhance their own political strength.

Other Americans, however, viewed the growing foreign-born population with alarm. Their fears led to the rise of what is known as "nativism," a defense of native-born people and a hostility to the foreign-born, usually combined with a desire to stop or slow immigration. The emerging nativism took many forms. Some of it was a result of simple racism. Many nativists (conveniently overlooking their own immigrant heritage) argued that the new immigrants were inherently inferior to older-stock Americans. Some viewed them with the same

NATIVISM AND ANTI-IMMIGRATION SENTIMENT

ANTI-IMMIGRATION SENTIMENT AND NA-TIVISM HAVE LONG BEEN PRESENT IN THE NATION, as indicated by the first two items below: an 1852 broadside announcing publication of *The American Patriot,* a nativist newspaper, and a cartoon from 1850. The broadside issues a dire warning: "Already the enemies of our dearest institutions, like the foreign spies in the Trojan horse of old, are within our gates. They are disgorging themselves upon us, at the rate of Hundreds of Thousands Every Year! They aim at nothing short of conquest and supremacy over us."

Fast forward to April 2010 when Arizona Senate Bill 1070 was signed into law by Governor Jan Brewer. Provisions of the law include the right of law enforcement agents to ask for a person's immigration documents during routine stops and a mandate that any illegal immigrant convicted of a crime or misdemeanor be turned over to federal immigration agents. Crictics claim that the law is a product of nativism and anti-immigration sentiment directed specifically at those of Hispanic origin, which will result in persecution of both legal and undocumented immigrants. Some of the most insightful crtiques of the law have come from political cartoonists. See two examples below.

ANTI-IMMIGRATION SENTIMENT—1850/1852

"IRISH AND GERMANS STEAL THE BALLOT BOX." (Courtesy, Granger Collection)

1. What complaints against immigrants are stated in the broadside? To whom in particular is *The American Patriot* opposed? Why is there such strong opposition to these immigrants?
2. What does the depiction of the immigrants in the cartoon suggest about them? What specific grievance against the immigrants is expressed?

REACTIONS TO ARIZONA SENATE BILL 1070—2010

"IMMIGRATION AND LIBERTY" BY DARYL CAGLE (Source: © 2010 Daryl Cagle, MSNBC, and PoliticalCartoons.com)

"YOUR ACTIVITIES AROUSE SUSPICION" BY NICK ANDERSON (Nick Anderson Editorial Cartoon used with the permission of Nick Anderson, the Washington Post Writers Group and the Cartoonist Group. All rights reserved.)

MAKE CONNECTIONS

1. What attitude toward the Arizona law is reflected in these two cartoons? Do the cartoons suggest the same attitude toward the law? What differences, if any, do you detect?
2. How do the cartoonists portray immigrants or those most affected by the Arizona law?
3. In what ways does the nativist sentiment reflected in the nineteenth-century documents differ from the attitude toward immigration behind the Arizona law?

Total immigration during five-year periods (in millions)

1,748
1,283
850
430

1841-1845 1846-1850 1851-1855 1856-1860
Year

IMMIGRATION, 1840–1860 Immigration continued to increase in the forty years before the Civil War. This chart illustrates the much higher levels of growth than in the previous forty years. The low point in this era was the first half of the 1840s, in which 430,000 new immigrants entered the United States. That was significantly higher than the largest number of the previous twenty years. In the early 1850s, the number of immigrants grew to nearly two million.

• *What events in Europe contributed to this increase?*

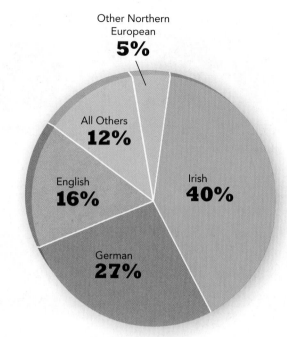

Other Northern European
5%

All Others
12%

English
16%

Irish
40%

German
27%

SOURCES OF IMMIGRATION, 1840–1860 Although the extent of immigration increased dramatically in the two decades after 1840, the sources of it remained remarkably stable. Note how closely the distribution of immigrant groups portrayed in this pie chart parallels that in the similar chart for the 1820–1840 period.

• *What were some of the differences between what German and Irish immigrants did once they arrived in America?*

contempt and prejudice—and the same low estimate of their potential abilities—with which they viewed African Americans and Indians. Many nativists avoided racist arguments but argued nevertheless that the newcomers were socially unfit to live alongside people of older stock, that they did not bring with them sufficient standards of civilization. Evidence for that, they claimed, was the wretched urban and sometimes rural slums in which they lived. (Many nativists seemed to assume that such wretchedness was something immigrants chose, rather than the result of their extreme poverty.) Others—especially workers—complained that because foreigners were willing to work for low wages, they were stealing jobs from the native labor force. Protestants, observing the success of Irish Catholics in establishing footholds in urban politics, warned that the Catholic Church and the pope were gaining a foothold in American government. Whig politicians were outraged because so many of the newcomers voted Democratic. Others complained that the immigrants corrupted politics by selling their votes. Many older-stock Americans of both parties feared that immigrants would bring new, radical ideas into national life.

Out of these tensions and prejudices emerged a number of new secret societies created to combat what nativists had come to call the "alien menace." Most of them originated in the Northeast. Some later spread to the West and even to the South. The first of these, the Native American Association, began agitating against immigration in 1837. In 1845, nativists held a convention in Philadelphia and formed the Native American Party (unaware that the term they used to describe themselves would one day become a common label for American Indians). Many of the nativist groups combined in 1850 to form the Supreme Order of the Star-Spangled Banner. It endorsed a list of demands that included banning Catholics or the foreign-born from holding public office, more restrictive naturalization laws, and literacy tests for voting. The order adopted a strict code of secrecy, which included the secret password, used in lodges across the country, "I know nothing." Ultimately, members of the movement became known as the "Know-Nothings."

NATIVE AMERICAN PARTY

Gradually, the Know-Nothings turned their attention to party politics, and after the election of 1852 they created a new political organization that they called the American Party. In the East, the new organization scored an immediate and astonishing success in the elections of 1854: the Know-Nothings cast a large vote in Pennsylvania and New York and won control of the state government in Massachusetts. Elsewhere, the progress of the Know-Nothings was more modest. Western members of the party, because of the presence of many German voters in the area, found it expedient not to oppose naturalized Protestants. After 1854, the strength of the Know-Nothings declined.

THE KNOW-NOTHINGS

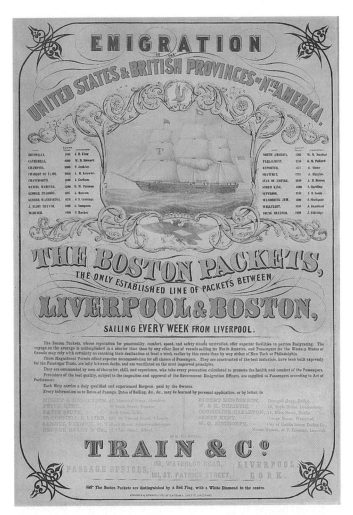

AN APPEAL TO EMIGRANTS This widely distributed advertising card was one of many appeals to potential English and Irish travelers to America in the 1830s and 1840s. Like other such companies, it tried to attract both affluent passengers (by boasting of "superior accommodations") and working-class people of modest means. (Courtesy of The Bostonian Society/Old State House)

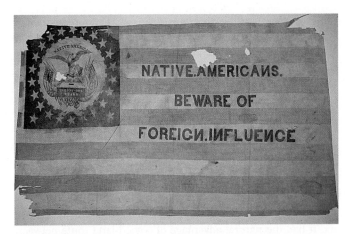

A "KNOW-NOTHING" FLAG The American Party, which began as a secret organization with the popular nickname "Know-Nothings" (from their refusal to divulge any information about their activities), was in the forefront of antebellum campaigns against immigration—as this flag (which refers to the older-stock white members of the party as "Native Americans") suggests. The Know-Nothings were particularly alarmed about the rising number of Catholic immigrants to the United States and warned that this "monster" (Catholicism) was "only waiting for the hour to approach to plant its flag of tyranny, persecution, and oppression among us." (Photo courtesy of Milwaukee County Historical Society)

TRANSPORTATION, COMMUNICATIONS, AND TECHNOLOGY

Just as the industrial revolution needed a growing population, it also required an efficient system of transportation and communications. Such a system was essential in creating regional, national, and ultimately international markets. Progress in this area required not just significant investment, but also important advances in technological knowledge.

THE CANAL AGE

From 1790 until the 1820s, the so-called turnpike era, Americans had relied largely on roads for internal transportation. But in a country as large as the United States was becoming, roads alone (and the mostly horse-drawn vehicles that used them) were not adequate for the nation's expanding needs. And so, in the 1820s and 1830s, Americans began to turn to other means of transportation as well.

The larger rivers, especially the Mississippi and the Ohio, had been important transportation routes for years, but most of the traffic on them consisted of flat barges—little more than rafts—that floated downstream laden with cargo and were broken up at the end of their journeys because they could not navigate back upstream. To return north, shippers had to send goods by land or by agonizingly slow upstream vessels that sometimes took up to four months to travel the length of the Mississippi.

These rivers became vastly more important by the 1820s, as STEAMBOATS steamboats grew in number and improved in design. The new riverboats carried the corn and wheat of northwestern farmers and the cotton and tobacco of southwestern planters to New Orleans in a fraction of the time of the old barges. From New Orleans, oceangoing ships took the cargoes on to eastern ports. Steamboats also developed a significant passenger traffic, and companies built increasingly lavish vessels to compete for this lucrative trade.

But neither the farmers of the West nor the merchants of the East were wholly satisfied with this pattern of trade. Farmers would pay less to transport their goods (and eastern consumers would pay less to consume them) if they could ship them directly eastward to market, rather than by the roundabout river-sea route; and northeastern merchants, too, could sell larger quantities of their manufactured goods if they could transport their merchandise more directly and economically to the West. New highways across the mountains provided a partial solution to the problem. But the costs of hauling goods overland, although lower than before, were still too high for anything except the most compact and valuable merchandise. The thoughts of some merchants and entrepreneurs began, therefore, to turn to an alternative: canals.

A team of four horses could haul one and a half tons of goods eighteen miles a day on the turnpikes. But the same four horses, walking along the "towpaths" next to canals while yoked to barges, could draw a boatload of a hundred tons twenty-four miles a day. By the 1820s, the economic advantages of canals had generated a booming interest in expanding the water routes to the West. Canal building was too expensive for private enterprise, and the job of digging canals fell largely to the states. The ambitious state governments of the Northeast took the lead in constructing them. New York was the first to act. It had the natural advantage of a good land route between the Hudson River and Lake Erie through the only real break in the Appalachian chain. But the engineering tasks were still imposing. The distance was more than 350 miles, several times the length of any of the existing canals in America. The route was interrupted by high ridges and a wilderness of woods. After a long public debate over whether the scheme was practical, canal advocates prevailed when De Witt Clinton, a late but ardent convert to the cause, became governor in 1817. Digging began on July 4, 1817.

ECONOMIC ADVANTAGES OF CANALS

The building of the Erie Canal was the greatest construction project the United States had ever undertaken. The canal itself was simple: a ditch forty feet wide and four feet deep, with towpaths along the banks. But hundreds of difficult cuts and fills, some of them enormous, were required to enable the canal to pass through hills and over valleys; stone aqueducts were necessary to carry it across streams; and eighty-eight locks, of heavy masonry with great wooden gates, were needed to permit ascents and descents. The Erie Canal was not just an engineering triumph, but an immediate financial success as well. It opened in October 1825, amid elaborate ceremonies and celebrations, and traffic was soon so heavy that within about seven years tolls had repaid the entire cost of construction. By providing a route to the Great Lakes, the canal gave New York direct access to Chicago and the growing markets of the West. New York could now compete with (and increasingly replace) New Orleans as a destination for agricultural goods (particularly wheat) and other products of the West, and as a source for manufactured goods to be sold in the region.

THE ERIE CANAL

The system of water transportation—and the primacy of New York—extended farther when the states of Ohio and Indiana, inspired by the success of the Erie Canal, provided

BUILDING THE ERIE CANAL This lithograph by Anthony Imbert suggests something of the enormous engineering challenges that the builders of the Erie Canal faced. This picture shows excavations at Lockport, New York, where a horse-powered crane and a large crew of Irish immigrant workers clear boulders from the channel. Imbert created these and other images to illustrate a book published in 1825 to celebrate the completion of the canal. (*Building the Erie Canal.* Lithograph by Anthony Imbert. From Cadwallader Colden's *Memoir on the Celebration of the Completion of the New York Canals.* The Metropolitan Museum of Art, Harris Brisbane Dick Fund, 1941. [41.51])

CANALS IN THE NORTHEAST, 1823–1860 The great success of the Erie Canal, which opened in 1825, inspired decades of energetic canal building in many areas of the United States, as this map illustrates. But none of the new canals had anything like the impact of the original Erie Canal, and thus none of New York's competitors—among them Baltimore, Philadelphia, and Boston—were able to displace it as the nation's leading commercial center.

• *What form of transportation ultimately displaced the canals?*

water connections between Lake Erie and the Ohio River. These canals helped connect them by an inland water route all the way to New York, although it was still necessary to transfer cargoes several times between canal, lake, and river craft. One of the immediate results of these new transportation routes was increased white settlement in the Northwest, because canals made it easier for migrants to make the westward journey and to ship their goods back to eastern markets.

Rival cities along the Atlantic seaboard took alarm at the prospect of New York's acquiring so vast a hinterland. But they had limited success in catching up. Boston, its way to the Hudson River blocked by the Berkshire Mountains, did not even try to connect itself to the West by canal; its hinterland would remain confined largely to New England. Philadelphia and Baltimore had the still more formidable Allegheny Mountains to contend with. They made a serious effort at canal building, nevertheless, but with discouraging results. Pennsylvania's effort ended in an expensive failure. Maryland constructed part of the Chesapeake and Ohio Canal beginning in 1828, but completed only the stretch between Washington, D.C., and Cumberland, Maryland, and thus never crossed the mountains. In the South, Richmond

and Charleston also aspired to build water routes to the Ohio Valley, but never completed them.

In the end, canals did not provide a satisfactory route to the West for any of New York's rivals. Some cities, however, saw their opportunity in a different and newer means of transportation. Even before the canal age had reached its height, the era of the railroad was already beginning.

THE EARLY RAILROADS

Eventually, railroads became the primary transportation system for the United States, and they remained so until the construction of the interstate highway system in the mid-twentieth century.

Railroads emerged from a combination of technological and entrepreneurial innovations. The technological breakthroughs included the invention of tracks, the creation of steam-powered locomotives, and the development of railroad cars that could serve as public carriers of passengers and freight. By 1804, both English and American inventors had experimented with steam engines for propelling land vehicles.

TECHNOLOGICAL
BASIS OF THE
RAILROAD

RACING ON THE RAILROAD Peter Cooper, who in later years was best known as a philanthropist and as the founder of the Cooper Union in New York City, was also a successful iron manufacturer. Cooper designed and built the first steam-powered locomotive in America in 1830 for the Baltimore and Ohio Railroad. On August 28 of that year, he raced his locomotive (the Tom Thumb) against a horse-drawn railroad car. This sketch depicts the moment when Cooper's engine overtook the horsecar. (Museum of the City of New York)

In 1820, John Stevens ran a locomotive and cars around a circular track on his New Jersey estate. And in 1825, the Stockton and Darlington Railroad in England opened a short length of track and became the first line to carry general traffic.

American entrepreneurs, especially in those northeastern cities that sought better communication with the West, quickly grew interested in the English experiment. The first company to begin actual operations was the Baltimore and Ohio, which opened a thirteen-mile stretch of track in 1830. In New York, the Mohawk and Hudson began running trains along the sixteen miles between Schenectady and Albany in 1831. By 1836, more than a thousand miles of track had been laid in eleven states.

But there was not yet a true railroad system. Even the longest of the lines was comparatively short in the 1830s, and most of them served simply to connect water routes, not to link one railroad to another. Even when two lines did connect, the tracks often differed in gauge (width), so that cars from one line often could not fit onto the tracks of another. Schedules were erratic, and wrecks were frequent. But railroads made some important advances in the 1830s and 1840s. The introduction of heavier iron rails improved the roadbeds. Steam locomotives became more flexible and powerful. Redesigned passenger cars became stabler, more comfortable, and larger.

Railroads and canals were soon competing bitterly. For a time, the Chesapeake and Ohio Canal Company blocked the advance of the Baltimore and Ohio Railroad through the narrow gorge of the upper Potomac, which it controlled; and the state of New York prohibited railroads from hauling freight in competition with the Erie Canal and its branches. But railroads had so many advantages that when they were able to compete freely with other forms of transportation they almost always prevailed.

COMPETITION BETWEEN RAILROADS AND CANALS

THE TRIUMPH OF THE RAILS

After 1840, railroads gradually supplanted canals and all other modes of transport. In 1840, there were 2,818 miles of railroad tracks in the United States; by 1850, there were 9,021. An unparalleled burst of railroad construction followed in the 1850s, tripling the amount of trackage in just ten years. The most comprehensive and efficient system was in the Northeast, which had twice as much trackage per square mile as the Northwest and four times as much as the South. But the expansion of the rails left no region untouched. Railroads were even reaching west of the Mississippi, which was spanned at several points by great iron bridges. One line ran from Hannibal to St. Joseph on the Missouri River, and another was under construction between St. Louis and Kansas City.

An important change in railroad development was the trend toward the consolidation of short lines into longer lines (known as "trunk lines"). By 1853, four major railroad trunk lines had crossed the Appalachian Mountains to connect the Northeast with the Northwest. The New York Central and the New York and Erie gave New York City access to the Lake Erie ports. The Pennsylvania railroad linked Philadelphia and Pittsburgh, and the Baltimore and Ohio connected Baltimore with the Ohio River at Wheeling. From the terminals of these lines, other railroads into the interior touched the Mississippi River at eight points. Chicago became the rail center of the West, served by fifteen lines and more than a hundred daily trains. The appearance of the great trunk lines tended to divert traffic from the main water routes—the Erie Canal and the Mississippi River. By lessening the dependence of the West on the Mississippi, the railroads helped weaken further the connection between the Northwest and the South.

CONSOLIDATION

Capital to finance the railroad boom came from many sources. Private American investors provided part of the necessary funding, and railroad companies borrowed large sums from abroad. But local governments—states, counties, cities, towns—also often contributed capital, because they were eager to have railroads serve them. The railroads obtained substantial additional assistance from the federal government in the form of public land grants. In 1850, Senator Stephen A. Douglas of Illinois and other railroad-minded politicians persuaded

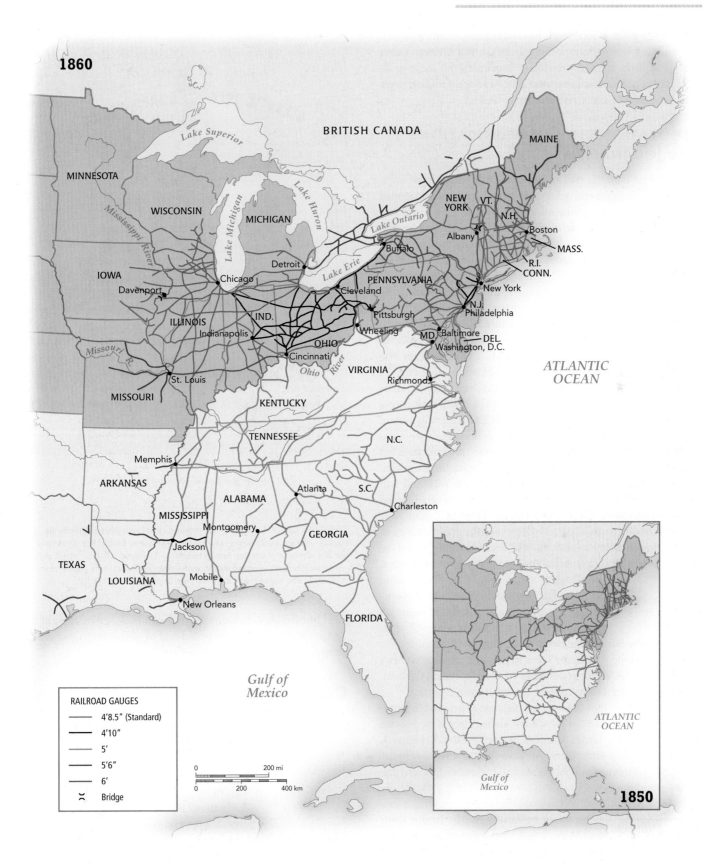

RAILROAD GROWTH, 1850–1860 These two maps illustrate the dramatic growth in the extent of American railroads in the 1850s. Note the particularly extensive increase in mileage in the upper Midwest (known at the time as the Northwest). Note too the relatively smaller increase in railroad mileage in the South. Railroads forged a close economic relationship between the upper Midwest and the Northeast, and weakened the Midwest's relationship to the South.

• *How did the growth of railroads in the North contribute to the South's growing sense of insecurity within the Union?*

Congress to grant federal lands to aid the Illinois Central, which was building from Chicago toward the Gulf of Mexico. Other states and their railroad promoters demanded the same privileges, and by 1860, Congress had allotted over 30 million acres to eleven states to assist railroad construction.

INNOVATIONS IN COMMUNICATIONS AND JOURNALISM

Critical to the railroads was an important innovation in communications: the magnetic telegraph. Telegraph lines extended along the tracks, connecting one station with another and aiding the scheduling and routing of trains. But the telegraph also permitted instant communication between distant cities, tying the nation together as never before. At the same time, it helped reinforce the schism between the North and the South. Like railroads, telegraph lines were far more extensive in the North than in the South, and they helped similarly to link the North to the Northwest (and thus to separate the Northwest further from the South).

THE TELEGRAPH The telegraph burst into American life in 1844, when Samuel F. B. Morse, after several years of experimentation, succeeded in transmitting from Baltimore to Washington the news of James K. Polk's nomination for the presidency. The relatively low cost of constructing wire systems made the Morse telegraph system seem the ideal answer to the problems of long-distance communication. By 1860, more than 50,000 miles of wire connected most parts of the country; and a year later, the Pacific telegraph, with 3,595 miles of wire, opened between New York and San Francisco. By then, nearly all the independent lines had joined in one organization, the Western Union Telegraph Company.

New forms of journalism also drew communities into a common communications system. In 1846, Richard Hoe invented the steam cylinder rotary press, making it possible to print newspapers rapidly and cheaply. The development of the telegraph, together with the introduction of the rotary press, made possible much speedier collection and distribution of news than ever before. In 1846, newspaper publishers from around the nation formed the Associated Press to promote cooperative news gathering by wire; no longer did they have to depend on the cumbersome exchange of newspapers for out-of-town reports.

THE ASSOCIATED PRESS

Major metropolitan newspapers began to appear in the larger cities of the Northeast. In New York alone, there were Horace Greeley's *Tribune,* James Gordon Bennett's *Herald,* Henry J. Raymond's *Times,* and others. All gave serious attention to national and even international events and had substantial circulations beyond the city.

FUELING SECTIONAL DISCORD

In the long run, journalism would become an important unifying factor in American life. In the 1840s and 1850s, however, the rise of the new journalism helped to feed sectional discord. Most of the major magazines and newspapers were in the North, reinforcing the South's sense of subjugation. Southern newspapers tended to have smaller budgets and reported largely local news. Few had any impact outside

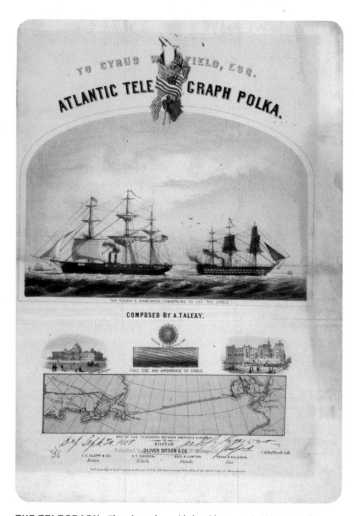

THE TELEGRAPH The telegraph provided rapid communication across the country—and eventually across oceans—for the first time. Samuel F. B. Morse was one of a number of nineteenth-century inventors who helped create the telegraph, but Morse was the most commercially successful of the rivals, hence his greater reputation than others who helped create it. (Library of Congress [LCUSZC4-5040])

their immediate communities. The combined circulation of the *Tribune* and the *Herald* exceeded that of all the daily newspapers published in the South put together.

COMMERCE AND INDUSTRY

By the middle years of the nineteenth century, the United States had developed the beginnings of a modern capitalist economy and an advanced industrial capacity. This emerging economy created enormous wealth and changed the face of all areas of the nation. But it did not, of course, affect everyone equally. Some classes and regions benefited from the economic development far more than others.

IMPACT OF THE MARKET ECONOMY

THE EXPANSION OF BUSINESS, 1820–1840

American business grew rapidly in the 1820s and 1830s, partly because of population growth and the transportation revolution, but also because of the daring, imagination, and ruthlessness of a new generation of entrepreneurs.

One important change came in the retail distribution of goods. In the larger cities, stores specializing in groceries, dry goods, hardware, and other lines appeared, although residents of smaller towns and villages still depended on general stores (stores that did not specialize). In these less populous areas, many people did much of their business by barter.

The organization of business was also changing. Individuals or limited partnerships continued to operate most businesses, and the dominating figures were still the great merchant capitalists, who generally had sole ownership of their enterprises. In some larger businesses, however, the individual merchant capitalist was giving way to the corporation. Corporations be-

ADVANTAGES OF THE CORPORATION

gan to develop particularly rapidly in the 1830s, when some legal obstacles to their formation were removed. Previously, a corporation could obtain a charter only by a special act of the state legislature—a cumbersome process that stifled corporate growth. By the 1830s, however, states were beginning to pass general incorporation laws, under which a group could secure a charter merely by paying a fee.

The new laws also permitted a system of limited liability, which meant that individual stockholders risked losing only the value of their own investment if a corporation should fail, and that they were not liable (as they had been in the past) for the corporation's larger losses. The rise of these new corporations made possible the accumula-

tion of much greater amounts of capital and hence made possible much larger manufacturing and business enterprises.

Investment alone, however, still provided too little capital to meet the demands of the most ambitious businesses. Such

INADEQUATE CREDIT

businesses relied heavily on credit, and their borrowing often created dangerous instability. Credit mechanisms remained very crude in the early nineteenth century. The government alone could issue official currency, but the official currency consisted only of gold and silver (or paper certificates backed literally by gold and silver), and there was thus too little of it to support the growing demand for credit. Under pressure from corporate promoters, many banks issued large quantities of bank notes—unofficial currency that circulated in much the same way that government currency did but was of much less stable value. But the notes had value only to the degree that the bank could sustain public confidence in their value; and some banks issued so many notes that their own reserves could not cover them. As a result, bank failures were frequent, and bank deposits were often insecure. The difficulty of obtaining credit for business investment remained, therefore, an impediment to economic growth.

THE MOST PROFOUND ECONOMIC DEVELOPMENT IN MID-NINETEENTH-CENTURY AMERICA WAS THE RISE OF THE FACTORY.

THE EMERGENCE OF THE FACTORY

The most profound economic development in mid-nineteenth-century America was the rise of the factory. Before the War of 1812, most of what manufacturing there was in the United

CHICAGO, 1858 This photograph of the busy freight depot and grain elevators of the Illinois Central Railroad illustrates the rapid growth of Chicago in the 1850s as the great trading center of the central part of the United States. (Chicago Historical Society)

States took place within private households or in small, individually operated workshops. Men and women built or made products by hand, or with simple machines such as hand-operated looms. Gradually, however, improved technology and increasing demand produced a fundamental change. It came first in the New England textile industry. There, entrepreneurs were beginning to make use of new and larger machines driven by water power that allowed them to bring textile operations together under a single roof. This factory system, as it came to be known, spread rapidly in the 1820s and began to make serious inroads into the old home-based system of spinning thread and weaving cloth.

Factories also penetrated the shoe industry, concentrated in eastern Massachusetts. Shoes were still largely handmade, but

TRANSFORMATION OF THE SHOE INDUSTRY manufacturers were beginning to employ workers who specialized in one or another of the various tasks involved in production. Some factories began producing large numbers of identical shoes in ungraded sizes and without distinction as to rights and lefts. By the 1830s, factory production was spreading from textiles and shoes into other industries and from New England to other areas of the Northeast.

Between 1840 and 1860, American industry experienced even more dramatic growth as the factory system spread rapidly. In 1840, the total value of manufactured goods produced in the United States stood at $483 million; ten years later the figure had climbed to over $1 billion; and in 1860 it reached close to $2 billion. For the first time, the value of manufactured goods was approximately equal to that of agricultural products.

Of the approximately 140,000 manufacturing establishments in the country in 1860, 74,000 were located in the Northeast. The

THE INDUSTRIAL NORTHEAST Northeast plants were so large that the region produced more than two-thirds of the nation's manufactured goods. Of the 1,311,000 workers in manufacturing in the United States, about 938,000 were employed in the mills and factories of New England and the mid-Atlantic states.

ADVANCES IN TECHNOLOGY

Even the most highly developed industries were still relatively immature by later standards. American cotton manufacturers, for example, produced goods of coarse grade; fine items continued to come from England. But machine technology advanced more rapidly in the United States in the mid-nineteenth century than in any other country in the world. The American economy was growing so rapidly that the rewards of technological innovation were very great. Change was so rapid, in fact, that some manufacturers built their new machinery out of wood; by the time the wood wore out, they reasoned, improved technology would have made the machine obsolete. By the beginning of the 1830s, American technology had become so advanced—particularly in textile manufacturing—that industrialists in Britain and Europe were beginning to travel to the United States to learn new techniques, instead of the other way around.

The manufacturing of machine tools—the tools used to make machinery parts—was an important contribution to manufacturing. The government supported much of the research and development of machine tools, often in connection with supplying the military. For example, a government armory in Springfield, Massachusetts, developed two important tools—the turret lathe (used for cutting screws and other metal parts) and the universal milling machine (which replaced the hand chiseling of complicated parts and dies)—early in the nineteenth century. The precision grinding machine (which became critical to, among other things, the construction of sewing machines) was designed in the 1850s to help the United States Army produce standardized rifle parts. The federal armories such as those at Springfield and Harpers Ferry, Virginia, became the breeding ground for many technological discoveries, and a magnet for craftsmen and factory owners looking for ideas that could be of use to them. By the 1840s, the machine tools used in the factories of the Northeast were already better than those in most European factories.

Interchangeable parts, which Eli Whitney and Simeon North

INTERCHANGEABLE PARTS had tried to introduce into gun factories, now found their way into many industries. Eventually, interchangeability would revolutionize watch and clock making, the manufacturing of locomotives and steam engines, and the making of many farm tools. It would also help make possible such newer devices as bicycles, sewing machines, typewriters, cash registers, and eventually the automobile.

Industrialization was also profiting from the introduction of new sources of energy. Coal was replacing wood and water power as fuel for many factories. The production of coal, most of it mined around Pittsburgh in western Pennsylvania, leaped from 50,000 tons in 1820 to 14 million tons in 1860. The new power source made it possible to locate mills away from running streams and thus permitted industry to expand still more widely.

The great technological advances in American industry owed

TECHNOLOGICAL INNOVATIONS much to American inventors, as the patent records of the time make clear. In 1830, the number of inventions patented was 544; by 1850, the figure had risen to 993; and in 1860, it stood at 4,778. In 1839, Charles Goodyear, a New England hardware merchant, discovered a method of vulcanizing rubber (treating it to give it greater strength and elasticity); by 1860, his process had found over 500 uses and had helped create a major American rubber industry. In 1846, Elias Howe of Massachusetts constructed a sewing machine; Isaac Singer made improvements on it, and the Howe-Singer machine was soon being used in the manufacture of ready-to-wear clothing.

For all the technological innovations that characterized the early factory system, most American industry remained wedded to the most traditional source of power: water. In the 1820s and 1830s, water power remained the most important source of power for manufacturing. The first important factory towns in New England—Lawrence, Lowell, and others—emerged where they did because of the natural waterfalls that could be channeled to provide power for the mills built along their banks. This sometimes required factories to close for periods in the winter when rivers were frozen. That was one reason factory owners began to look for alternative forms of energy that could be used throughout the year, which led them by the late 1830s to rely more and more heavily on steam and other transportable forms of energy that could be fueled by wood, coal, or (later) petroleum.

MEN AND WOMEN AT WORK

However sophisticated industrial firms became technologically and administratively, manufacturers still relied above all on a supply of labor. In the 1820s and 1830s, factory labor came primarily from the native-born population. After 1840, the growing immigrant population became the most important new source of workers.

RECRUITING A NATIVE WORKFORCE

Recruiting a labor force was not an easy task in the early years of the factory system. Ninety percent of the American people in the 1820s still lived and worked on farms, and many urban residents were skilled artisans—independent crafts workers who owned and managed their own shops as small businessmen; they were not likely to flock to factory jobs. The available unskilled workers were not numerous enough to form a reservoir from which the new industries could draw.

The beginnings of an industrial labor supply came instead from the transformation of American agriculture in the nine-

TRANSFORMATION OF AMERICAN AGRICULTURE

teenth century. The opening of vast, fertile new farmlands in the Midwest, the improvement of transportation systems, the development of new farm machinery—all combined to increase food production dramatically. New farming methods were also less labor-intensive than the old ones; the number of workers required to produce large crops in the West was much smaller than the number required to produce smaller crops in the less fertile Northeast. No longer did each region have to feed itself entirely from its own farms; it could import food from other regions. As as result, farmers and their families began to abandon some of the relatively unprofitable farming areas of the East. In the Northeast, especially in New England, where poor land had always placed harsh limits on farm productivity, rural people began leaving the land to work in the factories.

Two systems of recruitment emerged to bring this new labor supply to the expanding textile mills. One, common in the mid-Atlantic states (especially in such major manufacturing centers as New York and Philadelphia), brought whole families from the farm to the mill. Parents tended looms alongside their children, some of whom were no more than four or five years old. The second system, common in Massachusetts, enlisted young women, mostly farmers' daughters in their late teens and early twenties. It was known as the Lowell or Waltham System, after the factory towns in which it first emerged. Many of these women worked for several years in the factories, saved their wages, and returned home to marry and raise children. Others married men they met in the factories or in town and remained part of the industrial world, but often stopped working in the mills to take up domestic roles instead.

WOMEN AT WORK This early photograph of female mill workers standing before their machines suggests something of the primitive quality of early factories—dimly lit, cramped, with conditions that offered little protection against accidents. All the women in this picture are wearing hair tightly pulled back, to prevent it from being caught in one of the machines. (Courtesy George Eastman House)

RULES FOR EMPLOYEES

STRICT RULES GOVERNED THE WORKING LIFE OF THE YOUNG WOMEN who worked in the textile mills in Lowell, Massachusetts, in the first half of the nineteenth century. Equally strict rules regulated their time away from work (what little leisure time they enjoyed) in the company-supervised boardinghouses in which they lived. The excerpts from the *Handbook to Lowell* from 1848 that follow suggest the tight supervision under which the Lowell mill girls worked and lived.

Many companies today publish employee handbooks that provide information about employee responsibilities, including working hours and days, and expectations of employee performance. They may also outline employee benefits, such as compensation, vacation policies, and medical benefits. Some companies issue formal rules of conduct and ethics by which their employees must abide. The example from the Simpson Manufacturing Company, which makes building products, provides an interesting comparison to the Lowell guidelines.

HANDBOOK TO LOWELL—1848

HANDBOOK TO LOWELL

Factory Rules

REGULATIONS TO BE OBSERVED by all persons employed in the factories of the Hamilton Manufacturing Company. The overseers are to be always in their rooms at the starting of the mill, and not absent unnecessarily during working hours. They are to see that all those employed in their rooms are in their places in due season, and keep a correct account of their time and work. They may grant leave of absence to those employed under them, when they have spare hands to supply their places and not otherwise, except in cases of absolute necessity.

All persons in the employ of the Hamilton Manufacturing Company are to observe the regulations of the room where they are employed. They are not to be absent from their work without the consent of the overseer, except in cases of sickness, and then they are to send him word of the cause of their absence. They are to board in one of the houses of the company and give information at the counting room, where they board, when they begin, or, whenever they change their boarding place; and are to observe the regulations of their boarding-house.

Those intending to leave the employment of the company are to give at least two weeks' notice thereof to their overseer.

All persons entering into the employment of the company are considered as engaged for twelve months, and those who leave sooner, or do not comply with all these regulations, will not be entitled to a regular discharge.

The company will not employ anyone who is habitually absent from public worship on the Sabbath, or known to be guilty of immorality.

A physician will attend once in every month at the counting-room, to vaccinate all who may need it, free of expense.

Anyone who shall take from the mills or the yard, any yarn, cloth or other article belonging to the company will be considered guilty of stealing and be liable to prosecution.

Payment will be made monthly, including board and wages. The accounts will be made up to the last Saturday but one in every month, and paid in the course of the following week.

These regulations are considered part of the contract, with which all persons entering into the employment of the Hamilton Manufacturing Company, engage to comply.

Boarding House Rules

REGULATIONS FOR THE BOARDING-HOUSES of the Hamilton Manufacturing Company. The tenants of the boarding-houses are not to board, or permit any part of their houses to be occupied by any person, except those in the employ of the company, without special permission.

They will be considered answerable for any improper conduct in their houses, and are not to permit their boarders to have company at unseasonable hours.

The doors must be closed at ten o'clock in the evening, and no person admitted after that time, without some reasonable excuse.

The keepers of the boarding-houses must give an account of the number, names and employment of their boarders, when required, and report the names of such as are guilty of any improper conduct, or are not in the regular habit of attending public worship.

The buildings, and yards about them, must be kept clean and in good order; and if they are injured, otherwise than from ordinary use, all necessary repairs will be made, and charged to the occupant.

The sidewalks, also, in front of the houses, must be kept clean, and free from snow, which must be removed from them immediately after it has ceased falling; if neglected, it will be removed by the company at the expense of the tenant.

It is desirable that the families of those who live in the houses, as well as the boarders, who have not had the kine pox, should be vaccinated, which will be done at the expense of the company, for such as wish it.

Some suitable chamber in the house must be reserved, and appropriated for the use of the sick, so that others may not be under the necessity of sleeping in the same room.

JOHN AVERY, Agent.

UNDERSTAND, ANALYZE, AND EVALUATE

1. What do these rules suggest about the everyday lives of the mill workers?
2. What do the rules suggest about the company's attitude toward the workers? Do the rules offer any protections to the employees, or are they all geared toward benefiting the employer?
3. Why would the company enforce such strict rules? Why would the mill workers accept them?

SIMPSON CODE OF CONDUCT—2004

SIMPSON MANUFACTURING: CODE OF BUSINESS CONDUCT AND ETHICS

November 18, 2004

At Simpson Manufacturing Co., Inc. and its subsidiaries (Company), we expect that all of our employees, officers and directors will treat each other, our customers, and our suppliers with goodwill, trust, and respect. As a Company, we value honesty, high ethical standards and compliance with laws, rules and regulations.

The following provides guidance on the application of these principles:

Compliance with Laws, Rules and Regulations

...

Equal Employment Opportunity (EEO) and Discrimination Laws: It continues to be the practice of the Company to employ positive business and personnel practices designed to ensure the full realization of equal employment opportunity. Further, we expect all employees to accomplish their work in a businesslike manner with a concern for the well-being of their co-workers. Harassment of any employee by any other employee is prohibited, regardless of their working relationship . . .

Securities Laws: All employees of the Company are prohibited from transacting in the Company's securities, for themselves, family members, friends or any other person, while in the possession of material, nonpublic (inside) information concerning the Company. In addition employees must not give inside information to anyone . . .

Antitrust Laws: We do not discuss our prices with our competitors. We do not enter into illegal agreements or engage in illegal practices in restraint of trade. For additional information on antitrust laws, contact the

President of your company or the President of Simpson Manufacturing.

Health and Safety

The Company seeks to provide a clean, safe and healthy place to work. All employees are expected to observe all safety rules and practices and to follow instructions concerning safe work practices.

Record Keeping and Reporting of Information

All records and reported information must be accurate, complete, honest and timely.

Conflicts of Interest

Every employee, officer and director, is expected to make decisions in the best interest of the Company and not for personal gain. A conflict of interest can arise when an employee, officer or director takes action or has a personal interest that may make it difficult to perform his or her work for the Company objectively and effectively. . . . Employees are prohibited from accepting meals, entertainment, travel, gratuities, merchandise or promotional material that could influence objectivity in making business decisions. Employees are generally prohibited from accepting any such item worth more than $50. Certain business events may require an employee's participation in excess of this amount. These must be approved by their supervisor.

Fair Dealing

Employees, officers and directors should endeavor to deal fairly with the Company's customers and suppliers and each other. No one should take unfair advantage of anyone else through manipulation or misrepresentation of material facts.

Quality

Products that meet our quality standards are essential to our success. Everyone in the Company is responsible for product quality and must be committed to ensuring the effectiveness of the Quality Management System. For more information on the Company's Quality Principles, please see your supervisor.

Protection and Proper Use of Company Assets

All employees, officers and directors should protect the Company's assets and ensure their efficient use.

Confidentiality

Employees, officers and directors should maintain the confidentiality of information entrusted to them by the Company, its customers, and its vendors and suppliers, except when disclosure is authorized or legally mandated. Confidential information includes all non-public information.

Encouraging the Reporting of Any Illegal or Unethical Behavior

Many areas of the law, such as securities and antitrust, are very complicated. The Company encourages employees to talk to supervisors, managers or other appropriate personnel when in doubt about the best course of action in a particular situation. Additionally, employees should report violations of laws, rules, regulations or the Code of Business Conduct and Ethics to the President of the Company or the subsidiary or an ombudsman appointed for this purpose. There will be no retaliation against anyone who presents this type of information in good faith.

MAKING CONNECTIONS

1. What attitude toward its employees is reflected in Simpson Manufacturing's Code of Business Conduct and Ethics? Is the attitude noticeably different from that evident in the *Handbook to Lowell*?
2. What image of its own status does the Simpson Manufacturing Code present?
3. What might account for the change in employee–employer relations evident in these two documents?

Labor conditions in these early years of the factory system were significantly better than those in English industry, better too than they would ultimately become in much of the United States. The employment of young children created undeniable hardships. But the misery was not as great as in European factories, since working children in America usually remained under the supervision of their parents. In England, by contrast, asylum authorities often hired out orphans to factory owners who showed little concern for their welfare and kept them in something close to slavery.

Even more different from the European labor pattern was the

THE LOWELL SYSTEM

"Lowell System," which relied heavily, indeed almost exclusively, on young unmarried women. In England and other areas of industrial Europe, the conditions of work for women were often horrifyingly bad. A British parliamentary investigation revealed, for example, that women workers in the coal mines endured unimaginably wretched conditions. Some had to crawl on their hands and knees, naked and filthy, through cramped, narrow tunnels, pulling heavy coal carts behind them. It was little wonder that English visitors to America considered the Lowell mills

a female paradise by contrast. The Lowell workers lived in clean boardinghouses and dormitories, which the factory owners maintained for them. They were well fed and carefully supervised. Because many New Englanders considered the employment of women to be vaguely immoral, the factory owners placed great emphasis on maintaining a proper environment for their employees, enforcing strict curfews and requiring regular church attendance. Employers quickly dismissed women suspected of immoral conduct. Wages for the Lowell workers were generous by the standards of the time. The women even found time to write and publish a monthly magazine, the *Lowell Offering*.

Yet even these relatively well-treated workers often found the transition from farm life to factory work difficult, even traumatic. Uprooted from everything familiar, forced to live among

WOMEN WORKERS

strangers in a regimented environment, many women suffered from severe loneliness and disorientation. Still more had difficulty adjusting to the nature of factory work—the repetition of fixed tasks hour after hour, day after day. That the women had to labor from sunrise to sunset was not in itself a new experience;

LOWELL, MASSACHUSETTS, 1832 Lowell was one of the leading manufacturing centers of New England in the 1830s, and one of the largest textile centers in America. Lowell relied heavily on women workers. Company owners—in deference to popular uneasiness about women working outside the home—created a paternalistic system of boardinghouses for them, where they could be carefully supervised. This map shows the clusters of boardinghouses adjacent to groups of factories. Note how concentrated the manufacturing center of the town was, and how the transportation system (rail and water) served the factories. Note also the many churches, which women workers were usually required to attend.

• *What happened to this labor system in the 1840s and 1850s?*

many of them had worked similarly long days on the farm. But that they now had to spend those days performing tedious, unvarying chores, and that their schedules did not change from week to week or season to season, made the adjustment to factory work especially painful. But however uncomfortable women may have found factory work, they had few other options. They were barred from such manual labor as construction or from work as sailors or on the docks. Most of society considered it unthinkable for women to travel the country alone, as many men did, in search of opportunities. Work in the mills was in many cases the only alternative to returning to farms that could no longer support them.

The paternalistic factory system of Lowell did not, in any case, survive for long. In the competitive textile market as it developed in the 1830s and **DECLINE OF THE LOWELL SYSTEM** 1840s—a market prey to the booms and busts that afflicted the American economy as a whole—manufacturers found it difficult to maintain the relatively high living standards and the reasonably attractive working conditions with which they had begun. Wages declined; the hours of work lengthened; the conditions of the boardinghouses deteriorated as the buildings decayed and overcrowding increased.

In 1834, mill workers in Lowell organized a union—the Factory Girls Association—which staged a strike to protest a 25 percent wage cut. Two years later, the association struck again—against a rent increase in the boardinghouses. Both strikes failed, and a recession in 1837 virtually destroyed the organization. Eight years later the Lowell women, led by the militant Sarah Bagley, created the Female Labor Reform Association and began demanding a ten-hour day (some women worked twelve-hour shifts) and for improvements in conditions in the mills. The new association not only made demands of management; it also turned to state government and asked for legislative investigation of conditions in the mills. By then, however, the character of the factory workforce was changing again. The young women who had worked in the mills were gradually moving into other occupations—teaching or domestic service—or marriage. And textile manufacturers were turning to a less contentious labor supply: immigrants.

THE IMMIGRANT WORKFORCE

The rapidly increasing supply of immigrant workers after 1840 was a boon to manufacturers and other entrepreneurs. At last they had access to a source of labor that was both large and inexpensive. These new workers, because of their vast numbers and their unfamiliarity with their new country, had less leverage than the women they at times displaced. As a result, they often

FOUR WOMEN WEAVERS This tintype shows four young women employed in the textile factories of Lowell, Massachusetts. Neatly dressed in matching uniforms, they conveyed the image the factory managers wanted the public to absorb: that women could work in the mills and still be protected from the rough-and-tumble world of industrialization. (American Textile History Museum, Lowell, MA)

encountered far worse working conditions. Construction gangs, made up increasingly of Irish immigrants, performed the heavy, **ECONOMIC ADVANTAGES OF IMMIGRANT LABOR** unskilled work on turnpikes, canals, and railroads under often intolerable conditions. Because most of these workers had no marketable skills and because of native prejudice against them, they received wages so low (and so intermittently, since the work was seasonal and uncertain) that they generally did not earn enough to support their families in even minimal comfort. Many of them lived in flimsy shanties, in grim conditions that endangered the health of their families (and reinforced native prejudices toward the "shanty Irish").

The arrival of Irish workers accelerated the deterioration of working conditions in New England. There was far less social pressure on owners to provide a decent environment for Irish workers than there had been for native women. Employers began paying piece rates (wages tied to how much a worker produced) rather than a daily wage and employed other devices to speed up production and use the labor force more profitably and efficiently. By the mid-1840s, the town of Lowell—once a model for foreign visitors of enlightened industrial development—had become a squalid slum. Similarly miserable working-class neighborhoods were emerging in other northeastern cities.

Conditions were still not as bad as in most factory towns in England and Europe, but in almost all industrial areas, factories themselves were becoming large, noisy, unsanitary, and often dangerous

HARSH WORK
CONDITIONS

places to work. The average workday was extending to twelve, often fourteen hours. Wages were declining, so that even skilled male workers could hope to earn only from $4 to $10 per week, while unskilled laborers were likely to earn only about $1 to $6 per week. Women and children, whatever their skills, also earned less than most men.

THE FACTORY SYSTEM AND THE ARTISAN TRADITION

It was not only the mill workers who suffered from the transition to the modern factory system. It was also the skilled artisans whose trades the factories were displacing. The artisan tradition was as much a part of the older, republican vision of America as the tradition of sturdy, independent, yeoman farmers. Independent craftsmen considered themselves embodiments of the American ideal; they clung to a vision of economic life that was in some ways very different from what the new capitalist class was promoting. Skilled artisans valued their independence; they also valued the stability and relative equality within their economic world.

The factory system threatened that world with obsolescence.

DE-SKILLING

Some artisans made successful transitions into small-scale industry. But others found themselves unable to compete with the new factory-made goods that sold for a fraction of the artisans' prices. In the face of this competition from industrial capitalists, craftsmen began early in the nineteenth century to form organizations—workingmen's political parties and the first American labor unions—to protect their endangered positions and to resist the new economic order. As early as the 1790s, printers and cordwainers (makers of high-quality boots and shoes) took the lead. Members of other skilled trades—carpenters, joiners, masons, plasterers, hatters, and shipbuilders—felt similarly vulnerable.

In such cities as Philadelphia, Baltimore, Boston, and New York, the skilled workers of each craft formed societies for

NATIONAL
TRADE UNIONS

mutual aid. During the 1820s and 1830s, the craft societies began to combine on a citywide basis and set up central organizations known as trade unions. With the widening of markets, the economies of cities were interconnected, so workers soon realized there were advantages in joining forces. They estab-

lished national unions or federations of local ones. In 1834, delegates from six cities founded the National Trades' Union; and in 1836, the printers and the cordwainers set up their own national craft unions.

This early craft union movement fared poorly. Labor leaders struggled against the handicap of hostile laws and hostile courts. The common law, as interpreted by the courts in the industrial states, viewed a combination among workers as, in itself, an illegal conspiracy. The Panic of 1837, a dramatic financial collapse that produced a severe recession, weakened the movement further.

FIGHTING FOR CONTROL

Workers at all levels of the emerging industrial economy attempted to improve their lots. They tried, with little success, to persuade state legislatures to pass laws setting a maximum workday. Two states—New Hampshire in 1847 and Pennsylvania in 1848—actually passed ten-hour laws, limiting the workday unless the workers agreed to an "express contract" calling for more time on the job. Such measures were virtually without impact, however, because employers could simply require prospective employees to sign the "express contract" as a condition of hiring. Three states—Massachusetts, New Hampshire, and Pennsylvania—passed laws regulating child labor. But again, the results were minimal. The laws simply limited the workday to ten hours for children unless their parents agreed to something longer; employers had little difficulty persuading parents to consent to additional hours.

Perhaps the greatest legal victory of industrial workers came in Massachusetts in 1842, when the supreme court of the state,

COMMONWEALTH
V. HUNT

in *Commonwealth v. Hunt*, declared that unions were lawful organizations and that the strike was a lawful weapon. Other state courts gradually accepted the principles of the Massachusetts decision. On the whole, however, the union movement of the 1840s and 1850s remained generally ineffective. Some workers were reluctant to think of themselves as members of a permanent laboring force and resisted joining unions. But even those unions that did manage to recruit significant numbers of industrial workers were usually not large enough or strong enough to stage strikes, and even less frequently strong enough to win them.

Artisans and skilled workers, despite their setbacks in the 1830s, had somewhat greater success than did factory workers. But their unions often had more in common with preindustrial guilds than with modern labor organizations. In most cases, their primary purpose was to protect the favored position of their members in the labor force by restricting admission to the skilled trades. The organizing effort that had floundered in the 1830s revived impressively in the 1850s. Among the new organizations skilled workers created were the National Typographical Union, founded in 1852, the Stone Cutters in 1853, the Hat Finishers in 1854, and the Molders and the Machinists, both in 1859.

Virtually all the early craft unions excluded women, even though female workers were numerous in almost every indus-

FEMALE PROTECTIVE UNIONS

try and craft. As a result, women began establishing their own protective unions by the 1850s, often with the support of middle-class female reformers. Like the male craft unions, the female protective unions had little power in dealing with employers. They did, however, serve an important role as mutual aid societies for women workers.

Despite these persistent efforts at organization and protest, the American working class in the 1840s and 1850s was notable for its relatively modest power. In England, workers were becoming a powerful, united, and often violent economic and political force. They were creating widespread social turmoil and helping to transform the nation's political structure. In America, nothing of the sort happened. Many factors combined to inhibit the growth of effective labor resistance. Among the most impor-

AMERICA'S DIVIDED WORKING CLASS

tant was the flood of immigrant laborers into the country. The newcomers were usually willing to work for lower wages than native workers. Because they were so numerous, manufacturers had little difficulty replacing disgruntled or striking workers with eager immigrants. Ethnic divisions and tensions—both between natives and immigrants and among the various immigrant groups themselves—often led workers to channel their resentments into internal bickering rather than into their shared grievances against employers. There was, too, the sheer strength of the industrial capitalists, who had not only economic but also political and social power and could usually triumph over even the most militant challenges.

"FREE LABOR"

Despite the many obstacles and challenges that faced northern workers in the first half of the nineteenth century, nothing was more important than the idea of personal freedom. Most workers had hard lives, but they were proud of their personal freedoms and considered themselves what some called the "sovereign individual"—people who could, at least in theory, make choices and change their lives.

Modern notions of freedom are much more robust than those of the early nineteenth century, when only a few men (and no women) were able to vote; when workers were sometimes bound to their employers for years; when women were subjugated to their husbands; and when, of course, millions of African Americans were living with almost no freedom. But even in the early years of American history, the belief in the freedom of the individual was strong. In the North in particular, personal liberty was growing exponentially for more and more Americans. By the mid-nineteenth century, most white Americans identified themselves as free individuals, no matter what their occupations or means.

Some of the great philosophers of nineteenth-century America argued that the "independency of the individual" required free people to escape from the market economy and find

freedom in solitude and the wonders of nature—as Henry David Thoreau tried to do in his famous retreat to live alone in a cabin on Walden Pond in Concord, Massachusetts (see pp. 324–325). But for most Americans, the opportunities for solitude and communion with nature were slim. For most northern workers, freedom meant the absence of slavery. It meant that they could leave jobs they did not want, move to new areas of the country, and seek opportunities to change their lives. Their material circumstances were sometimes far worse than those of many slaves in the South. Still, they believed that their lives were better than those who lacked freedom. And when the great debate over slavery began in the 1840s and 1850s, northern laborers—however bad their own lots—abhorred slavery, both because it was the antithesis of freedom and because they feared that slavery threatened the jobs of free laborers.

Not only slaves were denied the freedom that most Americans valued. The more than 200,000 free black men and women living in the North (and a few in the South) remained ineligible to vote and were not considered legal citizens. Many of the free blacks in the North were people who had been skilled crafts workers as slaves and who bought or were given their freedom. But their lots were in many ways worse than when they were working in the South. In the northern cities to which many free blacks moved, there were many white craftsmen already who saw black workers as rivals. Most free blacks worked in menial jobs and as domestic servants.

PATTERNS OF INDUSTRIAL SOCIETY

The industrial revolution made the United States—and particularly its more economically developed regions—dramatically wealthier almost every year. It was also making society more unequal, and it transformed social relationships and everyday life at almost every level—from the workplace to the family.

THE RICH AND THE POOR

The commercial and industrial growth of the United States greatly elevated the average income of the American people. But this increasing wealth was being distributed highly unequally.

INCREASING INEQUALITY IN WEALTH

Substantial groups of the population shared hardly at all in the economic growth: slaves, Indians, landless farmers, and many of the unskilled workers on the fringes of the manufacturing system. But even among the rest of the population, disparities of income were marked. Wealth had always been unequally distributed in the United States, to be sure. Even in the era of the Revolution, according to some estimates, 45 percent of the wealth was concentrated in the hands of about 10 percent of the population. But by the mid-nineteenth century, that concentration had become far more pronounced. In Boston in 1845, for example, 4 percent of the citizens are estimated to have owned more than 65 percent of the wealth; in Philadelphia in 1860, 1 percent of the population possessed more than half the wealth. Among the American people overall in 1860, according to scholarly estimates, 5 percent of the families possessed more than 50 percent of the wealth.

There had been wealthy classes in America almost from the beginning of European settlement. But the extent and character of wealth were changing in response to the commercial revolution of the mid-nineteenth century. Merchants and industrialists were accumulating enormous fortunes; and because there was now a significant number of rich people living in cities, a distinctive culture of wealth began to emerge. In large cities, people of great wealth gathered together in neighborhoods of great opulence. They founded clubs and developed elaborate social rituals. They looked increasingly for ways to display their wealth—in the great mansions they built, the showy carriages in which they rode, the lavish household goods they accumulated, the clothes they wore, the elegant social establishments they patronized. New York, which had more wealthy families than anywhere else, developed a particularly elaborate high society. The construction of the city's great Central Park, which began in the 1850s, was in part a result of pressure from the members of high society, who wanted an elegant setting for their daily carriage rides.

There was also a significant population of genuinely destitute people emerging in the growing urban centers of the nation. These were people who were not merely poor, in the

THE URBAN POOR

NEW YORK, WHICH HAD MORE WEALTHY FAMILIES THAN ANYWHERE ELSE, DEVELOPED A PARTICULARLY ELABORATE HIGH SOCIETY.

sense of having to struggle to sustain themselves—most Americans were poor in that sense. They were almost entirely without resources, often homeless, dependent on charity or crime or both for survival.

Some of these "paupers," as contemporaries called them, were recent immigrants who had failed to find work or to adjust to life in the New World. Some were widows and orphans, stripped of the family structures that allowed most working-class Americans to survive. Some were people suffering from alcoholism or mental illness, unable to work. Others were victims of native prejudice—barred from all but the most menial employment because of race or ethnicity. The Irish were particular victims of such prejudice.

Among the worst off were free blacks. African American communities in antebellum northern cities were small by later standards, but most major urban areas had significant black populations. Some of these African Americans were descendants of families that had lived in the North for generations. Others were former slaves who had escaped from the South or been released by their masters or had bought their freedom; some former slaves, once free, then worked to buy the freedom of relatives left behind. In material terms, at least, life was not always much better for them in the North than it had been in slavery. Most had access only to very menial jobs, which usually paid too little to allow workers to support their families or educate their children; in bad times, many had

AFRICAN AMERICAN POVERTY

THE SHOP AND WAREHOUSE OF DUNCAN PHYFE Duncan Phyfe was a celebrated and (as this watercolor by John Rubens Smith suggests) prosperous furniture maker in New York for many decades, serving the growing population of affluent households in search of refinement and display. The elegant Georgian details on Phyfe's shop on Fulton Street suggest how even places of business were adapting to the new conception of opulence. (The Metropolitan Museum of Art, Rogers Fund, 1922 (22.28.1) Photograph © 1982 The Metropolitan Museum of Art/Art Resource)

CENTRAL PARK To affluent New Yorkers, the construction of the city's great Central Park was important because it provided them with an elegant setting for their daily carriage rides—an activity ostensibly designed to expose the riders to fresh air but that was really an occasion for them to display their finery to their neighbors. (Museum of the City of New York)

access to no jobs at all. In most parts of the North, blacks could not vote, could not attend public schools, indeed could not use any of the public services available to white residents. Most blacks preferred life in the North, however arduous, to life in the South because it permitted them at least some level of freedom.

SOCIAL MOBILITY

One might expect the contrasts between conspicuous wealth and conspicuous poverty in antebellum America to have encouraged more class conflict than actually occurred. But a number of factors operated to limit resentments. For one thing, however much the relative economic position of American workers may have been declining, the absolute living standard of most laborers was improving. Life, in material terms at least, was usually better for factory workers than it had been on the farms or in the European societies from which they had migrated. They ate better, they were often better clothed and housed, and they had greater access to consumer goods.

There was also a significant amount of mobility within the working class, which helped to limit discontent. Opportunities for social mobility, for working one's way up the economic ladder, were relatively modest. A few workers did manage to move

SOCIAL MOBILITY

from poverty to riches by dint of work, ingenuity, and luck—a very small number, but enough to support the dreams of those who watched them. And a much larger number of workers managed to move at least one notch up the ladder—for example, becoming in the course of a lifetime a skilled, rather than an unskilled, laborer. Such people could envision their children and grandchildren moving up even further.

More common than social mobility was geographic mobility, which was even more extensive in the United States than in Europe, where it was considerable. America had a huge expanse of uncultivated land in the West, much of it open for settlement for the first time in the 1840s and 1850s. Some workers saved money, bought land, and moved west to farm it. The historian Frederick Jackson Turner later referred to the availability of western lands as a "safety valve" for discontent, a basic explanation for the relative lack of social conflict in the antebellum United States. But few urban workers, and even fewer poor ones, could afford to make such a move or had the expertise to know how to work land even if they could. Much more common was the movement of laborers from one industrial town to another. Restless, questing, sometimes hopeful, sometimes despairing, these frequently moving people were often the victims of layoffs, looking for better opportunities elsewhere. Their searches may seldom have led to a marked improvement in their circumstances, but the rootlessness of this large segment of the workforce—one of the most distressed segments—made effective organization and protest difficult.

There was, finally, another "safety valve" for working-class discontent: politics. Economic opportunity may not have greatly expanded in the nineteenth century, but opportunities to participate in politics did. And to many white, male working people, access to the ballot seemed to offer a way to help guide their society and to feel like a significant part of their communities.

MIDDLE-CLASS LIFE

For all the visibility of the very rich and the very poor in antebellum society, the fastest-growing group in America was the middle class. The expansion of the middle class was in part a result of the growth of the industrial economy and the increasing commercial life that accompanied it. Economic development opened many more opportunities for people to own or work in businesses, to own shops, to engage in trade, to enter professions, and to administer organizations. In earlier times, when ownership of land had been the only real basis of wealth, society had been divided between people with little or no land (people Europeans generally called peasants) and a landed gentry (which in Europe usually meant an inherited aristocracy). Once commerce and industry became a source of wealth, these rigid distinctions broke down; and many people could become prosperous without owning land, but by providing valuable services to the new economy or by owning capital other than land.

RAPIDLY EXPANDING MIDDLE CLASS

Middle-class life in the years before the Civil War rapidly established itself as the most influential cultural form of urban America. Middle-class families lived in solid and often substantial homes, which, like the wealthy, they tended to own. Workers and artisans were increasingly becoming renters—a relatively new phenomenon in American cities that spread widely in the early nineteenth century.

Middle-class women tended to remain in the home and care for the children and the household, although increasingly they were also able to hire servants—usually young, unmarried immigrant women who put in long hours of arduous work for very little money. One of the aspirations of middle-class women in an age when doing the family's laundry could take an entire day was to escape from some of the drudgery of housework.

New household inventions altered, and greatly improved, the character of life in middle-class homes. Perhaps the most important was the invention of the cast-iron stove, which began to replace fireplaces as the principal vehicle for cooking and also as an important source of heat. These wood- or coal-burning devices were hot, clumsy, and dirty by the standards of the twenty-first century; but compared to the inconvenience and danger of cooking on an open hearth, they

NEW HOUSEHOLD INVENTIONS

seemed a great luxury. Stoves gave cooks more control over the preparation of food and allowed them to cook several things at once.

Middle-class diets were changing rapidly in the antebellum years, and not just because of the wider range of cooking the stove made possible. The expansion and diversification of American agriculture, and the ability of farmers to ship goods to urban markets by rail from distant regions, greatly increased the variety of food available in cities. Fruits and vegetables were difficult to ship over long distances in an age with little refrigeration, but families had access to a greater variety of meats, grains, and dairy products than they had had in the past. A few households acquired iceboxes in the years before the Civil War, and the sight of wagons delivering large chunks of ice to wealthy and middle-class homes began to become a familiar part of urban life. Iceboxes allowed their owners to keep fresh meat and dairy products for as long as several days without spoilage. Most families, however, did not yet have any kind of refrigeration. Preserving food for them meant curing meat with salt and preserving fruits in sugar. Diets were generally much heavier and starchier than they are today, and middle-class people tended to be considerably stouter than would be fashionable in the twenty-first century.

Middle-class homes came to differentiate themselves from those of workers and artisans in other ways as well. They were more elaborately decorated and furnished, with household goods made available for the first time through factory production. Houses that had once had bare walls and floors now had carpeting, wallpaper, and curtains. The spare, simple styles of eighteenth-century homes gave way to the much more elaborate, even baroque household styles of the early Victorian era—styles increasingly characterized by crowded, even cluttered rooms, dark colors, lush fabrics, and heavy furniture and draperies. Middle-class homes also became larger. It became less common for children to share beds and less common for all family members to sleep in the same room. Parlors and dining rooms separate from the kitchen—once a luxury reserved largely for the wealthy—became the norm for the middle class as well. Some urban middle-class homes had indoor plumbing and indoor toilets by the 1850s—a significant advance over the outdoor wells and privies that had been virtually universal only a few years earlier (and that remained common among working-class people).

GROWING CLASS DISTINCTIONS

THE CHANGING FAMILY

The new industrializing society of the northern regions of the United States produced profound changes in the nature and function of the family. At the heart of the transformation was the movement of families from farms to urban areas, where jobs, not land, were the most valued commodities. The patriarchal system of the countryside, whereby fathers controlled their

> ECONOMIC OPPORTUNITY MAY NOT HAVE GREATLY EXPANDED IN THE NINETEENTH CENTURY, BUT OPPORTUNITIES TO PARTICIPATE IN POLITICS DID.

children's futures by controlling the distribution of land to them, could not survive the move to a city or town. Sons and daughters were much more likely to leave the family in search of work than they had been in the rural world.

Another important change was the shift of income-earning work out of the home and into the shop, mill, or factory. In the early decades of the nineteenth century (and for many years before that), the family itself had been the principal unit of economic activity. Family farms, family shops, and family industries were the norm throughout most of the United States. Men, women, and children worked together, sharing tasks and jointly earning the income that sustained the family. But as farming spread to the fertile lands of the Northwest and as the size and

DECLINING ECONOMIC ROLE OF THE FAMILY

profitability of farms expanded, agricultural work became more commercialized. Farm owners in need of labor began to rely less on their families (which often were not large enough to satisfy the demand) and more on hired male workers. These farmhands performed many of the tasks that on smaller farms had once been the jobs of the women and children of the family. As a result, farm women tended to work increasingly at domestic tasks—cooking, sewing, garden-

ing, and dairying—a development that spared them from some heavy labor but that also removed them from the principal income-producing activities of the farm. (See Chapter 11 for a discussion of family relations in the agrarian South.)

In the industrial economy of the rapidly growing cities, there was an even more significant decline in the traditional economic function of the family. The urban household itself became less important as a center of production. Instead, most income earners left home each day to work elsewhere. A sharp distinction began to emerge between the public world of the workplace—the world of commerce and industry—and the private world of the family. The world of the family was now more often dominated not by production, but by housekeeping, child rearing, and other primarily domestic concerns. It was also a world dominated by women.

FALLING BIRTH RATES

Accompanying (and perhaps in part caused by) the changing economic function of the family was a decline in the birth rate. In 1800, the average American woman could be expected to give birth to approximately seven children during her childbearing years. By 1860, the average woman bore five children. The birth rate fell most quickly in urban areas and among

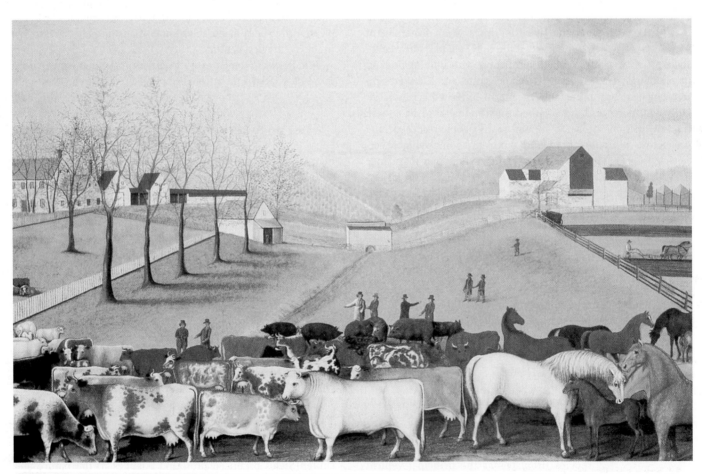

PASTORAL AMERICA, 1848 This painting by the American artist Edward Hicks suggests the degree to which Americans continued to admire the "Peaceable Kingdom" (the name of another, more famous Hicks work) of the agrarian world. Hicks titled this work *An Indian Summer View of the Farm w. Stock of James C. Cornell of Northampton Bucks County Pennsylvania. That Took the Premium in the Agricultural Society, October the 12, 1848.* It portrays the diversified farming of a prosperous Pennsylvania family, shown here in the foreground with their cattle, sheep, and workhorses. In the background stretches a field ready for plowing and another ready for harvesting. (Edward Hicks, The Cornell Farm.

middle-class women. Mid-nineteenth-century Americans had access to some birth-control devices, which undoubtedly contributed in part to the change. There was also a significant rise in abortions, which remained legal in some states until after the Civil War and which, according to some estimates, may have terminated as many as 20 percent of all pregnancies in the 1850s. But the most important cause of the declining birth rate was almost certainly changes in sexual behavior—including increased abstinence.

WOMEN AND THE "CULT OF DOMESTICITY"

The emerging distinction between the public and private worlds, between the workplace and the home, led to increasingly sharp distinctions between the social roles of men and women. Those distinctions affected not only factory workers and farmers, but members of the growing middle class as well. There had, of course, always been important differences between the male and female spheres in American society. Women had long been denied many legal and political rights enjoyed by men; within the family, the husband and father had traditionally ruled, and the wife and mother had generally bowed to his demands and

desires. It had long been practically impossible for most women to obtain divorces, although divorces initiated by men were often easier to arrange. (Men were also far more likely than women to win custody of children in case of a divorce.) In most states, husbands retained almost absolute authority over both the property and persons of their wives. Wife beating was illegal in only a few areas, and the law did not acknowledge that rape could occur within marriage. Women traditionally had very little access to the worlds of business or politics. Indeed, in most communities custom dictated that women never speak in public before mixed audiences.

Most women also had much less access to education than men, a situation that survived into the mid-nineteenth century. Although they were encouraged to attend school at the elementary level, they were strongly discouraged—and in most cases effectively barred—from pursuing higher education. Oberlin in Ohio became the first college in America to accept female students; it permitted four to enroll in 1837, despite criticism that coeducation was a rash experiment approximating free love. Oberlin authorities were confident that "the mutual influence of the sexes upon each other is decidedly happy in the cultivation of both mind & manners." But few other institutions shared

FEMALE EDUCATION

NATHAN HAWLEY AND FAMILY Nathan Hawley, seated at center in this 1801 painting, was typical of many early-nineteenth-century fathers in having a very large family. Nine members are visible here. Hawley at the time was the warden of the Albany County jail in New York, and the painting was by William Wilkie, one of the inmates there. The painting suggests that Hawley was a man of modest but not great means. His family is fashionably dressed, and there are paintings on the walls—signs of style and affluence. But the house is very simply furnished, without drapes for the windows, with a simple painted floor cloth in the front room, and a bare floor in the back. (Nathan Hawley and Family; William Wilkie ca.1801. Albany, New York. Watercolor on Paper; 15 3/4" × 20" Signed lower right: William Wilkie fecit; inscribed in lower margin: NATHAN HAWLEY and FAMILY, Novr. 3d. 1801. Albany Institute of History and Art Purchase 1951.58)

SHAKESPEARE IN AMERICA

PERFORMANCES of Shakespeare began in America as early as 1750, but public interest in his plays reached its peak in the 1830s, 1840s, and 1850s, when theater was the most popular performing art throughout the United States, and Shakespeare the most popular playwright. Many, perhaps most, performances of Shakespearean plays were irreverent, inaccurate, and romanticized. Tragedies were rewritten with happy endings. Comedies were interlaced with contemporary, regional humor. Texts were reworked with American dialect, and plays were abbreviated and sandwiched into programs containing other popular work of the time. So familiar were many Shakespearean plots that audiences took delight in seeing them parodied in productions such as "Julius Sneezer," "Hamlet and Egglet," and "Much Ado About a Merchant of Venice."

People from all walks of life went regularly to the theater and mingled with one another in ways that would become unusual in later eras. Seating was often divided by class—a tier of boxes for the wealthiest patrons, orchestra seats for the middle class, and high balconies for those too poor to sit anywhere else (and for virtually all nonwhite members of the audience). But despite these distinctions, going to the theater was a vibrantly democratic experience.

One result was that American audiences were often noisy, rambunctious, and—at least in the eyes of many actors—obnoxious. Men and women shouted out reactions to the plays, taunted actors, and occasionally—as in an 1832 performance of *Richard III* in New York—climbed onto the stage and joined the performance, mingling with the actors during a battle scene and charging across the stage as if they were soldiers.

The leading Shakespearean actors of the antebellum era became figures of enormous public interest and at times could spur great popular passion. Evidence of that came from events in New York City in 1849. The celebrated American actor Edwin Forrest gave a performance of *Macbeth* on the same evening that a renowned English actor, William Macready, was performing the same play elsewhere in the city. Many New Yorkers believed that the aloof, aristocratic Macready, and through him the city's wealthy elites, were attempting to humiliate Forrest. Forrest supporters crowded into Macready's performance and hooted him off the stage. Three days later, Macready tried again at the Astor Place Opera House. Ten thousand people, most of them Forrest enthusiasts, gathered outside and tried to force their way into the theater. Militia, called out for the occasion, fired into the crowd, killing at least 22 and wounding more than 150. It was one of the bloodiest civil conflicts of the first half of the nineteenth century.

THE PARK THEATER This 1821 watercolor by John Searle shows the interior of the Park Theater in New York, which had recently been rebuilt after a fire. The play is a farce by the English playwright William T. Moncrieff. The faces in the audience are all portraits of real New Yorkers at the time.
(© Collection of the New-York Historical Society)

Shakespeare remained popular throughout the Civil War. In 1864, enthusiastic crowds greeted a performance in New York of *Julius Caesar*, featuring three members of America's most celebrated theatrical family: Junius Brutus

---

their views. Coeducation remained extraordinarily rare until long after the Civil War; and only a very few women's colleges—such as Mount Holyoke, founded in Massachusetts by Mary Lyon in 1837—emerged.

No longer income producers, middle-class women became

NEW ROLES FOR WOMEN

guardians of the "domestic virtues." Their role as mothers, entrusted with the nurturing of the young, seemed more central to the family than it had in the past. And their role as wives—as companions and helpers to their husbands—grew more important as well. Middle-class women also became more important as consumers. They learned to place a high value on keeping a

clean, comfortable, and well-appointed home, on entertaining, and on dressing elegantly and stylishly.

Occupying their own "separate sphere," some women began to develop a distinctive female culture. Friendships among

WOMEN'S SEPARATE SPHERE

women became increasingly intense; women began to form their own social networks (and, ultimately, to form female clubs and associations that were of great importance to the advancement of various reforms). A distinctive feminine literature began to emerge to meet the demands of middle-class women. There were women's magazines, of which the most prominent was *Godey's Lady's Book,* edited after 1837

THE ASTOR PLACE RIOT This later watercolor of the Astor Place riot in 1849 conveys something of the violence and bedlam that the great rivalry between Edwin Forrest and William Macready produced. Here, anti-English mobs demonstrate outside the theater in which the English actor Macready is performing. During the rioting, they set the theater on fire, and the turmoil subsided only when the Seventh Regiment guard was called out. (*The Great Riot at the Astor Place Opera House*, New York, Thursday Evening, May 10, 1849. Published by N. Currier, 1849. Museum of the City of New York, The Harry T. Peters Collection)

THE BOOTHS IN *JULIUS CAESAR* The Booths were America's leading acting family in the 1860s, and this photograph by Mathew Brady captures a rare event: the appearance together in a play of Edwin Booth, the most famous and talented member of the family, and two of his acting brothers, John Wilkes (left, remembered today as Lincoln's assassin but well known at the time as a popular actor) and Junius Brutus Booth Jr. (right). They are performing Shakespeare's *Julius Caesar* in New York. (Library of Congress)

Booth, an aging giant who had been the foremost tragic actor of his generation, and his sons Edwin and John Wilkes. Edwin Booth went on to become America's most revered actor of the last half of the nineteenth century, renowned in particular for his performances of *Hamlet* and other great Shakespearean roles. His brother, John Wilkes, is best remembered for leaping to the stage of Ford's Theater in Washington on April 14, 1865, after having fatally shot Abraham Lincoln. His famous exclamation at the time, "Sic semper tyrannis," was the motto of the state of Virginia. But it was better known as the phrase Brutus supposedly uttered after killing Julius Caesar, an event most familiar to nineteenth-century audiences—and to Booth himself—from performances of Shakespeare's play.

By the end of the nineteenth century, Shakespeare's work was starting to be associated with the educated upper classes. The great Shakespearean actors of these later years had no large followings among workers and ordinary people. They were favorites of the aristocracy, who sought to protect them and the plays they performed from being debased by common audiences they considered incapable of understanding them. A clear distinction had grown up between "high culture," of which Shakespeare was now a part, and "lowbrow culture," from which Shakespeare was gradually excluded. That distinction has survived into our own time. •

UNDERSTAND, ANALYZE, AND EVALUATE

1. What does the Astor Place riot suggest about the theater in mid-nineteenth-century America?

2. In the late nineteenth century, performances of Shakespeare ceased to be "entertainment for the masses" and became instead part of "high culture." What does this shift suggest about American society in general during this period?

3. What public entertainments today have the same widespread appeal—across lines of class, age, and gender—that the performances of Shakespeare had in the mid-nineteenth century?

by Sarah Hale. The magazine scrupulously avoided dealing with public controversies or political issues and focused instead on fashions, shopping and homemaking advice, and other purely domestic concerns. Politics and religion were inappropriate for the magazine, Hale explained in 1841, because "other subjects are more important for our sex and more proper for our sphere."

By the standards of a later era, the increasing isolation of women from the public world seems to be a form of oppression and discrimination. And it is true that few men considered women fit for business, politics, or the professions. On the other hand, most middle-class men—and many middle-class women as well—considered the new female sphere a

BENEFITS AND COSTS

vehicle for expressing special qualities that made women in some ways superior to men. Women were to be the custodians of morality and benevolence, just as the home—shaped by the influence of women—was to be a refuge from the harsh, competitive world of the marketplace. It was women's responsibility to provide religious and moral instruction to their children and to counterbalance the acquisitive, secular impulses of their husbands. Thus the "cult of domesticity," as some scholars have called it, brought both benefits and costs to middle-class women. It allowed them to live lives of greater material comfort than in the past, and it placed a higher value on their "female virtues" and on their roles as wife and mother. At the same time, it left women increasingly detached from the public world, with few outlets for their other interests and energies.

The costs of that detachment were particularly clear among unmarried women of the middle class. By the 1840s, the ideology of domesticity had grown so powerful that few genteel women would any longer consider working (as many had in the past) in shops or mills, and few employers would consider hiring them. But unmarried women nevertheless required some income-producing activity. They had few choices. Some could become teachers or nurses, professions that seemed to call for the same female qualities that made women important within the home; and both of those professions began in the 1840s and 1850s to attract significant numbers of women, although not until the Civil War did females begin to dominate them. Otherwise, unmarried females were largely dependent on the generosity of relatives or hired as governesses for children or companions for widows and other women.

Middle-class people gradually came to consider work by women outside the household to be unseemly, something characteristic of the lower classes—as indeed it was. But working-class women could not afford to stay home and cultivate the "domestic virtues." They had to produce income for their families. They continued to work in factories and mills, but under conditions far worse than those that the original, more "respectable" women workers had once enjoyed. They also frequently found employment in middle-class homes. Domestic service became one of the most frequent sources of female employment. In other words, now that production had moved outside the household, women who needed to earn money had to move outside their own households to do so.

WORKING-CLASS WOMEN

Leisure Activities

Leisure time was scarce for all but the wealthiest Americans in the mid-nineteenth century. Most people worked long hours. Saturday was a normal working day. Vacations—paid or unpaid—were rare. For most people, Sunday was the only respite from work and was generally reserved for religion and rest. Almost no commercial establishments did any business at all on Sunday, and even within the home many families frowned upon playing games or engaging in other kinds of entertainment on the Sabbath. For working-class and middle-class people, therefore, holidays took on a special importance. That was one reason for the strikingly elaborate Fourth of July celebrations throughout the country. The celebrations were not just expressions of patriotism. They were a way of enjoying one of the few holidays from work available to virtually all Americans.

In rural America, where most people still lived, the erratic pattern of farmwork gave many people some relief from the relentless working schedules of city residents. For urban people, however, leisure was something to be seized in what few free moments they had. Men gravitated to taverns for drinking,

talking, and game-playing. Women gathered in one another's homes for conversation, card games, or to share work on such household tasks as sewing. For educated people, whose numbers were rapidly expanding, reading became one of the principal leisure activities. Newspapers and magazines proliferated rapidly, and books—novels, histories, autobiographies, biographies, travelogues, and others—became staples of affluent homes. Women were particularly avid readers, and women writers created a new genre of fiction specifically for females—the "sentimental novel," which often offered idealized visions of women's lives and romances (see pp. 342–343).

There was also a vigorous culture of public leisure, even if many families had to struggle to find time or means to participate in it. In larger cities, theaters were becoming increasingly popular; and while some of them catered to particular social groups, others attracted audiences that crossed class lines. Wealthy people, middle-class people, workers and their families: all could sometimes be found watching a performance of Shakespeare or a melodrama based on a popular novel or an American myth. Minstrel shows—in which white actors mimicked (and ridiculed) African-American culture—became increasingly popular (see pp. 432–433). Public sporting events—boxing, horse racing, cockfighting (already becoming controversial), and others—often attracted considerable crowds. Baseball—not yet organized into professional leagues—was beginning to attract large crowds when played in city parks or fields on the edges of towns (see pp. 392–393). A particularly exciting event in many communities was the arrival of the circus—a traveling entertainment with roots in the middle ages that continued to entertain, delight, and bamboozle children and adults alike.

MINSTREL SHOWS

Popular tastes in public spectacle tended toward the bizarre and the fantastic. Most men and women lived in a constricted world of familiar things. Relatively few people traveled; and in the absence of film, radio, television, or even much photography, they hungered for visions of unusual phenomena that contrasted with their normal experiences. People going to the theater or the circus or the museum wanted to see things that amazed and even frightened them. Perhaps the most celebrated provider of such experiences was the famous and unscrupulous showman P. T. Barnum, who opened the American Museum in New York in 1842—not a showcase for art or nature, but a great freak show populated by midgets (the most famous named Tom Thumb), Siamese twins, magicians, and ventriloquists. Barnum was a genius in publicizing his ventures with garish posters and elaborate newspaper announcements. Only later, in the 1870s, did he launch the famous circus for which he is still best remembered. But he was always a pioneer in exploiting public tastes for the wild and exotic.

P. T. BARNUM

One of the ways Barnum tried to draw visitors to his museum was by engaging lecturers. He did so because he understood that the lecture was one of the most popular forms of entertainment in nineteenth-century America. Men and women flocked in enormous numbers to lyceums (see pp. 366–367), churches, schools, and auditoriums to hear lecturers explain the latest advances in science, to describe their visits to exotic places, to provide vivid historical narratives, or to rail against the evils of alcohol or slavery. Messages of social uplift and reform attracted rapt audiences, particularly among women eager for guidance as they adjusted to the often jarring changes in the character of family life in the industrializing world.

THE AGRICULTURAL NORTH

Even in the rapidly urbanizing and industrializing Northeast, and more so in what nineteenth-century Americans called the Northwest (and what Americans today call the Midwest), most people remained tied to the agricultural world. But agriculture, like industry and commerce, was becoming increasingly a part of the new capitalist economy, linked to the national and international market. Where agriculture could not compete in this new commercial world, it declined. Where it could compete, it simultaneously flourished and changed.

RISE OF COMMERCIAL AGRICULTURE

NORTHEASTERN AGRICULTURE

The story of agriculture in the Northeast after 1840 is one of decline and transformation. The reason for the decline was simple: the farmers of the section could no longer compete with the new and richer soil of the Northwest. Centers of production were gradually shifting westward for many of the farm goods that had in the past been most important to northeastern agriculture: wheat, corn, grapes, cattle, sheep, and hogs.

Some eastern farmers responded to these changes by moving west themselves and establishing new farms. Still others moved to mill towns and became laborers. Some farmers, however, remained on the land and managed to hold their own. As the eastern urban centers increased in population, many farmers turned to the task of supplying food to nearby cities; they raised vegetables (truck farming) or fruit and sold it in local towns. New York, for example, led all other states in apple production.

TRUCK FARMING IN THE NORTHEAST

The rise of cities also stimulated the rise of profitable dairy farming. Approximately half the dairy products of the country were produced in the East; most of the rest came from the West, where Ohio was the leading dairy state. Partly because of the expansion of the dairy industry, the Northeast led other sections in the production of hay. New York was the leading hay state in the nation; Pennsylvania and New England grew large crops as well. The Northeast also exceeded other areas in producing potatoes.

But while agriculture in the region remained an important part of the economy, it was steadily becoming less important than the industrial growth of the Northeast itself. As a result, the rural population in many parts of the Northeast continued to decline.

THE OLD NORTHWEST

There was some industry in the states of the Northwest, more than in the South; and in the two decades before the Civil War, the region experienced steady industrial growth. By 1860, it had 36,785 manufacturing establishments employing 209,909 workers. There was a flourishing industrial and commercial area along the shore of Lake Erie, with Cleveland at its center. Another manufacturing region was in the Ohio River valley; the meatpacking city of Cincinnati was its nucleus. Farther west, the rising city of Chicago, destined to become the great metropolis of the region, was emerging as the national center of the agricultural machinery and meatpacking industries.

INDUSTRIALIZATION IN THE OLD NORTHWEST

Most of the major industrial activities of the West either served agriculture (as in the case of farm machinery) or relied on agricultural products (as in flour milling, meatpacking, whiskey distilling, and the making of leather goods). As this suggests, industry was, on the whole, much less important in the Northwest than farming.

Some areas of the Northwest were not yet dominated by whites. Indians remained the most numerous inhabitants of much of the upper third of the Great Lakes states until after the Civil War. In those areas, hunting and fishing, along with some sedentary agriculture, remained the principal economic activities of both whites and Native Americans. But the tribes did not become integrated into the new commercialized economy that was emerging elsewhere in the Northwest.

For the white (and occasionally black) settlers who populated the lands farther south, the Northwest was primarily an agricultural region. Its rich and plentiful lands made farming a lucrative and expanding activity there, in contrast to the declining agrarian Northeast. Thus the typical citizen of the Northwest was not an industrial worker or poor, marginal farmer, but the owner of a reasonably prosperous family farm. The average size of western farms was 200 acres, the majority of them owned by the people who worked them.

Rising farm prices around the world provided a strong incentive for these western farmers to engage in commercial agriculture. That usually meant concentrating on a single crop for market (corn, wheat, cattle, sheep, hogs, and others). In the early years of white settlement in the Northwest, farm prices rose because of the debilitation of European agriculture in the aftermath of the Napoleonic Wars and the growing urban population (and hence the growing demand for food) of industrializing areas of Europe. The Northwest, with good water routes on the Mississippi for getting its crops to ocean-going vessels, profited from this international trade.

AGRICULTURAL SPECIALIZATION

But industrialization, in both the United States and Europe, provided the greatest boost to agriculture. With the growth of factories and cities in the Northeast, the domestic market for farm goods increased dramatically. The growing national and worldwide demand for farm products resulted in steadily rising farm prices. For most farmers, the 1840s and early 1850s were years of increasing prosperity.

To meet the increasing demand for its farm products, residents of the Northwest worked strenuously, and often frantically, to increase their productive capacities. Many tried to take advantage of the large areas of still uncultivated land and to enlarge the area of white settlement during the 1840s. By 1850, the growing western population was moving into the prairie regions both east and west of the Mississippi: into areas of Indiana, Michigan, Illinois, Missouri, Iowa, and Minnesota. Residents cleared forest lands or made use of fields the Indians had cleared many years earlier. And they began to develop a timber industry to make use of the forests that remained. Wheat was the staple crop of the region, but other crops—corn, potatoes, and oats—and livestock were also important.

The Northwest increased production not only by expanding the area of settlement, but also by adopting new agricultural technologies that greatly reduced the labor necessary for producing a crop and slowed the exhaustion of the region's rich soil. Farmers began to cultivate new varieties of seed, notably Mediterranean wheat, which was hardier than the native type; and they imported better breeds of animals, such as hogs and sheep from England and Spain, to take the place of native stock. Most important were improved tools and farm machines, which American inventors and manufacturers produced in rapidly increasing numbers. During the 1840s, more efficient grain drills, harrows, mowers, and hay rakes came into wide use. The cast-iron plow, an earlier innovation, remained popular because its parts could be replaced when broken. An even better tool appeared in 1847, when John Deere established at Moline, Illinois, a factory to manufacture steel plows, which were more durable than those made of iron.

NEW AGRICULTURAL TECHNOLOGIES

Two new machines heralded a coming revolution in grain production. The most important was the automatic reaper, the invention of Cyrus H. McCormick of Virginia. The reaper enabled one worker to harvest as much wheat (or any other small grain) in a day as five could harvest using older methods. McCormick, who had patented his device in 1834, established a factory at Chicago, in the heart of the grain belt, in 1847. By 1860, more than 100,000 reapers were in use on western farms. Almost as important to the grain grower was the thresher—a machine that separated the grain from the wheat stalks. Threshers appeared in large numbers after 1840. Before that, farmers generally flailed grain by hand (seven bushels a day was a good average for a farm) or used farm animals to tread it (twenty bushels a day on the average). A threshing machine, such as those manufactured by the Jerome I. Case factory in

McCORMICK REAPER

> **❝ I DON'T BELIEVE IN A LAW TO PREVENT A MAN FROM GETTING RICH; IT WOULD DO MORE HARM THAN GOOD. ❞**
>
> **ABRAHAM LINCOLN**

Racine, Wisconsin, could thresh twenty-five bushels or more in an hour.

The Northwest considered itself the most democratic section of the country. But its democracy was based on a defense of economic freedom and the rights of property—a white, middle-class vision of democracy that was becoming common in many other parts of the country as well. Abraham Lincoln, an Illinois Whig, voiced the economic opinions of many of the people of his section. "I take it that it is best for all to leave each man free to acquire property as fast as he can," said Lincoln. "Some will get wealthy. I don't believe in a law to prevent a man from getting rich; it would do more harm than good. . . . When one starts poor, as most do in the race of life, free society is such that he knows he can better his condition; he knows that there is no fixed condition of labor for his whole life."

RURAL LIFE

Life for farming people was very different from life in towns and cities. It also varied greatly from one farming region to another. In the more densely populated farm areas east of the Appalachians and in the easternmost areas of the Northwest, farmers were usually part of relatively vibrant communities and made extensive use of the institutions of those communities—the churches, schools, stores, and taverns. As white settlement moved farther west, farmers became more isolated and had to struggle to find any occasions for contact with people outside their own families.

Religion drew farm communities together perhaps more than any other force, particularly since so many farm areas were populated by people of common ethnic (and therefore religious) backgrounds. Town or village churches were popular meeting places, both for services and for social events—most of them dominated by women. Even in areas with no organized churches, farm families—and, again, women in particular—gathered in one another's homes for prayer meetings, Bible readings, and other religious activities. Weddings, baptisms, and funerals also brought communities together in celebration or mourning.

IMPORTANCE OF RELIGION IN RURAL COMMUNITIES

But religion was only one of many reasons for interaction. Farm people joined together frequently to share tasks that a single family would have difficulty performing on its own; festive barn raisings were among the most frequent. Women prepared large suppers while the men worked on the barn and the children played. Large numbers of families also gathered together at harvest time to help bring in crops, husk corn, or thresh wheat. Women came together to share domestic tasks as well, holding "bees" in which groups of women joined together to make quilts, baked goods, preserves, and other products.

But despite the many social gatherings farm families managed to create, they lived in a world with much less contact with popular culture and public social life than people who lived in towns and cities. Rural people, often even more than urban ones, treasured their links to the outside world—letters from relatives and friends in distant places, newspapers and magazines from cities they had never seen, catalogs advertising merchandise that their local stores never had. Yet many also valued their separation from urban culture and cherished the relative autonomy that farm life gave them. One reason many rural Americans looked back nostalgically on country life once they moved to the city was that they sensed that in the urban world they did not have as much control over the patterns of their daily lives as they had once known.

LOOKING BACK

Between the 1820s and the 1850s, the American economy experienced the beginnings of an industrial revolution—a change so profound that in the United States, as in Europe, it transformed almost every area of life in fundamental ways.

The American industrial revolution was a result of many things: population growth (through both natural increase and immigration), advances in transportation and communication, new technologies that spurred the development of factories capable of mass producing goods, the recruiting of a large industrial labor force, and the creation of corporate bodies capable of managing large enterprises. The new economy created great wealth, expanding the ranks of the wealthy and helping to create a large new middle class. It also created high levels of inequality, which were particularly visible in the growth of a large industrial working class.

Culture in the industrializing areas of the North changed too, and there were important changes in the structure and behavior of the family, in the role of women, and in the way people used their leisure time and encountered popular culture. The changes were often alluring, often disorienting, and often both. They helped widen the gap in experience and understanding between the generation of the Revolution and the generation of the mid-nineteenth century. They also helped widen the gap between North and South. •

SIGNIFICANT EVENTS

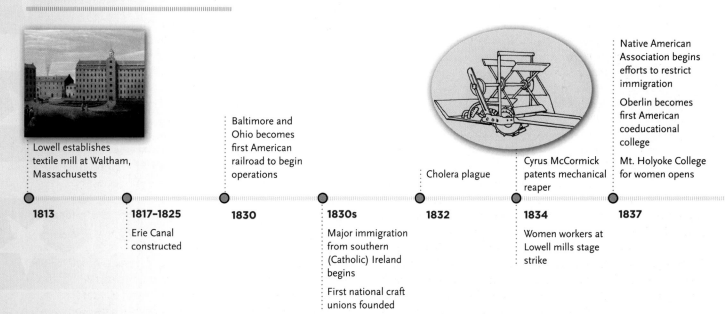

Lowell establishes textile mill at Waltham, Massachusetts

1813

1817–1825
Erie Canal constructed

Baltimore and Ohio becomes first American railroad to begin operations

1830

1830s
Major immigration from southern (Catholic) Ireland begins

First national craft unions founded

Cholera plague

1832

Cyrus McCormick patents mechanical reaper

1834
Women workers at Lowell mills stage strike

Native American Association begins efforts to restrict immigration

Oberlin becomes first American coeducational college

Mt. Holyoke College for women opens

1837

KEY TERMS/PEOPLE/PLACES/EVENTS

RECALL AND REFLECT

1. What were the political responses to immigration in mid-nineteenth-century America? Do you see any parallels to responses to immigration today?

2. Why did the rail system supplant the canal system as the nation's major transportation network?

3. How did the industrial workforce change between the 1820s and the 1840s? What were the effects on American society of changes in the workforce?

4. How did America's industrial revolution and the factory system change family life and women's social and economic roles?

5. How did agriculture in the North change as a result of growing industrialization and urbanization?

Samuel F. B. Morse sends first telegraph message

Rotary press invented, making possible rapid printing of newspapers

Nativists form Supreme Order of the Star-Spangled Banner to oppose immigration

1842

Massachusetts Supreme Court, in *Commonwealth v. Hunt,* declares unions and strikes legal

1844

1845

Irish potato famine begins, spurring major emigration to America

Native American Party formed to combat immigration

Female Labor Reform Association established at Lowell

1846

1847

John Deere begins manufacturing steel plows

1848

Failed revolution in Germany spurs emigration to America

1850

1852

American Party (Know-Nothings) formed

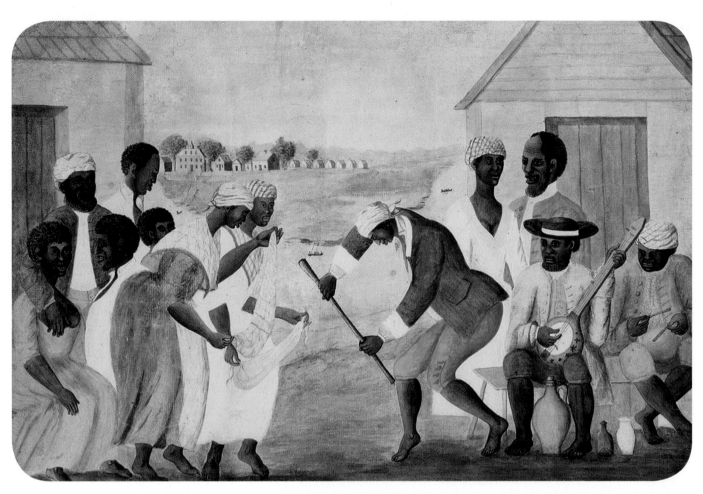

THE OLD PLANTATION This painting, by an unidentified folk artist of the early nineteenth century, suggests the importance of music in the lives of plantation slaves in America. The banjo, which the black musician at right is playing, was originally an African instrument. (The Granger Collection, New York)

11 COTTON, SLAVERY, AND THE OLD SOUTH

THE SOUTH, LIKE THE NORTH, EXPERIENCED DRAMATIC growth in the middle years of the nineteenth century. Southerners fanned out into the territories of the Southwest and established new communities, new states, and new markets. The southern agricultural economy grew increasingly productive and increasingly prosperous. Trade in such staples as sugar, rice, tobacco, and above all cotton made the South a major force in international commerce and created substantial wealth within the region. It also tied the South securely to the emerging capitalist world of the United States and its European trading partners.

Yet despite its expansion and growth, the South experienced a much less fundamental transformation in these years than did the North. The South had

SETTING THE STAGE

begun the nineteenth century a primarily agricultural region; it remained overwhelmingly agrarian in 1860. It had begun the century with few important cities and little industry; so it remained sixty years later. In 1800, a plantation system dependent on slave labor had dominated the southern economy; by 1860, that system had only strengthened its grip on the region. As the South grew and expanded, it became increasingly unlike the North and increasingly sensitive to what it considered to be threats to its distinctive way of life. One historian has written, "The South grew, but it did not develop."

❝ THE SOUTH GREW, BUT IT DID NOT DEVELOP. ❞

LOOKING AHEAD

1. How did slavery shape the southern economy and society, and how did it make the South different from the North?
2. What was the myth and what was the reality of white society in the South? Why was the myth so pervasive and widely believed?
3. How did slaves resist their enslavement? How successful were their efforts? What was the response of whites?

THE COTTON ECONOMY

The most important economic development in the mid-nineteenth-century South was the shift of economic power from the "upper South" (the original southern states along the Atlantic coast) to the "lower South" (the expanding agricultural regions in the new states of the Southwest). That shift reflected above all the growing dominance of cotton in the southern economy.

THE RISE OF KING COTTON

Much of the upper South continued in the nineteenth century to rely, as it always had, on the cultivation of tobacco. But the market for that crop was notoriously unstable. Tobacco prices were subject to frequent depressions, including a prolonged one that began in the 1820s and extended

DECLINE OF THE TOBACCO ECONOMY

into the 1850s. Tobacco also rapidly exhausted the land on which it grew; it was difficult for most growers to remain in business in the same place for very long. By the 1830s, therefore, many farmers in the old tobacco-growing regions of Virginia, Maryland, and North Carolina were shifting to other crops—notably wheat—while the center of tobacco cultivation was moving westward, into the Piedmont area.

The southern regions of the coastal South—South Carolina, Georgia, and parts of Florida—continued to rely on the cultivation of rice, a more stable and lucrative crop. Rice, however, demanded substantial irrigation and needed an exceptionally long growing season (nine months), so cultivation of that staple remained restricted to a relatively small area. Sugar growers along the Gulf Coast, similarly, enjoyed a reasonably profitable market for their crop. But sugar cultivation required intensive (and debilitating) labor and a long growing time. Only relatively wealthy planters could afford to engage in it, and they faced major competition from the great sugar plantations of the Caribbean. Sugar cultivation, therefore, did not spread much beyond a small area in southern Louisiana and eastern Texas. Long-staple (Sea Island) cotton was another lucrative crop, but like rice and sugar, it could grow only in a limited area—the coastal regions of the Southeast.

The decline of the tobacco economy in the upper South, and the limits of the sugar, rice, and long-staple cotton economies farther south, might have forced the region to shift its attention in the nineteenth century to other nonagricultural pursuits, had it not been for the growing importance of a new product that

SHORT-STAPLE COTTON

soon overshadowed all else: short-staple cotton. This was a hardier and coarser strain of cotton that could grow successfully in a variety of climates and in a variety of soils. It was harder to process than the long-staple variety; its seeds were more difficult to remove from the fiber. But the 1793 invention of the cotton gin (see pp. 191–192) had largely solved that problem.

Demand for cotton was growing rapidly. The growth of the textile industry in Britain in the 1820s and 1830s, and in New England in the 1840s and 1850s, created an enormous new demand for the crop. As a result, ambitious men and women rapidly moved into previously uncultivated lands—many of them newly open to planter settlement after the relocation of the tribes in the 1820s and 1830s—to establish new cotton-growing regions.

Beginning in the 1820s, therefore, cotton production spread rapidly. From the western areas of South Carolina and Georgia, production moved steadily westward—first into Alabama and Mississippi, then into northern Louisiana, Texas, and Arkansas. By the 1850s, cotton had become the linchpin of the southern

THE NEW ORLEANS COTTON EXCHANGE Edgar Degas, the French impressionist, painted this scene of cotton traders examining samples in the New Orleans cotton exchange in 1873. By this time the cotton trade was producing less impressive profits than those that had made it the driving force of the booming southern economy of the 1850s. Degas' mother came from a Creole family of cotton brokers in New Orleans, and two of the artist's brothers (depicted here reading a newspaper and leaning against a window) joined the business in America. (Giraudon/Art Resource)

economy. In 1820, the South had produced about 500,000 bales of cotton. By 1850 it was producing nearly 3 million bales a year, and by 1860 nearly 5 million. There were periodic fluctuations in cotton prices, resulting generally from overproduction; periods of boom frequently gave

SPREAD OF COTTON PRODUCTION

way to abrupt busts. But the cotton economy continued to grow, even if in fits and starts. By the time of the Civil War, cotton constituted nearly two-thirds of the total export trade of the United States and was bringing in nearly $200 million a year. The annual value of the rice crop, in contrast, was $2 million. It was little wonder that southern politicians now proclaimed: "Cotton is king!"

Cotton production dominated the more recently settled areas of what came to be known as the "lower South" (or, in a later era, the "Deep South"). Many people began to call this region the "Cotton Kingdom." Settlement of the area resembled in some ways the rush of gold seekers to a new strike. The prospect of tremendous profits from growing cotton drew white settlers to the lower South by the thousands. Some were wealthy planters from the older states who transferred their assets and slaves to a cotton plantation. Most were small slaveholders or slaveless farmers who hoped to move into the planter class.

A similar shift, if an involuntary one, occurred in the slave

EXPANSION OF SLAVERY

population. Between 1820 and 1860, the number of slaves in Alabama leaped from 41,000 to 435,000, and in Mississippi from 32,000 to 436,000. In the same period, the increase in Virginia was only from 425,000 to 490,000. Between 1840 and 1860, according to some estimates, 410,000 slaves moved from the upper South to the cotton states—either accompanying masters who were themselves migrating to the Southwest or (more often) sold to planters already there. Indeed, the sale of slaves to the Southwest became an important economic activity in the upper South and helped the troubled planters of that region compensate for the declining value of their crops.

SOUTHERN TRADE AND INDUSTRY

In the face of this booming agricultural expansion, other forms of

WEAK MANUFACTURING SECTOR

economic activity developed slowly in the South. The business classes of the region—the manufacturers and merchants—were not unimportant. There was growing activity in flour milling and in textile and iron manufacturing, particularly in the upper South. The Tredegar Iron Works in Richmond, for example, compared favorably with the best iron mills in the Northeast. But industry remained an insignificant force in comparison with the agricultural

66 **COTTON IS KING!** 99

66 **FROM THE RATTLE WITH WHICH THE NURSE TICKLES THE EAR OF THE CHILD BORN IN THE SOUTH TO THE SHROUD THAT COVERS THE COLD FORM OF THE DEAD, EVERYTHING COMES TO US FROM THE NORTH.** 99

ALBERT PIKE

economy. The total value of southern textile manufactures in 1860 was $4.5 million—a threefold increase over the value of those goods twenty years before, but only about 2 percent of the value of the raw cotton exported that year.

To the degree that the South developed a nonfarm commercial sector, it was largely to serve the needs of the plantation economy. Particularly important were the brokers, or "factors," who marketed the planters' crops. These merchants tended to live in such towns as New Orleans, Charleston, Mobile, and Savannah, where they worked to find buyers for cotton and other crops and where they purchased goods for the planters they served. The South had only a very rudimentary financial system, and the factors often also served the planters as bankers, providing them with credit. Planters frequently accumulated substantial debts, particularly during periods when cotton prices were in decline; and the southern merchant-bankers thus became figures of considerable influence and importance in the region. There were also substantial groups of professional people in the South—lawyers, editors, doctors, and others. In most parts of the region, however, they too were closely tied to and dependent on the plantation economy. However important manufacturers, merchants, and professionals might have been to southern society, they were relatively unimportant in comparison with the manufacturers, merchants, and professionals of the North, on whom southerners were coming more and more (and increasingly unhappily) to depend.

The primitive character of the region's banking system

INADEQUATE REGIONAL TRANSPORTATION SYSTEM

matched a lack of development in other basic services and structures necessary for industrial development. Perhaps most notable was the South's inadequate transportation system. In the North in the antebellum period, enormous sums were invested in roads, canals, and above all railroads to knit the region together into an integrated market. In the South there were no such investments. Canals were almost nonexistent; most roads were crude and unsuitable for heavy transport; and railroads, although they expanded substantially in the 1840s and 1850s, failed to tie the region together effectively. Such towns as Charleston, Atlanta, Savannah, and Norfolk had direct connections with Memphis, and thus with the Northwest; and Richmond was connected, via the Virginia Central, with the Memphis and Charleston Railroad. In addition, several independent lines furnished a continuous connection between the Ohio River and New Orleans. Most of the South, however, remained unconnected to the national railroad system. Most lines in the region were short and local. The principal means of transportation was water. Planters generally shipped their crops to market along rivers or by sea; most manufacturing was in or near port towns.

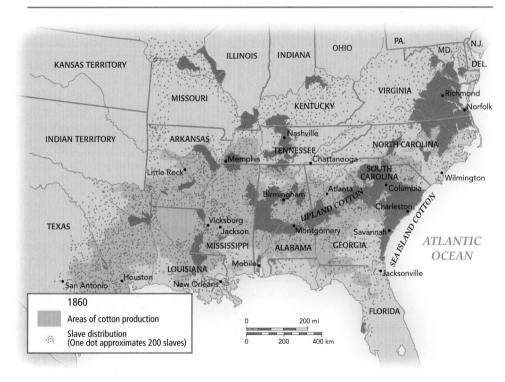

SLAVERY AND COTTON IN THE SOUTH, 1820 AND 1860 These two maps show the remarkable spread of cotton cultivation in the South in the decades before the Civil War. Both maps show the areas of cotton cultivation (the green-colored areas) as well as areas with large slave populations (the brown-dotted areas). Note how in the top map, which represents 1820, cotton production is concentrated largely in the East, with a few areas scattered among Alabama, Mississippi, Louisiana, and Tennessee. Slavery is most concentrated along the Georgia and South Carolina coast, areas in which long-staple cotton was grown, with only a few other areas of highly dense slave populations. By 1860, the South had changed dramatically. Cotton production had spread throughout the lower South, from Texas to northern Florida, and slavery had moved with it. Slavery was also much denser in the tobacco-growing regions of Virginia and North Carolina, which had also grown.

• *How did this economic shift affect the white South's commitment to slavery?*

Perceptive southerners recognized the economic subordination of their region to the North. "From the rattle with which the nurse tickles the ear of the child born in the South to the shroud that covers the cold form of the dead, everything comes to us from the North." the Arkansas journalist Albert Pike lamented. Perhaps the most prominent advocate of southern economic independence was James B. D. De Bow, a resident of New Orleans. He published a magazine advocating southern commercial and agricultural expansion, *De Bow's Review,* which survived from its founding in 1846 until 1880. De Bow made his journal into a tireless advocate of southern economic independence from the North, warning constantly of the dangers of the "colonial" relationship between the sections. One writer noted in the pages of his magazine: "I think it would be safe to estimate the amount which is lost to us annually by our vassalage to the

DE BOW'S REVIEW

PLANTATIONS IN LOUISIANA, 1858 This map provides a detailed view of plantation lands along a stretch of the Mississippi River between New Orleans and Baton Rouge, Louisiana. Note the long, narrow shapes of these landholdings—known as "long lots." This system was designed to give as many planters as possible frontage on the river, which they needed to transport their crops to market and to receive goods in return. The river also deposited rich soil on the lands near its banks, which made cultivation of crops easier. Note how towns, stores, and churches all are near the riverbank, so planters and others living on plantations nearby could reach them easily by boat.

• *How is this landscape different from that of the newly opened federal lands in the West?*

North at $100,000,000. Great God!" Yet *De Bow's Review* was itself evidence of the dependency of the South on the North. It was printed in New York, because no New Orleans printer had facilities adequate for the task; it was filled with advertisements from northern manufacturing firms; and its circulation was always modest in comparison with those of northern publications. In Charleston, for example, it sold an average of 173 copies per issue; *Harper's Magazine* of New York, in contrast, regularly sold 1,500 copies to South Carolinians.

SOURCES OF SOUTHERN DIFFERENCE

Despite this growing concern about the region's "colonial dependency," the South made few serious efforts to build an economy that might challenge its dependency. An important question about antebellum southern history, therefore, is why the region did so little to develop a larger industrial and commercial economy of its own. Why did it remain so different from the North?

Part of the reason was the great profitability of the region's agricultural system, particularly of cotton production. In the Northeast, many people had turned to manufacturing as the agricultural economy of the region declined. In the South, the agricultural economy was booming, and ambitious people eager to profit from the emerging capitalist economy had little incentive to look beyond it. Another reason was that wealthy southerners had so much capital invested in their land and, particularly, their slaves that they had little left for other investments. Some historians have suggested that the southern climate—with its long, hot, steamy summers—was less suitable for industrial development than the climate of the North. Still others have claimed that southern work habits (perhaps a reflection of the debilitating effects of the climate) impeded industrialization; some white southerners appeared—at least to many northern observers—not to work very hard, to lack the strong work ethic that fueled northern economic development.

REASONS FOR COLONIAL DEPENDENCY

But the southern failure to create a flourishing commercial or industrial economy was also in part the result of a set of values distinctive to the South that discouraged the growth of cities and industry. Many white southerners liked to think of themselves as representatives of a special way of life: one based on traditional values of chivalry, leisure, and elegance. White southerners were, they argued, "cavaliers"—people happily free from the base, acquisitive instincts of the "yankees" to their north. Southern white people were, they believed, more concerned with a refined and gracious way of life than with rapid growth and development. Appealing as the "cavalier" image was to southern whites, however, it conformed to the reality of southern society in very limited ways.

THE CAVALIER IMAGE

WHITE SOCIETY IN THE SOUTH

Only a small minority of southern whites owned slaves. In 1850, when the total white population of the South was over 6 million, the number of slaveholders was only 347,525. In 1860, when the white population was just above 8 million, the number of slaveholders had risen to only 383,637. These figures are somewhat misleading, since each slaveholder was normally the head of a family averaging five members. But even with all members of slaveowning families included in the figures, those owning slaves still amounted to perhaps no more than one-quarter of the white population. And of the minority of whites holding slaves, only a small proportion owned them in substantial numbers.

THE PLANTER CLASS

How, then, did the South come to be seen—both by the outside world and by many southerners themselves—as a society dominated by great plantations and wealthy landowning planters? In large part, it was because the planter aristocracy—the cotton magnates, the sugar, rice, and tobacco nabobs, the whites who owned at least forty or fifty slaves and 800 or more acres—exercised power and influence far in excess of their numbers. They stood at the apex of society, determining the political, economic, and even social life of their region. Enriched by vast annual incomes, dwelling in palatial homes, surrounded by broad acres and many black servants, they became a class to which all other southerners deferred. The wealthiest planters also maintained homes in towns or cities and spent several months of the year there, engaged in a glittering social life. Others traveled widely, especially to Europe, as an antidote to the isolation of plantation life. And many used their plantations to host opulent social events.

PLANTER ARISTOCRACY

White southerners liked to compare their planter class to the old upper classes of England and Europe: true aristocracies, long entrenched. In fact, however, the southern upper class was in most cases not at all similar to the landed aristocracies of the Old World. In some areas of the upper South—the Tidewater region of Virginia, for example—some of the great aristocrats were indeed people whose families had occupied positions of wealth and power for generations. In most of the South, however, a long-standing landed aristocracy, although central to the "cavalier" image, was largely a myth. Even the most important planters in the cotton-growing areas of the South were, typically, new to their wealth and power. As late as the 1850s, many of the great landowners in the lower South were still first-generation settlers, who had arrived with only modest resources, struggled for years to clear land and develop a plantation in what was at first a rugged wilderness, and only relatively recently had started to live in the comfort and luxury for which they became famous. Large areas of the "Old South" (as Americans later called the South of the pre–Civil War era) had been settled and cultivated for less than two decades at the time of the Civil War.

Nor was the world of the planter nearly as leisured and genteel as the "cavalier" myth would suggest. Growing staple crops was a business that was in its own way just as competitive and just as risky as the industrial enterprises of the North. Planters had to supervise their operations carefully if they hoped to make a profit. They were, in many respects, just as much competitive capitalists as the industrialists of the North whose lifestyles they claimed to hold in contempt. Even many affluent planters lived rather modestly, their wealth so heavily invested in land and slaves that there was little left for personal comfort. And white planters, even some substantial ones, tended to move frequently as new and presumably more productive areas opened up to cultivation.

PLANTATION MANAGEMENT

Indeed, it may have been the very newness and precariousness of the plantation way of life, and the differences between the reality of that life and the image of it, that made many southern planters determined to portray themselves as genteel aristocrats. Having struggled so hard to reach and maintain their positions, they were all the more determined to defend them. Perhaps that was why the defense of slavery and of the South's "rights" was stronger in the new, booming regions of the lower South and weaker in the more established and less flourishing areas of the Tidewater.

Wealthy southern whites sustained their image of themselves as aristocrats in many ways. They avoided such "coarse" occupations as trade and commerce; those who did not become planters often gravitated toward the military, a "suitable" career for men raised in a culture in which medieval knights (as portrayed in the novels of Walter Scott) were a powerful and popular image. The aristocratic ideal also found reflection in the definition of a special role for southern white women.

ARISTOCRATIC VALUES

"HONOR"

Above all, perhaps, white males adopted an elaborate code of chivalry, which obligated them to defend their "honor," often through dueling—which survived in the South long after it had largely vanished in the North. Southern white males placed

A GEORGIA PLANTATION This map of the Hopeton Plantation in Georgia shows both how much plantations were connected to the national and world markets, and how much they tried to be self-sufficient. Note the large areas of land devoted to the growing of cotton, rice, and sugarcane, all of them crops for the market. Note also the many crops grown for the local market or for consumption by residents of the plantation—potatoes, vegetables, corn, and others. The top left of the map shows the distribution of living quarters, with slaves' quarters grouped together very near the owner's residence.

• Why would a plantation in this part of the South be so much more diversified in the market crops it raised than the cotton plantations in the Mississippi Delta?
• Why would planters want their slaves living nearby? Why might slaves be unhappy about being so close to their owners?

enormous stock in conventional forms of courtesy and respect in their dealings with one another—perhaps as a way of distancing themselves from the cruelty and disrespect that were so fundamental to the slave system they controlled. Violations of such forms often brought what seemed to outsiders a disproportionately heated and even violent response.

The idea of honor in the South was only partly connected to the idea of ethical behavior and bravery. It was also tied to the importance among white males of the public appearance of dignity and authority—of saving face in the presence of others. Anything that seemed to challenge the dignity, social station, or "manhood" of a white southern male might be the occasion for a challenge to duel, or at least for a stern public rebuke. When the South Carolina congressman Preston Brooks strode into the chamber of the United States Senate and savagely beat Senator Charles Sumner of Massachusetts with a cane to retaliate for what he considered an insult to a relative, he was acting wholly in accord with the idea of southern honor. In the North, he was reviled as a savage. In the South, he became a popular hero. But

Brooks was only the most public example of a code of behavior that many white southern men followed. Avenging insults was a social necessity in many parts of southern society, and avenging insults to white southern women was perhaps the most important obligation of a white southern "gentleman."

CULT OF
HONOR

THE "SOUTHERN LADY"

In some respects, affluent white women in the South occupied roles very similar to those of middle-class white women in the North. Their lives generally centered in the home, where they served as companions to and hostesses for their husbands and as nurturing mothers for their children. Even less frequently than in the North did "genteel" southern white women engage in public activities or find income-producing employment.

But the life of the "southern lady" was also in many ways very different from that of her northern counterpart. For one thing,

ST. JOHN PLANTATION, LOUISIANA This Greek Revival "big house" of the St. John Plantation in St. Martin Parish, Louisiana, still stands today. In 1861, when the artist Adrien Persac painted this view, it occupied the center of a 5,000-acre sugar plantation and was the setting of the self-consciously elegant life of the planter and his family. To the right is a brick sugar factory and the cabins of the plantation's slaves, who performed the arduous work of sugar harvesting and production. (Louisiana State University Museum of Art)

SUBORDINATE STATUS OF WOMEN

the cult of honor in the region meant in theory that southern white men gave particular importance to the "defense" of women. In practice, this generally meant that white men were even more dominant and white women even more subordinate in southern culture than they were in the North. George Fitzhugh, one of the South's most important social theorists, wrote in the 1850s: "Women, like children, have but one right, and that is the right to protection. The right to protection involves the obligation to obey."

More important in determining the role of southern white women, however, were the social and economic realities in which they lived. The vast majority of females in the region lived on farms, relatively isolated from people outside their own families, with virtually no access to the "public world" and thus few opportunities to look beyond their roles as wives and mothers. Because the family was the principal economic unit on most farms, the dominance of husbands and fathers

66 WOMEN, LIKE CHILDREN, HAVE BUT ONE RIGHT, AND THAT IS THE RIGHT TO PROTECTION. THE RIGHT TO PROTECTION INVOLVES THE OBLIGATION TO OBEY. 99

GEORGE FITZHUGH

over wives and children was even greater than in those northern families in which income-producing activities had moved out of the home and into the factory or office. For many white women, living on farms of modest size meant a fuller engagement in the economic life of the family than was becoming typical for middle-class women in the North. These women engaged in spinning, weaving, and other production; they participated in agricultural tasks; they helped supervise the slave workforce. On some of the larger plantations, however, even these limited roles were sometimes considered unsuitable for white women; and the "plantation mistress" became, in some cases, more an ornament for her husband than an active part of the economy or the society.

Southern white women also had less access to education than their northern counterparts. Nearly a quarter of all white women over twenty were completely illiterate; relatively few women had more than a rudimentary exposure to schooling. Even wealthy planters were not much interested in

CLEAR STARCHING IN LOUISIANA This 1837 etching by Auguste Hervieu offers a strikingly unromanticized view of plantation women in the South. The white plantation mistress, soberly dressed, speaks harshly to two black household servants, presumably criticizing the way they are doing the laundry. The slaves cower, carefully hiding whatever resentment they might feel behind a submissive pose. Nothing in this picture suggests anything like the kind of ease and luxury often associated with plantation life in popular mythology at the time and since. (General Research Division, New York Public Library, Astor, Lenox and Tilden Foundations)

extensive schooling for their daughters. The few female "academies" in the South trained women primarily to be suitable wives.

Southern white women had other special burdens as well.
OTHER BURDENS The southern white birth rate remained nearly 20 percent higher than that of the nation as a whole, and infant mortality in the region remained higher than elsewhere; nearly half the children born in the South in 1860 died before they reached five years of age. The slave labor system had a mixed impact on white women. It helped spare many of them from certain kinds of arduous labor, but it also threatened their relationships with their husbands. Male slaveowners had frequent sexual relationships with the female slaves on their plantations; the children of those unions became part of the plantation labor force and served as a constant reminder to white women of their husbands' infidelity. Black women (and men) were obviously the most important victims of such practices. But white women suffered too.

A few southern white women rebelled against their roles and against the prevailing assumptions of their region. Some became outspoken abolitionists and joined northerners in the crusade to abolish slavery. Some agitated for other reforms within the South itself. Most white women, however, found few outlets for whatever discontent they may have felt with their lives. Instead, they generally convinced themselves of the benefits of their position and—even more fervently than southern white men—defended the special virtues of the southern way of life. Upper-class white women in the South were particularly

> THE NEW FEMALE "ACADEMIES" IN THE SOUTH TRAINED WOMEN PRIMARILY TO BE SUITABLE WIVES.

energetic in defending the class lines that separated them from poorer whites.

THE PLAIN FOLK

The typical white southerner was not a great planter and slaveholder, but a modest yeoman farmer. Some of these "plain folk," as they have become known, owned a few slaves, with whom they worked and lived far more closely than did the larger planters. Most (in fact, three-quarters of all white families) owned no slaves. Some plain folk, most of whom owned their own land, devoted themselves largely to subsistence farming; others grew cotton or other crops for the market, but usually could not produce enough to allow them to expand their operations or even get out of debt. During the 1850s, the number of nonslaveholding landowners increased much faster than the number of slaveholding landowners. While there were occasional examples of poor farmers moving into the ranks of the planter class, such cases were rare. Most yeomen knew that they had little prospect of substantially bettering their lot.

One reason was the southern educational system, which provided poor whites with few opportunities to learn and thus limited their chances of advancement. For the sons of wealthy planters, the region provided ample opportunities to gain an education. In 1860 there were 260 southern colleges and universities, public and private, with 25,000 students enrolled in them,
LIMITED EDUCATIONAL OPPORTUNITIES or more than half the total number of students in the United States. But universities were within the reach of only the upper class. The elementary and secondary schools of the South were not only fewer but also inferior to those of the Northeast (although not much worse than the crude schools of the Northwest), and a higher proportion of whites were illiterate than in other parts of the country.

That a majority of the South's white population consisted of modest farmers largely excluded from the dominant plantation society raises another important question about the antebellum South. Why did the plain folk have so little power in the public world of the Old South? Why did they not oppose the aristocratic social system in which they shared so little? Why did they not resent the system of slavery, from which they generally did not benefit?

Some nonslaveowning whites did oppose the planter elite, but for the most part in limited ways and in a relatively few, isolated areas. These were southern highlanders, the "hill people,"
HILL PEOPLE who lived in the Appalachian ranges east of the Mississippi, in the Ozarks to the west of the river, and in other "hill country" or "backcountry" areas cut off from the commercial world of the plantation system. Of all southern whites, they were the most isolated from the mainstream of the region's life. They practiced a simple form of subsistence agriculture, owned practically no slaves, and had a proud sense of seclusion. They were, in most respects,

unconnected to the new commercial economy that dominated the great cotton-planting region of the South. They produced almost no surplus for the market, had little access to money, and often bartered for the goods they could not grow themselves.

To such men and women, slavery was unattractive for many of the same reasons it was unappealing to workers and small farmers in the North: because it threatened their sense of their own independence. Hill country farmers lived in a society defined by individual personal freedom and unusual isolation from modern notions of property. They also held to older political ideals, which for many included the ideal of fervent loyalty to the nation as a whole.

Such whites frequently expressed animosity toward the planter aristocracy of the other regions of the South. The mountain region was the only part of the South to defy the trend toward sectional conformity, and it was the only part to resist the movement toward secession when it finally developed. Even during the Civil War itself, many hill country southerners refused to support the Confederacy; some went so far as to fight for the Union.

Far greater in number, however, were the nonslaveowning whites who lived in the midst of the plantation system. Many, perhaps most of them, accepted that system because they were

CLOSE
RELATIONS WITH
THE PLANTATION
ARISTOCRACY

tied to it in important ways. Small farmers depended on the local plantation aristocracy for many things: access to cotton gins, markets for their modest crops and their livestock, credit or other financial assistance in time of need. In many areas, there were also extensive kinship networks linking lower- and upper-class whites. The poorest resident of a county might easily be a cousin of the richest aristocrat. Taken together, these mutual ties helped mute what might otherwise have been pronounced class tensions.

Small farmers felt tied to the plantation society in other ways as well. For white men, at least, the South was an unusually democratic society, in the sense that participation in politics—both through voting and through attending campaign meetings and barbecues—was even more widespread than in the North, where participation was also high. Just as political participation gave workers in the North a sense of connection to the social order, so it did for farmers in the South—even though officeholders in the South, even more than in the North, were almost always members of the region's elites. In the 1850s, moreover, the boom in the cotton economy allowed many small farmers to improve their economic fortunes. Some bought more land, became slaveowners, and moved into at least the fringes of plantation society. Others simply felt more secure in their positions as independent yeomen and hence more likely to embrace the fierce regional loyalty that was spreading throughout the white South in these years.

Small farmers, even more than great planters, were also committed to a traditional, male-dominated family structure. Their household-centered economies required the participation of all family members and, they believed, a stable system of

COMMITMENT
TO
PATERNALISM

gender relations to ensure order and stability. Men were the unquestioned masters of their homes; women and children, who were both family and workforce, were firmly

under the master's control. As the northern attack on slavery increased in the 1840s and 1850s, it was easy for such farmers to believe—and easy for ministers, politicians, and other propagandists for slavery to persuade them—that an assault on one hierarchical system (slavery) would open the way to an assault on another such system (patriarchy).

There were other white southerners, however, who did not share in the plantation economy in even limited ways and yet continued to accept its premises. These were the members of a particularly degraded class—numbering perhaps a half million in 1850—known to other classes variously and demeaningly as "crackers," "sand hillers," or "poor white trash" (a phrase used as a chapter title in Harriet Beecher Stowe's *Uncle Tom's Cabin*). Occupying the infertile lands of the pine barrens, the red hills, and the swamps, they lived in miserable cabins amid genuine destitution. Many owned no land (or owned land on which virtually nothing could be grown) and supported themselves by foraging or hunting. Others worked at times as common laborers for their neighbors, although the slave system limited their opportunities. Their degradation resulted partly from dietary deficiencies and disease. Some resorted at times to eating clay (hence the tendency of affluent whites to refer to them disparagingly as "clay eaters"); and they suffered from pellagra, hookworm, and malaria. Planters and small farmers alike held them in contempt. They formed a true underclass. In some material respects, their plight was worse than that of the African American slaves (who themselves often looked down on the poor whites).

Yet, even among these southerners—the true outcasts of white society in the region—there was no real opposition to the

LIMITED CLASS
CONFLICT

plantation system or slavery. In part, undoubtedly, this was because these men and women were so benumbed by poverty that they had little strength to protest. But their relative passivity resulted also from perhaps the single greatest unifying factor among the southern white population, the one force that was most responsible for reducing tensions among the various classes: their perception of race. However poor and miserable these white southerners might have been, they could still consider themselves members of a ruling race; they could still look down on the black population of the region and feel a bond with their fellow whites born of a determination to maintain their racial supremacy. As Frederick Law Olmsted, a northerner who visited the South and chronicled southern society in the 1850s, wrote: "From childhood, the one thing in their condition which has made life valuable to the mass of whites has been that the niggers are yet their inferiors."

SLAVERY: THE "PECULIAR INSTITUTION"

White southerners often referred to slavery as the "peculiar institution." By that they meant not that the institution was odd, but that it was distinctive, special. The description was apt, for American slavery was indeed distinctive. The South in the mid-nineteenth century was the only area in the Western world—except for Brazil, Cuba, and Puerto Rico—where slavery still existed. Slavery, more than any other single factor, isolated the South from the rest of American society. And as that isolation increased, so did the commitment of southerners to defend the institution.

Within the South itself, the institution of slavery had paradoxical results. On the one hand, it isolated blacks from whites, drawing a sharp and inviolable racial line dividing one group of southerners from another. As a result, African Americans under slavery began to develop a society and culture of their own, one in many ways unrelated to the white civilization around them. On the other hand, slavery created a unique bond between blacks and whites—masters and slaves—in the South. The two groups may have maintained separate spheres, but each sphere was deeply influenced by, indeed dependent on, the other.

VARIETIES OF SLAVERY

Slavery was an institution established and regulated in detail by law. The slave codes of the southern states forbade slaves to hold property, to leave their masters' premises without permission, to be out after dark, to congregate with other slaves except at church, to carry firearms, or to strike a white person, even in self-defense. The codes of some states prohibited whites from teaching slaves to read or write and denied slaves the right to

LEGAL BASIS OF SLAVERY

testify in court against white people. The laws contained no provisions to legalize slave marriages or divorces. If an owner killed a slave while punishing him, the act was generally not considered a crime. Slaves, however, faced the death penalty for killing or even resisting a white person and for inciting revolt. The codes also contained extraordinarily rigid provisions for de-

fining a person's race. Anyone with even a trace of African ancestry was defined as black. And anyone even rumored to possess any such trace was presumed to be black unless he or she could prove otherwise—which was, of course, almost impossible to do.

These and dozens of other restrictions might seem to suggest that slaves lived under a uniformly harsh and dismal regime. Had the laws been rigidly enforced, that might have been the case. In fact, however, enforcement was spotty and uneven. Some slaves did acquire property, did learn to read and write, and did assemble with other slaves, in spite of laws to the contrary. Although the major slave offenses generally fell under the jurisdiction of the courts (and thus of the slave codes), white owners handled most

REALITY OF SLAVERY

transgressions and inflicted widely varying punishments. In other words, despite the rigid provisions of law, there was in reality considerable variety within the slave system. Some blacks lived in almost prisonlike conditions, rigidly and harshly controlled by their masters. Many (probably most) others enjoyed some flexibility and (at least in comparison to the regimen prescribed by law) a significant degree of autonomy.

Most masters possessed very few slaves, and their experience with (and image of) slavery was a reflection of the special nature of slavery on the small farm. White farmers with few slaves generally supervised their workers directly and often worked closely alongside them. On such farms, blacks and whites developed a form of intimacy unknown on larger plantations. The paternal relationship between such masters and their slaves could, like relationships between fathers and children, be warm and affectionate. It could also be tyrannical and cruel. In either case, it was a relationship based on the relative powerlessness of the slaves.

Although the majority of slaveowners were small farmers, the majority of slaves lived on plantations of medium or large size, with sizable slave workforces. Substantial planters often

HAULING THE WHOLE WEEKS PICKING This watercolor by William Henry Brown, painted in approximately 1842, portrays a slave family loading cotton onto a wagon, presumably after a hard day of picking. Even young children participate in the chores. Brown was an artist known for his silhouettes, a form popular in the nineteenth century. (One of his later subjects was Abraham Lincoln.) This picture, however, is part of a five-foot cutout he made as a gift to a family he was visiting. (Historic New Orleans Collection)

hired overseers and even assistant overseers to represent them. "Head drivers," trusted and responsible slaves often assisted by several subdrivers, acted under the overseer as foremen.

Larger planters generally used one of two methods of assigning slave labor. One was the task system (most common in rice culture), under which slaves were assigned a particular task in the morning, for example, hoeing one acre; after completing the job, they were free for the rest of the day. The other, far more common, was the gang system (employed on the cotton, sugar, and tobacco plantations), under which slaves were simply divided into groups, each of them directed by a driver, and compelled to work for as many hours as the overseer considered a reasonable workday.

TASK AND GANG SYSTEMS

LIFE UNDER SLAVERY

Slaves generally received at least enough necessities to enable them to live and work. Their masters usually furnished them with an adequate, if mostly coarse, diet, consisting mainly of cornmeal, salt pork, molasses, and on special occasions fresh meat or poultry. Many slaves cultivated gardens for their own use. They received cheap clothing and shoes. They lived in crude cabins, called slave quarters, usually clustered together in a complex near the master's house. The plantation mistress or a doctor retained by the owner provided some medical care; but slave women themselves—as "healers" and midwives, or simply as mothers—were the more important source.

Slaves worked hard, beginning with light tasks as children. Their workdays were longest at harvest time. Slave women worked particularly hard. They generally labored in the fields with the men, and they assumed as well the crucial chores traditionally reserved for women—cooking, cleaning, and child rearing. Because slave families were often divided, with husbands and fathers frequently living on neighboring plantations (or, at times, sold to plantation owners far away), black women often found themselves acting in effect as single parents. Within the slave family, therefore, women had special burdens but also a special authority.

SPECIAL POSITION OF WOMEN

Slaves were, as a group, much less healthy than southern whites. After 1808, when the international slave trade became illegal in America, the proportion of blacks to whites steadily declined. In 1820, there was one African American to every four whites; in 1840, one to every five. The slower increase of the black population was a result of its comparatively high death rate. Slave mothers had large families, but the enforced poverty in which virtually all African Americans lived ensured that fewer of their children would survive to adulthood than the children of white parents. Even those who did survive typically died at a younger age than the average white person.

HIGH SLAVE MORTALITY RATES

Even so, according to some scholars, the actual material conditions of slavery may have been better than those of some northern factory workers and better than those of both peasants and industrial workers in much of nineteenth-century Europe.

The conditions of American slaves were certainly less severe than those of slaves in the Caribbean and South America crops, which required more arduous labor. Sugar production in the Caribbean islands, in particular, involved extraordinarily back-breaking work and a high risk of fatal tropical diseases. Caribbean and South American planters continued to use the African slave trade well into the nineteenth century to replenish their labor supply, so they had less incentive than American planters (who no longer had access to that trade) to protect their existing laborers. Growing cotton, the principal activity for most slaves in the United States, was much less debilitating than growing sugar; and planters had strong economic incentives to maintain a healthy slave population. One result of this was that America became the only country where a slave population actually increased through natural reproduction (although it grew much more slowly than the white population).

Most masters did make some effort to preserve the health—and thus the usefulness—of their slaves. One example was the frequent practice of protecting slave children from hard work until early adolescence. Masters believed that doing so would

NURSING THE MASTER'S CHILD Louisa, a slave on a Missouri plantation owned by the Hayward family in the 1850s, is photographed here holding the master's infant son. Black women typically cared for white children on plantations, sometimes with great affection and sometimes—as this photograph may suggest—dutifully and without enthusiasm. (Missouri Historical Society)

THE CHARACTER OF SLAVERY

NO issue in American history has produced a richer literature or a more spirited debate than the nature of American slavery. The debate began even before the Civil War, when abolitionists strove to expose slavery to the world as a brutal, dehumanizing institution, while southern defenders of slavery tried to depict it as a benevolent, paternalistic system. But by the late nineteenth century, as historian David Blight noted in *Race and Reunion* (2002), with white Americans eager for sectional conciliation, both northern and southern chroniclers of slavery began to accept a romanticized and unthreatening picture of the Old South and its "peculiar institution."

The first major scholarly examination of slavery was Ulrich B. Phillips's *American Negro Slavery* (1918), which portrayed slavery as an essentially benign institution in which kindly masters looked after submissive, childlike, and generally contented African Americans. Phillips's apologia for slavery remained the authoritative work on the subject for nearly thirty years.

Challenges to Phillips began to emerge in the 1940s, as concern about racial injustice increasingly engaged the attention of white Americans. In 1941, Melville J. Herskovits challenged Phillips's contention that black Americans retained little of their African cultural inheritance. In 1943, Herbert Aptheker published a chronicle of slave revolts as a way of refuting Phillips's claim that blacks were submissive and content.

A somewhat different challenge to Phillips emerged in the 1950s from historians who emphasized the brutality of the institution. Kenneth Stampp's *The Peculiar Institution* (1956) and Stanley Elkins's *Slavery* (1959) described a labor system that did serious physical and psychological damage to its victims. Stampp, and especially Elkins, portrayed slavery as something like a prison, in which men and women had virtually no space in which to develop their own social and cultural lives.

In the 1970s, new scholarship on slavery focused on slaves' striking success in building a culture of their own despite their enslavement. John Blassingame in 1973 argued that "the most remarkable aspect of the whole process of enslavement is the extent to which the American-born slaves were able to retain their ancestors' culture." Herbert Gutman, in *The Black Family in Slavery and Freedom* (1976), challenged the prevailing belief that slavery had weakened and even destroyed the African American family. On the contrary, he argued, the black family survived slavery with impressive strength. Eugene Genovese's *Roll, Jordan, Roll* (1974) and other works revealed how African Americans manipulated the paternalist assumptions at the heart of slavery to build a large cultural space of their own within the system where they could develop their own family life, social traditions, and reli-

---

make young slaves more loyal and would also ensure better health as adults. Another example was the use of hired labor, when available, for the most unhealthy or dangerous tasks. A traveler in Louisiana noted, for example, that Irishmen were employed to clear malarial swamps and to handle cotton bales at the bottom of chutes extending from the river bluff down to a boat landing. If an Irish worker died of disease or in an accident, a master could hire another for a dollar a day or less. But a master would lose an investment of perhaps $1,000 or more if a prime field hand died. Still, cruel masters might forget their pocketbooks in the heat of anger. Slaves were often left to the discipline of overseers, who had less of an economic stake in their well-being; overseers were paid in proportion to the amount of work they could get out of the slaves they supervised.

Household servants had a somewhat easier life—physically at least—than did field hands. On a small plantation, the same slaves might do both field work and housework. But on a large estate, there would generally be a separate domestic staff: nursemaids, housemaids, cooks, butlers, coachmen. These people lived close to the master and his family, eating the leftovers from the family table and in some cases even sleeping in the "big house." Between the blacks and whites of such households affectionate, almost familial relationships might sometimes develop. More often,

HOUSE SLAVES

however, house servants resented their isolation from their fellow slaves and the lack of privacy that came with living in such close proximity to the master's family. Among other things, that proximity meant that their transgressions were more visible than those of field hands, and so they received punishments more often than did other slaves. When emancipation came after the Civil War, it was often the house servants who were the first to leave the plantations of their former owners.

Female household servants were especially vulnerable to sexual abuse by their masters and white overseers, who sometimes pressured them into supposedly consensual sexual relationships and sometimes raped them. In addition to unwanted sexual attention from white men, female slaves often received vindictive treatment from white women. Plantation mistresses naturally resented the sexual liaisons between their husbands and female slaves. Punishing their husbands was not usually possible, so they often punished the slaves instead—with arbitrary beatings, increased workloads, and various forms of psychological torment.

SEXUAL ABUSE

SLAVERY IN THE CITIES

The conditions of slavery in the cities differed significantly from those in the countryside. On relatively isolated plantations, slaves

Recent works by Walter Johnson and Ira Berlin mark at least a partial return to the "damage" thesis. In *Soul by Soul* (2000), a study of the New Orleans slave market, Johnson contends that for whites, purchasing slaves was a way of fulfilling the middle-class fantasy of success and independence, but for the slaves themselves the trade was destructive and dehumanizing. Ira Berlin's *Many Thousands Gone* (2000), *Generation of Captivity* (2003), and *The Making of African America* (2010) similarly emphasize the dehumanizing character of the slave market and argue that slavery was less a social system than a commodification of human beings. •

UNDERSTAND, ANALYZE, AND EVALUATE

1. Why have scholarly studies of slavery interpreted the system so differently? Do the differing interpretations reflect general social attitudes of the period in which the studies were written?
2. Why might the conclusions drawn by Robert Fogel and Stanley Engerman in *Time on the Cross* have provoked vehement criticism?
3. What might be some reasons for the resurgence of focus on the "damage" thesis of slavery, as in the works by Walter Johnson and Ira Berlin?

gious patterns. That same year, Robert Fogel and Stanley Engerman published their controversial *Time on the Cross*, a highly quantitative study that supported some of the claims of Gutman and Genovese about black achievement, but that went much further in portraying slavery as a successful and reasonably humane (if ultimately immoral) system. Slave workers, they argued, were better treated and lived in greater comfort than most northern industrial workers of the same era.

Other scholarship on slavery has focused on the role of women within it. Elizabeth Fox-Genovese's *Within the Plantation Household* (1988) examined the lives of both white and black women on the plantation. Rejecting the claims of some feminist historians that black and white women shared a common female identity born of their shared subordination to men, she portrayed slave women as defined by their dual roles as members of the plantation workforce and anchors of the black family.

had little contact with free blacks and lower-class whites, and masters maintained fairly direct and effective control; a deep and seemingly unbridgeable chasm yawned between slavery and freedom. In the city, however, a master often could not supervise his slaves closely and at the same time use them profitably. Even if they slept at night in carefully watched backyard barracks, slaves moved about during the day alone, performing errands of various kinds. Thus urban slaves gained numerous opportunities to mingle with free blacks and with whites. In the cities, the line between slavery and freedom became increasingly indistinct.

There was a considerable market in the South for common laborers, particularly since, unlike in the North, there were few European immigrants to perform menial chores. Even the poorest whites tended to prefer working on farms to doing ordinary labor, and so masters often hired out slaves for such tasks. Slaves on contract worked in mining and lumbering (often far from cities); but others worked on the docks and on construction sites, drove wagons, and performed other unskilled jobs in cities and towns. Slave women and children worked in the region's few textile mills. Particularly skilled workers such as blacksmiths or carpenters were also often hired out.

AUTONOMY OF URBAN SLAVES

Many white southerners considered slavery to be incompatible with city life, and as southern cities grew the number of slaves in them declined, relatively if not absolutely. Fearing conspiracies and insurrections, many urban slaveowners sold off much of their male property to the countryside. The remaining black women outnumbered black men. The same cities also had more white men than women—a situation that helped account for the birth of many mulattoes. Even while slavery in the cities was declining, the forced segregation of urban blacks, both free and slave, from white society increased. Segregation was a means of social control intended to make up for the loosening of the discipline of slavery itself in urban areas.

FREE AFRICAN AMERICANS

There were about 250,000 free African Americans in the slaveholding states by the start of the Civil War, more than half of them in Virginia and Maryland. In some cases, they were slaves who had somehow earned money with which they managed to buy their own and their families' freedom, usually by developing a skill they could market independently of their masters. It was

> MANY WHITE SOUTHERNERS CONSIDERED SLAVERY TO BE INCOMPATIBLE WITH CITY LIFE.

usually urban blacks, with their greater freedom of movement and activity, who could take that route. One example was Elizabeth Keckley, a slave woman who bought freedom for herself and her son with proceeds from sewing. She later became a seamstress, personal servant, and companion to Mary Todd Lincoln in the White House. But few masters had any incentive, or inclination, to give up their slaves, so this route was open to relatively few people.

Some slaves were sometimes set free by a master who had moral qualms about slavery, or by a master's will after his death—for example, the more than 400 slaves belonging to John Randolph of Roanoke, freed in 1833. From the 1830s on, however, state laws governing slavery became more rigid. That was

TIGHTENED RESTRICTIONS ON FREE BLACKS

in part a response to the fears Nat Turner's revolt (see p. 314) created among white southerners: free blacks, removed from close supervision by whites, might generate more violence and rebellion than slaves. It was also in part because the community of free blacks in southern cities was becoming larger and, to whites, more threatening—a dangerous example to blacks still in slavery. The rise of abolitionist agitation in the North—and the fear that it would inspire slaves to rebel—also persuaded southern whites to tighten their system. The new laws made it more and more difficult, and in some cases practically impossible, for owners to set free (or "manumit") their slaves; all southern states forbade free African Americans from entering. Arkansas even forced the freed slaves living there to leave.

A few free blacks (generally those on the northern fringes of the slaveholding regions) attained wealth and prominence. Some owned slaves themselves, usually relatives whom they had bought in order to ensure their ultimate emancipation. In a few cities—New Orleans, Natchez, Charleston—free black communities managed to flourish relatively unmolested by whites and with some economic stability. Most free blacks, however, lived in abject poverty, under conditions worse than those of African Americans in the North. Law or custom closed many occupations to them, forbade them to assemble without white supervision, and placed numerous other restraints on them. They were only quasi-free, but they had all the burdens of freedom: the necessity to support themselves, to find housing, to pay taxes. Yet, great as were the hardships of freedom, these blacks preferred them to slavery.

THE SLAVE TRADE

The transfer of slaves from one part of the South to another was one of the most important and terrible consequences of the development of the Southwest. Sometimes slaves moved

SLAVE MARKETS

to the new cotton lands in the company of their original owners, who were migrating themselves. More often, however, the transfer occurred through the medium of professional slave traders. Traders transported slaves over long distances on trains or on river or ocean steamers. On shorter journeys, the slaves moved on foot, trudging in coffles of hundreds along dusty highways—

THE BUSINESS OF SLAVERY The offices of slave dealers were familiar sights on the streets of pre–Civil War southern cities and towns. They provide testimony to the way in which slavery was not just a social system, but a business, deeply woven into the fabric of southern economic life. (*Library of Congress*)

just as their ancestors had marched to the ports in Africa from which they had embarked to America. Eventually they arrived at some central market such as Natchez, New Orleans, Mobile, or Galveston, where purchasers gathered to bid for them. At the auction, the bidders checked the slaves like livestock, watching them as they were made to walk or trot, inspecting their teeth, feeling their arms and legs, looking for signs of infirmity or age. Some traders tried to deceive buyers by blacking gray hair, oiling withered skin, and concealing physical defects in other ways. A sound young field hand would fetch a price that, during the 1840s and 1850s, varied from $500 to $1,700, depending mainly on fluctuations in the price of cotton. An attractive, sexually desirable woman might bring much more.

The domestic slave trade, essential to the growth and prosperity of the whole system, was also one of its most horrible aspects. The trade dehumanized all who were involved in it. It separated children from parents, and parents from each other. Even families kept together by scrupulous masters might be broken up in the division of the estate after the master's death. Planters might deplore the trade, but they eased their consciences by holding the traders in contempt and assigning them a low social position.

The foreign slave trade was as bad or worse. Although federal law had prohibited the importation of slaves from 1808 on, some

THE FOREIGN SLAVE TRADE

continued to be smuggled into the United States as late as the 1850s. The numbers can only be estimated. There were not enough such imports to satisfy all planters, and the southern commercial conventions, which met annually to consider means of making the South economically independent, began to discuss the legal reopening of the trade. "If it is right to buy slaves in Virginia and carry them to New Orleans," William L. Yancey of Alabama asked his fellow delegates at the 1858 meeting, "why is it not right to buy them in Cuba, Brazil, or Africa and carry them there?" The convention that year voted to recommend the repeal of all laws against slave imports, but the repeal never occurred. Within the South, only the delegates from the states of the upper South, which profited from the domestic trade, opposed the foreign competition.

The continued smuggling of slaves was not without resistance. In 1839, a group of 53 slaves in Cuba took charge of a ship, the *Amistad,* that was transporting them to another port in Cuba. Their goal was to sail back to their homelands in Africa. The slaves had no experience with sailing, and they tried to compel the crew to steer them across the Atlantic. Instead, the ship sailed up the Atlantic coast until it was captured by a ship of the United States Revenue Service. Many Americans, including President Van Buren, thought the slaves should be returned to Cuba. But at the request of a group of abolitionists, former president John Quincy Adams went before the Supreme Court to argue that they should be freed. Adams argued that the foreign slave trade was illegal and thus the *Amistad* rebels could not be

returned to slavery. The Court accepted his argument in 1841, and most of the former slaves were returned to Africa, with funding from American abolitionists.

Two years later, another group of slaves revolted on board a ship and took control of it—this time an American vessel bound from Norfolk, Virginia, to New Orleans—and steered it (and its 135 slaves) to the British Bahamas, where slavery was illegal and the slaves were given sanctuary. Such shipboard revolts were rare, but they were symbols of the continued effort by Africans to resist slavery.

SLAVE RESISTANCE

Few issues have sparked as much debate among historians as the effects of slavery on the blacks themselves. (See "Debating the Past," pp. 310–311.) Slaveowners, and many white Americans after emancipation, liked to argue that the slaves were generally content, "happy with their lot." That may well have been true in some cases. But it is clear that the vast majority of southern blacks were not content with being slaves, that they yearned for freedom even though most realized there was little they could do to secure it. Evidence for that conclusion can be found, if

HARRIET TUBMAN WITH ESCAPED SLAVES Harriet Tubman (c. 1820–1913) was born into slavery in Maryland. In 1849, when her master died, she escaped to Philadelphia to avoid being sold out of state. Over the next ten years, she assisted first members of her own family and then up to 300 other slaves to escape from Maryland to freedom. During the Civil War, she served alternately as a nurse and as a spy for Union forces in South Carolina. She is shown here, on the left, with some of the slaves she had helped to free. (Sophia Smith Collection, Smith College)

nowhere else, from the reaction of slaves when emancipation finally came. Virtually all reacted to freedom with joy and celebration; relatively few chose to remain in the service of the whites who had owned them before the Civil War (although most African Americans remained for many years subservient to whites in one way or another).

Rather than contented acceptance, the dominant response of blacks to slavery was a complex one: a combination of adaptation and resistance. At the extremes, slavery could produce two very different reactions, each of which served as the basis for a powerful stereotype in white society. One extreme was what became known as the "Sambo"—the shuffling, grinning, head-scratching, deferential slave who acted out the role that he recognized the white world expected of him. More often than not, the "Sambo" pattern of behavior was a charade, a façade assumed in the presence of whites. The other extreme was the slave rebel—the African American who could not bring himself or herself to either acceptance or accommodation but remained forever rebellious. Actual slave revolts were extremely rare, but the knowledge that they were possible struck terror into the hearts of white southerners everywhere. In 1800, Gabriel Prosser gathered 1,000 rebellious slaves outside Richmond; but two Africans gave the plot away, and the Virginia militia stymied the uprising before it could begin. Prosser and thirty-five others were executed. In 1822, the Charleston free black Denmark Vesey and his followers—rumored to total 9,000—made preparations for revolt; but again word leaked out, and suppression and retribution followed. In 1831, Nat Turner, a slave preacher, led a band of African Americans who armed themselves with guns and axes and, on a summer night, went from house to house in Southampton County, Virginia. They killed sixty white men, women, and children before being overpowered by state and federal troops. More than a hundred blacks were executed in the aftermath. Nat Turner's was the only actual large-scale slave insurrection in the nineteenth-century South, but fear of slave conspiracies and renewed violence pervaded the section as long as slavery lasted.

PROSSER AND TURNER REBELLIONS

For the most part, however, resistance to slavery took other, less drastic forms such as running away. A small number managed to escape to the North or to Canada, especially after sympathetic whites began organizing the so-called underground railroad to assist them in flight. But the odds against a successful escape, particularly from the Deep South, were almost impossibly high. The hazards of distance and the slaves' ignorance of geography were serious obstacles. So were the white "slave patrols," which stopped wandering blacks on sight throughout the South demanding to see travel permits. Without such a permit, slaves were presumed to be runaways and were taken captive. Slave patrols often employed bloodhounds to track African Americans who attempted to escape

ACTUAL SLAVE REVOLTS WERE EXTREMELY RARE, BUT THE KNOWLEDGE THAT THEY WERE POSSIBLE STRUCK TERROR INTO THE HEARTS OF WHITE SOUTHERNERS EVERYWHERE.

through the woods. Despite all the obstacles to success, however, blacks continued to run away from their masters in large numbers. Some did so repeatedly, undeterred by the whippings and other penalties inflicted on them when captured.

But perhaps the most important method of resistance was simply a pattern of everyday behavior by which blacks defied their masters. That whites so often considered blacks to be lazy and shiftless suggests one means of resistance: refusal to work hard.

Some slaves stole from their masters or from neighboring whites. Some performed isolated acts of sabotage: losing or breaking tools (southern planters gradually began to buy unusually heavy hoes because so many of the lighter ones got broken) or performing tasks improperly. Many African Americans resisted by building into their normal patterns of behavior subtle methods of rebellion.

SLAVE RESISTANCE

THE CULTURE OF SLAVERY

Resistance was only part of the slave response to slavery. Another was an elaborate process of adaptation. The process did not imply contentment with bondage. It represented a recognition that there was no realistic alternative. One of the ways blacks adapted was by developing their own, separate culture, one that enabled them to sustain a sense of racial pride and unity.

LANGUAGE AND MUSIC

In many areas, slaves retained a language of their own, sometimes incorporating African speech patterns into English. Having arrived in America speaking many different African languages, the first generations of slaves had as much difficulty communicating with one another as they did with white people. To overcome these barriers, they learned a simple, common language (known to linguists as "pidgin"). It retained some African words, but it drew primarily, if selectively, from English. And while slave language grew more sophisticated as blacks spent more time in America—and as new generations grew up never having known African tongues—some features of this early pidgin survived in black speech for many generations.

PIDGIN

Music was especially important in slave society. In some ways, it was as important to African Americans as language. Most important were voices and song. Field workers often used songs to pass the time in the fields; since they sang them in the presence of whites, they usually attached relatively innocuous words to them. But African Americans also

IMPORTANCE OF SLAVE SPIRITUALS

created more emotionally rich and politically challenging music in the relative privacy of their religious services. It was there that the tradition of the spiritual emerged in the early nineteenth century.

AFRICAN AMERICAN RELIGION

A separate slave religion was not supposed to exist. Almost all African Americans were Christians by the early nineteenth century. Some had converted voluntarily, and some were coerced by their masters and by the Protestant missionaries who evangelized among them. Masters expected their slaves to worship under the supervision of white ministers. Indeed, autonomous black churches were banned by law; and many slaves became members of the same denominations as their owners—usually Baptist or Methodist. In the 1840s and 1850s, as slavery expanded in the South, missionary efforts increased. Vast numbers of African Americans became members of Protestant churches in those years.

Nevertheless, blacks throughout the South developed their own version of Christianity, at times incorporating into it such

> IN THEIR PRAYERS AND SONGS AND SERMONS, BLACK CHRISTIANS TALKED AND SANG OF THE DAY WHEN THE LORD WOULD "CALL US HOME," "DELIVER US TO FREEDOM," "TAKE US TO THE PROMISED LAND."

practices as voodoo or other polytheistic religious traditions of Africa. Or they simply bent religion to the special circumstances of bondage. Natural leaders emerging within the slave community rose to the rank of preacher.

African American religion was often more emotional than that of its white counterparts and reflected the influence of African customs and practices. Slave prayer meetings routinely involved fervent chanting, spontaneous exclamations from the congregation, and ecstatic conversion experiences. Black religion was also more joyful and affirming than that of many white denominations. And above all, African American religion emphasized the dream of freedom and deliverance. In their prayers and songs and sermons, black Christians talked and sang of the day when the Lord would "call us home," "deliver us to freedom," "take us to the Promised Land." And while their white masters generally chose to interpret such language merely as the expression of hopes for life after death, many African Americans themselves used the images of Christian salvation to express their own dream of freedom in the present world. Christian images, and biblical injunctions, were central to Gabriel Prosser, Denmark Vesey, Nat Turner, and others who planned or engaged in open resistance to slavery.

SLAVE RELIGION

In cities and towns in the South, some African Americans had their own churches, where free blacks occasionally worshiped alongside slaves. In the countryside, however, slaves usually attended the same churches as their masters—sometimes a chapel on the plantation itself, sometimes a church serving a larger farm community. Seating in such churches was usually segregated. Slaves sat in the rear or in balconies. They held their own services later, often in secret, usually at night.

SLAVES AT REST This photograph of a group of slaves resting in front of their cabins on a plantation in the 1850s is relatively unusual. It shows both the modesty of their homes and the domesticity that slaves created for themselves. (Fotosearch/Getty Images)

THE SLAVE FAMILY

The slave family was the other crucial institution of black culture in the South. Like religion, it suffered from certain legal restrictions—most notably the lack of legal marriage. Nevertheless, what we now call the "nuclear family" consistently emerged as the dominant kinship model among African Americans.

Such families did not always operate according to white customs. Black women generally began bearing children at younger ages than most whites, often as early as age fourteen or fifteen. Slave communities did not condemn premarital pregnancy in the way white society did, and African American couples would often begin living together before marrying. It was customary, however, for couples to marry—in a ceremony involving formal vows—soon after conceiving a child. Often, marriages occurred between slaves living on neighboring

SLAVE MARRIAGES

THE SLAVES' MUSIC

FOR African Americans living as slaves on southern plantations, there was little leisure time—and little opportunity for the kinds of cultural activities that were beginning to appeal to other groups of Americans. But slaves managed nevertheless to create a culture of their own. And among its most distinctive and pervasive features was music.

Indeed, to white observers at least, nothing was more striking about slave life than the role music played within it. African Americans sang frequently, sometimes alone, even more often in groups. They sang while they worked together in the fields, as they shucked corn, slaughtered hogs, or repaired fences. They sang whenever they had social gatherings—on Sundays or on the rare other holidays from work. They sang when they gathered for chores in the evenings. They sang during their religious services. And they sang with a passion, at times even an ecstasy, that was completely unfamiliar to whites—and sometimes troubling to them.

Their songs were rarely written down and often seemed entirely spontaneous; but much slave music was really derived from African and Caribbean traditions passed on through generations and from snatches of other songs the performers had heard before and from which they improvised variations. In its emotionalism, its pulsing rhythms, and its lack of conventional formal structure, it resembled nothing its white listeners had ever heard before.

Slaves sang whether or not there were any musical instruments to accompany them, but they often created instruments for themselves out of whatever materials were at hand. "Us take pieces of sheep's rib or cow's jaw or a piece of iron, with an old kettle or a hollow gourd and some horsehair to make the drum," one former slave recalled years later. "They'd take the buffalo horn and scrape it out to make the flute." When they could, they would build banjos, an instrument that had originated in Africa. Their masters sometimes gave them violins and guitars. When the setting permitted it, African Americans danced to their music—dances very different from and much more spontaneous than the formal steps that nineteenth-century whites generally learned. They also used music to accompany one of their other important cultural traditions: storytelling. Black music on the plantations took a number of forms. The most common was religious songs, the precursors of modern gospel music, which expressed—in terms that their white masters, who usually did not listen to the words very carefully, usually found acceptable—a faith in their eventual freedom and salvation and often spoke of Africans as a chosen people waiting for redemption. At other times, the songs would express a bitterness toward white slaveholders. The great black abolitionist Frederick Douglass remembered one:

> We raise de wheat,
> Dey gib us de corn;
> We bake de bread,
> Dey gib us de crust;
> We sif the meal,
> Dey gib us de huss;
> We peel de meat,
> Dey gib us de skin;
> And dat's de way
> Dey take us in;
> We skim de pot,
> Dey gib us de liquor,

plantations. Husbands and wives sometimes visited each other with the permission of their masters, but often such visits had to be in secret, at night. Family ties were no less strong than those of whites, and many slave marriages lasted throughout the course of long lifetimes.

When marriages did not survive, it was often because of circumstances over which blacks had no control. Up to a third of all black families were broken apart by the slave trade; an average slave might expect during a lifetime to see ten or more relatives sold. And that accounted for some of the other distinctive characteristics of the black family, which adapted itself to the cruel realities of its own uncertain future. Extended kinship networks—which grew to include not only spouses and their children, but also aunts, uncles, grandparents, even distant cousins—were strong and important and often helped compensate for the breakup of

IMPORTANCE OF KINSHIP NETWORKS

nuclear families. A slave forced suddenly to move to a new area, far from his or her family, might create fictional kinship ties and become "adopted" by a family in the new community. Even so, the impulse to maintain contact with a spouse and children remained strong long after the breakup of a family. One of the most frequent causes of flight from the plantation was a slave's desire to find a husband, wife, or child who had been sent elsewhere.

It was not only by breaking up families through sale that whites intruded on black family life. Black women, usually powerless to resist the sexual advances of their masters, often bore the children of whites—children whom the whites almost never recognized as their own and who were consigned to slavery from birth.

In addition to establishing social and cultural institutions of their own, slaves adapted themselves to slavery by forming complex relationships with their masters. However much blacks resented their lack of freedom, they often found it difficult to

SLAVE MUSIC This folk painting illustrates the importance of music to slaves (and at times also to their masters). The banjo in the hands of the man in the center was an instrument that originated in Africa. (Private Collection/Peter Newark/Bridgeman Art Library International)

both because they often enjoyed listening to it and because the more intelligent understood that without this means of emotional and spiritual release, active resistance to slavery might be more frequent.

The powerful music that emerged from slavery helped shape the lives of African Americans on the plantations. It also helped lay the foundations for music that almost all Americans later embraced: gospel, blues, jazz, rhythm and blues, rock, and rap. •

UNDERSTAND, ANALYZE, AND EVALUATE

1. Does the prominent place of music in slave culture support the thesis that slavery was essentially a benign institution?
2. The English dramatist William Congreve in *The Mourning Bride* wrote:

   > Music hath charms to soothe the savage breast,
   > To soften rocks, or bend a knotted oak.

   How might this quote apply to the place of music in African American slave culture?
3. What more recent musical forms continue the tradition of the slaves' religious songs or spirituals? In what way do these more recent forms serve purposes similar to that of the slaves' religious songs? Does music continue to shape a distinct African American culture?

And say dat's good enough for nigger.
Your butter and the fat;
Poor nigger, you can't ever get that.

To African Americans, music was a treasured avenue of escape from the hardships of slavery. It was also a vehicle through which they could express anger, resentment, and hope. Their masters generally tolerated their slaves' music—and even valued it,

maintain an entirely hostile attitude toward their owners. Not only were they dependent on whites for the material means of existence—food, clothing, and shelter; they also often derived from their masters a sense of security and protection. There was, in short, a paternal relationship between

PATERNAL NATURE OF SLAVERY

slave and master—sometimes harsh, sometimes kindly, but almost invariably important. Paternalism, in fact, became (even if not always consciously) a vital instrument of white control. By creating a sense of mutual dependence, whites helped reduce resistance to an institution that, in essence, served only the interests of the ruling race.

LOOKING BACK

While the North was creating a complex and rapidly developing commercial-industrial economy, the South was expanding its agrarian economy without making many fundamental changes in its character. Great migrations took many southern whites, and even more African American slaves, into new agricultural areas in the Deep South, where they created a booming "cotton kingdom"

that raised crops for export around the world. The cotton economy created many great fortunes and some modest ones. It also entrenched the planter class as the dominant force within southern society—both as owners of vast numbers of slaves, and as patrons, creditors, landlords, and marketers for the large number of poor whites who lived on the edge of the planter world.

The differences between the North and the South were a result of differences in natural resources, social structure, climate, and culture. Above all, they were the result of the existence within the South of an unfree labor system that prevented the kind of social fluidity that an industrializing society usually requires and that kept a large proportion of the southern population in debilitating bondage. •

KEY TERMS/PEOPLE/PLACES/EVENTS

CULT OF HONOR 304
DE BOW'S REVIEW 301
DENMARK VESEY 314
GABRIEL PROSSER 314

GANG SYSTEM 309
NAT TURNER 314
PIDGIN 314
"SAMBO" 314

SLAVE CODES 308
TASK SYSTEM 309

SIGNIFICANT EVENTS

1800
Gabriel Prosser organizes unsuccessful slave revolt in Virginia

1808
Importation of slaves to United States banned

1820s
Prolonged depression in tobacco prices begins

English market for cotton textiles boosts prices and causes explosion in cotton production in the Southwest

1822
Denmark Vesey thwarted in plans for slave rebellion in Charleston

RECALL AND REFLECT

1. Why did cotton become the leading crop of the South?

2. Why did industry fail to develop in the South to the extent that it did in the North?

3. How did slavery function economically and socially?

4. What was the effect of slavery on white slaveowners? on slaves? on nonslaveowning whites? on free blacks?

5. Through what means did slaves maintain a distinct African American culture?

John Randolph of Roanoke
frees 400 slaves

De Bow's Review founded
in New Orleans

1831
Nat Turner slave rebellion
breaks out in Virginia

1833

1837
Cotton prices
plummet

1846

1849
Rise in cotton
prices spurs
production boom

***GIRLS' EVENING SCHOOL* (C. 1840), ANONYMOUS** Schooling for women, which expanded significantly in the mid-nineteenth century, included training in domestic arts (as indicated by the sewing table at right), as well as in reading, writing, and other basic skills. (The Granger Collection, New York)

12 | ANTEBELLUM CULTURE AND REFORM

THE UNITED STATES IN THE MID-NINETEENTH CENTURY was a rapidly changing society—growing in size, population, and economic complexity. Many Americans were excited by the new possibilities these changes produced. Others, however, were painfully aware of the challenges to traditional values and institutions, the social instability, the increasing inequality, and the uncertainty about the future that accompanied change.

One result of these conflicting attitudes was the emergence of a broad array of movements intended to "reform" the nation. These reform efforts generally reflected one of two basic impulses. The first was an optimistic faith in human nature, a belief that within every individual resided a spirit that was basically good and that society should attempt to unleash. A second impulse was a desire for order and control. With their traditional values and institutions under assault and often eroding, many Americans yearned above all for a restoration of stability and discipline to their nation. Often, this impulse embodied a conservative nostalgia for better, simpler times. But it also inspired forward-

SETTING THE STAGE

looking efforts to create new institutions of social control, suited to the realities of the new age.

The reforms that flowed from these two impulses came in many guises and mobilized many different groups. In the course of the 1840s, however, one issue—slavery—came to overshadow all others. And one group of reformers—the abolitionists—became the most visible of all. At that point, the reform impulse, which at first had been a force that tended to unify the sections, became another wedge between the North and the South.

LOOKING AHEAD

1. How did an American national culture of art, literature, philosophy, and communal living develop in the nineteenth century?
2. What were the issues on which social and moral reformers tried to "remake the nation"? How successful were their efforts?
3. Why did the crusade against slavery become the preeminent issue of the reform movement?

THE ROMANTIC IMPULSE

"In the four quarters of the globe," wrote the English wit Sydney Smith in 1820, "who reads an American book? or goes to an

NATIONAL CULTURAL ASPIRATIONS

American play? or looks at an American picture or statue?" The answer, he assumed, was obvious: no one. American intellectuals were painfully aware of the low regard in which Europeans held their artistic and intellectual life, and in the middle decades of the nineteenth century they continued to work for both an elevation and a liberation of their nation's culture—for the creation of an American artistic world independent of Europe, one that would express their nation's special virtues.

At the same time, however, some of the nation's cultural leaders were beginning to strive for another kind of liberation, one that would gradually come almost to overshadow their self-conscious nationalism. That impulse—which was, ironically, largely an import from Europe—was the spirit of romanticism. In literature, in philosophy, in art, even in politics and economics, American intellectuals were committing themselves to the liberation of the human spirit.

NATIONALISM AND ROMANTICISM IN AMERICAN PAINTING

When Sydney Smith asked in 1820 who looked at an American painting, he was expressing the almost universal belief among European artists that they—and they alone—stood at the center of the world of art. But in the United States, a great many people were, in fact, looking at American paintings in the antebellum era—and they were doing so not because the paintings introduced them to the great traditions of Europe, but because they believed Americans were creating important new artistic traditions of their own.

The most important and popular American paintings of the first half of the nineteenth century set out to evoke the wonder of the nation's landscape. Unlike their European counterparts, American painters did not favor gentle scenes of carefully cultivated countrysides. They sought instead to capture the undiluted power of nature by portraying some of the nation's wildest and most spectacular areas—to evoke what many nineteenth-century people called the "sublime," the feeling of awe and wonderment and even fear of the grandeur of nature. The first great

HUDSON RIVER SCHOOL

school of American painters emerged in New York. Frederic Church, Thomas Cole, Thomas Doughty, and Asher Durand—who were, along with others, known as the Hudson River School—painted the spectacular vistas of the rugged and still largely unsettled Hudson Valley. Like Emerson and Thoreau, whom many of the painters read and admired, they considered nature—more than civilization—the best source of wisdom and spiritual fulfillment. In portraying the Hudson Valley, they seemed to announce that in America, unlike in Europe, "wild nature" still existed; and that America, therefore, was a nation of greater

promise than the played-out lands of the Old World. Yet there was also a sense of nostalgia in many of the Hudson River paintings, an effort to preserve and cherish a kind of nature that many Americans feared was fast disappearing.

In later years, some of the Hudson River painters traveled farther west, in search of more profound spiritual experiences. They found an even more rugged and spectacular natural world. Their enormous canvases of great natural wonders—the Yosemite Valley, Yellowstone, the Rocky Mountains—touched a passionate chord among the American public. Some of the most famous of their paintings—particularly the works of Albert Bierstadt and Thomas Moran—traveled around the country attracting enormous crowds.

LITERATURE AND THE QUEST FOR LIBERATION

American readers in the first decades of the nineteenth century were relatively indifferent to the work of their nation's own writers. The most popular novelist in America in these years was the British writer Sir Walter Scott, whose swashbuckling historical novels set in eighteenth-century England and Scotland won him an impassioned readership in both Britain and America. When Americans read books written in their own country, many people were likely to turn to the large number of "sentimental novels," written mostly by and for women. (See "Patterns of Popular Culture," pp. 342–343.)

But even during the heyday of Scott in the 1820s, the effort to create a distinctively American literature—which Washington Irving and others had advanced in the first decades of the century—made considerable progress with the emergence of the first great American novelist: James Fenimore Cooper. The author of more than thirty novels in the space of three decades, Cooper was known to his contemporaries as a master of adventure and suspense. What most distinguished his work, however,

COOPER AND THE AMERICAN WILDERNESS

was its evocation of the American wilderness. Cooper had grown up in central New York, at a time when the edge of white settlement was not far away; and he retained throughout his life a fascination with man's relationship to nature and with the challenges (and dangers) of America's expansion westward. His most important novels were known as the "Leatherstocking Tales." Among them were *The Last of the Mohicans* (1826) and *The Deerslayer* (1841). They explored the American frontiersman's experience with Indians, pioneers, violence, and the law.

Cooper's novels were a continuation of the early-nineteenth-century effort to produce a truly American literature. But they also served as a link to the concerns of later intellectuals. For in the "Leatherstocking Tales" could be seen not only a celebration of the American spirit and landscape but also an evocation, through the central character of Natty Bumppo, of the ideal of the independent individual with a natural inner goodness. There was also evidence of another impulse that would motivate American reform: the fear of disorder. Many of Cooper's less savory characters illustrated the vicious, grasping nature of some of the nation's western settlers and suggested a need for social discipline even in the wilderness.

Other important American writers emerged on the heels of Cooper. They displayed even more clearly the grip of romanticism on the nation's intellectual life. Walt Whitman, the self-proclaimed poet of American democracy, was the son of a Long Island carpenter and lived for many years roaming from place to place, doing odd jobs, while writing poetry. Finally, in 1855, he hired a printer and published a first volume of work: *Leaves of Grass*. His poems were an unrestrained celebration of democracy, of the liberation of the individual, and of the pleasures of the flesh as well as of the spirit. They also expressed Whitman's personal yearning for emotional and physical release and personal fulfillment—a yearning perhaps rooted in part in his own experience as a homosexual living in a society profoundly intol-

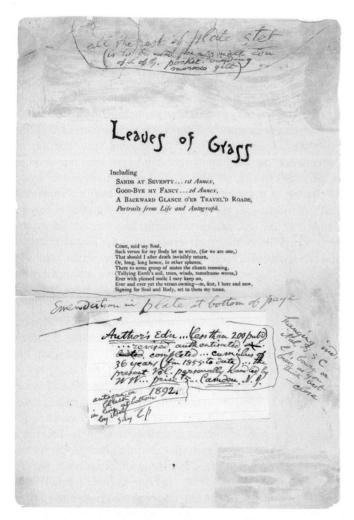

TITLE PAGE FOR WHITMAN'S *LEAVES OF GRASS* For more than thirty years after the publication of the original *Leaves of Grass* in 1855, Walt Whitman constantly revised and expanded the collection of poems and issued numerous subsequent editions. This sample title page, with notations by Whitman indicating changes and additions he wanted made, is for the final such edition, published in 1892, the year of Whitman's death. In a public statement he wrote to announce publication, he said that "the book *Leaves of Grass*, which he has been working on at great intervals and partially issued for the past thirty-five or forty years, is now completed. . . . Faulty as it is, he decides it is by far his special and entire self-chosen poetic utterance." (Rare Book and Special Collections Division, Library of Congress)

erant of unconventional sexuality. In his large body of poems, Whitman not only helped liberate verse from traditional, restrictive conventions but also helped express the soaring spirit of individualism that characterized his age.

The new literary concern with the unleashing of human emotions did not always produce such optimistic works, as the work of Herman Melville suggests. Born in New York in 1819, Melville ran away to sea as a youth and spent years sailing the world before returning home to become the greatest American novelist of his era. The most important of his novels was *Moby Dick*, published in 1851. His portrayal of Ahab, the powerful, driven captain of a whaling vessel, was a story of courage and of the strength of individual will; but it was also a tragedy of pride and revenge. Ahab's maniacal search for Moby Dick, a great white whale that had maimed him, suggested how the search for personal fulfillment and triumph could not only liberate but destroy as well. The result of Ahab's great quest was his own annihilation, reflecting Melville's conviction that the human spirit was a troubled, often self-destructive force.

HERMAN MELVILLE

Even more bleak were the works of one of the few southern writers of the time to embrace the search for the essence of the human spirit: Edgar Allan Poe. In the course of his short and unhappy life (he died in 1849 at the age of forty), Poe produced stories and poems that were primarily sad and macabre. His first book, *Tamerlane and Other Poems* (1827), received little recognition. But later works, including his most famous poem, "The Raven" (1845), established him as a major, if controversial, literary figure. Poe evoked images of individuals rising above the narrow confines of intellect and exploring the deeper world of the spirit and the emotions. Yet that world, he seemed to say, contained much pain and horror. Other American writers were contemptuous of Poe's work and his message, but he was ultimately to have a profound effect on European poets such as Baudelaire.

LITERATURE IN THE ANTEBELLUM SOUTH

Poe, however, was something of an exception in the world of southern literature. Like the North, the South experienced a literary flowering in the mid-nineteenth century, and produced writers and artists who were concerned with defining the nature of American society and of the American nation. But white southerners tended to produce very different images of what that society was and should be.

Southern novelists of the 1830s (among them Beverly Tucker, William Alexander Caruthers, and John Pendleton Kennedy), some of them writers of great talent, many of them residents of Richmond, produced historical romances or romantic eulogies of the plantation system of the upper South. In the 1840s, the southern literary capital moved to Charleston, home of the most distinguished of the region's men of letters: William Gilmore Simms. For a time, his work expressed a broad nationalism that transcended his regional background; but by the 1840s he too had become a strong defender of southern institutions—especially slavery—against the encroachments of the North.

SOUTHERN ROMANTICISM

There was, he believed, a unique quality to southern life that it was the duty of intellectuals to defend.

One group of southern writers, however, produced works that were more broadly American and less committed to a glorification of the peculiarities of southern life. These were writers from the fringes of plantation society, who depicted the world of the backwoods rural areas. Augustus B. Longstreet, Joseph G. Baldwin, Johnson J. Hooper, and others focused not on aristocratic "cavaliers," but on ordinary people and poor whites. Instead of romanticizing their subjects, they were deliberately and sometimes painfully realistic. And they seasoned their sketches with a robust, vulgar humor that was new to American literature. These southern realists established a tradition of American regional humor that was ultimately to find its most powerful voice in Mark Twain.

THE TRANSCENDENTALISTS

One of the outstanding expressions of the romantic impulse in America came from a group of New England writers and philosophers known as the transcendentalists. Borrowing heavily from German philosophers such as Kant, Hegel, and Schelling, and from the English writers Coleridge and Carlyle, the transcendentalists embraced a theory of the individual that rested on a distinction (first suggested by Kant) between what they called "reason" and "understanding"—words they used in ways that seem unfamiliar, even strange, to modern ears. Reason, as they defined it, had little to do with rationality. It was, rather, the individual's innate capacity to grasp beauty and truth through giving full expression to the instincts and emotions; and as such, it was the highest human faculty. Understanding, the transcendentalists argued, was the use of intellect in the narrow, artificial ways imposed by society; it involved the repression of instinct and the victory of externally imposed learning. Every person's goal, therefore, should be liberation from the confines of "understanding" and the cultivation of "reason." Each individual should strive to "transcend" the limits of the intellect and allow the emotions, the "soul," to create an "original relation to the Universe."

Transcendentalist philosophy emerged first among a small group of intellectuals centered in Concord, Massachusetts. Their leader and most eloquent voice was Ralph Waldo Emerson. A Unitarian minister in his youth, Emerson left the church in 1832 to devote himself entirely to writing and teaching the elements of transcendentalism. He was a dazzling figure to his contemporaries—a lecturer whose public appearances

RALPH WALDO EMERSON

> **❝ NOTHING IS AT LAST SACRED BUT THE INTEGRITY OF YOUR OWN MIND. ❞**
>
> **RALPH WALDO EMERSON**

drew rapturous crowds; a conversationalist who drew intellectuals to his Concord home almost daily. He was the most important intellectual of his age.

Emerson produced a significant body of poetry, but he was most renowned for his essays and lectures. In "Nature" (1836), one of his best-known essays, Emerson wrote that in the quest for self-fulfillment, individuals should work for a communion with the natural world: "in the woods, we return to reason and faith. . . . Standing on the bare ground—my head bathed by the blithe air, and uplifted into infinite space,—all mean egotism vanishes. . . . I am part and particle of God." In other essays, he was even more explicit. "Nothing is at last sacred," he wrote in "Self-Reliance" (1841), perhaps his most famous essay, "but the integrity of your own mind." The quest for self-reliance, he explained, was really a search for communion with the unity of the universe, the wholeness of God, the great spiritual force that he described as the "Oversoul." Each person's innate capacity to become, through his or her private efforts, a part of this essence was perhaps the classic expression of the romantic belief in the "divinity" of the individual.

Emerson was also a committed nationalist, an ardent proponent of American cultural independence. In a famous 1837 lecture, "The American Scholar," he boasted that "our day of dependence, our long apprenticeship to the learning of other lands, draws to a close." His belief that truth and beauty could be derived as much from instinct as from learning suggested that Americans, lacking the rich cultural heritage of European nations, could still aspire to artistic and literary greatness. Artistic and intellectual achievement need not rely on tradition and history; it could come from the instinctive creative genius of individuals. "Let the single man plant himself indomitably on his instincts and there abide," Emerson once said, "and the huge world will come round to him."

Almost as influential as Emerson was another leading Concord transcendentalist, Henry David Thoreau. Thoreau went even further than his friend Emerson in repudiating the repressive forces of society, which produced, he said, "lives of quiet desperation." Individuals should work for self-realization by resisting pressures to conform to society's expectations and responding instead to their own instincts. Thoreau's own effort to free himself—immortalized in his most famous book, *Walden* (1854)—led him to build a small cabin in the Concord woods on the edge of Walden Pond, where he lived alone for two years as simply as he could. "I went to the woods," he explained, "because I wished to live deliberately, to front only the essential facts of life, and see if I could not learn what it had to teach, and not, when I came to die, discover that I had not lived." Living simply, Thoreau believed, was a desirable

> **❝ I WENT TO THE WOODS BECAUSE I WISHED TO LIVE DELIBERATELY, TO FRONT ONLY THE ESSENTIAL FACTS OF LIFE, AND SEE IF I COULD NOT LEARN WHAT IT HAD TO TEACH, AND NOT, WHEN I CAME TO DIE, DISCOVER THAT I HAD NOT LIVED. ❞**
>
> **HENRY DAVID THOREAU**

alternative to the rapidly modernizing world around him—a world, he believed, that the disruptive and intrusive railroad unhappily symbolized.

Thoreau's rejection of what he considered the artificial constraints of society extended as well to his relationship with government. In 1846, he went to jail (briefly) rather than agree to pay a poll tax. He would not, he insisted, give financial support to a government that permitted the existence of slavery. In his 1849 essay "Resistance to Civil Government," he explained his refusal by claiming that the individual's personal morality had the first claim on his or her actions, that a government which required violation of that morality had no legitimate authority. The proper response was "civil disobedience," or "passive resistance"—a public refusal to obey unjust laws.

THOREAU AND CIVIL DISOBEDIENCE

THE DEFENSE OF NATURE

The transcendentalists, and others, feared the impact of the new capitalist enthusiasms on the integrity of the natural world. "The mountains and cataracts, which were to have made poets and painters," wrote the essayist Oliver Wendell Holmes, "have been mined for anthracite and dammed for water power."

Nature was not just a setting for economic activity, as many farmers, miners, and others believed; and it was not simply a body of data to be catalogued and studied, as many scientists thought. It was the source of human inspiration—the vehicle through which individuals could best realize the truth within their own souls. Genuine spirituality, they argued, came not from formal religion but through communion with the natural world. "In wildness is the preservation of the world." Thoreau once wrote. Humans separated from nature, he believed, would lose a substantial part of their humanity.

In making such claims, the transcendentalists were among the first Americans to anticipate the environmental movement of the twentieth century. They had no scientific basis for their defense of the wilderness, no knowledge of modern ecology, little sense of the twentieth-century notion of the interconnectedness of species. But they did believe in, and articulate, an essential unity between humanity and nature—a spiritual unity, they believed, without which civilization would be impoverished. They looked at nature, they said, "with new eyes," and with those eyes they saw that "behind nature, throughout nature, spirit is present."

VISIONS OF UTOPIA

Although transcendentalism was above all an individualistic philosophy, it helped spawn the most famous of all nineteenth-century experiments in communal living: Brook Farm, which the Boston transcendentalist George Ripley established as an experimental community in West Roxbury, Massachusetts, in 1841.

BROOK FARM

There, according to Ripley, individuals would gather to create a new form of social organization. All residents would share equally in the labor of the community so that all could share too in the leisure, because leisure was the first necessity for cultivation of the self. (Ripley was one of the first Americans to attribute positive connotations to the idea of leisure; most of his contemporaries equated it with laziness and sloth.) Participation in manual labor served another purpose as well: it helped individuals bridge the gap between the world of the intellect and learning, and the world of instinct and nature. The obvious tension between the ideal of individual freedom and the demands of a communal society took their toll on Brook Farm. Many residents became disenchanted and left; when a fire destroyed the central building of the community in 1847, the experiment dissolved.

Among the original residents of Brook Farm was the writer Nathaniel Hawthorne, who expressed his disillusionment with the experiment and, to some extent, with transcendentalism in a series of notable novels. In *The Blithedale Romance* (1852), he wrote scathingly of Brook Farm itself, portraying the disastrous consequences of the experiment on the individuals who had submitted to it.

The failure of Brook Farm did not, however, prevent the formation of other experimental communities. Some borrowed, as Ripley had done, from the ideas of the French philosopher Charles Fourier, whose ideas of socialist communities organized as cooperative "phalanxes" received wide attention in America. Others drew from the ideas of the Scottish industrialist and philanthropist Robert Owen. Owen himself founded an experimental community in Indiana in 1825, which he named New Harmony. It was to be a "Village of Cooperation," in which every resident worked and lived in total equality. The community was an economic failure, but the vision that had inspired it continued to enchant Americans. Dozens of other "Owenite" experiments began in other locations in the following years.

NEW HARMONY

REDEFINING GENDER ROLES

One of the principal concerns of many of the new utopian communities (and of the new social philosophies on which they rested) was the relationship between men and women. Transcendentalism and other movements of this period fostered expressions of a kind of feminism that would not gain a secure foothold in American society until the late twentieth century.

One of those most responsible for raising issues of gender was Margaret Fuller. A leading transcendentalist and a close associate of Emerson, she suggested the important relationship between the discovery of the "self" that was so central to antebellum reform and the questioning of gender roles: "Many women are considering within themselves what they need and what they have not," she wrote in a famous feminist

> ## 66 IN WILDNESS IS THE PRESERVATION OF THE WORLD. 99
>
> **HENRY DAVID THOREAU**

DANCING CLASSES AT NEW LANARK, 1825 Robert Owen (1771–1858) was a "free thinker" and an early socialist who sought to build a new community that would allow men and women to work in an egalitarian environment. Owen insisted that the residents at New Lanark should enjoy recreation and leisure as well as labor. (Eileen Tweedy/The Art Archive)

Mr OWEN'S INSTITUTION, NEW LANARK.
(Quadrille Dancing.)

work, *Woman in the Nineteenth Century* (1844). "I would have Woman lay aside all thought, such as she habitually cherishes, of being taught and led by men." Fuller herself, before her premature death in a shipwreck in 1850, lived a life far different from the domestic ideal of her time. She had intimate relationships with many men; became a great admirer of European socialists and a great champion of the Italian revolution of 1848, which she witnessed during travels there; and established herself as an intellectual leader whose power came in part from her perspective as a woman.

A redefinition of gender roles was crucial to one of the most enduring of the utopian colonies of the nineteenth century: the Oneida Community, established in 1848 in upstate New York by

REDEFINED GENDER ROLES AT THE ONEIDA COMMUNITY

John Humphrey Noyes. The Oneida "Perfectionists," as residents of the community called themselves, rejected traditional notions of family and marriage. All residents, Noyes declared, were "married" to all other residents; there were to be no permanent conjugal ties. But Oneida was not, as its horrified critics often claimed, an experiment in unrestrained "free love." It was a place where the community carefully monitored sexual behavior; where women were to be protected from unwanted childbearing; in which children were raised communally, often seeing little of their own parents. The Oneidans took special pride in what they considered the liberation of their women from the demands of male "lust" and from the traditional bonds of family.

> **❝ I WOULD HAVE WOMAN LAY ASIDE ALL THOUGHT, SUCH AS SHE HABITUALLY CHERISHES, OF BEING TAUGHT AND LED BY MEN. ❞**
>
> **MARGARET FULLER**

The Shakers, even more than the Oneidans, made a redefinition of traditional sexuality and gender roles central to their society. Founded by "Mother" Ann Lee in the 1770s, the society of the Shakers survived throughout the nineteenth century and into the twentieth. (A tiny remnant survives today.) But the Shakers attracted a particularly large following in the antebellum period and established more than twenty communities throughout the Northeast and Northwest in the 1840s. They derived their name from a unique religious ritual, a sort of ecstatic dance, in which members of a congregation would "shake" themselves free of sin while performing a loud chant.

The most distinctive feature of Shakerism, however, was its commitment to complete celibacy—which meant, of course, that no one could be born to Shakerism; all Shakers had to choose the faith voluntarily. Shaker communities attracted about 6,000 members in the 1840s, more women than

THE SHAKERS

men; and members lived in conditions in which contact between men and women was very limited. Shakers openly endorsed the idea of sexual equality; they even embraced the idea of a God who was not clearly male or female. Within the Shaker society as a whole, it was women who exercised the most power. Mother Ann Lee was succeeded as leader of the movement by Mother Lucy Wright. Shakerism, one observer wrote in the 1840s, was a refuge from the "perversions of marriage" and "the gross abuses which drag it down."

The Shakers were not, however, motivated only by a desire to escape the burdens of traditional gender roles. They were trying as well to create a society separated and protected from the chaos and disorder that they believed had come to characterize American life as a whole. They were less interested in personal freedom than in social discipline. And in that, they were like some other dissenting religious sects and utopian communities of their time. Another example was the Amana Community, founded by German immigrants in 1843; its members settled in Iowa in 1855 and attempted to realize Christian ideals by creating an ordered, socialist society.

THE MORMONS

Among the most important efforts to create a new and more ordered society within the old was that of the Church of Jesus

JOSEPH SMITH   Christ of Latter Day Saints—the Mormons. Mormonism began in upstate New York as a result of the efforts of Joseph Smith, a young, energetic, but economically unsuccessful man, who had spent most of his twenty-four years moving restlessly through New England and the Northeast. Then, in 1830, he published a remarkable document—the Book of Mormon, named for the ancient prophet who he claimed had written it. It was, Smith said, a translation of a set of golden tablets he had found in the hills of New York, revealed to him by an angel of God. The Book of Mormon told the story of an ancient and successful civilization in America, peopled by one of the lost tribes of Israel who had found their way to the New World centuries before Columbus. Its members waited patiently for the appearance of the Messiah, and they were rewarded when Jesus came to America after his resurrection. Subsequent generations, however, strayed from the path of righteousness that Jesus had laid out for them. Ultimately, their civilization collapsed, and God punished the sinful by making their skin dark. These darkened people, Smith believed, were the descendants of the American Indians, although the modern tribes had no memory of their origins. But while the ancient Hebrew kingdom in America had ultimately vanished, Smith believed, its history as a righteous society could serve as a model for a new holy community in the United States.

JOSEPH SMITH REVIEWING HIS TROOPS After being driven from earlier homes in Missouri, Mormons under the leadership of the religion's founder, Joseph Smith, created a model city in Nauvoo, Illinois—where they also organized an army of more than 4,000 men. This painting by the Mormon artist Carl Christensen portrays Smith, astride the white horse in front, reviewing a vast array of troops—with the pastoral and productive landscape of Nauvoo arrayed in the background. The existence of this large private army aroused great alarm in surrounding non-Mormon communities and contributed to the clashes that led to both the murder of Smith himself and the expulsion of the Mormons from Illinois. (*Joseph Mustering the Nauvoo Legion* by C. C. A. Christensen. Courtesy Brigham Young University Museum of Art. All rights reserved.)

In 1831, gathering a small group of believers around him, Smith began searching for a sanctuary for his new community of "saints," an effort that would continue unhappily for more than twenty years. Time and again, the Mormons attempted to establish their "New Jerusalem." Time and again, they met with persecution from surrounding communities suspicious of their radical religious doctrines—which included polygamy (the right of men to take several wives), a rigid form of social organization, and, particularly damaging to their image, an intense secrecy, which gave rise to wild rumors among their critics of conspiracy and depravity.

Driven from their original settlements in Independence, Missouri, and Kirtland, Ohio, the Mormons moved on to the new town of Nauvoo, Illinois, which by the early 1840s had become an imposing and economically successful community. In 1844, however, Joseph Smith was arrested, charged with treason (for allegedly conspiring against the government to win foreign support for a new Mormon colony in the Southwest), and imprisoned in Carthage, Illinois. There an angry mob attacked the jail, forced Smith from his cell, and shot and killed him. The Mormons now abandoned Nauvoo and, under the leadership of Smith's successor, Brigham Young, traveled across the desert—a society of 12,000 people, in one of the largest single group migrations in American history—and established a new community in Utah, the present Salt Lake City. There, at last, the Mormons were able to create a lasting settlement.

ESTABLISHMENT
OF SALT LAKE
CITY

Like other experiments in social organization of the era, Mormonism reflected a belief in human perfectibility. God had once been a man, the church taught, and thus every man or woman could aspire to become—as Joseph Smith had become—a saint. But unlike other new communities, such as the Oneidans, the Mormons did not embrace the doctrine of individual liberty. Instead, they created a highly organized, centrally directed, almost militarized social structure, a refuge against the disorder and uncertainty of the secular world. They placed particular emphasis on the structure of the family. Mormon religious rituals even included a process by which men and women went through baptism ceremonies in the name of deceased ancestors; as a result, they believed, they would be reunited with those ancestors in heaven. The intense Mormon interest in genealogy, which continues today, is a reflection of this belief in the possibility of reuniting present generations with those of the past.

The original Mormons were, for the most part, men and women who felt displaced in their rapidly changing society—people left behind or troubled by the material growth and social progress of their era. In the new religion, they found genuine faith. In the society Mormonism created, they found security and order.

REMAKING SOCIETY

The simultaneous efforts to liberate the individual and impose order on a changing world also helped create a wide range of new movements to remake society—movements in which, to a striking degree, women formed the real rank and file and often the leadership as well. By the 1830s, such movements had taken the form of organized reform societies. "In no country in the world," Tocqueville had observed, "has the principle of association been more successfully used, or more unsparingly applied to a multitude of different objects, than in America."

The new organizations did indeed work on behalf of a wide range of issues: temperance; education; peace; the care of the poor, the handicapped, and the mentally ill; the treatment of criminals; the rights of women; and many more. Few eras in American history have witnessed as wide a range of reform efforts as emerged in the mid-nineteenth century. And few eras have exposed more clearly the simultaneous attraction of Americans to the ideas of personal liberty and social order.

NEW REFORM
MOVEMENTS

REVIVALISM, MORALITY, AND ORDER

The philosophy of reform arose from several distinct sources. One was the optimistic vision of those who, like the transcendentalists, rejected Calvinist doctrines and preached the divinity of the individual. These included not only Emerson, Thoreau, and their followers, but also a much larger group of Americans who embraced the doctrines of Unitarianism and Universalism and absorbed European romanticism.

A second, and in many respects more important, source was Protestant revivalism—the movement that had begun with the Second Great Awakening early in the century and had, by the 1820s, evolved into a powerful force for social reform. Although the New Light revivalists were theologically far removed from the transcendentalists and Unitarians, they had come to share the optimistic belief that every individual was capable of salvation. According to Charles Grandison Finney, an evangelistic Presbyterian minister who became the most influential revival leader of the 1820s and 1830s, traditional Calvinist doctrines of predestination and individual human helplessness were both obsolete and destructive. Each person, he preached, contained within himself or herself the capacity to experience spiritual rebirth and achieve salvation. A revival of faith need not depend on a miracle from God; it could be created by individual effort.

Finney enjoyed particular success in upstate New York, where he helped launch a series of passionate revivals in towns along the Erie Canal—a region so prone to religious awakenings that it was known as the "burned-over district." It was no coincidence that the new revivalism should prove so powerful there,

> **66 IN NO COUNTRY IN THE WORLD HAS THE PRINCIPLE OF ASSOCIATION BEEN MORE SUCCESSFULLY USED, OR MORE UNSPARINGLY APPLIED TO A MULTITUDE OF DIFFERENT OBJECTS, THAN IN AMERICA. 99**
>
> **ALEXIS DE TOCQUEVILLE**

for this region of New York was experiencing—largely as a result of the construction of the canal—a major economic transformation. And with that transformation had come changes in the social fabric so profound that many men and women felt baffled and disoriented. (It was in roughly this same area of New York that Joseph Smith first organized the Mormon church.)

REVIVALISM IN THE BURNED-OVER DISTRICT

In Rochester, New York, the site of his greatest success, Finney staged a series of emotionally wrenching religious meetings that aroused a large segment of the community. He had particular success in mobilizing women, on whom he tended to concentrate his efforts—both because women found the liberating message of revivalism particularly appealing and because, Finney discovered, they provided him with access to their male relatives. Gradually, he developed a large following among the relatively prosperous citizens of the region. They were enjoying the economic benefits of the new commercial growth, but they were also uneasy about some of the social changes accompanying it (among them the introduction into their community of a new, undisciplined pool of transient laborers). For them, revivalism became not only a means of personal salvation but a mandate for the reform (and control) of their society. Finney's revivalism became a call for a crusade against personal immorality. "The church," he maintained, "must take right ground on the subject of Temperance, the Moral Reform, and all the subjects of practical morality which come up for decision from time to time."

FINNEY'S DOCTRINE OF PERSONAL REGENERATION

THE TEMPERANCE CRUSADE

Evangelical Protestantism added major strength to one of the most influential reform movements of the era: the crusade against drunkenness. No social vice, argued some reformers (including, for example, many of Finney's converts in cities such as Rochester), was more responsible for crime, disorder, and poverty than the excessive use of alcohol. Women, who were particularly active in the temperance movement, claimed that alcoholism placed a special burden on wives: men spent money on alcohol that their families needed for basic necessities, and drunken husbands often abused their wives and children.

In fact, alcoholism was an even more serious problem in antebellum America than it has been in the twentieth and twenty-first centuries. The supply of alcohol was growing rapidly, particularly in the West; farmers there grew more grain than they could sell in the still-limited markets in this prerailroad era, so they distilled much of it into whiskey. But in the East, too, commercial distilleries and private stills were widespread. The appetite for alcohol was growing along with the supply: in isolated western areas, where drinking provided a social pastime in small towns and helped ease the loneliness and isolation on farms; in pubs and saloons in eastern cities, where drinking was the principal leisure activity for many workers. The average male in the 1830s drank nearly three times as much alcohol as the average person does today. And as that figure suggests, many people drank habitually and excessively, with bitter consequences for themselves and others. Among the many supporters of the temperance movement were people who saw it as a way to overcome their own problems with alcoholism.

Although advocates of temperance had been active since the late eighteenth century, the new reformers gave the movement an energy and influence it had never previously known. In 1826, the American Society for the Promotion of Temperance emerged as a coordinating agency among various groups; it attempted to use many of the techniques of revivalism in preaching abstinence. Then, in 1840, six reformed alcoholics in Baltimore organized the Washington Temperance Society and began to draw large crowds—in which workers (many of them attempting to overcome their own alcoholism) were heavily represented—to hear their impassioned and intriguing confessions of past sins. By then, temperance advocates had grown dramatically in numbers; more than a million people had signed a formal pledge to forgo hard liquor.

AMERICAN SOCIETY FOR THE PROMOTION OF TEMPERANCE

As the movement gained in strength, it also became divided in purpose. Some temperance advocates now urged that abstinence include not only liquor but beer and wine as well. Not everyone agreed. Some began to demand state legislation to restrict the sale and consumption of alcohol (Maine passed such a law in 1851); others insisted that temperance must rely on the conscience of the individual. Whatever their disagreements, by promoting abstinence reformers were attempting to promote the moral self-improvement of individuals. They were also trying to impose discipline on society.

The search for social discipline was particularly clear in the battle over prohibition laws, which pitted established Protestants against new Catholic immigrants, to many of whom drinking was an important social ritual and an integral part of the life of their communities. The arrival of the immigrants was profoundly disturbing to established residents of many communities, and the restriction of alcohol seemed to them a way to curb the disorder they believed the new population was creating.

CULTURAL DIVISIONS OVER ALCOHOL

HEALTH FADS AND PHRENOLOGY

For some Americans, the search for individual and social perfection led to an interest in new theories of health and knowledge. Threats to public health were critical to the sense of insecurity that underlay many reform movements, especially after the terrible cholera epidemics of the 1830s and 1840s. Cholera is a severe bacterial infection of the intestines, usually a result of consuming contaminated food or water. In the nineteenth century, long before the discovery of antibiotics, less than half of those who contracted the disease survived. Thousands of people died of cholera during its occasional outbreaks, and in certain cities—New Orleans in 1833 and St. Louis in 1849—the effects were truly catastrophic. Nearly a quarter of

THE DRUNKARD'S PROGRESS This 1846 lithograph by Nathaniel Currier shows what temperance advocates argued was the inevitable consequence of alcohol consumption. Beginning with an apparently innocent "glass with a friend," the young man rises step by step to the summit of drunken revelry, then declines to desperation and suicide while his abandoned wife and child grieve. (Library of Congress)

the population of New Orleans died in the 1833 epidemic. Many municipalities, pressured by reformers, established city health boards to try to find solutions to the problems of epidemics. But the medical profession of the time, unaware of the nature of bacterial infections, had no answers; and the boards therefore found little to do.

Instead, many Americans turned to nonscientific theories for improving health. Affluent men and, especially, women flocked to health spas for the celebrated "water cure," which purported to improve health through immersing people in hot or cold baths or wrapping them in wet sheets. Although the water cure in fact delivered few of the benefits its promoters promised, it did have some therapeutic value; some forms of hydrotherapy are still in use today. Other people adopted new dietary theories. Sylvester Graham, a Connecticut-born Presbyterian minister and committed reformer, won many followers with his prescriptions for eating fruits, vegetables, and bread made from coarsely ground flour—a prescription not unlike some dietary theories today—instead of meat. (The "Graham cracker" is made from a kind of flour named for him.) Graham accompanied his dietary prescriptions with moral warnings about the evils of excess and luxury.

Perhaps strangest of all to modern sensibilities was the widespread belief in the new "science" of phrenology, which appeared first in Germany and became popular in the United States begin-

ning in the 1830s through the efforts of Orson and Lorenzo Fowler, publishers of the *Phrenology Almanac*.

PHRENOLOGY

Phrenologists argued that the shape of an individual's skull was an important indicator of his or her character and intelligence. They made elaborate measurements of bumps and indentations to calculate the size (and, they claimed, the strength) of different parts of the brain, each of which, they argued, controlled a specific kind of intelligence or behavior. For a time, phrenology seemed to many Americans an important vehicle for improving society. It provided a way of measuring an individual's fitness for various positions in life and seemed to promise an end to the arbitrary process by which people matched their talents to occupations and responsibilities. The theory is now universally believed to have no scientific value at all.

MEDICAL SCIENCE

In an age of rapid technological and scientific advances, the science of medicine sometimes seemed to lag behind. In part, that was because of the greater difficulty of experimentation in medicine, which required human subjects as compared to other areas of science and technology that relied on inanimate objects. In part, it was because of the character of the medical profession, which—in the absence of any significant regulation—attracted many poorly educated people and many quacks, in

"SPOUT BATH AT WARM SPRINGS" Among the many fads and theories about human health to gain currency in the 1830s and 1840s, one of the most popular was the idea that bathing in warm, sulphurous water was restorative. Visitors to "warm springs" all over the United States and Europe "took the baths," drank the foul-smelling water, and sometimes stayed for weeks as part of a combination vacation and "cure." This 1837 drawing is by Sophie Dupont, a visitor to a popular spa. She wrote to a friend that the water, "notwithstanding its odour of half spoiled eggs and its warmth, is not very nauseous to the taste." (Courtesy of Hagley Museum and Library)

PHRENOLOGY This lithograph illustrates some of the ideas of the popular "science" of phrenology in the 1830s. Drawing from the concepts of the German writer Johann Gaspar Spurzheim, American phrenologists promoted the belief that a person's character and talents could be understood by the formation of his or her skull; that the brain was, in fact, a cluster of autonomous organs, each controlling some aspect of human thought or behavior. In this diagram, the areas of the brain that supposedly control "identity," "acquisitiveness," "secretiveness," "marvelousness," and "hope" are clearly identified. The theory has no scientific basis. (Library of Congress)

addition to trained physicians. Efforts to regulate the profession were beaten back in the 1830s and 1840s by those who considered the licensing of physicians to be a form of undemocratic monopoly. The prestige of the profession, therefore, remained low, and it was for many people a career of last resort.

The biggest problem facing American medicine, however, was the absence of basic knowledge about disease. The great medical achievement of the eighteenth century—the development of a vaccination against smallpox by Edward Jenner—came from no broad theory of infection, but from a brilliant adaptation of folk practices among country people. The development of anesthetics came not from medical doctors at first, but from a New England dentist, William Morton, who was looking for ways to help his patients endure the extraction of teeth. Beginning in 1844, Morton began experimenting with using sulphuric ether. John Warren, a Boston surgeon, soon began using ether to sedate surgical patients. Even these advances met with stiff resistance from traditional physicians, some of whom continued to believe that all medical knowledge derived from timeless truths and ancient scholars and who mistrusted innovation and experimentation. Others rejected scientific advances because of unorthodox, and untested "medical" techniques popularized by entrepreneurs, many of them charlatans.

In the absence of any broad acceptance of scientific methods and experimental practice in medicine, it was very difficult for even the most talented doctors to succeed in treating disease. Even so, halting progress toward the discovery of the germ the-

ory did occur in antebellum America. In 1843, the Boston essayist, poet, and physician Oliver Wendell Holmes published his findings from a study of large numbers of cases of "puerperal fever" (septicemia in children) and concluded that the disease could be transmitted from one person to another. This discovery of contagion met with a storm of criticism, but was later vindicated by the clinical success of the Hungarian physician Ignaz Semmelweis, who noticed that the infection seemed to be spread by medical students who had been working with corpses. Once he began requiring students to wash their hands and disinfect their instruments, the infections virtually disappeared.

DISCOVERY OF CONTAGION

REFORMING EDUCATION

One of the outstanding reform movements of the mid-nineteenth century was the effort to produce a system of universal public education. As of 1830, no state yet had such a system, although some states—such as Massachusetts—had supported a limited version for many years. In the 1830s, however, interest in public education grew rapidly. It was a reflection of the new belief in the innate capacity of every person and of society's obligation to tap that capacity; but it was a reflection, too, of the desire to expose students to stable social values as a way to resist instability.

The greatest of the educational reformers was Horace Mann, the first secretary of the Massachusetts Board of Education, which was established in 1837. To Mann and his followers, education was the only way to "counterwork this tendency to the domination of capital and the servility of labor." The only way to protect democracy, Mann believed, was to create an educated electorate. He reorganized the Massachusetts school system, lengthened the academic year (to six months), doubled teachers' salaries (although he did nothing to eliminate the large disparities between the salaries of male and female teachers), enriched the curriculum, and introduced new methods of professional training for teachers.

Other states experienced similar expansion and development. They built new schools, created teachers' colleges, and offered large new groups of children access to education. Henry Barnard helped produce a new educational system in Connecticut and Rhode Island. Pennsylvania passed a law in 1835 appropriating state funds for the support of universal education. Governor William Seward of New York extended public support of schools throughout the state in the early 1840s. By the 1850s, the principle of tax-supported elementary schools had been accepted in all the states; and all were making at least a start toward putting the principle into practice.

RAPID GROWTH OF PUBLIC EDUCATION

Yet the quality of the new education continued to vary widely. In some places—Massachusetts, for example, where Mann established the first American state-supported teachers' college in 1839 and where the first professional association of teachers was created in 1845—educators were usually capable men and women, often highly trained, and with an emerging sense of themselves as career professionals. In other areas, however, teachers were often barely literate, and limited funding for education restricted opportunities severely. In the newly settled regions of the West, where the white population was highly dispersed, many children had no access to schools at all. In the South, the entire black population was barred from formal education (although approximately 10 percent of the slaves managed to achieve literacy anyway), and only about a third of all white children of school age actually enrolled in schools in 1860. In the North the percentage was 72 percent, but even there, many students attended classes only briefly and casually.

The interest in education was visible too in the growing movement to educate American Indians in the antebellum period. Some reformers held racist assumptions about the unredeemability of nonwhite peoples; but even many who accepted that idea about African Americans continued to believe that Indians could be "civilized" if only they could be taught the ways of the white world. Efforts to educate Native Americans and encourage them to assimilate were particularly prominent in such areas of the Far West as Oregon. Substantial numbers of whites were beginning to settle there in the 1840s. Nevertheless, the great majority of Native Americans remained outside the reach of educational reform, either by choice or by circumstance or both.

Despite limitations and inequities, the achievements of the school reformers were impressive by any standard. By the beginning of the Civil War, the United States had one of the highest literacy rates of any nation of the world: 94 percent of the population of the North and 83 percent of the white population of the South (58 percent of the total southern population).

ACHIEVEMENTS OF EDUCATIONAL REFORM

The conflicting impulses that underlay the movement for school reform were visible in some of the different educational institutions that emerged. In New England, for example, the transcendentalist Bronson Alcott established a controversial experimental school in Concord that reflected his strong belief in the importance of complete self-realization. He urged children to learn from their own inner wisdom, not from the imposition of values by the larger society. Children were to teach themselves, rather than rely on teachers.

A similar emphasis on the potential of the individual sparked the creation of new institutions to help the handicapped, institutions that formed part of a great network of charitable activities known as the Benevolent Empire. Among them was the Perkins School for the Blind in Boston, the first such school in America. Nothing better exemplified the romantic impulse of the era than the belief of those who founded Perkins that even society's supposedly least-favored members—the blind and otherwise handicapped—could be helped to discover inner strength and wisdom.

THE BENEVOLENT EMPIRE

More typical of educational reform, however, were efforts to use schools to impose a set of social values on children—the values that reformers believed were appropriate for their new, industrializing society. These values included thrift, order, discipline, punctuality, and respect for authority. Horace Mann, for example, spoke frequently of the role of public schools in extending democracy and expanding individual opportunity. But he spoke, too, of their role in creating social order. "The unrestrained passions of men are not only homicidal, but suicidal," he said, suggesting a philosophy very different from that of Alcott and other transcendentalists, who emphasized instinct and emotion. "Train up a child in the way he should go, and when he is old he will not depart from it."

> 66 TRAIN UP A CHILD IN THE WAY HE SHOULD GO, AND WHEN HE IS OLD HE WILL NOT DEPART FROM IT. 99
>
> **HORACE MANN**

REHABILITATION

Similar impulses helped create another powerful movement of reform: the creation of "asylums" (as they now began to be called) for criminals and for the mentally ill. On

THE ASYLUM
MOVEMENT

the one hand, in advocating prison and hospital reform, Americans were reacting to one of society's most glaring ills. Criminals of all kinds, debtors unable to pay their debts, the mentally ill, even senile paupers—all were crowded together indiscriminately into prisons and jails, which in some cases were literally holes in the ground; one jail in Connecticut was an abandoned mine shaft. Beginning in the 1820s, numerous states replaced these antiquated facilities with new "penitentiaries" and mental institutions designed to provide a proper environment for inmates. New York built the first penitentiary at Auburn in 1821. In Massachusetts, the reformer Dorothea Dix began a national movement for new methods of treating the mentally ill. Imprisonment of debtors and paupers gradually disappeared, as did such traditional practices as legal public hangings.

But the creation of "asylums" for social deviants was not sim-

PRISON
REFORM

ply an effort to curb the abuses of the old system. It was also an attempt to reform and rehabilitate the inmates. New forms of rigid prison discipline were designed to rid criminals of the "laxness" that had presumably led them astray. Solitary confinement and the imposition of silence on work crews (both adopted in Pennsylvania and New York in the 1820s) were meant to give prisoners opportunities to meditate on their wrongdoings (hence the term "penitentiary": a place for individuals to cultivate penitence). Some reformers argued that the discipline of the asylum could serve as a model for other potentially disordered environments—for example, factories and schools. But penitentiaries and mental hospitals often fell victim to overcrowding, and the original reform ideal gradually faded. Many prisons ultimately degenerated into little more than warehouses

for criminals, with scant emphasis on rehabilitation. The idea, in its early stages, had been more optimistic.

The "asylum" movement was not, however, restricted to criminals and people otherwise considered "unfit." The idea that a properly structured institution could prevent moral failure or rescue individuals from failure and despair helped spawn the creation of new orphanages designed as educational institutions. Such institutions, reformers believed, would provide an environment in which children who might otherwise be drawn into criminality could be trained to become useful citizens. Similar institutions emerged to provide homes for "friendless" women—women without families or homes, but otherwise "respectable," for whom the institutions might provide an opportunity to build a new life. (Such homes were in part an effort to prevent such women from turning to prostitution.) There were also new facilities for the poor: almshouses and workhouses, which created closely supervised environments for those who had failed to work their way up in society. Such an environment, reformers believed, would train them to live more productive lives.

THE INDIAN RESERVATION

Some of these same beliefs underlay the emergence in the 1840s and 1850s of a new "reform" approach to the problems of Native Americans: the idea of the reservation. For several decades, the dominant thrust of U.S. policy toward the Indians in areas of white settlement had been relocation. The principal motive behind relocation had always been a simple one: getting the tribes out of the way of white civilization. But among some whites there had also been another, if secondary, intent: to move the Indians to a place where they would be protected from whites and allowed to develop to a point where assimilation might be

PERKINS SCHOOL FOR THE BLIND The Perkins School in Boston was the first school for the blind in the United States and was committed to the idea that the blind could be connected effectively to the world through the development of new skills, such as reading through the relatively new technique of Braille. This woodcut shows Perkins's main building in the mid-1850s, by which time the school was already over twenty years old. It continues to educate the blind today. (Perkins School for the Blind History Museum)

THE RISE OF FEMINISM

IN THE 1840S, a group of women who had started out as abolitionists began to advocate for the rights of women themselves. "All men and women are created equal," they declared. They argued that women should have the same opportunities as men and should no longer be restricted to the domestic sphere. This effort reached its peak at the 1848 Convention in Seneca Falls, New York, where a Declaration of Sentiments was proclaimed.

Just as the women's rights movement of the nineteenth century grew out of the abolitionist movement, so the feminist movement of the twentieth century built upon the civil rights movement. The modern feminist movement often marks its beginning with the publication of Betty Friedan's *The Feminine Mystique* in 1963 and the formation of the National Organization for Women (NOW) in 1966. Despite the more than one hundred years separating the two documents below, the basic sentiments of the Seneca Falls Declaration bear many similarities to the ideas that have shaped feminist thinking of the twentieth and twenty-first centuries.

SENECA FALLS—1848

THE DECLARATION OF SENTIMENTS, SENECA FALLS CONFERENCE, 1848

When, in the course of human events, it becomes necessary for one portion of the family of man to assume among the people of the earth a position different from that which they have hitherto occupied, but one to which the laws of nature and of nature's God entitle them, a decent respect to the opinions of mankind requires that they should declare the causes that impel them to such a course.

We hold these truths to be self-evident: that all men and women are created equal; that they are endowed by their Creator with certain inalienable rights; that among these are life, liberty, and the pursuit of happiness; that to secure these rights governments are instituted, deriving their just powers from the consent of the governed. Whenever any form of government becomes destructive of these ends, it is the right of those who suffer from it to refuse allegiance to it, and to insist upon the institution of a new government, laying its foundation on such principles, and organizing its powers in such form, as to them shall seem most likely to effect their safety and happiness. . . . Such has been the patient sufferance of the women under this government, and such is now the necessity which constrains them to demand the equal station to which they are entitled. The history of mankind is a history of repeated injuries and usurpations on the part of man toward woman, having in direct object the establishment of an absolute tyranny over her . . .

Now, in view of this entire disfranchisement of one-half the people of this country, . . . because women do feel themselves aggrieved, oppressed, and fraudulently deprived of their most sacred rights, we insist that they have immediate admission to all the rights and privileges which belong to them as citizens of the United States.

From Elizabeth Cady Stanton, *A History of Woman Suffrage*, vol. 1 (Rochester, NY: Fowler and Wells, 1889), pp. 70–71.

UNDERSTAND, ANALYZE, AND EVALUATE

1. The Seneca Falls Declaration is modeled on the U.S. Declaration of Independence. Why do you think the women who wrote the Seneca Falls Declaration used that model? How did they adapt the U.S. Declaration of Independence to fit their specific demands?

2. What is the primary grievance expressed in the document? How long did it take for this grievance to be addressed? Why did it take so long?

NATIONAL ORGANIZATION FOR WOMEN—1966

THE NATIONAL ORGANIZATION FOR WOMEN'S 1966 STATEMENT OF PURPOSE

We, men and women who hereby constitute ourselves as the National Organization for Women, believe that the time has come for a new movement toward true equality for all women in America, and toward a fully equal partnership of the sexes, as part of the worldwide revolution of human rights now taking place within and beyond our national borders.

The purpose of NOW is to take action to bring women into full participation in the mainstream of American society now, exercising all the privileges and responsibilities thereof in truly equal partnership with men.

We believe the time has come to . . . confront, with concrete action, the conditions that now prevent women from enjoying the equality of opportunity and freedom of choice which is their right, as individual Americans, and as human beings.

NOW is dedicated to the proposition that women, first and foremost, are human beings, who, like all other people in our society, must have the chance to develop their fullest human potential. We believe that women can achieve such equality only by accepting to the full the challenges and responsibilities they share with all other people in our society, as part of the decision-making mainstream of American political, economic and social life.

. . .

WE BELIEVE that the power of American law, and the protection guaranteed by the U.S. Constitution to the civil rights of all individuals, must be effectively applied and enforced to isolate and remove patterns of sex discrimination, to ensure equality of opportunity in employment and education, and equality of civil and political rights and responsibilities on behalf of women, as well as for Negroes and other deprived groups.

. . .

WE BELIEVE THAT women will do most to create a new image of women by acting now, and by speaking out in behalf of their own equality, freedom, and human dignity—not in pleas for special privilege, nor in enmity toward men, who are also victims of the current, half-equality between the sexes—but in an active, self-respecting partnership with men. By so doing, women will develop confidence in their own ability to determine actively, in partnership with men, the conditions of their life, their choices, their future and their society.

This Statement of Purpose was written by Betty Friedan, author of The Feminine Mystique.

National Organization for Women Statement of Purpose (1966), reprinted with permission.

MAKE CONNECTIONS

1. How does the NOW statement of purpose echo the sentiments of the Seneca Falls Declaration?
2. What image of women's status does each document create? How do these images differ?
3. What rights that are asked for in the Declaration of 1848 had women gained by 1966? Has the vision outlined in the NOW statement of purpose been achieved today?

possible. Even Andrew Jackson, whose animus toward Indians was legendary, once described the removals as part of the nation's "moral duty . . . to protect and if possible to preserve and perpetuate the scattered remnants of the Indian race."

It was a small step from the idea of relocation to the idea of the reservation: the idea of creating an enclosed region in which Indians would live in isolation from white society. The reservations served white economic purposes above all—moving Native Americans out of good lands that white settlers wanted. But they were also supposed to serve a reform purpose. Just as prisons, asylums, and orphanages would provide society with an opportunity to train and uplift misfits and unfortunates within white society, so the reservations might provide a way to undertake what one official called "the great work of regenerating the Indian race." Native Americans on reservations, reformers argued, would learn the ways of civilization in a protected setting.

The Emergence of Feminism

The reform ferment of the antebellum period had a particular meaning for American women. They played central roles in a wide range of reform movements and a particularly important role in the movements on behalf of temperance and the abolition of slavery. In the process, they expressed their awareness of the problems that women themselves faced in a male-dominated society. The result was the creation of the first important American feminist movement, one that laid the groundwork for more than a century of agitation for women's rights.

Women in the 1830s and 1840s faced not only all the traditional restrictions imposed on members of their sex by society, but also a new set of barriers that had emerged from the doctrine of "separate spheres" and the transformation of the family. Many women who began to involve themselves in reform movements in the 1820s and 1830s came to look on such restrictions

REFORM
MOVEMENTS
AND THE RISE
OF FEMINISM

with rising resentment. Some began to defy them. Sarah and Angelina Grimké, sisters born in South Carolina who had become active and outspoken abolitionists, ignored attacks by men who claimed that their activities were inappropriate for their sex. "Men and women were CREATED EQUAL," they argued. "They are both moral and accountable beings, and whatever is right for man to do, is right for women to do." Other reformers—Catharine Beecher, Harriet Beecher Stowe (her sister), Lucretia Mott, Elizabeth Cady Stanton, and Dorothea Dix—also chafing at the restrictions placed on them by men, similarly pressed at the boundaries of "acceptable" female behavior.

Finally, in 1840, the patience of several women snapped. A group of American female delegates arrived at a world antislavery convention in London, only to be turned away by the men who controlled the proceedings. Angered at the rejection, several of the delegates—notably Lucretia Mott and Elizabeth

THE "DECLARATION OF SENTIMENTS" Frederick Douglass joined female abolitionists in signing the famous "Declaration of Sentiments" that emerged out of the Women's Rights Convention at Seneca Falls, New York, in 1848—one of the founding documents of American feminism. (National Park Service, U.S. Department of the Interior)

Cady Stanton—became convinced that their first duty as reformers should now be to elevate the status of women. Over the next several years, Mott, Stanton, Susan B. Anthony, and others began drawing pointed parallels between the plight of women

SENECA FALLS

and the plight of slaves; and in 1848, they organized a convention in Seneca Falls, New York, to discuss the question of women's rights. Out of the meeting emerged a "Declaration of Sentiments" (patterned on the 1776 Declaration of Independence), which stated that "all men and women are created equal," that women no less than men have certain inalienable rights. Their most prominent demand was for the right to vote, thus launching a movement for woman suffrage that would continue until 1920. But the document was in many ways more important for its rejection of the whole notion that men and women should be assigned separate "spheres" in society.

It should not be surprising, perhaps, that many of the women involved in these feminist efforts were Quakers. Quakerism had long embraced the ideal of sexual equality and had tolerated, indeed encouraged, the emergence of women as preachers and community leaders. Women taught to expect the absence of gender-based restrictions in their own communities naturally resented the restrictions they encountered when they moved outside them. Quakers had also been among the leaders of the antislavery movement, and Quaker women played a leading role within those efforts. Of the women who drafted the Declaration of Sentiments, all but Elizabeth Cady Stanton were Quakers.

Progress toward feminist goals was limited in the antebellum years, but individual women did manage to break the social barriers to advancement.

> " WHATEVER IS RIGHT FOR MAN TO DO, IS RIGHT FOR WOMEN TO DO. "
>
> **SARAH AND ANGELINA GRIMKÉ**

Elizabeth Blackwell, born in England, gained acceptance and

LIMITED
PROGRESS FOR
WOMEN

fame as a physician. Her sister-in-law Antoinette Brown Blackwell became the first ordained woman minister in the United States; and another sister-in-law, Lucy Stone, took the revolutionary step of retaining her maiden name after marriage (as did the abolitionist Angelina Grimké). Stone became a successful and influential lecturer on women's rights. Emma Willard, founder of the Troy Female Seminary in 1821, and Catharine Beecher, who founded the Hartford Female Seminary in 1823, worked on behalf of women's education. Some women expressed their feminist sentiments even in their choice of costume—by wearing a distinctive style of dress (introduced in the 1850s) that combined a short skirt with full-length pantalettes—an outfit that allowed freedom of movement without loss of modesty. Introduced by the famous actress Fanny Kemble, it came to be called the "bloomer" costume, after one of its advocates, Amelia Bloomer. (It provoked so much controversy that feminists finally abandoned it, convinced that the furor was drawing attention away from their more important demands.)

There was an irony in this rise of interest in the rights of women. Feminists benefited greatly from their association with other reform movements, most notably abolitionism; but they also suffered from them. For the demands of women were usually assigned—even by some women themselves—a secondary position to what many considered the far greater issue of the rights of slaves.

THE CRUSADE AGAINST SLAVERY

The antislavery movement was not new to the mid-nineteenth century. There had been efforts even before the Revolution to limit, and even eliminate, the institution. Those efforts had helped remove slavery from most of the North by the end of the eighteenth century and had led to the legal prohibition of the international slave trade in 1808. There were powerful antislavery movements in Europe that cried out forcefully against human bondage, perhaps most notably from Britain, where the great antislavery leader, William Wilberforce, had led the effort to abolish the slave trade, and later slavery itself, from the British Empire. But American antislavery sentiment remained relatively muted in the first decades after independence. Not until 1830 did it begin to gather the force that would ultimately enable it to overshadow virtually all other efforts at social reform.

EARLY OPPOSITION TO SLAVERY

In the early years of the nineteenth century, those who opposed slavery were, for the most part, a calm and genteel lot, expressing moral disapproval but engaging in few overt activities. To the extent that there was an organized antislavery movement, it centered on the concept of colonization—the effort to encour-

age the resettlement of African Americans in Africa or the

AMERICAN
COLONIZATION
SOCIETY

Caribbean. In 1817, a group of prominent white Virginians organized the American Colonization Society (ACS), which worked carefully to challenge slavery without challenging property rights or southern sensibilities. The ACS proposed a gradual manumission (or freeing) of slaves, with masters receiving compensation through funds raised by private charity or appropriated by state legislatures. The Society would then transport liberated slaves out of the country and help them to establish a new society of their own elsewhere.

The ACS was not without impact. It received some funding from private donors, some from Congress, some from the legislatures of Virginia and Maryland. And it arranged the shipment of several groups of African Americans out of the country, some of them to the west coast of Africa, where in 1830 they established the nation of Liberia (which became an independent republic in 1846—its capital, Monrovia, was named for the American president who had presided over the initial settlement).

But the ACS was in the end a negligible force. Neither private nor public funding was nearly enough to carry out the vast projects its supporters envisioned. In the space of a decade, they

FAILURE OF
COLONIZATION

managed to "colonize" fewer slaves than were born in the United States in a month. No amount of funding, in fact, would have

been enough; there were far too many black men and women in America in the nineteenth century to be transported to Africa by any conceivable program. And in any case, the ACS met resistance from African Americans themselves, many of whom were now three or more generations removed from Africa and had no wish to move to a land of which they knew almost nothing. (The Massachusetts free black Paul Cuffe had met similar resistance from members of his own race in the early 1800s when he proposed a colonization scheme of his own.)

By 1830, in other words, the early antislavery movement was rapidly losing strength. Colonization was proving not to be a viable method of attacking the institution, particularly since the cotton boom in the Deep South was increasing the commitment of planters to their "peculiar" labor system. Those opposed to slavery had reached what appeared to be a dead end.

GARRISON AND ABOLITIONISM

At this crucial juncture, with the antislavery movement seemingly on the verge of collapse, a new figure emerged to transform it into a dramatically different phenomenon. He was William Lloyd Garrison. Born in Massachusetts in 1805, Garrison was an assistant in the 1820s to the New Jersey Quaker Benjamin Lundy, who published the leading antislavery newspaper of the time—the *Genius of Universal Emancipation*—in

GARRISON AND
THE *LIBERATOR*

Baltimore. Garrison shared Lundy's abhorrence of slavery, but he soon grew impatient with his employer's moderate tone and mild

proposals for reform. In 1831, therefore, he returned to Boston to found his own weekly newspaper, the *Liberator*.

Garrison's simple philosophy was genuinely revolutionary. Opponents of slavery, he said, should view the institution from the point of view of the black man, not the white slaveowner. They should not, as earlier reformers had done, talk about the evil influence of slavery on white society; they should talk about the damage the system did to Africans. And they should, therefore, reject "gradualism" and demand the immediate, unconditional, universal abolition of slavery. Garrison spoke with particular scorn about the advocates of colonization. They were not emancipationists, he argued; on the contrary, their real aim was to strengthen slavery by ridding the country of those African Americans who were already free. The true aim of foes of slavery, he insisted, must be to extend to African Americans all the rights of American citizenship. As startling as the drastic nature of his proposals was the relentless, uncompromising tone with which he promoted them. "I am aware," he wrote in the first issue of the *Liberator,* "that many object to the severity of my language; but is there not cause for severity? I will be as harsh as truth, and as uncompromising as justice. . . . I am in earnest—I will not equivocate—I will not excuse—I will not retreat a single inch—AND I WILL BE HEARD."

Garrison soon attracted a large group of followers throughout the North, enough to enable him to found the New England

AMERICAN ANTISLAVERY SOCIETY

Antislavery Society in 1832 and a year later, after a convention in Philadelphia, the American Antislavery Society. Membership in the new organizations mushroomed. By

> **❝ I WILL BE AS HARSH AS TRUTH, AND AS UNCOMPROMISING AS JUSTICE. ❞**
>
> **WILLIAM LLOYD GARRISON**

1835, there were more than 400 chapters of the societies; by 1838, there were 1,350 chapters, with more than 250,000 members. Antislavery sentiment was developing a strength and assertiveness greater than at any other point in the nation's past history.

BLACK ABOLITIONISTS

Abolitionism had a particular appeal to the free blacks of the North, who in 1850 numbered about 250,000, mostly concentrated in cities. They lived in conditions of poverty and oppression often worse than those of their slave counterparts in the South. An English traveler who had visited both sections of the country wrote in 1854 that he was "utterly at a loss to imagine the source of that prejudice which subsists against [African Americans] in the Northern states, a prejudice unknown in the South, where the relations between the Africans and the European [white American] are so much more intimate." This confirmed an earlier observation by the French observer Alexis de Tocqueville that "the prejudice which repels the Negroes seems to increase in proportion as they are emancipated." Northern blacks were often victimized by mob violence; they had virtually no access to education; they could vote in only a few states; and they were barred from all but the most menial of occupations. Most worked either as domestic servants or as sailors in the American merchant marine, and their wages were such that they lived, for the most part, in squalor. Some were kidnapped by whites and forced back into slavery.

FUGITIVE SLAVE LAW CONVENTION Abolitionists gathered in Cazenovia, New York, in August 1850 to consider how to respond to the law recently passed by Congress requiring northern states to return fugitive slaves to their owners. Frederick Douglass is seated just to the left of the table in this photograph of some of the participants. The gathering was unusual among abolitionist gatherings in including substantial numbers of **African Americans.** (Madison County Historical Society, Oneida, NY)

For all their problems, however, northern blacks were aware of, and fiercely proud of, their freedom. And they remained acutely sensitive to the plight of those members of their race

FREE BLACKS' COMMITMENT TO ABOLITION

who remained in bondage, aware that their own position in society would remain precarious as long as slavery existed. Many in the 1830s came to support Garrison, to subscribe to his newspaper, and to sell subscriptions to it in their own communities. Indeed, the majority of the *Liberator*'s early subscribers were free African Americans.

There were also important African American leaders who expressed the aspirations of their race. One of the most militant was David Walker, a free black from Boston, who in 1829 published a harsh pamphlet: *Walker's Appeal . . . to the Colored Citizens*. In it he declared: "America is more our country than it is the whites'—we have enriched it with our blood and tears." He warned: "The whites want slaves, and want us for their slaves, but some of them will curse the day they ever saw us." Slaves should, he declared, cut their masters' throats, should "kill, or be killed!"

Most African American critics of slavery, however, were less violent in their rhetoric. Sojourner Truth, a freed black woman, spent several years involved in a strange religious cult in upstate New York. She emerged as a powerful and eloquent spokeswoman for the abolition of slavery.

The greatest African American abolitionist of all—and one of

FREDERICK DOUGLASS

the most electrifying orators of his time, black or white—was Frederick Douglass. Born a slave in Maryland, Douglass escaped to Massachusetts in 1838, became an outspoken leader of antislavery sentiment, and spent two years lecturing in England, where members of that country's vigorous antislavery movement lionized him. On his return to the United States in 1847, Douglass purchased his freedom from his Maryland owner and founded an antislavery newspaper, the *North Star,* in Rochester, New York. He achieved wide renown as well for his autobiography, *Narrative of the Life of Frederick Douglass* (1845), in which he presented a damning picture of slavery. Douglass demanded for African Americans not only freedom but full social and economic equality as well. "What, to the American slave, is your 4th of July?" Douglass harshly asked in an Independence Day speech in Rochester, New York, in 1854. "I answer: a day that reveals to him, more than all other days in the year, the gross injustice and cruelty to which he is the constant victim. . . . There is not a nation on earth guilty of practices, more shocking and bloody, than are the people of these United States at this very hour."

Black abolitionists had been active for years before Douglass emerged as a leader of their cause; they had held their first national convention in 1830. But with Douglass's leadership, they became a more influential force; and they began, too, to forge alliances with white antislavery leaders such as Garrison.

ANTI-ABOLITIONISM

Abolitionism was a powerful force, but it provoked a powerful opposition as well. Almost all white southerners, of course, looked on the movement with fear and contempt. But so too did many northern whites. Indeed, even in the North, abolitionists were never more than a small, dissenting minority.

To its critics, the abolitionist crusade was a dangerous and frightening threat to the existing social system. Some whites correctly warned that it would produce a terrible war between the sections. Others feared, also correctly, that it might lead to a great influx of free blacks into the North. The strident, outspoken abolition movement seemed to many northern whites a sign of the disorienting social changes their society was experiencing—yet another threat to stability and order. To other northerners, mostly men of business, abolition was a threat to lucrative trade with the South.

The result was an escalating wave of violence directed against abolitionists in the 1830s. When Prudence Crandall attempted to admit several African American girls to her private school in Connecticut, local citizens had her arrested, threw filth into her

VIOLENT REPRISALS

well, and forced her to close down the school. A mob in Philadelphia attacked the abolitionist headquarters, the "Temple of Liberty," in 1834, burned it to the ground, and began a bloody

WILLIAM LLOYD GARRISON Garrison was the first member of the antislavery movement to call publicly for "immediate and complete emancipation" of slaves. That was in 1831, and for the next three decades he remained a stern and uncompromising enemy of slavery. After the Civil War, however, Garrison displayed little interest in the plight of the blacks he had tried to emancipate. Instead, he turned to women's suffrage, Indian rights, and the prohibition of alcohol. (FPG/Getty Images)

THE ABOLITION OF SLAVERY

THE Thirteenth Amendment to the Constitution, ratified in 1865, following the Civil War, abolished slavery in the United States. But the effort to abolish slavery did not begin or end in North America. Emancipation in the United States was part of a worldwide antislavery movement that had begun in the late eighteenth century and continued through the end of the nineteenth.

The movement to end slavery reflected the ideals of the Enlightenment, which inspired new concepts of individual freedom and political equality. As Enlightenment ideas spread throughout the Western world in the seventeenth and eighteenth centuries, introducing human rights and individual liberty to the concept of civilization, people on both sides of the Atlantic began to ask whether slavery was compatible with these new ideas. Some Enlightenment thinkers, including some of the founders of the American republic, believed that freedom was appropriate for white people, but not for people of color. But others came to believe that all human beings had an equal claim to liberty, and their views became the basis for an escalating series of antislavery movements.

Opponents of slavery first targeted the slave trade—the vast commerce in human beings that had grown up in the seventeenth and eighteenth centuries and had come to involve large parts of Europe, Africa, the Caribbean, and North and South America. In the

"AM I NOT A MAN AND A BROTHER" This bronze medallion commemorates the victory of British antislavery activists in extinguishing slavery from throughout the British Empire in 1834. It also records the close links between their movement and the American abolitionist movement led by William Lloyd Garrison. The image on this medallion of a man in chains became a popular one in American antislavery circles in the following years. (The Art Archive)

aftermath of the revolutions in America, France, and Haiti in the late eighteenth and early nineteenth centuries, the attack on the slave trade gained momentum. The English reformer William Wilberforce spent years attacking Britain's connection with the slave trade, arguing against it on moral and religious grounds. After the Haitian revolution, he argued as well that the continuation of slavery would create more slave revolts. In 1807, he persuaded Parliament to pass a law ending the slave trade within the entire British Empire. The British example—combined with political, economic, and military pressure from London—persuaded many other nations to make the international slave trade illegal: the United States in 1808, France in 1814, Holland in 1817, and Spain in 1845. Trading in slaves continued within countries and colonies where slavery remained legal (including the United States), and some illegal slave trading continued throughout the Atlantic world. But the sale of slaves steadily declined after 1807. The last known shipment of slaves across the Atlantic—from Africa to Cuba—occurred in 1867.

Ending the slave trade was a great deal easier than ending slavery itself. But pressure to abolish slavery grew steadily throughout the nineteenth century, with Wilberforce once more helping lead the international outcry against the institution. In Haiti, the slave revolts that began in 1791 eventually abolished not only slavery but also French rule. In some parts of South America, slavery came to an end with the overthrow of Spanish rule in the 1820s. Simón Bolívar, the great leader of Latin American independence, considered

race riot. Another mob seized Garrison on the streets of Boston in 1835 and threatened to hang him. Authorities saved him from death only by locking him in jail. Elijah Lovejoy, the editor of an abolitionist newspaper in Alton, Illinois, was a repeated victim of mob violence. Three times, angry whites invaded his offices and smashed his presses. Three times, Lovejoy installed new machines and began publishing again. When a mob attacked his office a fourth time, late in 1837, he tried to defend his press. The attackers set fire to the building and, as Lovejoy fled, shot and killed him.

That so many men and women continued to embrace abolitionism in the face of such vicious opposition from within their own communities suggests much about the nature of the movement. Abolitionists were not people who made their political commitments lightly or casually. They were strong-willed, passionate crusaders, displaying enormous courage and moral strength, and displaying, too, at times a level of fervor that many of their contemporaries found disturbing. Abolitionists were widely denounced, even by some who shared their aversion to slavery, as wild-eyed fanatics bent on social revolution. The anti-abolitionist mobs, in other words, were only the most violent expression of a sentiment that many other white Americans shared.

ABOLITIONISM DIVIDED

By the mid-1830s, the abolitionist crusade had become impossible to ignore. It had also begun to experience serious internal abolishing slavery an important part of his mission. He freed those slaves who joined his armies, and he insisted on prohibitions of slavery in several of the constitutions he helped frame. In 1833, the British parliament passed a law abolishing slavery throughout the British Empire and compensated slaveowners for freeing their slaves. France abolished slavery in its empire in 1848. In the Caribbean, Spain followed Britain in slowly eliminating slavery from its colonies. Puerto Rico abolished slavery in 1873 and Cuba became the last colony in the Caribbean to end slavery, in 1886, in the face of increasing slave resistance and the declining profitability of slave-based plantations. Brazil was the last nation in the Americas to end the system, in 1888. The Brazilian military began to turn against slavery after the valiant participation of slaves in Brazil's war with Paraguay in the late 1860s; eventually, educated Brazilian civilians began to oppose the system too, arguing that it obstructed economic and social progress.

In the United States, the power of world opinion—and the example of Wilberforce's movement in England—became an important spur to the abolitionist movement as it gained strength in the 1820s and 1830s. American abolitionism, in turn, helped reinforce the movements abroad. Frederick Douglass, the former slave turned abolitionist, became a major figure in the international antislavery movement and was a much-admired and much-sought-after speaker in England and Europe in the 1840s and 1850s. No other nation paid as terrible a price for abolishing slavery as did the United States during its Civil War, but American emancipation was nevertheless a part of a worldwide movement toward ending legalized human bondage. •

UNDERSTAND, ANALYZE, AND EVALUATE

1. Why did opponents of slavery focus first on ending the slave trade, rather than abolishing slavery itself? Why was ending the slave trade easier than ending slavery?
2. How do William Wilberforce's arguments against slavery compare with those of the abolitionists in the United States?
3. How could a nation that declared "all men are created equal" justify slavery?

strains and divisions. One reason was the violence of the anti-abolitionists, which persuaded some members of the movement that a more moderate approach was necessary. Another reason was the growing radicalism of William Lloyd Garrison, who shocked even many of his own allies (including Frederick Douglass) by attacking not only slavery but the government itself. The Constitution, he said, was "a covenant with death and an agreement with hell." The nation's churches, he claimed, were bulwarks of slavery. In 1840, finally, Garrison precipitated a formal division within the American Antislavery Society by insisting that women, who had always been central to the organization's work, be permitted to participate in the movement on terms of full equality.

MODERATES VERSUS EXTREMISTS

He continued after 1840 to arouse controversy with new and even more radical stands: an extreme pacifism that rejected even defensive wars; opposition to all forms of coercion—not just slavery but prisons and asylums; and finally, in 1843, a call for northern disunion from the South. The nation could, he suggested, purge itself of the sin of slavery by expelling the slave states from the Union.

From 1840 on, therefore, abolitionism moved in many channels and spoke with many different voices. The Garrisonians remained influential, with their uncompromising moral stance. Others operated in more moderate ways, arguing that abolition could be accomplished only as the result of a long, patient, peaceful struggle—"immediate abolition gradually accomplished," as they called it. At first, such moderates depended on "moral suasion." They would appeal to the conscience of the slaveholders and convince them that their institution was sinful. When that produced no results, they turned to political action, seeking to induce the northern states and the federal government to aid the cause wherever possible. They joined the Garrisonians in helping runaway slaves find refuge in the North or in Canada through the so-called underground railroad (although their efforts were never as highly organized as the term suggests). They helped fund the legal battle over the Spanish slave vessel *Amistad*.

Later, after the Supreme Court (in *Prigg v. Pennsylvania*, 1842) ruled that states need not aid in enforcing the 1793 law requiring the return of fugitive slaves to their owners, abolitionists secured the passage of "personal liberty laws" in several northern states. These laws forbade state officials to assist in the capture and return of runaways. Above all, the antislavery societies petitioned Congress to abolish slavery in places where the federal government had jurisdiction—in the territories and in the District of Columbia—and to prohibit the interstate slave trade. But political abolitionism had severe limits. Few members of the movement believed that Congress could constitutionally interfere with a "domestic" institution such as slavery within the individual states themselves.

The abolitionists never formed a political party. Antislavery sentiment underlay the formation in 1840 of the Liberty Party, which chose the Kentucky antislavery leader James G. Birney as its presidential candidate. But this party, and its successors, never campaigned for outright abolition (an illustration of the important fact that "antislavery" and "abolitionism" were not always the same thing). They stood instead for "free soil," for keeping slavery out of the territories. Some free-soilers were concerned about the welfare of African Americans; others cared nothing about the slaves but simply wanted to keep the West a country for whites. Garrison dismissed free-soilism as "white-manism." But the free-soil position would ultimately do what abolitionism never could accomplish: attract the support of large numbers, even a majority, of the white population of the North.

The frustrations of political abolitionism drove some critics of slavery to embrace more drastic measures. A few began to

SENTIMENTAL NOVELS

"**AMERICA** is now wholly given over to a damned mob of scribbling women," Nathaniel Hawthorne complained in 1855, "and I should have no chance of success while the public taste is occupied with their trash." Hawthorne, one of the leading novelists of his time, was complaining about the most popular form of fiction in mid-nineteenth-century America—not his own dark and serious works, but the "sentimental novel," a genre of literature written and read mostly by middle-class women.

In an age when affluent women occupied primarily domestic roles, and in which finding a favorable marriage was the most important thing many women could do to secure or improve their lots in life, the sentimental novel gave voice to both female hopes and female anxieties. The plots of sentimental novels were usually filled with character-improving problems and domestic trials, but most of them ended with the heroine securely and happily married. They were phenomenally successful, many of them selling over 100,000 copies each—far more than almost any other books of the time.

Sentimental heroines were almost always beautiful and endowed with specifically female qualities—"all the virtues," one novelist wrote, "that are founded in the sensibility of the heart: Pity, the attribute of angels, and friendship, the balm of life, delight to dwell in the female breast." Women were highly sensitive creatures, the sentimental writers believed, incapable of disguising their feelings, and subject to fainting, mysterious illnesses, trances, and, of course, tears—things rarely expected of men. But they were also capable of a kind of nurturing love and natural sincerity that was hard to find in the predominantly male public world. In Susan Warner's *The Wide, Wide World* (1850), for example, the heroine, a young girl named Ellen Montgomery, finds herself suddenly thrust into the "wide, wide world" of male competition after her father loses his fortune. She is unable to adapt to it, but she is saved in the end when she is taken in by wealthy relatives, who will undoubtedly prepare her for a successful marriage. They restore to her the security and comfort to which she had been born and without which she seemed unable to thrive.

Sentimental novels accepted uncritically the popular assumptions about women's special needs and desires, and they offered stirring tales of how women satisfied them. But sentimental novels did not stop with romanticized images of female fulfillment through protection and marriage. They hinted as well at the increasing role of women in reform movements. Many such books portrayed women dealing with social and moral problems—and using their highly developed female sensibilities to help other women escape from their troubles. Women were particularly suitable for such reform work, the writers implied, because they were specially gifted at helping and nurturing others.

The most famous sentimental novelist of the nineteenth century was Harriet Beecher Stowe. Most of her books—*The Minister's Wooing, My Wife and I, We and Our Neighbors*, and others—portrayed the travails and ultimate triumphs of women as they became wives, mothers, and hostesses. But Stowe was and remains best known for her 1852 antislavery novel, *Uncle Tom's Cabin*, one of the most influential books ever published in America. As a story about slavery, and about an aging black man—Uncle Tom—who is unfailingly submissive to his white masters, it is in many ways very different from

advocate violence; a group of prominent abolitionists in New England, for example, funneled money and arms to John Brown to enable bloody uprisings in Kansas and Virginia (see pp. 364–365, 370). Others attempted to arouse widespread public anger through propaganda. Abolitionist descriptions of slavery—for example, Theodore Dwight Weld and Angelina Grimké's *American Slavery as It Is: Testimony of a Thousand Witnesses* (1839)—presented what the authors claimed were careful, factual pictures of slavery, but what were in fact highly polemical, often wildly distorted images.

The most powerful document of abolitionist propaganda, however, was a work of fiction: Harriet Beecher Stowe's *Uncle Tom's Cabin*. It appeared first, in 1851–1852, as a serial in an antislavery weekly. Then, in 1852, it was published as a book. It rocked the nation, selling more than 300,000 copies within a year of publication, and was later issued

HARRIET BEECHER STOWE

again and again to become one of the most remarkable best-sellers in American history.

Stowe's novel emerged not just out of abolitionist politics, but also out of a popular tradition of sentimental novels written by, and largely for, women. (See "Patterns of Popular Culture," above.) Stowe combined the emotional conventions of the sentimental novel with the political ideas of the abolition movement, and to sensational effect. Her novel, by embedding the antislavery message within a familiar and popular literary form, succeeded in bringing the message of abolitionism to an enormous new audience—not only those who read the book but also those who watched dramatizations of its story by countless theater companies throughout the nation. The novel's emotional portrayal of good, kindly slaves victimized by a cruel system; of the loyal, trusting Uncle Tom; of the vicious overseer Simon Legree (described as a New Englander so as to prevent the book from seeming to be an attack on southern whites); of the escape of the

"A SAD STORY" This nineteenth-century engraving shows a reader gazing sadly and wistfully away from a popular sentimental novel of the time. The magazine that published this picture wrote a disapproving story to accompany it, which began: "The young girl whose tender heart is so powerfully stirred with imaginative sorrow by the reading of some fictitious tale of distress might in our judgment have been provided by wise parents with a more wholesome form of entertainment." (Culver Pictures, Inc.)

UNCLE TOM'S CABIN Uncle Tom's Cabin did much to inflame public opinion in both the North and the South in the last years before the Civil War. When Abraham Lincoln was introduced to Stowe once in the White House, he reportedly said to her: "So you are the little lady that has brought this great war." At the time, however, Stowe was equally well known as one of the most successful American writers of sentimental novels. (Bettmann/Corbis)

Another way in which women were emerging from their domestic sphere was in becoming consumers of the expanding products of America's industrializing economy. The female characters in sentimental novels searched not just for love, security, and social justice; they also searched for luxury and for the pleasure of buying some favored item. Susan Warner illustrated this aspect of the culture of the sentimental novel—and the desires of the women who read them—in *The Wide, Wide World,* in her description of the young Ellen Montgomery in an elegant bookstore, buying a Bible: "Such beautiful Bibles she had never seen; she pored in ecstasy over their varieties of type and binding, and was very evidently in love with them all." •

UNDERSTAND, ANALYZE, AND EVALUATE

1. How did the lives of the heroines of the sentimental novels compare with the lives of real women of the nineteenth century? What made them so popular?
2. How did the sentimental novels encourage women's participation in public life? Did the novels reinforce prevailing attitudes toward women or broaden the perception of women's "proper role"?
3. *Uncle Tom's Cabin* is probably one of the best-known works of American fiction. Why was this novel so much more powerful than other sentimental novels? Why has it endured?

her other novels. But *Uncle Tom's Cabin* is a sentimental novel, too. Stowe's critique of slavery is based on her belief in the importance of domestic values and family security. Slavery's violation of those values, and its denial of that security, is what made it so abhorrent to her. The simple, decent Uncle Tom faces many of the same dilemmas that the female heroines of other sentimental novels encounter in their struggles to find security and tranquillity in their lives.

beautiful Eliza; of the heart-rending death of Little Eva—all became a part of American popular legend. Reviled throughout the South, Stowe became a hero to many in the North. And in both regions, her novel helped to inflame sectional tensions to a new level of passion. Few books in American history have had so great an impact on the course of public events.

Even divided, therefore, abolitionism remained a powerful influence on the life of the nation. Only a relatively small

ABOLITIONISM'S ENDURING INFLUENCE

number of people before the Civil War ever accepted the abolitionist position that slavery must be entirely eliminated in a single stroke. But the crusade that Garrison had launched, and that thousands of committed men and women kept alive for three decades, was a constant, visible reminder of how deeply the institution of slavery was dividing America.

LOOKING BACK

The rapidly changing society of antebellum America produced a remarkable upsurge of cultural nationalism and reform. Writers, artists, intellectuals, and others drew heavily from new European notions of personal liberation—a set of ideas often known as romanticism. But they also strove to create a truly American culture,

unbeholden to European models. The literary and artistic life of the nation expressed the rising interest in personal liberation—in giving individuals the freedom to explore their own souls and to find in nature a full expression of their divinity. It also called attention to some of the nation's glaring social problems.

Reformers, too, made use of the romantic belief in the divinity of the individual. They flocked to religious revivals, worked on behalf of such "moral" reforms as temperance, supported education, and stirred the beginnings of feminism. Above all, in the North, they rallied against slavery. Out of this growing antislavery movement emerged a new and powerful phenomenon: abolitionism, which rejected moderate reform and insisted on nothing less than immediate emancipation of the slaves. The abolitionist crusade galvanized much of the North. It also contributed greatly to the growing schism between North and South. •

KEY TERMS/PEOPLE/PLACES/EVENTS

Amistad 341
Charles Grandison Finney 328
Edgar Allan Poe 323
Elizabeth Cady Stanton 336
Frederick Douglass 339
Harriet Beecher Stowe 342
Henry David Thoreau 324
Herman Melville 323

Horace Mann 332
Hudson River School 322
James Fenimore Cooper 322
Joseph Smith 327
Lucretia Mott 336
Margaret Fuller 325
Nathaniel Hawthorne 325
Ralph Waldo Emerson 324

Sarah and Angelina Grimké 336
Seneca Falls 336
Shakers 326
Susan B. Anthony 336
Transcendentalism 324
Walt Whitman 323
William Lloyd Garrison 337

SIGNIFICANT EVENTS

American Colonization Society founded — 1817

New York constructs first penitentiary — 1821

Robert Owen founds New Harmony community in Indiana — 1825

American Society for the Promotion of Temperance founded — 1826

James Fenimore Cooper publishes *The Last of the Mohicans* — 1826

David Walker publishes *Appeal . . . to the Colored Citizens* — 1829

Joseph Smith publishes the *Book of Mormon* — 1830

American Colonization Society helps create Liberia for emigrating American slaves — 1830

William Lloyd Garrison begins publishing the *Liberator* — 1831

American Antislavery Society founded — 1833

Horace Mann becomes first secretary of Massachusetts Board of Education — 1837

Liberty Party formed — 1840

RECALL AND REFLECT

1. What is "romanticism" and how was it expressed in American literature and art?

2. How did religion affect reform movements, and what was the effect of these movements on religion?

3. What were the aims of the women's movement of the nineteenth century? How successful were women in achieving these goals?

4. What arguments and strategies did the abolitionists use in their struggle to end slavery? Who opposed them and why?

1841
Brook Farm founded in Roxbury, Massachusetts

1844
Mormon leader Joseph Smith killed

1845
Frederick Douglass publishes autobiography

1847
Mormons found Salt Lake City

1848
Women's rights convention held at Seneca Falls, New York

Oneida Community founded in New York

1850
Nathaniel Hawthorne publishes *The Scarlet Letter*

1851
Herman Melville publishes *Moby Dick*

1852
Harriet Beecher Stowe publishes *Uncle Tom's Cabin*

1854
Henry David Thoreau publishes *Walden*

1855
Walt Whitman publishes *Leaves of Grass*

"BLEEDING KANSAS" The battle over the fate of slavery in Kansas was one of the most turbulent events of the 1850s. This 1855 poster invites antislavery forces to a meeting to protest the actions of the "bogus" pro-slavery territorial legislature, which had passed laws that, among other things, made it illegal to speak or write against slavery. "Squatter sovereignty" was another term for "popular sovereignty," the doctrine that gave residents of a prospective state the power to decide the fate of slavery there. (Bettmann/Corbis)

13 | THE IMPENDING CRISIS

UNTIL THE 1840S, THE TENSIONS BETWEEN THE NORTH AND the South remained relatively contained. Had no new sectional controversies arisen, the United States might have avoided a civil war and the two sections might have resolved their differences peacefully over time. But new controversies did arise, all of them centered on slavery.

From the North came the increasingly powerful abolitionist movement, which rejected compromise and conciliation and attempted, with great success, to make the elimination of slavery a moral issue that would not be open to compromise. From the South came an increasingly belligerent defense of slavery. Slavery, its proponents argued, was not a necessary evil, but a positive good—the best possible system for white southerners, who needed a labor force, and the best possible system as well for black southerners, whom the defenders of slavery insisted needed the paternalistic supervision of white masters.

The West brought these differences to a head most forcefully. As the nation annexed extensive new lands—Texas, the

SETTING THE STAGE

Southwest territories, California, Oregon country, and others—a single question arose again and again: What would be the status of slavery in the territories? Two compromises—one in 1850 and another in 1854—failed to contain the conflict. The result was a dangerous and persistent crisis that produced such bitterness, such anger, and such despair on both sides that it could no longer be contained. By the time Abraham Lincoln became president in 1860, the nation was beginning to break apart and the momentum toward civil war was becoming almost impossible to reverse.

LOOKING AHEAD

1. How did the annexation of western territories intensify the conflict over slavery and lead to deeper divisions between the North and the South?

2. What compromises attempted to resolve the conflicts over the expansion of slavery into new territories? To what degree were these compromises successful? Why did they eventually fail to resolve the differences between the North and the South?

3. What were the major arguments for and against slavery and its expansion into new territories?

LOOKING WESTWARD

The United States acquired more than a million square miles of new territory in the 1840s—the greatest wave of expansion since the Louisiana Purchase nearly forty years before. By the end of the decade, the nation possessed all the territory of the present-day United States except Alaska, Hawaii, and a few relatively small areas acquired later through border adjustments. Many factors accounted for this great new wave of expansion, the most important of which were the hopes and ambitions of the many thousands of white Americans who moved into or invested in these new territories. Advocates of expansion justified their goals with a carefully articulated set of ideas—an ideology known as "Manifest Destiny," which became one of the factors driving white Americans to look to the West.

MANIFEST DESTINY

Manifest Destiny reflected both the burgeoning pride that characterized American nationalism in the mid-nineteenth century and the idealistic vision of social perfection that fueled so much of the reform energy of the time. It rested on the idea that America was destined—by God and by history—to expand its boundaries over a vast area, an area that included, but was not necessarily restricted to, the continent of North America. American expansion was not selfish, its advocates insisted; it was an altruistic attempt to extend American liberty to new realms. John L. O'Sullivan, the influential Democratic editor who gave the movement its name, wrote in 1845 that the American claim to new territory

> is by the right of our manifest destiny to overspread and to possess the whole of the continent which Providence has given us for the development of the great experiment of liberty and federative self government entrusted to us.

Manifest Destiny represented more than pride in the nation's political system. Running throughout many of the arguments for expansion was an explicitly racial justification. Throughout the 1840s, many Americans defended the idea of westward expansion by citing the superiority of the "American race"—white people of northern European origins. The "nonwhite"

RACIAL JUSTIFICATION

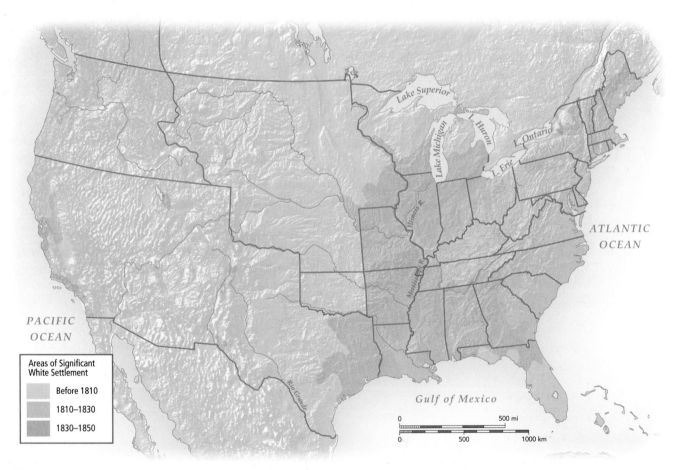

EXPANDING SETTLEMENT, 1810–1850 This map shows the dramatic expansion of the territorial boundaries of the United States in the decades after the Louisiana Purchase. By 1850, the nation had reached its present boundaries (with the exception of Alaska and Hawaii, which it acquired later). Much of this acquisition occurred in the 1840s. It also shows the spread of white settlement within the territories and states.

• *What events contributed to the annexation of new land to the United States in those years?*

peoples of the territories could not be absorbed into the republican system. The Indians, the Mexicans, and others in the western regions were racially unfit to be part of an "American" community, Manifest Destiny advocates insisted. Westward expansion was, therefore, a movement to spread both a political system and a racially defined society. O'Sullivan called "racial purity" (or "whiteness") the "key" to the triumph of the nation.

By the 1840s, the idea of Manifest Destiny had spread throughout the nation, publicized by the new "penny press" (inexpensive newspapers aimed at a mass audience) and fanned by the rhetoric of nationalist politicians. Advocates of Manifest Destiny disagreed, however, about how far and by what means the nation should expand. Some had relatively limited territorial

THE LONE STAR FLAG Almost from the moment Texas won its independence from Mexico in 1836, it sought admission to the United States as a state. Controversies over the status of slavery in the territories prevented its admission until 1845, and so for nine years it was an independent republic. The tattered banner pictured here was one of the republic's original flags. (Frank Lerner, from Showers-Brown Collection, Star of the Republic Museum)

goals; others envisioned a vast new "empire of liberty" that would include Canada, Mexico, Caribbean and Pacific islands, and ultimately, a few dreamed, much of the rest of the world. Some believed America should use force to achieve its expansionist goals, while others felt that the nation should expand peacefully or not at all.

Not everyone embraced the idea of Manifest Destiny. Henry Clay and other prominent politicians feared, correctly as it

OPPOSITION TO FURTHER EXPANSION

turned out, that territorial expansion would reopen the painful controversy over slavery and threaten the stability of the Union. But their voices were barely audible over the clamor of enthusiasm for expansion in the 1840s, which began with the issues of Texas and Oregon.

AMERICANS IN TEXAS

The United States had once claimed Texas—which until the 1830s was part of the Republic of Mexico—as a part of the Louisiana Purchase, but it had renounced the claim in 1819. Twice thereafter the United States had offered to buy Texas, only to meet with indignant Mexican refusals.

But in the early 1820s, the Mexican government launched an ill-advised experiment that would eventually cause it to lose its great northern province: it encouraged American immigration into Texas. The Mexicans hoped to strengthen the economy of the territory and increase their own tax revenues. They also liked the idea of the Americans sitting between Mexican settlement and the large and sometimes militant Indian tribes to the north. They convinced themselves, too, that settlers in Texas would serve as an effective buffer against United States expansion into the region; the Americans, they thought, would soon become loyal to the Mexican government. An 1824 colonization law designed to attract American settlers promised the newcomers cheap land and a four-year exemption from taxes.

Thousands of Americans, attracted by the rich soil in Texas, took advantage of Mexico's welcome. Since much of the available land was suitable for growing cotton, the great majority of the immigrants were southerners, many of whom brought slaves with them. By 1830, there were about 7,000 Americans living in Texas, more than twice the number of Mexicans there.

Most of the settlers came to Texas through the efforts of American intermediaries, who received sizable land grants from Mexico in return for promising to bring settlers into the

STEPHEN AUSTIN

region. The most successful of them was Stephen F. Austin, a young immigrant from Missouri who had established the first legal American settlement in Texas in 1822. Austin and other intermediaries were effective in recruiting American immigrants to Texas, but they also created centers of power in the region that competed with the Mexican government. In 1826, one of these American intermediaries led a revolt to establish Texas as an independent nation (which he proposed calling Fredonia). The Mexicans quickly crushed the revolt and, four years later, passed new laws barring any further American immigration into the region. They were too late. Americans kept flowing into the territory, and in 1833 Mexico dropped the futile immigration ban. By 1835 over 30,000 Americans, white and black, had settled in Texas.

TENSIONS BETWEEN THE UNITED STATES AND MEXICO

Friction between the American settlers and the Mexican government continued to grow. It arose from the continuing ties of the immigrants to the United States, and it arose, too, from their desire to legalize slavery, which the Mexican government had made illegal in Texas (as it was in Mexico) in 1830. But the Americans were divided over how to address their unhappiness with Mexican rule. Austin and his followers wanted to reach a peaceful settlement that would give Texas more autonomy within the Mexican republic. Other Americans wanted to fight for independence.

In the mid-1830s, instability in Mexico itself drove General Antonio Lopez de Santa Anna to seize power as a dictator and impose a new, more conservative and autocratic regime on the nation and its territories. A new law increased the powers of the national government of Mexico at the expense of the state governments, a measure that Texans from the United States assumed Santa Anna was aiming specifically at them. The Mexicans even imprisoned Stephen Austin in Mexico City for a time, claiming that he was encouraging revolts among his fellow Americans in Texas. Sporadic fighting between Americans and Mexicans in Texas began in 1835 and escalated as the Mexican government sent more troops into the territory. In 1836, the American settlers defiantly proclaimed their independence from Mexico.

Santa Anna led a large army into Texas, where the American settlers were having difficulties organizing an effective defense of their new "nation." Several different factions claimed to be the legitimate government of Texas, and the rebels could not even agree on who their commanders were. Mexican forces annihilated an American garrison at the Alamo mission in San Antonio after a famous, if futile, defense by a group of Texas patriots, a group that included, among others, the renowned frontiersman and former Tennessee congressman Davy Crockett. Another garrison at Goliad suffered substantially the same fate when the Mexicans executed most of the force after it had surrendered. By March of 1836, the rebellion appeared to have collapsed. Americans were fleeing east toward Louisiana to escape Santa Anna's army.

But General Sam Houston managed to keep a small force together. And on April 23, 1836, at the Battle of San Jacinto SAN JACINTO (near the present-day city of Houston), he defeated the Mexican army and took Santa Anna prisoner. During the surrender, American troops killed many of the Mexican soldiers in retribution for the executions at Goliad. Santa Anna, under pressure from his captors, signed a treaty giving Texas independence. The Mexican government repudiated the treaty, and Mexican troops briefly occupied San Antonio in 1842 but were unable to win Texas back.

A number of Mexican residents of Texas (known as *Tejanos*) had fought with the Americans in the revolution. But soon after Texas won its independence, their positions grew difficult. The Americans did not trust them, fearing that they were agents of the Mexican government, and in effect drove many of them out of the new republic. Most of those who stayed had to settle for a politically and economically subordinate status within the fledgling nation.

AUSTIN, TEXAS, 1840 Four years after Texas declared its independence from Mexico, the new republic's capital, Austin, was still a small village, most of whose buildings were rustic cabins, as this hand-colored lithograph from the time suggests. The imposing house atop the hill at right was a notable exception. It was the residence of **President Mirabeau Lamar.** (The Center for American History, The University of Texas at Austin)

Above all, American Texans hoped for annexation by the United States. One of the first acts of the new president of Texas, Sam Houston, was to send a delegation to Washington with an offer to join the Union. There were supporters of expansion in the United States who welcomed these overtures; indeed, expansionists in the United States had been supporting and encouraging the revolt against Mexico for years. But there was also opposition. Many American northern-

OPPOSITION TO ANNEXATION

ers opposed acquiring a large new slave territory, and others opposed increasing the southern votes in Congress and in the electoral college. Unfortunately for the Texans, one of the opponents was President Jackson, who feared annexation might cause a dangerous sectional controversy and even a war with Mexico. He therefore did not support annexation and even delayed recognizing the new republic until 1837. Presidents Martin Van Buren and William Henry Harrison also refrained from pressing the issue during their terms of office.

Spurned by the United States, Texas cast out on its own. Its leaders sought money and support from Europe. Some of them dreamed of creating a vast southwestern nation, stretching to the Pacific, that would rival the United States—a dream that appealed to European nations eager to counter the growing power of America. England and France quickly recognized and concluded trade treaties with Texas. In response, President Tyler persuaded Texas to apply for statehood again in 1844. But when Secretary of State Calhoun presented an annexation treaty to Congress as if its only purpose were to extend slavery, northern senators rebelled and defeated it. Rejection of the treaty only spurred advocates of Manifest Destiny to greater efforts toward their goal. The Texas question quickly became the central issue in the election of 1844.

OREGON

Control of what was known as Oregon country, in the Pacific Northwest, was another major political issue in the 1840s. Its half-million square miles included the present states of Oregon, Washington, and Idaho, parts of Montana and Wyoming, and half of British Columbia. Both Britain and the

DISPUTED CLAIMS

United States claimed sovereignty in the region—the British on the basis of explorations in the 1790s by George Vancouver, a naval officer; the Americans on the basis of simultaneous claims by Robert Gray, a fur trader. Unable to resolve their conflicting claims diplomatically, they agreed in an 1818 treaty to allow citizens of each country equal access to the territory. This arrangement, known as "joint occupation," continued for twenty years.

In fact, by the time of the treaty neither Britain nor the United States had established much of a presence in Oregon country. White settlement in the region consisted largely of

> ❝ **WHEN A PEOPLE REFUSE OR NEGLECT TO FILL THE DESIGNS OF PROVIDENCE, THEY OUGHT NOT TO COMPLAIN OF THE RESULTS.** ❞
>
> **MARCUS WHITMAN**

American and Canadian fur traders; and the most significant white settlements were the fur trading post established by John Jacob Astor's company at Astoria and other posts built by the British Hudson Bay Company north of the Columbia River—where residents combined fur trading with farming and recruited Indian labor to compensate for their small numbers.

But American interest in Oregon grew substantially in the 1820s and 1830s. Missionaries considered the territory an attractive target for evangelical efforts, especially after the strange appearance of four Nez Percé and Flathead Indians in St. Louis in 1831. White Americans never discovered what had brought the Indians (who spoke no English) from Oregon to Missouri, and all four died before they could find out. But some missionaries considered the visit a divinely inspired invitation to extend their efforts westward. They were also motivated by a desire to counter the Catholic missionaries from Canada, whose presence in Oregon, many believed, threatened American hopes for annexation. The missionaries had little success with the tribes they attempted to convert, and some—embittered by Indian resistance to their efforts—began encouraging white immigration into the region, arguing that by repudiating Christianity the Indians had abdicated their right to the land. "When a people refuse or neglect to fill the designs of Providence, they ought not to complain of the results," said the missionary Marcus Whitman, who, with his wife, Narcissa, had established an important, if largely unsuccessful, mission among the Cayuse Indians east of the Cascade Mountains.

Significant numbers of white Americans began emigrating

CONFLICT BETWEEN SETTLERS AND INDIANS

to Oregon in the early 1840s, and they soon substantially outnumbered the British settlers there. They also devastated much of the Indian population, in part through a measles epidemic that spread through the Cayuse. The tribe blamed the Whitman mission for the plague, and in 1847 they attacked it and killed thirteen whites, including Marcus and Narcissa. But such resistance did little to stem the white immigration. By the mid-1840s, American settlements had spread up and down the Pacific coast; and the new settlers (along with advocates of Manifest Destiny in the East) were urging the United States government to take possession of the disputed Oregon territory.

WESTWARD MIGRATION

The migrations into Texas and Oregon were part of a larger movement that took hundreds of thousands of white and black Americans into the far western regions of the continent between 1840 and 1860. Southerners flocked mainly to Texas. But the largest number of migrants came from the Old Northwest—white men and women, and a few African Americans, who undertook arduous journeys in search of new opportunities. Most traveled in family groups, until the early 1850s, when the great

PROMOTING THE WEST Cyrus McCormick was one of many American businessmen with an interest in the peopling of the American West. The reaper he invented was crucial to the cultivation of the new agricultural regions, and the rapid settlement of those regions was, in turn, essential to the health of his company. In this poster, the McCormick Reaper Company presents a romantic, idealized image of vast, fertile lands awaiting settlement, an image that drew many settlers westward. (Chicago Historical Society)

California gold rush attracted many single men (see pp. 359–361). Most were relatively prosperous young people. Poor people could not afford the expensive trip, and those who wished to migrate usually had to do so by joining more established families or groups as laborers—men as farm or ranch hands, women as domestic servants, teachers, or, in some cases, prostitutes. The character of the migrations varied according to the destination of the migrants. Groups headed for areas where mining or lumbering was the principal economic activity consisted mostly of men. Those heading for farming regions traveled mainly as families.

All the migrants were in search of a new life, but they harbored many different visions of what a new life would bring. Some—particularly after the discovery of gold in California in 1848—hoped for quick riches. Others planned to take advantage of the vast public lands the federal government was selling at modest prices to acquire property for farming or speculation. Still others hoped to establish themselves as merchants and serve the new white communities developing in the West. Some (among them the Mormons) were on religious missions or were attempting to escape the epidemic diseases plaguing many cities in the East. But the vast majority of migrants were looking for economic opportunities. They formed a vanguard for the expanding capitalist economy of the United States.

LIFE ON THE TRAIL

Most migrants—about 300,000 between 1840 and 1860—traveled west along the great overland trails. They generally gathered in one of several major depots in Iowa and Missouri (Independence, St. Joseph, or Council Bluffs), joined a wagon train led by hired guides, and set off with their belongings piled in covered wagons, livestock trailing behind. The major route west was the 2,000-mile Oregon Trail, which stretched from Independence across the Great Plains and through the South Pass of the Rocky Mountains. From there, migrants moved north into Oregon or south (along the California Trail) OREGON TRAIL to the northern California coast. Other migrations moved along the Santa Fe Trail, southwest from Independence into New Mexico.

However they traveled, overland migrants faced considerable hardships—although the death rate for travelers was only slightly higher than the rate for the American population as a whole. The mountain and desert terrain in the later portions of the trip were particularly difficult. Most journeys lasted five or six months (from May to November), and there was always pressure to get through the Rockies before the snows began, not always an easy task given the very slow pace of most wagon trains (about fifteen miles a day). And although some migrants were moving west at

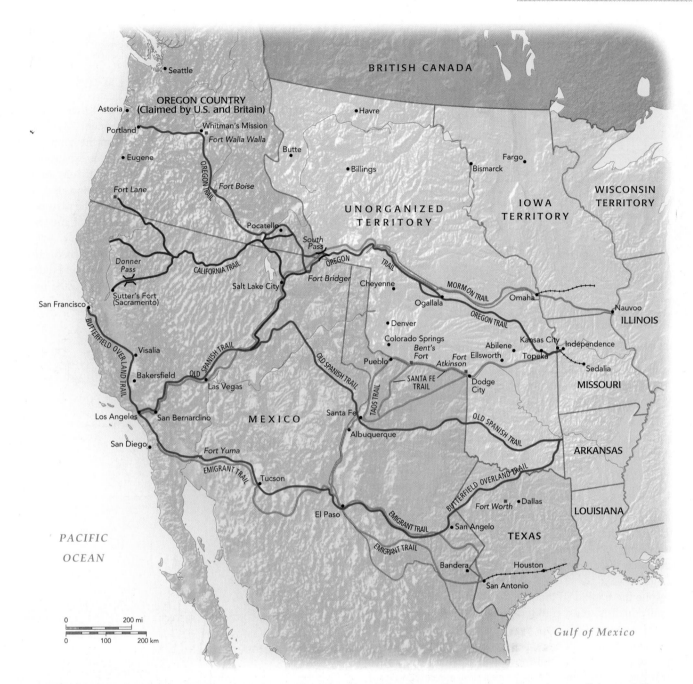

WESTERN TRAILS IN 1860 As settlers began the long process of exploring and establishing farms and businesses in the West, major new trails began to facilitate travel and trade between the region and the more thickly settled areas to the east. Note how many of the trails led to California and how few of them led into any of the far northern regions of United States territory. Note too the important towns and cities that grew up along these trails.

• *What forms of transportation later performed the functions that these trails performed prior to the Civil War?*

least in part to escape the epidemic diseases of eastern cities, they were not immune from plagues. Thousands of people died on the trail of cholera during the great epidemic of the early 1850s.

In the years before the Civil War, fewer than 400 migrants (about one-tenth of 1 percent) died in conflicts with the tribes. In fact, Indians were usually more helpful than dangerous to the white migrants. They often served as guides through difficult terrain or aided travelers in crossing streams or herding livestock. They maintained an extensive trade with the white travelers in horses, clothing, and fresh food. But stories of the occasional conflicts between migrants and Indians on the trail created widespread fear among white travelers, even though more Indians than white people (and relatively few of either) died in those conflicts.

Life on the trail was obviously very different from life on a farm or in a town. But the society of the trail re-created many of

CROSSING THE SIERRAS A wagon train struggles across the rugged trails over the Sierra Nevada Mountains, as migrants travel in California. The image is a black and white photograph that was colored by paint. Only a few years later, the same trip could be achieved much easier because of the transcontinental railroad. (The Granger Collection, New York)

the patterns of conventional American society. Families divided tasks along gender lines: the men driving and, when necessary,

LIFE ON THE TRAIL

repairing the wagons or hunting game; the women cooking, washing clothes, and caring for children. Almost everyone, male or female, walked the great majority of the time, to lighten the load for the horses drawing the wagons; and so the women, many of whose chores came at the end of the day, generally worked much harder than the men, who usually rested when the caravan halted.

Despite the traditional image of westward migrants as rugged individualists, most travelers found the journey a highly collective experience. That was partly because many expeditions consisted of groups of friends, neighbors, or relatives who had decided to pull up stakes and move west together. And it was partly because of the intensity of the experience: many weeks of difficult travel with no other human contacts except, occasionally, with Indians. Indeed, one of the most frequent causes of disaster for travelers was the breakdown of the necessarily communal character of the migratory companies. It was a rare expedition in which there were not some internal conflicts before the trip was over.

EXPANSION AND WAR

The growing number of white Americans in the lands west of the Mississippi put great pressure on the government in Washington to annex Texas, Oregon, and other territory. In the 1840s, these expansionist pressures helped push the United

States into a war that—however dubious its origins—became a triumph for the advocates of Manifest Destiny.

THE DEMOCRATS AND EXPANSION

In preparing for the presidential election of 1844, the two leading candidates—Henry Clay and former president Martin Van Buren—both tried to avoid taking a stand on the controversial issue of the annexation of Texas. Sentiment for expansion was mild within the Whig Party, and Clay had no difficulty securing the nomination despite his noncommittal position. But many southern Democrats supported annexation, and the party passed over Van Buren to nominate a strong supporter of annexation, the previously unheralded James K. Polk.

Polk was not as obscure as his Whig critics claimed. He had

JAMES K. POLK

represented Tennessee in the House of Representatives for fourteen years, four of

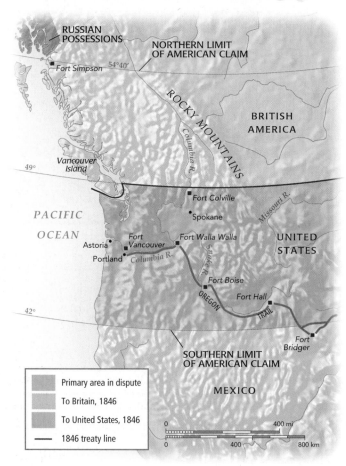

THE OREGON BOUNDARY, 1846 One of the last major boundary disputes between the United States and Great Britain involved the territory known as Oregon—the large region on the Pacific coast north of California (which in 1846 was still part of Mexico). For years, America and Britain had overlapping claims on the territory. The British claimed land as far south as the present state of Oregon, while the Americans claimed land extending well into what is now Canada. Tensions over the Oregon border at times rose to the point that many Americans were demanding war, some using the slogan "54–40 or fight," referring to the latitude of the northernmost point of the American claim.

• *How did President James K. Polk defuse the crisis?*

them as Speaker, and had subsequently served as governor. But by 1844, he had been out of public office—and for the most part out of the public mind—for three years. What made his victory possible was his support for the position, expressed in the Democratic platform, "that the re-occupation of Oregon and the re-annexation of Texas at the earliest practicable period are great American measures." By combining the Oregon and Texas questions, the Democrats hoped to appeal to both northern and southern expansionists. Polk carried the election by 170 electoral votes to 105, although his popular majority was less than 40,000.

Polk entered office with a clear set of goals and with plans for attaining them. John Tyler accomplished the first of Polk's goals for him. Interpreting the election returns as a mandate for the annexation of Texas, the outgoing president won congressional approval for it in February 1845. That December, Texas became a state.

Polk himself resolved the Oregon question. The British minister in Washington brusquely rejected a compromise Polk offered that would establish the United States–Canadian border at the 49th parallel; he did not even refer the proposal to London. Incensed, Polk again asserted the American claim to all of Oregon. There was loose talk of war on both sides of the

COMPROMISE OVER OREGON

Atlantic—talk that in the United States often took the form of the bellicose slogan "54–40 or fight!" (a reference to where the Americans hoped to draw the northern boundary of their part of Oregon). But neither country really wanted war. Finally, the British government accepted Polk's original proposal. On June 15, 1846, the Senate approved a treaty that fixed the boundary at the 49th parallel, where it remains today.

THE SOUTHWEST AND CALIFORNIA

One of the reasons the Senate and the president had agreed so readily to the British offer to settle the Oregon question was that new tensions were emerging in the Southwest—tensions that ultimately led to a war with Mexico. As soon as the United States admitted Texas to statehood in 1845, the Mexican government broke diplomatic relations with Washington. Mexican-American relations grew still worse when a dispute developed over the boundary between Texas and Mexico. Texans claimed the Rio Grande as their western and southern border, a claim that would have added much of what is now New Mexico to Texas. Mexico, although still not conceding the loss of Texas, argued nevertheless that the border had always been the Nueces River, to the north of the Rio Grande. Polk accepted the Texas

TEXAS BOUNDARY IN DISPUTE

SACRAMENTO IN THE 1850S The busy river port of Sacramento served the growing agricultural and mining economies of north central California in the 1850s—years in which the new state began the dramatic population growth that a century later would make it the nation's largest. (California State Library, Sacramento)

claim, and in the summer of 1845 he sent a small army under General Zachary Taylor to Texas to protect it against a possible Mexican invasion.

Part of the area in dispute was New Mexico, whose Spanish and Indian residents lived in a multiracial society that by the 1840s had endured for nearly a century and a half. In the 1820s, the Mexican government had invited American traders into the region (just as it invited American settlers into Texas), hoping to speed development of the province. And New Mexico, like Texas, began to become more American than Mexican. A flourishing commerce soon developed between Santa Fe and Independence, Missouri.

AMERICAN
INTERESTS IN
CALIFORNIA

Americans were also increasing their interest in an even more distant province of Mexico: California. In this vast region lived members of several western Indian tribes and perhaps 7,000 Mexicans, mostly descendants of Spanish colonists. Gradually, however, white Americans began to arrive: first maritime traders and captains of Pacific whaling ships, who stopped to barter goods or buy supplies; then merchants, who established stores, imported merchandise, and developed a profitable trade with the Mexicans and Indians; and finally pioneering farmers, who entered California from the east, by land, and settled in the Sacramento Valley. Some of these new settlers began to dream of bringing California into the United States.

President Polk soon came to share their dream and committed himself to acquiring both New Mexico and California for the United States. At the same time that he dispatched troops to Texas, he sent secret instructions to the commander of the Pacific naval squadron to seize the California ports if Mexico declared war. Representatives of the president quietly informed Americans in California that the United States would respond sympathetically to a revolt against Mexican authority there.

THE MEXICAN WAR, 1846–1848 Shortly after the settlement of the Oregon border dispute with Britain, the United States entered a war with Mexico over another contested border. This map shows the movement of Mexican and American troops during the fighting, which extended from the area around Santa Fe south to Mexico City and west to the coast of California. Note the American use of its naval forces to facilitate a successful assault on Mexico City, and other attacks on the coast of California. Note, too, how unsuccessful the Mexican forces were in their battles with the United States. Mexico won only one battle—a relatively minor one at San Pasqual near San Diego—in the war.

• *How did President Polk deal with the popular clamor for the United States to annex much of present-day Mexico?*

THE MEXICAN WAR

Having appeared to prepare for war, Polk turned to diplomacy and dispatched a special minister, John Slidell, to try to buy off the Mexicans. But Mexican leaders rejected Slidell's offer to purchase the disputed territories. On January 13, 1846, as soon as he heard the news, Polk ordered Taylor's army in Texas to move across the Nueces River, where it had been stationed, to the Rio Grande. For months, the Mexicans refused to fight. But finally, according to disputed American accounts, some Mexican troops crossed the Rio Grande and attacked a unit of American soldiers. Polk now told Congress: "War exists by the act of Mexico herself." On May 13, 1846, Congress declared war by votes of 40 to 2 in the Senate and 174 to 14 in the House.

FAILURE OF
THE SLIDELL
MISSION

The war had many opponents in the United States. Whig critics charged from the beginning (and not without justification) that Polk had deliberately maneuvered the country into the conflict and had staged the border incident that had precipitated the declaration. Many other critics argued that the hostilities with Mexico were draining resources and attention away from the more important issue of the Pacific Northwest. Even when the United States finally reached its agreement with Britain on the Oregon question, opponents claimed that Polk had settled for less than he should have because he was preoccupied with Mexico. Opposition intensified as the war continued and as the public became aware of the casualties and expense.

OPPOSITION TO
THE WAR

To others, the war was a moral crime. Ulysses Grant, then an officer in the Mexican War, called it "one of the most unjust ever waged." Abraham Lincoln criticized the war on the grounds that it gave the president too much power. "Allow the President to invade a neighboring country whenever he shall deem it necessary . . . ," he said, "and you allow him to make war at pleasure." Pacifists were particularly dismayed. Henry David Thoreau was so horrified by the war that he refused to pay taxes (which he said financed the conflict) and spent time in jail.

American forces did well against the Mexicans, but victory did not come as quickly as Polk had hoped. The president

THE BATTLE OF MONTEREY The Battle of Monterey in 1846 was one of the most important conflicts of the Mexican War. Troops under the command of General Zachary Taylor defeated the Mexican forces, but not without significant American casualties. The surrender of the Mexican army on September 26 was a result of the Americans surrounding the Mexican soldiers. It was an important step in the American victory in the Mexican War. (Historicus, Inc.)

ordered Taylor to cross the Rio Grande, seize parts of northeastern Mexico, beginning with the city of Monterrey, and then march on to Mexico City itself. Taylor captured Monterrey in September 1846, but he let the Mexican garrison evacuate without pursuit. Polk now began to fear that Taylor lacked the tactical skill for the planned advance against Mexico City. He also feared that, if successful, Taylor would become a powerful political rival (as, in fact, he did).

In the meantime, Polk ordered other offensives against New Mexico and California. In the summer of 1846, a small army under Colonel Stephen W. Kearny captured Santa Fe with no

BEAR FLAG REVOLUTION

opposition. Then Kearny proceeded to California, where he joined a conflict already in progress that was being staged jointly by American settlers, a well-armed exploring party led by John C. Frémont, and the United States Navy: the so-called Bear Flag Revolution. Kearny brought the disparate American forces together under his command, and by the autumn of 1846 he had completed the conquest of California.

The United States now controlled the two territories for which it had gone to war. But Mexico still refused to concede defeat. At this point, Polk and General Winfield Scott, the commanding general of the army and its finest soldier, launched a

bold new campaign. Scott assembled an army at Tampico, which the navy transported down the Mexican coast to Veracruz. With an army that never numbered more than 14,000, Scott advanced 260 miles along the Mexican National Highway toward Mexico City, kept American casualties low, and never lost a battle before finally seizing the Mexican capital. A new Mexican government took power and announced its willingness to negotiate a peace treaty.

President Polk was now unclear about his objectives. He continued to encourage those who demanded that the United States annex much of Mexico itself. At the same time, concerned about the approaching presidential election, he was growing anxious to finish the war quickly. Polk had sent a special presidential envoy, Nicholas Trist, to negotiate a settlement. On February 2, 1848, Trist reached agreement with the new Mexican government on

TREATY OF GUADALUPE HIDALGO

the Treaty of Guadalupe Hidalgo, by which Mexico agreed to cede California and New Mexico to the United States and acknowledge the Rio Grande as the boundary of Texas. In return, the United States promised to assume any financial claims its new citizens had against Mexico and to pay the Mexicans $15 million. Trist had obtained most of Polk's original demands, but he had not satisfied the new, more expansive

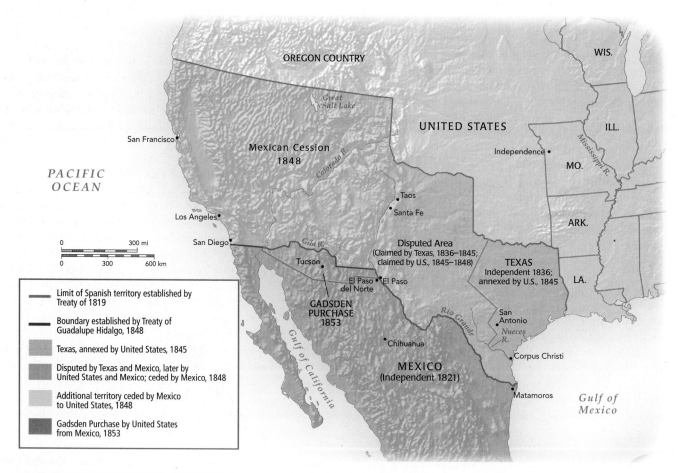

SOUTHWESTERN EXPANSION, 1845–1853 The annexation of much of what is now Texas in 1845, the much larger territorial gains won in the Mexican War in 1848, and the purchase of additional land from Mexico in 1853 completed the present continental border of the United States.

• *What great event shortly after the Mexican War contributed to a rapid settlement of California by migrants from the eastern United States?*

dreams of acquiring additional territory in Mexico itself. Polk angrily claimed that Trist had violated his instructions, but he soon realized that he had no choice but to accept the treaty to silence a bitter battle growing between ardent expansionists demanding the annexation of "All Mexico!" and antislavery leaders charging that the expansionists were conspiring to extend slavery to new realms. The president submitted the Trist treaty to the Senate, which approved it by a vote of 38 to 14. The war was over, and America had gained a vast new territory. But it had also acquired a new set of troubling and divisive issues.

THE SECTIONAL DEBATE

James Polk tried to be a president whose policies transcended sectional divisions. But conciliating the sections was becoming an almost impossible task. Polk gradually earned the enmity of northerners and westerners alike, who believed his policies (particularly his enthusiasm for territorial expansion in the Southwest) favored the South at their expense.

SLAVERY AND THE TERRITORIES

In August 1846, while the Mexican War was still in progress, Polk asked Congress to appropriate $2 million for purchasing peace with Mexico. Representative David Wilmot of Pennsylvania, an antislavery Democrat, introduced an amendment to the appropriation bill prohibiting slavery in any territory acquired from Mexico. The so-called **WILMOT PROVISO** Wilmot Proviso passed the House but failed in the Senate. It would be called up, debated, and voted on repeatedly for years. Southern militants, in the meantime, contended that all Americans had equal rights in the new territories, including the right to move their "property" (slaves) there.

As the sectional debate intensified, President Polk supported a proposal to extend the Missouri Compromise line through the new territories to the Pacific coast, banning slavery north of the line and permitting it south of the line. **COMPETING PLANS** Other politicians supported a plan, originally known as "squatter sovereignty" and later by the more dignified phrase "popular sovereignty," which would allow the people of each territory (acting through their legislature) to decide the status of slavery there. The debate over these various proposals dragged on for many months, and the issue remained unresolved when Polk left office in 1849.

The presidential campaign of 1848 dampened the controversy for a time as both Democrats and Whigs tried to avoid the slavery question. When Polk, in poor health, declined to run again, the Democrats nominated Lewis Cass of Michigan, a dull, aging party regular. The Whigs nominated General Zachary Taylor of Louisiana, hero of the Mexican War but a man with no political experience. Opponents of slavery found the choice of candidates unsatisfying, and out of their discontent emerged the new Free-Soil Party, which drew from the existing Liberty Party and the antislavery wings of the Whig and Democratic Parties and which endorsed the Wilmot Proviso. Its candidate was former president Martin Van Buren.

Taylor won a narrow victory. But while Van Buren failed to carry a single state, he polled an impressive 291,000 votes (10 percent of the total), and the Free-Soilers elected ten members to **FREE-SOIL PARTY** Congress. The emergence of the Free-Soil Party as an important political force, like the emergence of the Know-Nothing and Liberty Parties before it, signaled the inability of the existing parties to contain the political passions slavery was creating.

THE CALIFORNIA GOLD RUSH

By the time Taylor took office, the pressure to resolve the question of slavery in the far western territories had become more urgent as a result of dramatic events in California. In January 1848, James Marshall, a carpenter working on one of rancher John Sutter's sawmills, found traces of gold in the foothills of the Sierra Nevada. Sutter tried to suppress the news, fearing a gold rush would destroy his own substantial empire in the region. But by May, word of the discovery had reached San Francisco; by late summer, it had reached the east coast of the United States and much of the rest of the world. Almost immediately, hundreds of thousands of people from around the world began flocking to California in a frantic search for gold. California's non-Indian population increased nearly twentyfold in four years: from 14,000 in 1848 to over 220,000 in 1852.

The atmosphere in California at the peak of the gold rush was one of crazed excitement and greed. For a short time, San Francisco was almost completely depopulated as residents raced to the mountains to search for gold; the city's principal newspaper (which had been criticizing the gold mania) had to stop publication because it could no longer find either staff or readers. "Nothing but the introduction of insane asylums can effect a cure," one visitor remarked of the gold mania.

Most pre–gold-rush migrants to the Far West had prepared carefully before making the journey. But the gold-rush migrants **FORTY-NINERS** (known as "Forty-niners") threw caution to the winds. They abandoned farms, jobs, homes, families; they piled onto ships and flooded the overland trails—many carrying only what they could pack on their backs. The overwhelming majority of the Forty-niners (perhaps 95 percent) were men, and the society they created on their arrival in California was unusually volatile because of the absence of women, children, and families.

The gold rush also attracted some of the first Chinese migrants to the western United States. News of the discoveries created great excitement in China, particularly in impoverished areas, where letters from Chinese already in California and reports from Americans visiting in China spread the word. It was, of course, extremely difficult for a poor Chinese peasant to get to America; but many young, adventurous people (mostly men) decided to go anyway—believing that they could quickly become rich and then return to China. Emigration brokers loaned many migrants money for passage to California, which the migrants would pay off out of their earnings there. The migration was almost entirely

LOOKING FOR GOLD Finding gold in California was not, for the most part, a task for lone prospectors. More common were teams of people who, together, built elaborate mining technologies. As this 1852 photograph shows, the mining teams were often interracial. The white miners on the left stand conspicuously apart from the Chinese workers on the right, but both groups were essential parts of the enterprise. (Art Resource, NY)

voluntary (unlike the forced movement of kidnapped "coolies" to such places as Peru and Cuba at about the same time). The Chinese in California were, therefore, free laborers and merchants, looking for gold or, more often, hoping to profit from other economic opportunities the gold boom was creating.

The gold rush created a serious labor shortage in California, as many male workers left their jobs and flocked to the gold fields. This shortage created opportunities for many people who needed work (including Chinese immigrants). It also led to an overt exploitation of Indians that resembled slavery in all but name. White vigilantes, who called themselves "Indian hunters," were already hunting down and killing

INDIAN SLAVERY

thousands of Indians before the gold rush (contributing to the process by which the Native American population of California declined from 150,000 to 30,000 between the 1850s and 1870). Now a new state law permitted the arrest of "loitering" or orphaned Indians and their assignment to a term of "indentured" labor.

The gold rush was of critical importance to the growth of California, but not for the reasons most of the migrants hoped. There was substantial gold in the hills of the Sierra Nevada, and many people got rich from it. But Only a tiny fraction of the Forty-niners ever found gold, or even managed to stake a claim to land on which they could look for gold. Some

ONLY A TINY FRACTION OF THE FORTY-NINERS EVER FOUND GOLD, OR EVEN MANAGED TO STAKE A CLAIM TO LAND ON WHICH THEY COULD LOOK FOR GOLD.

disappointed migrants returned home after a while. But many stayed in California and swelled both the agricultural and urban populations of the territory. By 1856, for example, San Francisco—whose population had been 1,000 before the gold rush (and at one point declined to about 100 as people left for the mines)—was the home of over 50,000 people. By the early 1850s, California's population, which had always been diverse, had become even more so. The gold rush had attracted not just white Americans, but also Europeans, Chinese, South Americans, Mexicans, free blacks, and slaves who accompanied southern migrants. Conflicts over gold intersected with racial and ethnic tensions to make the territory an unusually turbulent place. As a result, pressure grew to create a more stable and effective government. The gold rush, therefore, became another factor putting pressure on the United States to resolve the status not only of California, but of all territories—and of slavery within them—as well.

RISING SECTIONAL TENSIONS

Zachary Taylor believed statehood could become the solution to the issue of slavery in the territories. As long as the new lands remained territories, the federal government was responsible for deciding the fate of slavery within them. But once they became states, he thought, their own governments would be able to settle the slavery question. At Taylor's urging, California quickly adopted a constitution that prohibited slavery, and in December 1849 Taylor asked Congress to admit California as a free state. New Mexico, he added, should also be granted statehood as soon as it was ready and should, like California, be permitted to decide for itself what it wanted to do about slavery.

Congress balked, in part because of several other controversies concerning slavery that were complicating the debate. One was the effort of antislavery forces to abolish slavery in the District of Columbia, a movement bitterly resisted by southerners. Another was the emergence of personal liberty laws in northern states, which barred courts and police officers from helping to return runaway slaves to their owners. In response, southerners demanded a stringent law that would require northern states to return fugitive slaves to their owners. But the biggest obstacle to the president's program was the white South's fear that two new free states would be added to the northern majority. The number of free and slave states was equal in 1849—fifteen each. But the admission of California would upset the balance; and New Mexico, Oregon, and Utah might upset it further, leaving the South in a minority in the Senate, as it already was in the House.

Tempers were now rising to dangerous levels. Even many otherwise moderate southern leaders were beginning to talk about secession from the Union. In the North, every state legislature but one adopted a resolution demanding the prohibition of slavery in the territories.

SECTIONAL CONFLICT OVER SLAVERY IN THE TERRITORIES

THE COMPROMISE OF 1850

Faced with this mounting crisis, moderates and unionists spent the winter of 1849–1850 trying to frame a great compromise.

The aging Henry Clay, who was spearheading the effort, believed that no compromise could last unless it settled all the issues in dispute between the sections. As a result, he took several measures that had been proposed separately, combined them into a single piece of legislation, and presented it to the Senate on January 29, 1850. Among the bill's provisions were the admission of California as a free state; the formation of territorial governments in the rest of the lands acquired from Mexico, without restrictions on slavery; the abolition of the slave trade, but not slavery itself, in the District of Columbia; and a new and more effective fugitive slave law. These resolutions launched a debate that raged for seven months—both in Congress and throughout the nation. The debate occurred in two phases, the differences between which revealed much about how American politics was changing in the 1850s.

CLAY'S PROPOSED SOLUTION

In the first phase of the debate, the dominant voices in Congress were those of old men—national leaders who still remembered Jefferson, Adams, and other founders—who argued for or against the compromise on the basis of broad ideals. Clay himself, seventy-three years old in 1850, appealed to shared national sentiments of nationalism. Early in March, another of the older leaders—John C. Calhoun, sixty-eight years old and so ill that he had to sit grimly in his seat while a colleague read his speech for him—joined the debate. He insisted that the North grant the South equal rights in the territories, that it agree to observe the laws concerning fugitive slaves, that it cease attacking slavery, and that it amend the Constitution to create dual presidents, one from the North and one from the South, each with a veto. Calhoun was making radical demands that had no chance of passage. But like Clay, he was offering what he considered a comprehensive, permanent solution to the sectional problem that would, he believed, save the Union. After Calhoun came the third of the elder statesmen, sixty-eight-year-old Daniel Webster, one of the great orators of his time. Still nourishing presidential ambitions, he delivered an eloquent address in the Senate, trying to rally northern moderates to support Clay's compromise.

But in July, after six months of this impassioned, nationalistic debate, Congress defeated the Clay proposal. And with that, the controversy moved into its second phase, in which a very different cast of characters predominated. Clay, ill and tired, left Washington to spend the summer resting in the mountains. Calhoun had died even before the vote in July. And Webster accepted a new appointment as secretary of state, thus removing himself from the Senate and from the debate.

In place of these leaders, a new, younger group now emerged. One spokesman was William H. Seward of New York, forty-nine years old, a wily political operator who staunchly opposed the proposed compromise. The ideals of union were to him less important than the issue of eliminating slavery. Another was Jefferson Davis of Mississippi, forty-two years old, a representative of the new, cotton South. To him, the slavery issue was less one of principles and ideals than one of economic self-interest. Most important of all, there was Stephen A. Douglas, a thirty-seven-year-old Democratic senator from Illinois. A westerner

NEW LEADERSHIP

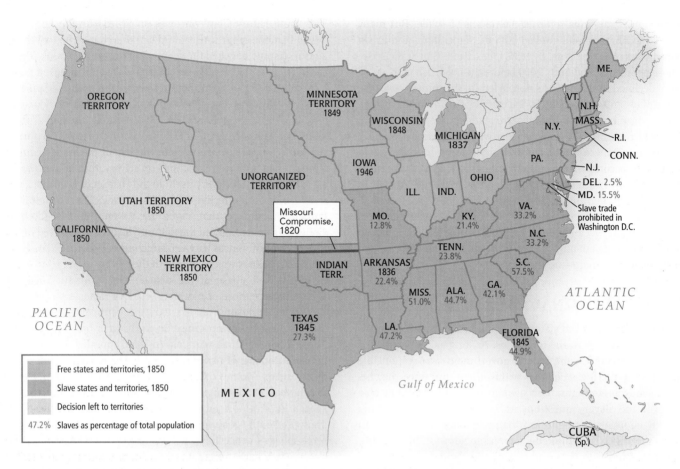

SLAVE AND FREE TERRITORIES UNDER THE COMPROMISE OF 1850 The acquisition of vast new western lands raised the question of the status of slavery in new territories organized for statehood by the United States. Tension between the North and the South on this question led in 1850 to a great compromise, forged in Congress, to settle this dispute. The compromise allowed California to join the Union as a free state and introduced the concept of "popular sovereignty" for other new territories.

• *How well did the compromise of 1850 work?*

from a rapidly growing state, he was an open spokesman for the economic needs of his section—and especially for the construction of railroads. His was a career devoted not to any broad national goals but to sectional gain and personal self-promotion.

The new leaders of the Senate were able, as the old leaders had not been, to produce a compromise. One spur to the compromise was the disappearance of the most powerful obstacle to it: the president. Zachary Taylor had been adamant that only after California and possibly New Mexico were admitted as states could other measures be discussed. But on July 9, 1850, Taylor suddenly died—the victim of a violent stomach disorder. He was succeeded by Millard Fillmore of New York—a dull, handsome, dignified man who understood the political importance of flexibility. He supported the compromise and used his powers of persuasion to swing northern Whigs into line.

The new leaders also benefited from their own pragmatic tactics.

THE COMPROMISE OF 1850 WAS NOT A PRODUCT OF WIDESPREAD AGREEMENT ON COMMON NATIONAL IDEALS. IT WAS, RATHER, A VICTORY OF BARGAINING AND SELF-INTEREST.

Douglas's first step, after the departure of Clay, was to break up the "omnibus bill" that Clay had envisioned as a great, com-

TEMPORARY COMPROMISE

prehensive solution to the sectional crisis and to introduce instead a series of separate measures to be voted on one by one. Thus representatives of different sections could support those elements of the compromise they liked and oppose those they did not. Douglas also gained support with complicated back-room deals linking the compromise to such nonideological matters as the sale of government bonds and the construction of railroads. As a result of his efforts, by mid-September Congress had enacted and the president had signed all the components of the compromise.

The Compromise of 1850, unlike the Missouri Compromise thirty years before, was not a product of widespread agreement on common national ideals. It was, rather, a victory of bargaining and self-interest. Still, members of Congress hailed the measure as a triumph of statesmanship; and Millard Fillmore, signing it, called it a just settlement of the sectional problem, "in its character final and irrevocable."

THE CRISES OF THE 1850s

For a few years after the Compromise of 1850, the sectional conflict seemed briefly to have succeeded amid booming prosperity and growth. But the tensions between North and South remained, and the crisis continued to smolder until—in 1854—it once more burst into the open.

THE UNEASY TRUCE

Both major parties endorsed the Compromise of 1850 in 1852, and both nominated presidential candidates unidentified with sectional passions. The Democrats chose the obscure New Hampshire politician Franklin Pierce, and the Whigs the military hero General Winfield Scott, a man of unknown political views. But the sectional question was a divisive influence in the election anyway, and the Whigs were the principal victims. They suffered the massive defection of antislavery members angered by the party's evasiveness on the issue. Many of them flocked to the Free-Soil Party, whose antislavery presidential candidate, John P. Hale, repudiated the Compromise of 1850. The divisions among the Whigs helped produce a victory for the Democrats in 1852.

Franklin Pierce, a charming, amiable man of no particular distinction, attempted to maintain party—and national—harmony by avoiding divisive issues, particularly by avoiding the issue of slavery. But it was an unachievable goal. Northern opposition to the Fugitive Slave Act intensified quickly after 1850, when southerners began appearing in northern states to pursue people they claimed were fugitives. Mobs formed in some northern cities to prevent enforcement of the law, and several northern states also passed their own laws barring the deportation of fugitive slaves. White southerners watched with growing anger and alarm as the one element of the Compromise of 1850 that they had considered a victory seemed to become meaningless as a result of northern defiance.

OPPOSITION TO THE FUGITIVE SLAVE ACT

"YOUNG AMERICA"

One of the ways Franklin Pierce hoped to dampen sectional controversy was through his support of a movement in the Democratic Party known as "Young America." Its adherents saw the expansion of American democracy throughout the world as a way to divert attention from the controversies over slavery. The great liberal and nationalist revolutions of 1848 in Europe stirred them to dream of a republican Europe with governments based on the model of the United States. They dreamed as well of expanding American commerce in the Pacific and acquiring new territories in the Western Hemisphere.

But efforts to extend the nation's domain could not avoid becoming entangled with the sectional crisis. Pierce had been pursuing unsuccessful diplomatic attempts to buy Cuba from Spain (efforts begun in 1848 by Polk). In 1854, however, a group of his envoys sent him a private document from Ostend, Belgium, making the case for seizing Cuba by force. When the Ostend Manifesto, as it became known, was leaked to the public, it enraged many antislavery northerners, who charged the administration with conspiring to bring a new slave state into the Union.

OSTEND MANIFESTO

The South, for its part, opposed all efforts to acquire new territory that would not support a slave system. The kingdom of Hawaii agreed to join the United States in 1854, but the treaty died in the Senate because it contained a clause prohibiting slavery in the islands. A powerful movement to annex Canada to the United States—a movement that had the support of many Canadians eager for access to American markets—similarly foundered, at least in part because of slavery.

SLAVERY, RAILROADS, AND THE WEST

What fully revived the sectional crisis was the same issue that had produced it in the first place: slavery in the territories. By the mid-1850s, the line of substantial white settlement had moved beyond the boundaries of Missouri, Iowa, and what became Minnesota into a great expanse of plains, which many white Americans had once believed was unfit for cultivation. Now it was becoming apparent that large sections of this region were, in fact, suitable for farming and ranching. In the states of the Old Northwest, therefore, prospective settlers urged the government to open the area to them, provide territorial governments, and—despite the solemn assurance the United States had earlier given the Indians of the sanctity of their reservations—dislodge the tribes located there so as to make room for white settlers. There was relatively little opposition from any segment of white society to this proposed violation of Indian rights. But the interest in further settlement raised two divisive issues that gradually became entwined with each other: railroads and slavery.

As the nation expanded westward, the problem of communication between the older states and the areas west of the Mississippi River became more and more critical. As a result, broad support began to emerge for building a transcontinental railroad. The problem was where to place it—and in particular, where to locate the railroad's eastern terminus, where the line could connect with the existing rail network east of the Mississippi. Northerners favored Chicago, the rapidly growing capital of the free states of the Northwest. Southerners supported St. Louis, Memphis, or New Orleans—all located in slave states. The transcontinental railroad, in other words, had become part of the struggle between the North and the South.

TRANSCONTINENTAL RAILROAD AND SLAVERY

Pierce's secretary of war, Jefferson Davis of Mississippi, removed one obstacle to a southern route. Surveys indicated that a railroad with a southern terminus would have to pass through an area in Mexican territory. But in 1853 Davis sent James

GADSDEN PURCHASE Gadsden, a southern railroad builder, to Mexico, where he persuaded the Mexican government to accept $10 million in exchange for a strip of land that today comprises part of Arizona and New Mexico and that would have facilitated a southern route for the transcontinental railroad. The so-called Gadsden Purchase only accentuated the sectional rivalry.

THE KANSAS-NEBRASKA CONTROVERSY

As a senator from Illinois, a resident of Chicago, and the acknowledged leader of northwestern Democrats, Stephen A. Douglas naturally wanted the transcontinental railroad for his own city and section. He also realized the strength of the principal argument against the northern route west of the Mississippi: that it would run mostly through country with a substantial Indian population. As a result, he introduced a bill in January 1854 to organize (and thus open to white settlement) a huge new territory, known as Nebraska, west of Iowa and Missouri.

Douglas knew the South would oppose his bill because it would prepare the way for a new free state; the proposed territory was in the area of the Louisiana Purchase north of the Missouri Compromise line (36°30′) and hence closed to slavery. In an effort to make the measure acceptable to southerners, Douglas inserted a provision that the status of slavery in the territory would be determined by the territorial legislature—that is, according to "popular sovereignty." In theory, the region could choose to open itself to slavery (although few believed it actually would). When southern Democrats demanded more, Douglas agreed to an additional clause explicitly repealing the Missouri Compromise. He also agreed to divide the area into two new territories—Nebraska and Kansas—instead of one. The new, second territory (Kansas) was more likely to become a slave state. In its

KANSAS-NEBRASKA ACT

final form the measure was known as the Kansas-Nebraska Act. President Pierce supported the bill, and after a strenuous debate, it became law in May 1854 with the unanimous support of the South and the partial support of northern Democrats.

Perhaps no piece of legislation in American history produced so many immediate, sweeping, and ominous consequences. It divided and destroyed the Whig Party, which nearly disappeared by 1856. It divided the northern Democrats (many of whom were appalled at the repeal of the Missouri Compromise, which they considered an almost sacred part of the fabric of the Union) and drove many of them from the party. Most important, it spurred the creation of a new party that was frankly sectional in composition and creed. People in both major parties who opposed Douglas's bill began to call themselves Anti-Nebraska Democrats and Anti-Nebraska Whigs. In 1854, they formed a new organization and named it the Republican Party. It instantly became a major force in American politics. In the elections of that year, the Republicans won enough seats in Congress to permit them, in combination with allies among the Know-Nothings, to organize the House of Representatives.

BIRTH OF THE REPUBLICAN PARTY

"BLEEDING KANSAS"

Events in Kansas itself in the next two years increased the political turmoil in the North. White settlers from both the North and the South began moving into the territory almost immediately after the passage of the Kansas-Nebraska Act. In the spring of 1855, elections were held for a territorial legislature. There were only about 1,500 legal voters in Kansas by then, but thousands of Missourians, some traveling in armed bands into Kansas, swelled the vote to over 6,000. The result was that proslavery forces elected a majority to the legislature, which immediately legalized slavery. Outraged free-staters elected their own

"BLEEDING KANSAS" During the bitter battles over slavery in 1856, the slave state of Missouri tried to prevent antislavery emigrants from passing through their territory en route to Kansas. Free-staters responded by organizing a large emigration through Iowa, circumventing Missouri. Those who entered Kansas by that route tended to arrive armed, some of them with large cannons—among them the one pictured here, which free-staters brought with them to Topeka that year. (Kansas State Historical Society)

delegates to a constitutional convention, which met at Topeka and adopted a constitution excluding slavery. They then chose their own governor and legislature and petitioned Congress for statehood. President Pierce denounced them as traitors and threw the full support of the federal government behind the pro-slavery territorial legislature. A few months later a pro-slavery federal marshal assembled a large posse, consisting mostly of Missourians, to arrest the free-state leaders, who had set up their headquarters in Lawrence. The posse sacked the town, burned the "governor's" house, and destroyed several printing presses. Retribution came quickly.

Among the most fervent abolitionists in Kansas was John Brown, a fiercely committed foe of slavery who considered himself an instrument of God's will to destroy slavery. He had moved to Kansas with his sons so that they could fight to make it a free state. After the events in Lawrence, he gathered six followers (including four of his sons) and in one night murdered five pro-slavery settlers, leaving their mutilated bodies to discourage other supporters of slavery from entering Kansas. This bloody episode, known as the Pottawatomie Massacre, led to more civil strife in Kansas—irregular, guerrilla warfare conducted by armed bands, some of

POTTAWATOMIE MASSACRE them more interested in land claims or loot than in ideologies. Northerners and southerners alike came to believe that the events in Kansas illustrated (and were caused by) the aggressive designs of the other section. "Bleeding Kansas" became a symbol of the sectional controversy.

Another symbol soon appeared, in the United States Senate. In May 1856, Charles Sumner of Massachusetts—a militant and passionate opponent of slavery—rose to give a speech titled "The Crime Against Kansas." In it, he gave particular attention to Senator Andrew P. Butler of South Carolina, an outspoken defender of slavery. The

South Carolinian was, Sumner claimed, the "Don Quixote" of slavery, having "chosen a mistress . . . who, though ugly to others, is always lovely to him, though polluted in the sight of the world, is chaste in his sight . . . the harlot slavery."

The pointedly sexual references and the viciousness of the speech enraged Butler's nephew, Preston Brooks, a member of the House of Representatives from South Carolina. Several days

PRESTON BROOKS AND CHARLES SUMNER after the speech, Brooks approached Sumner at his desk in the Senate chamber during a recess, raised a heavy cane, and began beating him repeatedly on the head and shoulders. Sumner, trapped in his chair, rose in agony with such strength that he tore the desk from the bolts holding it to the floor. Then he collapsed, bleeding and unconscious. So severe were his injuries that he was unable to return to the Senate for four years. Throughout the North, he became a hero—a martyr to the barbarism of the South. In the South, Preston Brooks became a hero, too. Censured by the House, he resigned his seat, returned to South Carolina, and stood successfully for reelection.

THE FREE-SOIL IDEOLOGY

What had happened to produce such deep hostility between the two sections? In part, the tensions were reflections of the two sections' differing economic and territorial interests. But they were also reflections of a hardening of ideas in both North and South. As the nation expanded and political power grew more dispersed, each section became concerned with ensuring that its vision of America's future would be the dominant one.

In the North, assumptions about the proper structure of society came to center on the belief in "free soil" and "free labor." Although abolitionists generated

> AS THE NATION EXPANDED AND POLITICAL POWER GREW MORE DISPERSED, EACH SECTION BECAME CONCERNED WITH ENSURING THAT ITS VISION OF AMERICA'S FUTURE WOULD BE THE DOMINANT ONE.

ANTI-ABOLITIONIST VIOLENCE This 1838 woodcut depicts the anti-abolitionist riot in Alton, Illinois, in which Elijah P. Lovejoy, publisher of an abolitionist newspaper, was slain on November 7, 1837. The death of Lovejoy aroused the antislavery movement throughout the United States. (Library of Congress)

LYCEUMS

TWO passions of the mid-nineteenth century—education and oratory—combined in the 1830s to create a movement that was both popular and, its creators believed, educational: the lyceum.

Although the name came from a building in ancient Greece where Aristotle had taught, the lyceum was not a place. It was an idea, the brainchild of Josiah Holbrook, a Yale graduate and schoolteacher who dreamed of bringing knowledge to adults. Holbrook himself gave a series of lectures in Millbury, Massachusetts, in 1826 to an audience of "farmers and mechanics," offering "instruction in the sciences and other branches of useful knowledge." From that modest experiment, the "lyceum movement" quickly spread through Massachusetts, New England, and other parts of the American North and Northwest. (The movement had only a small impact in the South.)

Making use of public libraries, vacant schools, and other existing spaces, lyceum organizers recruited some of the leading scholars, politicians, and orators of their time to provide entertainment and instruction to adult audiences. The topics of lectures were as various as the speakers. The lyceum in Salem, Massachusetts, for example, sponsored lectures in 1838 on "Causes of the American Revolution," "The Sun," "The Legal Rights of Women," and "The Satanic School of Literature and Reform." The Lowell Institute in Boston provided lectures by the geologist Benjamin Silliman (who spoke there ninety-six times), the naturalist Louis Agassiz, the Russian traveler George Kennan, and the writer-physician Oliver Wendell Holmes (who appeared many times to give a popular lecture on "The Common Law"). Organizers estimated that 13,000 people attended the Lowell lectures in the 1837–1838 season alone. Lectures were open to all (for a small admission charge), but those who attended had to be "neatly dressed and of orderly behavior," and no one could leave the hall while a lecture was in progress. Lyceums may have entertained, but their purpose was to educate.

As the nation became increasingly preoccupied with sectional divisions and battles over slavery, the lyceums became important forums for discussion of public controversies. In Springfield, Illinois, in 1838, Abraham Lincoln spoke at the Young Men's Lyceum to denounce the lynchings of several slaves in Mississippi and an attack on a free black man in St. Louis—examples, he said, of the "mobocratic spirit" and a challenge to the "reverence for the laws" that should be the "political religion of the nation." In the years that followed, prominent abolitionists—William Lloyd Garrison, Wendell Phillips, Frederick Douglass, and others—became among the most popular lyceum orators in the North. Douglass, a former slave turned antislavery orator, traveled widely speaking at lyceums as far-flung as central Ohio, the island of Nantucket, Massachusetts, and England (where he created a sensation within the British lyceum movement). Douglass mesmerized audiences with his scathing descriptions of life under slavery, and his lyceum lectures helped make him one of the best-known and, in the North, most widely admired public figures of his time.

---

some support for their argument that slavery was a moral evil and must be eliminated, most white northerners came to believe that the existence of slavery was dangerous not because of what it did to blacks but because of what it threatened to do to whites. At the heart of American democracy, they argued, was the right of all citizens to own property, to control their own labor, and to have access to opportunities for advancement.

"FREE-SOIL" IDEOLOGY

According to this northern vision, the South was the antithesis of democracy—a closed, static society, in which slavery preserved an entrenched aristocracy and in which common whites had no opportunity to improve themselves. While the North was growing and prospering, the South was stagnating, rejecting the values of individualism and progress. The South was, northern free-laborites further maintained, engaged in a conspiracy to extend slavery throughout the nation and thus to destroy the openness of northern capitalism and replace it with the closed, aristocratic system of the South. The only solution to this "slave power conspiracy" was to fight the spread of slavery and extend the nation's democratic, free-labor ideals to all sections of the country.

"SLAVE POWER CONSPIRACY"

This ideology, which lay at the heart of the new Republican Party, also strengthened the commitment of Republicans to the Union. Since the idea of continued growth and progress was central to the free-labor vision, the prospect of dismemberment of the nation—a diminution of America's size and economic power—was unthinkable.

THE PRO-SLAVERY ARGUMENT

In the South, in the meantime, a very different ideology—entirely incompatible with the free-labor ideology—was emerging among southern whites on the issue of slavery. It was a result of many things: the Nat Turner uprising in 1831, which terrified southern whites and made them more determined than ever to make slavery secure; the expansion of the cotton economy into the Deep South, which made slavery unprecedentedly lucrative; and the growth of the Garrisonian abolitionist movement, with its strident attacks on southern society. The popularity of Harriet Beecher Stowe's *Uncle Tom's Cabin* was perhaps the most glaring evidence of the success of those attacks, but other abolitionist writings had been antagonizing white southerners for years.

At their heart, lyceums always remained what they had been at the start: a place for men and women to educate and improve themselves by listening to knowledgeable speakers talk about what they knew. They both reflected and helped strengthen the growing interest in education in mid-nineteenth-century America. They helped drive the expansion and improvement of the public school system in many areas, and they marked the beginning of many decades of efforts to extend the benefits of education to adults. They helped popularize the lecture system of instruction, which remains a staple of university education even today. In the fevered years preceding the Civil War, however, lyceums also helped spread explosive ideas about slavery, freedom, and union that fanned the popular passions of the age. •

UNDERSTAND, ANALYZE, AND EVALUATE

1. What role did lyceums play in the campaign against slavery?
2. Why was the lyceum movement so much more successful and popular in the North than in the South?
3. Is there an equivalent today of the lyceum? If so, how do its popularity and influence compare with that of the lyceum?

LYCEUM LECTURE, 1841 This drawing portrays an 1841 lyceum lecture at Clinton Hall in New York City by James Pollard Espy, a meteorologist. "An army of men of talent," the New York *Mirror* commented at the time, observing the great popularity of the lyceum series, "has held the town captive." (Museum of the City of New York)

In response to these pressures, a number of white southerners produced a new intellectual defense of slavery. Professor Thomas R. Dew of the College of William and Mary helped begin that effort in 1832. Twenty years later, supporters of slavery summarized their views in an anthology titled *The Pro-Slavery Argument*. John C. Calhoun stated the essence of the case in 1837: Southerners should stop apologizing for slavery as a necessary evil and defend it as "a good—a positive good." It was good for the slaves, white southerners argued, because they enjoyed better conditions than industrial workers in the North. Slavery was good for southern society as a whole because it was the only way the two races could live together in peace. It was good for the entire country because the southern economy, based on slavery, was the key to the prosperity of the nation.

THE PRO-SLAVERY ARGUMENT

Above all, southern apologists argued, slavery was good because it served as the basis for the southern way of life— a way of life superior to any other in the United States, perhaps in the world. White southerners looking at the North saw a spirit of greed, debauchery, and instability. "The masses of the North are venal, corrupt, covetous, mean and selfish," wrote one southerner. Others wrote with horror of the factory system and the crowded, pestilential cities filled with unruly immigrants. The South, by contrast, was a stable, orderly society, operating at a slow and human pace. It was free from the feuds between capital and labor plaguing the North. It protected the welfare of its workers. And it allowed the aristocracy to enjoy a refined and accomplished cultural life. It was, in short, an ideal social order in which all elements of the population were secure and content.

The defense of slavery rested, too, on increasingly elaborate arguments about the biological inferiority of African Americans, who were, many white Southerners claimed, inherently unfit to take care of themselves, let alone exercise the rights of citizenship. And just as abolitionist arguments drew strength from Protestant theology in the North, the pro-slavery defense mobilized the Protestant clergy in the South to give the institution a religious and biblical justification.

> 66 **THE MASSES OF THE NORTH ARE VENAL, CORRUPT, COVETOUS, MEAN AND SELFISH.** 99

BUCHANAN AND DEPRESSION

ELECTION OF 1856

In this unpromising climate, the presidential campaign of 1856 began. Democratic Party leaders wanted a candidate who, unlike President Pierce, was not closely associated with the explosive question of "Bleeding Kansas." They chose James Buchanan of Pennsylvania, a reliable Democratic stalwart who as minister to England had been safely out of the country during the recent controversies. The Republicans, participating in their first presidential contest, denounced the Kansas-Nebraska Act and the expansion of slavery but also endorsed a Whiggish program of internal improvements, thus combining the idealism of antislavery with the economic aspirations of the North. As eager as the Democrats to present a safe candidate, the Republicans nominated John C. Frémont, who had made a national reputation as an explorer of the Far West and who had no political record. The Native American, or Know-Nothing, Party was beginning to break apart, but it nominated former president Millard Fillmore, who also received the endorsement of a small remnant of the Whig Party.

After a heated, even frenzied campaign, Buchanan won a narrow victory over Frémont and Fillmore. A slight shift of votes in Pennsylvania and Illinois would have elected the Republican candidate. Particularly significant was that Frémont had attracted virtually no votes at all in the South while outpolling all other candidates in the North. At the time of his inauguration, Buchanan was, at age sixty-five, the oldest president, except for William Henry Harrison, ever to have taken office. Whether because of age and physical infirmities or because of a more fundamental weakness of character, he was a painfully timid and indecisive president at a critical moment in history.

In the year Buchanan took office, a financial panic struck the country, followed by a depression that lasted several years. In the North, the depression strengthened the Republican Party because distressed manufacturers, workers, and farmers came to believe that the hard times were the result of the unsound policies of southern-controlled Democratic administrations. They expressed their frustrations by moving into an alliance with antislavery elements and thus into the Republican Party.

THE DRED SCOTT DECISION

On March 6, 1857, the Supreme Court of the United States projected itself into the sectional controversy with one of the most controversial and notorious decisions in its history—its ruling in the case of *Dred Scott v. Sandford,* handed down two days after Buchanan was inaugurated. Dred Scott was a Missouri slave, once owned by an army surgeon who had taken Scott with him into Illinois and Wisconsin, where slavery was forbidden. In 1846, after the surgeon died, Scott sued his master's widow for freedom on the grounds that his residence in free territory had liberated him from slavery. The claim was well grounded in Missouri law, and in 1850 the circuit court in which Scott filed the suit declared him free. By now, John Sanford, the brother of the surgeon's widow, was claiming ownership of Scott, and he appealed the circuit court ruling to the state supreme court, which reversed the earlier decision. When Scott appealed to the federal courts, Sanford's attorneys claimed that Scott had no standing to sue because he was not a citizen, but private property.

The Supreme Court (which misspelled Sanford's name in its decision) was so divided that it was unable to issue a single ruling on the case. The thrust of the various rulings, however, was a stunning defeat for the antislavery movement. Chief Justice Roger Taney, who wrote one of the majority opinions, declared

TANEY'S SWEEPING OPINION

that Scott could not bring a suit in the federal courts because he was not a citizen. African Americans had no claim to citizenship, Taney argued, and in fact virtually no rights under the Constitution. Slaves were property, and the Fifth Amendment prohibited Congress from taking property without "due process of law." Consequently, Taney concluded, Congress possessed no authority to pass a law depriving persons of their slave property in the territories. The Missouri Compromise, therefore, had always been unconstitutional.

The ruling did nothing to challenge the right of an individual state to prohibit slavery within its borders, but the statement that the federal government was powerless to act on the issue was a drastic and startling one. Few judicial opinions have ever created as much controversy. Southern whites were elated: the highest tribunal in the land had sanctioned some of the most extreme southern arguments. In the North, the decision produced widespread fury and dismay. The decision, the *New York Tribune* wrote, "is entitled to just so much moral weight as would be the judgment of a majority of those congregated in any Washington bar-room." Republicans threatened that when they won control of the national government, they would reverse the decision—by "packing" the Court with new members.

DEADLOCK OVER KANSAS

President Buchanan timidly endorsed the *Dred Scott* decision. At the same time, he tried to resolve the controversy over Kansas by supporting its admission to the Union as a slave state. In response, the pro-slavery territorial legislature called an election for delegates to a constitutional convention. The free-state residents refused to participate, claiming that the legislature had discriminated against them in drawing district lines. As a result, the pro-slavery forces won control of the convention, which met in 1857 at Lecompton, framed a constitution legalizing slavery, and refused to give voters a chance to reject it. When an election for a new territorial legislature was called, the antislavery groups turned out to vote and won a majority. The new legislature promptly submitted the Lecompton constitution to the voters, who rejected it by more than 10,000 votes.

Both sides had resorted to fraud and violence, but it was clear nevertheless that a majority of the people of Kansas opposed slavery. Buchanan, however, pressured Congress to admit Kansas under the Lecompton constitution. Stephen A. Douglas and other western Democrats refused to support the president's proposal, which died in the House of Representatives. Finally, in April 1858, Congress approved a compromise: The Lecompton constitution would be submitted to the voters of Kansas again. If

LECOMPTON
CONSTITUTION
REJECTED

it was approved, Kansas would be admitted to the Union; if it was rejected, statehood would be postponed. Again, Kansas voters decisively rejected the Lecompton constitution. Not until the closing months of Buchanan's administration in early 1861, after several southern states had already withdrawn from the Union, did Kansas enter the Union—as a free state.

THE EMERGENCE OF LINCOLN

Given the gravity of the sectional crisis, the congressional elections of 1858 took on a special importance. Of particular note was the United States Senate election in Illinois, which pitted Stephen A. Douglas, the most prominent northern Democrat, against Abraham Lincoln, who was largely unknown outside Illinois but who quickly emerged as one of the most skillful politicians in the Republican Party.

Lincoln was a successful lawyer who had long been involved in state politics. He had served several terms in the Illinois legislature and one undistinguished term in Congress. But he was

LINCOLN-
DOUGLAS
DEBATES

not a national figure like Douglas, so he tried to increase his visibility by engaging Douglas in a series of debates. The Lincoln-Douglas debates attracted enormous crowds and received wide attention in newspapers across the country. By the time the debates ended, Lincoln's increasingly eloquent and passionate attacks on slavery had made him nationally prominent.

At the heart of the debates was a basic difference on the issue of slavery. Douglas appeared to have no moral position on the issue. "One of the reserved rights of the states," he said. "was the right to regulate the relations between master and servant, on the slavery question." But Douglas went further, endorsing what was still the dominant sentiment among whites (both North and South) of his time: "I am opposed to negro citizenship in any and every form. I believe this government was made on the white basis. I believe it was made by white men for the benefit of white men and their posterity forever." Lincoln's opposition to slavery was more fundamental. If the nation could accept that African Americans were not entitled to basic human rights, he argued, then it could accept that other groups—immigrant laborers, for example—could be deprived of rights, too. And if slavery were to extend into the western territories, he claimed, opportunities for poor white laborers to better their lots there would be lost. The nation's future, he argued (reflecting the central idea of the Republican Party), rested on the spread of free labor.

Lincoln believed slavery was morally wrong, but he was not an abolitionist. That was in part because he could not envision an easy alternative to slavery in the areas where it already existed. He shared the prevailing view among northern whites that African Americans were not prepared (and perhaps never

LINCOLN'S
POSITION

would be) to live on equal terms with whites. But even while Lincoln accepted the inferiority of black people, he continued to believe that they were entitled to basic rights. "I have no purpose to introduce political and social equality between the white and the

THE HARPERS FERRY ARSENAL John Brown's famous raid on Harpers Ferry in 1859 centered on this arsenal, from which he and his followers tried, in vain, to foment slave rebellion throughout the South. (National Park Service, Harpers Ferry. U.S. Department of the Interior)

black races. . . . But I hold that . . . there is no reason in the world why the negro is not entitled to all the natural rights enumerated in the Declaration of Independence, the right to life, liberty, and the pursuit of happiness. I hold that he is as much entitled to these as the white man." Lincoln and his party wanted to "arrest the further spread" of slavery—that is, prevent its expansion into the territories; but they would not directly challenge it where it already existed and would instead trust that the institution would gradually die there of its own accord.

Douglas's position satisfied his followers sufficiently to win him reelection to the Senate in 1858, but it aroused little enthusiasm and did nothing to enhance his national political ambitions. Lincoln, by contrast, lost the election but emerged with a growing following both in and beyond the state. And outside Illinois, the elections went heavily against the Democrats, who lost ground in almost every northern state. The Democratic Party retained control of the Senate but lost its majority in the House, with the result that the congressional sessions of 1858 and 1859 were bitterly deadlocked.

JOHN BROWN'S RAID

The battles in Congress, however, were overshadowed by a spectacular event that enraged and horrified the entire South and greatly hastened the rush toward disunion. In the fall of 1859,

JOHN BROWN'S RAID

John Brown, the antislavery zealot whose bloody actions in Kansas had inflamed the crisis there, staged an even more dramatic episode, this time in the South itself. With private encouragement and financial aid from some prominent eastern abolitionists, he made elaborate plans to seize a mountain fortress in Virginia from which, he believed, he could foment a slave insurrection in the South. On October 16, he and a group of eighteen followers attacked and seized control of a United States arsenal in Harpers Ferry, Virginia. But the slave uprising Brown hoped to inspire did not occur, and he quickly found himself besieged by citizens, local militia companies, and, before long, United States troops under the command of Robert E. Lee. After ten of his men were killed, Brown surrendered. He was promptly tried in a Virginia court for treason against the state, found guilty, and sentenced to death. He and six of his followers were hanged.

No other single event did more than the Harpers Ferry raid to convince white southerners that they could not live safely in the Union. John Brown's raid, many southerners believed (incorrectly) had the support of the Republican Party, and it suggested to them that the North was now committed to producing a slave insurrection.

THE ELECTION OF LINCOLN

The presidential election of 1860 had the most momentous consequences of any in American history. It was also among the most complex.

The Democratic Party was torn apart by a battle between southerners, who demanded a strong endorsement of slavery, and westerners, who supported the idea of popular sovereignty.

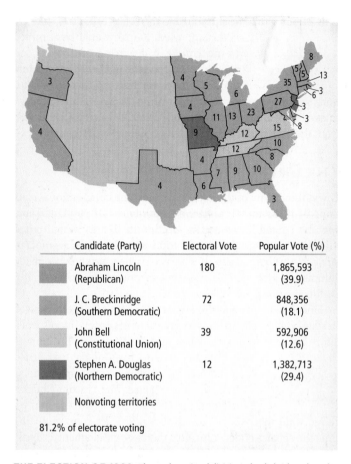

Candidate (Party)	Electoral Vote	Popular Vote (%)
Abraham Lincoln (Republican)	180	1,865,593 (39.9)
J. C. Breckinridge (Southern Democratic)	72	848,356 (18.1)
John Bell (Constitutional Union)	39	592,906 (12.6)
Stephen A. Douglas (Northern Democratic)	12	1,382,713 (29.4)
Nonvoting territories		

81.2% of electorate voting

THE ELECTION OF 1860 The stark sectional divisions that helped produce the Civil War were clearly visible in the results of the 1860 presidential election. Abraham Lincoln, the antislavery Republican candidate, won virtually all the free states. Stephen Douglas, a northern Democrat with no strong position on the issue of slavery, won only one border and one free state, and John Bell, a supporter of both slavery and union, won three border states. John Breckinridge, a strong pro-slavery southern Democrat, carried the entire Deep South. Lincoln won less than 40 percent of the popular vote but, because of the four-way division in the race, managed to win a clear majority of the electoral vote.

• *What impact did the election of Lincoln have on the sectional crisis?*

The party convention met in April in Charleston, South Carolina. When the convention endorsed

DIVIDED DEMOCRATS

popular sovereignty, delegates from eight states in the lower South walked out. The remaining delegates could not agree on a presidential candidate and finally adjourned after agreeing to meet again in Baltimore in June. The decimated convention at Baltimore nominated Stephen Douglas for president. In the meantime, disenchanted southern Democrats met in Richmond and nominated John C. Breckinridge of Kentucky. Later, a group of conservative ex-Whigs met in Baltimore to form the Constitutional Union Party, with John Bell of Tennessee as their presidential candidate. They endorsed the Union and remained silent on slavery.

The Republican leaders, in the meantime, were trying to broaden their appeal so as to attract every major interest group in the North. They warned that the South was blocking the North's economic aspirations. The platform endorsed such traditional Whig measures as a high tariff, internal improvements, a homestead bill, and a Pacific railroad to be built with federal financial assistance. It supported the right of each state to decide the status of slavery within its borders. But it also insisted that neither Congress nor territorial legislatures could legalize slavery in the territories. The Republican convention chose Abraham Lincoln as the party's presidential nominee. Lincoln was appealing because of his growing reputation for eloquence, because of his firm but moderate position on slavery, and because his relative obscurity ensured that he would have none of the drawbacks of other, more prominent (and therefore more controversial) Republicans. He was a representative of the West, a considerable asset in a race against Douglas.

> **THE ELECTION OF LINCOLN BECAME THE FINAL SIGNAL TO MANY WHITE SOUTHERNERS THAT THEIR POSITION IN THE UNION WAS HOPELESS.**

In the November election, Lincoln won the presidency with a majority of the electoral votes but only about two-fifths of the fragmented popular vote. The Republicans, moreover, failed to win a majority in Congress. Even so, the election of Lincoln became the final signal to many white southerners that their position in the Union was hopeless. And within a few weeks of Lincoln's victory, the process of disunion began—a process that would quickly lead to a prolonged and bloody war between two groups of Americans, each heir to more than a century of struggling toward nationhood, each now convinced that it shared no common ground with the other.

DISUNION

LOOKING BACK

In the decades following the War of 1812, a vigorous sense of nationalism pervaded much of American life, helping to smooth over the growing differences among the very different societies emerging in the regions of the United States. By the 1850s, however, the forces that had worked to hold the nation together in the past were falling victim to new and much more divisive pressures that were working to split the nation apart.

Driving the sectional tensions of the 1850s was a battle over national policy toward the western territories, which were clamoring to become states of the Union—and over the place of slavery within them. Should slavery be permitted in the new states? And who should decide whether to permit it or not? There were strenuous efforts to craft compromises and solutions to this dilemma: the Compromise of 1850, the Kansas-Nebraska Act of 1854, and others. But despite these efforts, positions on slavery continued to harden in both the North and the South until ultimately each region came to consider the other its enemy. Bitter battles in the territory of Kansas over whether to permit slavery

SIGNIFICANT EVENTS

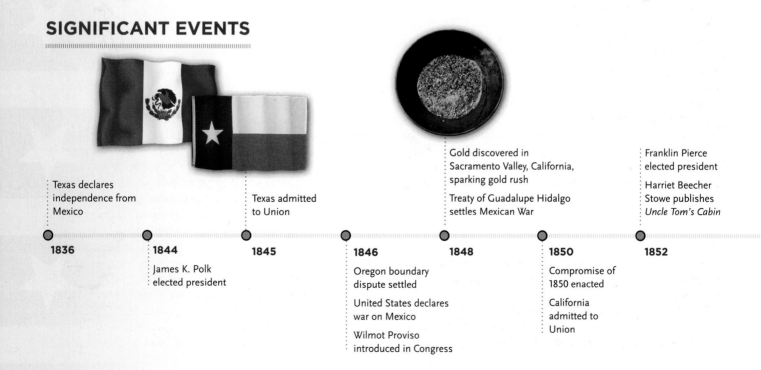

1836	1844	1845	1846	1848	1850	1852

Texas declares independence from Mexico

James K. Polk elected president

Texas admitted to Union

Oregon boundary dispute settled

United States declares war on Mexico

Wilmot Proviso introduced in Congress

Gold discovered in Sacramento Valley, California, sparking gold rush

Treaty of Guadalupe Hidalgo settles Mexican War

Compromise of 1850 enacted

California admitted to Union

Franklin Pierce elected president

Harriet Beecher Stowe publishes *Uncle Tom's Cabin*

there; growing agitation by abolitionists in the North and pro-slavery advocates in the South; the Supreme Court's controversial *Dred Scott* decision in 1857; the popularity of *Uncle Tom's Cabin;* and the emergence of the new Republican Party openly and centrally opposed to slavery: all worked to destroy the hopes for compromise and push the South toward secession.

In 1860, all pretense of common sentiment collapsed when no political party presented a presidential candidate capable of attracting national support. The Republicans nominated Abraham Lincoln of Illinois, a little-known politician recognized for his eloquent condemnations of slavery in a Senate race two years earlier. The Democratic Party split apart, with its northern and southern wings each nominating different candidates. A third party, devoted to the Constitution and the Union, forlornly nominated a candidate of its own who found almost no constituency at all. Lincoln won the election easily, but with less than forty percent of the vote. And almost immediately after his victory, the states of the South began preparing to secede from the Union.   •

KEY TERMS/PEOPLE/PLACES/EVENTS

ABRAHAM LINCOLN 369
COMPROMISE OF 1850 361
DRED SCOTT DECISION 368
"FORTY-NINERS" 359
FREE-SOIL PARTY 359
GADSDEN PURCHASE 364
GENERAL ANTONIO LOPEZ DE
    SANTA ANNA 350
HARPERS FERRY 370

JAMES K. POLK 354
JOHN BROWN 370
KANSAS-NEBRASKA ACT 364
MANIFEST DESTINY 348
OREGON TRAIL 352
POPULAR SOVEREIGNTY 359
SAM HOUSTON 350
STEPHEN A. DOUGLAS 361
STEPHEN F. AUSTIN 349

TEJANOS 350
THE ALAMO 350
TREATY OF GUADALUPE HIDALGO 358
WILMOT PROVISO 359
WINFIELD SCOTT 358
"YOUNG AMERICA" 363
ZACHARY TAYLOR 356

RECALL AND REFLECT

1. How were the boundary disputes over Oregon and Texas resolved? Why were the resolutions in the two cases so different?

2. How did Polk's decisions and actions as president intensify the sectional conflict?

3. What was the issue at stake in "Bleeding Kansas," and how did events in Kansas reflect the growing sectional division between North and South?

4. What was the *Dred Scott* decision? What was the decision's impact on the sectional crisis?

5. How did the growing sectional crisis affect the nation's major political parties?

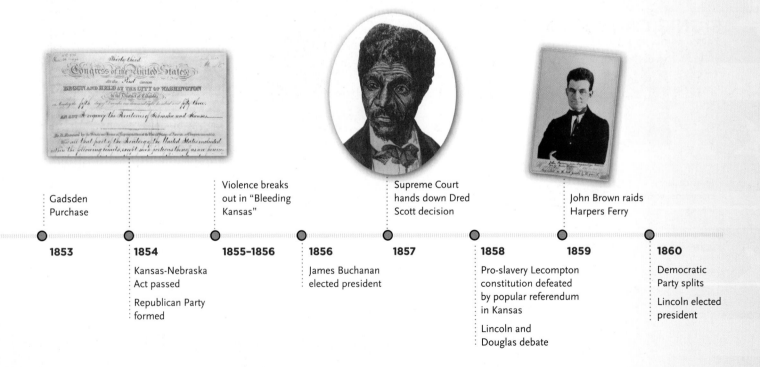

Gadsden Purchase		Violence breaks out in "Bleeding Kansas"			Supreme Court hands down Dred Scott decision			John Brown raids Harpers Ferry		
1853	**1854**	**1855–1856**	**1856**	**1857**		**1858**	**1859**		**1860**
	Kansas-Nebraska Act passed		James Buchanan elected president			Pro-slavery Lecompton constitution defeated by popular referendum in Kansas			Democratic Party splits
	Republican Party formed					Lincoln and Douglas debate			Lincoln elected president

UNION SOLDIERS AT REST The Civil War was one of the bloodiest conflicts in American history. But there were many times at which the armies were not in battle. This photograph of union soldiers was taken at a large supply base in northern Virginia in 1862—one of many sites in which soldiers spent long, idle periods. (Library of Congress, Prints & Photographs Division [LC-USZ62-82754])

14 | THE CIVIL WAR

BY THE END OF 1860, the cords that had once bound the Union together seemed to have snapped. The romantic vision of America's great national destiny had ceased to be a unifying force; North and South now defined that destiny in different and apparently irreconcilable terms. The stable two-party system could not dampen sectional conflict any longer; that system had collapsed in the 1850s, to be replaced by a new one that accentuated, rather than muted, regional controversy. Above all, the federal government was no longer the remote, unthreatening presence it once had been; the need to resolve the status of the territories had made it necessary for Washington to deal with sectional issues in a direct and forceful way. The divisive forces that had always existed within the United States could no longer be counterbalanced by unifying forces.

The election of Abraham Lincoln in 1860—the result of a four-way race in which no candidate achieved close to a majority of the popular vote—was itself evidence of the growing divisions within

SETTING THE STAGE

the nation. That the victor was a man who was clearly from the antislavery camp made his election a powerful factor in the movement toward war. In the aftermath of Lincoln's victory, Southern states began to proclaim their secession from the Union, and the new administration was faced with the fateful choice between letting the Union dissolve or engaging in war.

The conflict that followed was one of the most savage in the history of warfare to that point. At least 618,000 Americans died in the Civil War—a level of casualties almost equal to the total number of American deaths in all the nation's other wars combined. But the war had many other effects on the character of the nation. Perhaps most important, it produced the end of slavery in the United States. Yet the abolition of slavery did not lead to equality or justice for African Americans. It did, however, mark a major turning point in their—and the nation's—history.

LOOKING AHEAD

1. How did the North's mobilization for war differ from mobilization in the South? What accounts for these differences?
2. What were the differences between the impact of the war in the North and the South?
3. What were the military strategies employed by the North and the South from the opening clashes in 1861 through the Union victory in 1865, and how did these strategies differ?

THE SECESSION CRISIS

Almost as soon as the news of Abraham Lincoln's election reached the South, the militant leaders of the region—
"SOUTHERN NATIONALISM" the champions of the new concept of "Southern nationalism," men known both to their contemporaries and to history as the "fire-eaters"—began to demand an end to the Union.

THE WITHDRAWAL OF THE SOUTH

South Carolina, long the hotbed of Southern separatism, seceded first. It called a special convention, which voted unanimously on December 20, 1860, to withdraw the state from the Union. By the time Lincoln took office, six other states from
ESTABLISHMENT OF THE CONFEDERACY the lower South—Mississippi (January 9, 1861), Florida (January 10), Alabama (January 11), Georgia (January 19), Louisiana (January 26), and Texas (February 1)—had seceded. In February 1861, representatives of the seven seceded states met at Montgomery, Alabama, and announced the formation of a new nation: the Confederate States of America. The response from the North was confused and indecisive. President James Buchanan told Congress in December 1860 that no state had the right to secede from the Union but suggested that the federal government had no authority to stop a state if it did.

The seceding states immediately seized the federal property—forts, arsenals, government offices—within their boundaries. But at first they did not have sufficient military power to seize two fortified offshore military installations: Fort Sumter, on an island in the harbor of Charleston, South Carolina, garrisoned by a small force under Major Robert Anderson; and Fort Pickens, in the harbor of Pensacola, Florida. South Carolina sent commissioners to Washington to ask for the surrender of Sumter; but Buchanan, timid though he was, refused to yield it. Indeed, in January 1861 he ordered an unarmed merchant ship to proceed to Fort Sumter with additional troops and supplies. Confederate guns on shore fired at the vessel—the first shots between North and South—and turned it back. Still, neither section was yet ready to concede that war had begun. And in Washington, efforts began once more to forge a compromise.

THE FAILURE OF COMPROMISE

Gradually, compromise forces gathered behind a proposal first submitted by Senator John J. Crittenden of Kentucky and
CRITTENDEN COMPROMISE known as the Crittenden Compromise. It called for several constitutional amendments, which would guarantee the permanent existence of slavery in the slave states and would satisfy Southern demands on such issues as fugitive slaves and slavery in the District of Columbia. But the heart of Crittenden's plan was a proposal to reestablish the Missouri Compromise line in all present and future territory of the United States: Slavery would be prohibited north of the line and permitted south of it. The remaining Southerners in the Senate seemed willing to accept the plan, but the Republicans were not. The compromise would have required the Republicans to abandon their most fundamental position: that slavery not be allowed to expand.

And so nothing had been resolved when Abraham Lincoln arrived in Washington for his inauguration—sneaking into the city in disguise on a night train to avoid assassination as he passed through the slave state of Maryland. In his inaugural address, which dealt directly with the secession crisis, Lincoln laid down several basic principles. Since the Union was older than the Constitution, no state could leave it. Acts of force or violence to support secession were insurrectionary. And the government would "hold, occupy, and possess" federal property in the seceded states—a clear reference to Fort Sumter.

FORT SUMTER

Conditions at Fort Sumter were deteriorating quickly. Union forces were running short of supplies; unless they received fresh provisions, the fort would have to be evacuated. Lincoln believed that if he surrendered Sumter, his commitment to maintaining the Union would no longer be credible. So he sent a relief expedition to the fort, carefully informing the South Carolina authorities that there would be no attempt to send troops or munitions unless the supply ships met with resistance.

The new Confederate government now faced a dilemma. Permitting the expedition to land would seem to be a tame submission to federal authority. Firing on the ships or the

AN EARLY CONFEDERATE FLAG This early Confederate naval flag was seized by Union forces when they captured New Orleans in April 1862. (The Museum of the Confederacy, Richmond, Virginia. Photography by Katherine Wetzel)

FORT SUMTER DURING THE BOMBARDMENT This graphic drawing shows the interior of Fort Sumter during its bombardment by Confederate forces in April 1861. Union forces faced the dual problem of heavy Confederate artillery and cannon fire, and dwindling supplies—since the Confederates had blockaded the Charleston harbor to prevent the North from resupplying the fort. (National Geographic Society)

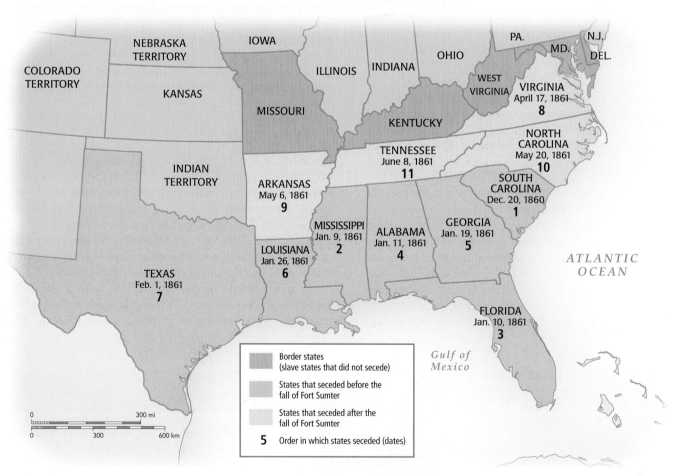

THE PROCESS OF SECESSION The election of Lincoln, the candidate of the antislavery Republican Party, to the presidency had the immediate result of inspiring many of the states in the Deep South to secede from the Union, beginning with South Carolina only a little more than a month after the November election. Other states nearer the northern border of the slaveholding region remained in the Union for a time, but the U.S. attempt to resupply Fort Sumter (and the bombardment of the fort by the new Confederate army) mobilized the upper South to secede as well. Only enormous pressure from the federal government kept the slaveholding states of Maryland, Delaware, Kentucky, and Missouri in the Union.

• *What accounted for the creation of the state of West Virginia in 1861?*

fort would seem (to the North at least) to be aggression. But Confederate leaders finally decided that to appear cowardly would be worse than to appear belligerent, and they ordered

THE WAR BEGINS

General P. G. T. Beauregard, commander of Confederate forces at Charleston, to take the island, by force if necessary. When Anderson refused to surrender the fort, the Confederates bombarded it for two days, April 12–13, 1861. On April 14, Anderson surrendered. The Civil War had begun.

Almost immediately, Lincoln began mobilizing the North for war. And equally promptly, four more slave states seceded from the Union and joined the Confederacy: Virginia (April 17, 1861), Arkansas (May 6), North Carolina (May 20), and Tennessee (June 8). The four remaining slave states—Maryland, Delaware, Kentucky, and Missouri—cast their lot with the Union (under heavy political and even military pressure from Washington).

Was there anything that Lincoln (or those before him) could have done to settle the sectional conflict peaceably? That question has preoccupied historians for more than a century without resolution. (See "Debating the Past," pp. 380–381.) There were, of course, actions that might have prevented a war: if, for example, Northern leaders had decided to let the South withdraw in peace. The real question, however, is not what hypothetical situations might have reversed the trend toward war but whether the preponderance of forces in the nation were acting to hold the nation together or to drive it apart. And by 1861, it seems clear that in both the North and the South, sectional antagonisms—whether justified or not—had risen to such a point that the existing terms of union had become untenable.

People in both regions had come to believe that two distinct and incompatible civilizations had developed in the United States and that those civilizations were incapable of living together in peace. Ralph Waldo Emerson, speaking for much of the North, said at the time: "I do not see how a barbarous community and a civilized community can constitute one state." And a slaveowner, expressing the sentiments of much of the South, said shortly after the election of Lincoln: "These [Northern] people hate us, annoy us, and would have us assassinated by our slaves if they dared. They are a different people from us, whether better or worse, and there is no love between us. Why then continue together?"

> ❝ I DO NOT SEE HOW A BARBAROUS COMMUNITY AND A CIVILIZED COMMUNITY CAN CONSTITUTE ONE STATE. ❞
>
> **RALPH WALDO EMERSON**

That the North and the South had come to believe these things helped lead to secession and

war. Whether these things were actually true—whether the North and the South were really as different and incompatible as they thought—is another question, one that the preparations for and conduct of the war help to answer.

THE OPPOSING SIDES

As the war began, only one thing was clear: all the important material advantages lay with the North. Its population was

UNION ADVANTAGES

more than twice as large as that of the South (and nearly four times as large as the nonslave population of the South), so the Union had a much greater manpower reserve for both its armies and its workforce. The North had an advanced industrial system and was able by 1862 to manufacture almost all its own war materials. The South had almost no industry at all and, despite impressive efforts to increase its manufacturing capacity, had to rely on imports from Europe throughout the war.

In addition, the North had a much better transportation system than did the South and, in particular, more and better railroads: twice as much trackage as the Confederacy and a much better integrated system of lines. During the war, moreover, the already inferior Confederate railroad system steadily deteriorated and by the beginning of 1864 had almost collapsed.

But in the beginning the North's material advantages were not as decisive as they appear in retrospect. The South was, for the most part, fighting a defensive war on its own land and thus had the advantage of local support and familiarity with the territory. The Northern armies, on the other hand, were fighting

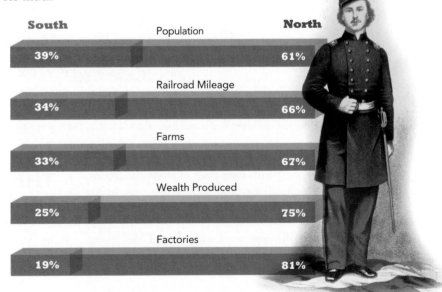

South		North
	Population	
39%		61%
	Railroad Mileage	
34%		66%
	Farms	
33%		67%
	Wealth Produced	
25%		75%
	Factories	
19%		81%

UNION AND CONFEDERATE RESOURCES Virtually all the material advantages—population, manufacturing, railroads, wealth, even agriculture—lay with the North during the Civil War, as this chart shows.

• *What advantages did the South have in the conflict?*

WAR BY RAILROAD Union soldiers pose beside a mortar mounted on a railroad car in July 1864, during the siege of Petersburg, Virginia. Railroads played a critical role in the Civil War, and the superiority of the North's rail system was an important factor in its victory. It was appropriate, perhaps, that the battle for Petersburg, the last great struggle of the war, was over control of critical railroad lines. (National Archives and Records Administration)

mostly within the South, with long lines of communications, amid hostile local populations, and with access only to the South's own inadequate transportation system. The commit-

SOUTHERN ADVANTAGES

ment of the white population of the South to the war was, with limited exceptions, clear and firm. In the North, opinion about the war was more divided and support for it remained shaky until near the end. A major Southern victory at any one of several crucial moments might have proved decisive by breaking the North's will to continue the struggle. Finally, many Southerners believed that the dependence of the English and French textile industries on American cotton would require those nations to intervene on the side of the Confederacy.

THE MOBILIZATION OF THE NORTH

In the North, the war produced considerable discord, frustration, and suffering. But it also produced prosperity and economic growth by giving a major stimulus to both industry and agriculture.

ECONOMIC MEASURES

With Southern forces now gone from Congress, the Republican Party could exercise virtually unchallenged authority. During the war, it enacted an aggressively nationalistic program to promote economic development, particularly in the West. The Homestead Act of 1862 permitted any citizen or prospective citizen to claim 160 acres of public land and to purchase it for

REPUBLICAN ECONOMIC POLICY

a small fee after living on it for five years. The Morrill Land Grant Act of the same year transferred substantial public acreage to the state governments, which were to

sell the land and use the proceeds to finance public education. This act led to the creation of many new state colleges and universities, the so-called land-grant institutions. Congress also passed a series of tariff bills that by the end of the war had raised duties to the highest level in the nation's history—a great boon to domestic industries eager for protection from foreign competition.

Congress also moved to complete the dream of a transcontinental railroad. It created two new federally chartered corporations: the Union Pacific Railroad Company, which was to build westward from Omaha, and the Central Pacific, which was to build eastward from California, settling the prewar conflict over the location of the line. The two projects were to meet in the middle and complete the link. The government provided free public lands and generous loans to the companies.

The National Bank Acts of 1863–1864 created a new national banking system. Existing or newly formed banks could join the

NATIONAL BANK ACTS

system if they had enough capital and were willing to invest one-third of it in government securities. In return, they could issue

U.S. Treasury notes as currency. The new system eliminated much of the chaos and uncertainty in the nation's currency and created a uniform system of national bank notes.

More difficult than promoting economic growth was financing the war itself. The government tried to do so in three ways: by levying taxes, issuing paper currency, and borrowing.

Congress levied new taxes on almost all goods and services; and in 1861 the government levied an income tax for the first

FINANCING THE WAR

time, with rates that eventually rose to 10 percent on incomes above $5,000. But taxation raised only a small proportion of

the funds necessary for financing the war, and strong popular resistance prevented the government from raising the rates. At least equally controversial was the printing of paper currency, or "greenbacks." The new currency was backed not by gold or silver, but simply by the good faith and credit of the government (much like today's currency). The value of the greenbacks fluctuated according to the fortunes of the Northern armies. Early in 1864, with the war effort bogged down, a greenback dollar was worth only 39 percent of a gold dollar. Even at the close of the war, it was worth only 67 percent of a gold dollar. Because of the difficulty of making purchases with this uncertain currency, the government used greenbacks sparingly. The Treasury issued only $450 million worth of paper currency—a small proportion of the cost of the war but enough to produce significant inflation.

By far the largest source of financing for the war was loans from the American people. In previous wars, the government had sold bonds only to banks and to a few wealthy investors. Now, however, the Treasury persuaded ordinary citizens to buy over $400 million worth of bonds—the first example of mass financing of a war in American history. Still, bond purchases by individuals constituted only a small part of the government's borrowing, which in the end totaled $2.6 billion. Most of the loans came from banks and large financial interests.

RAISING THE UNION ARMIES

Over 2 million men served in the Union armed forces during the course of the Civil War. But at the beginning of 1861, the

SENDING THE BOYS OFF TO WAR In this painting by Thomas Nast, New York's Seventh Regiment parades down Broadway in April 1861, to the cheers of exuberant, patriotic throngs, shortly before departing to fight in what most people then assumed would be a brief war. Thomas Nast is better known for his famous political cartoons of the 1870s. (Seventh Regiment Armory, New York City)

THE CAUSES OF THE CIVIL WAR

IN his second inaugural address in March 1865, Abraham Lincoln looked back at the beginning of the Civil War four years earlier. "All knew," he said, that slavery "was somehow the cause of the war." Few historians doubt the basic truth of Lincoln's

"ON TO FREEDOM" This painting by Theodore Kaufmann shows a group of fugitive slaves escaping from the South in the late years of the Civil War. Thousands of former slaves crossed the Union lines, where they were given their freedom. Many of them joined the Union Army. (The Granger Collection, New York)

statement, but they have disagreed sharply about whether slavery was the only, or even the principal, cause of the war.

This debate began even before the war itself. In 1858, Senator William H. Seward of New York took note of two competing explanations of the sectional tensions that were then inflaming the nation. On one side, he claimed, stood those who believed the sectional hostility to be "accidental, unnecessary, the work of interested or fanatical agitators." Opposing them stood those (like Seward himself) who believed there to be "an irrepressible conflict between opposing and enduring forces."

The "irrepressible conflict" argument dominated historical discussion of the war from the 1860s to the 1920s. Because the North and the South had reached positions on the issue of slavery that were both irreconcilable and seemingly unalterable, some historians claimed, the conflict had become "inevitable." James Rhodes, in his seven-volume *History of the United States from the Compromise of 1850* . . . (1893–1900), placed greatest emphasis on the moral conflict over slavery, but he suggested as well that the struggle also reflected fundamental differences between the Northern and Southern economic systems. Charles and Mary Beard in *The Rise of American Civilization*

regular army of the United States consisted of only 16,000 troops, many of them stationed in the West to protect white settlers from Indians. So the Union, like the Confederacy, had to raise its army mostly from scratch. Lincoln called for an increase of 23,000 in the regular army, but the bulk of the fighting, he knew, would have to be done by volunteers in state militias. When Congress convened in July 1861, it authorized enlisting 500,000 volunteers for three-year terms (as opposed to the customary three-month terms). This voluntary system of recruitment produced adequate forces only briefly. After the first flush of enthusiasm for the war, enlistments declined. By March 1863, Congress was forced to pass a national draft law. Virtually all young adult males were eligible to be drafted; but a man could escape service by hiring someone to go in his place or by paying the government a fee of $300. Only about 46,000 men were ever actually conscripted, but the draft greatly increased voluntary enlistments.

To a people accustomed to a remote and inactive national government, conscription was strange and threatening. Opposition to the law was widespread, particularly among laborers, immigrants, and Democrats opposed to the war (known as "Peace Democrats" or "Copperheads" by their opponents). Occasionally, opposition to the draft erupted into violence. Demonstrators against the draft rioted in New York City for four days in July 1863, after the first names were selected for conscription. It was among the most violent urban uprisings in American history. More than 100 people died. Irish workers were at the center of the violence. They were angry because black strikebreakers had been used against them in a recent longshoremen's strike; and they blamed African Americans generally for the war, which they thought was being fought for the benefit of slaves who would soon be competing with white workers for jobs. The rioters lynched a number of African Americans, burned down

DRAFT RIOTS

(2 vols., 1927) also viewed the war as an irrepressible economic, rather than moral, conflict. Ultimately, however, most of those who believed the Civil War to have been "irrepressible" returned to an emphasis on social and cultural factors. Allan Nevins, in *The Ordeal of the Union* (8 vols., 1947–1971), argued that the "problem of slavery" lay at the root of the cultural differences between the North and the South, but that the "fundamental assumptions, tastes, and cultural aims" of the two regions were diverging in other ways as well.

More recent proponents of the "irrepressible conflict" argument have taken different views of the Northern and Southern positions on the conflict but have been equally insistent on the role of culture and ideology in creating them. Eric Foner, in *Free Soil, Free Labor, Free Men* (1970) and other writings, emphasized the importance of the "free-labor ideology" to Northern opponents of slavery. Most Northerners (including Abraham Lincoln), Foner claimed, opposed slavery largely because they feared it might spread to the North and threaten the position of free white laborers. Eugene Genovese, writing of Southern slaveholders in *The Political Economy of Slavery* (1965), argued that just as Northerners were becoming convinced of a Southern threat to their economic system, so Southerners believed that the North had aggressive and hostile designs on the Southern way of life. Like Foner, therefore, Genovese saw cultural differences as the source of an all but inevitable conflict.

Other historians have argued that the Civil War might have been avoided, that the differences between North and South were not so fundamental as to have necessitated war. The idea of the war as avoidable gained wide recognition among historians in the 1920s and 1930s, when a group known as the "revisionists" began to offer new accounts of the origins of the conflict. One of the leading revisionists was James G. Randall, who saw in the social and economic systems of the North and the South no differences so fundamental as to require a war. Avery Craven, another leading revisionist, argued similarly in *The Coming of the Civil War* (1942) that slave laborers were not much worse off than Northern industrial workers, that the institution was already on the road to "ultimate extinction," and that war could therefore have been averted had skillful and responsible leaders worked to produce compromise.

More recent students of the Civil War have emphasized the role of political agitation and ethnocultural conflicts in the coming of the war. Michael Holt, in *The Political Crisis of the 1850s* (1978), emphasized the role of political parties and especially the collapse of the second party system, rather than the irreconcilable differences between sections, in explaining the conflict, although he avoided placing blame on any one group. Along with Paul Kleppner, Joel Silbey, and William Gienapp, Holt was one of the creators of an "ethnocultural" interpretation of the war. These scholars argue that the Civil War began in large part because the party system—the most effective instrument for containing and mediating sectional differences—collapsed in the 1850s and produced

a new Republican Party that aggravated, rather than calmed, the divisions in the nation. William Gienapp, in *The Origins of the Republican Party, 1852–1856* (1987), argued that the disintegration of the party system in the early 1850s was less a result of the debate over slavery in the territories than of such ethnocultural issues as temperance and nativism. Gienapp and the other ethnoculturalists would not entirely dispute Lincoln's claim that slavery was "somehow the cause of the war." But they do challenge the arguments of Eric Foner and others that the "free labor ideal" of the North—and the challenge slavery, and its possible expansion into the territories, posed to that ideal—was the principal reason for the conflict. Slavery became important, they suggest, less because of irreconcilable differences of attitude than because of the collapse of parties and other structures that might have contained the conflict. •

UNDERSTAND, ANALYZE, AND EVALUATE

1. Some arguments regarding the Civil War as inevitable focus on economic differences between the North and the South. What were these differences and how might they have led—inevitably—to war?

2. Some revisionist scholars attribute the Civil War to a "blundering generation" of political leaders. Who were these leaders and what blunders did they make? Could better decisions have avoided war?

3. According to the ethnoculturalists, what was the role of political parties in the coming of the Civil War?

---

homes and businesses (mostly those of free blacks), and even destroyed an orphanage for African American children. Only the arrival of federal troops subdued the rioters.

WARTIME POLITICS

When Abraham Lincoln arrived in Washington early in 1861, many politicians—noting his lack of national experience and his folksy, unpretentious manner—considered him a minor politician from the prairies, a man whom the real leaders of his party would easily control. But the new president moved quickly to establish his own authority. He assembled a cabinet representing every faction of the Republican Party and every segment of Northern opinion—men of exceptional prestige and influence and in some cases arrogance, several of whom believed that they, not Lincoln, should be president. Lincoln moved boldly as well to use the war powers of the presidency, ignoring what

he considered inconvenient parts of the Constitution because, he said, it would be foolish to lose the whole by being afraid to disregard a part. He sent troops into battle without asking Congress for a declaration of war. (Lincoln insisted on calling the conflict a domestic insurrection, which required no formal declaration of war; to ask for a declaration would, he believed, constitute implicit recognition of the Confederacy as an independent nation.) He increased the size of the regular army without receiving legislative authority to do so. He unilaterally proclaimed a naval blockade of the South.

Lincoln's greatest political problem was the widespread popular opposition to the war, mobilized by factions in the Democratic Party. The Peace Democrats feared that the agricultural Northwest was losing influence to the industrial East and that Republican nationalism was eroding states' rights. Lincoln used extraordinary methods to suppress them. He ordered

WARTIME
REPRESSION

SUSPENDING THE WRIT OF HABEAS CORPUS

A WRIT OF HABEAS CORPUS is a court order directing that anyone arrested be brought before the court to see whether there is sufficient evidence to hold the person for trial. The writ does not determine guilt or evidence; rather, it allows a judge to decide whether a prisoner is being legally detained. The right of habeas corpus is guaranteed by the Constitution in Article 1, Section 9: "The privilege of the writ of habeas corpus shall not be suspended, unless when in cases of rebellion or invasion the public safety may require it."

Soon after the beginning of the Civil War, a mob in Baltimore attacked Union troops moving through the city. President Abraham Lincoln then suspended habeas corpus in the area around Washington, D.C., thus permitting military authorities to arrest persons suspected of being disloyal to the Union even without evidence of guilt. Following Union losses on the battlefield and facing upcoming elections and the enactment of a military conscription act, on September 24, 1862, Lincoln issued a proclamation suspending habeas corpus throughout the nation (the "1862" document).

President Lincoln was not the only president to suspend the writ of habeas corpus. On October 17, 2006, President George W. Bush signed into law the Military Commissions Act of 2006, which suspended the right of habeas corpus to persons "determined by the United States" to be "enemy combatants" or persons "awaiting such determination." Section 7 of the act includes the clause relating to habeas corpus matters. An excerpt of Section 7 along with a fact sheet explaining and defending the law appear as the "2006" documents.

LINCOLN—1862

Proclamation Suspending the Writ of Habeas Corpus

BY THE PRESIDENT OF THE UNITED STATES OF AMERICA:

A PROCLAMATION

Whereas, it has become necessary to call into service not only volunteers but also portions of the militia of the States by draft in order to suppress the insurrection existing in the United States, and disloyal persons are not adequately restrained by the ordinary processes of law from hindering this measure and from giving aid and comfort in various ways to the insurrection;

Now, therefore, be it ordered, first, that during the existing insurrection and as a necessary measure for suppressing the same, all Rebels and Insurgents, their aiders and abettors within the United States, and all persons discouraging volunteer enlistments, resisting militia drafts, or guilty of any disloyal practice, affording aid and comfort to Rebels against the authority of United States, shall be subject to martial law and liable to trial and punishment by Courts Martial or Military Commission:

Second. That the Writ of Habeas Corpus is suspended in respect to all persons arrested, or who are now, or hereafter during the rebellion shall be, imprisoned in any fort, camp, arsenal, military prison, or other place of confinement by any military authority by the sentence of any Court Martial or Military Commission.

In witness whereof, I have hereunto set my hand, and caused the seal of the United States to be affixed.

Done at the City of Washington this twenty fourth day of September, in the year of our Lord one thousand eight hundred and sixty-two, and of the Independence of the United States the 87th.

ABRAHAM LINCOLN

By the President:

WILLIAM H. SEWARD, Secretary of State.

UNDERSTAND, ANALYZE, AND EVALUATE

1. What justification does Lincoln give for his suspension of habeas corpus?
2. Whose rights were affected by the proclamation? That is, to whom was habeas corpus denied? Why?

MILITARY COMMISSIONS ACT OF 2006

SEC. 7. HABEAS CORPUS MATTERS.

. . . (1) No court, justice, or judge shall have jurisdiction to hear or consider an application for a writ of habeas corpus filed by or on behalf of an alien detained by the United States who has been determined by the United States to have been properly detained as an enemy combatant or is awaiting such determination.

(2) Except as provided in paragraphs (2) and (3) of section 1005(e) of the Detainee Treatment Act of 2005 (10 U.S.C. 801 note), no court, justice, or judge shall have jurisdiction to hear or consider any other action against the United States or its agents relating to any aspect of the detention, transfer, treatment, trial, or conditions of confinement of an alien who is or was detained by the United States and has been determined by the United States to have been properly detained as an enemy combatant or is awaiting such determination.

This fact sheet released by the Bush White House when the president signed the bill into law explains and defends the law:

The bill I'm about to sign also provides a way to deliver justice to the terrorists we have captured. In the months after 9/11, I authorized a system of military commissions to try foreign terrorists accused of war crimes. These commissions were similar to those used for trying enemy combatants in the Revolutionary War and the Civil War and World War II. Yet the legality of the system I established was challenged in the court, and the Supreme Court ruled that the military commissions needed to be explicitly authorized by the United States Congress.

And so I asked Congress for that authority, and they have provided it. With the Military Commission Act, the legislative and executive branches have agreed on a system that meets our national security needs. These military commissions will provide a fair trial, in which the accused are presumed innocent, have access to an attorney, and can hear all the evidence against them. These military commissions are lawful, they are fair, and they are necessary.

MAKE CONNECTIONS

1. Lincoln suspended the writ of habeas corpus by presidential proclamation; President Bush's suspension of habeas corpus was part of the Military Commissions Act passed by Congress. Does this mean that Bush's suspension of habeas corpus was constitutional?

2. How does President Bush defend and justify his suspension of habeas corpus? How does he make use of the past to help make his case?

3. To whom does the Military Commissions Act of 2006 deny habeas corpus? Whose suspension of habeas corpus was more extensive—Lincoln's or Bush's?

HANGING A NEGRO IN CLARKSON STREET.

THE NEW YORK CITY DRAFT RIOT, 1863 Opposition to the Civil War draft was widespread in the North and in July 1863 produced a violent four-day uprising in New York City in which as many as 100 people died. The riot began on July 13 with a march by 4,000 men, mostly poor Irish laborers, who were protesting the provisions by which some wealthy people could be exempted from conscription. "Rich man's war, poor man's fight," the demonstrators cried (just as some critics of the war chanted at times in the South). Many New Yorkers also feared that the war would drive black workers north to compete for their jobs. The demonstration turned violent when officials began drawing names for the draft. The crowd burned the draft building and then split into factions. Some rioters attacked symbols of wealth such as exclusive shops and mansions. Others terrorized black neighborhoods and lynched some residents. This contemporary engraving depicts one such lynching. Only by transferring five regiments to the city from Gettysburg (less than two weeks after the great battle there) was the government able to restore order. (The Granger Collection)

military arrests of civilian dissenters and suspended the right of habeas corpus (the right of an arrested person to a speedy trial). At first, Lincoln used these methods only in sensitive areas such as the border states; but in 1862, he proclaimed that all persons who discouraged enlistments or engaged in disloyal practices were subject to martial law. In all, more than 13,000 persons were arrested and imprisoned for varying periods. The most prominent Copperhead in the country—Ohio Congressman Clement L. Vallandigham—was seized by military authorities and exiled to the Confederacy after he made a speech claiming that the purpose of the war was to free the blacks and enslave the whites. Lincoln defied all efforts to curb his authority to suppress opposition, even those of the Supreme Court. When Chief Justice Taney issued a writ (*Ex parte Merryman*) requiring him to release an imprisoned Maryland secessionist leader, Lincoln simply ignored it. (After the war, in 1866, the Supreme Court ruled in *Ex parte Milligan* that military trials in areas where the civil courts existed were unconstitutional.)

Repression was not the only tool the North used to strengthen support for the war. In addition to arresting "disloyal" Northerners, Lincoln's administration used new tools of persuasion to build popular opinion in favor of the war. In addition to pro-war pamphlets, posters, speeches, and songs, the war mobilized a significant corps of photographers—organized by the renowned Mathew Brady, one of the first important photographers in American history—to take pictures of the war. The photographs that resulted from this effort—new to warfare—were among the grimmest ever made to that point, many of them displaying the vast numbers of dead on the Civil War battlefields. For some, the images of death contributed to a revulsion from the war. But for most Northerners, they gave evidence of the level of sacrifice that had been made for the preservation of the Union and thus spurred the nation on to victory. (Southerners used similar propaganda in the Confederacy, although less effectively.)

The presidential election of 1864 occurred, therefore, in the midst of considerable political dissension. The Republicans had suffered heavy losses in the congressional elections of 1862, and in response leaders of the party tried to create a broad coalition of all the groups that supported the war. They called the new organization the Union Party, but in reality it was little more than the Republican Party and a small faction of War Democrats. The Union Party nominated Lincoln for another term as president and Andrew Johnson of Tennessee, a War Democrat who had opposed his state's decision to secede, for the vice presidency.

The Democrats nominated George B. McClellan, a celebrated former Union general who had been relieved of his command by Lincoln. The party adopted a platform denouncing the war and calling for a truce. McClellan repudiated that demand, but the Democrats were clearly the peace party in the campaign, trying to profit from growing war weariness and from the Union's discouraging military position in the summer of 1864.

At this crucial moment, however, several Northern military victories, particularly the capture of Atlanta, Georgia, early in September, rejuvenated Northern morale and boosted

1864 ELECTION Republican prospects. Lincoln won reelection comfortably, with 212 electoral votes to McClellan's 21; the president carried every state except Kentucky, New Jersey, and Delaware. But Lincoln's lead in the popular vote was a modest 10 percent. Had Union victories not occurred when they did, and had Lincoln not made special arrangements to allow Union troops to vote, the Democrats might have won.

THE POLITICS OF EMANCIPATION

Despite their surface unity in 1864 and their general agreement on most economic matters, the Republicans disagreed sharply on the issue of slavery. Radicals—led in Congress by such men as Representative Thaddeus Stevens of Pennsylvania and Senators Charles Sumner of Massachusetts and Benjamin Wade of Ohio—wanted to use the war to abolish slavery immediately and completely. Conservatives favored a slower, more gradual, and, they believed, less disruptive process for ending slavery. In the beginning, at least, they had the support of the president.

Despite Lincoln's cautious view of emancipation, momentum began to gather behind it early in the war. In 1861, Congress passed the Confiscation Act, which declared that all slaves used for "insurrectionary" purposes (that is, in support of the Confederate military effort) would be considered freed. Subsequent laws in the spring of 1862 abolished slavery in the District of Columbia and in the western territories, and compensated owners. In July 1862, the Radicals pushed through Congress the second Confiscation Act, which again declared free the slaves of persons aiding and supporting the insurrection (whether or not the slaves themselves were doing so) and which also authorized the president to employ African Americans, including freed slaves, as soldiers. As the war progressed, much of the North seemed slowly to accept emancipation as a central war aim; nothing less would justify the enormous sacrifices of the struggle, many Northerners believed. As a result, the Radicals increased their influence within the Republican Party—a development that did not go unnoticed by the president, who decided to seize the leadership of the rising antislavery sentiment himself.

CONFISCATION ACTS

On September 22, 1862, after the Union victory at the Battle of Antietam, the president announced his intention to use his war powers to issue an executive order freeing all slaves in the Confederacy. And on January 1, 1863, he formally signed the Emancipation Proclamation, which declared forever free slaves in all areas of the Confederacy except those already under Union control: Tennessee, western Virginia, and southern Louisiana. The proclamation did not apply to the border slave states, which had never seceded from the Union and therefore were not subject to the president's war powers.

EMANCIPATION PROCLAMATION

The immediate effect of the proclamation was limited, since it applied only to slaves still under Confederate control. But the document was of great importance nevertheless, because it clearly and irrevocably established that the war was being fought not only to preserve the Union but also to eliminate slavery. Eventually, as federal armies occupied much of the South, the proclamation became a practical reality and led directly to the freeing of thousands of slaves. Even in areas not directly affected by the proclamation, the antislavery impulse gained strength.

The U.S. government's tentative measures against slavery were not, at first, a major factor in the liberation of slaves. Instead, the war helped African Americans to liberate themselves, and they did so in increasing numbers as the war progressed. Many slaves were taken from their plantations and put to work building defenses and other chores. Once transported to the front, many of them found ways to escape across Northern lines, where they were treated as "contraband"—goods seized from people who had no right to them. They could not be returned to their masters. By 1862, the Union army often penetrated deep into the Confederacy. Almost everywhere they went, escaped slaves flocked to join them by the thousands, often whole families. Some of them joined the Union Army, others simply stayed with the troops until they could find their way to free states. When the Union captured New Orleans and much of southern Louisiana, slaves refused to work for their former masters, even though the Union occupiers had not made any provisions for liberating African Americans.

By the end of the war, slavery had been abolished in two Union slave states—Maryland and Missouri—and in three Confederate states occupied by Union forces—Tennessee, Arkansas, and Louisiana. The final step came in 1865, when Congress approved and the necessary states ratified the Thirteenth Amendment, abolishing slavery as an institution in all parts of the United States. After more than two centuries, legalized slavery finally ceased to exist in the United States.

AFRICAN AMERICANS AND THE UNION CAUSE

About 186,000 emancipated African Americans served as soldiers, sailors, and laborers for the Union forces, joining a significant number of free blacks from the North. The services of African Americans to the Union military were significant in many ways, not least because of the substantial obstacles many black men had to surmount in order to enlist.

In the first months of the war, African Americans were largely excluded from the military. A few black regiments eventually took shape in some of the Union-occupied areas of the Confederacy, largely because they were a ready source of manpower in these defeated regions. But once Lincoln issued the Emancipation Proclamation, black enlistment increased rapidly and the Union military began actively to recruit African American soldiers and sailors in both the North and, where possible, the South.

BLACK ENLISTMENT

Some of these men were organized into fighting units, of which the best known was probably the Fifty-fourth Massachusetts Infantry, which (like most black regiments) had a white commander: Robert Gould Shaw, a member of an aristocratic Boston family. Shaw and more than half his regiment died during a battle near Charleston, South Carolina, in the summer of 1863.

Most black soldiers, however, were assigned menial tasks behind the lines, such as digging trenches and transporting water. Even though fewer African Americans than whites died in combat, the black mortality rate was actually higher than the rate for white soldiers because so many died of disease from working long, arduous hours in unsanitary conditions. Conditions for blacks and whites were unequal in other ways as well. African American soldiers were paid a third less than were white soldiers (until Congress changed the law in mid-1864). But however dangerous, onerous, or menial the tasks black soldiers were given, most of them felt enormous pride in their service—pride they retained throughout their lives

MISTREATMENT OF BLACK SOLDIERS

AFRICAN AMERICAN TROOPS Although most of the black soldiers who enlisted in the Union army during the Civil War performed noncombat jobs behind the lines, there were also black combat regiments—members of one of which are pictured here—who fought with great success and valor in critical battles. (Library of Congress)

and often through the lives of their descendants. Many moved from the army into politics and other forms of leadership (in both the North and, after the war, the Reconstruction South).

Black fighting men captured by the Confederates were, unlike white prisoners, not returned to the North in exchange for Southern soldiers being returned to the South. They were sent back to their masters (if they were escaped slaves) or often executed. In 1864, Confederate soldiers killed over 260 African Americans after capturing them in Tennessee.

THE WAR AND ECONOMIC DEVELOPMENT

The Civil War did not, as some historians used to claim, transform the North from an agrarian to an industrial society. Industrialization was already far advanced when the war began, and in some areas, the war retarded growth—by cutting manufacturers off from their Southern markets and sources of raw material, and by diverting labor and resources to military purposes.

On the whole, however, the war sped the economic development of the North. That was in part a result of the political dominance of the Republican Party and its promotion of nationalistic economic legislation. But it was also because the war itself required the expansion of certain sectors of the economy. Coal production increased by nearly 20 percent during the war. Railroad facilities improved—mainly through the adoption of a standard gauge (track width) on new lines. The loss of

farm labor to the military forced many farmers to increase the mechanization of agriculture.

The war was a difficult experience for many American workers. Industrial laborers experienced a substantial loss of purchasing power, as prices in the North rose by more than 70 percent during the war, while wages rose only about 40 percent. That was partly because liberalized immigration laws permitted a flood of new workers into the labor market and

HARD TIMES FOR WORKERS

helped keep wages low. It was also because the increasing mechanization of production eliminated the jobs of many skilled workers. One result of these changes was a substantial increase in union membership in many industries and the creation of several national unions, for coal miners, railroad engineers, and others—organizations bitterly opposed and rigorously suppressed by employers.

WOMEN, NURSING, AND THE WAR

Responding not only to the needs of employers for additional labor, but to their own, often desperate, need for money, women found themselves, either by choice or by necessity, thrust into new and often unfamiliar roles during the war. They took over positions vacated by men and worked as teachers, retail sales clerks, office workers, and mill and factory hands.

Above all, women entered nursing, a field previously dominated by men. The U.S. Sanitary Commission, an organization

THE U.S. SANITARY COMMISSION Mathew Brady took this photograph of female nurses and Union soldiers standing before an infirmary at Brandy Station, Virginia, near Petersburg, in 1864. The infirmary was run by the U.S. Sanitary Commission, the government-supported nursing corps that became important to the medical care of wounded soldiers during the Civil War. (National Archives and Records Administration)

U.S. SANITARY COMMISSION of civilian volunteers led by Dorothea Dix, mobilized large numbers of female nurses to serve in field hospitals. By the end of the war, women were the dominant force in nursing; by 1900, nursing had become an almost entirely female profession. Female nurses not only cared for patients but also performed other tasks considered appropriate for women: cooking, cleaning, and laundering.

Female nurses encountered considerable resistance from male doctors, many of whom considered women too weak for medical work and who, in any case, found the sight of women taking care of strange men inappropriate. TRADITIONAL GENDER ROLES REINFORCED The Sanitary Commission tried to counter such arguments by attributing to nursing many of the domestic ideals that American society attributed to women's work in the home. Women as nurses would play the same maternal, nurturing, instructive role they played as wives and mothers. "The right of woman to her sphere, which includes housekeeping, cooking, and nursing, has never been disputed," one Sanitary Commission official insisted. But not all women who worked for the commission were content with a purely maternal role; some challenged the dominance of men in the organization and even stood up against doctors whom they considered incompetent, increasing the resentment felt toward them by many men. In the end, though, the work of female nurses was so indispensable to the military that the complaints of male doctors were irrelevant.

Nurses, and many other women, found the war a liberating experience, in which (as one Sanitary Commission nurse later wrote) the American woman "had developed potencies and possibilities of which she had been unaware and which surprised her, as it did those who witnessed her marvelous achievement." Some women, especially those who had been committed to feminist causes earlier, came to see the war as an opportunity to win support for their own goals. Elizabeth Cady Stanton and Susan B. Anthony, who together founded the National Woman's Loyal League in 1863, worked simultaneously for the abolition of slavery and the awarding of suffrage to women. Clara Barton, who was active during the war in collecting and distributing medical supplies and who later became an important figure in the nursing profession (and a founder of the American Red Cross), said in 1888: "At the war's end, woman was at least fifty years in advance of the normal position which continued peace would have assigned her." That may have been an exaggeration; but it captured the degree to which many women looked back on the war as a crucial moment in the redefinition of female roles and in the awakening of a sense of independence and new possibilities.

> 66 AT THE WAR'S END, WOMAN WAS AT LEAST FIFTY YEARS IN ADVANCE OF THE NORMAL POSITION WHICH CONTINUED PEACE WOULD HAVE ASSIGNED HER. 99
>
> **CLARA BARTON**

Whatever nursing may have done for the status of women, it had an enormous impact on the medical profession and on NURSING AND MEDICINE the treatment of wounded soldiers during the war. The U.S. Sanitary Commission not only organized women to serve at the front; it also funneled medicine and supplies to badly overtaxed field hospitals. The commission also (as its name suggests) helped spread ideas about the importance of sanitary conditions in hospitals and clinics and probably contributed to the relative decline of death by disease in the Civil War. Nevertheless, twice as many soldiers died of diseases—malaria, dysentery, typhoid, gangrene, and others—as died in combat during the war. Even minor injuries could lead to fatal infections.

THE MOBILIZATION OF THE SOUTH

Many Southerners boasted loudly of the differences between their new nation and the nation they had left. The differences were real. But there were also important similarities between the Union and the Confederacy, which became clear as the two sides mobilized for war: similarities in their political systems, in the methods they used for financing the war and conscripting troops, and in the way they fought.

THE CONFEDERATE GOVERNMENT

The Confederate constitution was largely identical to the Constitution of the United States, but with several significant exceptions: it explicitly acknowledged the sovereignty of the individual states (although not the right of secession), and it specifically sanctioned slavery and made its abolition (even by one of the states) practically impossible.

The constitutional convention at Montgomery named a provisional president and vice president: Jefferson Davis of Mississippi and Alexander H. Stephens of Georgia, who were later chosen by the general electorate, without opposition, for six-year terms. Davis had been a moderate secessionist before the war; Stephens had argued against secession. The Confederate government, like the Union government, was dominated throughout the war by moderate leaders. Also like the Union's, it was dominated less by the old aristocracy of the East than by the newer aristocrats of the West, of whom Davis was the most prominent example.

Davis was, in the end, an unsuccessful president. He was a reasonably able administrator and the dominating figure in his government, encountering little interference from the generally tame members of his unstable cabinet and serving as his own secretary of war. But he rarely provided genuinely national leadership. One shrewd Confederate official wrote: "All the revolutionary vigor is with the enemy. . . . With us timidity-hair splitting."

DAVIS'S LEADERSHIP

There were no formal political parties in the Confederacy, but its congressional and popular politics were rife with dissension nevertheless. Some white Southerners (and of course most African Americans who were aware of the course of events) opposed secession and war. Many white people in poorer

SOUTHERN DIVISIONS

"backcountry" and "upcountry" regions, where slavery was limited, refused to recognize the new Confederate government or to serve in the Southern army; some worked or even fought for the Union. Most white Southerners supported the war; but as in the North, many were openly critical of the government and the military, particularly as the tide of battle turned against the South and the Confederate economy decayed.

MONEY AND MANPOWER

Financing the Confederate war effort was a monumental and ultimately impossible task. It involved creating a national revenue system in a society unaccustomed to significant tax burdens. It depended on a small and unstable banking system that had little capital to lend. Because most wealth in the South was invested in slaves and land, liquid assets were scarce; and the Confederacy's only gold—seized from U.S. mints located in the South—was worth only about $1 million.

The Confederate congress tried at first not to tax the people directly but to requisition funds from the individual states. Most of the states, however, were also unwilling to tax their citizens and paid their shares, when they paid them at all, with bonds or notes of dubious worth. In 1863, the congress enacted an income tax—which planters could pay "in kind" (as a percentage of their produce). But taxation never provided the Confederacy with very much revenue; it produced only about 1 percent of the government's total income. Borrowing was not much more successful. The Confederate government issued bonds in such vast amounts that the public lost faith in them and stopped buying them. Efforts to borrow money in Europe using cotton as collateral fared no better.

FUNDING PROBLEMS

As a result, the Confederacy had to pay for the war through the least stable, most destructive form of financing: paper currency, which it began issuing in 1861. By 1864, the Confederacy had issued the staggering total of $1.5 billion in paper money, more than twice what the Union had produced. And unlike the Union, the Confederacy did not establish a uniform currency system; the national government, states, cities, and private banks all issued their own notes, producing widespread chaos and confusion. The result was a disastrous inflation, far worse than anything the North experienced. Prices in the North rose 80 percent in the course of the war; in the South they rose 9,000 percent, with devastating effects on the South's morale.

Like the United States, the Confederacy first raised a military by calling for volunteers. And as in the North, by the end of 1861 voluntary enlistments were declining. In April 1862, therefore, the congress enacted a Conscription Act, which subjected all white males between the ages of eighteen and thirty-five to military service for three years. As in the North, a draftee could avoid service if he furnished a substitute. But since the price of substitutes was high, the provision aroused such

PRICES IN THE NORTH ROSE 80 PERCENT IN THE COURSE OF THE WAR; IN THE SOUTH THEY ROSE 9,000 PERCENT.

RAISING THE
CONFEDERATE
ARMY

opposition from poorer whites that it was repealed in 1863. Even more controversial was the exemption from the draft of one white man on each plantation with twenty or more slaves, a provision that caused smaller farmers to make the same complaint some Northerners made: "It's a rich man's war but a poor man's fight." Many more white Southerners were exempted from military service than were Northerners.

Even so, conscription worked for a time. At the end of 1862, about 500,000 men were in the Confederate military. (A total of approximately 900,000 served in the course of the entire war.) That number did not include the many slave men and slave women recruited by the military to perform such services as cooking, laundry, and manual labor, hence freeing additional white manpower for fighting. After 1862, however, conscription began producing fewer men—in part because the Union had by then begun to seize large areas of the Confederacy and thus had cut off much of the population from conscription or recruitment.

Early in 1864, the government faced a critical manpower shortage. In a desperate move, the Confederate congress began trying to draft men as young as seventeen and as old as fifty.

CONFEDERATE VOLUNTEERS Young Southern soldiers posed for this photograph in 1861, shortly before the First Battle of Bull Run. The Civil War was the first major military conflict in the age of photography, and it launched the careers of many of America's early photographers. (Cook Collection, Valentine Richmond History Center)

MANPOWER
SHORTAGE

But in a nation suffering from intense war weariness, where many had concluded that defeat was inevitable, nothing could attract or retain an adequate army any longer. In 1864–1865 there were 100,000 desertions. In a frantic final attempt to raise men, the Confederate congress authorized the conscription of 300,000 slaves, but the war ended before the government could attempt this incongruous experiment.

STATES' RIGHTS VERSUS CENTRALIZATION

The greatest sources of division in the South, however, were differences of opinion over the doctrine of states' rights. States' rights had become such a cult among many white Southerners that they resisted all efforts to exert national authority, even those necessary to win the war. They restricted Davis's ability to impose martial law and suspend habeas corpus. They obstructed conscription. Recalcitrant governors such as Joseph Brown of Georgia and Zebulon M. Vance of North Carolina tried at times to keep their own troops apart from the Confederate forces and insisted on hoarding surplus supplies for their own states' militias.

CENTRALIZATION

Even so, the Confederate government did make substantial strides in centralizing power in the South. By the end of the war, the Confederate bureaucracy was larger than its counterpart in Washington. The central government experimented, successfully for a time, with a "food draft"—which permitted soldiers to feed themselves by seizing crops from farms in their path. The government impressed slaves, often over the objections of their owners, to work as laborers on military projects. The Confederacy seized control of the railroads and shipping; it imposed regulations on industry; it limited corporate profits. States' rights sentiment was a significant handicap, but the South nevertheless took important steps in the direction of centralization—becoming in the process increasingly like the region whose institutions it was fighting to escape.

ECONOMIC AND SOCIAL EFFECTS OF THE WAR

The war had a devastating effect on the economy of the South. It cut off Southern planters and producers from the markets in the North on which they had depended; it made the sale of cotton overseas much more difficult; it robbed farms and industries that did not have large slave populations of a male workforce, leaving some of them unable to function effectively. While in the North production of all goods, agricultural and industrial, increased somewhat during the war, in the South production declined by more than a third.

Most of all, perhaps, the fighting itself wreaked havoc on the Southern economy. Almost all the major battles of the war occurred within the Confederacy; both armies spent most of their time on Southern soil. As a result of the savage fighting, the South's already inadequate railroad system was nearly destroyed; much of its most valuable farmland and many of its most successful plantations were ruined by Union troops (especially in the last year of the war).

Once the Northern naval blockade became effective in 1862, the South experienced massive shortages of almost everything. The region was overwhelmingly agricultural, but since it had concentrated so single-mindedly on producing cotton and other export crops, it did not grow enough food to meet its own needs. And despite the efforts of women ECONOMIC WOES and slaves to keep farms functioning, the departure of white male workers seriously diminished the region's ability to keep up what food production there had been. Large numbers of doctors were conscripted to serve the needs of the military, leaving many communities without any medical care. Blacksmiths, carpenters, and other craftsmen were similarly in short supply.

As the war continued, the shortages, the inflation, and the suffering created increasing instability in Southern society. There were major food riots, some led by women, in Georgia, North Carolina, and Alabama in 1863, as well as a large demonstration in Richmond that quickly turned violent. Resistance to conscription, food impressment, and taxation increased throughout the Confederacy, as did hoarding and black-market commerce.

Despite the economic woes of the South, the war transformed Confederate society in many of the same ways that it was changing the society of the Union. The changes were particularly significant for Southern women. Because so many men left the farms and plantations to fight, the task of keeping families together and maintaining agricultural production fell increasingly to women. Slaveowners' wives often became responsible for managing large slave work forces; the wives of NEW ROLES FOR WOMEN more modest farmers learned to plow fields and harvest crops. Substantial numbers of females worked as schoolteachers or in government agencies in Richmond. Even larger numbers chose nursing, both in hospitals and in temporary facilities set up to care for wounded soldiers.

The long-range results of the war for Southern women are more difficult to measure but equally profound. The experience of the 1860s almost certainly forced many women to question the prevailing Southern assumption that females were unsuited for certain activities, that they were not fit to participate actively in the public sphere. A more concrete legacy was the decimation of the male population and the creation of a major gender imbalance in the region. After the war, there were many thousands more women in the South than there were men. In Georgia, for example, women outnumbered men by 36,000 in 1870; in North Carolina by 25,000. The result, of course, was a large number of unmarried or widowed women who, both during and after the war, had no choice but to find employment—thus, by necessity rather than choice, expanding the number of acceptable roles for women in Southern society.

Even before emancipation, the war had far-reaching effects on the lives of slaves. Confederate leaders were even more terrified of slave revolts during the war than they had been in peacetime, and they enforced slave codes and other regulations with particular severity. Even so, many slaves—especially those near the front—found ways to escape their masters and cross behind Union lines in search of freedom. Those who had no

ATLANTA AFTER THE BURNING General Sherman captured Atlanta on September 2, 1864, evacuated most of the population, and set fire to the city. This photograph shows the extent of the devastation. The destruction of Atlanta was the beginning of Sherman's famous "March to the Sea." It also signaled the beginning of a new kind of warfare, waged not just against opposing armies but also against the economies and even the populations of the enemy. *(Corbis)*

realistic avenue for escape seemed, to their owners at least, to be particularly resistant to authority during the war. That was in part because on many plantations, the masters and overseers for whom they were accustomed to working were away at war; they found it easier to resist the authority of the women and boys left behind to manage the farms.

STRATEGY AND DIPLOMACY

Militarily, the initiative in the Civil War lay mainly with the North, since it needed to destroy the Confederacy, while the South needed only to avoid defeat. Diplomatically, however, the initiative lay with the South. It needed to enlist the recognition and support of foreign governments; the Union wanted to preserve the status quo prior to the war.

THE COMMANDERS

The most important Union military commander was Abraham Lincoln, whose previous military experience consisted only of

LINCOLN'S
LEADERSHIP brief service in his state militia during the Black Hawk War. Lincoln was a successful commander in chief because he realized that numbers and resources were on his side, and because he took advantage of the North's material advantages. He realized, too, that the proper objective of his armies was the destruction of the Confederate armies, not the occupation of Southern territory. It was important that Lincoln had a good grasp of strategy, because many of his generals did not. The problem of finding adequate commanders for the troops in the field plagued him throughout the first three years of the war.

From 1861 to 1864, Lincoln tried time and again to find a chief of staff capable of orchestrating the Union war effort. He turned first to General Winfield Scott, the aging hero of the Mexican War. But Scott was unprepared for the magnitude of the new conflict and retired on November 1, 1861. Lincoln replaced him with the young George B. McClellan, commander of the Union armies in the East, the Army of the Potomac; but the proud, arrogant McClellan had a wholly inadequate grasp of strategy and returned to the field in March 1862. For most of the rest of the year, Lincoln had no chief of staff. And when

ULYSSES S. GRANT One observer said of Grant (seen here posing for a photograph during the Wilderness campaign of 1864): "He habitually wears an expression as if he had determined to drive his head through a brick wall, and was about to do it." It was an apt metaphor for Grant's military philosophy, which relied on constant, unrelenting assault. One result was that Grant was willing to fight when other Northern generals held back. Another was that Grant presided over some of the worst carnage of the Civil War. (Library of Congress)

ROBERT E. LEE Lee was a moderate by the standards of Southern politics in the 1850s. He opposed secession and was ambivalent about slavery. But he could not bring himself to break with his region, and he left the U.S. Army to lead Confederate forces beginning in 1861. He was (and remains) the most revered of all the white Southern leaders of the Civil War. For decades after his surrender at Appomattox, he was a symbol to white Southerners of the "Lost Cause." (Bettmann/Corbis)

BASEBALL AND THE CIVIL WAR

LONG before the great urban stadiums, long before the lights and the cameras and the multimillion-dollar salaries, long before the Little Leagues and the high school and college teams, baseball was the most popular game in America. And during the Civil War, it was a treasured pastime for soldiers, and for thousands of men (and some women) behind the lines, in both North and South.

The legend that baseball was invented by Abner Doubleday, who probably never even saw the game, came from Albert G. Spalding, a patriotic sporting-goods manufacturer eager to prove that the game had purely American origins and to dispel the notion that it came from England. In fact, baseball was derived from a variety of earlier games, especially the English pastimes of cricket and rounders. American baseball took its own distinctive form beginning in the 1840s, when Alexander Cartwright, a shipping clerk, formed the New York Knickerbockers, laid out a diamond-shaped field with four bases, and declared that batters with three strikes were out and that teams with three outs were retired.

Cartwright moved west in search of gold in 1849, ultimately grew rich, and settled finally in Hawaii (where he brought the game to Americans in the Pacific). But the game did not languish in his absence. Henry Chadwick, an English-born journalist, spent much of the 1850s popularizing the game (and regularizing its rules). By 1860, baseball was being played by college students and Irish workers, by urban elites and provincial farmers, by people of all classes and ethnic groups from New England to Louisiana. It was also attracting the attention of women. Students at Vassar College formed "ladies" teams in the 1860s, and in Philadelphia, free black men formed the first of what was to become a great network of African American baseball teams, the Pythians. From the beginning, they were barred from playing against most white teams.

When young men marched off to war in 1861, some took their bats and balls with them. Almost from the start of the fighting, soldiers in both armies took advantage of idle moments to lay out baseball diamonds and organize games. There were games in prison camps; games on the White House lawn (where Union soldiers were sometimes billeted); and games on battlefields that were sometimes interrupted by gunfire and cannonfire. "It is astonishing how indifferent a person can become to danger," a soldier wrote home to Ohio in 1862. "The report of musketry is heard but a very little distance from us, . . . yet over there on the other side of the road is most of our company, playing Bat Ball." After a skirmish in Texas, another Union soldier lamented that, in addition to casualties, his company had lost "the only baseball in Alexandria, Texas." Far from discouraging baseball, military commanders—and the United States Sanitary Commission, the Union army's medical arm—actively encouraged the game during the war. It would, they believed, help keep up the soldiers' morale.

Away from the battlefield, baseball continued to flourish. In New York City, games between local teams drew crowds of ten or twenty thousand. The National Association of Baseball Players (founded in 1859) had recruited ninety-one clubs in ten northern states by 1865; a North

---

he finally appointed General Henry W. Halleck to the post, he found him an ineffectual strategist who left all substantive decision making to the president. Not until March 1864 did Lincoln finally find a general he trusted to command the war effort: Ulysses S. Grant, who shared Lincoln's belief in making enemy armies and resources, not enemy territory, the target of military efforts. Lincoln gave Grant a relatively free hand, but the general always submitted at least the broad outlines of his plans to the president for advance approval.

Lincoln's (and later Grant's) handling of the war effort faced constant scrutiny from the Committee on the Conduct of the War, a joint investigative committee of the two houses of Congress and the most powerful voice the legislative branch has ever had in formulating war policies. Established in December 1861 and chaired by Senator Benjamin F. Wade of Ohio, it complained constantly of the insufficient ruthlessness of Northern generals, which Radicals on the committee attributed (largely inaccurately) to a secret sympathy among the officers for slavery. The committee's efforts often seriously interfered with the conduct of the war.

Southern command arrangements centered on President Davis, who, unlike Lincoln, was a trained professional soldier. Nevertheless, he failed to create an effective command system. Early in 1862, Davis named General Robert E. Lee as his principal military adviser. But in fact, Davis had no intention of sharing control of strategy with anyone. After a few months, Lee left Richmond to command forces in the field, and for the next two years Davis planned strategy alone. In February 1864, he named General Braxton Bragg as a military adviser; but Bragg never provided much more than technical advice. Not until February 1865 did the Confederate Congress create the formal position of general in chief. Davis named Lee to the post but made clear that he expected to continue to make all basic decisions. In any case, the war ended before this last command structure had time to take shape.

ROBERT E. LEE

At lower levels of command, men of markedly similar backgrounds controlled the war in both the North and the South. Many of the professional officers on both sides were graduates of the United States Military Academy at West Point and the United States Naval Academy at Annapolis, and thus had been

Western Association of Baseball Players, organized in Chicago in 1865, indicated that the game was becoming well established in the West as well. In Brooklyn, William Cammeyer drained a skating pond on his property, built a board fence around it, and created the first enclosed baseball field in America—the Union grounds. He charged 10 cents admission. The professionalization of the game was under way.

Despite the commercialization and spectacle that came to be associated with baseball in the years after the Civil War, the game remained for many Americans what it was to millions of young men fighting in the most savage war in the nation's history—an American passion that at times, even if briefly, erased the barriers dividing groups from one another. "Officers and men forget, for a time, the differences in rank," a Massachusetts private wrote in 1863, "and indulge in the invigorating sport with a schoolboy's ardor." •

RIFLES AND BATS Soldiers pose on the battlefield in full uniform and carrying their rifles, with a pile of baseball bats on the grass in front of them. Baseball was a popular recreation for troops on both sides of the Civil War. (Dennis Goldstein, Atlanta)

trained in similar ways. Many were closely acquainted, even friendly, with their counterparts on the other side. And all were imbued with the classic, eighteenth-century models of warfare that the service academies still taught. The most successful officers were those who, like Grant and William Tecumseh Sherman, were able to see beyond their academic training and envision a new kind of warfare in which destruction of resources was as important as battlefield tactics.

Amateur officers played an important role in both armies as commanders of volunteer regiments. In both North and South, such men were usually economic or social leaders in their communities who appointed themselves officers and rounded up troops to lead. This system was responsible for recruiting considerable numbers of men into the armies of the two nations. Only occasionally, however, did it produce officers of real ability.

THE ROLE OF SEA POWER

The Union had an overwhelming advantage in naval power, and it gave its navy two important roles in the war. One was enforcing a blockade of the Southern coast, which the president ordered on April 19, 1861. The other was assisting the Union armies in field operations.

The blockade of the South was never fully effective, but it had a major impact on the Confederacy nevertheless. The United States Navy could generally keep oceangoing ships out of Confederate ports. For a time, small blockade runners continued to slip through. But gradually, federal forces tightened the blockade by seizing the ports themselves. The last important port in Confederate hands—Wilmington, North Carolina—fell to the Union early in 1865.

THE UNION BLOCKADE

The Confederates made bold attempts to break the blockade with new weapons. Foremost among them was an ironclad warship, constructed by plating with iron a former United States frigate, the *Merrimac*, which the Yankees had scuttled in Norfolk harbor when Virginia seceded. On March 8, 1862, the refitted *Merrimac*, renamed the *Virginia*, left Norfolk to attack a blockading squadron of wooden ships at nearby Hampton Roads. It destroyed

IRONCLADS

two of the ships and scattered the rest. But the Union government had already built ironclads of its own. And one of them, the *Monitor,* arrived off the coast of Virginia only a few hours after the *Virginia's* dramatic foray. The next day, it met the *Virginia* in the first battle between ironclad ships. Neither vessel was able to sink the other, but the *Monitor* put an end to the *Virginia's* raids and preserved the blockade. The Confederacy experimented as well with other naval innovations, such as small torpedo boats and hand-powered submarines. But despite occasional small successes with these new weapons, the South never managed to overcome the Union's naval advantages.

As a supporter of land operations, the Union navy was particularly important in the western theater of war—the vast region between the Appalachian Mountains and the Mississippi River—where the major rivers were navigable by large vessels. The navy transported supplies and troops and joined in attacking Confederate strong points. With no significant navy of its own, the South could defend only with fixed land fortifications, which proved no match for the mobile land-and-water forces of the Union.

EUROPE AND THE DISUNITED STATES

Judah P. Benjamin, the Confederate secretary of state for most of the war, was a clever and intelligent man, but he confined most of his energy to routine administrative tasks. William Seward, his counterpart in Washington, gradually became one of the great American secretaries of state. He had invaluable assistance from Charles Francis Adams, the American minister to London, who had inherited the considerable diplomatic talents of his father, John Quincy Adams, and his grandfather, John Adams.

At the beginning of the war, the ruling classes of England and France, the two nations whose support was most crucial to both sides, were generally sympathetic to the Confederacy, for several reasons. The two nations imported much Southern cotton for their textile industries; they were eager to weaken the United States, an increasingly powerful commercial rival; and some admired the supposedly aristocratic social order of the South, which they believed resembled the hierarchical structures of their own societies. But France was unwilling to take sides in the conflict unless England did so first. And in England, the government was reluctant to act because there was powerful popular support for the Union. Important English liberals such as John Bright and Richard Cobden considered the war a struggle between free and slave labor and urged their followers to support the Union cause. The politically conscious but largely unenfranchised workers in Britain expressed their sympathy for the North frequently and unmistakably—in mass meetings, in resolutions, and through their champions in Parliament. After Lincoln issued the Emancipation Proclamation, these groups worked particularly avidly for the Union.

Southern leaders hoped to counter the strength of the British antislavery forces by arguing that access to Southern cotton was vital to the English and French textile industries. But this "King Cotton diplomacy," on which the Confederacy had staked so many

KING COTTON DIPLOMACY

of its hopes, failed. English manufacturers had a surplus of both raw cotton and finished goods on hand in 1861 and could withstand a temporary loss of access to American cotton. Later, as the supply of American cotton began to diminish, both England and France managed to keep some of their mills open by importing cotton from Egypt, India, and other sources. Equally important, English workers, the people most seriously threatened by the cotton shortage, did not clamor to have the blockade broken. Even most of the 500,000 English textile workers thrown out of jobs as a result of mill closings continued to support the North. In the end, therefore, no European nation offered diplomatic recognition to the Confederacy or intervened in the war. No nation wanted to antagonize the United States unless the Confederacy seemed likely to win, and the South never came close enough to victory to convince its potential allies to support it.

Even so, there was considerable tension, and on occasion near hostilities, between the United States and Britain, beginning in the first days of the war. Great Britain declared itself neutral as soon as the fighting began, followed by France and other nations. The Union government was furious: neutrality implied that the two sides to the conflict had equal stature. Washington was insisting that the conflict was simply a domestic insurrection, not a war between two legitimate governments.

A more serious crisis, the so-called Trent affair, began in late 1861. Two Confederate diplomats, James M. Mason and John Slidell, had slipped through the then-ineffective Union blockade to Havana, Cuba, where they boarded an English steamer, the *Trent,* for England. Waiting in Cuban waters was the American frigate *San Jacinto,* commanded by the impetuous Charles Wilkes. Acting without authorization, Wilkes stopped the British vessel, arrested the diplomats, and carried them in triumph to Boston. The British government demanded the release of the prisoners, reparations, and an apology. Lincoln and Seward, aware that Wilkes had violated maritime law and unwilling to risk war with England, stalled the negotiations until American public opinion had cooled off, then released the diplomats with an indirect apology. A second diplomatic crisis lasted for years. Unable to construct large vessels itself, the Confederacy bought six ships, known as commerce destroyers, from British shipyards. The best known of them were the *Alabama,* the *Florida,* and the *Shenandoah.* The United States protested that this sale of military equipment to a belligerent violated the laws of neutrality, and the protests became the basis, after the war, of damage claims by the United States against Great Britain.

TRENT AFFAIR

THE AMERICAN WEST AND THE WAR

Except for Texas, which joined the Confederacy, all the western states and territories remained officially loyal to the Union—but not without controversy and conflict. Southerners and Southern sympathizers were active throughout the West. And, in some places, there was actual combat between Unionists and secessionists.

There was particularly vicious fighting in Kansas and Missouri, the scene of so much bitterness before the war. The same pro-slavery and free-state forces who had fought one an-other in the 1850s continued to do so, with even more deadly

GUERRILLA WAR IN THE WEST

results. William C. Quantrill, an Ohio na-tive who had spent much of his youth in the West, became a captain in the Confederate army after he organized a band of guerrilla fighters (mostly teenage boys) with which he terrorized areas around the Kansas-Missouri border. Quantrill and his band were an exceptionally murderous group, notorious for killing almost everyone in their path. Their most infamous act was a siege of Lawrence, Kansas, during which they slaughtered 150 civilians, adults and children alike. Union troops killed Quantrill shortly after the end of the war. Union sympathiz-ers in Kansas, organized in bands known as the Jayhawkers, were only marginally less savage, as they moved across western Missouri exacting reprisals for the actions of Quantrill and other Confederate guerrillas. One Jayhawk unit was jointly commanded by the son of John Brown and the brother of Susan B. Anthony, men who brought the fervor of abolitionists to their work. Even without a major battle, the border areas of Kansas and Missouri were among the bloodiest and most terrorized places in the United States during the Civil War.

Not long after the war began, Confederate agents tried to negotiate alliances with the Five Civilized Tribes living in Indian Territory (later Oklahoma), in hopes of recruiting their support against Union forces in the West. The Indians themselves were divided. Some wanted to support the South, both because they resented the way the United States government had treated them and because some tribal leaders were themselves slave-holders. But other Indians supported the North out of a general hostility to slavery (in both the South and their own nation).

One result of these divisions was a civil war within Indian Territory itself. Another was that Indian regiments fought for both the Union and the Confederacy during the war. But the tribes themselves never formally allied themselves with either side.

THE COURSE OF BATTLE

In the absence of direct intervention by the European powers, the two contestants in America were left to resolve the conflict

HIGH CASUALTIES

between themselves. They did so in four long years of bloody combat that produced more carnage than any war in American history, before or since. More than 618,000 Americans died in the Civil War, far more than the 115,000 who perished in World War I or the 318,000 who died in World War II—more, indeed, than died in all other American wars combined prior to Vietnam. There were nearly 2,000 deaths for every 100,000 of population during the Civil War. In World War I, the com-parable figure was 109 deaths; in World War II, 241 deaths. Massive death, and along with it massive grief, shadowed both North and South during and after the war.

Despite the gruesome cost, the Civil War has become the most romanticized and the most intently studied of all American wars. In part, that is because the conflict produced—in addition to terrible fatalities—a series of military campaigns of classic strategic interest and a series of military leaders who displayed unusual brilliance and daring.

THE TECHNOLOGY OF BATTLE

Much of what happened on the battlefield in the Civil War was a result of new technologies that transformed the nature of combat. The Civil War has often been called the first "modern" war and the first "total" war. The great conflict between the North and the South was unlike any war fought before it, and it suggested what warfare would be like in the future.

The most obvious change in the character of warfare in the 1860s was the nature of the armaments that both sides used in

REPEATING WEAPONS

battle. Among the most important was the introduction of repeating weapons. Samuel Colt had patented a repeating pistol (the revolver) in 1835, but more important for military purposes was the repeating rifle, introduced in 1860 by Oliver Winchester. Also important were greatly improved cannons and artillery, a result of advances in iron and steel technology of the previous decades.

These devastating advances in the effectiveness of arms and artillery changed the way soldiers in the field fought. It was now impossibly deadly to fight battles as they had been fought for centuries, with lines of infantry soldiers standing erect in the field firing volleys at their opponents until one side with-drew. Fighting in that way now produced almost inconceivable slaughter, and soldiers quickly learned that the proper position for combat was staying low to the ground and behind cover. For the first time in the history of organized warfare infantry did not fight in formation, and the battlefield became a more chaotic place. Gradually, the deadliness of the new weapons encouraged armies on both sides to spend a great deal of time building elaborate fortifications and trenches to protect themselves from enemy fire. The sieges of Vicksburg and Petersburg, the defense of Richmond, and many other sieges led to the construction of vast fortifications around cities and attacking armies. (They were the predecessors to the great net-work of trenches that became so central a part of World War I.)

Other weapons technologies were less central to the fighting of the war, but important nevertheless. There was sporadic use of the relatively new technology of hot-air balloons, employed intermittently to provide a view of enemy formations in the field. (During one battle, a Union balloonist took a telegraph line aloft with him in his balloon and tapped out messages about troop movements to the commanders below.) Ironclad ships such as the *Merrimac* (or *Virginia*) and the *Monitor,* tor-pedoes, and submarine technology all suggested the dramatic changes that would soon overtake naval warfare, although none played a major role in the Civil War.

Critical to the conduct of the war, however, were two other relatively new technologies: the railroad and the telegraph.

IMPORTANCE OF THE RAILROAD

The railroad was particularly important in a war in which millions of soldiers were

THE CONSOLIDATION OF NATIONS

THE American Civil War was an event largely rooted in conditions particular to the United States. But it was also a part of a worldwide movement in the nineteenth century to create large, consolidated nations. A commitment to preserving the Union—to consolidating, rather than dismantling, the nation—was one of the principal motives for the North's commitment to fighting a war against the seceding states. Similar efforts at expansion, consolidation, and unification were occurring in many other nations around the same time.

The consolidation of nation-states was, of course, not new to the nineteenth century. The revolutions in America and France in the late eighteenth century—and the subsequent strengthening of the French concept of nationhood under Napoleon in the early nineteenth century—inspired new nationalist enthusiasms in other parts of Europe. Nationalist sentiment also grew among peoples who shared language, culture, ethnicity, and tradition and who came to believe that a consolidated nation was the best vehicle for strengthening their common bonds.

THE UNIFICATION OF ITALY This painting shows a climactic moment in the history of Italian unification. Garibaldi, the great leader of independence forces in southern Italy, greets King Victor Emmanuel of the Piedmont, the leader of independence forces in the North. Garibaldi greeted him by saying, "Saluto il primo Re d'Italia" ("I hail the first king of Italy"). The moment was significant both practically—it demonstrated Garibaldi's willingness to accept Victor Emmanuel's authority—and symbolically, as the triumph of nationalist sentiment in this once-decentralized country. (Museo del Risorgimento, Milan/Index S.A.S.)

In 1848, a wave of nationalist revolutions erupted in Italy, France, and Austria, challenging the imperial powers that many Europeans believed were subjugating national cultures. Those revolutions failed, but they helped lay the groundwork for the two most important national consolidations of nineteenth-century Europe.

One of these consolidations occurred in Germany, which was divided into numerous small, independent states in the early nineteenth century but where popular sentiment for German unification had been growing for decades. It was spurred in part by new histories of the German *Volk* (people) and by newly constructed images of German traditions, visible in such literature as the Grimms' fairy tales—an effort to record and popularize German folk traditions and make them the basis of a shared sense of a common past. In 1862, King Wilhelm I of Prussia—the leader of one of the most powerful of the scattered German states—appointed an aristocratic landowner, Otto von Bismarck, as his prime minister. Bismarck exploited the growing nationalism throughout the various German states and helped develop a strong popular base for unification. He did so in part by launching Prussian wars against Denmark, Austria, and France—wars Prussia easily won, inspiring pride in German power that extended well beyond Prussia itself. The Franco-Prussian War of 1870 was particularly important, because Prussia fought it to take possession of the French provinces of Alsace and Lorraine—provinces the Prussians claimed were part of the German "national community" because its people, although legally French citizens, were ethnically and linguistically German. In 1871, capitalizing on the widespread nationalist sentiment the war had created throughout the German-speaking states, Bismarck persuaded the German king to proclaim himself emperor (or *Kaiser*) of a new empire that united all German peoples except those in Austria and Switzerland.

The second great European movement for national unification occurred in Italy, which had long been divided into small kingdoms, city-states, and regions controlled by the Vatican. Beginning in the early nineteenth century, Italian nationalists formed what became known as the Young Italy movement, under the leadership of Giuseppe Mazzini. The movement demanded an end to foreign control in Italy and the unification of the Italian people into a single nation. Peoples with common language, culture, and tradition, Mazzini believed, should be free to unite and govern themselves. More important than this growing popular nationalism as a cause of Italian unification were the efforts of powerful and ambitious leaders. The most powerful Italian state in the mid-nineteenth century was the kingdom of the Piedmont and Sardinia, in the northwestern part of the peninsula. Its king, Victor Emmanuel II, appointed his own version of Bismarck—Camillo di Cavour—as prime minister in 1852. Cavour joined forces with nationalists in other areas of Italy to drive the Spanish and the Austrians out of Italian territory. Having first won independence for northern Italy, Cavour joined forces with the southern nationalist leader Giuseppe Garibaldi, who helped win independence in the south and then agreed to a unification of the entire Italian nation under Victor Emmanuel in 1860.

Other nations in these years were also trying to create, preserve, and strengthen nation-states. Some failed to do so—Russia, for example, despite the reform efforts of several tsars, never managed to create a stable nation-state from among its broad and diverse peoples. But others succeeded—Meiji Japan, for example, instituted a series of reforms in the 1880s and 1890s that created a powerful new Japanese nation-state.

In fighting and winning the Civil War, the nationalists of the Northern parts of the United States not only preserved the unity of their nation. They also became part of a movement toward the consolidation of national cultures and national territories that extended through many areas of the globe. •

UNDERSTAND, ANALYZE, AND EVALUATE

1. How did the problems facing Bismarck differ from those facing Lincoln?
2. Which man—Mazzini, Cavour, or Garibaldi—in the struggle to achieve the unification of Italy most closely parallels Lincoln and the fight to preserve the Union?
3. Does Mazzini's argument—that peoples with common language, culture, and tradition should be free to unite and govern themselves—apply to the North's attempt to preserve the Union, or does it better fit the South's attempt to secede and form a separate nation?

being mobilized and transferred to the front, and in which a single field army could number as many as 250,000 men. Transporting such enormous numbers of soldiers, and the supplies necessary to sustain them, would have been almost impossible without railroads, which made it possible for these large armies to be assembled and moved from place to place. But they also limited mobility. Railroad lines and stations are, of course, in fixed positions. Commanders, therefore, were forced to organize their campaigns at least in part around the location of the railroads whether the location was optimal or not.

The impact of the telegraph on the war was limited both by the scarcity of qualified telegraph operators and by the dif-

THE TELEGRAPH

ficulty of bringing telegraph wires into the fields where battles were being fought. Things improved somewhat after the new U.S. Military Telegraph Corps, headed by Thomas Scott and Andrew Carnegie, trained and employed over 1,200 operators. Gradually, too, both the Union and Confederate armies learned to string telegraph wires along the routes of their troops so that field commanders were able to stay in close touch with one another during battles. Both the North and the South sent spies behind enemy lines who tried to tap the telegraph lines of their opponents and send important information back about troop movements and formations.

THE OPENING CLASHES, 1861

The Union and the Confederacy fought their first major battle of the war in northern Virginia. A Union army of over 30,000 men under the command of General Irvin McDowell was stationed just outside Washington. About thirty miles away, at the town of Manassas, was a slightly smaller Confederate army under P. G. T. Beauregard. If the Northern army could destroy the Southern one, Union leaders believed, the war might end at once. In mid-July, McDowell marched his inexperienced troops toward Manassas. Beauregard moved his troops behind Bull Run, a small stream north of Manassas, and called for reinforcements, which reached him the day before the battle. The two armies were now approximately the same size.

On July 21, in the First Battle of Bull Run, or First Battle of Manassas, McDowell almost succeeded in dispersing the

FIRST BATTLE OF BULL RUN

Confederate forces. But the Southerners stopped a last strong Union assault and then began a savage counterattack. The Union troops, exhausted after hours of hot, hard fighting, suddenly panicked. They broke ranks and retreated chaotically. McDowell was unable to reorganize them, and he had to order a retreat to Washington—a disorderly withdrawal complicated by the presence along the route of many civilians who had ridden down from the capital, picnic baskets in hand, to watch the battle from nearby hills. The Confederates, as disorganized by victory as the Union forces were by defeat, and short of supplies and transportation, did not pursue. The battle was a severe blow to Union morale and to the president's confidence in his officers. It also dispelled the illusion that the war would be a quick one.

Elsewhere in 1861, Union forces were achieving some small but significant victories. In Missouri, rebel forces gathered behind Governor Claiborne Jackson and other state officials who wanted to secede from the Union. Nathaniel Lyon, who commanded a small regular army force in St. Louis, moved his troops into southern Missouri to face the secessionists. On August 10, at the Battle of Wilson's Creek, Lyon was defeated and killed—but not before he had seriously weakened the striking power of the Confederates. Union forces were subsequently able to hold most of the state.

WILSON'S CREEK

Meanwhile, a Union force under George B. McClellan moved east from Ohio into western Virginia. By the end of 1861, it had "liberated" the anti-secession mountain people of the region. They created their own state government loyal to the Union and were admitted to the Union as West Virginia in 1863. The occupation of western Virginia was of limited military value, since the mountains cut the area off from the rest of Virginia. It was, however, an important symbolic victory for the North.

THE WESTERN THEATER

After the First Battle of Bull Run, military operations in the East settled into a long and frustrating stalemate. The first decisive operations in 1862 occurred in the West. Union forces were trying to seize control of the southern Mississippi River, which would divide the Confederacy and give the North easy transportation into the heart of the South. Northern soldiers advanced on the river from both the north and south, moving downriver from Kentucky and upriver from the Gulf of Mexico toward New Orleans.

In April, a Union squadron of ironclads and wooden vessels commanded by David G. Farragut gathered in the Gulf of Mexico, then smashed past weak Confederate forts near the mouth of the Mississippi, and from there sailed up to New Orleans, which was defenseless because the Confederate high command had expected the attack to come from the north. The city surrendered on April 25—the first major Union victory and an important turning point in the war. From then on, the mouth of the Mississippi was closed to Confederate trade; and the South's largest city and most important banking center was in Union hands.

NEW ORLEANS CAPTURED

Farther north in the western theater, Confederate troops under the command of Albert Sidney Johnston were stretched out in a long defensive line centered at two forts in Tennessee, Fort Henry and Fort Donelson, on the Tennessee and Cumberland Rivers, respectively. But the forts were well behind the main Southern flanks, a fatal weakness that Union commanders recognized and exploited. Early in 1862, Ulysses S. Grant attacked Fort Henry, whose defenders, awed by the ironclad riverboats accompanying the Union army, surrendered with almost no resistance on February 6. Grant then moved both his naval and ground forces to Fort Donelson, where the Confederates put up a stronger fight but finally, on February 16, had to surrender. By cracking the Confederate center,

Grant had gained control of river communications and forced Confederate forces out of Kentucky and half of Tennessee.

With about 40,000 men, Grant now advanced south along the Tennessee River to seize control of railroad lines vital to the Confederacy. From Pittsburg Landing, he marched to nearby Shiloh, Tennessee, where a force almost equal to his own, commanded by Albert Sidney Johnston and P. G. T. Beauregard, caught him by surprise. The result was the Battle of Shiloh, April 6–7. In the first day's fighting (during which Johnston was killed), the Southerners drove Grant back to the river. But the next day, reinforced by 25,000 fresh troops, Grant recovered the lost ground and forced Beauregard to withdraw. After the narrow Union victory at Shiloh, Northern forces occupied Corinth, Mississippi, the hub of several important railroads, and established control of the Mississippi River as far south as Memphis.

SHILOH

Braxton Bragg, who succeeded Johnston as commander of the Confederate army in the West, gathered his forces at Chattanooga, in eastern Tennessee, which the Confederacy still controlled. He hoped to win back the rest of the state and then move north into Kentucky. But first he had to face a Union army (commanded by Don Carlos Buell and later William S. Rosecrans), whose assignment was to capture Chattanooga. The two armies maneuvered for advantage inconclusively in northern Tennessee and southern Kentucky for several months until they finally met, December 31–January 2, in the Battle of Murfreesboro, or Stone's River. Bragg was forced to withdraw to the south, his campaign a failure. By the end of 1862, Union forces had made considerable progress in the West. But the major conflict remained in the East, where they were having much less success.

THE VIRGINIA FRONT, 1862

Union operations were being directed in 1862 by George B. McClellan, commander of the Army of the Potomac and the most controversial general of the war. McClellan was a superb trainer of men, but he often appeared reluctant to commit his troops to battle. Opportunities for important engagements came and went, and McClellan seemed never to take advantage of them—claiming always that his preparations were not yet complete or that the moment was not right. During the winter of 1861–1862, McClellan concentrated on training his army of 150,000 men near Washington. Finally, he designed a spring campaign whose purpose was to capture the Confederate capital at Richmond. But instead of heading overland directly toward Richmond, McClellan chose a complicated, roundabout route that he thought would circumvent the Confederate defenses. The navy would carry his troops down the Potomac to a peninsula east of Richmond, between the York and James Rivers. The army would approach the city from there. It became known as the Peninsular campaign.

GEORGE McCLELLAN

McClellan began the campaign with only part of his army. Approximately 100,000 men accompanied him down the Potomac. Another 30,000—under General Irvin McDowell—

THE WAR IN THE WEST, 1861–1863 While the Union armies in Virginia were meeting with repeated frustrations, the Union armies in the West were scoring notable successes in the first two years of the war. This map shows a series of Union drives in the western Confederacy. Admiral David Farragut's ironclads led to the capture of New Orleans—a critical Confederate port—in April 1862, while forces farther north under the command of Ulysses S. Grant drove the Confederate army out of Kentucky and western Tennessee. These battles culminated in the Union victory at Shiloh, which led to Union control of the upper Mississippi River.

• Why was control of the Mississippi so important to both sides?

remained behind to protect Washington. McClellan insisted that Washington was safe as long as he was threatening Richmond, and finally persuaded Lincoln to promise to send him the additional men. But before the president could do so, a Confederate army under Thomas J. ("Stonewall") Jackson changed his plans. Jackson staged a rapid march north through the Shenandoah Valley, as if he were planning to cross the Potomac and attack Washington. Alarmed, Lincoln dispatched McDowell's corps to head off Jackson. In the brilliant Valley campaign of May 4–June 9, 1862, Jackson defeated two sepa-

rate Union forces and slipped away before McDowell could catch him.

Meanwhile, Confederate troops under Joseph E. Johnston were attacking McClellan's advancing army outside Richmond.

SEVEN PINES   But in the two-day Battle of Fair Oaks, or Seven Pines (May 31–June 1), they could not repel the Union forces. Johnston, badly wounded, was replaced by Robert E. Lee, who then recalled Stonewall Jackson from the Shenandoah Valley. With a combined force of 85,000 to face McClellan's 100,000, Lee launched a new offensive, known as

July 1861–July 1862

Kernstown
March 23, 1862

Winchester
May 25, 1862

Jackson's Valley
campaign
May–June 1862

First Battle of Bull Run
(Manassas)
July 21, 1861

Washington

Front
Royal
May 23, 1862

Cross Keys
June 8, 1862

MARYLAND

Shenandoah Valley

Port Republic
June 9, 1862

McDowell
May 8, 1862

Rappahannock R.

James R.

Chesapeake Bay

Fair Oaks
May 31–June 1, 1862

Richmond

VIRGINIA

Battle of the Seven Days
June 25–July 1, 1862
McClellan forced to
retreat by Lee,
reinforced by Jackson

Williamsburg
May 5, 1862

Yorktown

Siege of Yorktown
April 5–May 4, 1862

Confederate forces
Union forces
Confederate victories
Union victories
Inconclusive
Union-held territory
at start of war
Confederate states

0   50 mi
0   50 km   100 km

August–December 1862

South Mountain
Sept. 14

Antietam
Sep. 17

WEST
VIRGINIA
Controlled
by Union
after 1861

Harpers Ferry
Sept. 15

MARYLAND

Chantilly
Sept. 1

Washington

Shenandoah R.

Second Battle
of Bull Run (Manassas)
Aug. 29–30

Cedar Mountain
Aug. 9

Chesapeake Bay

Fredericksburg
Dec. 13

VIRGINIA

0   25 mi
0   25   50 km

1863

PENNSYLVANIA

Carlisle

Chambersburg

York

Gettysburg
July 1–3

WEST
VIRGINIA
Admitted to
Union in 1863

Frederick

MARYLAND

Washington

Brandy Station
June 9

Fredericksburg

Chancellorsville
May 1–5
Jackson killed

Rappahannock R.

Chesapeake Bay

0   25 mi
0   25   50 km

THE VIRGINIA THEATER, 1861–1863 Much of the fighting during the first two years of the Civil War took place in what became known as the Virginia theater—although the campaigns in this region eventually extended north into Maryland and Pennsylvania. The Union hoped for a quick victory over the newly created Confederate army. But as these maps show, the Southern forces consistently thwarted such hopes. The map at top left shows the battles of 1861 and the first half of 1862, almost all of them won by the Confederates. The map at lower left shows the last months of 1862, during which the Southerners again defeated the Union in most of their engagements—although Northern forces drove the Confederates back from Maryland in September. The map on the right shows the troop movements that led to the climactic battle of Gettysburg in 1863.

• *Why were the Union forces unable to profit more from their material advantages during these first years of the war?*

the Battle of the Seven Days (June 25–July 1). Lee wanted to cut McClellan off from his base on the York River and then destroy the isolated Union army. But McClellan fought his way across the peninsula and set up a new base on the James. There, with naval support, the Army of the Potomac was safe.

McClellan was now only twenty-five miles from Richmond, with a secure line of water communications, and thus in a good position to renew the campaign. Time and again, however, he found reasons for delay. Instead of replacing McClellan with a more aggressive commander, Lincoln finally ordered the army to move to northern Virginia and join a smaller force under John Pope. The president hoped to begin a new offensive against Richmond on the direct overland route that he himself had always preferred.

As the Army of the Potomac left the peninsula by water, Lee moved north with the Army of Northern Virginia to strike Pope before McClellan could join him. Pope was as rash as McClellan was cautious, and he attacked the approaching Confederates without waiting for the arrival of all of McClellan's troops. In the ensuing Second Battle of Bull Run, or Second Battle of Manassas (August 29–30), Lee threw back the assault and routed Pope's army, which fled to Washington. With hopes for an overland campaign against Richmond now in disarray, Lincoln removed Pope from command and put McClellan in charge of all the Union forces in the region.

Lee soon went on the offensive again, heading north through western Maryland, and McClellan moved out to meet him. McClellan had the good luck to get a copy of Lee's orders, which revealed that a part of the Confederate army, under Stonewall Jackson, had separated from the rest to attack Harpers Ferry. But instead of attacking quickly before the Confederates could recombine, McClellan delayed and gave Lee time to pull most of his forces together behind Antietam Creek, near the town of Sharpsburg.

ANTIETAM

There, on September 17, in the bloodiest single-day engagement of the war, McClellan's 87,000-man army repeatedly attacked Lee's force of 50,000, with enormous casualties on both sides. Six thousand soldiers died, and 17,000 sustained injuries. Late in the day, just as the Confederate line seemed ready to break, the last of Jackson's troops arrived from Harpers Ferry to reinforce it. McClellan might have broken through with one more assault. Instead, he allowed Lee to retreat into Virginia. Technically, Antietam was a Union victory, but in reality, it was an opportunity squandered. In November, Lincoln finally removed McClellan from command for good.

McClellan's replacement, Ambrose E. Burnside, was a short-lived mediocrity. He tried to move toward Richmond by crossing the Rappahannock at Fredericksburg, the strongest defensive point on the river. There, on December 13, he launched a series of attacks against Lee, all of them bloody, all of them hopeless. After losing a large part of his army, Burnside withdrew to the north bank of the Rappahannock. He was relieved at his own request.

THE PROGRESS OF THE WAR

Why did the Union—with its much larger population and its much better transportation and technology than the Confederacy—make so little progress in the first two years of the war? Had there been a decisive and dramatic victory by either side early in the war—for example, a major victory by the Union at the First Battle of Bull Run—the conflict might have ended quickly by destroying the Confederacy's morale. But no such decisive victory occurred in the first two years of the war.

Many Northerners blamed the military stalemate on timid or incompetent Union generals, and there was some truth to that view. But the more important reason for the drawn-out conflict

THE FIRST CONNECTICUT ARTILLERY Photographed on an unidentified battlefield, the First Connecticut Artillery stands posing before its array of cannons—and the stumps of trees cut down to allow them unimpeded shots at the enemy. (US Army Military History Institute, Carlisle, PA)

was that it was not a traditional war of tactics and military strategy. It was, even if the leaders of both sides were not yet fully aware of it, a war of attrition. Winning or losing battles here and there would not determine the outcome of the war. What would bring the war to a conclusion was the steady destruction of the resources that were necessary for victory. More than two bloody years of fighting was still to come. But those last years were a testimony to the slow, steady deterioration of the Confederacy's ability to maintain the war and to the consistent growth of the resources that allowed the Union armies to grow steadily stronger.

1863: YEAR OF DECISION

At the beginning of 1863, General Joseph Hooker was in command of the still formidable Army of the Potomac, whose 120,000 troops remained north of the Rappahannock, opposite Fredericksburg. But despite his reputation as a fighter (his popular nickname was "Fighting Joe"), Hooker showed little resolve as he launched his own campaign in the spring. Taking part of his army, Hooker crossed the river above Fredericksburg and moved toward the town and Lee's army. But at the last minute, he apparently lost his nerve and drew back to a defensive position in a desolate area of brush and scrub trees known as the Wilderness. Lee had only half as many men as Hooker did, but

BATTLE OF CHANCELLORSVILLE

he boldly divided his forces for a dual assault on the Union army. In the Battle of Chancellorsville, May 1–5, Stonewall Jackson attacked the Union right and Lee himself charged the front. Hooker barely managed to escape with his army. Lee had defeated the Union objectives, but he had not destroyed the Union army. And his ablest officer, Jackson, was wounded during the battle and subsequently died of pneumonia.

While the Union forces were suffering repeated frustrations in the East, they were continuing to achieve important

VICKSBURG

victories in the West. In the spring of 1863, Ulysses S. Grant was driving at Vicksburg, Mississippi, one of the Confederacy's two remaining strongholds on the southern Mississippi River. Vicksburg was well protected, surrounded by rough country on the north and low, marshy ground on the west, and with good artillery coverage of the river itself. But in May, Grant boldly moved men and supplies—overland and by water—to an area south of the city, where the terrain was better. He then attacked Vicksburg from the rear. Six weeks later, on July 4, Vicksburg—whose residents were by then literally starving as a result of a prolonged siege—surrendered. At almost the same time, the other Confederate strong point on the river, Port Hudson, Louisiana, also surrendered—to a Union force that had moved north from New Orleans. The Union had achieved one of its basic military aims: control of the whole length of the Mississippi. The Confederacy was split in two, with Louisiana, Arkansas, and Texas cut off from the other seceded states. The victories on the Mississippi were among the great turning points of the war.

During the siege of Vicksburg, Lee proposed an invasion of Pennsylvania, which would, he argued, divert Union troops north and remove the pressure on the lower Mississippi. Further, he

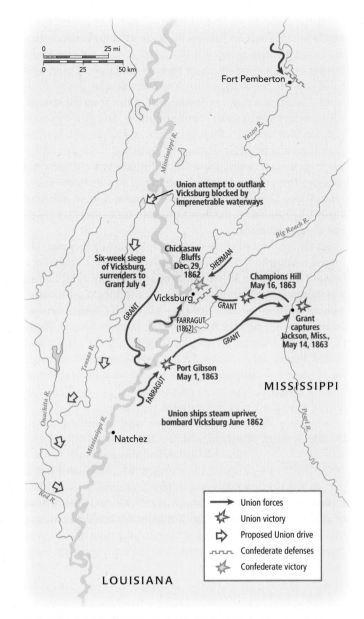

THE SIEGE OF VICKSBURG, MAY–JULY 1863 In the spring of 1863, Grant began a campaign to win control of the final piece of the Mississippi River still controlled by the Confederacy. To do that required capturing the Southern stronghold at Vicksburg—a well-defended city sitting above the river. Vicksburg's main defenses were in the North, so Grant boldly moved men and supplies around the city and attacked it from the south. Eventually, he cut off the city's access to the outside world, and after a six-week siege, its residents finally surrendered.

• *What impact did the combined victories at Vicksburg and Gettysburg have on Northern commitment to the war?*

argued, if he could win a major victory on Northern soil, England and France might come to the Confederacy's aid. The war-weary North might even quit the war before Vicksburg fell.

In June 1863, Lee moved up the Shenandoah Valley into Maryland and then entered Pennsylvania. The Union Army of the Potomac, commanded first by Hooker and then by George C. Meade, also moved north, parallel with the Confederates' movement, staying between Lee and Washington. The two armies finally encountered each other at the small town of Gettysburg,

GETTYSBURG, JULY 1–3, 1863 Gettysburg was the most important single battle of the Civil War. The map on the left shows the distribution of Union and Confederate forces at the beginning of the battle, July 1, after Lee had driven the Northern forces south of town. The map on the right reveals the pattern of the attacks on July 2 and 3. Note, in particular, Pickett's bold and costly charge, whose failure on July 3 was the turning point in the battle and, some chroniclers have argued, the war.

• *Why did Robert E. Lee believe that an invasion of Pennsylvania would advance the Confederate cause?*

Pennsylvania. There, on July 1–3, 1863, they fought the most celebrated battle of the war.

Meade's army established a strong, well-protected position on the hills south of the town. The confident and combative

GETTYSBURG

Lee attacked, even though his army was outnumbered 75,000 to 90,000. His first assault on the Union forces on Cemetery Ridge failed. A day later he ordered a second, larger effort. In what is remembered as Pickett's Charge, a force of 15,000 Confederate soldiers advanced for almost a mile across open country while being swept by Union fire. Only about 5,000 made it up the ridge, and this remnant finally had to surrender or retreat. By now Lee had lost nearly a third of his army. On July 4, the same day as the surrender of Vicksburg, he withdrew from Gettysburg—another major turning point in the war. Never again were the weakened Confederate forces able to threaten Northern territory seriously.

Before the end of 1863, there was a third important turning point, this one in Tennessee. After occupying Chattanooga on September 9, Union forces under William Rosecrans began an unwise pursuit of Bragg's retreating Confederate forces. Bragg was waiting for them just across the Georgia line, with reinforcements from Lee's army. The two armies engaged in

the Battle of Chickamauga (September 19–20), one of the few battles in which the Confederates enjoyed a numerical superiority (70,000 to 56,000). Union forces could not break the Confederate lines and retreated back to Chattanooga.

Bragg now began a siege of Chattanooga itself, seizing the heights nearby and cutting off fresh supplies to the Union forces.

BATTLE OF
CHATTANOOGA

Grant came to the rescue. In the Battle of Chattanooga (November 23–25), the reinforced Union army drove the Confederates back into Georgia. Northern troops then occupied most of eastern Tennessee. Union forces had now achieved a second important objective: control of the Tennessee River. Four of the eleven Confederate states were now effectively cut off from the Southern nation. No longer could the Confederacy hope to win independence through a decisive military victory. They could hope to win only by holding on and exhausting the Northern will to fight.

THE LAST STAGE, 1864–1865

By the beginning of 1864, Ulysses S. Grant had become general in chief of all the Union armies. At long last, the president had found a commander whom he could rely on to pursue the war doggedly and tenaciously. Grant was not a subtle strategic or tactical general; he believed in using the North's overwhelming advantage in troops and material resources to overwhelm the South. He was not afraid to absorb massive casualties as long as he was inflicting similar casualties on his opponents.

Grant planned two great offensives for 1864. In Virginia, the Army of the Potomac (technically under Meade's command, but really now under Grant's) would advance toward Richmond and force Lee into a decisive battle. In Georgia, the western army, under William T. Sherman, would advance east toward Atlanta and destroy the remaining Confederate force farther south, which was now under the command of Joseph E. Johnston. The northern campaign began when the Army of the Potomac, 115,000 strong, plunged into the rough, wooded Wilderness area of northwestern Virginia in pursuit of Lee's 75,000-man army. After avoiding an engagement for several weeks, Lee turned Grant back in the Battle of the Wilderness (May 5–7). But Grant was undeterred. Without stopping to rest or reorganize, he resumed his march toward Richmond. He met Lee again in the bloody, five-day Battle of Spotsylvania

GRANT'S STRATEGY

Court House, in which 12,000 Union troops and a large but unknown number of Confederates died or were wounded. Despite the enormous losses, Grant kept moving. But victory continued to elude him.

Lee kept his army between Grant and the Confederate capital and on June 1–3 repulsed the Union forces again, just northeast of Richmond, at Cold Harbor. The month-long Wilderness campaign had cost Grant 55,000 men (killed, wounded, and captured) to Lee's 31,000. And Richmond still had not fallen.

Grant now changed his strategy. He moved his army east of Richmond, bypassing the capital altogether, and headed south toward the railroad center at Petersburg. If he could seize Petersburg, he could cut off the capital's communications with the rest of the Confederacy. But Petersburg had strong defenses; and once Lee came to the city's relief, the assault became a prolonged siege, which lasted nine months.

In Georgia, meanwhile, Sherman was facing less ferocious resistance. With 90,000 men, he confronted Confederate forces of 60,000 under Johnston, who was unwilling to risk a direct engagement. As Sherman advanced, Johnston tried to delay him by maneuvering. The two armies fought only one real

VIRGINIA CAMPAIGNS, 1864–1865 From the Confederate defeat and retreat from Gettysburg until the end of the war, most of the eastern fighting took place in Virginia. By now, Ulysses S. Grant was commander of all Union forces and had taken over the Army of the Potomac. Although Confederate forces won a number of important battles during the Virginia campaign, the Union army grew steadily stronger and the Southern forces steadily weaker. Grant believed that the Union strategy should reflect the North's greatest advantage: its superiority in men and equipment.

• *What effect did this decision have on the level of casualties?*

MOBILE BAY, 1864 This painting by Robert Weir portrays a famous naval battle at the entrance to Mobile Bay between a Union sloop-of-war, the *U.S.S. Richmond*, part of a fleet commanded by Admiral David Farragut, and a Confederate iron-clad, the *C.S.S. Tennessee*. Although Confederate mines were scattered across the entrance to the harbor, Farragut ordered his ships into battle with the memorable command: "Damn the torpedoes! Full speed ahead!" The Union forces defeated the Confederate flotilla and three weeks later captured the forts defending the harbor—thus removing from Confederate control the last port on the Gulf Coast available to the blockade runners who were attempting to supply the South's war needs. (Mariners' Museum, Newport News, Virginia)

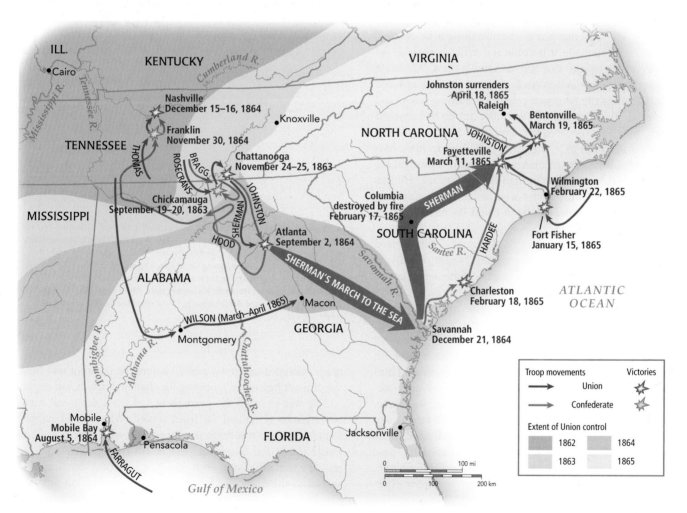

SHERMAN'S MARCH TO THE SEA, 1864–1865 While Grant was wearing Lee down in Virginia, General William Tecumseh Sherman was moving east across Georgia. After a series of battles in Tennessee and northwest Georgia, Sherman captured Atlanta and then marched unimpeded to Savannah, on the Georgia coast—deliberately devastating the towns and plantations through which his troops marched. Note that after capturing Savannah by Christmas 1864, Sherman began moving north through the Carolinas. A few days after Lee surrendered to Grant at Appomattox, Confederate forces farther south surrendered to Sherman.

• *What did Sherman believe his devastating March to the Sea would accomplish?*

battle—at Kennesaw Mountain, northwest of Atlanta, on June 27—where Johnston scored an impressive victory. Even so,

CAPTURE OF ATLANTA

he was unable to stop the Union advance toward Atlanta. President Davis replaced Johnston with the combative John B. Hood, who twice daringly attacked Sherman's army but accomplished nothing except seriously weakening his own forces. Sherman took Atlanta on September 2. News of the victory electrified the North and helped unite the previously divided Republican Party behind President Lincoln.

Hood now tried unsuccessfully to draw Sherman out of Atlanta by moving back up through Tennessee and threatening an invasion of the North. Sherman did not take the bait. But he did send Union troops to reinforce Nashville. In the Battle of Nashville, on December 15–16, 1864, Northern forces practically destroyed what was left of Hood's army.

Meanwhile, Sherman had left Atlanta to begin his soon-to-be-famous March to the Sea. Living off the land, destroying supplies it could not use, his army cut a sixty-mile-wide swath of

MARCH TO THE SEA

desolation across Georgia. "War is all hell," Sherman had once said. By that he meant not that war is a terrible thing to be avoided, but that it should be made as horrible and costly as possible for the opponent. He sought not only to deprive the Confederate army of war materials and railroad communications but also to break the will of the Southern people, by burning towns and plantations along his route. By December 20, he had reached Savannah, which surrendered two days later. Sherman offered it to President Lincoln as a Christmas gift. Early in 1865, having left Savannah largely undamaged, Sherman continued his destructive march northward through South Carolina. He was virtually unopposed until he was well inside North Carolina, where a small force under Johnston could do no more than cause a brief delay.

In April 1865, Grant's Army of the Potomac—still engaged in the prolonged siege at Petersburg—finally captured a vital railroad junction southwest of the town. Without rail access to the South, cut off from other Confederate forces, Lee could no longer hope to defend Richmond. With the remnant of his army, now about 25,000 men, Lee began moving west in the forlorn hope of finding a way around the Union forces so that he could head south and link up with Johnston in North

APPOMATTOX COURT HOUSE

Carolina. But the Union army pursued him and blocked his escape route. Finally recognizing that further bloodshed was futile, Lee arranged to meet Grant at a private home in the small town of Appomattox Court House, Virginia. There, on April 9, he surrendered what was left of his forces. Nine days later, near Durham, North Carolina, Johnston surrendered to Sherman.

In military terms, at least, the long war was now effectively over, even though Jefferson Davis refused to accept defeat. He fled south from Richmond and was finally captured in Georgia. A few Southern diehards continued to fight, but even their resis-

> **❝ WAR IS ALL HELL ❞**
>
> **WILLIAM TECUMSEH SHERMAN**

A LETTER FROM THE FRONT Charles Wellington Reed, a nineteen-year-old Union soldier who was also a talented artist, sent illustrated letters to the members of his family throughout the war. In this 1863 letter to his mother, he portrays the Ninth Massachusetts Battery leaving Centreville, Virginia, on its way to Gettysburg. Two weeks later, Reed fought in the famous battle and eventually received the Congressional Medal of Honor for his bravery there. "Such a shrieking, hissing, seathing I never dreamed was imaginable," he wrote of the fighting at the time. (Manuscript Division, Library of Congress)

tance collapsed before long. Well before the last shot was fired, the difficult process of reuniting the shattered nation had begun.

The war ensured the permanence of the Union, but many other issues remained far from settled. What would happen to the freedmen (the term used for slaves who were now liberated)? Could the South and the North reconcile? Would the massive industrial growth in the North during the Civil War spread to the South, or would the South remain an agrarian region with much less wealth than in the North? The end of the war was the beginning of more than a generation of struggle to determine the legacy of the Civil War.

LOOKING BACK

The American Civil War began with high hopes and high ideals on both sides. In both the North and the South, thousands of men enthusiastically enlisted in local regiments; marched down the streets of their towns and cities dressed in uniforms of blue or gray to the cheers of family, friends, and neighbors; and went off to war. Four years later, more than 600,000 of them were dead and many more maimed and traumatized for life. A fight for "principles" and "ideals"—a fight few people had thought would last more than a few months—had become one of the longest wars, and by far the bloodiest war, in American history, before or since.

During the first two years of fighting, the Confederate forces seemed to have all the advantages. They were fighting on their own soil. Their troops seemed more committed to the cause than those of the North. Their commanders were exceptionally talented, while Union forces were for a time erratically led. Gradually, however, the Union's advantages began to assert themselves. The Union had a stabler political system led by one of the greatest leaders in the nation's history (as opposed to the Confederacy's untested government led by a relatively weak president). It had a much larger population, a far more developed industrial economy, superior financial institutions, and a better railroad system. By the middle of 1863, the tide of war had changed; and over the next two years, Union forces gradually wore down the Confederate armies before finally triumphing in 1865.

The North's victory was not just a military one. The war strengthened the North's economy, giving a spur to industry and railroad development. It greatly weakened the South's, by destroying millions of dollars of property and depleting the region's young male population. Southerners had gone to war in part because of their fears of growing Northern dominance. The war itself, ironically, confirmed and strengthened that dominance. There was no doubt by 1865 that the future of the United States lay in the growth of industry and commerce, which would occur for many years primarily outside the South.

IMPACT OF THE NORTH'S VICTORY

But most of all, the Civil War was a victory for the millions of African American slaves, over whose plight the conflict had largely begun in the first place. The war produced Abraham Lincoln's epochal Emancipation Proclamation and, later, the Thirteenth Amendment to the Constitution, which abolished slavery. It also encouraged hundreds of thousands of slaves to free themselves, to desert their masters and seek refuge behind Union lines—at times to fight in the Union armies. The future of the freed slaves was not to be an easy one, but 3.5 million people who had once lived in bondage emerged from the war as free men and women. •

RECALL AND REFLECT

1. Assess the advantages of the North and those of the South at the beginning of the Civil War. How did the advantages of each side change over the course of the war?

2. How did the Confederate government differ from the federal government of the United States?

3. How did the Civil War affect the West?

4. How did the war affect the lives of women in the North and in the South?

5. Compare Lincoln and Davis as heads of government and commanders in chief.

6. Why did Lincoln issue the Emancipation Proclamation, and what were its effects?

SIGNIFICANT EVENTS

Confederate States of America formed

Battles of Shiloh, Second Bull Run, Antietam, Fredericksburg

Robert E. Lee named commander of Confederate armies

1860

South Carolina secedes from Union

1861

Jefferson Davis named president of Confederacy

Conflict at Fort Sumter, South Carolina (April 12–14), begins Civil War

First Battle of Bull Run

1862

Homestead Act and Morrill Land Grant Act passed

Confederacy enacts military draft

KEY TERMS/PEOPLE/PLACES/EVENTS

Battles of Chancellorsville, Gettysburg, Chattanooga

Lincoln issues Emancipation Proclamation (January 1)

Sherman captures Atlanta (September 2)

Lee surrenders to Grant at Appomattox Courthouse (April 9)

1863

Vicksburg surrenders (July 4)

Union enacts military draft

Antidraft riots break out in New York City

West Virginia admitted to Union

1864

Grant named commander of Union armies

Battle of the Wilderness (May 5–7)

Sherman's "March to the Sea" begins

Lincoln reelected president

1865

Thirteenth Amendment, abolishing slavery, ratified

THE GENIUS OF FREEDOM This 1874 lithograph portrays a series of important moments in the history of African Americans in the South during Reconstruction—among them the participation of black soldiers in the Civil War, a speech by a black representative in the North Carolina legislature, and the movement of African American workers from slavery into a system of free labor. It also portrays some of the white leaders (among them Lincoln and Charles Sumner) who had promoted the cause of the freedmen. (Chicago Historical Society)

15 | RECONSTRUCTION AND THE NEW SOUTH

FEW PERIODS IN THE HISTORY OF THE UNITED STATES have produced as much bitterness or created such enduring controversy as the era of Reconstruction—the years following the Civil War, when Americans attempted to reunite their shattered nation. To many white Southerners, Reconstruction was a vicious and destructive experience—a time when vindictive Northerners inflicted humiliation and revenge on the prostrate South and unnecessarily delayed a genuine reunion of the sections. Northern defenders of Reconstruction, in contrast, argued that their policies and forceful federal intervention were the only way to keep unrepentant Confederates from restoring Southern society as it had been before the war.

To most African Americans at the time, and to many people of all races since, Reconstruction was notable for other reasons. Neither a vicious tyranny, as white Southerners charged, nor a thoroughgoing reform, as many Northerners claimed, it was, rather, a small but important first step in the effort by former slaves to secure civil rights and economic power. Reconstruction did not provide African

SETTING THE STAGE

Americans with either the legal protections or the material resources to assure them real equality. When it came to an end, finally, in the late 1870s, the freed slaves found themselves abandoned by the federal government to face a system of economic peonage and legal subordination. Yet for all its shortcomings, Reconstruction did help African Americans create institutions and legal precedents that in the twentieth century became the basis for their efforts to win freedom and equality.

LOOKING AHEAD

1. What were the various plans for Reconstruction proposed by Lincoln, Johnson, and Congress? Which plan was enacted and why?
2. What were the effects of Reconstruction for blacks and whites in the South?
3. What were the political achievements and failures of the Grant administration?

THE PROBLEMS OF PEACEMAKING

In 1865, as it became clear that the war was almost over, no one in Washington had yet formed a plan for what would happen to the defeated South. Lincoln could not negotiate a treaty with the Confederate government; he continued to insist that the Confederate government had no legal right to exist. Yet neither could he simply readmit the Southern states into the Union as if nothing had happened.

THE AFTERMATH OF WAR AND EMANCIPATION

The Civil War was a catastrophe for the South with no parallel in America's experience as a nation. Towns had been gutted, plantations burned, fields neglected, bridges and railroads destroyed. Many white Southerners, stripped of their slaves through emancipation and stripped of the capital they

THE DEVASTATED SOUTH

had invested in now-worthless Confederate bonds and currency, had almost no personal property. Many families had to rebuild their fortunes without the help of adult males, massive numbers of whom had died in the war. Some white Southerners faced starvation and homelessness.

The more than 258,000 Confederate soldiers who had died in the war constituted over 20 percent of the adult white male population of the region; thousands more returned home wounded or sick. Almost all surviving white Southerners had lost people close to them in the fighting. A cult of ritualized mourning developed throughout the region in the late 1860s, particularly among white women—many of whom wore mourning clothes (and jewelry) for two years or longer. At the same time, white Southerners began to romanticize the "Lost Cause" and its leaders, and to look back nostalgically at the South as it had existed before the terrible disruptions of war. Such Confederate heroes as Robert E. Lee, Stonewall Jackson, and (later) Jefferson Davis were treated with extraordinary reverence, almost as religious figures. Communities throughout the South built elaborate monuments to their war dead in town squares. The tremendous

MYTH OF THE "LOST CAUSE"

RICHMOND, 1865 By the time Union forces captured Richmond in early 1865, the Confederate capital had been under siege for months and much of the city lay in ruins, as this photograph reveals. On April 4, President Lincoln, accompanied by his son Tad, visited Richmond. As he walked through the streets of the shattered city, hundreds of former slaves emerged from the rubble to watch him pass. "No triumphal march of a conqueror could have equalled in moral sublimity the humble manner in which he entered Richmond," a black soldier serving with the Union army wrote. "It was a great deliverer among the delivered. No wonder tears came to his eyes." (Library of Congress)

A MONUMENT TO THE LOST CAUSE This monument in the town square of Monroe, Georgia, was typical of many such memorials erected all across the South after the Civil War. They served both to commemorate the Confederate dead and to remind white Southerners of what was by the 1870s already widely known and romanticized as the "Lost Cause." (©Lee Snider/Corbis)

sense of loss that pervaded the white South reinforced the determination of many whites to protect what remained of their now-vanished world.

If conditions were bad for many Southern whites, they were worse for most Southern blacks—the 4 million men and women emerging from bondage. Some of them had also seen service during the war—as servants to Confederate officers or as teamsters and laborers for the Southern armies. Nearly 200,000 had fought for the Union, and 38,000 had died. Others had worked as spies or scouts for Union forces in the South. Many more had flocked to the Union lines to escape slavery. Even before Emancipation, thousands of slaves in many parts of the South had taken advantage of wartime disruptions to leave their owners and move off in search of freedom. As soon as the war ended, hundreds of thousands more former

slaves—young and old, healthy and sick—left their plantations. Some went in search of family members who had been sold by their former masters. But many others had nowhere to go. Some trudged to the nearest town or city, roamed the countryside camping at night on the bare ground, or gathered around Union occupation forces, hoping for assistance. Virtually none owned any land or property. Most had no possessions except the clothes they wore.

In 1865, in short, Southern society was in vast disarray. Blacks and whites, men and women faced a future of great uncertainty. Yet all Southerners faced this future with some very clear aspirations. For both blacks and whites, Reconstruction became a struggle to define the meaning of freedom. But the former slaves and the defeated whites had very different conceptions of what freedom meant.

COMPETING NOTIONS OF FREEDOM

For African Americans, freedom meant above all an end to slavery and to all the injustices and humiliation they associated with it. But it also meant the acquisition of rights and protections that would allow them to live as free men and women in the same way white people did. "If I cannot do like a white man," one African American man told his former master, "I am not free."

African Americans differed with one another on how to achieve that freedom. Some demanded a redistribution of economic resources, especially land, because, as a convention of Alabama freedmen put it in a formal resolution, "The property which they hold was nearly all earned by the sweat of our brows." Others asked simply for legal equality, confident that given the same opportunities as white citizens they could advance successfully in American society. But whatever their particular demands, virtually all former slaves were united in their desire for independence from white control. Freed from slavery, blacks throughout the South began almost immediately to create autonomous African American communities. They pulled out of white-controlled churches and established their own. They created fraternal, benevolent, and mutual-aid societies. When they could, they began their own schools.

> FREEDOM FOR
> THE EX-SLAVES

For most white Southerners, freedom meant something very different. It meant the ability to control their own destinies without interference from the North or the federal government. And in the immediate aftermath of the war, they attempted to exercise this version of freedom by trying to restore their society to its antebellum form. Slavery had been abolished in the former Confederacy by the Emancipation Proclamation, and everywhere else (as of December 1865) by the Thirteenth Amendment. But many white planters wanted to continue slavery in an altered form by keeping black workers legally tied to the plantations. When many white Southerners fought for what they considered freedom, they were fighting above all to preserve local and regional autonomy and white supremacy.

The federal government kept troops in the South after the war to preserve

> **" IF I CANNOT DO LIKE A WHITE MAN, I AM NOT FREE. "**

A FREEDMEN'S BUREAU SCHOOL African American students and teachers stand outside a school for former slaves, one of many run by the Freedmen's Bureau throughout the defeated Confederacy in the first years after the war. (U.S. Army Military History Institute, Carlisle, Pennsylvania. Photo by Jim Enos)

order and protect the freedmen. In March 1865, Congress established the Freedmen's Bureau, an agency of the army directed by General Oliver O. Howard. The Freedmen's Bureau distributed food to millions of former slaves. It established schools staffed by missionaries and teachers who had been sent to the South by Freedmen's Aid Societies and other private and church groups in the North. It made modest efforts to settle blacks on lands of their own. (The bureau also offered considerable assistance to poor whites, many of whom were similarly destitute and homeless after the war.) But the Freedmen's Bureau was not a permanent solution. It had authority to operate for only one year; and in any case it was far too small to deal effectively with the enormous problems facing Southern society. By the time the war ended, other proposals for reconstructing the defeated South were emerging.

THE FREEDMEN'S BUREAU

ISSUES OF RECONSTRUCTION

Reconstruction was determined not just by social realities or ideals. It was also determined by partisan politics. The terms by which the Southern states rejoined the Union had important implications for both major political parties. The Republican victories in 1860 and 1864 had been a result in large part of the division of the Democratic Party and, later, the removal of the South from the electorate. Readmitting the South, leaders of both parties believed, would reunite the Democrats and weaken the Republicans. In addition, the Republican Party had taken advantage of the South's absence from Congress to pass a program of nationalistic economic legislation—railroad subsidies,

protective tariffs, banking and currency reforms, and other measures to benefit Northern business leaders and industrialists. Should the Democratic Party regain power with heavy Southern support, these programs would be in jeopardy. Complicating these practical questions were emotional concerns. Many Northerners believed the South should be punished in some way for the suffering and sacrifice its rebellion had caused. Many Northerners believed, too, that the South should be transformed, made over in the North's urbanized image—its supposedly backward, feudal, undemocratic society civilized and modernized.

Even among the Republicans in Congress, there was considerable disagreement about the proper approach to Reconstruction—disagreement that reflected the same factional divisions that had created disputes over emancipation during the war. Conservatives insisted that the South accept the abolition of slavery, but proposed few other conditions for the readmission of the seceded states. The Radicals, led by Representative Thaddeus Stevens of Pennsylvania and Senator Charles Sumner of Massachusetts, urged that the civil and military leaders of the Confederacy be punished, that large numbers of Southern whites be disenfranchised, that the legal rights of former slaves be protected, and that the property of wealthy white Southerners who had aided the Confederacy be confiscated and distributed among the freedmen. Some Radicals favored granting suffrage to the former slaves. Others hesitated, since few Northern states permitted blacks to vote. Between the Radicals and the Conservatives stood a faction of uncommitted Republicans, the Moderates, who rejected the punitive goals of the Radicals but supported extracting at least some concessions from the South on African American rights.

CONSERVATIVE AND RADICAL REPUBLICANS

PLANS FOR RECONSTRUCTION

President Lincoln's sympathies lay with the Moderates and Conservatives of his party. He believed that a lenient Reconstruction policy would encourage Southern unionists and other former Whigs to join the Republican Party and would thus prevent the readmission of the South from strengthening the Democrats. More immediately, the Southern unionists could become the nucleus of new, loyal state governments in the South. Lincoln was not uninterested in the fate of the freedmen, but he was willing to defer questions about their future for the sake of rapid reunification.

Lincoln's Reconstruction plan, which he announced in December 1863, offered a general amnesty to white Southerners—other than high officials of the Confederacy—who would pledge loyalty to the government and accept the elimination of slavery. Whenever 10 percent of the number of voters in 1860 took the oath in any state, those loyal voters could set up a state government. Lincoln also hoped to extend suffrage to African Americans who were educated, owned property, and had served in the Union army. Three Southern states—Louisiana, Arkansas, and Tennessee, all under Union occupation—reestablished loyal governments under the Lincoln formula in 1864.

LINCOLN'S 10% PLAN

The Radical Republicans were astonished at the mildness of Lincoln's program. They persuaded Congress to deny seats to representatives from the three "reconstructed" states and refused to count the electoral vote of those states in the election of 1864. But for the moment, the Radicals were uncertain about what form their own Reconstruction plan should take. Their

WADE-DAVIS BILL first effort to resolve that question was the Wade-Davis Bill, passed by Congress in July 1864. It authorized the president to appoint a provisional governor for each conquered state. When a majority (not Lincoln's 10 percent) of the white males of the state pledged their allegiance to the Union, the governor could summon a state constitutional convention, whose delegates were to be elected by those who would swear (through the so-called Ironclad Oath) that they had never borne arms against the United States—another departure from Lincoln's plan. The new state constitutions would have to abolish slavery, disenfranchise Confederate civil and military leaders, and repudiate debts accumulated by the state governments during the war. After a state had met these conditions, Congress would readmit it to the Union. Like the president's proposal, the Wade-Davis Bill left up to the states the question of political rights for blacks. Congress passed the bill a few days before it adjourned in 1864, and Lincoln disposed of it with a pocket veto. His action enraged the Radical leaders, and the pragmatic Lincoln became convinced he would have to accept at least some of the Radical demands. He began to move toward a new approach to Reconstruction.

THE DEATH OF LINCOLN

What plan Lincoln might have produced no one can say. On the night of April 14, 1865, the president and his wife attended a play at Ford's Theater in Washington. As they sat in the presidential box, John Wilkes Booth, a member of a distinguished family of actors and a zealous advocate of the Southern cause, entered the box from the rear and shot Lincoln in the head. The president was carried unconscious to a house across the street, where early the next morning, surrounded by family, friends, and political associates (among them a tearful Charles Sumner), he died.

The circumstances of Lincoln's death earned him immediate martyrdom. It also produced something close to hysteria throughout the North. There were accusations that Booth had acted as part of a great conspiracy—accusations that contained some truth. Booth did indeed have associates, one of whom stabbed and wounded Secretary of State Seward the night of the assassination, another of whom abandoned at the last moment a plan to murder Vice President Johnson. Booth himself escaped on horseback into the Virginia countryside, where, on April 26, he was cornered by Union troops and shot to death in a blazing barn. A military tribunal convicted eight other people of participating in the conspiracy (at least two of them on the basis of virtually no evidence). Four were hanged.

To many Northerners, however, the murder of the president seemed evidence of an even greater conspiracy—one masterminded and directed by the unrepentant leaders of the defeated

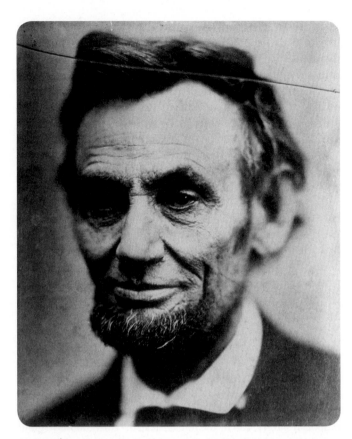

ABRAHAM LINCOLN This haunting photograph of Abraham Lincoln, showing clearly the weariness and aging that four years as a war president had created, was taken in Washington only four days before his assassination in 1865. (Library of Congress)

South. Militant Republicans exploited such suspicions relentlessly for months, ensuring that Lincoln's death would help doom his plans for a relatively easy peace.

JOHNSON AND "RESTORATION"

Leadership of the Moderates and Conservatives fell to Lincoln's successor, Andrew Johnson, who was not well suited, by either circumstance or personality, for the task. A Democrat until he had joined the Union ticket with Lincoln in 1864, he became a

ANDREW JOHNSON'S PERSONALITY Republican president at a moment when partisan passions were growing. Johnson himself was an intemperate and tactless man, filled with resentments and insecurities. He was also openly hostile to the freed slaves and unwilling to support any plans that guaranteed them civil equality or enfranchisement. He once declared, "White men alone must manage the South."

Johnson revealed his plan for Reconstruction—or "Restoration," as he preferred to call it—soon after he took office, and he implemented it during the summer of 1865, when Congress was in recess. Like Lincoln, he offered amnesty to those Southerners who would take an oath of allegiance. (High-ranking Confederate officials and any white Southerner with land worth $20,000 or more would have to apply to the president for individual pardons. Johnson, a self-made man, apparently liked the thought of the great planter aristocrats humbling themselves before him.) In most other respects, however, his plan resembled that of the Wade-Davis Bill. For each state, the president appointed a provisional governor, who was to invite qualified voters to elect delegates to a constitutional convention. Johnson did not specify how many qualified voters were necessary, but he implied that he would require a majority (as had the Wade-Davis Bill). In order to win readmission to Congress, a state had to revoke its ordinance of secession, abolish slavery, ratify the Thirteenth Amendment, and repudiate the Confederate and state war debts. The final procedure before restoration was for a state to elect a state government and send representatives to Congress.

By the end of 1865, all the seceded states had formed new governments—some under Lincoln's plan, some under Johnson's—and were prepared to rejoin the Union as soon as Congress recognized them. But Radical Republicans vowed not to recognize the Johnson governments, just as they had previously

NORTHERN ATTITUDES HARDEN

refused to recognize the Lincoln regimes; for by now, Northern opinion had hardened and become more hostile toward the South than it had been a year earlier when Congress passed the Wade-Davis Bill. Many Northerners were disturbed by the apparent reluctance of some delegates to the Southern conventions to abolish slavery, and by the refusal of all the conventions to grant suffrage to any blacks. They were astounded that states claiming to be "loyal" should elect prominent leaders of the recent Confederacy as state officials and representatives to Congress. Particularly hard to accept was Georgia's choice of Alexander H. Stephens, former Confederate vice president, as a United States senator.

RADICAL RECONSTRUCTION

Reconstruction under Johnson's plan—often known as "presidential Reconstruction"—continued only until Congress reconvened in December 1865. At that point, Congress refused to seat the representatives of the "restored" states and created a new Joint Committee on Reconstruction to frame a Reconstruction policy of its own. The period of "congressional," or "Radical," Reconstruction had begun.

THE BLACK CODES

Meanwhile, events in the South were driving Northern opinion in more radical directions. Throughout the South in 1865 and early 1866, state legislatures were enacting sets of laws known as the Black Codes, designed to give whites substantial control over former slaves. The codes authorized local officials to apprehend unemployed African Americans, fine them for vagrancy, and hire them out to private employers to satisfy the fine. Some of the codes forbade blacks to own or lease farms or to take any jobs other than as plantation workers or domestic servants.

Congress first responded to the Black Codes by passing an act extending the life of the Freedmen's Bureau and widening its powers so that it could nullify work agreements forced on

JOHNSON'S VETOES

freedmen under the Black Codes. Then, in April 1866, Congress passed the first Civil Rights Act, which declared African Americans to be citizens of the United States and gave the federal government power to intervene in state affairs to protect the rights of citizens. Johnson vetoed both bills, but Congress overrode him on each of them.

THE FOURTEENTH AMENDMENT

In April 1866, the Joint Committee on Reconstruction proposed a new amendment to the Constitution, which Congress approved in early summer and sent to the states for ratification. Eventually, it became one of the most important of all the provisions in the Constitution.

The Fourteenth Amendment offered the first constitutional definition of American citizenship. Everyone born in the United States, and everyone naturalized, was automatically a citizen and entitled to all the "privileges and immunities" guaranteed by the Constitution, including equal protection of the laws by both the state and national governments. There could

CITIZENSHIP FOR BLACKS

be no other requirements (for example, being white) for citizenship. The amendment also imposed penalties—reduction of representation in Congress and in the electoral college—on states that denied suffrage to any adult male inhabitants. (The wording reflected the prevailing view in Congress and elsewhere that the franchise was properly restricted to men.) Finally, it prohibited former members of Congress or other former federal officials who had aided the Confederacy from holding any state or federal office unless two-thirds of Congress voted to pardon them.

Congressional Radicals offered to readmit to the Union any state whose legislature ratified the Fourteenth Amendment. Only Tennessee did so. All the other former Confederate states, along with Delaware and Kentucky, refused, leaving the amendment temporarily without the necessary approval of three-fourths of the states.

But by now, the Radicals were growing more confident and determined. Bloody race riots in New Orleans and other Southern cities—riots in which African Americans were the principal victims—were among the events that strengthened their hand. In the 1866 congressional elections, Johnson actively campaigned for Conservative candidates, but he did his own cause more harm than good with his intemperate speeches. The voters returned an overwhelming majority of Republicans, most of them Radicals, to Congress. In the Senate, there were now 42 Republicans to 11 Democrats; in the House, 143 Republicans to 49 Democrats. (The South remained largely unrepresented in both chambers.) Congressional Republicans were now strong enough to enact a plan of their own even over the president's objections.

AMERICAN CITIZENS (TO THE POLLS) The artist T. W. Wood painted this watercolor of voters standing in line at the polls during the 1866 elections. A prosperous Yankee, a working-class Irishman, and a Dutch coach driver stand next to the newest addition to the American electorate: an African American, whose expression conveys his excitement at being able to join the community of voters. Wood meant this painting to celebrate the democratic character of American life after the Civil War. (T. W. Wood Art Gallery, Vermont College, Montpelier)

THE CONGRESSIONAL PLAN

The Radicals passed three Reconstruction bills early in 1867 and

THREE RECONSTRUCTION BILLS

overrode Johnson's vetoes of all of them. These bills finally established, nearly two years after the end of the war, a coherent plan for Reconstruction.

Under the congressional plan, Tennessee, which had ratified the Fourteenth Amendment, was promptly readmitted. But Congress rejected the Lincoln-Johnson governments of the other ten Confederate states and, instead, combined those states into five military districts. A military commander governed each district and had orders to register qualified voters (defined as all adult black males and those white males who had not participated in the rebellion). Once registered, voters would elect conventions to prepare new state constitutions, which had to include provisions for black suffrage. Once voters ratified the new constitutions, they could elect state governments. Congress had to approve a state's constitution, and the state legislature had to ratify the Fourteenth Amendment. Once that happened, and once enough states ratified the amendment to make it part of the Constitution, then the former Confederate states could be restored to the Union.

By 1868, seven of the ten former Confederate states (Arkansas, North Carolina, South Carolina, Louisiana, Alabama, Georgia, and Florida) had fulfilled these conditions (including ratification of the Fourteenth Amendment, which now became part of the Constitution) and were readmitted to

the Union. Conservative whites held up the return of Virginia and Texas until 1869 and Mississippi until 1870. By then, Congress had added one more requirement for readmission—

FIFTEENTH AMENDMENT

ratification of another constitutional amendment, the Fifteenth, which forbade the states and the federal government to

deny suffrage to any citizen on account of "race, color, or previous condition of servitude."

To stop the president from interfering with their plans, the congressional Radicals passed two remarkable laws of dubious constitutionality in 1867. One, the Tenure of Office Act, forbade the president to remove civil officials, including members of his own cabinet, without the consent of the Senate. The principal purpose of the law was to protect the job of Secretary of War Edwin M. Stanton, who was cooperating with the Radicals. The other law, the Command of the Army Act, prohibited the president from issuing military orders except through the commanding general of the army (General Grant), who could not be relieved or assigned elsewhere without the consent of the Senate.

The congressional Radicals also took action to stop the Supreme Court from interfering with their plans. In 1866, the Court had declared in the case of *Ex parte Milligan* that military tribunals were unconstitutional in places where civil courts were functioning, a decision that seemed to threaten the system of military government the Radicals were planning for the South. Radicals in Congress immediately proposed several bills that would require two-thirds of the justices to support any decision overruling a law of Congress, would deny the Court jurisdiction

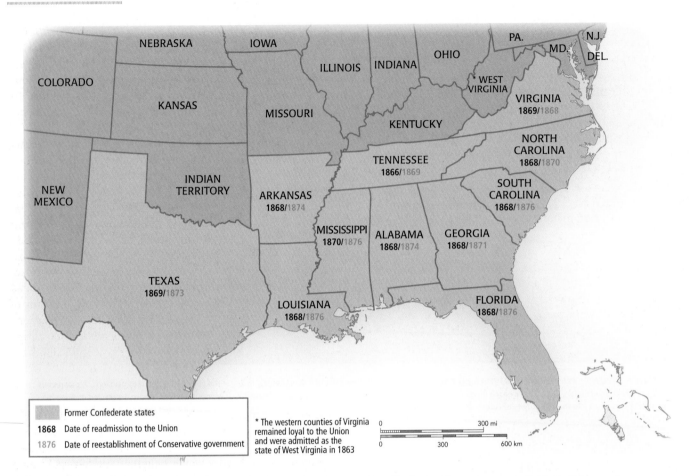

NEBRASKA

IOWA

PA.

N.J.

MD.

DEL.

COLORADO

ILLINOIS

INDIANA

OHIO

WEST
VIRGINIA

KANSAS

MISSOURI

VIRGINIA
1869/1868

KENTUCKY

NORTH
CAROLINA
1868/1870

NEW
MEXICO

INDIAN
TERRITORY

ARKANSAS
1868/1874

TENNESSEE
1866/1869

SOUTH
CAROLINA
1868/1876

MISSISSIPPI
1870/1876

ALABAMA
1868/1874

GEORGIA
1868/1871

TEXAS
1869/1873

LOUISIANA
1868/1876

FLORIDA
1868/1876

Former Confederate states

1868 Date of readmission to the Union

1876 Date of reestablishment of Conservative government

* The western counties of Virginia
remained loyal to the Union
and were admitted as the
state of West Virginia in 1863

0   300 mi

0   300   600 km

RECONSTRUCTION, 1866–1877 This map shows the former Confederate states and provides the date when each was readmitted to the Union as well as a subsequent date when each state managed to return political power to traditional white, conservative elites—a process white Southerners liked to call "redemption."

• *What had to happen for a state to be readmitted to the Union? What had to happen before a state could experience "redemption"?*

in Reconstruction cases, would reduce its membership to three, and would even abolish it. The justices apparently took notice. Over the next two years, the Court refused to accept jurisdiction in any cases involving Reconstruction (and the congressional bills concerning the Court never passed).

THE IMPEACHMENT OF THE PRESIDENT

President Johnson had long since ceased to be a serious obstacle to the passage of Radical legislation, but he was still the official charged with administering the Reconstruction programs. As such, the Radicals believed, he remained a serious impediment to their plans. Early in 1867, they began looking for a way to impeach him and remove him from office. Republicans found grounds for impeachment, they believed, when Johnson dismissed Secretary of War Stanton despite Congress's refusal to agree, thus deliber-

TENURE OF
OFFICE ACT

ately violating the Tenure of Office Act in hopes of testing the law before the courts. Elated Radicals in the House quickly impeached the president and sent the case to the Senate for trial.

The trial before the Senate lasted throughout April and May 1868. The Radicals put heavy pressure on all the Republican senators, but the Moderates (who were losing faith in the

Radical program) vacillated. On the first three charges to come

JOHNSON
ACQUITTED

to a vote, seven Republicans joined the Democrats and independents to support acquittal. The vote was 35 to 19, one short of

the constitutionally required two-thirds majority. After that, the Radicals dropped the impeachment effort.

THE SOUTH IN RECONSTRUCTION

When white Southerners spoke bitterly in later years of the effects of Reconstruction, they referred most frequently to the governments Congress helped impose on them—governments they claimed were both incompetent and corrupt, that saddled the region with enormous debts, and that trampled on the rights of citizens. When black Southerners and their defenders condemned Reconstruction, in contrast, they spoke of the failure of the national and state governments to go far enough to guarantee freedmen even the most elemental rights of citizenship—a failure that resulted in a harsh new system of economic subordination. (See "Debating the Past," pp. 428–429.)

THE RECONSTRUCTION GOVERNMENTS

In the ten states of the South that were reorganized under the congressional plan, approximately one-fourth of the white males were at first excluded from voting or holding office. That produced black majorities among voters in South Carolina, Mississippi, and Louisiana (states where blacks were also a majority of the population), and in Alabama and Florida (where they were not). But the government soon lifted most suffrage restrictions so that nearly all white males could vote. After that, Republicans maintained control only with the support of many Southern whites.

Critics called these Southern white Republicans "scalawags." Many were **"SCALAWAGS"** former Whigs who had never felt comfortable in the Democratic Party—some of them wealthy (or once wealthy) planters or businessmen interested in the economic development of the region. Others were farmers who lived in remote areas where there had been little or no slavery and who hoped the Republican program of internal improvements would help end their economic isolation. Despite their diverse social positions, scalawags shared a belief that the Republican Party would serve their economic interests better than the Democrats.

White men from the North also served as Republican leaders in the South. Critics of Reconstruction referred to them pejoratively as "carpetbaggers," which con-
"CARPETBAGGERS," veyed an image of penniless adventurers who arrived with all their possessions in a carpetbag (a common kind of cheap suitcase covered with carpeting material). In fact, most of the so-called carpetbaggers were well-educated people of middle-class origin, many of them doctors, lawyers, and teachers. Most were veterans of the Union army who looked on the South as a new frontier, more promising than the West. They had settled there at war's end as hopeful planters or as business and professional people.

> **❝ WE CLAIM EXACTLY THE SAME RIGHTS, PRIVILEGES AND IMMUNITIES AS ARE ENJOYED BY WHITE MEN—WE ASK NOTHING MORE AND WILL BE CONTENT WITH NOTHING ELSE. ❞**

But the most numerous Republicans in the South were the **FREEDMEN** black freedmen, most of whom had no previous experience in politics and who tried, therefore, to build institutions through which they could learn to exercise their power. In several states, African American voters held their own conventions to chart their future course. One such "colored convention," as Southern whites called them, assembled in Alabama in 1867 and announced: "We claim exactly the same rights, privileges and immunities as are enjoyed by white men—we ask nothing more and will be content with nothing else." The black churches that freedmen created after emancipation also helped give unity and political self-confidence to the former slaves. African Americans played a significant role in the politics of the Reconstruction South. They served as delegates to the constitutional conventions. They held public offices of practically every kind. Between 1869 and 1901, twenty African Americans served in the U.S. House of Representatives, two in the Senate (Hiram Revels of Mississippi and Blanche K. Bruce of Mississippi). African Americans served, too, in state legislatures and in various other state offices. Southern whites complained loudly (both at the time and for generations to come) about "Negro rule" during Reconstruction, but no such thing ever actually existed in any of the states. No black man was ever elected governor of a Southern state (although Lieutenant Governor P. B. S. Pinchback briefly performed gubernatorial duties in Louisiana). African Americans never controlled any of the state legislatures, although they held a majority in the lower house in South Carolina for a short time. In the South as a whole, the percentage of black officeholders was always far lower than the percentage of blacks in the population.

The record of the Reconstruction governments is mixed. Critics at the time and since denounced them for corruption

THE BURDENED SOUTH This Reconstruction-era cartoon expresses the South's sense of its oppression at the hands of Northern Republicans. President Grant (whose hat bears Abraham Lincoln's initials) rides in comfort in a giant carpetbag, guarded by bayonet-wielding soldiers, as the South staggers under the burden in chains. More evidence of destruction and military occupation is visible in the background. (Culver Pictures, Inc.)

THE LOUISIANA CONSTITUTIONAL CONVENTION, 1868 This lithograph commemorates the brief moment during which black voters actually dominated the politics of Louisiana. When the state held a constitutional convention in 1868, a majority of the delegates were African Americans (many of them freeborn blacks who had moved to Louisiana from the North). The constitution they passed guaranteed political and civil rights to black citizens. When white conservatives regained control of the state several years later, they passed a new constitution of their own, repealing most of those guarantees. (Library of Congress)

The end of Reconstruction did not end corruption in Southern state governments. In many states, in fact, corruption increased.

And the state expenditures of the Reconstruction years were huge only in comparison with the meager budgets of the antebellum era. They represented an effort to provide the South with desperately needed services that antebellum governments had never offered: public education, public works programs, poor relief, and other costly new commitments. There were, to be sure, graft and extravagance in Reconstruction governments; there were also positive and permanent accomplishments.

EDUCATION

Perhaps the most important of those accomplishments was a dramatic improvement in the education of African Americans and white Southerners with scant learning. In the first years of Reconstruction, much of the impetus for educational reform in the South came from outside groups—from the Freedmen's Bureau, from Northern private philanthropic organizations, from many Northern women, black and white, who traveled to the South to teach in freedmen's schools—and from black Southerners themselves. Over the opposition of many Southern whites, who feared that education would give African Americans "false notions of equality," these reformers established a large network of schools for former slaves—4,000 schools by 1870, staffed by 9,000 teachers (half of them black), teaching 200,000 students (about 12 percent of the total school-age population of the freedmen). In the 1870s, Reconstruction governments also began to build a comprehensive public school system in the South. By 1876, more than half of all white children and about 40 percent of all black children were attending schools in the South. Several black "academies," offering more advanced education, also began operating. Gradually, these academies grew into an important network of black colleges and universities, which included such distinguished schools as Fisk and Atlanta Universities and Morehouse College.

Already, however, Southern education was becoming divided into two separate systems, one black and one white. Early efforts to integrate the schools of the region were a dismal failure. The Freedmen's Bureau schools, for example, were open to students of all races, but almost no whites attended them. New Orleans set up an integrated school system under the Reconstruction government; again, whites almost universally stayed away. The one federal effort to mandate school integration—the Civil Rights Act of 1875—had its provisions for educational desegregation removed before it was passed. As soon as the Republican governments of Reconstruction were replaced, the new Southern Democratic regimes quickly abandoned all efforts to promote integration.

SEGREGATED
SCHOOLS

and financial extravagance, and there is some truth to both charges. Officeholders in many states enriched themselves through graft and other illicit activities. State budgets expanded to hitherto unknown totals, and state debts soared to previously undreamed-of heights. In South Carolina, for example, the public debt increased from $7 million to $29 million in eight years.

But the corruption in the South, real as it was, was hardly unique to the Reconstruction governments. Corruption was at least as rampant in the Northern states. And in both North and South, it was a result of the same thing: a rapid economic expansion of government services (and revenues) that put new strains on (and new temptations before) elected officials everywhere.

LANDOWNERSHIP AND TENANCY

The most ambitious goal of the Freedmen's Bureau, and of some Republican Radicals in Congress, was to make Reconstruction the vehicle for a fundamental reform of landownership in the South. The effort failed. In the last years of the war and the first years of Reconstruction, the Freedmen's Bureau did oversee the redistribution of substantial amounts of land to freedmen in a few areas—notably the Sea Islands of South Carolina and

FAILURE OF LAND REDISTRIBUTION

Georgia, and areas of Mississippi that had once belonged to the family of Jefferson Davis. By June 1865, the bureau had settled nearly 10,000 black families on their own land—most of it drawn from abandoned plantations—arousing dreams among former slaves throughout the South of "forty acres and a mule." By the end of that year, however, the experiment was already collapsing. Southern plantation owners were returning and demanding the restoration of their property, and President Johnson was supporting their demands. Despite the resistance of the Freedmen's Bureau, the government eventually returned most of the confiscated land to the original white owners.

Very few Northern Republicans believed that the federal government had the right to confiscate property. Even so, distribution of landownership in the South changed considerably in the postwar years. Among whites, there was a significant decline in landownership, from 80 percent before the war to 67 percent by the end of Reconstruction. Some whites lost their land because of unpaid debt or increased taxes; some left the marginal lands they had owned to move to more fertile areas, where they rented.

During the same period, the number of African Americans who owned land rose from virtually none to more than 20 percent. Many black landowners acquired their property through hard work or luck or both. But some relied unwisely on assistance from white-dominated financial or philanthropic institutions. One of them was the Freedman's Bank, established in 1865 by antislavery whites in an effort to promote landownership among African Americans. They persuaded thousands of freedmen to deposit their modest savings in the bank, but then invested heavily in unsuccessful enterprises. It was ill prepared, therefore, for the national depression of the 1870s and it failed in 1874.

Still, most blacks, and a growing minority of whites, did not own their own land during Reconstruction; and some who

THE SOUTHERN PLANTATION BEFORE AND AFTER EMANCIPATION This map shows the distribution of lands and dwellings on the Barrow Plantation in Oglethorpe County, Georgia, before and after the emancipation of slaves at the close of the Civil War. The map on the left shows the plantation in 1861, as the war began. Like the Hopeton Plantation shown on p. 304, the Barrow plantation was highly centralized before the war, with all slaves living together in a complex of dwellings near the master's house. Twenty years later, as the map on the right shows, the same landscape was very differently divided. Housing was now widely dispersed, as former slaves became tenants or sharecroppers and began working their own small pieces of land and living independently. Churches had sprung up away from the landowner's house as well.

• *Why did former slaves move so quickly to relocate their homes and churches away from their former masters?*

acquired land in the 1860s had lost it by the 1890s. These people worked for others in one form or another. Many African

SHARECROPPING

American agricultural laborers—perhaps 25 percent of the total—simply worked for wages. Most, however, became tenants of white landowners—working their own plots of land and paying their landlords either a fixed rent or a share of their crop (see p. 434).

The new system represented a repudiation by former slaves of the gang-labor system of the antebellum plantation, in which slaves had lived and worked together under the direction of a master. As tenants and sharecroppers, African Americans enjoyed at least a physical independence from their landlords and had the sense of working their own land, even if in most cases they could never hope to buy it. But tenantry also benefited landlords in some ways, relieving them of any responsibility for the physical well-being of their workers.

THE CROP-LIEN SYSTEM

In some respects, the postwar years were a period of remarkable economic progress for African Americans. If the material benefits they had received under slavery are calculated as income, then prewar blacks had earned about a 22 percent share of the profits of the plantation system. By the end of Reconstruction, they were earning 56 percent. Measured another way, the per capita income of Southern blacks rose 46 percent between 1857 and 1879, while the per capita income of Southern whites declined 35 percent. This represented one of the most significant redistributions of income in American history.

But these figures are somewhat misleading. While the black share of profits was increasing, the total profits of Southern agriculture were declining—a result of the dislocations of the war and a reduction in the world market for cotton. In addition, while African Americans were earning a greater return on each hour of labor than they had under slavery, they were working fewer hours. Women and children were less likely to labor in the fields than in the past. Adult men tended to work shorter days. In all, the black labor force worked about one-third fewer hours during Reconstruction than slaves had been compelled to work under slavery—a reduction that brought the working schedule of blacks roughly into line with that of white farm laborers. Nor did the income redistribution of the postwar years lift many African Americans out of poverty. Black per capita income rose from about one-quarter of white per capita income to about one-half in the first few years after the war. And after this initial increase, it rose hardly at all.

For blacks and poor whites alike, whatever gains there might have been as a result of land and income redistribution were often overshadowed by the ravages of the crop-lien system. Few of the traditional institutions of credit in the South—the "factors" and banks—returned after the war. In their stead emerged a

NEW SYSTEM OF CREDIT

new system of credit, centered in large part on local country stores, some of them owned by planters, others by independent merchants. Blacks and whites, landowners and tenants—all depended on these stores for such necessities as food, clothing, seed, and farm implements. And since farmers did not have the same steady cash flow as other workers, customers usually had to rely on credit from these merchants in order to purchase what they needed. Most local stores had no competition (and went to great lengths to ensure that things stayed that way). As a result, they were able to set interest rates as high as 50 or 60 percent. Farmers had to give the merchants a lien (or claim) on their crops as collateral for the loans (thus the term "crop-lien

A VISIT FROM THE OLD MISTRESS Winslow Homer's 1876 painting of an imagined visit by a Southern white woman to a group of her former slaves was an effort to convey something of the tension in relations between the races in the South during Reconstruction. The women, once intimately involved in one another's lives, look at each other guardedly, carefully maintaining the space between them. Some white Southerners attacked the painting for portraying white and black women on a relatively equal footing. Some black Southerners criticized it for depicting poor rural African Americans instead of the more prosperous professional blacks who were emerging in Southern cities. "There were plenty of well-dressed negroes if he would but look for them," one wrote. (National Museum of American Art, Smithsonian Institution. Gift of William T. Evans/Art Resource, NY)

system"). Farmers who suffered a few bad years in a row, as often happened, could become trapped in a cycle of debt from which they could never escape.

This burdensome credit system had a number of effects on the region, almost all of them unhealthy. One effect was that some former slaves who had acquired land during the early years of Reconstruction gradually lost it as they fell into debt. So, to a lesser extent, did white small landowners. Another effect was that Southern farmers became almost wholly dependent on cash crops—and most of all on cotton—because only such marketable commodities seemed to offer any possibility of escape from debt. Thus Southern agriculture, never sufficiently diversified even in the best of times, became more one-dimensional than ever. The relentless planting of cotton, moreover, was contributing to an exhaustion of the soil. The crop-lien system, in other words, was not only helping to impoverish small farmers; it was also contributing to a general decline in the Southern agricultural economy.

The African American Family in Freedom

One of the most striking features of the black response to Reconstruction was the effort to build or rebuild family structures and to protect them from the interference they had experienced under slavery. A major reason for the rapid departure of so many emancipated slaves from plantations was the desire to find lost relatives and reunite families. Thousands of African Americans wandered through the South—often over vast distances—looking for husbands, wives, children, or other relatives from whom they had been separated. In the few black

WASH DAY ON THE PLANTATION One of the most common occupations of women recently emancipated from slavery was taking in laundry from white families who no longer had slaves as household servants. This photograph of a group of African American women illustrates how arduous a task laundry was. (Library of Congress)

newspapers that circulated in the South, there were many advertisements by people searching for information about their relatives. Former slaves rushed to have marriages, previously without legal standing, sanctified by church and law. Black families resisted living in the former slave quarters and moved instead to small cabins scattered widely across the countryside, where they could enjoy at least some privacy. Within the black family, the definition of male and female roles quickly came to resemble that within white families. Many women and children ceased working in the fields. Such work, they believed, was a badge of slavery. Instead, many women restricted themselves largely to domestic tasks—cooking, cleaning, gardening, sewing, raising children, attending to the needs of their husbands. Some black husbands refused to allow their wives to work as servants in white homes. "When I married my wife I married her to wait on me," one freedman told a former master who was attempting to hire his wife as a servant. "She got all she can do right here for me and the children."

Still, middle-class notions of domesticity were often difficult to sustain in the impoverished circumstances of most former slaves. Economic necessity required many black women to engage in income-producing activities, including activities that they and their husbands resisted: working as domestic servants, taking in laundry, or helping in the field. By the end of Reconstruction, half of all black women over the age of sixteen were working for wages. And unlike white working women, most black female income-earners were married.

CHANGING GENDER ROLES

> ECONOMIC NECESSITY REQUIRED MANY BLACK WOMEN TO ENGAGE IN INCOME-PRODUCING ACTIVITIES: WORKING AS DOMESTIC SERVANTS, TAKING IN LAUNDRY, OR HELPING IN THE FIELD.

THE GRANT ADMINISTRATION

Exhausted by the political turmoil of the Johnson administration, American voters in 1868 yearned for a strong, stable figure to guide them through the troubled years of Reconstruction. They turned trustingly to General Ulysses S. Grant, the hero of the war and, by 1868, a revered national idol.

THE SOLDIER PRESIDENT

Grant could have had the nomination of either party in 1868. But believing that Republican Reconstruction policies were more popular in the North, he accepted the Republican nomination. The Democrats nominated former governor Horatio Seymour of New York. The campaign was a bitter one, and Grant's triumph was surprisingly narrow. Without the 500,000 new black Republican voters in the South, he would have had a minority of the popular vote.

U. S. GRANT

Grant entered the White House with no political experience, and his performance was clumsy and ineffectual from the start. Except for Hamilton Fish, whom Grant appointed secretary of state and who served for eight years with great distinction, most members of the cabinet were ill equipped for their tasks. Grant relied chiefly, and increasingly, on established party leaders—the group most ardently devoted to patronage. His administration used the spoils system even more blatantly than most of its predecessors, embittering reform-minded members of his party. Grant also alienated the many Northerners who were growing disillusioned with Radical Reconstruction policies, which the president continued to support. Some Republicans suspected, correctly, that there was also corruption in the Grant administration itself.

By the end of Grant's first term, therefore, members of a substantial faction of the party—who referred to themselves as Liberal Republicans—had come to oppose what they called "Grantism." In 1872, hoping to prevent Grant's reelection, they bolted the party and nominated their own presidential candidate: Horace Greeley, veteran editor and publisher of the *New York Tribune*. The Democrats, somewhat reluctantly, named Greeley their candidate as well, hoping that the alliance with the Liberals would enable them to defeat Grant. But the effort was in vain. Grant won a substantial victory, polling 286 electoral votes to Greeley's 66, and nearly 56 percent of the popular total.

LIBERAL REPUBLICANS

THE GRANT SCANDALS

During the 1872 campaign, the first of a series of political scandals came to light that would plague Grant and the Republicans for years. It involved the Crédit Mobilier construction company, which had helped build the Union Pacific Railroad. The heads of Crédit Mobilier had used their positions as Union Pacific stockholders to steer large fraudulent contracts to their construction company, thus bilking the Union Pacific (and the federal government, which provided large subsidies to the railroad) of millions. To prevent investigations, the directors had given Crédit Mobilier stock to key members of Congress. But in 1872, Congress launched an investigation, which revealed that some highly placed Republicans—including Schuyler Colfax, now Grant's vice president—had accepted stock.

CRÉDIT MOBILIER

One dreary episode followed another in Grant's second term. Benjamin H. Bristow, Grant's third Treasury secretary, discovered that some of his officials and a group of distillers operating as a "whiskey ring" were cheating the government out of taxes by filing false reports. Then a House investigation revealed that William W. Belknap, secretary of war, had accepted bribes to retain an Indian-post trader in office (the so-called

GRANT THE TRAPEZE ARTISTS This cartoon by the eminent cartoonist Joseph Keppler shows President Ulysses S. Grant swinging on a trapeze holding on to the "whiskey ring" and the "navy ring" (references to two of the many scandals that plagued his presidency). Using a strap labeled "corruption," he holds aloft some of the most notorious figures in those scandals. The cartoon was published in 1880, when Grant was unsuccessfully attempting to win the Republican nomination to run for another term as president. (Library of Congress)

Indian ring). Other, lesser scandals added to the growing impression that "Grantism" had brought rampant corruption to government.

THE GREENBACK QUESTION

Compounding Grant's, and the nation's, problems was a financial crisis, known as the Panic of 1873. It began with the failure

PANIC OF 1873 of a leading investment banking firm, Jay Cooke and Company, which had invested too heavily in postwar railroad building. There had been panics before—in 1819, 1837, and 1857—but this was worse than any earlier economic crisis. The depression it produced lasted four years.

Debtors now pressured the government to redeem federal war bonds with greenbacks, paper currency of the sort printed

during the Civil War, which would increase the amount of money in circulation. But Grant and most Republicans wanted a "sound" currency—based solidly on gold reserves—which would favor the interests of banks and other creditors. There was approximately $356 million in paper currency issued during the Civil War that was still in circulation. In 1873, the Treasury issued more in response to the panic. But in 1875, Republican leaders in Congress, in an effort to crush the greenback movement for good, passed the Specie Resumption Act. It provided that after January 1, 1879, the greenback dollars, whose value constantly fluctuated, would be redeemed by the government and replaced with new certificates, firmly pegged to the price of gold. The law satisfied creditors, who had worried that debts would be repaid in paper currency of uncertain value. But "resumption" made things more difficult for debtors, because the gold-based money supply could not easily expand.

In 1875, the "greenbackers," as the inflationists were called, formed their own political organization: the National Greenback Party. It was active in the next three presidential elections, but it

NATIONAL GREENBACK PARTY failed to gain widespread support. It did, however, keep the money issue alive. The question of the proper composition of the currency was to remain one of the most controversial and enduring issues in late-nineteenth-century American politics.

REPUBLICAN DIPLOMACY

The Johnson and Grant administrations achieved their greatest successes in foreign affairs. The accomplishments were the work not of the presidents themselves, who displayed little aptitude for diplomacy, but of two outstanding secretaries of state: William H. Seward, who had served Lincoln and who remained in office until 1869; and Hamilton Fish, who served throughout the two terms of the Grant administration.

An ardent expansionist, Seward acted with as much daring as the demands of Reconstruction politics and the Republican

"SEWARD'S FOLLY" hatred of President Johnson would permit. Seward accepted a Russian offer to sell Alaska to the United States for $7.2 million, despite criticism from many Americans who considered Alaska a frozen wasteland and derided it as "Seward's Folly." In 1867, Seward also engineered the American annexation of the tiny Midway Islands, west of Hawaii.

Hamilton Fish's first major challenge was resolving the long-standing controversy with England over the American claims that the British government had violated neutrality laws during the Civil War by permitting English shipyards to build ships (among them the *Alabama*) for the Confederacy. American demands that England pay for the damage these vessels had

ALABAMA CLAIMS caused became known as the "*Alabama* claims." In 1871, after a number of failed efforts, Fish forged an agreement, the Treaty of Washington, which provided for international arbitration and in which Britain expressed regret for the "escape" of the *Alabama* from England.

THE ABANDONMENT OF RECONSTRUCTION

As the North grew increasingly preoccupied with its own political and economic problems, interest in Reconstruction began to wane. The Grant administration continued to protect Republican governments in the South, but less because of any interest in ensuring the position of freedmen than because of a desire to prevent the reemergence of a strong Democratic Party in the region. But even the presence of federal troops was not enough to prevent white Southerners from overturning the Reconstruction regimes. By the time Grant left office, Democrats had taken back (or, as white Southerners called it, "redeemed") the governments of seven of the eleven former Confederate states. For three other states—South Carolina, Louisiana, and Florida—the end of Reconstruction had to wait for the withdrawal of the last federal troops in 1876, a withdrawal that was the result of a long process of political bargaining and compromise at the national level. (One former Confederate state, Tennessee, had never been part of the Reconstruction process because it had ratified the Fourteenth Amendment and rejoined the Union in 1866.)

THE SOUTHERN STATES "REDEEMED"

In the states where whites constituted a majority—the states of the upper South—overthrowing Republican control was relatively simple. By 1872, all but a handful of Southern whites had regained suffrage. Now a clear majority of the electorate, they needed only to organize and vote for their candidates.

In other states, where African Americans were a majority or the black and white populations were almost equal, whites used intimidation and violence to undermine the Reconstruction regimes. Secret societies—the Ku Klux Klan, the Knights of the White Camellia, and others—used terrorism to frighten or physically bar blacks from voting or otherwise exercising citizenship. Paramilitary organizations—the Red Shirts and White Leagues—armed themselves to "police" elections and worked to force all white males to join the Democratic Party and to exclude all African Americans from meaningful political activity.

The Ku Klux Klan was the largest and most effective of these organizations. Formed in 1866 and led by former Confederate KU KLUX KLAN general Nathan Bedford Forrest, it gradually absorbed many of the smaller terrorist organizations in the South. Its leaders devised rituals, costumes, secret languages, and other airs of mystery to create a bond among its members and make the organization seem even more terrifying to those it was attempting to intimidate. The Klan's "midnight rides"—bands of men clad in white sheets and masks, their horses covered with white robes and with hooves muffled—created terror in black communities throughout the South.

Many white Southerners considered the Klan and the other secret societies and paramilitary groups proud, patriotic societies. Together such groups served, in effect, as a military force (even if a decentralized and poorly organized one) continuing the battle against Northern rule. They worked in particular to advance the interests of those with the most to gain from a restoration of white supremacy—above all the planter class and the Southern Democratic Party. Even stronger than the Klan in discouraging black political power, however, was the simple weapon of economic pressure. Some planters refused to rent land to Republican blacks; storekeepers refused to extend them credit; employers refused to give them work.

THE KU KLUX KLAN ACTS

The Republican Congress tried for a time to turn back this new wave of white repression. In 1870 and 1871, it passed two ENFORCEMENT ACTS Enforcement Acts, also known as the Ku Klux Klan Acts, which were in many ways the most radical measures of the era. The Enforcement Acts prohibited the states from discriminating against voters on the basis of race and gave the federal government power to supersede the state courts and prosecute violations of the law. It was the first time the federal government had ever claimed the power to prosecute crimes by individuals under federal law. Federal district attorneys were now empowered to take action against conspiracies to deny African Americans such rights as voting, holding office, and serving on juries. The new laws also authorized the president to use the military to protect civil rights and to suspend the right of habeas corpus when violations of the rights seemed particularly egregious. In October 1871, President Grant used this provision of the law when he declared a "state of lawlessness" in nine counties in South Carolina and sent in federal troops to occupy the area. Hundreds of suspected Klan members were arrested; some were held for long periods without trial; some were eventually convicted under the law and sent to jail.

The Enforcement Acts were seldom used as severely as they were in South Carolina, but they were effec- DECLINE OF THE KLAN tive in the effort by blacks and Northern whites to weaken the Klan. By 1872, Klan violence against blacks was in decline throughout the region.

WANING NORTHERN COMMITMENT

The Ku Klux Klan Acts marked the peak of Republican commitment to enforce the new rights Reconstruction was extending to black citizens. But that commitment did not last for very long. Southern blacks were gradually losing the support of many of their former backers in the North. As early as 1870, after the adoption of the Fifteenth Amendment, some northern reformers convinced themselves that their long campaign on behalf of black people was now over—that with the vote, African Americans ought to be able to take care of themselves. Over the next several years, former Radical leaders such as Charles Sumner and Horace Greeley now began calling themselves Liberals, cooperating with Democrats and, at times, outdoing even the Democrats in denouncing what they viewed as black and carpetbag misgovernment. Within the South itself, many white Republicans joined the Liberals and eventually moved into the Democratic Party.

The Panic of 1873 further undermined support for Reconstruction. The economic crisis spurred Northern industrialists and their allies to find an explanation for the poverty and instability around them. They found it in a new idea known as "Social Darwinism" (see pp. 481–485), a harsh theory that argued that individuals who failed did so because of their own weakness and "unfitness." Those influenced by Social

IMPACT OF SOCIAL DARWINISM

Darwinism came to view the large number of unemployed vagrants in the North—and poor African Americans in the South—as irredeemable misfits. Social Darwinism also encouraged a broad critique of government intervention in social and economic life, which further weakened commitment to the Reconstruction program. Support for land redistribution, never great, and willingness to spend money from the depleted federal treasury to aid the freedmen, waned quickly after 1873. State and local governments also found themselves short of funds, and rushed to cut back on social services—which in the South meant the end of almost all services to the former slaves.

In the congressional elections of 1874, the Democrats won control of the House of Representatives for the first time since 1861. Grant took note of the changing temper of the North and made use of military force to prop up the Republican regimes that were still standing in the South. By the end of 1876, only three southern states were left in the hands of the Republicans— South Carolina, Louisiana, and Florida. In state elections that year, Democrats (after using terrorist tactics) claimed victory in all three. But the Republicans challenged the results and claimed victory as well, and they were able to remain in office because of the presence of federal troops. Without federal troops, it was now clear, the last of the Republican regimes would quickly fall.

THE COMPROMISE OF 1877

Grant had hoped to run for another term in 1876, but most Republican leaders—shaken by recent Democrat successes,

HAYES VERSUS TILDEN

afraid of the scandals with which Grant was associated, and concerned about the president's declining health—resisted. Instead, they sought a candidate not associated with the problems of the Grant years, one who might entice Liberals back and unite the party again. They settled on Rutherford B. Hayes of Ohio, a former Union army officer, governor, and congressman, champion of civil service reform. The Democrats united behind Samuel J. Tilden, the reform governor of New York who had been instrumental in challenging the corrupt Tweed Ring of New York City's Tammany Hall.

Although the campaign was a bitter one, there were few differences of principle between the candidates, both of whom

THOSE INFLUENCED BY SOCIAL DARWINISM CAME TO VIEW THE LARGE NUMBER OF UNEMPLOYED VAGRANTS IN THE NORTH—AND POOR AFRICAN AMERICANS IN THE SOUTH—AS IRREDEEMABLE MISFITS.

were conservatives committed to moderate reform. The November election produced an apparent Democratic victory. Tilden carried the South and several large Northern states, and his popular margin over Hayes was nearly 300,000 votes. But disputed returns from Louisiana, South Carolina, Florida, and Oregon, whose total electoral vote was 20, threw the election in doubt. Tilden had undisputed claim to 184 electoral votes, only one short of a majority. But Hayes could still win if he managed to receive all 20 disputed votes.

The Constitution had established no method to determine the validity of disputed returns. It was clear that the decision lay with Congress, but it was not clear with which house or through what method. (The Senate was Republican, the House, Democratic.) Members of each party naturally supported a solution that would yield them the victory.

Finally, late in January 1877, Congress tried to break the deadlock by creating a special electoral commission to judge the disputed votes. The commission was to be composed of five senators, five representatives, and five justices of the Supreme Court. The congressional delegation would

SPECIAL ELECTORAL COMMISSION

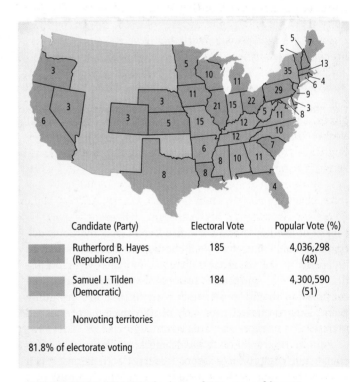

Candidate (Party)	Electoral Vote	Popular Vote (%)
Rutherford B. Hayes (Republican)	185	4,036,298 (48)
Samuel J. Tilden (Democratic)	184	4,300,590 (51)
Nonvoting territories		

81.8% of electorate voting

THE ELECTION OF 1876 The election of 1876 was one of the most controversial in American history. As in the elections of 1824, 1888, and 2000, the winner of the popular vote—Samuel J. Tilden—was not the winner of the electoral college, which he lost by one vote. The final decision as to who would be president was not made until the day before the official inauguration in March.

• *How did the Republicans turn this apparent defeat into a victory?*

RECONSTRUCTION

DEBATE over the nature of Reconstruction has created so much controversy over the decades that one scholar, writing in 1959, described the issue as a "dark and bloody ground." For many years, a relatively uniform and highly critical view of Reconstruction prevailed among historians. William A. Dunning offered the principal scholarly expression of this view in *Reconstruction, Political and Economic*

THE FREEDMEN'S BUREAU For four years after the Civil War, the Freedmen's Bureau served newly freed slaves, helping them to get housing, food, education, and other services. This image shows African American men and women waiting for rations, most of them old and sick. (The New York Public Library/Art Resource, NY)

(1907), the first major historical interpretation of Reconstruction. Dunning portrayed Reconstruction as a corrupt outrage perpetrated on the prostrate South by a vicious and vindictive group of Northern Republican Radicals. Unscrupulous carpetbaggers flooded the South to profit from the misery of the defeated region. Ignorant, illiterate blacks were thrust into positions of power for which they were entirely unfit. The Reconstruction experiment survived only because of the determination of the Republican Party to keep itself in power. Some later writers, notably Howard K. Beale, added an economic motive—to protect Northern business interests.

Dunning's interpretation shaped the views of several generations of historians and helped shape popular depictions of Reconstruction such as those expressed in the 1915 film *The Birth of a Nation* and then the 1936 book and 1939 movie *Gone with the Wind*.

The great African American scholar W. E. B. Du Bois was among the first to challenge the Dunning view. In *Black Reconstruction* (1935), Du Bois argued that Reconstruction politics in the Southern states had been an effort on the part of the masses, black and white, to create a more democratic society. The misdeeds of the Reconstruction governments, he claimed, had been greatly exaggerated, and their achievements overlooked. In the 1940s, the historians

consist of five Republicans and five Democrats. The Court delegation would include two Republicans, two Democrats, and an independent. But the independent seat ultimately went to a justice whose real sympathies were with the Republicans. The commission voted along straight party lines, 8 to 7, awarding every disputed vote to Hayes. Congress accepted their verdict on March 2. Two days later, Hayes was inaugurated.

Behind the resolution of the deadlock, however, lay a series of elaborate compromises among leaders of both parties. When a Democratic filibuster threatened to derail the commission's report, Republican Senate leaders met secretly with Southern Democratic leaders to work out terms by which the Democrats would allow the election of Hayes. According to traditional accounts, Republicans and Southern Democrats met at Washington's Wormley Hotel. In return for a Republican

pledge that Hayes would withdraw the last federal troops from the South, thus permitting the overthrow of the last Republican governments there, the Southerners agreed to abandon the filibuster.

Actually, the story behind the "Compromise of 1877" is more complex. Hayes was already on record favoring withdrawal of the troops, so Republicans needed to offer more than that if they hoped for Democratic support. The real agreement, the one that won over the Southern Democrats, was reached well before the Wormley meeting. As the price of their cooperation, the Southern Democrats (among them some former Whigs) exacted several pledges from the Republicans in addition to withdrawal of the troops: the appointment of at least one Southerner to the Hayes cabinet, control of federal patronage in their areas,

COMPROMISE OF 1877

C. Vann Woodward, David Herbert Donald, Thomas B. Alexander, and others began to reexamine the Reconstruction governments in the South and to suggest that their records were not nearly as bad as most historians had previously assumed.

By the early 1960s, a new view of Reconstruction was emerging. The revisionist approach was summarized by John Hope Franklin in *Reconstruction After the Civil War* (1961) and Kenneth Stampp in *The Era of Reconstruction* (1965), who claimed that the postwar Republicans had been engaged in a genuine, if flawed, effort to solve the problem of race in the South by providing much-needed protection to the freedmen. The Reconstruction governments, for all their faults, had been bold experiments in interracial politics. The congressional Radicals were not saints, but they had displayed a genuine concern for the rights of slaves. Andrew Johnson was not a martyred defender of the Constitution, but an inept, racist politician who resisted reasonable compromise and brought the government to a crisis. African Americans had played only a small part in Reconstruction governments and had generally acquitted themselves well. The Reconstruction regimes had, in fact, brought important progress to the South, establishing the region's first public school system and other important social changes. Corruption in the South had been no worse than corruption in the North at that time. What was tragic about Reconstruction, the revisionist view claimed, was not what it did to Southern whites but, rather, what it did not do for Southern blacks. By stopping short of the reforms necessary to ensure blacks genuine equality, Reconstruction had consigned them to more than a century of injustice and discrimination.

In later years, scholars began to question the revisionist view in an attempt to draw attention to the achievements of Reconstruction. Eric Foner, in *Nothing but Freedom* (1983) and *Reconstruction: America's Unfinished Revolution* (1988), emphasized how far the former slaves moved toward freedom and independence in a short time and how large a role African Americans themselves played in shaping Reconstruction. During Reconstruction, blacks won a certain amount of legal and political power in the South; even though they held that power only temporarily, they used it to strengthen their economic and social positions and to win a position of limited but genuine independence. Though they failed to achieve equality, they won a measure of individual and community autonomy that they used as building blocks of the freedom that emancipation alone had not guaranteed. Leon Litwack argued similarly in *Been in the Storm So Long* (1979) that former slaves used the relative latitude they enjoyed under Reconstruction to build a certain independence for themselves within Southern society. They strengthened their churches; they reunited their families; by refusing to work in the "gang-labor" system of the plantations, they forced the creation of a new labor system in which they had more control over their own lives. Writing from the perspective of women's history, Amy Dru Stanley and Jacqueline Jones have both argued that the freed slaves displayed considerable independence in constructing their households on their own terms and asserting their control over family life, reproduction, and work. According to Jones in *Labor of Love, Labor of Sorrow* (1985), women in particular sought the opportunity "to labor on behalf of their own families and kin within the protected spheres of household and community."

Some historians have begun to argue that Reconstruction was not restricted to the South alone. Heather Richardson, in *West from Appomattox* (2007) and *The Death of Reconstruction* (2001), shows how the entire nation changed during and as a result of the Civil War and Reconstruction—with the South, perhaps, changing least of all. The age of Reconstruction was also the age of western expansion and industrialization. •

UNDERSTAND, ANALYZE, AND EVALUATE

1. According to the essay, *The Birth of a Nation* and *Gone with the Wind* are popular depictions of Reconstruction that reflect Dunning's interpretation of the era. Can you find other popular depictions that reflect other interpretations of Reconstruction?

2. A new view of Reconstruction began to emerge in the 1960s, the era of the civil rights movement. Why do you think the civil rights movement might have encouraged historians and others to reexamine Reconstruction?

3. Which view of Reconstruction do you find more persuasive—the view of Reconstruction as a tragic era of exploitation of the South by the North or the view that sees Reconstruction as an era of achievement and progress?

---

generous internal improvements, and federal aid for the Texas and Pacific Railroad. Many powerful Southern Democrats supported industrializing their region. They believed Republican programs of federal support for business would aid the South more than the states' rights policies of the Democrats.

In his inaugural address, Hayes announced that the South's most pressing need was the restoration of "wise, honest, and peaceful local self-government"—a signal that he planned to withdraw federal troops and let white Democrats take over the state governments. That statement, and Hayes's subsequent actions, supported the widespread charges that he was paying off the South for acquiescing in his election and strengthened those who referred to him as "his Fraudulency." Hayes tried to counter such charges by projecting an image of stern public (and private) rectitude. But the election had already created such

bitterness that even Hayes's promise to serve only one term could not mollify his critics.

The president and his party had hoped to build up a "new Republican" organization in the South drawn from Whiggish conservative white groups and committed to some modest acceptance of African American rights. But all such efforts failed.

REPUBLICAN
FAILURE IN
THE SOUTH

Although many white Southern leaders sympathized with Republican economic policies, popular resentment of Reconstruction and its attack on white supremacy was so deep that supporting the party was politically impossible. At the same time, the withdrawal of federal troops signaled that the national government was giving up its attempts to control Southern politics and to improve the lot of African Americans in Southern society.

THE LEGACIES OF RECONSTRUCTION

Reconstruction made some important contributions to the efforts of former slaves to achieve dignity and equality in American life. And it was not as disastrous an experience for Southern whites as most of them believed at the time. But Reconstruction was in the end largely a failure, for in those years the United States abandoned its first serious effort to resolve the nation's oldest and deepest social problem—the problem of race. Moreover, the experience so disappointed, disillusioned, and embittered white Americans that it would be nearly a century before they would try again in any serious way.

Why did this great assault on racial injustice not achieve

IDEOLOGICAL LIMITS

more? In part, it was because of the weaknesses and errors of the people who directed it. But in greater part, it was because at-

> RECONSTRUCTION WAS IN THE END LARGELY A FAILURE, FOR IN THOSE YEARS THE UNITED STATES ABANDONED ITS FIRST SERIOUS EFFORT TO RESOLVE THE NATION'S OLDEST AND DEEPEST SOCIAL PROBLEM—THE PROBLEM OF RACE.

tempts to produce solutions ran up against conservative obstacles so deeply embedded in the nation's life that they could not be dislodged. Veneration of the Constitution sharply limited the willingness of national leaders to infringe on the rights of states and individuals. A profound respect for private property and free enterprise prevented any real assault on economic privilege in the South. Above all, perhaps, a pervasive belief among many of even the most liberal whites that African Americans were inherently inferior served as an obstacle to equality. Given the context within which Americans of the 1860s and 1870s were working, what is surprising, perhaps, is not that Reconstruction did so little, but that it did even as much as it did.

Considering the odds confronting them, therefore, African Americans had reason for pride in the gains they were able to make during Reconstruction. And future generations had reason for gratitude for two great charters of freedom—the Fourteenth and Fifteenth Amendments to the Constitution—which, although largely ignored at the time, would one day serve as the basis for a "Second Reconstruction" that would renew the drive to bring freedom and equality to all Americans.

THE NEW SOUTH

The agreement between southern Democrats and northern Republicans that helped settle the disputed election of 1876 was supposed to be the first step toward developing a stable, permanent Republican Party in the South. In that respect, at least, it failed. In the years following the end of Reconstruction, white southerners established the Democratic Party as the only viable political organization for the region's whites. Even so, the South did change in the years after Reconstruction in some of the ways the framers of the Compromise of 1877 had hoped.

THE "REDEEMERS"

By the end of 1877—after the last withdrawal of federal troops—every southern state government had been "redeemed" by white

BOURBON RULE

Democrats. Many white southerners rejoiced at the restoration of what they liked to call "home rule." But in reality, political power in the region was soon more restricted than at any time since the Civil War. Once again, the South fell under the control of a powerful, conservative oligarchy, whose members were known variously as the "Redeemers" (to themselves and their supporters) or the "Bourbons" (a term for aristocrats used by some of their critics).

In a few places, this post-Reconstruction ruling class was much the same as the ruling class of the antebellum period. In Alabama, for example, the old planter elite—despite challenges from new merchant and industrial forces—retained much of its

"IS *THIS* A REPUBLICAN FORM OF GOVERNMENT?" The New York artist and cartoonist Thomas Nast marked the end of Reconstruction in 1876 with this biting cartoon in *Harper's Weekly*, expressing his dismay at what he considered the nation's betrayal of the former slaves, who still had not received adequate guarantees of their rights. The caption of the cartoon continued: "Is *this* protecting life, liberty, or property? Is *this* equal protection of the laws?" (Courtesy of The Newberry Library, Chicago) former power and continued largely to dominate the state for decades. In most areas, however, the Redeemers constituted a genuinely new ruling class. They were merchants, industrialists, railroad developers, and financiers. Some of them were former planters, some of them northern immigrants who had become absorbed into the region's life, some of them ambitious, upwardly mobile white southerners from the region's lower social tiers. They combined a commitment to "home rule" and social conservatism with a commitment to economic development.

The various Bourbon governments of the New South behaved in many respects quite similarly to one another. Conservatives had complained that the Reconstruction governments fostered widespread corruption, but the Redeemer regimes were, if anything, even more awash in waste and fraud. (In this, they were little different from governments in every region of the country.) At the same time, virtually all the new Democratic regimes lowered taxes, reduced spending, and drastically diminished state services—including many of the most important accomplishments of Reconstruction. In one state after another, for example, state support for public school systems was reduced or eliminated. "Schools are not a necessity," an economy-conscious governor of Virginia commented.

By the late 1870s, significant dissenting groups were challenging the Bourbons: protesting the cuts in services and denouncing the commitment of the Redeemer governments to paying off the prewar and Reconstruction debts in full, at the original (usually high) rates of interest. In Virginia, for example, a vigorous "Readjuster" movement emerged, demanding that the state revise its debt payment procedures so as to make more money available for state services. In 1879, the Readjusters won control of the legislature, and in the next few years they captured the governorship and a U.S. Senate seat. Other states produced similar movements, some of them adding demands as well for greenbacks, debt relief, and other economic reforms. (A few such independent movements included significant numbers of African Americans in their ranks, but all consisted primarily of lower-income whites.) By the mid-1880s, however, conservative southerners—largely by exploiting racial prejudice—had effectively destroyed most of the dissenting movements.

THE READJUSTER CHALLENGE

INDUSTRIALIZATION AND THE "NEW SOUTH"

Some white southern leaders in the post-Reconstruction era hoped to see their region become the home of a vigorous industrial economy. The South had lost the war, such leaders argued, because its economy had been unable to compete with the modernized manufacturing capacity of the North. Now the region must

HENRY GRADY

 WE HAVE SOWN TOWNS AND CITIES IN THE PLACE OF THEORIES AND PUT BUSINESS ABOVE POLITICS. . . . WE HAVE FALLEN IN LOVE WITH WORK. 🙶

HENRY GRADY

"out-Yankee the Yankees" and build a "New South." Henry Grady, editor of the *Atlanta Constitution,* and other prominent spokesmen for a New South seldom challenged white supremacy, but they did advocate other important changes in southern values. Above all, they promoted the virtues of thrift, industry, and progress—qualities that prewar southerners had often denounced in northern society. "We have sown towns and cities in the place of theories," Grady boasted to a New England audience in the 1880s, "and put business above politics. . . . We have fallen in love with work." But even the most fervent advocates of the New South creed were generally unwilling to break entirely with the southern past. That was evident in, among other things, the popular literature of the region. At the same time that white southern writers were extolling the virtues of industrialization in newspaper editorials and speeches, they were painting nostalgic portraits of the Old South in their literature. Few southerners advocated a literal return to the old ways, but most whites eagerly embraced romantic talk of the "Lost Cause." And they responded warmly to the local-color fiction of such writers as Joel Chandler Harris, whose folktales—the most famous being *Uncle Remus* (1880)—portrayed the slave society of the antebellum years as a harmonious world marked by engaging dialect and close emotional bonds between the races. The writer Thomas Nelson Page similarly extolled the old Virginia aristocracy. The growing popularity of minstrel shows also reflected the romanticization of the Old South (see "Patterns of Popular Culture"). The white leaders of the New South, in short, faced their future with one foot still in the past.

Even so, southern industry expanded dramatically in the years after Reconstruction and became a more important part of the region's economy than ever before. Most visible was the growth in textile manufacturing, which increased ninefold in the last twenty years of the century. In the past, southern planters had usually shipped their cotton out of the region to manufacturers in the North or in Europe. Now textile factories appeared in the South itself—many of them drawn to the South from New England by the abundance of water power, the ready supply of cheap labor, the low taxes, and the accommodating conservative governments. The tobacco-processing industry, similarly, established an important foothold in the region, largely through the work of James B. Duke of North Carolina, whose American Tobacco Company established for a time a virtual monopoly over the processing of raw tobacco into marketable materials. In the lower South, and particularly in Birmingham, Alabama, the iron (and, later, steel) industry grew rapidly. By 1890, the southern iron and steel industry represented nearly a fifth of the nation's total capacity.

Railroad development increased substantially in the post-Reconstruction years—at a rate far greater than that of the nation at large. Between 1880 and 1890, trackage in the South

The Minstrel Show

THE minstrel show was one of the most popular forms of entertainment in America in the second half of the nineteenth century. It was also a testament to the high awareness of race (and the high level of racism) in American society both before and after the Civil War. Minstrel performers were mostly white, usually disguised as black. But African American performers also formed their own minstrel shows and transformed them, at least to a degree, into vehicles for training black entertainers and developing new forms of music and dance.

MINSTRELSY AT HIGH TIDE The Primrose & West minstrel troupe—a lavish and expensive entertainment that drew large crowds in the 1800s—was one of many companies to offer this brand of entertainment to eager audiences all over the country. Although minstrelsy began with white musicians performing in blackface, the popularity of real African American minstrels encouraged the impresarios of the troupe to include groups of white and black performers alike. (©Collection of the New-York Historical Society)

Before and during the Civil War, when minstrel shows consisted almost entirely of white performers, performers blackened their faces with cork and presented grotesque stereotypes of the slave culture of the American South. Among the most popular of the stumbling, ridiculously ignorant characters invented for these shows were such figures as "Zip Coon" and "Jim Crow" (whose name later resurfaced as a label for late-nineteenth-century segregation laws). A typical minstrel show presented a group of seventeen or more men seated in a semicircle facing the audience. The man in the center ran the show, played the straight man for the jokes of others, and led the music—lively dances and sentimental ballads played on banjos, castanets, and other instruments and sung by soloists or the entire group.

After the Civil War, white minstrels began to expand their repertoire. Drawing from the famous and successful freak shows of P. T. Barnum and other entertainment entrepreneurs, some began to include Siamese twins, bearded ladies, and even a supposedly 8-foot 2-inch "Chinese giant" in their shows. They also incorporated sex, both by including women in some shows and, even more popularly, by recruiting female impersonators. One of the most successful minstrel performers of the 1870s was Francis Leon, who delighted crowds with his female portrayal of a flamboyant "prima donna."

One reason white minstrels began to move in these new directions was that they were now facing competition from black performers, who could provide more authentic versions of

---

more than doubled. And the South took a major step toward integrating its transportation system with that of the rest of the country when, in 1886, it changed the gauge (distance between the two rails) of its trackage to correspond with the standards of the North. Yet southern industry developed within strict limits, and its effects on the region were never even remotely comparable to the effects of industrialization on the North. The southern share of national manufacturing doubled in the last twenty years of the century, to 10 percent of the total. But that percentage was the same the South had claimed in 1860; the region, in other words, had done no more than regain what it had lost during

Railroad Development

the war and its aftermath. The region's per capita income increased 21 percent in the same period. But at the end of the century, average income in the South was only 40 percent of that in the North; in 1860 it had been more than 60 percent. And even in those areas where development had been most rapid—textiles, iron, railroads—much of the capital had come from the North. In effect, the South was developing a colonial economy.

The growth of industry in the South required the region to recruit a substantial industrial workforce for the first time. From the beginning, a high percentage of the factory workers (and an especially high percentage of textile workers) were women. Heavy male casualties in the Civil War had helped

THE ELECTRIC 3 MINSTRELS For every large troupe such as Primrose & West there were dozens of smaller traveling minstrel bands such as Callan, Haley, and Callan's shown here on the road in the 1880s. In concert, these men performed in exaggerated blackface. Posing for photographs, they tried to exhibit sober, middle-class respectability. (Brown Brothers)

black music, dance, and humor, and usually bring more talent to the task than white performers. The Georgia Minstrels, organized in 1865, was one of the first all-black minstrel troupes, and it had great success in attracting white audiences in the Northeast for several years. By the 1870s, touring African American minstrel groups were numerous. The black minstrels used many of the conventions of the white shows. There were dances, music, comic routines, and sentimental recitations. Some black performers even chalked their faces to make themselves look as dark as the white blackface performers with whom they were competing. Black minstrels sometimes denounced slavery (at least indirectly) and did not often speak demeaningly of the capacities of their race. But they could not entirely escape caricaturing African American life as they struggled to meet the expectations of their white audiences.

While the black minstrel shows had few openly political aims, they did help develop some important forms of African American entertainment and transform them into a part of the national culture. Black minstrels introduced new forms of dance, derived from the informal traditions of slavery and black community life: the "buck and wing,"

the "stop time," and the "Virginia essence," which established the foundations for the tap and jazz dancing of the early twentieth century. They also improvised musically and began experimenting with forms that over time contributed to the growth of ragtime, jazz, and rhythm and blues.

Eventually, black minstrelsy—like its white counterpart—evolved into other forms of theater, including the beginnings of serious black drama. At Ambrose Park in Brooklyn in the 1890s, for example, the celebrated black comedian Sam Lucas (a veteran of the minstrel circuit) starred in the play *Darkest America*, which one black newspaper later described as a "delineation of Negro life, carrying the race through all their historical phases from the plantation, into reconstruction days and finally painting our people as they are today, cultured and accomplished in the social graces, [holding] the mirror faithfully up to nature."

But interest in the minstrel show did not die altogether. In 1927, Hollywood released *The Jazz Singer*, the first feature film with sound. It was about the career of a white minstrel performer, and its star was one of the most popular singers of the twentieth century: Al Jolson, whose career had begun on the blackface minstrel circuit years before. •

UNDERSTAND, ANALYZE, AND EVALUATE

1. How did minstrel shows performed by white minstrels reinforce prevailing attitudes toward African Americans?
2. Minstrel shows performed by black minstrels often conformed to existing stereotypes of African Americans. Why?
3. Can you think of any popular entertainments today that carry remnants of the minstrel shows of the nineteenth century?

create a large population of unmarried women who desperately needed employment. Factories also hired entire families, many of whom were moving into towns from failed farms. Workdays were long (often twelve hours a day) and wages were far below the northern equivalent; indeed, one of the greatest attractions of the South to industrialists was that employers were able to pay workers there as little as one-half what northern workers received.

Life in most mill towns was rigidly controlled by the owners and managers of the factories, who rigorously suppressed attempts at protest or union organization. Company stores sold goods to workers at inflated prices and issued credit at exorbi-

tant rates (much like country stores in agrarian areas), and mill owners ensured that no competitors were able to establish themselves in the community. At the same time, however, the conditions of the mill town helped create a strong sense of community and solidarity among workers (even if they seldom translated such feelings into militancy).

Some industries, textiles for example, offered virtually no opportunities to African American workers. Others—including tobacco, iron, and lumber—did provide some employment for blacks, usually the most menial and lowest-paid positions. Some mill towns, therefore, were places where black and white culture came into close contact. That proximity contributed less to the growth of racial harmony than to the determination of white leaders to take additional measures to protect white supremacy.

At times, industrialization proceeded on the basis of no wage-paying employment. Through the "convict-lease" system, "Convict-Lease" System southern states leased gangs of convicted criminals to private interests as a cheap labor supply. The system exposed the convicts to brutal and at times fatal mistreatment. It paid them nothing (the leasing fees went to the states, not the workers). And it denied employment in railroad construction and other projects to the free labor force.

TENANTS AND SHARECROPPERS

Despite significant growth in southern industry, the region remained primarily agrarian. The most important economic reality in the post-Reconstruction South, therefore, was the impoverished state of agriculture. The 1870s and 1880s saw an acceleration of the trends that had begun in the immediate postwar years: the imposition of systems of tenantry and debt peonage on much of the region; the reliance on a few cash crops rather than on a diversified agricultural system; and increasing absentee ownership of valuable farmlands (many of them purchased by merchants and industrialists who paid little attention to whether the land was being properly used). During Reconstruction, perhaps a third or more of the farmers in the South were tenants; by 1900, the figure had increased to 70 per-

cent. That was in large part the result of the crop-lien system, the system by which farmers borrowed money against their future crops and often fell deeper and deeper into debt.

Tenantry took several forms. Farmers who owned tools, equipment, and farm animals—or who had the money to buy them—usually paid an annual cash rent for their land. But many farmers (including most black ones) had no money or equipment. Landlords would supply them with land, a crude house, a few tools, seed, and sometimes a mule. In return, farmers would promise the landlord a large share of the annual crop—hence the term "sharecropping." After paying their landlords and their local merchants (who were often the same people), sharecroppers seldom had anything left to sell on their own.

AFRICAN AMERICANS AND THE NEW SOUTH

The "New South creed" was not the property of whites alone. Many African Americans were attracted to the vision of progress BLACK MIDDLE CLASS and self-improvement as well. Some blacks succeeded in elevating themselves into a distinct middle class—most of them economically inferior to the white middle class, but nevertheless significant. These were former slaves (and, as the decades passed, their offspring) who managed to acquire property, build small businesses, or enter professions. A few African Americans accumulated substantial fortunes by establishing banks and insurance

FAMILY PORTRAIT An African American family poses for a portrait in a cotton field in South Carolina in the 1880s. The images shown here are part of a stereograph, a relatively new and highly popular photographic technique that creates the illusion of a three-dimensional image when viewed through a special device. (Robert N. Dennis Collection of Stereoscopic Views)

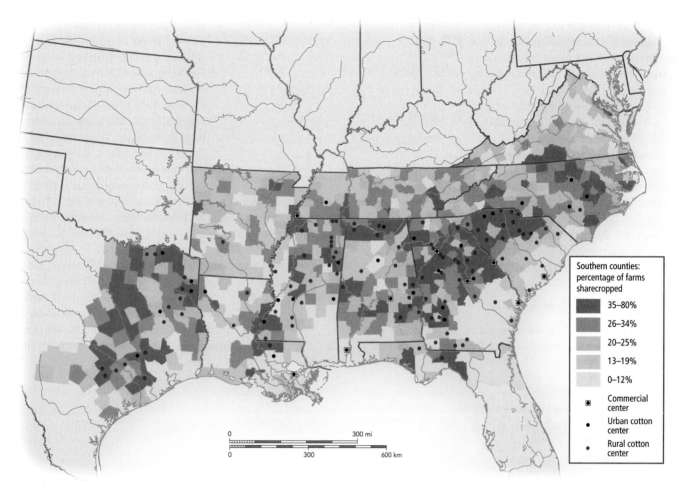

THE CROP-LIEN SYSTEM IN 1880 In the years after the Civil War, more and more southern farmers—white and black—became tenants or sharecroppers on land owned by others. This map shows the percentage of farms that were within the so-called crop-lien system, the system by which people worked their lands for someone else, who had a claim (or "lien") on a part of the farmers' crops. Note the high density of sharecropping and tenant farming in the most fertile areas of the Deep South, the same areas where slaveholding had been most dominant before the Civil War.

• *How did the crop-lien system contribute to the shift in southern agriculture toward one-crop farming?*

companies to serve the black community. One of those was Maggie Lena, a black woman who became the first female bank president in the United States when she founded the St. Luke Penny Savings Bank in Richmond in 1903. Most middle-class blacks experienced more modest gains by becoming doctors, lawyers, nurses, or teachers serving African American communities.

A cardinal tenet of this rising group of African -Americans was that education was vital to the future of their race. With the support of northern missionary societies and, to a far lesser extent, a few southern state governments, they expanded the network of black colleges and institutes that had taken root during Reconstruction into an important educational system.

The chief spokesman for this commitment to education, and for a time the major spokesman for African Americans in the South (and beyond), was Booker T. Washington, founder and president of the Tuskegee Institute in Alabama. Born into slavery, Washington had worked his way out of poverty after acquiring an education (at Virginia's famous Hampton

BOOKER T. WASHINGTON

Institute). He urged other blacks to follow the same road to self-improvement.

Washington's message was both cautious and hopeful. African Americans should attend school, learn skills, and establish a solid footing in agriculture and the trades. Industrial, not classical, education should be their goal. They should, moreover, refine their speech, improve their dress, and adopt habits of thrift and personal cleanliness; they should, in short, adopt the standards of the white middle class. Only thus, he claimed, could they win the respect of the white population, the prerequisite for any larger social gains. African Americans should forgo agitating for political rights, he said, and concentrate on self-improvement and preparation for equality. In a famous speech in Georgia in 1895, Washington outlined a philosophy of race relations that became widely known as the Atlanta Compromise. "The wisest among my race understand," he said, "that the agitation of questions of social equality is the extremest folly." Rather, blacks should engage in "severe and constant struggle" for economic gains; for, as he

THE ATLANTA COMPROMISE

explained, "no race that has anything to contribute to the markets of the world is long in any degree ostracized." If African Americans were ever to win the rights and privileges of citizenship, they must first show that they were "prepared for the exercise of these privileges." Washington offered a powerful challenge to those whites who wanted to discourage African Americans from acquiring an education or winning any economic gains. He helped awaken the interest of a new generation to the possibilities for self-advancement through self-improvement. But his message was also an implicit promise that African Americans would not overtly challenge the system of segregation that whites were then in the process of erecting.

> 66 **NO RACE THAT HAS ANYTHING TO CONTRIBUTE TO THE MARKETS OF THE WORLD IS LONG IN ANY DEGREE OSTRACIZED.** 99
>
> **BOOKER T. WASHINGTON**

THE BIRTH OF JIM CROW

Few white southerners had ever accepted the idea of racial equality. That the former slaves acquired any legal and political rights at all after emancipation was in large part the result of federal support. That support all but vanished after 1877. Federal troops withdrew. Congress lost interest. And the Supreme Court effectively stripped the Fourteenth and Fifteenth Amendments of much of their significance. In the so-called civil rights cases of 1883, the Court ruled that the Fourteenth Amendment prohibited state governments from discriminating against people because of race but did not restrict private organizations or individuals from doing so. Thus railroads, hotels, theaters, and workplaces could legally practice segregation.

Eventually, the Court also validated state legislation that institutionalized the separation of the races. In *Plessy v. Ferguson* (1896), a case involving a Louisiana law that required separate seating arrangements for the races on railroads, the Court held that separate accommodations did not deprive blacks of equal

PLESSY V. FERGUSON

TUSKEGEE INSTITUTE, 1881 From these modest beginnings, Booker T. Washington's Tuskegee Institute in Alabama became the preeminent academy offering technical and industrial training to black men. It deliberately de-emphasized the traditional liberal arts curricula of most colleges. Washington considered such training an unnecessary frill and encouraged his students to work on developing practical skills. (Bettmann/Corbis)

rights if the accommodations were equal, a decision that survived for years as part of the legal basis for segregated schools. In *Cumming v. County Board of Education* (1899), the Court ruled that laws establishing separate schools for whites were valid even if there were no comparable schools for African Americans.

Even before these decisions, white southerners were working to strengthen white supremacy and to separate the races to the greatest extent possible. One illustration of this movement from subordination to segregation was black voting rights. In some states, disenfranchisement had begun almost as soon as Reconstruction ended. But in other areas, black voting continued for some time after Reconstruction—largely because conservative whites believed they could control the black electorate and use it to beat back the attempts of poor white farmers to take control of the Democratic Party. In the 1890s, however, franchise restrictions became much more rigid. During those years, some small white farmers began to demand complete black disenfranchisement—both because of racial prejudice and because they objected to the black vote being used against them by the conservative planters (known as "Bourbons"). At the same time, many members of the conservative elite began to fear that poor whites might unite politically with poor African Americans to challenge them. They too began to support further franchise restrictions.

In devising laws to disenfranchise black males, the southern states had to find ways to evade the Fifteenth Amendment, which prohibited states from denying anyone the right to vote because of race. Two devices emerged before 1900 to accomplish this goal. One was the poll tax or some form of property qualification; few African Americans were prosperous enough to meet such requirements. Another was the "literacy" or "understanding" test, which required voters to demonstrate an ability to read and to interpret the Constitution. Even those African Americans who could read had trouble passing the difficult test white officials gave them. Such restrictions were often applied unequally. Literacy tests for whites, for example, were sometimes much easier than those for blacks. Even so, the laws affected poor white voters as well as African Americans. By the late 1890s, the black vote had decreased by 62 percent, the white vote by 26 percent. One result was that some states passed so-called grandfather laws, permitting men who could not meet the literacy and property qualifications to be enfranchised if

RESTRICTING THE FRANCHISE

A LYNCH MOB, 1893 A large, almost festive crowd gathers to watch the lynching of a black man accused of the murder of a three-year-old white girl. Lynchings remained frequent in the South until as late as the 1930s, but they reached their peak in the 1890s and the first years of the twentieth century. Lynchings such as this one—published well in advance and attracting whole families who traveled great distances to see them—were relatively infrequent. Most lynchings were the work of smaller groups, operating with less visibility. (Library of Congress)

THE ORIGINS OF SEGREGATION

NOT until after World War II, when the emergence of the civil rights movement forced white Americans to confront the issue of racial segregation, did historians pay much attention to the origins of the institution. Most had assumed that the separation of the races had emerged naturally and even inevitably out of the abolition of slavery. It had been a response to the failure of Reconstruction, the weakness and poverty of the African American community, and the pervasiveness of white racism. It was, as W. J. Cash argued in *The Mind of the South* (1941), the way things had always been.

The first major challenge to these assumptions, indeed the first serious scholarly effort to explain the origins of segregation, was C. Vann Woodward's *The Strange Career of Jim Crow* (1956), which not only reshaped scholarship, but also had a significant political impact. As a southern liberal, Woodward wanted to convince both scholars and the larger public that the racial institutions they considered part of a long, unbroken tradition were in fact the product of a particular set of historical circumstances.

In the aftermath of emancipation, and indeed for two decades after Reconstruction, Woodward argued, race relations in the South had remained relatively fluid. Blacks and whites did not often interact as equals, but black southerners enjoyed a degree of latitude in social and even political affairs. Blacks and whites often rode together in the same railroad cars, ate in the same restaurants, and used the same public facilities. African Americans voted in significant numbers. By the end of the nineteenth century, however, a great wave of racist legislation—the Jim Crow laws, which established the basis of segregation—had hardened race relations and destroyed the alternatives that many whites and blacks had considered viable only a few years before. The principal reason, Woodward argued, was the Populist political insurgency of the 1890s, which frightened many white southerners into thinking that African Americans might soon be a major political power in the region. Southern conservatives, in particular, used the issue of white supremacy to attack the Populists and to prevent African Americans from forming an alliance with them. The result was segregation and the disenfranchisement of African Americans (along with many poor whites).

Woodward's argument suggested that laws are important in shaping social behavior—that laws had made segregation and, by implication, other laws could unmake it. Historian Joel Williamson disagreed and in *After Slavery* (1965), his study of South Carolina, he argued that the laws of the 1890s simply ratified a set of conditions that had been firmly established by the end of Reconstruction. As early as the mid-1870s, Williamson claimed, the races had already begun to live in two separate societies, and by the end of the decade, segregation was largely in place, continuing in a different form a pattern of racial separation established under slavery. The laws of the 1890s did little more than codify an already established system.

With the publication of *North of Slavery* in 1965, Leon Litwack exposed the existence of widespread segregation, supported by an early version of Jim Crow laws, in the North before the Civil War. In almost every northern state, he revealed, free blacks experienced a kind of segregation not very different from what freed slaves would experience in the South after the Civil War. A few years later, Ira Berlin argued in *Slaves Without Masters* (1974) that in the antebellum South, white people had created a wide range of discriminatory laws aimed at free blacks and ensuring segregation. The Jim Crow regime, such

their ancestors had voted before Reconstruction began, thus barring the descendants of slaves from the polls while allowing poor whites access to them. In many areas, however, ruling elites were quite content to see poor whites, a potential source of opposition to their power, barred from voting.

The Supreme Court proved as compliant in ruling on the disenfranchising laws as it was in dealing with the civil rights cases. The Court eventually voided the grandfather laws, but it validated the literacy test (in the 1898 case of *Williams v. Mississippi*) and displayed a general willingness to let the southern states define their own suffrage standards as long as evasions of the Fifteenth Amendment were not too glaring.

Laws restricting the franchise and segregating schools were only part of a network of state statutes—known as the Jim Crow laws—that by the first years of the twentieth century had institutionalized an elaborate system of segregation reaching into almost every area of southern life. Blacks and whites could not ride

WHITE
CONTROL
PERPETUATED

in the same railroad cars, sit in the same waiting rooms, use the same washrooms, eat in the same restaurants, or sit in the same theaters. Blacks had no access to many public parks, beaches, and picnic areas; they could not be patients in many hospitals. Much of the new legal structure did no more than confirm what had already been widespread social practice in the South since well before the end of Reconstruction. But the Jim Crow laws also stripped African Americans of many of the modest social, economic, and political gains they had made in the more fluid atmosphere of the late nineteenth century. The laws served, too, as a means for whites to retain control of social relations between the races in the newly growing cities and towns of the South, where traditional patterns of deference and subjugation were more difficult to preserve than in the countryside. What had been maintained by custom in the rural South was to be maintained by law in the urbanizing South.

THE NEGRO GALLERY.

(Collection of the Louisiana Museum)

segregation, Rabinowitz suggested, was not integration, but exclusion.

In the early 1980s, a number of scholars began examining segregation anew in light of the rising American interest in South Africa, whose system of apartheid seemed to them to be similar in many ways to the by-then largely dismantled Jim Crow system in the South. John Cell's *The Highest Stage of White Supremacy* (1982) used the comparison to construct a revised explanation of how segregation emerged in the American South. The segregation laws, Cell argued, were a continuation of southern whites' unchanging determination to retain control over the African American population.

The emergence of large black communities in urban areas and of a significant black labor force in factories presented a new challenge to white southerners. In the city, blacks and whites were in more direct competition than they had been in the countryside. There was more danger of social mixing. The city therefore required different, and more rigidly institutionalized, systems of control. The Jim Crow laws were a response not just to an enduring commitment to white supremacy, but also to a new urban reality that required a rigid legal and institutional basis for white supremacy. •

works suggested, emerged naturally out of precedents established before the Civil War, in both the North and the South.

Other scholars challenged these interpretations by attempting to link the rise of legal segregation to changing social and economic circumstances in the South. Howard Rabinowitz's *Race Relations in the Urban South* (1978) linked the rise of segregation to the new challenge of devising a form of race relations suitable to life in the growing southern cities, into which rural blacks were moving in substantial numbers. The creation of separate public facilities—schools, parks, waiting rooms, etc.—was not so much an effort to drive blacks out of white facilities as it was an attempt to create a set of facilities where none had previously existed for a black community. The alternative to

UNDERSTAND, ANALYZE, AND EVALUATE

1. Do laws shape social behavior, or is social behavior codified into law? What examples support your view?
2. How have historians linked segregation to urbanization?
3. Was segregation, whether emerging naturally or imposed by law, inevitable?

More than legal efforts were involved in this process. The 1890s witnessed a dramatic increase in white violence against blacks, which, along with the Jim Crow laws, served to inhibit black agitation for equal rights. The worst such violence—lynching of blacks by white mobs, either because the victims were accused of crimes or because they had seemed somehow to violate their expected

LYNCHINGS   station—reached appalling levels. In the nation as a whole in the 1890s, there was an average of 187 lynchings each year, more than 80 percent of them in the South. The vast majority of victims were black.

The most celebrated lynchings occurred in cities and towns, where large, well-organized mobs—occasionally with the tacit cooperation of local authorities—seized black prisoners from the jails and hanged them in great public rituals. Such public lynchings were often planned well in advance and elaborately organized. They attracted large audiences from surrounding regions. Entire families traveled many miles to witness the spec-

tacles. But such great public lynchings were relatively rare. Much more frequent, and more dangerous to African Americans because less visible or predictable, were lynchings performed by small vigilante mobs, often composed of friends or relatives of the victim (or supposed victim) of a crime. Those involved in lynchings often saw their actions as a legitimate form of law enforcement; and indeed, some victims of lynchings had in fact committed crimes. But lynchings were also a means by which whites controlled the black population through terror and intimidation. Thus, some lynch mobs killed African Americans whose only "crime" had been presumptuousness. Others chose as victims outsiders in the community, whose presence threatened to disturb the normal pattern of race relations. Black men who had made any sexual advances toward white women (or who white men thought had done so) were particularly vulnerable to lynchings; the fear of black sexuality, and the unspoken fear among many men that white women might be attracted to that sexuality, was always an important part of the belief system that supported segregation. Whatever the reasons or circumstances, the victims of lynch mobs were denied the protection of the laws and the opportunity to prove their innocence.

The rise of lynchings shocked the conscience of many white Americans in a way that other forms of racial injustice did not. Almost from the start there was a substantial anti-lynching movement. In 1892 Ida B. Wells, a committed black journalist, launched what became an international anti-lynching movement with a series of impassioned articles after the lynching of three of her friends in Memphis, Tennessee, her home. The movement gradually gathered strength in the first years of the twentieth century, attracting substantial support from whites (particularly white women) in both the North and South. Its goal was a federal anti-lynching law, which would allow the national government to do what state and local governments in the South were generally unwilling to do: punish those responsible for lynchings.

But the substantial white opposition to lynchings stood as an exception to the general white support for suppression of African Americans. Indeed, just as in the antebellum period, the shared commitment to white supremacy helped dilute class animosities between poorer whites and the Bourbon oligarchies. Economic issues tended to play a secondary role to race in WHITE UNITY southern politics, distracting people from the glaring social inequalities that afflicted blacks and whites alike. The commitment to white supremacy, in short, was a burden for poor whites as well as for blacks.

LOOKING BACK

Reconstruction, long remembered by many white Americans as a vindictive outrage or a tragic failure, was in fact a profoundly important moment in American history. Despite the bitter political battles in Washington and throughout the South, culminating in the unsuccessful effort to impeach President Andrew Johnson, the most important result of the effort to reunite the nation after its long and bloody war was a reshaping of the lives of ordinary people in all regions of the nation.

In the North, Reconstruction solidified the power of the Republican Party and ensured that public policy would support the continued growth of an advanced industrial economy. The rapid growth of the northern economy continued and accelerated, drawing more and more of its residents into an expanding commercial world.

In the South, Reconstruction did more than simply bring slavery to an end. It fundamentally rearranged the relationship between the region's white and black citizens. Only for a while did Reconstruction permit African Americans to participate actively and effectively in southern politics. After a few years of widespread black voting and significant black officeholding, the forces of white supremacy forced most African Americans to the margins of the southern political world, where they would mostly remain until the 1960s.

But in other ways, the lives of southern blacks changed dramatically. Overwhelmingly, they left the plantations. Some sought work in towns and cities. Some left the region altogether. But the great majority began farming on small farms of their own—not as landowners, except in rare cases, but as tenants

SIGNIFICANT EVENTS

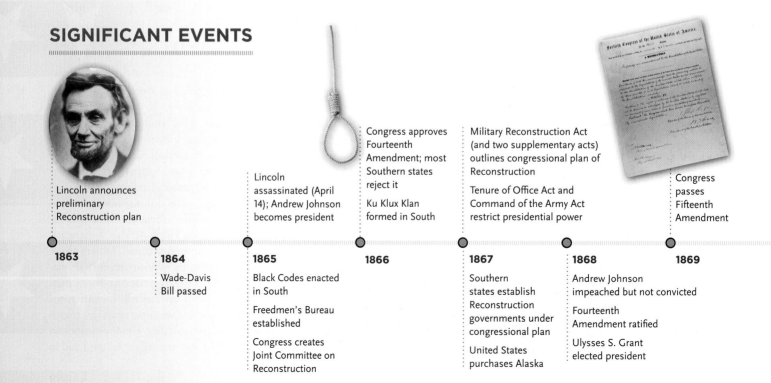

Lincoln announces preliminary Reconstruction plan

Lincoln assassinated (April 14); Andrew Johnson becomes president

Congress approves Fourteenth Amendment; most Southern states reject it

Ku Klux Klan formed in South

Military Reconstruction Act (and two supplementary acts) outlines congressional plan of Reconstruction

Tenure of Office Act and Command of the Army Act restrict presidential power

Congress passes Fifteenth Amendment

1863

1864
Wade-Davis Bill passed

1865
Black Codes enacted in South

Freedmen's Bureau established

Congress creates Joint Committee on Reconstruction

1866

1867
Southern states establish Reconstruction governments under congressional plan

United States purchases Alaska

1868
Andrew Johnson impeached but not convicted

Fourteenth Amendment ratified

Ulysses S. Grant elected president

1869

and sharecroppers on land owned mostly by whites. The result was a form of economic bondage, driven by debt, only scarcely less oppressive than the legal bondage of slavery. But within this system, African Americans managed to carve out a much larger sphere of social and cultural autonomy than they had ever been able to create under slavery. Black churches organized in great numbers. African American schools emerged in some communities, and black colleges began to appear in the region. Some former slaves owned businesses and flourished. In southern cities and towns, a fledgling black middle class began to emerge.

The system of tenantry, which emerged in the course of Reconstruction, continued after its end to dominate the south-ern economy. Strenuous efforts by "New South" advocates to advance industry and commerce in the region produced signifi-cant results in a few areas. But the South on the whole remained what it had always been, an overwhelmingly rural society with a sharply defined class structure. It was also a region with a deep commitment among its white citizens to the subordination of African Americans—a commitment solidified in the 1890s and the early twentieth century when white southerners erected an elaborate legal system of segregation (the "Jim Crow" laws). The promise of the great Reconstruction amendments to the Constitution—the Fourteenth and Fifteenth—remained largely unfulfilled in the South as the century drew to its close. •

KEY TERMS/PEOPLE/PLACES/EVENTS

ANDREW JOHNSON 415
ATLANTA COMPROMISE 435
BLACK CODES 416
BOOKER T. WASHINGTON 435
CARPETBAGGERS 419
CHARLES SUMNER 414
COMPROMISE OF 1877 427
CROP-LIEN SYSTEM 422

ENFORCEMENT ACTS 426
FOURTEENTH AMENDMENT 416
FREEDMEN'S BUREAU 414
HAMILTON FISH 425
IDA B. WELLS 440
JIM CROW LAWS 436
KU KLUX KLAN 426
PANIC OF 1873 425

PLESSY v. FERGUSON 436
RADICAL REPUBLICANS 414
REDEEMERS 430
SCALAWAGS 419
SHARECROPPING 422
THADDEUS STEVENS 414
WADE-DAVIS BILL 415
WILLIAM SEWARD 425

RECALL AND REFLECT

1. What were the principal questions facing the nation at the end of the Civil War?

2. What were the achievements of Reconstruction? Where did it fail and why?

3. What new problems arose in the South as the North's inter-est in Reconstruction waned?

4. What was the Compromise of 1877, and how did it affect Reconstruction?

5. How did the New South differ from the South before the Civil War?

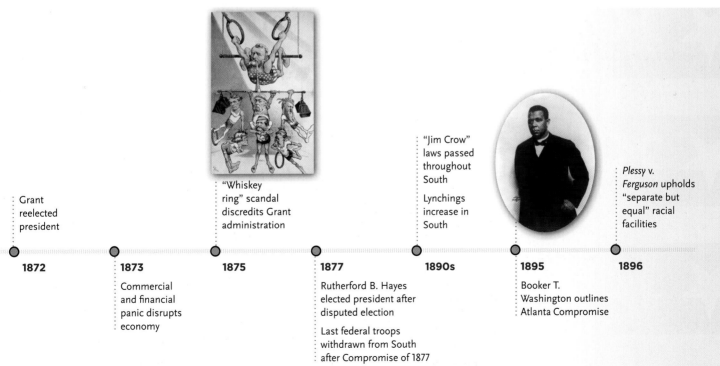

Grant reelected president

1872

1873
Commercial and financial panic disrupts economy

"Whiskey ring" scandal discredits Grant administration

1875

1877
Rutherford B. Hayes elected president after disputed election

Last federal troops withdrawn from South after Compromise of 1877

"Jim Crow" laws passed throughout South

Lynchings increase in South

1890s

1895
Booker T. Washington outlines Atlanta Compromise

Plessy v. Ferguson upholds "separate but equal" racial facilities

1896

APPENDIXES

TOPOGRAPHICAL MAP OF THE UNITED STATES

Vancouver Island

Puget Sound

COAST RANGE

CASCADE RANGE

ROCKY MOUNTAINS

Columbia R.

COLUMBIA PLATEAU

Snake R.

Marias R.

Milk R.

Missouri R.

Assiniboine R.

Lake Winnipegosis

Yellowstone R.

Tongue R.

Powder R.

Bighorn R.

Little Missouri R.

Belle Fourche R.

BLACK HILLS

Cheyenne R.

Missouri R.

James R.

SIERRA NEVADA

Humboldt R.

Great Salt Lake

Yampa R.

White R.

Niobrara R.

N. Platte R.

Lodgepole R.

Platte R.

Republican R.

Sacramento R.

Central Valley

San Joaquin R.

Green R.

Gunnison R.

ROCKY MOUNTAINS

Arkansas R.

Smoky Hill R.

COAST RANGES

DEATH VALLEY

Virgin R.

San Juan R.

Colorado R.

COLORADO PLATEAU

Rio Grande

Pecos R.

Cimarron R.

N. Canadian R.

MOHAVE DESERT

Colorado R.

Gila R.

Gila R.

Verde R.

Canadian R.

Red R.

PACIFIC OCEAN

Brazos R.

Colorado R.

Nueces R.

Rio Grande

ARCTIC OCEAN

RUSSIA

Bering Strait

BROOKS RANGE

ALASKA

Yukon R.

CANADA

Mt. McKinley

ALASKA RANGE

Bering Sea

ALEUTIAN ISLANDS

Gulf of Alaska

0   250   500 miles

0   250   500 kilometers

Kauai

Niihau

Oahu

Molokai

Lanai

Kahoolawe

Maui

HAWAII

PACIFIC OCEAN

Hawaii

0   50   100 miles

0   50   100 kilometers

MEXICO

A-2 •

NADA

Lake Nipigon

e of Woods

Lake Superior

Lake Huron

Lake Michigan

Lake Ontario

Lake Erie

St. Croix R.

Mississippi R.

Cedar R.

Iowa R.

Des Moines R.

Rock R.

Fox R.

Kankakee R.

Illinois R.

Scioto R.

Wabash R.

Ohio R.

Missouri R.

Osage R.

Cumberland R.

Tennessee R.

Mississippi R.

White R.

Arkansas R.

Ouachita R.

Red R.

Sabine R.

Yazoo R.

Tombigbee R.

Pearl R.

Alabama R.

Chattahoochee R.

Mobile R.

Altamaha R.

Saluda R.

Savannah R.

Roanoke R.

James R.

Potomac R.

Kanawha R.

Shenandoah R.

Susquehanna R.

Allegheny R.

Delaware R.

Hudson R.

Mohawk R.

St. Lawrence R.

Connecticut R.

Kennebec R.

Lake Champlain

CENTRAL

PLAINS

OZARK PLATEAU

AL PLAIN

ADIRONDACK MTS.

APPALACHIAN MOUNTAINS

ALLEGHENY MTS.

BLUE RIDGE MTS.

SHENANDOAH VALLEY

ATLANTIC COASTAL PLAIN

Chesapeake Bay

ATLANTIC OCEAN

Galveston Bay

Gulf of Mexico

Lake Okeechobee

BAHAMAS

CUBA

| 0 | 150 | 300 miles |
| 0 | 150 | 300 kilometers |

Land Elevation

Feet		Meters
Over 13,000		Over 3,000
6,560–13,000		2,000–3,000
3,280–6,560		1,000–2,000
660–3,280		2001–1,000
0–660		0–200
Below sea level		Below sea level

ATLANTIC OCEAN

PUERTO RICO

Caribbean Sea

| 0 | 50 | 100 miles |
| 0 | 50 | 100 kilometers |

UNITED STATES TERRITORIAL EXPANSION, 1783–1898

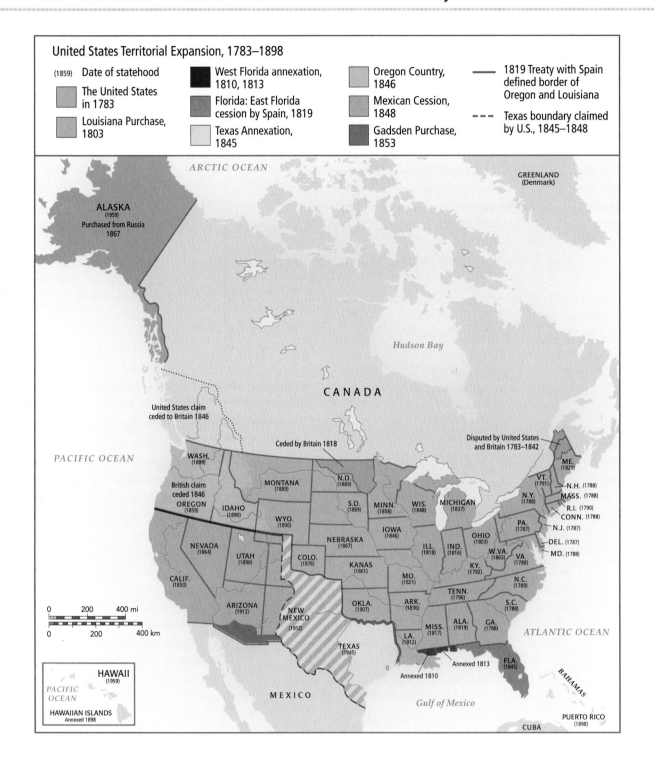

United States Territorial Expansion, 1783–1898

(1859) Date of statehood

The United States in 1783

Louisiana Purchase, 1803

West Florida annexation, 1810, 1813

Florida: East Florida cession by Spain, 1819

Texas Annexation, 1845

Oregon Country, 1846

Mexican Cession, 1848

Gadsden Purchase, 1853

1819 Treaty with Spain defined border of Oregon and Louisiana

Texas boundary claimed by U.S., 1845–1848

THE DECLARATION OF INDEPENDENCE

The Unanimous Declaration of the Thirteen United States of America

When, in the course of human events, it becomes necessary for one people to dissolve the political bands which have connected them with another, and to assume, among the powers of the earth, the separate and equal station to which the laws of nature and of nature's God entitle them, a decent respect to the opinions of mankind requires that they should declare the causes which impel them to the separation.

We hold these truths to be self-evident, that all men are created equal; that they are endowed by their Creator with certain unalienable rights; that among these, are life, liberty, and the pursuit of happiness. That, to secure these rights, governments are instituted among men, deriving their just powers from the consent of the governed; that, whenever any form of government becomes destructive of these ends, it is the right of the people to alter or to abolish it, and to institute a new government, laying its foundation on such principles, and organizing its powers in such form, as to them shall seem most likely to effect their safety and happiness. Prudence, indeed, will dictate that governments long established, should not be changed for light and transient causes; and, accordingly, all experience hath shown, that mankind are more disposed to suffer, while evils are sufferable, than to right themselves by abolishing the forms to which they are accustomed. But, when a long train of abuses and usurpations, pursuing invariably the same object, evinces a design to reduce them under absolute despotism, it is their right, it is their duty, to throw off such government and to provide new guards for their future security. Such has been the patient sufferance of these colonies, and such is now the necessity which constrains them to alter their former systems of government. The history of the present King of Great Britain is a history of repeated injuries and usurpations, all having, in direct object, the establishment of an absolute tyranny over these States. To prove this, let facts be submitted to a candid world:

He has refused his assent to laws the most wholesome and necessary for the public good.

He has forbidden his governors to pass laws of immediate and pressing importance, unless suspended in their operation till his assent should be obtained; and, when so suspended, he has utterly neglected to attend to them.

He has refused to pass other laws for the accommodation of large districts of people, unless those people would relinquish the right of representation in the legislature; a right inestimable to them, and formidable to tyrants only.

He has called together legislative bodies at places unusual, uncomfortable, and distant from the depository of their public records, for the sole purpose of fatiguing them into compliance with his measures.

He has dissolved representative houses repeatedly for opposing, with manly firmness, his invasions on the rights of the people.

He has refused, for a long time after such dissolutions, to cause others to be elected; whereby the legislative powers, incapable of annihilation, have returned to the people at large for their exercise; the state remaining, in the meantime, exposed to all the danger of invasion from without, and convulsions within.

He has endeavored to prevent the population of these States; for that purpose, obstructing the laws for naturalization of foreigners, refusing to pass others to encourage their migration hither, and raising the conditions of new appropriations of lands.

He has obstructed the administration of justice, by refusing his assent to laws for establishing judiciary powers.

He has made judges dependent on his will alone, for the tenure of their officers, and the amount and payment of their salaries.

He has erected a multitude of new offices, and sent hither swarms of officers to harass our people, and eat out their substance.

He has kept among us, in time of peace, standing armies, without the consent of our legislatures.

He has affected to render the military independent of, and superior to, the civil power.

He has combined, with others, to subject us to a jurisdiction foreign to our Constitution, and unacknowledged by our laws; giving his assent to their acts of pretended legislation:

For quartering large bodies of armed troops among us:

For protecting them by a mock trial, from punishment, for any murders which they should commit on the inhabitants of these States:

For cutting off our trade with all parts of the world:

For imposing taxes on us without our consent:

For depriving us, in many cases, of the benefit of trial by jury:

For transporting us beyond seas to be tried for pretended offences:

For abolishing the free system of English laws in a neighboring province, establishing therein an arbitrary government, and enlarging its boundaries, so as to render it at once an example and fit instrument for introducing the same absolute rule into these colonies:

For taking away our charters, abolishing our most valuable laws, and altering, fundamentally, the powers of our governments:

For suspending our own legislatures, and declaring themselves invested with power to legislate for use in all cases whatsoever.

He has abdicated government here, by declaring us out of his protection, and waging war against us.

He has plundered our seas, ravaged our coasts, burnt our towns, and destroyed the lives of our people.

He is, at this time, transporting large armies of foreign mercenaries to complete the works of death, desolation, and tyranny, already begun, with circumstances of cruelty and perfidy scarcely paralleled in the most barbarous ages, and totally unworthy the head of a civilized nation.

He has constrained our fellow citizens, taken captive on the high seas, to bear arms against their country, to become the executioners of their friends, and brethren, or to fall themselves by their hands.

He has excited domestic insurrections amongst us, and has endeavored to bring on the inhabitants of our frontiers, the merciless Indian savages, whose known rule of warfare is an undistinguished destruction of all ages, sexes, and conditions.

In every stage of these oppressions, we have petitioned for redress, in the most humble terms; our repeated petitions have been answered only by repeated injury. A prince, whose character is thus marked by every act which may define a tyrant, is unfit to be the ruler of a free people.

Nor have we been wanting in attention to our British brethren. We have warned them, from time to time, of attempts made by their legislature to extend an unwarrantable jurisdiction over us. We have reminded them of the circumstances of our emigration and settlement here. We have appealed to their native justice and magnanimity, and we have conjured them, by the ties of our common kindred, to disavow these usurpations, which would inevitably interrupt our connections and correspondence. They, too, have been deaf to the voice of justice and consanguinity. We must, therefore, acquiesce in the necessity, which denounces our separation, and hold them as we hold the rest of mankind, enemies in war, in peace, friends.

We, therefore, the representatives of the United States of America, in general Congress assembled, appealing to the Supreme Judge of the world for the rectitude of our intentions, do, in the name, and by the authority of the good people of these colonies, solemnly publish and declare, that these united colonies are, and of right ought to be, free and independent states: that they are absolved from all allegiance to the British Crown, and that all political connection between them and the state of Great Britain is, and ought to be, totally dissolved; and that, as free and independent states, they have full power to levy war, conclude peace, contract alliances, establish commerce, and to do all other acts and things which independent states may of right do. And, for the support of this declaration, with a firm reliance on the protection of Divine Providence, we mutually pledge to each other our lives, our fortunes, and our sacred honor.

The foregoing Declaration was, by order of Congress, engrossed, and signed by the following members:

JOHN HANCOCK

New Hampshire
Josiah Bartlett
William Whipple
Matthew Thornton

Massachusetts Bay
Samuel Adams
John Adams
Robert Treat Paine
Elbridge Gerry

Rhode Island
Stephen Hopkins
William Ellery

Connecticut
Robert Sherman
Samuel Huntington
William Williams
Oliver Wolcott

New York
William Floyd
Philip Livingston
Francis Lewis
Lewis Morris

New Jersey
Richard Stockton
John Witherspoon
Francis Hopkinson
John Hart
Abraham Clark

Pennsylvania
Robert Morris
Benjamin Rush
Benjamin Franklin
John Morton
George Clymer
James Smith
George Taylor
James Wilson
George Ross

Delaware
Caesar Rodney
George Read
Thomas McKean

Maryland
Samuel Chase
William Paca
Thomas Stone
Charles Carroll,
  of Carrollton

Virginia
George Wythe
Richard Henry Lee
Thomas Jefferson
Benjamin Harrison
Thomas Nelson, Jr.
Francis Lightfoot Lee
Carter Braxton

North Carolina
William Hooper
Joseph Hewes
John Penn

South Carolina
Edward Rutledge
Thomas Heyward, Jr.
Thomas Lynch, Jr.
Arthur Middleton

Georgia
Button Gwinnett
Lyman Hall
George Walton

Resolved, That copies of the Declaration be sent to the several assemblies, conventions, and committees, or councils of safety, and to the several commanding officers of the continental troops; that it be proclaimed in each of the United States, at the head of the army.

THE CONSTITUTION OF THE UNITED STATES OF AMERICA[1]

We the People of the United States, in Order to form a more perfect Union, establish Justice, insure domestic Tranquility, provide for the common defence, promote the general Welfare, and secure the Blessings of Liberty to ourselves and our Posterity, do ordain and establish this CONSTITUTION for the United States of America.

Article I

SECTION 1.

All legislative Powers herein granted shall be vested in a Congress of the United States, which shall consist of a Senate and House of Representatives.

SECTION 2.

The House of Representatives shall be composed of Members chosen every second Year by the People of the several States, and the Electors in each State shall have the Qualifications requisite for Electors of the most numerous Branch of the State Legislature.

No Person shall be a Representative who shall not have attained to the Age of twenty-five Years, and been seven Years a Citizen of the United States, and who shall not, when elected, be an Inhabitant of that State in which he shall be chosen.

[Representatives and direct Taxes[2] shall be apportioned among the several States which may be included within this Union, according to their respective Numbers, which shall be determined by adding to the whole Number of free Persons, including those bound to Service for a Term of Years, and excluding Indians not taxed, three fifths of all other Persons.][3] The actual Enumeration shall be made within three Years after the first Meeting of the Congress of the United States, and within every subsequent Term of ten Years, in such Manner as they shall by Law direct. The Number of Representatives shall not exceed one for every thirty Thousand, but each State shall have at Least one Representative; and until such enumeration shall be made, the State of New Hampshire shall be entitled to chuse three, Massachusetts eight, Rhode-Island and Providence Plantations one, Connecticut five, New York six, New Jersey four, Pennsylvania eight, Delaware one, Maryland six, Virginia ten, North Carolina five, South Carolina five, and Georgia three.

When vacancies happen in the Representation from any State, the Executive Authority thereof shall issue Writs of Election to fill such Vacancies.

The House of Representatives shall chuse their Speaker and other Officers; and shall have the sole Power of Impeachment.

SECTION 3.

The Senate of the United States shall be composed of two Senators from each State, chosen by the Legislature thereof, for six Years; and each Senator shall have one Vote.

Immediately after they shall be assembled in Consequence of the first Election, they shall be divided as equally as may be into three Classes. The Seats of the Senators of the first Class shall be vacated at the Expiration of the second Year, of the second Class at the Expiration of the fourth Year, and of the third Class at the Expiration of the sixth Year, so that one-third may be chosen every second Year; and if Vacancies happen by Resignation, or otherwise, during the Recess of the Legislature of any State, the Executive thereof may make temporary Appointments until the next Meeting of the Legislature, which shall then fill such Vacancies.

No Person shall be a Senator who shall not have attained to the Age of thirty Years, and been nine Years a Citizen of the United States, and who shall not, when elected, be an Inhabitant of that State for which he shall be chosen.

The Vice President of the United States shall be President of the Senate, but shall have no vote, unless they be equally divided.

The Senate shall chuse their other Officers, and also a President pro tempore, in the absence of the Vice President, or when he shall exercise the office of President of the United States.

The Senate shall have the sole Power to try all Impeachments. When sitting for that purpose they shall be on Oath or Affirmation. When the President of the United States is tried, the Chief Justice shall preside: And no person shall be convicted without the Concurrence of two thirds of the Members present.

Judgment in Cases of Impeachment shall not extend further than to removal from Office, and disqualification to hold and enjoy any Office of honor, Trust, or Profit under the United States: but the Party convicted shall nevertheless be liable and subject to Indictment, Trial, Judgment, and Punishment, according to Law.

SECTION 4.

The Times, Places and Manner of holding Elections for Senators and Representatives, shall be prescribed in each State by the Legislature thereof; but the Congress may at any time by Law make or alter such Regulations, except as to the Places of Chusing Senators.

The Congress shall assemble at least once in every Year, and such Meeting shall be on the first Monday in December, unless they shall by Law appoint a different day.

SECTION 5.

Each House shall be the Judge of the Elections, Returns and Qualifications of its own Members, and a Majority of each shall constitute a Quorum to do Business; but a smaller number may adjourn from day to day, and may be authorized to compel the Attendance of absent Members, in such Manner, and under such Penalties, as each House may provide.

---

[1] This version, which follows the original Constitution in capitalization and spelling, was published by the United States Department of the Interior, Office of Education, in 1935.

[2] Altered by the Sixteenth Amendment.

[3] Negated by the Fourteenth Amendment.

Each House may determine the Rules of its Proceedings, punish its Members for disorderly Behaviour, and, with the Concurrence of two thirds, expel a Member.

Each House shall keep a Journal of its Proceedings, and from time to time publish the same, excepting such Parts as may in their Judgment require Secrecy; and the Yeas and Nays of the Members of either House on any question shall, at the Desire of one fifth of those Present, be entered on the Journal.

Neither House, during the Session of Congress, shall, without the Consent of the other, adjourn for more than three days, nor to any other Place than that in which the two Houses shall be sitting.

Section 6.

The Senators and Representatives shall receive a Compensation for their Services, to be ascertained by Law, and paid out of the Treasury of the United States. They shall in all Cases, except Treason, Felony, and Breach of the Peace, be privileged from Arrest during their Attendance at the Session of their respective Houses, and in going to and returning from the same; and for any Speech or Debate in either House, they shall not be questioned in any other Place.

No Senator or Representative shall, during the Time for which he was elected, be appointed to any civil Office under the Authority of the United States, which shall have been created, or the Emoluments whereof shall have been increased, during such time; and no Person holding any Office under the United States shall be a Member of either House during his continuance in Office.

Section 7.

All Bills for raising Revenue shall originate in the House of Representatives; but the Senate may propose or concur with Amendments as on other bills.

Every Bill which shall have passed the House of Representatives and the Senate, shall, before it become a Law, be presented to the President of the United States; If he approve he shall sign it, but if not he shall return it, with his Objections, to that House in which it shall have originated, who shall enter the Objections at large on their Journal, and proceed to reconsider it. If after such Reconsideration two thirds of that House shall agree to pass the bill, it shall be sent, together with the objections, to the other House, by which it shall likewise be reconsidered, and if approved by two thirds of that House, it shall become a Law. But in all such Cases the Votes of both Houses shall be determined by Yeas and Nays, and the Names of the Persons voting for and against the Bill shall be entered on the Journal of each House respectively. If any Bill shall not be returned by the President within ten Days (Sundays excepted) after it shall have been presented to him, the Same shall be a Law, in like Manner as if he had signed it, unless the Congress by their Adjournment prevent its Return, in which Case it shall not be a Law.

Every Order, Resolution, or Vote to which the Concurrence of the Senate and House of Representatives may be necessary (except on a question of Adjournment) shall be presented to the President of the United States; and before the Same shall take Effect, shall be approved by him, or being disapproved by him,

shall be repassed by two thirds of the Senate and House of Representatives, according to the Rules and Limitations prescribed in the Case of a Bill.

Section 8.

The Congress shall have Power To lay and collect Taxes, Duties, Imposts and Excises, to pay the Debts and provide for the common Defence and general Welfare of the United States; but all Duties, Imposts and Excises shall be uniform throughout the United States;

To borrow money on the credit of the United States;

To regulate Commerce with foreign Nations, and among the several States, and with the Indian Tribes;

To establish an uniform rule of Naturalization, and uniform Laws on the subject of Bankruptcies throughout the United States;

To coin Money, regulate the Value thereof, and of foreign Coin, and fix the Standard of Weights and Measures;

To provide for the Punishment of counterfeiting the Securities and current Coin of the United States;

To establish Post Offices and post Roads;

To promote the Progress of Science and useful Arts, by securing for limited Times to Authors and Inventors the exclusive Right to their respective Writings and Discoveries;

To constitute Tribunals inferior to the Supreme Court;

To define and punish Piracies and Felonies committed on the high Seas, and Offenses against the Law of Nations;

To declare War, grant Letters of Marque and Reprisal, and make Rules concerning Captures on Land and Water;

To raise and support Armies, but no Appropriation of Money to that Use shall be for a longer Term than two Years;

To provide and maintain a Navy;

To make Rules for the Government and Regulation of the land and naval forces;

To provide for calling forth the Militia to execute the Laws of the Union, suppress Insurrections and repel Invasions;

To provide for organizing, arming, and disciplining the Militia, and for governing such Part of them as may be employed in the Service of the United States, reserving to the States respectively, the Appointment of the Officers, and the Authority of training the Militia according to the discipline prescribed by Congress;

To exercise exclusive Legislation in all Cases whatsoever, over such District (not exceeding ten Miles square) as may, by Cession of particular States, and the acceptance of Congress, become the Seat of the Government of the United States, and to exercise like Authority over all Places purchased by the Consent of the Legislature of the State in which the Same shall be, for the Erection of Forts, Magazines, Arsenals, Dockyards, and other needful Buildings;—And

To make all Laws which shall be necessary and proper for carrying into Execution for foregoing Powers, and all other Powers vested by this Constitution in the Government of the United States, or in any Department or Officer thereof.

Section 9.

The Migration or Importation of such Persons as any of the States now existing shall think proper to admit, shall not be prohibited by the Congress prior to the Year one thousand eight hundred and eight, but a tax or duty may be imposed on such Importation, not exceeding ten dollars for each Person.

The privilege of the Writ of Habeas Corpus shall not be suspended, unless when in Cases of Rebellion or Invasion the public Safety may require it.

No bill of Attainder or ex post facto Law shall be passed.

No capitation, or other direct, Tax shall be laid unless in Proportion to the Census or Enumeration herein before directed to be taken.

No Tax or Duty shall be laid on Articles exported from any State.

No Preference shall be given by any Regulation of Commerce or Revenue to the Ports of one State over those of another: nor shall Vessels bound to, or from, one State, be obliged to enter, clear, or pay Duties in another.

No Money shall be drawn from the Treasury, but in Consequence of Appropriations made by Law; and a regular Statement and Account of the Receipts and Expenditures of all public Money shall be published from time to time.

No title of Nobility shall be granted by the United States: And no Person holding any Office of Profit or Trust under them, shall, without the Consent of the Congress, accept of any present, Emolument, Office, or title, of any kind whatever, from any King, Prince, or foreign State.

Section 10.

No State shall enter into any Treaty, Alliance, or Confederation; grant Letters of Marque and Reprisal; coin Money; emit Bills of Credit; make any Thing but gold and silver Coin a Tender in Payment of Debts; pass any Bill of Attainder, ex post facto Law, or Law impairing the Obligation of Contracts, or grant any title of Nobility.

No State shall, without the Consent of the Congress, lay any Imposts or Duties on Imports or Exports, except what may be absolutely necessary for executing its inspection Laws; and the net Produce of all Duties and Imposts, laid by any State on Imports or Exports, shall be for the use of the Treasury of the United States; and all such Laws shall be subject to the Revision and Control of the Congress.

No state shall, without the Consent of Congress, lay any duty of Tonnage, keep Troops, or Ships of War in time of Peace, enter into any Agreement or Compact with another State, or with a foreign Power, or engage in War, unless actually invaded, or in such imminent Danger as will not admit of delay.

Article II

Section 1.

The executive Power shall be vested in a President of the United States of America. He shall hold his Office during the Term of four years, and, together with the Vice President, chosen for the same Term, be elected, as follows:

Each State shall appoint, in such Manner as the Legislature thereof may direct, a Number of Electors, equal to the whole Number of Senators and Representatives to which the State may be entitled in the Congress: but no Senator or Representative, or Person holding an Office of Trust or Profit under the United States, shall be appointed an Elector.

[The Electors shall meet in their respective States, and vote by Ballot for two persons, of whom one at least shall not be an Inhabitant of the same State with themselves. And they shall make a List of all the Persons voted for, and of the Number of Votes for each; which List they shall sign and certify, and transmit sealed to the Seat of the Government of the United States, directed to the President of the Senate. The President of the Senate shall, in the Presence of the Senate and House of Representatives, open all the Certificates, and the Votes shall then be counted. The Person having the greatest Number of Votes shall be the President, if such Number be a Majority of the whole Number of Electors appointed; and if there be more than one who have such Majority, and have an equal Number of Votes, then the House of Representatives shall immediately chuse by Ballot one of them for President; and if no Person have a Majority, then from the five highest on the list the said House shall in like Manner chuse the President. But in chusing the President, the Votes shall be taken by States, the Representation from each State having one Vote; a quorum for this Purpose shall consist of a Member or Members from two-thirds of the States, and a Majority of all the States shall be necessary to a Choice. In every Case, after the Choice of the President, the Person having the greatest Number of Votes of the Electors shall be the Vice President. But if there should remain two or more who have equal votes, the Senate shall chuse from them by Ballot the Vice President.][4]

The Congress may determine the Time of chusing the Electors, and the Day on which they shall give their Votes; which Day shall be the same throughout the United States.

No person except a natural-born Citizen, or a Citizen of the United States, at the time of the Adoption of this Constitution, shall be eligible to the Office of President; neither shall any Person be eligible to that Office who shall not have attained to the Age of thirty-five years, and been fourteen Years a Resident within the United States.

In Case of the Removal of the President from Office, or of his Death, Resignation, or Inability to discharge the Powers and Duties of the said Office, the same shall devolve on the Vice President, and the Congress may by Law provide for the Case of Removal, Death, Resignation, or Inability, both of the President and Vice President, declaring what Officer shall then act as President, and such Officer shall act accordingly, until the disability be removed, or a President shall be elected.

The President shall, at stated Times, receive for his Services a Compensation, which shall neither be increased nor diminished during the Period for which he shall have been elected, and he shall not receive within that Period any other Emolument from the United States, or any of them.

Before he enter on the execution of his Office, he shall take the following Oath or Affirmation:—"I do solemnly swear (or affirm) that I will faithfully execute the Office of President of the

---

[4]Revised by the Twelfth Amendment.

United States, and will, to the best of my Ability, preserve, protect, and defend the Constitution of the United States."

SECTION 2.

The President shall be Commander in Chief of the Army and Navy of the United States, and of the Militia of the several States, when called into the actual Service of the United States; he may require the Opinion, in writing, of the principal Officer in each of the executive Departments, upon any subject relating to the Duties of their respective Offices, and he shall have Power to Grant Reprieves and Pardons for Offenses against the United States, except in Cases of Impeachment.

He shall have Power, by and with the Advice and Consent of the Senate, to make Treaties, provided two-thirds of the Senators present concur; and he shall nominate, and by and with the Advice and Consent of the Senate, shall appoint Ambassadors, other public Ministers and Consuls, Judges of the supreme Court, and all other Officers of the United States, whose Appointments are not herein otherwise provided for, and which shall be established by Law: but the Congress may by Law vest the Appointment of such inferior Officers, as they think proper, in the President alone, in the Courts of Law, or in the Heads of Departments.

The President shall have Power to fill up all Vacancies that may happen during the Recess of the Senate, by granting Commissions which shall expire at the End of their next Session.

SECTION 3.

He shall from time to time give to the Congress Information of the State of the Union, and recommend to their Consideration such Measures as he shall judge necessary and expedient; he may, on extraordinary occasions, convene both Houses, or either of them, and in Case of Disagreement between them, with respect to the Time of Adjournment, he may adjourn them to such Time as he shall think proper; he shall receive Ambassadors and other public Ministers; he shall take care that the Laws be faithfully executed, and shall Commission all the Officers of the United States.

SECTION 4.

The President, Vice President and all civil Officers of the United States, shall be removed from Office on Impeachment for, and Conviction of, Treason, Bribery, or other high Crimes and Misdemeanors.

Article III

SECTION 1.

The judicial Power of the United States, shall be vested in one supreme Court, and in such inferior Courts as the Congress may from time to time ordain and establish. The Judges, both of the supreme and inferior Courts, shall hold their Offices during good Behaviour, and shall, at stated Times, receive for their Services, a Compensation, which shall not be diminished during their Continuance in Office.

SECTION 2.

The judicial Power shall extend to all Cases, in Law and Equity, arising under this Constitution, the Laws of the United States, and Treaties made, or which shall be made, under their Authority;—to all Cases affecting ambassadors, other public ministers and consuls;—to all cases of admiralty and maritime Jurisdiction;—to Controversies to which the United States shall be a Party;—to Controversies between two or more States;—between a State and Citizens of another State;[5]—between Citizens of different States—between Citizens of the same State claiming Lands under Grants of different States, and between a State, or the Citizens thereof, and foreign States, Citizens, or Subjects.

In all Cases affecting Ambassadors, other public Ministers and Consuls, and those in which a State shall be Party, the supreme Court shall have original Jurisdiction. In all the other Cases before mentioned, the supreme Court shall have appellate Jurisdiction, both as to Law and Fact, with such Exceptions, and under such Regulations as the Congress shall make.

The trial of all Crimes, except in Cases of Impeachment, shall be by Jury; and such Trial shall be held in the State where the said Crimes shall have been committed; but when not committed within any State, the Trial shall be at such Place or Places as the Congress may by Law have directed.

SECTION 3.

Treason against the United States, shall consist only in levying War against them, or in adhering to their Enemies, giving them Aid and Comfort. No Person shall be convicted of Treason unless on the Testimony of two Witnesses to the same overt Act, or on Confession in open Court.

The Congress shall have power to declare the Punishment of Treason, but no Attainder of Treason shall work Corruption of Blood, or Forfeiture except during the Life of the Person attained.

Article IV

SECTION 1.

Full Faith and Credit shall be given in each State to the public Acts, Records, and judicial Proceedings of every State. And the Congress may by general Laws prescribe the Manner in which such Acts, Records and Proceedings shall be proved, and the Effect thereof.

SECTION 2.

The Citizens of each State shall be entitled to all Privileges and Immunities of Citizens in the several States.

A Person charged in any State with Treason, Felony, or other Crime, who shall flee from Justice, and be found in another State, shall on demand of the executive Authority of the State from which he fled, be delivered up, to be removed to the State having Jurisdiction of the crime.

No Person held to Service or Labour in one State, under the Laws thereof, escaping into another, shall, in Consequence of any Law or Regulation therein, be discharged from such Service or Labour, but shall be delivered up on Claim of the Party to whom such Service or Labour may be due.

---

[5]Qualified by the Eleventh Amendment.

Section 3.

New States may be admitted by the Congress into this Union; but no new State shall be formed or erected within the Jurisdiction of any other State; nor any State be formed by the Junction of two or more States, or parts of States, without the Consent of the Legislatures of the States concerned as well as of the Congress.

The Congress shall have Power to dispose of and make all needful Rules and Regulations respecting the Territory or other Property belonging to the United States; and nothing in this Constitution shall be so construed as to Prejudice any Claims of the United States, or of any particular State.

Section 4.

The United States shall guarantee to every State in this Union a Republican Form of Government, and shall protect each of them against Invasion; and on Application of the Legislature, or of the Executive (when the Legislature cannot be convened) against domestic violence.

Article V

The Congress, whenever two-thirds of both Houses shall deem it necessary, shall propose Amendments to this Constitution, or, on the Application of the Legislatures of two-thirds of the several States, shall call a Convention for proposing Amendments, which, in either Case, shall be valid to all Intents and Purposes, as part of this Constitution, when ratified by the Legislatures of three-fourths of the several States, or by Conventions in three-fourths thereof, as the one or the other Mode of Ratification may be proposed by the Congress; Provided that no Amendment which may be made prior to the Year One thousand eight hundred and eight shall in any Manner affect the first and fourth Clauses in the Ninth Section of the first Article; and that no State, without its Consent, shall be deprived of its equal Suffrage in the Senate.

Article VI

All Depts contracted and Engagements entered into, before the Adoption of this Constitution, shall be as valid against the United States under this Constitution, as under the Confederation.

This Constitution, and the Laws of the United States which shall be made in Pursuance thereof; and all Treaties made, or which shall be made, under the Authority of the United States, shall be the supreme Law of the Land; and the Judges in every State shall be bound thereby, any Thing in the Constitution or Laws of any State to the Contrary notwithstanding.

The Senators and Representatives before mentioned, and the Members of the several State Legislatures, and all executive and judicial Officers, both of the United States and of the several States, shall be bound by Oath or Affirmation to support this Constitution; but no religious Tests shall ever be required as a qualification to any Office or public Trust under the United States.

Article VII

The Ratification of the Conventions of nine States shall be sufficient for the Establishment of this Constitution between the States so ratifying the same.

Done in convention by the Unanimous Consent of the States present the Seventeenth Day of September in the Year of our Lord one thousand seven hundred and Eighty seven, and of the Independence of the United States of America the Twelfth. In Witness whereof We have hereunto subscribed our Names.[6]

George Washington,
President and deputy from Virginia

New Hampshire
John Langdon
Nicholas Gilman

Massachusetts
Nathaniel Gorham
Rufus King

Connecticut
William Samuel Johnson
Roger Sherman

New York
Alexander Hamilton

Delaware
George Read
Gunning Beford, Jr.
John Dickinson
Richard Bassett
Jacob Broom

New Jersey
William Livingston
David Brearley
William Paterson
Jonathan Dayton

Pennsylvania
Benjamin Franklin
Thomas Mifflin
Robert Morris
George Clymer
Thomas FitzSimons
Jared Ingersoll
James Wilson
Gouverneur Morris

North Carolina
William Blount
Richard Dobbs Spaight
Hugh Williamson

Maryland
James McHenry
Daniel of St. Thomas
    Jenifer
Daniel Carroll

Virginia
John Blair
James Madison, Jr.

South Carolina
John Rutledge
Charles Cotesworth
    Pinckney
Charles Pinckney
Pierce Butler

Georgia
William Few
Abraham Baldwin

Articles in Addition to, and Amendment of, the Constitution of the United States of America, Proposed by Congress, and Ratified by the Legislatures of the Several States, Pursuant to the Fifth Article of the Original Constitution[7]

---

[6]These are the full names of the signers, which in some cases are not the signatures on the document.

[7]This heading appears only in the joint resolution submitting the first ten amendments.

[Article I]

Congress shall make no law respecting an establishment of religion, or prohibiting the free exercise thereof; or abridging the freedom of speech, or of the press; or the right of the people peaceably to assemble, and to petition the Government for a redress of grievances.

[Article II]

A well regulated Militia, being necessary to the security of a free State, the right of the people to keep and bear Arms shall not be infringed.

[Article III]

No Soldier shall, in time of peace, be quartered in any house, without the consent of the Owner, nor in time of war, but in a manner to be prescribed by law.

[Article IV]

The right of the people to be secure in their persons, houses, papers, and effects, against unreasonable searches and seizures, shall not be violated, and no Warrants shall issue, but upon probable cause, supported by Oath or affirmation, and particularly describing the place to be searched, and the persons or things to be seized.

[Article V]

No person shall be held to answer for a capital or otherwise infamous crime, unless on a presentment or indictment of a Grand Jury, except in cases arising in the land or naval forces, or in the Militia, when in actual service in time of War or public danger; nor shall any person be subject for the same offence to be twice put in jeopardy of life or limb; nor shall be compelled in any criminal case to be a witness against himself, nor be deprived of life, liberty, or property, without due process of law; nor shall private property be taken for public use, without just compensation.

[Article VI]

In all criminal prosecutions, the accused shall enjoy the right to a speedy and public trial, by an impartial jury of the State and district wherein the crime shall have been committed, which district shall have been previously ascertained by law, and to be informed of the nature and cause of the accusation; to be confronted with the witnesses against him; to have compulsory process for obtaining witnesses in his favour, and to have the Assistance of Counsel for his defence.

[Article VII]

In suits at common law, where the value in controversy shall exceed twenty dollars, the right of trial by jury shall be preserved, and no fact tried by a jury, shall be otherwise reexamined in any Court of the United States, than according to the rules of the common law.

[Article VIII]

Excessive bail shall not be required, nor excessive fines imposed, nor cruel and unusual punishments inflicted.

[Article IX]

The enumeration in the Constitution, of certain rights, shall not be construed to deny or disparage others retained by the people.

[Article X]

The powers not delegated to the United States by the Constitution, nor prohibited by it to the States, are reserved to the States respectively, or to the people. [Amendments I–X, in force 1791.]

[Article XI][8]

The Judicial power of the United States shall not be construed to extend to any suit in law or equity, commenced or prosecuted against one of the United States by Citizens of another State, or by Citizens or Subjects of any Foreign State.

[Article XII][9]

The Electors shall meet in their respective States and vote by ballot for President and Vice-President, one of whom, at least, shall not be an inhabitant of the same State with themselves; they shall name in their ballots the person voted for as President, and in distinct ballots the person voted for as Vice-President, and they shall make distinct lists of all persons voted for as President, and of all persons voted for as Vice-President, and of the number of votes for each, which lists they shall sign and certify, and transmit sealed to the seal of the government of the United States, directed to the President of the Senate;— The President of the Senate shall, in the presence of the Senate and House of Representatives, open all the certificates and the votes shall then be counted;—The person having the greatest number of votes for President, shall be the President, if such number be a majority of the whole number of Electors appointed; and if no person have such majority, then from the persons having the highest numbers not exceeding three on the list of those voted for as President, the House of Representatives shall choose immediately, by ballot, the President. But in choosing the President, the votes shall be taken by states, the representation from each state having one vote; a quorum for this purpose shall consist of a member or members from two-thirds of the states, and a majority of all the states shall be necessary to a choice. And if the House of Representatives shall not choose a President whenever the right of choice shall devolve upon them, before the fourth day of March next following, then the Vice-President shall act as President, as in the case of the death or other constitutional disability of the President.—The person having the greatest number of votes as Vice-President, shall be the Vice-President,

---

[8] Adopted in 1798.

[9] Adopted in 1804.

if such number be a majority of the whole number of Electors appointed, and if no person have a majority, then from the two highest numbers on the list, the Senate shall choose the Vice-President; a quorum for the purpose shall consist of two-thirds of the whole number of Senators, and a majority of the whole number shall be necessary to a choice. But no person constitutionally ineligible to the office of President shall be eligible to that of Vice-President of the United States.

[Article XIII][10]

SECTION 1.
Neither slavery nor involuntary servitude, except as a punishment for crime whereof the party shall have been duly convicted, shall exist within the United States, or any place subject to their jurisdiction.

SECTION 2.
Congress shall have power to enforce this article by appropriate legislation.

[Article XIV][11]

SECTION 1.
All persons born or naturalized in the United States, and subject to the jurisdiction thereof, are citizens of the United States and of the State wherein they reside. No State shall make or enforce any law which shall abridge the privileges or immunities of citizens of the United States; nor shall any State deprive any person of life, liberty, or property, without due process of law; nor deny to any person within its jurisdiction the equal protection of the laws.

SECTION 2.
Representatives shall be apportioned among the several States according to their respective numbers, counting the whole number of persons in each State, excluding Indians not taxed. But when the right to vote at any election for the choice of electors for President and Vice-President of the United States, Representatives in Congress, the Executive and Judicial officers of a State, or the members of the Legislature thereof, is denied to any of the male inhabitants of such State, being twenty-one years of age, and citizens of the United States, or in any way abridged, except for participation in rebellion, or other crime, the basis of representation therein shall be reduced in the proportion which the number of such male citizens shall bear to the whole number of male citizens twenty-one years of age in such State.

SECTION 3.
No person shall be a Senator or Representative in Congress, or elector of President and Vice-President, or hold any office, civil or military, under the United States, or under any State, who, having previously taken an oath, as a member of Congress, or as an officer of the United States, or as a member of any State leg-islature, or as an executive or judicial officer of any State, to support the Constitution of the United States, shall have engaged in insurrection or rebellion against the same, or given aid or comfort to the enemies thereof. But Congress may by a vote of two-thirds of each House, remove such disability.

SECTION 4.
The validity of the public debt of the United States, authorized by law, including debts incurred for payment of pensions and bounties for services in suppressing insurrection or rebellion, shall not be questioned. But neither the United States nor any State shall assume or pay any debts or obligation incurred in aid of insurrection or rebellion against the United States, or any claim for the loss or emancipation of any slave; but all such debts, obligations, and claims shall be held illegal and void.

SECTION 5.
The Congress shall have the power to enforce, by appropriate legislation, the provisions of this article.

[Article XV][12]

SECTION 1.
The right of citizens of the United States to vote shall not be denied or abridged by the United States or by any State on account of race, color, or previous condition of servitude—

SECTION 2.
The Congress shall have power to enforce this article by appropriate legislation.

[Article XVI][13]

The Congress shall have power to lay and collect taxes on incomes, from whatever source derived, without apportionment among the several States, and without regard to any census or enumeration.

[Article XVII][14]

The Senate of the United States shall be composed of two Senators from each State, elected by the people thereof, for six years; and each Senator shall have one vote. The electors in each State shall have the qualifications requisite for electors of the most numerous branch of the State legislatures.

When vacancies happen in the representation of any State in the Senate, the executive authority of such State shall issue writs of election to fill such vacancies: *Provided,* That the legislature of any State may empower the executive thereof to make temporary appointments until the people fill the vacancies by election as the legislature may direct.

This amendment shall not be so constructed as to affect the election or term of any Senator chosen before it becomes valid as part of the Constitution.

---

[10]Adopted in 1865.

[11]Adopted in 1868.

[12]Adopted in 1870.

[13]Adopted in 1913.

[14]Adopted in 1913.

[Article XVIII][15]

SECTION 1.

After one year from the ratification of this article the manufacture, sale, or transportation of intoxicating liquors within, the importation thereof into, or the exportation thereof from the United States and all territory subject to the jurisdiction thereof for beverage purposes is hereby prohibited.

SECTION 2.

The Congress and the several States shall have concurrent power to enforce this article by appropriate legislation.

SECTION 3.

This article shall be inoperative unless it shall have been ratified as an amendment to the Constitution by the legislatures of the several States, as provided in the Constitution, within seven years from the date of the submission hereof to the States by the Congress.

[Article XIX][16]

The right of citizens of the United States to vote shall not be denied or abridged by the United States or by any State on account of sex.

Congress shall have power to enforce this article by appropriate legislation.

[Article XX][17]

SECTION 1.

The terms of the President and Vice-President shall end at noon on the 20th day of January, and the terms of Senators and Representatives at noon on the 3d day of January, of the years in which such terms would have ended if this article had not been ratified; and the terms of their successors shall then begin.

SECTION 2.

The Congress shall assemble at least once in every year, and such meeting shall begin at noon on the 3d day of January, unless they shall by law appoint a different day.

SECTION 3.

If, at the time fixed for the beginning of the term of the President, the President elect shall have died, the Vice-President elect shall become President. If a President shall not have been chosen before the time fixed for the beginning of his term or if the President elect shall have failed to qualify, then the Vice-President elect shall act as President until a President shall have qualified; and the Congress may by law provide for the case wherein neither a President elect nor a Vice-President elect shall have qualified, declaring who shall then act as President, or the manner in which one who is to act shall be selected, and such person shall act accordingly until a President or Vice-President shall have qualified.

SECTION 4.

The Congress may by law provide for the case of the death of any of the persons from whom the House of Representatives may choose a President whenever the right of choice shall have developed upon them, and for the case of the death of any of the persons from whom the Senate may choose a Vice-President whenever the right of choice shall have developed upon them.

SECTION 5.

Sections 1 and 2 shall take effect on the 15th day of October following the ratification of this article.

SECTION 6.

This article shall be inoperative unless it shall have been ratified as an amendment to the Constitution by the legislatures of three-fourths of the several States within seven years from the date of its submission.

[Article XXI][18]

SECTION 1.

The eighteenth article of amendment to the Constitution of the United States is hereby repealed.

SECTION 2.

The transportation or importation into any State, Territory, or possession of the United States for delivery or use therein of intoxicating liquors, in violation of the laws thereof, is hereby prohibited.

SECTION 3.

This article shall be inoperative unless it shall have been ratified as an amendment to the Constitution by conventions in the several States, as provided in the Constitution, within seven years from the date of the submission hereof to the States by the Congress.

[Article XXII][19]

No person shall be elected to the office of the President more than twice, and no person who has held the office of President, or acted as President, for more than two years of a term to which some other person was elected President shall be elected to the office of the President more than once.

But this Article shall not apply to any person holding the office of President when this Article was proposed by the Congress, and shall not prevent any person who may be holding the office of President, or acting as President, during the term within which this Article becomes operative from holding the office of President or acting as President during the remainder of such term.

This article shall be inoperative unless it shall have been ratified as an amendment to the Constitution by the legislatures of three-fourths of the several states within seven years from the date of its submission to the states by the Congress.

---

[15]Adopted in 1918.

[16]Adopted in 1920.

[17]Adopted in 1933.

[18]Adopted in 1933.

[19]Adopted in 1961.

[Article XXIII][20]

SECTION 1.

The District constituting the seat of Government of the United States shall appoint in such manner as the Congress may direct:

A number of electors of President and Vice-President equal to the whole number of Senators and Representatives in Congress to which the District would be entitled if it were a State, but in no event more than the least populous State; they shall be in addition to those appointed by the States, but they shall be considered, for the purposes of the election of President and Vice-President, to be electors appointed by a State; and they shall meet in the District and perform such duties as provided by the twelfth article of amendment.

SECTION 2.

The Congress shall have power to enforce this article by appropriate legislation.

[Article XXIV][21]

SECTION 1.

The right of citizens of the United States to vote in any primary or other election for President or Vice President, for electors for President or Vice President, or for Senator or Representative in Congress, shall not be denied or abridged by the United States or any state by reason of failure to pay any poll tax or other tax.

SECTION 2.

The Congress shall have the power to enforce this article by appropriate legislation.

[Article XXV][22]

SECTION 1.

In case of the removal of the President from office or of his death or resignation, the Vice President shall become President.

SECTION 2.

Whenever there is a vacancy in the office of the Vice President, the President shall nominate a Vice President who shall take office upon confirmation by a majority vote of both Houses of Congress.

SECTION 3.

Whenever the President transmits to the President Pro Tempore of the Senate and the Speaker of the House of Representatives his written declaration that he is unable to discharge the powers and duties of his office, and until he transmits to them a written declaration to the contrary, such powers and duties shall be discharged by the Vice President as Acting President.

SECTION 4.

Whenever the Vice President and a majority of either the principal officers of the executive departments or of such other body as Congress may by law provide, transmit to the President Pro Tempore of the Senate and the Speaker of the House of Representatives their written declaration that the President is unable to discharge the powers and duties of his office, the Vice President shall immediately assume the powers and duties of the office as Acting President.

Thereafter, when the President transmits to the President Pro Tempore of the Senate and the Speaker of the House of Representatives his written declaration that no inability exists, he shall resume the powers and duties of his office unless the Vice President and a majority of either the principal officers of the executive departments or of such other body as Congress may by law provide, transmit within four days to the President Pro Tempore of the Senate and the Speaker of the House of Representatives their written declaration that the President is unable to discharge the powers and duties of his office. Thereupon Congress shall decide the issue, assembling within forty-eight hours for that purpose if not in session. If the Congress, within twenty-one days after receipt of the latter written declaration, or, if Congress is not in session, within twenty-one days after Congress is required to assemble, determines by two-thirds vote of both Houses that the President is unable to discharge the powers and duties of his office, the Vice President shall continue to discharge the same as Acting President; otherwise, the President shall resume the powers and duties of his office.

[Article XXVI][23]

SECTION 1.

The right of citizens of the United States, who are eighteen years of age or older, to vote shall not be denied or abridged by the United States or by any State on account of age.

SECTION 2.

The Congress shall have power to enforce this article by appropriate legislation.

[Article XXVII][24]

No law varying the compensation for the services of Senators and Representatives shall take effect until an election of Representatives shall have intervened.

---

[20] Adopted in 1961.

[21] Adopted in 1964.

[22] Adopted in 1967.

[23] Adopted in 1971.

[24] Adopted in 1992.

PRESIDENTIAL ELECTIONS

Year	Candidates	Parties	Popular Vote	Percentage of Popular Vote	Electoral Vote	Percentage of Voter Participation
1789	**GEORGE WASHINGTON (Va.)***				69	
	John Adams				34	
	Others				35	
1792	**GEORGE WASHINGTON (Va.)**				132	
	John Adams				77	
	George Clinton				50	
	Others				5	
1796	**JOHN ADAMS (Mass.)**	Federalist			71	
	Thomas Jefferson	Democratic Republican			68	
	Thomas Pinckney	Federalist			59	
	Aaron Burr	Dem.-Rep.			30	
	Others				48	
1800	**THOMAS JEFFERSON (Va.)**	Dem.-Rep.			73	
	Aaron Burr	Dem.-Rep.			73	
	John Adams	Federalist			65	
	C. C. Pinckney	Federalist			64	
	John Jay	Federalist			1	
1804	**THOMAS JEFFERSON (Va.)**	Dem.-Rep.			162	
	C. C. Pinckney	Federalist			14	
1808	**JAMES MADISON (Va.)**	Dem.-Rep.			122	
	C. C. Pinckney	Federalist			47	
	George Clinton	Dem.-Rep.			6	
1812	**JAMES MADISON (Va.)**	Dem.-Rep.			128	
	De Witt Clinton	Federalist			89	
1816	**JAMES MONROE (Va.)**	Dem.-Rep.			183	
	Rufus King	Federalist			34	
1820	**JAMES MONROE (Va.)**	Dem.-Rep.			231	
	John Quincy Adams	Dem.-Rep.			1	
1824	**JOHN Q. ADAMS (Mass.)**	Dem.-Rep.	108,740	30.5	84	26.9
	Andrew Jackson	Dem.-Rep.	153,544	43.1	99	
	William H. Crawford	Dem.-Rep.	46,618	13.1	41	
	Henry Clay	Dem.-Rep.	47,136	13.2	37	
1828	**ANDREW JACKSON (Tenn.)**	Democratic	647,286	56.0	178	57.6
	John Quincy Adams	National Republican	508,064	44.0	83	
1832	**ANDREW JACKSON (Tenn.)**	Democratic	687,502	55.0	219	55.4
	Henry Clay	National Republican	530,189	42.4	49	
	John Floyd	Independent			11	
	William Wirt	Anti-Mason	33,108	2.6	7	
1836	**MARTIN VAN BUREN (N.Y.)**	Democratic	765,483	50.9	170	57.8
	W. H. Harrison	Whig			73	
	Hugh L. White	Whig	739,795	49.1	26	
	Daniel Webster	Whig			14	
	W. P. Magnum	Independent			11	
1840	**WILLIAM H. HARRISON (Ohio)**	Whig	1,274,624	53.1	234	80.2
	Martin Van Buren	Democratic	1,127,781	46.9	60	
	J. G. Birney	Liberty	7,069		—	
1844	**JAMES K. POLK (Tenn.)**	Democratic	1,338,464	49.6	170	78.9
	Henry Clay	Whig	1,300,097	48.1	105	
	J. G. Birney	Liberty	62,300	2.3	—	

*State of residence at time of election.

Year	Candidates	Parties	Popular Vote	Percentage of Popular Vote	Electoral Vote	Percentage of Voter Participation
1848	**ZACHARY TAYLOR (La.)**	Whig	1,360,967	47.4	163	72.7
	Lewis Cass	Democratic	1,222,342	42.5	127	
	Martin Van Buren	Free-Soil	291,263	10.1	—	
1852	**FRANKLIN PIERCE (N.H.)**	Democratic	1,601,117	50.9	254	69.6
	Winfield Scott	Whig	1,385,453	44.1	42	
	John P. Hale	Free-Soil	155,825	5.0	—	
1856	**JAMES BUCHANAN (Pa.)**	Democratic	1,832,955	45.3	741	78.9
	John C. Frémont	Republican	1,339,932	33.1	114	
	Millard Fillmore	American	871,731	21.6	8	
1860	**ABRAHAM LINCOLN (Ill.)**	Republican	1,865,593	39.8	180	81.2
	Stephen A. Douglas	Democratic	1,382,713	29.5	12	
	John C. Breckinridge	Democratic	848,356	18.1	72	
	John Bell	Union	592,906	12.6	39	
1864	**ABRAHAM LINCOLN (Ill.)**	Republican	2,213,655	55.0	212	73.8
	George B. McClellan	Democratic	1,805,237	45.0	21	
1868	**ULYSSES S. GRANT (Ill.)**	Republican	3,012,833	52.7	214	78.1
	Horatio Seymour	Democratic	2,703,249	47.3	80	
1872	**ULYSSES S. GRANT (Ill.)**	Republican	3,597,132	55.6	286	71.3
	Horace Greeley	Democratic; Liberal Republican	2,834,125	43.9	66	
1876	**RUTHERFORD B. HAYES (Ohio)**	Republican	4,036,298	48.0	185	81.8
	Samuel J. Tilden	Democratic	4,300,590	51.0	184	
1880	**JAMES A. GARFIELD (Ohio)**	Republican	4,454,416	48.5	214	79.4
	Winfield S. Hancock	Democratic	4,444,952	48.1	155	
1884	**GROVER CLEVELAND (N.Y.)**	Democratic	4,874,986	48.5	219	77.5
	James G. Blaine	Republican	4,851,981	48.2	182	
1888	**BENJAMIN HARRISON (Ind.)**	Republican	5,439,853	47.9	233	79.3
	Grover Cleveland	Democratic	5,540,309	48.6	168	
1892	**GROVER CLEVELAND (N.Y.)**	Democratic	5,556,918	46.1	277	74.7
	Benjamin Harrison	Republican	5,176,108	43.0	145	
	James B. Weaver	People's	1,041,028	8.5	22	
1896	**WILLIAM McKINLEY (Ohio)**	Republican	7,104,779	51.1	271	79.3
	William J. Bryan	Democratic-People's	6,502,925	47.7	176	
1900	**WILLIAM McKINLEY (Ohio)**	Republican	7,207,923	51.7	292	73.2
	William J. Bryan	Dem.-Populist	6,358,133	45.5	155	
1904	**THEODORE ROOSEVELT (N.Y.)**	Republican	7,623,486	57.9	336	65.2
	Alton B. Parker	Democratic	5,077,911	37.6	140	
	Eugene V. Debs	Socialist	402,283	3.0	—	
1908	**WILLIAM H. TAFT (Ohio)**	Republican	7,678,098	51.6	321	65.4
	William J. Bryan	Democratic	6,409,104	43.1	162	
	Eugene V. Debs	Socialist	420,793	2.8	—	
1912	**WOODROW WILSON (N.J.)**	Democratic	6,293,454	41.9	435	58.8
	Theodore Roosevelt	Progressive	4,119,538	27.4	88	
	William H. Taft	Republican	3,484,980	23.2	8	
	Eugene V. Debs	Socialist	900,672	6.0	—	
1916	**WOODROW WILSON (N.J.)**	Democratic	9,129,606	49.4	277	61.6
	Charles E. Hughes	Republican	8,538,221	46.2	254	
	A. L. Benson	Socialist	585,113	3.2	—	
1920	**WARREN G. HARDING (Ohio)**	Republican	16,152,200	60.4	404	49.2
	James M. Cox	Democratic	9,147,353	34.2	127	
	Eugene V. Debs	Socialist	919,799	3.4	—	
1924	**CALVIN COOLIDGE (Mass.)**	Republican	15,725,016	54.0	382	48.9
	John W. Davis	Democratic	8,386,503	28.8	136	
	Robert M. LaFollette	Progressive	4,822,856	16.6	13	
1928	**HERBERT HOOVER (Calif.)**	Republican	21,391,381	58.2	444	56.9
	Alfred E. Smith	Democratic	15,016,443	40.9	87	
	Norman Thomas	Socialist	267,835	0.7	—	

Year	Candidates	Parties	Popular Vote	Percentage of Popular Vote	Electoral Vote	Percentage of Voter Participation
1932	**FRANKLIN D. ROOSEVELT (N.Y.)**	Democratic	22,821,857	57.4	472	56.9
	Herbert Hoover	Republican	15,761,841	39.7	59	
	Norman Thomas	Socialist	881,951	2.2	—	
1936	**FRANKLIN D. ROOSEVELT (N.Y.)**	Democratic	27,751,597	60.8	523	61.0
	Alfred M. Landon	Republican	16,679,583	36.5	8	
	William Lemke	Union	882,479	1.9	—	
1940	**FRANKLIN D. ROOSEVELT (N.Y.)**	Democratic	27,244,160	54.8	449	62.5
	Wendell L. Willkie	Republican	22,305,198	44.8	82	
1944	**FRANKLIN D. ROOSEVELT (N.Y.)**	Democratic	25,602,504	53.5	432	55.9
	Thomas E. Dewey	Republican	22,006,285	46.0	99	
1948	**HARRY S. TRUMAN (Mo.)**	Democratic	24,105,695	49.5	304	53.0
	Thomas E. Dewey	Republican	21,969,170	45.1	189	
	J. Strom Thurmond	State-Rights Democratic	1,169,021	2.4	38	
	Henry A. Wallace	Progressive	1,156,103	2.4	—	
1952	**DWIGHT D. EISENHOWER (N.Y.)**	Republican	33,936,252	55.1	442	63.3
	Adlai E. Stevenson	Democratic	27,314,992	44.4	89	
1956	**DWIGHT D. EISENHOWER (N.Y.)**	Republican	35,575,420	57.6	457	60.6
	Adlai E. Stevenson	Democratic	26,033,066	42.1	73	
	Other	—	—		1	
1960	**JOHN F. KENNEDY (Mass.)**	Democratic	34,227,096	49.9	303	62.8
	Richard M. Nixon	Republican	34,108,546	49.6	219	
	Other	—			15	
1964	**LYNDON B. JOHNSON (Tex.)**	Democratic	43,126,506	61.1	486	61.7
	Barry M. Goldwater	Republican	27,176,799	38.5	52	
1968	**RICHARD M. NIXON (N.Y.)**	Republican	31,770,237	43.4	301	60.6
	Hubert H. Humphrey	Democratic	31,270,533	42.7	191	
	George Wallace	American Indep.	9,906,141	13.5	46	
1972	**RICHARD M. NIXON (N.Y.)**	Republican	47,169,911	60.7	520	55.2
	George S. McGovern	Democratic	29,170,383	37.5	17	
	Other	—	—		1	
1976	**JIMMY CARTER (Ga.)**	Democratic	40,828,587	50.0	297	53.5
	Gerald R. Ford	Republican	39,147,613	47.9	241	
	Other	—	1,575,459	2.1	—	
1980	**RONALD REAGAN (Calif.)**	Republican	43,901,812	50.7	489	52.6
	Jimmy Carter	Democratic	35,483,820	41.0	49	
	John B. Anderson	Independent	5,719,722	6.6	—	
	Ed Clark	Libertarian	921,188	1.1	—	
1984	**RONALD REAGAN (Calif.)**	Republican	54,455,075	59.0	525	53.3
	Walter Mondale	Democratic	37,577,185	41.0	13	
1988	**GEORGE BUSH (Texas)**	Republican	47,946,422	54.0	426	50.2
	Michael S. Dukakis	Democratic	41,016,429	46.0	112	
1992	**WILLIAM J. CLINTON (Ark.)**	Democratic	44,908,233	43.3	370	55.2
	George Bush	Republican	39,102,282	37.7	168	
	Ross Perot	Independent	19,721,433	19.0	—	
1996	**WILLIAM J. CLINTON (Ark.)**	Democratic	47,401,185	49.3	379	
	Robert Dole	Republican	39,197,469	40.7	159	49.0
	Ross Perot	Reform	8,085,294	8.4	—	
2000	**GEORGE W. BUSH (Texas)**	Republican	50,459,211	47.89	271	51.0
	Albert Gore, Jr.	Democratic	51,003,894	48.41	266	
	Ralph Nader	Green	2,834,410	2.69	—	
2004	**GEORGE W. BUSH (Texas)**	Republican	62,028,285	50.73	286	
	John Kerry	Democratic	59,028,109	48.27	251	60.0
	Ralph Nader	Independent	463,647	0.38	—	
2008	**BARACK OBAMA (Ill.)**	Democratic	65,070,489	53	364	61.7
	John McCain	Republican	57,154,810	46	174	

Note: All data from www.fec.gov (federal election commission) www.fec.gov/pubrec/fe2004/2004presgen.shtml

FOR FURTHER READING

Chapter 1

Alvin M. Josephy, ed., *America in 1492: The World of the Indian Peoples Before the Arrival of Columbus* (1993) and Brian M. Fagan, *The Great Journey: The Peopling of Ancient America* (1987) provide introductions to pre-Columbian history, as does Charles Mann, *1491: New Revelations of the Americas Before Columbus* (2005). William M. Denevan, ed., *The Native Population of the Americas in 1492* (1976) and Russell Thornton, *American Indian Holocaust and Survival: A Population History Since 1492* (1987) are important contributions to the debate over the size and character of the American population before Columbus. Alfred Crosby, *The Columbian Exchange: Biological and Cultural Consequences of 1492* (1972) explores the results of European-Indian contact in both the Americas and Europe. Hugh Thomas, *Rivers of Gold: The Rise of the Spanish Empire from Columbus to Magellan* (2004) is a good popular history of the Spanish Empire. D. W. Meinig, *The Shaping of America, Vol. I: Atlantic America, 1492–1800* (1986) is an account of the early contacts between Europeans and the New World. Gary Nash, *Red, White and Black: The Peoples of Early America* (1982) provides a brief, multiracial survey of colonial America. Philip Curtin, *The Atlantic Slave Trade: A Census* (1969) has become the indispensable starting point for understanding African forced migration to the Americas. John Thornton, *Africa and Africans in the Making of the Atlantic World* (1998) examines the impact of slavery and the slave trade on the entire Atlantic world from the fifteenth through the eighteenth centuries. One outstanding collection of essays that summarizes modern scholarship on colonial America is Jack P. Greene and J. R. Pole, eds., *Colonial British America: Essays in the New History of the Early Modern Era* (1984). *Columbus and the Age of Discovery* (1991) is a seven-part documentary film series on Christopher Columbus, his era, and his legacy.

Chapter 2

William Cronon, *Changes in the Land: Indians, Colonists, and the Ecology of New England* (1983) examines the social and environmental effects of English settlement in colonial America. Richard White, *The Middle Ground: Indians, Empires, and Republics in the Great Lakes Region, 1650–1815* (1991) is an important study of the accommodations that Indians and early European settlers made in the continental interior. James H. Merrell, *The Indians' New World* (1991) and *Into the American Woods: Negotiators on the Pennsylvania Frontier* (1999) are among the best examinations of the impact of European settlement on eastern tribes. Nathaniel Philbrick, *Mayflower, A Story of Community, Courage, and War* (2006) is a vivid story of the Plymouth migration. Perry Miller, *The New England Mind: From Colony to Province* (1953) is a classic exposition of the Puritan intellectual milieu. David Hall, *Worlds of Wonder, Days of Judgment* (1990) is a good counterpoint to Miller. Michael Kammen, *Colonial New York* (1975) illuminates the diversity and pluralism of New York under the Dutch and the English. Russell Shorto, *The Island at the Center of the World* (2003) is a portrait of Dutch Manhattan. Edmund Morgan, *American Slavery, American Freedom* (1975) is a compelling narrative of political and social development in early Virginia. Peter Wood, *Black Majority* (1974) describes the early importance of slavery in the founding of South Carolina. Richard S. Dunn, *Sugar and Slaves: The Rise of the Planter Class in the English West Indies, 1624–1713* (1972) is important for understanding the origins of British colonial slavery. David J. Weber, *The Spanish Frontier in North America* (1992) and James C. Brooks, *Captains and Cousins: Slavery, Kinship, and Community in the Southwest Borderlands* (2002) examine the northern peripheries of the Spanish Empire.

Chapter 3

Edward Countryman, *Americans: A Collision of Histories* (1996) includes a vivid picture of the many cultures that encountered one another in early America. Bernard Bailyn, *Voyagers to the West: A Passage in the Peopling of America on the Eve of the Revolution* (1986) reveals the complexity and scope of European emigration to North America. Bailyn's *The Origin of American Politics* (1968) is an introduction to colonial politics. David Hackett Fischer, *Albion's Seed* (1989) suggests four major folkways for English migrants to America. Jack P. Greene, *Pursuits of Happiness: The Social Development of Early Modern British Colonies and the Formation of American Culture* (1986) is a broad portrait of life in early American communities. Laurel Thatcher Ulrich, *Good Wives: Image and Reality in the Lives of Women in Northern New England, 1650–1750* (1982) examines women's roles in colonial New England, and Mary Beth Norton, *In the Devil's Snare: The Salem Witchcraft Crisis of 1692* (2002) explores the role of gender in a sensational seventeenth-century controversy. John Demos, *The Unredeemed Captive: A Family Story of Early America* (1994) is a vivid, unconventional account of the experiences of a New England girl captured by Indians. Ira Berlin, *Many Thousands Gone: The First Two Centuries of Slavery in North America* (1998), Philip Morgan, *Slave Counterpoint: Black Culture in the Eighteenth-Century Chesapeake and Lowcountry* (1998), and Jill Lepore, *New York Burning: Liberty, Slavery, and Conspiracy in Eighteenth-Century New York* (2005) are important studies of slavery in the colonial era. Robin Blackburn, *The Making of New World Slavery: From the Baroque to the Modern, 1492–1800* (1997) includes an important examination of the character of the institution in colonial America. Kathleen M. Brown, *Good Wives, Nasty Wenches, and Anxious Patriarchs: Gender, Race and Power in Colonial Virginia* (1996) places gender at the center of the development of slavery in the Chesapeake. Rhys Isaac, *The Transformation of Virginia, 1740–1790* (1982) uses the methods of cultural anthropology in an influential study of the world of the colonial Virginia gentry.

Chapter 4

Fred Anderson, *The Crucible of War: The Seven Years' War and the Fate of Empire in British North America, 1754–1766* (2000) is an account of the critical years in which the British Empire transformed itself through its colonial wars in America. David Armitage, *The Ideological Origins of the British Empire* (2000) examines the ideas of those who promoted and sought to justify Britain's imperial ambitions. Francis Jennings, *The Ambiguous Iroquois Empire* (1984) examines the critical role of the Iroquois in the conflicts over empire in North America. Richard Bushman, *King and People in Colonial Massachusetts* (1987) traces the fracture between Massachusetts colonists and the imperial government. Gary Nash, *The Urban Crucible: The Northern Seaports and the Origins of the American Revolution* (1979) argues that increasing class stratification in northern cities contributed to the coming of the American Revolution. T. H. Breen, *The Marketplace of Revolution* (2004) argues that consumer politics played a major role in creating the Revolution. Jon Butler, *Becoming America: The Revolution Before 1776* (2000) argues for the emergence of a distinctive American culture in the eighteenth century. Robert R. Palmer, *The Age of Democratic Revolution: Vol. 1, The Challenge* (1959) and J. G. A. Pocock, *The Machiavellian Moment* (1975) both place the American Revolution in the context of a transatlantic political culture. Bernard Bailyn, *The Ideological Origins of the American Revolution* (1967) emphasizes the importance of English republican political thought for the revolutionary ideology of the American colonists.

Chapter 5

Robert Middlekauf, The Glorious Cause: The American Revolution, 1763–1789 (1985), a volume in the Oxford History of the United States, is a thorough, general history of the Revolution. Edward Countryman, *The American Revolution* (1985) is a useful, briefer overview. Gordon Wood, *The Radicalism of the American Revolution* (1992) emphasizes the profound political change that the Revolution produced. Charles Royster, *A Revolutionary People at War: The Continental Army and American Character* (1979) suggests the importance of military service for American men. David Hackett Fisher, *Washington's Crossing* (2004) uses this famous event to illuminate the meaning of the Revolution. Robert Gross, *The Minutemen and Their World* (1976) is an excellent social history of Revolutionary Concord. Mary Beth Norton, *Liberty's Daughters: The Revolutionary Experience of American Women, 1750–1800* (1980) demonstrates that the Revolution had a significant impact on the lives of American women as well. Eric Foner, *Tom Paine and Revolutionary America* (1976) connects the leading pamphleteer of the Revolution with urban radicalism in Philadelphia. Pauline Maier, *American Scripture* (1997) is a penetrating study of the making of the Declaration of Independence, and of its impact on subsequent generations of Americans. Devid McCullough, *1776* (2005) is a vivid account of Independence. Colin Calloway, *The American Revolution in Indian Country* (1995) is a study of an often-neglected aspect of the war. Sylvia R. Frey, *Water from the Rock: Black Resistance in a Revolutionary Age* (1991) argues that the American Revolution was a major turning point in the history of slavery in the American South. Gary B. Nash, *The Forgotten Fifth: African Americans in the Age of Revolution* (2006) is an account of the

impact of the Revolution on black Americans. Alan Taylor, *The Divided Ground: Indians, Settlers, and the Northern Borderlands of the American Revolution* (2006) describes how the Iroquois nations tried to navigate the war to their advantage.

Chapter 6

Charles Beard, *An Economic Interpretation of the Constitution of the United States* (1913) is one of the seminal works of modern American historical inquiry, although its interpretation is no longer widely accepted. Gordon Wood, *The Creation of the American Republic* (1969) is the leading analysis of the intellectual path from the Declaration of Independence to the American Constitution. Wood is also the author of *The Radicalism of the American Revolution* (1991) and *Empire of Liberty: A History of the Early Republic, 1789–1815* (2009). Jack Rakove, *Original Meanings: Politics and Ideas in the Making of the Constitution* (1996) connects the politics of the 1780s with the political ideas embedded in the Constitution. Stanley Elkins and Eric McKitrick, *The Age of Federalism* (1993) provides a detailed overview of political and economic development in the 1790s. Joyee Appleby, *Capitalism and a New Social Order: The Republican Vision of the 1790s* (1984) highlights liberal and capitalist impulses unleashed after the ratification of the Constitution. Drew McCoy, *The Elusive Republic: Political Economy in Jeffersonian America* (1980) is an account of the politics of the era of the Constitution. Joseph Ellis is the author of several books on the founders: *After the Revolution: Profiles of Early American Culture* (1979), which examines some of the framers of the new nation; *American Sphinx: The Character of Thomas Jefferson* (1997); *Founding Brothers: The Revolutionary Generation* (2000); *Passionate Sage: The Character and Legacy of John Adams* (1993); and *American Creation* (2007), a portrait of the nation from Independence to the Louisiana Purchase. David McCullough, *John Adams* (2001) is a sympathetic biography, Ron Chernow, *Alexander Hamilton* (2004) and *George Washington* (2010) and Edmund Morgan, *Benjamin Franklin* (2002) are biographies of the founders.

Chapter 7

Joseph J. Ellis, *American Sphinx: The Character of Thomas Jefferson* (1997) is a perceptive study of the man, and his *After the Revolution: Profiles of Early American Culture* (2002) offers portraits of some of his allies and opponents. Henry Adams, *History of the United States During the Administration of Jefferson and Adams*, 9 vols. (1889–1891) is one of the great literary achievements of early American historiography. Frank Bergon, ed., *The Journals of Lewis and Clark* (1989) is a concise abridgment of these fascinating accounts of their explorations. James Ronda, *Lewis and Clark among the Indians* (1984) examines the exploration from a Native American perspective. Thomas C. Cochran, *Frontiers of Change: Early Industrialization in America* (1981) summarizes economic development in the early republic. Jeanne Boydston, *Home and Work: Housework, Wages, and the Ideology of Labor in the Early Republic* (1990) argues that the cultural status of women declined as the market revolution began to transform the American economy. Drew McCoy, *The Elusive Republic: Political Economy in Jeffersonian America* (1980) traces the Jeffersonian struggle to keep the United States free from European-style corruption and decay. Paul Finkleman, *Slavery and the Founders: Race and Liberty in the Age of Jefferson* (1996) considers the problem of slavery in the early republic. Gary Wills, *James Madison* (2002) is an interpretive essay on this important early president. Donald Hickey, *The War of 1812: A Forgotten Conflict* (1989) is an account of the war. J. C. A. Stagg, *Mr. Madison's War: Politics, Diplomacy, and Warfare in the Early American Republic, 1783–1830* (1983) argues that James Madison led the United States to war against Great Britain in order to preserve vital American commercial interests, but that he underestimated New England opposition to the war.

Chapter 8

Daniel Walker Howe, *What Hath God Wrought: The Transformation of America, 1815–1848* (2007) is a synthetic study of the period following the War of 1812. Sean Wilentz, *The Rise of American Democracy: Jefferson to Lincoln* (2005) is a history of the rise of a "democratic creed" in early America. Frederick Jackson Turner, *The Frontier in American History* (1920) is the classic statement of American exceptionalism. John Mack Faragher, *Women and Men on the Overland Trail* (1979) was an early and influential book in the "new western history" that challenged Turner; his *Sugar Creek* (1987) portrays the society of the Old Northwest in the early nineteenth century. Robert V. Remini, *Andrew Jackson and the Course of American Empire: 1767–1821* (1977) emphasizes Andrew Jackson's importance in American territorial expansion in the South prior to 1821 and in the development of American nationalism. Morton J. Horwitz, *The Transformation of American Law, 1780–1865* (1977), an American legal history, connects changes in the law to changes in the American economy. Ernest R. May, *The Making of the Monroe Doctrine* (1975) presents the history of a leading principle of American foreign policy.

Chapter 9

Daniel Walker Howe, *What Hath God Wrought: The Transformation of America, 1815–1848* (2007) and Sean Wilentz, *The Rise of American Democracy: From Jefferson to Lincoln* (2005) are two important, broad studies of the "age of Jackson." Arthur M. Schlesinger Jr., *The Age of Jackson* (1945), a classic study, represents Jacksonian politics as an eastern, urban democratic movement of working men and upper-class intellectuals. Bray Hammond, *Banks and Politics in America from the Revolution to the Civil War* (1957) challenges Schlesinger by arguing that the Bank War was essentially a struggle between different groups of capitalist elites. Harry L. Watson, *Liberty and Power: The Politics of Jacksonian America* (1990) provides an important newer synthesis of Jacksonian politics. Donald B. Cole, *Martin Van Buren and the American Political System* (1984) examines the emergence of modern notions of party through the career of Van Buren. Richard Hofstadter, *The Idea of a Party System: The Rise of Legitimate Opposition in the United States, 1740–1840* (1969) traces the growing acceptance of the idea of partisan competition. Daniel Walker Howe, *The Political Culture of the American Whigs* (1979) analyzes the careers of several leading Whig politi-

cians, including the Whig triumvirate of Calhoun, Clay, and Webster. William V. Freehling, *Prelude to Civil War: The Nullification Controversy in South Carolina* (1966) argues that South Carolina planters' anxiety over the fate of slavery was at the heart of the nullification crisis. Francis P. Prucha, *American Indian Policy in the Formative Years* (1962) is an overview of early Indian policy by the leading scholar of the subject. Michael Rogin, *Fathers and Children: Andrew Jackson and the Destruction of American Indians* (1975) offers a more radical and idiosyncratic perspective on Jackson's career as an Indian fighter using the methods of psychoanalysis. Sean Wilentz, *Chants Democratic: New York City and the Rise of the American Working Class, 1788–1850* (1984) is an important study of working-class ideology during the Jacksonian period.

Chapter 10

Charles G. Sellers, *The Market Revolution: Jacksonian America, 1815–1846* (1991) demonstrates the overwhelming impact of the market revolution on American social and political development. George R. Taylor, *The Transportation Revolution* (1951) is an account of economic development in the antebellum period. Peter Bernstein, *The Wedding of the Waters* (2005) is an account of the creation of the Eric Canal. Christopher Clark, *The Roots of Rural Capitalism; Western Massachusetts, 1780–1860* (1990) is an examination of the impact of emerging capitalism on a rural area. Paul Johnson, *A Shopkeeper's Millennium: Society and Revivals in Rochester, New York, 1815–1837* (1978) explores the changing character of class relations in upstate New York in an age of rapid economic development. Alice Kessler-Harris, *Out to Work: A History of Wage-Earning Women in the United States* (1982) is a broad history of women in the wage labor force. Thomas Dublin, *Transforming Women's Work: New England Lives in the Industrial Revolution* (1994) looks particularly at the mill towns of the Northeast. Mary Ryan, *Cradle of the Middle Class: The Family in Oneida County, New York, 1790–1865* (1981) demonstrates the relationship between the market revolution and the changing character of middle-class family structure. Christine Stansell, *City of Women: Sex and Class in New York, 1789–1860* (1983) explores the female world of antebellum New York City. John Bodnar, *The Transplanted: A History of Immigrants in America* (1985) is a useful survey. Paul W. Gates, *The Farmer's Age: Agriculture, 1815–1860* (1966) is an important overview. Alan Taylor, *William Cooper's Town: Power and Persuasion on the Frontier in the Early American Republic* (1995) examines the early years of Cooperstown, New York, and the impact on it of the rise of the market and of democratic politics.

Chapter 11

Peter Kolchin, *American Slavery, 1619–1877* (1993) is a synthesis of the history of slavery in the United States from the settlement of Virginia through Reconstruction. Ira Berlin, *Many Thousands Gone* (2000) and *Generations of Captivity* (2003) are other histories of slavery. Walter Johnson, *Soul by Soul: Life Inside the Antebellum Slave Market* (2001) examines the slave trade. James Oakes, *Slavery and Freedom* (1990) provides an overview of southern politics and society in the antebellum period. Eugene

Genovese's classic study, *Roll, Jordan, Roll: The World the Slaves Made* (1974) argues that masters and slaves forged a system of mutual obligations within a fundamentally coercive social system Genovese's *The Political Economy of Slavery* (1965) argues that slavery blocked southern economic development. Mclvin Patrick Ely, *Israel on the Appomattox* (2004) is a chronicle of a free black community in Virginia prior to the Civil War. James Oakes, *The Ruling Race: A History of American Slaveholders* (1982) argues that slaveowners were hardheaded businessmen and capitalists. Frederick Douglass's *Narrative of the Life of Frederick Douglass*, first published in 1845, is a classic autobiography. Elizabeth Fox-Genovese, *Within the Plantation Household* (1988) argues against the idea that black and white women shared a community of interests on southern plantations. Charles Joyner, *Down by the Riverside: A South Carolina Slave Community* (1984) is a fine study of slavery in a single community. Adam Rothman, *Slave Country* (2007) examines the expansion of the South, and of slavery within it. Charles C. Bolton, *Poor Whites of the Antebellum South: Tenants and Laborers in Central North and Northeast Mississippi* (1994) and Stephanic McCurry, *Masters of Small Worlds: Yeoman Households, Gender Relations, and the Political Culture of the Antebellum South Carolina Low Country* (1997) are good studies of neglected groups in the southern population. Bertram Wyatt-Brown, *Southern Honor: Ethics and Behavior in the Old South* (1982) argues that concepts of honor lay at the core of southern white identity in the antebellum period. Steven Hahn. *The Roots of Southern Populism: Yeoman Farmers and the Transformation of the Georgia Upcountry, 1850–1890* (1983) argues that white farmers in upcountry regions of the antebellum South maintained economically self-sufficient communities on the periphery of the market.

Chapter 12

Steven Mintz, *Moralists and Moralizers: America's Pre–Civil War Reformers* (1995) and Ronald G. Walters, *American Reformers, 1815–1860* (1978) are overviews David Reynolds, *Walt Whitman's America* (1995) is both a cultural biography of Whitman and an evocation of the society Whitman celebrated. Leo Marx, *The Machine in the Garden* (1964) is an influential study of the tension between technological progress and the veneration of nature in the era of early industrialization. Nancy F. Cott, *The Bonds of Womanhood: "Woman's Sphere" in New England, 1780–1835* (1977) argues that nineteenth-century feminism emerged from the separation of home and work in the early nineteenth-century. Klaus J. Hansen, *Mormonism and the American Experience* (1981) examines the emergence of the most important new religion in nineteenth-century America. Ellen C. Dubois, *Feminism and Suffrage: The Emergence of an Independent Women's Movement in America, 1848–1869* (1978) examines the origins of the suffrage movement. David Brion Davis, *The Problem of Slavery in the Age of Revolution, 1770–1823* (1975) is an influential study of the rise of antislavery sentiment in the Western world. James Brewer Stewart, *Holy Warriors* (1976) is a good summary of the trajectory of abolitionism from the American Revolution through the emancipation. Ronald G. Walters, *The Antislavery Appeal: American Abolitionists After*

1830 (1976) emphasizes the religious motivations of antebellum abolitionism.

Chapter 13

Richard White, *It's Your Misfortune and None of My Own: A History of the American West* (1991) is a presentation of the social and economic history of the region. Anders Stephanson, *Manifest Destiny* (1995) briefly traces the origins of American expansion ideology. Robert M. Johannsen, *To the Halls of Montezuma: The Mexican War in the American Imagination* (1985) examines public attitudes toward the conflict. Paul D. Lack, *The Texas Revolutionary Experience: A Political and Social History, 1835–1836* (1992) chronicles Texas's route to independence from Mexico. Malcolm Rorabaugh, *Days of Gold: The California Gold Rush and the American Nation* (1997) is an account of this seminal event in the history of the West. Susan Lee Johnson, *Roaring Camp: The Social World of the Gold Rush* (2000) examines the experiences of men and women involved in the frenzy. David M. Pletcher, *The Diplomacy of Annexation: Texas, Oregon, and the Mexican War* (1973) chronicles war and diplomacy in the 1840s. Reginald Horsman, *Race and Manifest Destiny* (1981) is a seminal study of racial views in antebellum America. William W. Freehling, *The Road to Disunion, Vol. 1: Secessionists at Bay, 1776–1854* (1990) and *Vol. 2: Secessionists Triumphant, 1854–1861* (2007) explore the successful containment of sectionalism prior to the 1850s. David Potter, *The Impending Crisis, 1848–1861* (1976) is a thorough summary of a turbulent decade. Eric Foner, *Free Soil, Free Labor, Free Men* (1970) traces the emergence of the Republican Party, Michael Holt, *The Political Crisis of the 1850s* (1978) challenges Foner by emphasizing ethnic and religious alignment in northern politics, and in *The Fate of Their Country* (2004), he emphasizes the role of partisan politics as a key to the coming of the war. Don E. Fehrenbacher, *The Dred Scott Case* (1978) explains the Supreme Court's most infamous decision. Manisha Sinha, *The Counterrevolution of Slavery* (2000) argues that South Carolina's apparently radical drive for secession was in fact a highly conservative effort in defense of slavery.

Chapter 14

James McPherson, *Battle Cry of Freedom* (1988) is a history of the Civil War. Shelby Foote, *The Civil War: A Narrative*, 3 vols. (1958–1974) recounts the military history of the war. David Donald, *Lincoln* (1995) is a biography of the sixteenth president. James M. McPherson, *Abraham Lincoln and the Second American Revolution* (1990) offers reflections on the life and significance of Lincoln. Eric Foner, *The Fiery Trial* (2010) is a history of Lincoln and slavery. Doris Kearns Goodwin, *Team of Rivals* (2005) examines Lincoln's diverse and sometimes fractious Cabinet. Douglas Southall Freeman, *Robert E. Lee*, 4 vols. (1934–1935) and William McFeely, *Grant* (1981) are the leading biographies of the two most important Civil War generals. Philip Shaw Paludan, *"A People's Contest": The Union at War, 1861–1865* (1988) is a good account of the social impact of the war in the North. Iver Bernstein, *The New York City Draft Riots* (1990) examines an important event away from the battlefield. Jennifer L. Weber, *Copperheads* (2006) examines Northern opponents of the Civil War. Alvin Josephy, *The Civil War in the West* (1992) remedies a long-neglected aspect of the war. Emory Thomas, *The Confederate Nation* (1979) is a one-volume history of the Confederacy. Drew Gilpin Faust is the author of *Mothers of Invention* (1996), which examines the lives of elite Southern women during the war, and *The Republic of Suffering: Death and the American Civil War* (2008). Ira Berlin et al., eds., *Free at last: A Documentary History of Slavery, Freedom and the Civil War* (1992) is a superb compilation of primary sources from slaves and slaveowners relating to the demise of slavery during the Civil War years. Ira Berlin et al., *Slaves No More: Three Essays on Emancipation and the Civil War* (1992), the companion volume to the documents in *Free at Last,* argues that slaves and freedmen played an active role in destroying slavery and redefining freedom. Catherine Clinton and Nina Silber, *Divided Houses* (1992) is a collection of essays in the "new social history" from various historians demonstrating the importance of gender to the history of the Civil War. Edward L. Ayres, *In the Presence of Mine Enemies: War in the Heart of America* (2003) is a social history of two neighboring communities—one in the Union, the other in the Confederacy—at war. William Freehling, *The South vs. the South* (2001) notes the important role of pro-Union Southerners in determining the outcome of the war.

Chapter 15

Eric Foner, *Reconstruction: America's Unfinished Revolution, 1863–1877* (1988), a modern synthesis of Reconstruction scholarship, emphasizes the radicalism of Reconstruction and the role of freed people in the process of political and economic renovation. Thomas Holt, *Black over White: Negro Political Leadership in South Carolina During Reconstruction* (1977) examines Reconstruction in the state where black political power reached its apex. C. Vann Woodward, *Origins of the New South* (1951) is a classic work on the history of the South after Reconstruction and argues that a rising middle class defined the economic and political transformation of the New South. Nicholas Lemann, *Redemption: The Last Battle of the Civil War* (2006) reveals the determination of white southerners to regain control of their society. Edward Ayers, *The Promise of the New South* (1992) offers a portrait of social and cultural life in the New South. Jacqueline Jones, *Labor of Love, Labor of Sorrow* (1985) examines the lives of African American women after Emancipation. Leon Litwack, *Been in the Storm So Long: The Aftermath of Slavery* (1979) is a study of the experiences of freed slaves. Steven Hahn, *A Nation Under Our Feet: Black Political Struggles in the Rural South from Slavery to the Great Migration* (2003) is a wide-ranging history. C. Vann Woodward, *The Strange Career of Jim Crow* (rev. 1974) claims that segregation emerged only gradually across the South after Reconstruction. The "Woodward Thesis" has been challenged by, among others, Joel Williamson, *After Slavery: The Negro in South Carolina During Reconstruction* (1965); John W. Cell, *The Highest Stage of White Supremacy: The Origins of Segregation in South Africa and the American South* (1982); and Howard N. Rabinowitz, *Race Relations in the Urban South, 1865–1890* (1978).

Chapter 16

Frederick Jackson Turner's *The Frontier in American History* (1920) is a classic argument on the centrality of the frontier experience to American democracy. His argument frames much of the later historical writing on the West, most of which rejects the "Turner thesis." Patricia Nelson Limerick's *The Legacy of Conquest: The Unbroken Past of the American West* (1987) argues that the West was not a frontier but rather an inhabited place conquered by Anglo-Americans. Richard White. *"It's Your Misfortune and None of My Own": A History of the American West* (1991) is a general history of the region that revises many myths about the West. Ronald Takaki, *Strangers from a Different Shore: A History of Asian Americans* (1989) surveys the experiences of Asian Americans as immigrants to America's western shore. Jean Pfaelzer, *Driven Out: The Forgotten War Against Chinese Americans* (2007) illustrates anti-Chinese sentiment. John Mack Faragher, *Women and Men on the Overland Trail* (1979) examines the social experience of westering migrants, and Peggy Pascoe, *Relations of Rescue: The Search for Female Authority in the American West, 1874–1939* (1990) describes the female communities of the West. William Cronon, *Nature's Metropolis and the Great West* (1991) describes the relationships among economies and environments in the West. Jon Gjerde, *The Minds of the West: Ethnocultural Evolution in the Rural Middle West, 1830–1914* (1997) examines the impact of ethnicity on the shaping of the agrarian West. Robert Wooster, *The Military and United States Indian Policy, 1865–1902* (1988) and Sally Denton, *American Massacre: The Tragedy at Mountain Meadows, September 1857* (2003) examine the military campaigns against the Indians in the nineteenth century. Frederick E. Hoxie, *A Final Promise: The Campaign to Assimilate the Indians, 1880–1920* (1984) examines U.S. policies toward Native Americans in the years after the end of the Indian Wars. John Mack Faragher, *Daniel Boone* (1992) is a study of one of the West's most fabled figures. Richard Slotkin, *The Fatal Environment: The Myth of the Frontier in the Age of Industrialization* (1985) and *Gunfighter Nation* (1992) are provocative cultural studies of the idea of the West. Henry Nash Smith, *Virgin Land* (1950) is a classic study of the West in American culture. Rebecca Solnit, *River of Shadows: Edward Muybridge and the Technological Wild West* (2003) considers the impact of photography on images of the West.

Chapter 17

Robert Wiebe's *The Search for Order, 1877–1920* (1968) is an analysis of America's evolution from a society of what he calls island communities to a national urban society. David Nasaw, *Andrew Carnegie* (2006) is a biography of one of the first and most famous industrial tycoons, who also became a noted philanthropist. Alfred D. Chandler Jr. describes the new business practices that made industrialization possible in *The Visible Hand: The Managerial Revolution in American Business* (1977) and *Scale and Scope: The Dynamics of Industrial Capitalism* (1990). Olivier Zunz analyzes the social underpinnings of the new corporate order in *Making America Corporate, 1870–1920* (1990) and *Why the American Century?* (1998). David F. Noble, *America by Design:*

Science, Technology, and the Rise of Corporate Capitalism (1977) and David Hounshell, *From the American System to Mass Production, 1800–1932* (1984) discuss the explosion of science and technology in the era of rapid industrialization. Douglas Brinkley, *Wheels for the World* (2003) is a history of the Ford Motor Company. Daniel Rodgers, *The Work Ethic in Industrial America, 1850–1920* (1978) is an intellectual history of the way Americans viewed industrial workers. David Montgomery, *The Fall of the House of Labor: The Workplace, the State, and American Labor Activism, 1865–1925* (1987) analyzes the way industrialization shaped (and was shaped by) the workers, their expertise, and the strong cultural traditions of the shop floor. Alice Kessler-Harris documents the tremendous movement of women into the workforce in the period in *Out of Work: A History of Wage-Earning Women in the United States* (1982). John L. Thomas, *Alternative America: Henry George, Edward Bellamy, Henry Demarest Lloyd, and the Adversary Tradition* (1983) examines some important critics of corporate capitalism.

Chapter 18

Lewis Mumford, author of *The City in History* (1961), was America's foremost critic and chronicler of urbanization through the mid-twentieth century. John Bodnar provides a synthetic history of immigration in *The Transplanted: A History of Immigrants in America* (1985), which challenges an earlier classic study by Oscar Handlin, *The Uprooted: The Epic Story of the Great Migrations That Made the American People* (1973, 2nd ed.). The new urban mass culture of America's cities is the subject of William Leach, *Land of Desire: Merchants, Power, and the Rise of a New American Culture* (1993), and Kathy Peiss, *Cheap Amusements: Working Women and Leisure in Turn-of-the-Century New York* (1986). Stuart Blumin, *The Emergence of the Middle Class: Social Experience in the American City, 1760–1900* (1989) examines urban society and culture. T. J. Jackson Lears, *No Place of Grace: Antimodernism and the Transformation of American Culture, 1880–1920* (1981) chronicles patterns of resistance to the new culture. Debby Applegate, *The Most Famous Man in America: The Biography of Henry Ward Beecher* (2006) examines a renowned clergyman who was also a spokesman for modernity. Roy Rosenzweig and Elizabeth Blackmar, *The Park and the People: A History of Central Park* (1992) studies the creation of America's most famous public park. Edwin G. Burrows and Mike Wallace, *Gotham: A History of New York City to 1898* (1998) is a thorough history of New York's remarkable growth. John F. Kasson, *Amusing the Millions: Coney Island at the Turn of the Century* (1978) is an illustrated history and interpretation of the amusement park's place in American culture.

Chapter 19

Morton Keller, *Affairs of State: Public Life in Late Nineteenth-Century America* (1977) is a study of politics and government after Reconstruction as is Brian Balogh, *A Government Out of Sight: The Mystery of National Authority in Nineteenth-Century America* (2009). Nell Irvin Painter's *Standing at Armageddon: The United States, 1877–1919* (1987) explores the multicultural dimensions of industrialization, emphasizing the particularly

cataclysmic effect of industrialization on minority populations and on race relations. Martin J. Sklar, *The Corporate Reconstruction of American Capitalism, 1890–1916* (1988) offers an interpretation of the evolution of American business practice and, by extension, American politics and society. Two books charting the growing capacities of the American state during this period are Theda Skocpol, *Protecting Soldiers and Mothers: The Political Origins of Social Policy in the United States* (1992); and Stephen Skowronek, *Building a New American State: The Expansion of National Administrative Capacities, 1877–1920* (1982). Richard Hofstadter's *The Age of Reform: From Bryan to FDR* (1955) and Lawrence Goodwyn's *The Populist Moment* (1978) offer sharply contrasting characterizations of the populist and progressive reform movements of this time. Other important studies of populism include John D. Hicks, *The Populist Revolt* (1931), a classic account, and Steven Hahn, *The Roots of Southern Populism: Yeoman Farmers and the Transformation of the Georgia Upcountry* (1983). Michael Kazin, *The Populist Persuasion: An American History* (1995) places populist ideas in a broad historical context. Walter LaFeber, *The New Empire: An Interpretation of American Expansion, 1860–1898* (1963) and Ernest May, *Imperial Democracy* (1961) are important introductions to the subject. David F. Healy, *U.S. Expansionism: Imperialist Urge in the 1890s* (1970) is a contrasting view. Walter LaFeber, *The Cambridge History of American Foreign Policy, Vol. 2: The Search for Opportunity, 1865–1913* (1993) is an overview. William Appleman Williams, *The Tragedy of American Diplomacy*, rev. ed. (1972), is a classic revisionist work on the origins and consequences of American imperialism, supplemented by his *Empire as a Way of Life: An Essay on the Causes and Character of America's Present Predicament* (1982). Anders Stephanson, *Manifest Destiny: American Expansionism and the Empire of Right* (1995) is a short history of Americans' ideology of expansionism. Warren Zimmermann, *First Great Triumph: How Five Americans Made Their Country a Great Power* (2002) describes a circle of powerful figures who together helped create an ideology of empire for the United States in the early twentieth century. Robert L. Beisner's *Twelve Against Empire* (1968) chronicles the careers of the leading opponents of imperial expansion. Emily S. Rosenberg, *Spreading the American Dream: American Economic and Cultural Expansion, 1890–1945* (1982) is a cultural interpretation. Gerald F. Linderman, *The Mirror of War: American Society and the Spanish-American War* (1974) examines the social meaning of the war within the United States. Stuart Creighton Miller, *"Benevolent Assimilation": The American Conquest of the Philippines, 1899–1903* (1982) describes the American war in the Philippines. Michael Hunt, *The Making of a Special Relationship: The United States and China to 1914* (1983) is an introduction to the subject.

Chapter 20

Richard Hofstadter, *The Age of Reform: From Bryan to FDR* (1955) is a classic, and now controversial, analysis of the origins of the populist and progressive movements. Robert Wiebe, *The Search for Order, 1877–1920* (1967) is an important organizational interpretation of the era. Gabriel Kolko makes a distinctly revisionist argument that business conservatism was at the heart of the progressive movement in *The Triumph of Conservatism* (1963). Alan Dawley, *Struggles for Justice: Social Responsibility and the Liberal State* (1991) and Michael McGerr, *A Fierce Discontent: The Rise and Fall of the Progressive Movement in America, 1870–1920* (2003) are contrasting synthetic accounts of progressive movements and their ideas. John Milton Cooper, *The Pivotal Decades: The United States, 1900–1920* (1990) is a good narrative history of the period. For powerful insights into pragmatism, an important philosophical underpinning to much reform, see Robert Westbrook, *John Dewey and American Democracy* (1991) and Louis Menand, *The Metaphysical Club: A Story of Ideas* (2001). Thomas L. Haskell, *The Emergence of Professional Social Science* (1977) is an important study of the social sciences and professionalism. Paul Stare, *The Social Transformation of American Medicine* (1982) is a pathbreaking study of the emergence of modern systems of health care. Richard Greenwald, *The Triangle Fire, the Protocols of Peace, and Industrial Democracy in Progressive Era New York* (2006) examines a critical event in stimulating reform.

Nancy Cott, *The Grounding of American Feminism* (1987) studies the shifting roles and beliefs of women. Kathryn Kish Sklar, *Florence Kelley and the Nation's Work: The Rise of Women's Political Culture, 1830–1900* (1995) examines the impact of female reformers on the progressive movement and the nation's political culture as a whole. Glenda Gilmore, Gender and Jim Crow: *Women and the Politics of White Supremacy in North Carolina, 1896–1920* (1996) examines the role of gender in the construction of segregation. Louis Harlan, *Booker T. Washington: The Making of a Black Leader* (1956) and *Booker T. Washington: The Wizard of Tuskegee* (1983) are parts of an outstanding multivolume biography, as are David Levering Lewis, *W. E. B. Du Bois: Biography of a Race* (1993) and *W. E. B. Du Bois: The Fight for Equality and the American Century* (2000).

John Milton Cooper Jr. compares the lives and ideas of the progressive movement's leading national politicians in *The Warrior and the Priest: Woodrow Wilson and Theodore Roosevelt* (1983). He is also the author of *Woodrow Wilson: A Biography* (2009). John Morton Blum, *The Republican Roosevelt* (1954) is a long-popular brief study. Donald E. Anderson, *William Howard Taft* (1973) is a useful account of this unhappy presidency. Arthur S. Link is Wilson's most thorough biographer and the author of *Woodrow Wilson*, 5 vols. (1947–1965). Thomas K. McCraw, *Prophets of Regulation* (1984) is an excellent examination of important figures in the making of modern state capacity. Michael McGerr, *The Decline of Popular Politics* (1986) is an examination of the decline of public enthusiasm for parties in the North in the late nineteenth and early twentieth centuries. Samuel P. Hays, *The Gospel of Efficiency: The Progressive Conservation Movement, 1890–1920* (1962) describes the organizational imperatives behind the conservation movement, and Stephen R. Fox, *The American Conservation Movement: John Muir and His Legacy* (1981) is another such study. John Opie, *Nature's Nation: An Environmental History of the United States* (1998) is an ambitious synthesis of environmental history.

Chapter 21

Ernest R. May, *The World War and American Isolation* (1959) is an authoritative account of America's slow and controversial entry into the Great War. Frank Freidel provides an account of the American soldier's battlefield experience during World War I in *Over There: The Story of America's First Great Overseas Crusade* (1964). David Kennedy, *Over Here: The First World War and American Society* (1980) is a study of the domestic impact of the war. Robert D. Cuff, *The War Industries Board: Business-Government Relations During World War II* (1973) is an account of mobilization for war in the United States. Ronald Schaffer, *America in the Great War: The Rise of the War Welfare State* (1991) examines the ways in which mobilization for war created new public benefits for various groups, including labor. Maureen Greenwald, *Women, War, and Work* (1980) describes the impact of World War I on women workers. John Keegan, *The First World War* (1998) is a military history. Thomas Knock, *To End All Wars: Woodrow Wilson and the Quest for a New World Order* (1992) is a study of the battle for peace. Arno Mayer, *Wilson vs. Lenin* (1959) and *Politics and Diplomacy of Peacemaking: Containment and Counterrevolution* (1965) are revisionist accounts of the peacemaking process. Margaret MacMillan, *Paris 1919: Six Months That Changed the World* (2002) is an account of the Paris Peace Conference. America's stormy debate over immigration and national identity before, during, and after World War I is captured by John Higham, *Strangers in the Land: Patterns of American Nativism* (1955). William M. Tuttle Jr., in *Race Riot: Chicago in the Red Summer of 1919* (1970), recounts the terrible riots of 1919 that showed America violently divided along racial and ideological lines. Paul L. Murphy, *World War I and the Origins of Civil Liberties* (1979) shows how wartime efforts to quell dissent created new support for civil liberties. Beverly Gage, *The Day Wall Street Exploded* (2009) tells the story of postwar terrorism and the responses to it.

Chapter 22

Frederick Lewis Allen, *Only Yesterday* (1931) is a classic popular history of the 1920s. Michael Parrish, *Anxious Decades: America in Prosperity and Depression, 1920–1941* (1992) is a good survey. Ellis Hawley, *The Great War and the Search for a Modern Order* (1979) describes the effect of World War I on American ideas, culture, and society. William E. Leuchtenburg, *The Perils of Prosperity* (rev. ed. 1994) reveals the class divisions and culture dislocation that accompanied economic prosperity in the 1920s. David Brody, *Workers in Industrial America* (1980) is a series of essays on welfare capitalism and other labor systems of the 1920s. T. J. Jackson Lears, *Fables of Abundance: A Cultural History of Advertising in America* (1994) and Roland Marchand, *Advertising the American Dream* (1985) are inquiries into the role of advertising in the new consumer culture. James J. Flink, *The Car Culture* (1975) examines ways in which the automobile transformed American life. David Farber, *Sloan Rules: Alfred P. Sloan and the Triumph of General Motors* (2002) describes the consolidation of the giant automobile corporation. Susan Smulyan, *Selling Radio: The Commercialization of American*

Broadcasting, 1920–1934 (1994) chronicles the emergence of commercial radio. Alan Brinkley, *The Publisher: Henry Luce and His American Century* (2010) describes the rise of an important magazine empire. Robert Lynd and Helen Merrell Lynd, *Middletown* (1929) is a classic sociological study of how an American city encountered the consumer culture and economy of the 1920s. Ann Douglas's *Terrible Honesty: Mongrel Manhattan in the 1920s* (1995) examines the cultural and political history of the New Era in New York City. Lynn Dumenil, *The Modern Temper: America in the 1920s* (1995) examines the reactions of Americans to modern culture. George Chauncey, *Gay New York: Gender, Urban Culture, and the Making of the Gay Male World, 1890–1940* (1994) is an excellent work in a relatively new field of history. The decline of the feminist movement in the 1920s is explored in Nancy Cott, *The Grounding of American Feminism* (1987). Gary Gerstle, *American Crucible* (2000) is an important study of the changing role of race and ethnicity in defining American nationhood in the twentieth century. Nathan I. Huggins chronicles the cultural and political efflorescence of black Harlem during these years in *Harlem Renaissance* (1971). George Marsden, *Fundamentalism and American Culture* (1980) is a study of some of the religious battles that came to a head in the 1920s. Edward J. Larson, *Summer for the Gods: The Scopes Trial and America's Continuing Debate over Science and Religion* (1997) is an analysis of the Scopes trial. Leonard Moore, *Citizen Klansmen: The Ku Klux Klan in Indiana, 1921–1928* (1991) is a view of the Klan. Kathleen M. Blee, *Women and the Klan: Racism and Gender in the 1920s* (1991) re-creates the female world of the Klan. Michael Lerner, *Dry Manhattan: Prohibition in New York City* (2007) describes the impact of the Eighteenth Amendment Kevin Boyle, *Arc of Justice: A Saga of Race, Civil Rights, and Murder in the Jazz Age* (2004) is a portrait of New Era racial norms. David Burner, *The Politics of Provincialism* (1967) is a study of the ordeal of the Democratic Party in the 1920s. Morton Keller, *Regulating a New Economy: Public Policy and Economic Change in America, 1900–1933* (1990) and *Regulating a New Society: Public Policy and Social Change in America, 1900–1933* (1994) are studies of New Era public policy.

Chapter 23

Donald Worster scathingly indicts agricultural capitalism for its destruction of the plains environment in *Dust Bowl: The Southern Plains in the 1930s* (1979). Timothy Egan, *The Worst Hard Time* (2006) is a portrait of the impact of the Dust Bowl. In *The Great Depression: Delayed Recovery and Economic Change in America, 1929–1939* (1987), Michael Bernstein argues that we should ask not so much why the economy crashed in 1929 but rather why the expected recovery from the crash was so slow. Richard Pells, *Radical Visions and American Dreams: Culture and Social Thought in the Depression Years* (1973) is an important survey of the cultural and intellectual history of the 1930s. Studs Terkel, *Hard Times* (1970) is an oral history of the Depression. Susan Ware analyzes the effect of the Great Depression on women in *Holding Their Own: American Women in the 1930s* (1982). The Communist Party's most popular period in the United States is the subject of Harvey Klehr's *The Heyday of*

American Communism: The Depression Decade (1984) and, from quite different viewpoints, Robin D. G. Kelley, *Hammer and Hoe: Alabama Communists during the Great Depression* (1990) and Michael Denning, *The Cultural Front: The Laboring of American Culture in the Twentieth Century* (1997). Joan Hoff Wilson, *Herbert Hoover: Forgotten Progressive* (1975) argues that President Hoover was in many ways a surprisingly progressive thinker about the American social order.

Chapter 24

William E. Leuchtenburg, *Franklin D. Roosevelt and the New Deal* (1963) is a history of the New Deal. Anthony Badger, *The New Deal: The Depression Years* (1989) is another overview. David Kennedy, *Freedom from Fear: The American People in Depression and War, 1929–1945* (1999) is a narrative history. Geoffrey Ward, *Before the Trumpet: Young Franklin Roosevelt, 1882–1905* (1985) and *A First-Class Temperament: The Emergence of Franklin Roosevelt* (1989) are biographical accounts of the pre-presidential FDR. Frank Freidel, *Franklin D. Roosevelt: A Rendezvous with Destiny* (1990) is a one-volume biography by one of FDR's most important biographers. Alan Brinkley, *Franklin Delano Roosevelt* (2009) is a short biography. Jonathan Alter, *The Defining Moment* (2006) and Anthony Badger, *FDR: The First Hundred Days* (2008) portray the first months of the New Deal. Ellis Hawley, *The New Deal and the Problem of Monopoly* (1967) is a classic examination of the economic policies of the Roosevelt administration in its first five years. Colin Gordon, *New Deals: Business, Labor, and Politics in America, 1920–1935* (1994) is a reinterpretation of the early New Deal years. Michael Janeway, *The Fall of the House of Roosevelt* (2004) is an account of the complex group of New Dealers who shaped not only Roosevelt's government, but policy and politics beyond the New Deal as well. The transformation of liberalism after 1937 is the subject of Alan Brinkley, *The End of Reform: New Deal Liberalism in Recession and War* (1995). Jennifer Klein, *For All These Rights: Business, Labor, and the Shaping of America's Public-Private Welfare State* (2003) sees the origin of the modern welfare state as a product in part of struggles between labor and capital. Linda Gordon, *Pitied but Not Entitled: Single Mothers and the History of Welfare* (1994) is a pioneering work on women as the recipients and also the authors of government welfare policies. Alice Kessler-Harris, *In Pursuit of Equity: Women, Men, and the Quest for Economic Citizenship in Twentieth-Century America* (2001) is a study of the intersection of gender and economic rights. The efforts of Chicago workers to protest and organize is the subject of Lizabeth Cohen, *Making a New Deal: Industrial Workers in Chicago, 1919–1939* (1990). Nelson Lichtenstein, *The Most Dangerous Man in Detroit: Walter Reuther and the Fate of American Labor* (1995) is a study of one of the early leaders of the CIO. Richard Lowitt, *The New Deal and the West* (1984) pays particular attention to water policy and agriculture in the New Deal years. Jordan Schwarz, *The New Dealers: Power Politics in the Age of Roosevelt* (1993) examines the proponents of state-funded economic development of the South and West. Alan Brinkley, *Voices of Protest: Huey Long, Father Coughlin, and the Great Depression* (1982) examines some of the most powerful challenges to the

New Deal. Bruce Shulman, *From Cotton Belt to Sunbelt* (1991) explores the New Deal's effort to transform the region Roosevelt and others considered the nation's number-one economic problem, the American South. Harvard Sitkoff, *A New Deal for Blacks* (1978) and Nancy J. Weiss, *Farewell to the Party of Lincoln: Black Politics in the Age of FDR* (1983) take contrasting positions on what the New Deal did for African Americans.

Chapter 25

Robert Dallek, *Franklin D. Roosevelt and American Foreign Policy, 1932–1945* (1979) is a comprehensive study of Roosevelt's foreign policy, Akira Iriye, *The Cambridge History of American Foreign Relations, Vol. 3: The Globalizing of America, 1913–1945* (1993) is another important study. In *Inevitable Revolutions* (1983), Walter LaFeber recounts America's attempts to halt revolutionary movements throughout the world. James MacGregor Burns, *Roosevelt: The Soldier of Freedom* (1970) and Warren F. Kimball, *The Juggler: Franklin Roosevelt as Wartime Statesman* (1991) are two studies of the wartime president. Wayne S. Cole, *Charles A. Lindbergh and the Battle Against American Intervention in World War II* (1974) and *Roosevelt and the Isolationists, 1932–1945* (1983) examine prewar isolationism. A. Scott Berg, *Lindbergh* (1998) is a biography of the aviation hero who became a controversial figure in the 1930s. Charles DeBenedetti, *Origins of the Modern American Peace Movement, 1915–1929* (1978) and *The Peace Reform in American History* (1980) examine antiwar movements in American history, including prior to World War II. Joseph Lash's *Roosevelt and Churchill* (1976) explores the dynamic relationship between the two leaders of the United States and England. Akira Iriye, *The Origins of the Second World War in Asia and the Pacific* (1988) examines the conflict between China and Japan that preceded American intervention in the Pacific war. Gordon Prange, *At Dawn We Slept* (1981) examines the controversial attack on Pearl Harbor from both the Japanese and American sides.

Chapter 26

John Morton Blum, *V Was for Victory: Politics and American Culture During World War II* (1976) and Richard Polenberg, *War and Society* (1972) are studies of the home front during World War II. David Kennedy, *Freedom from Fear: The American People in Depression and War, 1929–1945* (1999) is a narrative of both the American military experience in the war and the war's impact on American politics and society. Alan Brinkley, *The End of Reform: New Deal Liberalism in Recession and War* (1995) examines the impact of the war on liberal ideology and political economy. Doris Kearns Goodwin, *No Ordinary Time: Franklin and Eleanor Roosevelt: The Home Front in World War II* (1994) is a portrait of the Roosevelts during the war. Susan Hartmann examines the transformation in women's work and family roles during and after the war in *The Homefront and Beyond: American Women in the 1940s* (1982). Richard M. Dalfiume, *Desegregation of the U.S. Armed Forces: Fighting on Two Fronts, 1939–1953* (1969) discusses race relations in the military during World War II and beyond. Maurice Isserman, *Which Side Were You On? The American Communist Party During World War II* (1982)

portrays the dramatic shifts in Communist Party strategy and status during the war. John W. Dower, *War Without Mercy: Race and Power in the Pacific War* (1986) examines the intense racism that shaped both sides of the war between the United States and Japan. Peter Irons, *Justice at War* (1983) and Roger Daniels, *Concentration Camps USA: Japanese-Americans and World War II* (1981) examine the internment of Japanese Americans. John Keegan, *Six Armies in Normandy: From D-Day to the Liberation of Paris, June 6–August 25, 1944* (1982) is an account of the Normandy invasion, as is Paul Fussell, *The Boy's Crusade: The American Infantry in Northwestern Europe, 1944–1945* (2003). David S. Wyman, *The Abandonment of the Jews: America and the Holocaust, 1941–1945* (1984) is sharply critical of American policy toward the victims of the Holocaust. Richard Rhodes, *The Making of the Atomic Bomb* (1987) is an account of one of the great scientific projects of the twentieth century. Gar Alperovitz, *The Decision to Use the Atomic Bomb and the Architecture of an American Myth* (1995) is an exhaustive and highly critical study of why the United States used atomic weapons in 1945. A sharply different view is visible in Herbert Feis, *The Atomic Bomb and the End of World War II* (1966) and Robert Maddox, *Hiroshima in History* (2007), John Hersey's *Hiroshima* (1946) reconstructs in minute detail the terrifying experience of the American atomic bomb attack on that Japanese city.

Chapter 27

Several books by John Lewis Gaddis, *Strategies of Containment* (1982), *The United States and the Origins of the Cold War, 1941–1947* (1972), and *The Cold War: A New History* (2005), provide an introduction to Cold War history. Walter LaFeber, *America, Russia, and the Cold War, 1945–1967* (7th ed. 1993) is a survey of American-Soviet relations. Melvyn P. Leffler, *A Preponderance of Power: National Security, the Truman Administration, and the Cold War* (1992) is a densely researched history of the policies of the 1940s, and his *For the Soul of Mankind: The United States, the Soviet Union, and the Cold War* (2008) is a reconsideration in light of the end of the Cold War. Warren I. Cohen, *The Cambridge History of American Foreign Relations, Vol. 4: America in the Age of Soviet Power, 1945–1991* (1991) is a general history. Michael Hogan, *The Marshall Plan* (1987) is a provocative interpretation of one of the pillars of the early containment doctrine. Philip Taubman, *Secret Empire: Eisenhower, the CIA, and the Hidden Story of America's Space Espionage* (2002) provides an unusual window into the impact of the Cold War on American intelligence efforts. David McCullough, *Truman* (1992) is a popular biography. Alonzo Hamby, *Man of the People: A Life of Harry S. Truman* (1995) is a scholarly one. Bruce Cumings, *The Origins of the Korean War* (1980) is a study of the context for America's first armed conflict of the Cold War. Ellen Schrecker, *Many Are the Crimes: McCarthyism in America* (1998) is an interpretation of McCarthyism, and David Oshinsky, *A Conspiracy So Immense: The World of Joe McCarthy* (1983) is a biography. Richard Fried, *Nightmare in Red* (1990) is a short overview of the Red Scare. Michael Ybarra, *Washington Gone Crazy: Senator Pat McCarran and the Great American Communist Hunt* (2004) is a study of another important figure in the Red Scare. Richard Pells, *The*

Liberal Mind in a Conservative Age: American Intellectuals in the 1940s and 1950s (1985) is a survey of postwar intellectual life.

Chapter 28

James T. Patterson, *Grand Expectations: Postwar America, 1945–1974* (1996) is a general history of the postwar era. John P. Diggins, *The Proud Decades: America in War and Peace, 1941–1960* (1989) and Godfrey Hodgson, *America in Our Time* (1976) are other important surveys. Kenneth T. Jackson, *The Crabgrass Frontier: The Suburbanization of the United States* (1985) is a classic history of a major social movement. Karal Ann Marling, *As Seen on TV: The Visual Culture of Everyday Life in the 1950s* (1995) is a study of the new medium. Lizabeth Cohen, *A Consumer's Republic: The Politics of Mass Consumption in Postwar America* (2003) examines the power of consumerism in postwar America. Elaine Tyler May, *Homeward Bound: American Families in the Cold War* (1988) is a challenging cultural history. Paul Boyer, *By the Bomb's Early Light: American Thought and Culture at the Dawn of the Atomic Age* (1985) examines the impact of the atomic bomb on American social thought. Stephen Ambrose, *Eisenhower the President* (1984) is a good biography, and Fred Greenstein, *The Hidden-Hand Presidency* (1982) is a challenge to earlier, dismissive views of Eisenhower's leadership style. Richard Kluger, *Simple Justice* (1975) is a classic history of the *Brown* decision, John Egerton, *Speak Now Against the Day: The Generation Before the Civil Rights Movement in the South* (1994) is a history of struggles over white supremacy in the first years after World War II.

Chapter 29

Allen J. Matusow, *The Unraveling of America: A History of Liberalism in the 1960s* (1984) is a history of this turbulent decade. David Farber, *The Age of Great Dreams: America in the 1960s* (1994) is a general history. Robert Dallek, *Lone Star Rising: Lyndon Johnson and His Times, 1908–1960* (1991), *Flawed Giant: Lyndon B. Johnson, 1960–1973* (1998), and *An Unfinished Life: John F. Kennedy, 1917–1963* (2003) are biographies. Raymond Arsenault, *Freedom Riders: 1961 and the Struggle for Justice* (2006) is a study of the civil rights movement. John Dittmer, *Local People: The Struggle for Civil Rights in Mississippi* (1994) is a study of the grassroots origins of the movement. William Chafe, *Civilities and Civil Rights: Greensboro, North Carolina, and the Black Struggle for Freedom* (1980) examines the southern civil rights movement and the white reaction to it. Taylor Branch, *Parting the Waters: America in the King Years, 1959–63* (1988), *Pillar of Fire: America in the King Years, 1963–65*, and *At Canaan's Edge: America in the King Years, 1965–68* (2006) are good histories of the movement (1998). Nicholas Lemann, *The Promised Land: The Great Black Migration and How It Changed America* (1991) is a study of the postwar African American migration to northern cities and of the Great Society's response to it. Graham T. Allison, *The Essence of Decision: Explaining the Cuban Missile Crisis* (1971) is an interpretation of the greatest crises of the Cold War. Ernest R. May and Philip D. Zelikow, *The Kennedy Tapes: Inside the White House During the Cuban Missile Crisis* (1997) provides the annotated transcripts of the taped meetings of

Kennedy's inner circle during the crisis. Robert D. Schulzinger, *A Time for War: The United States and Vietnam, 1945–1975* (1997) is a general history of the war. Neil Sheehan, *A Bright Shining Lie: John Paul Vann and America in Vietnam* (1988) is a picture of the war as experienced by a significant military figure of the 1960s. Christian J. Appy, *Working-Class War: American Combat Soldiers and Vietnam* (1993) examines the class basis of the army that fought in Vietnam. Larry Berman, *Planning a Tragedy* (1982) and *Lyndon Johnson's War* (1989); Leslie Gelb and Richard Betts, *The Irony of Vietnam: The System Worked* (1979); and David Halberstam, *The Best and the Brightest* (1972) are interpretations of the American decision to intervene and stay in Vietnam. Dan T. Carter, *The Politics of Rage: George Wallace, the Origins of the New Conservatism, and the Transformation of American Politics* (1995) is a study of the career of George Wallace. David Farber, *Chicago '68* (1988) examines the turbulent Democratic Convention and, through it, the passions that shaped a traumatic year in American history. Mark Kurlansky, *1968: The Year That Rocked the World* (2003) is a broader history of that turbulent year.

Chapter 30

John Morton Blum, *Years of Discord: American Politics and Society, 1961–1974* (1991) is an overview. James Miller, *"Democracy in the Streets": From Port Huron to the Siege of Chicago* (1987) is a history of the New Left through its leading organization, SDS, Kristin Luker, *Abortion and the Politics of Motherhood* (1984) is an account of this central battle over the nature of feminism. Margaret Cruikshank, *The Rise of a Gay and Lesbian Liberation Movement* (1992) and David Eisenbach, *Gay Power: An American Revolution* (2006) recount another important struggle of the 1960s and beyond. Ronald Takaki, *Strangers from a Distant Shore: A History of Asian Americans* (1989) examines the growing Asian community in postwar America. Stephen Ambrose, *Nixon: The Triumph of a Politician, 1962–1972* (1989) and *Nixon, Ruin and Recovery, 1973–1990* (1992) provides a chronicle of this important presidency. Joan Hoff, *Nixon Reconsidered* (1994) is a sympathetic account of Nixon's presidency before Watergate. Margaret MacMillan, *Nixon and Mao: The Week That Changed the World* (2007) examines Nixon's most famous diplomatic effort. Stanley J. Kutler, *The Wars of Watergate* (1990) is a scholarly study of the great scandal, and Jonathan Schell, *The Time of Illusion* (1975) is a contemporary account. David Greenberg, *Nixon's Shadow* (2003) is a perceptive examination of Nixon's place in American culture. Marilyn Young, *The Vietnam Wars, 1945–1990* (1991) provides, among other things, a full account of the last years of American involvement in Vietnam and of the conflicts in the region that followed the American withdrawal.

Chapter 31

Bruce J. Schulman, *The Seventies: The Great Shift in American Culture, Society, and Politics* (2001) and James T. Patterson, *Restless Giant: The United States from Watergate to Bush v. Gore* (2005) are broad histories of the era. James M. Cannon, *Time and Chance: Gerald Ford's Appointment with History* (1994) is a journalist's account of the Ford presidency, and Yanek Mieczkowski, *Gerald Ford and the Challenges of the 1970s* (2005) is a scholarly study. Gaddis Smith, *Morality, Reason, and Power* (1986) examines the Carter foreign policy. Steven Gillon, *The Democrats' Dilemma: Walter Mondale and the Liberal Legacy* (1992) is a discussion of the travails of the Democrats in the 1970s. Jerome L. Himmelstein, *To the Right: The Transformation of American Conservatism* (1990) and Godfrey Hodgson, *The World Turned Upside Down: A History of the Conservative Ascendancy in America* (1996) are introductions to the subject as is Kevin Kruse, *White Flight: Atlanta and the Making of Modern Conservatism* (2005). Lou Cannon, *President Reagan: The Role of a Lifetime* (1990) and Haynes Johnson, *Sleepwalking Through History* (1991) are accounts by journalists who covered the Reagan White House. Gill Troy, *Morning in America: How Ronald Reagan Invented the 1980s* (2005) is a scholarly study. John Lewis Gaddis, *The United States and the End of the Cold War* (1992) and *We Now Know: Rethinking Cold War History* (1997) examine the transformation of the world order after 1989. Richard Rhodes, *Arsenals of Folly* (2007) is a passionate account of the nuclear arms race. Herbert Parmet, *George Bush: The Life of a Lone Star Yankee* (1997) is the first major scholarly study of the 41st president.

Chapter 32

John Lewis Gaddis, *The United States and the End of the Cold War* (1992), *We Now Know: Rethinking Cold War History* (1997), and *Surprise, Security, and the American Experience* (2004) are early examinations of the post–Cold War transformation of the world order. Clinton's own memoir, *My Life* (2004) is a valuable account of his presidency. Theda Skocpol, *Boomerang: Clinton's Health Security Effort and the Turn Against Government in U.S. Politics* (1996) is an account of one of the major setbacks of Clinton's first term. Jeffrey Toobin, *A Vast Conspiracy* (1999) is an account of the scandals that rocked the Clinton presidency. Toobin is also the author of an account of the disputed 2000 presidential election, *Too Close to Call* (2001). Haynes Johnson, *The Best of Times: America in the Clinton Years* (2001) is an account of the politics and culture of the 1990s. John F. Harris, *The Survivor: President Clinton and His Times* (2005) is a valuable overview of this presidency. David Halberstam, *War in a Time of Peace. Bush, Clinton, and the Generals* (2001) examines the foreign policy and military ventures of the Bush and Clinton years. Samantha Power, *"A Problem from Hell": America and the Age of Genocide* (2003) is a study of a major question in the United States. George Packer, *The Assassin's Gate: America in Iraq* (2006); Jane Mayer, *The Dark Side* (2007); Lawrence Wright, *The Looming Tower: Al-Qaeda and the Road to 9/11* (2006) are among the many studies of the post-9/11 years and the war in Iraq. *Computer: A History of the Information Machine* (1996), by Martin Campbell-Kelly and William Aspray, is an introduction to the development of one of the critical technologies of the late twentieth century. William Julius Wilson, *The Truly Disadvantaged* (1987) and *When Work Disappears* (1996) are important studies of the inner-city poor from one of America's leading sociologists. David A. Hollinger, *Postethnic America: Beyond Multiculturalism* (1995) is a comment on the debates over multiculturalism.

TIMELINE IMAGE CREDITS

In Order from Left to Right

Ch 1: Library of Congress; Getty Images; Library of Congress; Museum of the City of New York. **Ch 2:** Library of Congress; Corbis; McGraw Hill Archive (DAL); Library of Congress. **Ch 3:** Alamy; Getty Images; Alamy; Library of Congress. **Ch 4:** The Granger Collection, NY; Library of Congress; Library of Congress; Alamy. **Ch 5:** Library of Congress; Punchstock; National Archives and Records Administration; Alamy. **Ch 6:** Getty Images; Library of Congress; New York Public Library; National Archives and Records Administration. **Ch 7:** Punchstock; Library of Congress; Library of Congress; Library of Congress. **Ch 8:** Library of Congress; Punchstock; Library of Congress; National Archives and Records Administration. **Ch 9:** Library of Congress; Library of Congress; Library of Congress; Library of Congress; Library of Congress. **Ch 10:** Library of Congress; McGraw Hill Archive (DAL); Getty Images; Library of Congress. **Ch 11:** Jupiter Images; Library of Congress; Library of Congress. **Ch 12:** Picture Quest; Library of Congress; Getty Images; Library of Congress; Library of Congress. **Ch 13:** Getty Images; Getty Images; National Archives and Records Administration; Library of Congress; Corbis. **Ch 14:** Library of Congress; Getty Images; Library of Congress; Corbis; Library of Congress. **Ch 15:** Library of Congress; Punchstock; National Archives and Records Administration; Library of Congress; Library of Congress. **Ch 16:** Alamy; Getty Images; Library of Congress; Library of Congress; National Archives and Records Administration. **Ch 17:** Library of Congress; Fotosearch; Library of Congress; Texas Energy Museum; Library of Congress. **Ch 18:** Alamy; Library of Congress; Library of Congress; Library of Congress. **Ch 19:** Library of Congress; National Archives and Records Administration; Library of Congress; Getty Images; Library of Congress. **Ch 20:** Library of Congress; Library of Congress; Library of Congress; Library of Congress. **Ch 21:** Library of Congress; Library of Congress; Library of Congress; Library of Congress. **Ch 22:** Getty Images; Punch Limited; Alamy; Library of Congress. **Ch 23:** Library of Congress; Punch Limited; Library of Congress; Library of Congress. **Ch 24:** Library of Congress; Library of Congress; Jupiter Images; Library of Congress. **Ch 25:** Library of Congress; Getty Images; Fotosearch; Library of Congress. **Ch 26:** Corbis; Library of Congress; Corbis; National Park Service. **Ch 27:** Library of Congress; Alamy; Getty Images; Public Domain; Library of Congress. **Ch 28:** Library of Congress; Library of Congress; Punch Limited; Library of Congress; NASA. **Ch 29:** Library of Congress; National Archives and Records Administration; Alamy; Library of Congress. **Ch 30:** Library of Congress; Getty Images; Getty Images; McGraw Hill Archive (DAL); Library of Congress. **Ch 31:** Alamy; Comstock; Getty Images; Library of Congress; Corbis. **Ch 32:** Corbis; Getty Images; SuperStock, Inc.; Getty Images.

INDEX